Science and Golf II

Other titles from E & FN Spon

Advanced Materials for Sports Equipment
K. Easterling

Amenity Landscape Management: A Resources Handbook
R. Cobham

Foods, Nutrition and Sports Performance
C. Williams and J.T. Devlin

Fungal Diseases of Amenity Turf Grasses
Third edition
J. Drew Smith, N. Jackson and A.R. Woolhouse

Journal of Sports Sciences
Published on behalf of the BASES and in association with ISAK
General editor: T. Reilly

Kinanthropometry IV
J.W. Duquet and J.A.P. Day

Science and Football II
T. Reilly, J. Clarys and A. Stibbe

Sports Geography
J. Bale

For more information about these and other titles published by us, please contact: The Promotion Department, E & FN Spon, 2–6 Boundary Row, London SE1 8HN. Telephone 071 522 9966.

Science and Golf II

PROCEEDINGS OF THE 1994 WORLD SCIENTIFIC CONGRESS OF GOLF

Edited by A.J. Cochran
Technical Consultant
Royal and Ancient Golf Club
St. Andrews
UK

and

M.R. Farrally
Department of Physical Education
University of St. Andrews
UK

E & FN SPON
An Imprint of Chapman & Hall

London · Glasgow · Weinheim · New York · Tokyo · Melbourne · Madras

Published by E & FN Spon, an imprint of Chapman & Hall, 2–6 Boundary Row, London SE1 8HN, UK

Chapman & Hall, 2–6 Boundary Row, London SE1 8HN, UK

Blackie Academic & Professional, Wester Cleddens Road, Bishopbriggs, Glasgow G64 2NZ, UK

Chapman & Hall GmbH, Pappelallee 3, 69469 Weinheim, Germany

Chapman & Hall Inc., One Penn Plaza, 41st Floor, New York, NY 10119, USA

Chapman & Hall Japan, Thomson Publishing Japan, Hirakawacho Nemoto Building, 6F, 1-7-11 Hirakawa-cho, Chiyoda-ku, Tokyo 102, Japan

Chapman & Hall Australia, Thomas Nelson Australia, 102 Dodds Street, South Melbourne, Victoria 3205, Australia

Chapman & Hall India, R. Seshadri, 32 Second Main Road, CIT East, Madras 600 035, India

First edition 1994

© 1994 E & FN Spon

Printed in Great Britain at the University Press, Cambridge

ISBN 0 419 18790 1

♾ Printed on permanent acid-free paper, manufactured in accordance with ANSI/NISO Z39.48-1992 and ANSI/NISO Z39.48-1984 (Permanence of Paper).

**World Scientific Congress of Golf
St. Andrews, Scotland
4–8th July 1994**

Held at the University of St. Andrews
and approved and grant-aided by the
United States Golf Association and the
Royal and Ancient Golf Club of St. Andrews

Administration Committee
A.J. Cochran
M.R. Farrally
D. Kemp
R. Price
J.I.C. Scott
A.S. Strachan

Scientific Committee
P.M. Canaway
A.J. Cochran
M.R. Farrally
L. Hardy
B.B. Lieberman
Y. Maki
R. Price
T. Reilly
M. Schofield
M. Sjogren
J. Snow
B. Stoddart
F.W. Thomas
G. Wiren

Steering Committee
A.J. Cochran
C. Dillman
M.R. Farrally
F.W. Thomas

Congress Director
M.R. Farrally
Department of Physical Education
University of St. Andrews

Congress Administrator
A. McFetridge-Kemp

Contents

Author's names and addresses   xvii

Foreword   xxv

PART ONE   THE GOLFER

1 How has biomechanics contributed to the
understanding of the golf swing?   3
C.J. Dillman and G.W. Lange

2 Usefulness of partial swings in the
rehabilitation of a golfer   14
L.J. Lemak, G.S. Fleisig, C.M. Welch, B. Marting
and J.E. Zvijac

3 Back pain in novice golfers, a one-year follow-up   20
G.A. Van Der Steenhoven, A. Burdorf
and E.G.M. Tromp-Klaren

4 Discrete pressure profiles of the feet and weight
transfer patterns during the golf swing   26
E.S. Wallace, P.N. Grimshaw and R.L. Ashford

5 Ground reaction forces and torques of
professional and amateur golfers   33
S.W. Barrentine, G.S. Fleisig, H. Johnson
and T.W. Woolley

6 The biomechanics of the shoe–ground interaction
in golf   40
G. Koenig, M. Tamres and R.W. Mann

7 A biomechanical analysis of the respiratory
pattern during the golf swing   46
K. Kawashima, S. Takeshita, H. Zaitsu and T. Meshizuka

8 Spine and hip motion analysis during the golf swing   50
M. McTeigue, S.R. Lamb, R. Mottram and F. Pirozzolo

9 **Centrifugal force and the planar golf swing**   59
B. Lowe and I.H. Fairweather

10 **Categorisation of golf swings**   65
M.A.J. Cooper and J.S.B. Mather

11 **Dynamic model and computer simulation of a**   71
golf swing
S.M. Nesbit, J.S. Cole, T.A. Hartzell, K.A. Oglesby
and A.F. Radich

12 **A concise method of specifying the geometry and**
timing of golf swings   77
D.L. Linning

13 **A study of the correlation between swing**   84
characteristics and club head velocity
R.L. Robinson

14 **Three-dimensional kinematic analysis of the**
golf swing   91
P.A. McLaughlin and R.J. Best

15 **One move to better ball flight**   97
K. Kanwar and R.V. Chowgule

16 **Common pre-swing and in-swing tendencies of**
amateur golfers   103
E. Alpenfels

17 **Golf development in Australia**   109
D. Wall

18 **Teaching methods and epistemic styles of**   117
golf instructors
R.J. Rancourt and R.Q. Searle

19 **Possibilities available in teaching using videos**
and computers   123
P.-A. Brostedt

20 **Research based golf: from the laboratory to the course**   127
D.J. Crews

21 **Contributions of psychological, psychomotor, and shot-making skills to prowess at golf** 138
P.R. Thomas and R. Over

22 **Factors affecting the salience of outcome, performance and process goals in golf** 144
K. Kingston and L. Hardy

23 **The self-regulatory challenges of golf** 150
D.S. Kirschenbaum

24 **Promotion of the flow state in golf: a goal perspective analysis** 156
J.L. Duda

25 **Mental preparation for golf: achieving optimal performance** 162
S. Murphy

26 **Visual performance differences among professional, amateur, and senior amateur golfers** 168
B. Coffey, A.W. Reichow, T. Johnson and S. Yamane

27 **Toward putting performance enhancement: a methodology using quantitative feedback** 174
P.H. Beauchamp, L.M. Landsberger, W.R. Halliwell, R. Koestner and M.E. Ford

28 **A study of golfers' abilities to read greens** 180
D. Pelz

29 **How to lower your putting score without improving** 186
B. Hoadley

30 **Comparing players in professional golf** 193
P.D. Larkey

31 **An analysis of 1992 performance statistics for players on the US PGA, Senior PGA and LPGA tours** 199
F. Wiseman, S. Chatterjee, D. Wiseman and N.S. Chatterjee

32 **The Ryder Cup: an analysis of relative performance 1980–1993**   205
T. Hale, V. Harper and J. Herb

33 **The ageing of a great player; Tom Watson's play in the US Open from 1980–1993**   210
L.J. Riccio

34 **A unified golf stroke value scale for quantitative stroke-by-stroke assessment**   216
L.M. Landsberger

35 **The search for the perfect handicap**   222
F.J. Scheid

36 **Outlier identification procedure for reduction of handicaps**   228
D.L. Knuth, F.J. Scheid and F.P. Engel

PART TWO   THE EQUIPMENT

37 **The state of the game, equipment and science**   237
F.W. Thomas

38 **Golf shafts – a technical perspective**   247
G.P. Horwood

39 **The dynamic performance of the golf shaft during the downswing**   259
J.H. Butler and D.C. Winfield

40 **An investigation of three dimensional deformation of a golf club during downswing**   265
A.M. Brylawski

41 **The attitude of the shaft during the swing of golfers of different ability**   271
J.S.B. Mather and M.A.J. Cooper

42 **Golf shaft flex point – an analysis of measurement techniques**   278
A. Chou and O.C. Roberts

43 Kick back effect of club-head at impact   **284**
M. Masuda and S. Kojima

44 Experimental determination of inertia ellipsoids   **290**
S.H. Johnson

**45 Contact forces, coefficient of restitution, and spin
rate of golf ball impact**   **296**
P.C. Chou, W. Gobush, D. Liang and J. Yang

**46 Measurement of dynamic characteristics of golf balls
and identification of their mechanical models**   **302**
S. Ujihashi

**47 An analytical model for ball–barrier impact
Part 1: Models for normal impact**   **309**
B.B. Lieberman and S.H. Johnson

**48 An analytical model for ball–barrier impact
Part 2: A model for oblique impact**   **315**
S. H. Johnson and B.B. Lieberman

49 The effects of driver head size on performance   **321**
T. Olsavsky

**50 Video monitoring system to measure initial launch
characteristics of golf ball**   **327**
W. Gobush, D. Pelletier and C. Days

**51 The relationship between golf ball construction and
performance**   **334**
M.J. Sullivan and T. Melvin

52 A new aerodynamic model of a golf ball in flight   **340**
A.J. Smits and D.R. Smith

**53 An indoor testing range to measure the aerodynamic
performance of golf balls**   **348**
M.V. Zagarola, B. Lieberman and A.J. Smits,

**54 Changes in golf ball performance over the last
25 years**   **355**
S. Aoyama

55 **Does it matter what ball you play?** 362
T. Hale, P. Bunyan and I. Sewell

56 **The golf equipment market 1984–1994** 369
S.K. Proctor

57 **Chemistry and properties of a high performance
golf ball coating** 376
T.J. Kennedy III and W. Risen, Jr

58 **Novel high acid ionomers for golf ball cover
applications** 383
M.J. Sullivan and R.A. Weiss

59 **A design system for iron golf clubs** 390
S. Mitchell, S.T. Newman, C.J. Hinde and R. Jones

PART THREE   THE GOLF COURSE AND THE GAME

60 **Environmental protection and beneficial
contributions of golf course turfs** 399
J.B. Beard

61 **The playing quality of golf greens** 409
S.W. Baker

62 **A method for classifying the quality of golf green turf** 419
T.A. Lodge and D.J. Pilbeam

63 **The effects of light-weight rolling on putting greens** 425
G.W. Hamilton, Jr, D.W. Livingston and A.E. Gover

64 **Golf ball impacts, greens and the golfer** 431
S.J. Haake

65 **Improving the performance of golf turf soils by
cultivation** 437
K.W. McAuliffe, R.J. Gibbs and A. Glasgow

66 **Soil macropore effects on the fate of phosphorus in a
turfgrass biosystem** 443
S.K. Starrett, N.E. Christians and T.A. Austin

67 **Experimental studies on black layer** 449
W.A. Adams and J.N.G. Smith

68 **The role of fungi on the development of
water-repellent soils on UK golf greens** 455
C.A. York and N.W. Lepp

69 **Subterranean insects and fungi: hidden costs
and benefits to the greenkeeper** 461
A.C. Gange

70 **A golf club on a volcano** 467
J.R. Gomez

71 **Response of creeping bentgrass (*Agrostis palustris*) to
natural organic fertilizers** 471
C.H. Peacock and J.M. Dipaola

72 **Characterization of localised dry spots on creeping
bentgrass turf in the United States** 477
T.K. Danneberger and R.A. Hudson

73 **Australian bunker sands – quantifying
playability** 483
R.B. Dewar, K.Y. Chan and G.W. Beehag

74 **Nutrient transport in runoff from two turfgrass
species** 489
D.T. Linde, T.L. Watschke and J.A. Borger

75 **Impact of golf courses on ground water
quality** 497
A.M. Petrovic

76 **Dislodgeable and volatile residues from
insecticide-treated turfgrass** 505
K.C. Murphy, R.J. Cooper and J.M. Clark

77 **Fate and mobility of pre-emergent herbicides in
turfgrass** 511
H.D. Niemczyk and A.A. Krause

78 **Reducing the environmental impact of golf course insect management** **519**
R.L. Brandenburg

79 **Health risk assessment from pesticide use in golf courses in Korea – Part two** **527**
Y.H. Moon, D.C. Shin and K.J. Lee

80 **Course design with precision and control** **534**
R.A. Ryder

81 **The role of management planning and ecological evaluation within the golf course environment** **540**
A.-M. Brennan

82 **The development and growth of the U.S. golf market** **546**
J.F. Beditz

83 **Development of golf courses: market research and appraisal** **554**
W.G. Deddis and J.S. Hanna

84 **Golf course development in Japan: its abnormal supply and demand** **562**
H. Zaitsu, S. Takeshita, T. Meshizuka and K. Kawashima

85 **Market appraisals for new golf projects** **569**
M.G. Williamson

86 **The database of golf in America: a guide to understanding U.S. golf markets** **576**
J.F. Rooney, Jr and H.J. White

87 **Targeting for success – the European golf market** **589**
K.R. Storey

88 **Spectators' views of PGA golf events** **596**
H. Hansen and R. Gauthier

89 **Golf for all? The problems of municipal provision** **602**
J.R. Lowerson

90 Golf, development and the human sciences: the swing is not the only thing   **611**
B. Stoddart

91 Discipline and flourish: golf as a civilising process?   **620**
D. Collinson and K. Hoskin

92 Golf, media and change in Australia   **626**
B. Parker

Index   635

Authors' names and addresses

The names and addresses in this list are those of the 'contact authors' of the papers in this book, who are not always the first-named authors.

W.A. Adams
Aberystwyth University of Wales
Institute of Biological Sciences
Sir George Stapledon Building
Aberystwyth
SY23 3DD

Tel. 0970 622302

E. Alpenfels
Pinehurst Resort and Country Club
Carolina Vista
P.O. Box 4000
N.C. 28374-4000
USA

Tel. 910 295 8121   Fax 910 295 8110

S. Aoyama
Titleist and Footjoy Worldwide
Fairhaven
MA 02719 0965
USA

Tel. 508 979 2000   Fax 508 979 3909

S. Baker
Sports Turf Institute
Bingley
West Yorkshire
BD16 1AU
UK

Tel. 0274 565131   Fax 0274 561891

J.B. Beard
International Sports Turf Institute
1812 Shadowood Drive
College Station
TX 77840
USA

Tel. 409 693 4066   Fax 409 693 4878

P. Beauchamp
Canadian Olympic Association
2380 Pierre Dupuy
Montreal, Que
H3C 3R4

Tel. 514 861 3371   Fax 514 861 2896

J. Beditz
National Golf Foundation
1150 South US One, Suite 401
Florida 33477
USA

Tel. 407 744 6006   Fax 407 744 6107

R. Brandenburg
Department of Entomology
North Carolina State University
College of Agriculture and Life Sciences
Box 7613
Raleigh, NC 27695 7613
USA

Tel. 919 515 2703

A.M. Brennan
Durrell Institute
of Conservation and Ecology
University of Kent
Canterbury
CT2 7NX
UK

Tel/Fax 0843 831291

P.A. Brostedt
Villagatan 4
114 32 Stockholm
Sweden

A. Brylawski
Lehigh University
Packard Lab
19 Memorial Drive West
Bethlehem
PA 18015 3085
USA

Fax 610 758 6224

J.H. Butler
True Temper Sports
8706 Dearfield Drive
Olive Branch
MS 38654
USA

Tel. 601 895 3535   Fax 601 895 8668

A. Chou
Titleist and Footjoy Worldwide
2839 Loker Ave. East
Carlsbad
CA 92008
USA

Tel. 619 929 8850   Fax 619 929 8731

P.C. Chou
Drexel University
Dept of Mechanical Engineering
32nd and Chestnut Streets
PA 19104
USA

Tel. 215 895 2288   Fax 215 895 1478

B. Coffey
College of Optometry
Pacific University
Forest Grove
Oregon 97116
USA

Tel. 503 224 2323   Fax 503 359 2261

D. Collinson
The University of Warwick
Warwick Business School
Coventry
CV4 7AL
UK

Tel. 0203 524306   Fax 0203 523719

M.A.J. Cooper
Dept of Mechanical Engineering
University of Nottingham
Nottingham NG7 2RD
UK

Tel. 0602 513819   Fax 0602 513800

D.J. Crews
Arizona State University
Dept of Exercise Science and Physical
Education
Box 870404
Tempe AZ 85287-1004
USA

Tel. 602 965 4718

K. Danneberger
The Ohio State University
Department of Agronomy
2021 Coffey Road
Columbus, OH 43210-1086
USA

Tel. 614 292 2001   Fax 614 292 7162

W.G. Deddis
University of Ulster
Department of Surveying
Newtownabbey
County Antrim
BT37 0QB
Northern Ireland

Tel. 0232 365131 ext. 2565
Fax 0232 362826

R. Dewar
Australian Turfgrass Research Institute
Research Laboratories
68 Victoria Avenue
Concord West
N.S.W 2138
Australia

Tel. 02 736 1233   Fax 02 743 6348

C.J. Dillman
Steadman Hawkins Sports Medicine
Foundation
181 West Meadow Drive
Suite 1000
Vail, Colorado 81657
USA

Tel. 303 479 9797 ext. 271
Fax 303 479 9753

J.L. Duda
Dept of Health Kinesiology and Leisure
Studies
1362 Lambert
West Lafayette
IN 47907-1362
USA

Fax 317 496 1239

G.S. Fleisig
American Sports Medicine Institute
1313 13th Street South
P.O. Box 550039
Birmingham
AL 35255-0039
USA

Tel. 205 918 0000   Fax 205 918 0800

A.C. Gange
Dept of Biology
Royal Holloway University of London
Egham
Surrey, TW20 0EX
UK

Tel. 0784 443773   Fax 0784 470756

W. Gobush
Titleist and Footjoy Worldwide
PO Box 965
Fairhaven
MA 02719 0965
USA

Tel. 508 979 2000   Fax 508 979 3909

J.R. Gomez
c/o Joaquin Mir, 11
Tafira Alta
35017 Las Palmas
De Gran Canaria
Canary Islands
Spain

Tel. 928 35 06 40   Fax 928 35 11 11

S. Haake
University of Sheffield
Dept of Mechanical and Process
Engineering
Mappin Street
Sheffield, S1 4DU
UK

Tel. 0742 768555   Fax 0742 753671

T. Hale
West Sussex Institute of Higher
Education
Bishop Otter College
College Lane
Chichester
W Sussex, PO19 4PE
UK

Tel. 0243 787911   Fax 0243 536011

G.W. Hamilton
Penn State University
University Park
PA 16802-3504
USA

Tel. 814 865 6541   Fax 814 863 7043

H. Hansen
University of Ottowa
Faculty of Health Sciences
School of Human Kinetics
125 University, PO Box 450 Stn A
Ottawa, KIN 6N5
Canada

Tel. 613 564 5920   Fax 613 564 7689

B. Hoadley
16 Williamson Court
Middletown
NJ 07748
USA

Tel. 908 671 6105

G. Horwood
TI Apollo Ltd
Oldbury, Warley
West Midlands
B69 2DF
UK

Tel. 021 544 7654   Fax 021 544 4519

S.H. Johnson
Lehigh University
Mechanical Engineering
Packard Lab
19 Memorial Drive West
Bethlehem
Pennsylvania 18015 3085
USA

R. Jones
Dept of Manufacturing Engineering
Loughborough University of Technology
Leicestershire, LE11 3TU
UK

Tel. 0509 263171   Fax 0509 267725

K. Kanwar
Chapsey Terrace
30 Altamount Road
Bombay 400 026
India

Tel. 91 22 3861526

K. Kawashima
Nihon University
Biomechanics Laboratory
College of Agricultural and Veterinary
Medicine, Fujisawa
Japan

Fax 81 466 82 4691

T. Kennedy
Spalding Sports Worldwide
425 Meadow Street, Chicopee
MA 01021 0901
USA

Tel. 413 536 1200   Fax 413 536 4831

K. Kingston
Dept of Sport Health and Physical
Education
University of Wales, Bangor
Gwynedd
LL57 2DG
UK

Tel. 0248 382756   Fax 0248 371053

D.S. Kirschenbaum
Center for Behavioral Medicine
676 North St Clair
Suite 1790, Chicago
Illinois 60611
USA

Fax 312 751 6976

D.L. Knuth
USGA
Far Hills
NJ 07931 0708
USA

Tel. 908 234 2300   Fax 908 234 9687

A.A. Krause
Plant Protection Institute
ul. Zwirki i Wigury 73
87-100 Torun
Poland

L.M. Landsberger
PO Box 491
Westmount Quebec
Canada H3Z 2T6

Tel. 514 848 8741   Fax 514 938 1705

P.D. Larkey
Carnegie Mellon University
School of Public Policy and Management
Pittsburgh
Pennsylvania 15213-3890
USA

Tel. 412 268 3034

L.J. Lemak
American Sports Medicine Institute
1313 13th Street South
Birmingham
AL 35255-0039
USA

Tel. 205 918 0000   Fax 205 918 0800

B.B. Lieberman
451 West Broadway
New York
NY 10012
USA

Tel. 212 257 5023   Fax 212 257 7983

D. Linning
26 Cinnamon Lane
Fearnhead
Warrington
WA2 0BB
UK

Tel. 0295 821957

T.A. Lodge
Sports Turf Research Institute
Bingley
West Yorkshire
BD16 1AU
UK

Tel. 0274 565131   Fax 0274 561891

B. Lowe
25 Arabin Street
Keilor
Victoria 3036
Australia

Tel. 61 3 336 4615   Fax 61 3 282 2444

M. Masuda
Shonan Institute of Technology
Department of Electrical Engineering
Tujido, Fujisawa 251
Japan

Tel. 81 466 34 4111   Fax 81 466 35 8897

J.S.B. Mather
Dept of Mechanical Engineering
University of Nottingham
Nottingham NG7 2RD

Tel. 0602 513773   Fax 0602 513800

K.W. McAuliffe
NZ Turf Culture Institute
Fitzherbert Science Centre
PO Box 347
Palmerston North
New Zealand

Tel./Fax 06 356 8090

P. McLaughlin
Centre for Rehabilitation
Victoria University of Technology
PO Box 14428
MMC Melbourne
Australia

Tel. 61 3 248 1115   Fax 61 3 248 1009

M. McTeigue
SportSense Inc.
1931 B Old Middlefield Way
Mountain View
CA 94043
USA

Tel. 407 624 8400   Fax 415 965 4123

T. Melvin
Spalding Sports Worldwide
425 Meadow Street
Chicopee
MA 01021 0901
USA

Tel. 413 536 1200   Fax 413 536 1404

T. Meshizuka
3-11-2-404 Soshigaya
Setagaya-ku
Tokyo 157
Japan

Tel. 03 3484 8915   Fax 03 3484 9821

Y. Moon
Dept of Preventive Medicine
Yonsei University College of Medicine
CPO Box 8044
Seoul 120
Korea

Fax 82 2 392 0239

K. Murphy
Turfgrass Science
University of Massachusetts
Stockbridge Hall
Amherst MA 01003
USA

Fax 413 545 1242

S.M. Murphy
Athlete Performance Division
United States Olympic Committee
One Olympic Plaza
Colorado Springs
Colorado 80909-5760
USA

Tel. 719 578 4516   Fax 719 632 5194

S.M. Nesbit
Layfette College
Engineering Division
Easton
PA 18042
USA

Tel. 215 250 5435

T. Olsavsky
Titleist and Footjoy Worldwide
2839 Loker Avenue East
Carlsbad
CA 92008
USA

Tel. 619 929 8850   Fax 619 929 8731

B. Parker
Australian Golf Digest
Australia

C.H. Peacock
North Carolina State University
Department of Crop Science
Raleigh
NC 27695 7620
USA

Tel. 919 515 2647   Fax 919 515 2647

D. Pelz
1200 Lakeway Drive
Suite 21, Austin
Texas 78734
USA

Tel. 512 261 6493   Fax 512 261 5391

A. Petrovic
Cornell University
Dept of Floriculture
20 Plant Science Building
Ithaca, NY 14853-5908
USA

Tel. 607 255 1789   Fax 607 255 9998

S. Proctor
Sports Marketing Surveys
Byfleet Business Centre
Chertsey Road
Byfleet
KT14 7AW
UK

Tel. 0932 350600   Fax 0932 350375

R.J. Rancourt
University of Ottawa
145 Jean-Jacques-Lussier
PO Box 450 Stn A
Ottawa, ON K1N 6N5
Canada

Fax 613 564 7689

L. Riccio
315 East Sixty-Ninth St
Apartment 9J
New York 10021
USA

Tel. 908 234 2300   Fax 908 234 9687

R. Robinson
East 3020 Packsaddle Drive
Coeur D'Alene
Idaho 83814
USA

Tel. 208 772 4342

J.F. Rooney
308 Geography Building
Oklahoma State University
Stillwater
Oklahoma 74078-0177
USA

Tel. 405 744 6250   Fax 405 744 5620

R.A. Ryder
Ryder Golf Services
50 Gally Hill Road
Church Crookham
GU13 0QF
UK

Tel. 0252 617542   Fax 0252 812082

F. Scheid
135 Elm Street
Kingston
MA 02364
USA

Tel. 617 585 6866   Fax 617 585 8201

A. Smits
Dept of Mechanical Engineering
Princeton University
PO Box CN5263
Princeton
NJ 08544 5263
USA

Tel. 609 258 5117   Fax 609 258 2276

S.K. Starrett
Iowa State University of Science and
Technology
College of Agriculture
Department of Horticulture
Horticulture Building
Ames, Iowa 50011-1100
USA

Tel. 515 294 2751   Fax 515 294 0730

B. Stoddart
Faculty of Communication
University of Canberra
Kirinari Street
PO Box 1
Belconnen ACT 2616
Australia

Tel. 61 6 201 2111   Fax 61 6 201 5119

S.K. Storey
Sports Marketing Surveys Ltd.
Byfleet Business Centre
Chertsey Road
Byfleet
KT14 7AW
UK

Tel. 0932 350600   Fax 0932 350375

M. Sullivan
Spalding Sports Worldwide
425 Meadow Street
PO Box 901
Chicopee
MA 01021 0901
USA

Tel. 413 536 1200   Fax 413 536 1404

M. Tamres
Department of Mechanical Engineering
Massachusetts Institute of Technology
Cambridge
MA 02139
USA

Tel. 617 253 5334   Fax 617 258 7018

F.W. Thomas
USGA
Far Hills
NJ 07931
USA

Tel. 908 234 2300   Fax 908 234 0138

P.R. Thomas
Griffith University
Faculty of Education
Queensland 4111
Australia

Tel. 61 7 875 7111   Fax 61 7 875 5910

S. Ujihashi
Tokyo Institute of Technology
2-12-1 Oh-okayama, Meguru-ku
Tokyo 152
Japan

Tel. 3 3726 1111 ext. 2158
Fax 3 3726 9174

G.A. Van der Steenhoven
State University of Leiden
PO Box 2360
2301 CJ LEIDEN
The Netherlands

Tel. 071 177461   Fax 071 177084

D. Wall
Australian Golf Union
153-155 Cecil Street
South Melbourne
Victoria 3205
Australia

Tel. 03 699 7944   Fax 03 690 8510

E. Wallace
Sport and Leisure Studies
University of Ulster
Newtownabbey
Co Antrim
BT37 0QB
Northern Ireland

Tel. 0232 365131   Telex 747493

T.L. Watschke
Penn State University
116 Agricultural Sciences and Industries
Building
University Park
PA 16802-3504
USA

Tel. 814 865 6541   Fax 814 863 7043

M.G. Williamson
TMS Advertising Ltd
10A Rutland Square
Edinburgh
EH1 2AS
UK

Tel. 031 228 8969   Fax 031 228 8979

F. Wiseman
Northeastern University
College of Business Administration
414 Hayden Hall
Boston
MA 02115
USA

Tel. 617 373 3260   Fax 617 373 2056

C. York
Sports Turf Research Institute
Bingley
West Yorkshire
BD16 1AU
UK

Tel. 0274 565131   Fax 0274 561891

M.V. Zagarola
Dept of Mechanical Engineering
Princeton University
PO Box CN5263
Princeton
NJ 08544 5263
USA

Tel. 609 258 5117   Fax 609 258 2282

Foreword

The papers contained within this book were presented at the World Scientific Congress of Golf held at the University of St Andrews from 4th to 8th July, 1994.

The papers and their authors represent a wide diversity not only of sciences themselves, but also of vocations – including golfers who also happen to be scientists, scientists who see interesting applications in golf, scientifically minded coaches and professional scientists working for equipment manufacturers. The common element is a burning interest in the game and the desire to find out more and establish hard evidence on their particular aspects of it.

In producing this book we have followed the same policy as at the first Congress, held in 1990, namely of issuing it in time for distribution at the Congress. This imposes quite strict deadlines on authors and reviewers and we wish to thank all of them for their co-operation.

The papers are grouped into three Parts, entitled The Golfer, The Equipment, and The Golf Course and the Game. Within each Part, similar topics are located as near to each other as possible.

Much of the work reported here was done primarily for interest's sake; but we believe that coaches, equipment designers, golf course maintainers, designers and planners and inquiring golfers generally, as well as scientific researchers, will find something in the book that is of **use** to them as well as of interest.

Alastair Cochran
Martin Farrally

The World Scientific Congress of Golf acknowledges financial support from the Royal and Ancient Golf Club of St Andrews and the United States Golf Association. It also receives patronage from the International Council of Sport Science and Physical Education through the World Commission of Sports Biomechanics.

Part One
The Golfer

1 How has biomechanics contributed to the understanding of the golf swing?

C.J. Dillman and G.W. Lange
Steadman-Hawkins Sports Medicine Foundation, Vail, Colorado, USA

Abstract
Research on the biomechanics of the golf swing has been carried out to understand and improve a golfer's performance. A summary of all research applied to the golf swing was provided in an attempt to interpret current scientific knowledge for its practical application. Most investigations have focused on wrist cocking and uncocking, ground reaction forces, and electromyography of the upper body. These studies alone, do not completely describe this most interesting and complex skill. For this reason, it is essential to adopt a more holistic approach to research on the golf swing through three-dimensional modelling of the golfer for determining the kinematics and kinetics of the entire link system.
Keywords: Biomechanics, EMG, Golf, Ground Reaction Forces, Wrist Action.

Introduction

In attempting to understand a complex movement such as the golf swing, scientists must describe the movement, analyze specific components, and then compare groups or equipment. The scientist's goal is to provide evidence that helps the golfer execute a swing to produce maximum distance, accuracy, control, and consistency in each golf shot[13]. It is the translation of a scientists evidence into a golfers performance that is often the most difficult. The purpose of this investigation is to show how biomechanical analysis of kinematics,

Science and Golf II: Proceedings of the World Scientific Congress of Golf. Edited by A.J. Cochran and M.R. Farrally. Published in 1994 by E & FN Spon, London. ISBN 0 419 18790 1

kinetics and muscle activity have contributed to the golfer's understanding of the swing.

The groundwork of golf analysis was established in a descriptive investigation presented by Rehling in 1955[20]. He presented feedback from 13 right-handed elite golfers describing body position, movement and weight shift during the swing. Elite golfers reported that the ball was played off the left heel (front foot) with the hips and shoulders parallel to the flag and the club held in an overlapping grip. Back swing was executed by rotating the hips in a clockwise direction while simultaneously moving the hands, arms, and shoulders. Throughout back swing the chin remained in the same position as address while weight was shifted onto the back foot. The downswing began with initiation from the left hand and weight shift toward the front foot. Through the hitting area, the left arm and clubhead formed a straight line to the ball, with the right arm straight and the shoulders parallel to the line of flight. Beyond impact, weight remains on the front foot while the golfer rotates to face the line of flight[20]. A more detailed description of this general series of motions has become the focus of numerous investigators driven by longer drives and lower handicaps.

Most golf research has generally focused on three major categories. The cocking and uncocking action of the wrists which determines, to a large extent, the final clubhead velocity. The forces at the feet (ground reaction forces) that are responsible for driving the swing. And the muscle activity in the upper body, measured through electromyography (EMG) that controls motion and prevents injury. A detailed description of all research applied to the golf swing will be presented for a better understanding of the current level of knowledge in golf analysis.

Wrist Action

Wrist action during the swing has been analyzed by a number of researchers[4,11,14,15,17,24,26,27]. The cocking and uncocking action of the wrists during downswing is critical to achieving maximum clubhead velocity. The first stage of downswing begins with the wrists, shoulders, arms, hands, and club moving together as a rigid body about a fixed axis of rotation[14]. The golfer must manage the club position by applying a negative torque throughout the first part of the downswing[11, 14, 17, 24]. The negative torque is applied with only gentle physical effort until the club was at approximately 60-70 degrees from the horizontal[27].

The time of downswing is approximately 230 to 250ms, with the transition from cocked to uncocked beginning 75ms after onset of downswing[14]. Therefore, in terms of impact, wrist uncocking occurs 100 to 80ms[17] or 125ms[14] prior to impact. It is also recognized that uncocking too early decreases the ability to produce large clubhead speeds[11,27]. Decrease in clubhead velocity results from not achieving maximum hand velocity prior to uncocking[4,27]. Budney and Bellow[4] argue that the delayed wrist uncocking may not be necessary for a powerful swing, but this is not supported by the other investigators[11,14, 15,26,27].

Once uncocking occurs, the wrists must act as a free hinge. Milburn[14] identified the free hinge system in low handicap golfers by measuring positive acceleration of the distal segment (clubhead) at the expense of negative acceleration of the proximal system. The ability to create the free hinge system allows for angular velocity up to 1690 degrees/s[15] and linear clubhead acceleration of 870 m/s^2 [17]. Neal and Wilson[17] recorded maximum acceleration 40ms prior to impact, and explained deceleration occurring up to impact by the "squaring up" of the clubhead. Williams[26] proposed a device to measure bend in the wrist during the swing called a Q-bend recorder. He proposed that the movement of the left wrist was important in squaring the clubhead for straight hits and effective contact[26].

Ground Reaction Forces

The contribution of wrist action in achieving maximum clubhead velocity and control is the result of a culmination of forces originating at the feet. The interaction between the shoe and the ground has been recognized as the vital link that allows a golfer to perform the body movements during the swing that lead to impact with the ball[28]. Investigations into the ground reaction forces have confirmed the observations of Rehling[20] regarding the shift of weight to the back foot (foot away from the pin) during backswing and a shift of weight forward toward impact[6,7,21,25,28].

An early investigation into the ground reaction forces during the golf swing of a single elite golfer was performed by Carlsoo[6] in 1967. Using two separate force plates, he found that horizontal forces during the back swing were directed toward the tee for the back foot and away from the tee for the front foot. The direction of forces reversed with the onset of downswing, and continued until impact. Similarly, Cooper et al[7] tested five elite golfers using different clubs and found that the forces causing clockwise rotation (back foot pushing backward and front foot forward) were reversed from 70 to 140 ms prior to impact. He also noted that the less lofted the club, the more stable a position the golfer assumed just after impact[7].

Maximum vertical forces greater than body weight have been recorded and attributed to centrifugal force caused by the swinging club[6]. These results were confirmed by several investigators[7,28]. At impact with the driver, the golfer had 75% of body weight on the front foot (foot toward the pin), which switched to almost 50% just after impact, and ended in follow through at 70-80% on the front foot. The weight transfer from front to back foot was also affected by the club used. Maximum force shift from back to front foot occurred after impact in the more lofted irons while it occurred prior to impact when using the driver. Maximum vertical force recorded was 150% of body weight for the driver and 133% for the 3-iron[7]. Williams and Cavanagh[28] reported maximum vertical force for a drive to be 1.6 times body weight. The force on the front foot at impact has been reported to be 100% of body weight[28] or 81 to 95% of body weight[21]. The total vertical force is probably greater than one body weight at the time of impact due to centrifugal force, and prompted Cooper et al[7] to conclude that weight shift is not complete to the left leg at contact, which doesn't support the idea of "hitting from the left side"[7]. Richards et al[21] contributed to the understanding of weight transfer by measuring where the center of vertical force should be placed under each foot for swings with a five iron. They found 44 to 46% of the vertical force was on the heels at the top of back swing and moved to 66% at contact for low handicap golfers and only 49% on the heels for high handicap golfers[21]. The results of these investigations have shed light on the differences between skilled and unskilled golfers.

Most investigators agree that there is some similarity in force production patterns across clubs and skill levels despite obvious differences in the resulting golf shots[21,25,28]. However, there are certain characteristics in a less skilled player that may not be observed in an elite player. Skilled players have been found to place their weight closer to their heels at the moment of contact[21], and to transfer vertical force from the back to front foot at a higher rate[25] and slightly farther forward than a less skilled player[21]. Less body rotation in high handicap golfers also results in a transfer of force to the anterior portion of the front foot[21]. The swing to swing variability of weight transfer pattern for players of differing ability has been observed to be the same despite the obvious differences in their swings[21,25,28]. Williams and Cavanagh[28] explain that performance may not be related to GRF's specifically, but to how these forces are transmitted through the rest of the body.

Electromyography

To understand which muscles are active and when during the golf swing, investigators have used electromyography (EMG). This is important in determining not only which muscles contribute to the swing, but also their potential for injury. The original work on EMG in golf was performed on "good" golfers by Slater-Hammel[23]. He found that the contraction movement coordination of each individual was extremely consistent, but there were wide variations between subjects. Primary activity in acceleration of the golf club was accomplished using the triceps brachii of the right and left arms, right latissimus dorsi, right pectoralis major, and posterior fibers of the left deltoid[23]. These original findings led to more in depth EMG studies of the shoulders, trunk and neck.

A great deal of the electromyographic emphasis in golf has been placed on the shoulder. During the swing, the rotator cuff dominates muscle activity. Within the rotator cuff, the subscapularis has been found to be the most active[9] especially during internal rotation[18]. The infraspinatus and supraspinatus were found to be active throughout the swing[9], but primarily at the extremes of shoulder range of motion[18]. The rotator cuff muscles must fire in synchrony to provide coordinated harmonious movement to protect the glenohumeral complex[9,18]. The latissimus dorsi and pectoralis major provide power bilaterally and show marked activation during acceleration[9,18]. The deltoid was found to be relatively quiet compared to the rotator cuff[9]. The anterior deltoid was found to be active during the forward swing and follow through for both the right and left shoulders[18]. Jobe et al[9] reported that the right deltoid was inactive, while the left deltoid was active preceding ball contact. The middle and posterior deltoids appear relatively non-contributory without any specific patterns. Regarding the deltoids, Pink[18] and Jobe et al[9] agree that because the golf swing doesn't require extremes of strength or range of motion, there is a relatively small contribution from the three deltoids bilaterally. No significant differences have been found for shoulder activity in highly skilled male and female golfers[10].

EMG activity has also been presented for the trunk muscles during the golf swing. Pink, Perry, and Jobe[19] tested the erector spinae and abdominal obliques of highly skilled golfers using surface electrodes. They found that the back swing revealed relatively low muscle activity (20-30% manual muscle test (MMT)) in the abdominal and paraspinal muscles bilaterally. This phase, they suggested, was simply positioning and preparing the body for an effective swing[19]. This is partially disputed by findings of Hosea et al[8] who reported that the left side muscles initiated the takeaway, while the right side abdominals and paraspinals were active from the top of back swing through impact. Pink et al[19] reported the right side erector spinae (75% MMT) and right (62% MMT) and left (54% MMT) abdominal obliques were active during forward swing. During acceleration, the left erector spinae was active (50% MMT) while the right side (64% MMT) abdominal obliques increased and the left side (42% MMT) decreased. Pink et al[19] characterized the downswing to a "forward fall" of which the precise arc of rotation and speed of motion was monitored and controlled, at least in part, by the right erector spinae and bilateral abdominal oblique muscles.

In the investigation by Hosea et al[8], amateurs were compared with professionals in terms of amount of EMG activity and biomechanical loads. They reported much higher EMG activity as a percentage of a maximum voluntary contraction (MVC) in the amateurs with less variability in the professionals. They also calculated peak shear, bending, torque, and compression in the lumbar spine corresponding to the EMG activity. Peak shear load was found to be much greater in the amateurs (81% greater), as was peak bending load (81% greater) and peak torque (50% greater). Only the peak compression load was greatest in the professionals. Peak shear, lateral bending, and torsional forces occurred during the forward swing and acceleration[8].

The temporal proportionality of EMG activation for the expert and novice golfers for shots of select distances with select clubs was explored by Abernathy, Neal, and Parker[1]. They concluded that relative timing is a variable feature of control at the electromyographic level. They also reported that low handicap golfers were remarkably consistent from trial to trial, as opposed to novices, especially when they were required to hit sub maximal, "touch shots" to a target[1].

EMG during the golf swing has also been used in an attempt to identify anxiety during the golf shot in low and high handicap players[2]. The investigators combined EMG activity from the flexor carpi radialis of each wrist, the left upper trapezius and total swing times. No significant differences were found between high and low handicap golfers, but more swing to swing variability was found in the high handicap golfers in the upper trapezius and swing times. They concluded that there was a relationship between variability in muscle activity, swing time and skill level.

Extraneous Golf Research

From a complex task such as the golf swing, there are multiple levels to conduct an analysis. A common concept in golf is that of the hub. This is generally considered the center of rotation of the swing. From a study by Saunders and Owens[22] comparing expert versus novice golfers, the authors demonstrated that novice players did not move backward or forward during the shot to the same extent as elite players. The greater range of lateral movement during the swing of elite players suggests that imagining the swing as a rotation about a fixed point may not be an appropriate practice, as this may inhibit the natural lateral movement associated with elite performance[22].

The actions involved in the golf swing make little difference without proper timing. Lampsa[12] modeled a golf swing to look at the effect of arm length, arm mass, club length, club angle and torso mass in order to maximize the distance of the drive. Only small increases in distance resulted from manipulation of these parameters. The author advised, for longer drives from the tee, the golfer should swing the club more optimally[12]. Neal, Abernathy, Moran, and Parker[16] attempted to identify timing patterns and strategies of kinematic components of the golf swing by manipulating club and target distance across skill levels. The authors found that "...the times spent in various phases of the golf swing are not kept in proportion, as the movement is scaled and modified to meet changing task demands". They concluded that no evidence was found to support the use of a simple linear scaling method of varying the total time for the golf swing[16].

The grip pressure of a golfer is important for proper club control and wrist action. Budney[3] measured grip pressure under the last three fingers of the left hand, the base of the first three fingers of the right hand and the left thumb. He found that during the downswing the left thumb and right hand apply an impulsive force to the club, reaching peak 50 or 60 milliseconds prior to impact. The last three fingers of the left hand were important to withstand centrifugal force[3] and, as stated earlier, to align the clubhead for effective contact with the ball[26].

Modifications to the clubs to create a matched set has also been explored. Budney and Bellow[5] reported on the effect club length, mass and mass distribution had on the golf swing. They found no relation between exertion and changes in mass distribution from club to club. It was also reported that the maximum driving force remained relatively the same for a specific golfer using a variety of golf clubs[5].

Conclusions

The ultimate goal for a golfer is to achieve proper speed, accuracy and consistency by bringing a large number of segments into action in the correct sequence[14]. The difficulty with research on such a complex task is that "the control of any given swing requires the brain to simultaneously control an extremely large number of independently active motor units and this, in theory at least, places an extremely high computational workload on the motor cortex". The problem is how so many degrees of freedom are controlled and how information pertaining to this control is stored to provide a basis for ongoing learning. The problem is compounded when one considers the total range of shots the expert golfer has apparent mastery over[16].

From the presented research on golf a few basic concepts are most notable. During the downswing, it is important to maintain a wrist cocked position in order to develop adequate clubhead speed. Weight transfer from the back to the front foot during the swing should remain closer to the heels at contact. The "hub" of highly skilled golfers moves laterally more than less skilled golfers. Finally, from the available research, EMG activity[1], swing times[2,16], hub movement[22], and weight transfer patterns[21] all exhibit less variability between swings for highly skilled golfers. These findings are only minimally applicable to correct understanding of the entire golf swing.

The research that is most essential to understanding the swing must take a more holistic approach. Before this can be accomplished a number of concepts must be explored. First, an accurate understanding of hip and shoulder rotation must be reported. From this, the transfer of forces between the hips and shoulders and their relative actions must be presented. This relationship, combined with the current knowledge of ground reaction forces would help to explain the segmental coordination of the legs, hips and torso. In order to gain a better understanding of the swing and make it applicable to the average golfer, all aspects of the swing should be summarized simultaneously. Without accurate measurement of all segments and their coordination, it is impossible to define what is correct or incorrect about a swing. This type of research would involve ground reaction force measurements combined with three- dimensional kinematics to measure segmental rotation and energy transfer, as well as temporal components for each segment during each phase of the swing. In order for a laboratory to accomplish this goal, force plates, multiple high speed (500 Hz or greater) cameras, and a large hitting area must be available. Complete analysis would provide a more understandable representation of the swing. Williams and Cavanagh[28] explained that performance may not be related to GRF's specifically, but how these forces are transmitted through the rest of the body. This implies that incorrect action of one segment may be accommodated for in various other segments making it important to look at each individual specifically. Individual characteristics may then be evaluated to determine productive or counter-productive actions and improve performance. A complete understanding of the golf swing can only be obtained if future research is directed in the following areas:

1)   Development of a three-dimensional biomechanical model of the golfer

2)   Utilization of this model in experimental studies to determine the kinematics and kinetics of its link system for various levels of golfers

3)   Employment of the model in computer simulation studies to determine the contributions of various elements to the overall swing in golf.

References

1. Abernethy, B, Neal, RJ, Moran, MJ, Parker, AW. Expert-Novice differences in muscle activity during the golf swing. In A.J. Cochran (ED.), **Science and Golf: Proceedings of the First World Scientific Congress of Golf,** University of St Andrews, Scotland. London: E&FN Spon. 25-29, 1990
2. Barclay, JK, WE McIlroy. Effect of skill level on muscle activity in the neck and forearm muscles during golf swing. In A.J. Cochran (ED.), **Science and Golf: Proceedings of the First World Scientific Congress of Golf,** University of St Andrews, Scotland. London: E&FN Spon. 49-53, 1990
3. Budney, D R, Measuring grip pressure during the golf swing. **Res. Q, 50:**272-277, 1979
4. Budney, D R and D G Bellow. Kinetic analysis of a golf swing. **Res. Q, 50(2):**171-179, 1979
5. Budney, D R and D G Bellow. On the swing mechanics of a matched set of golf clubs. **Res. Q, 53(3):**185-192, 1982
6. Carlsoo, S, A kinetic analysis of the golf swing. **J. Sport Med. Phys. Fit.,** 7:80-81, 1967
7. Cooper, J M, BT Bates, J Bedi, and J Scheuchenzuber. Kinematic and kinetic analysis of the golf swing, In **Biomechanics IV: Proceddings of the Fourth International Seminar on Biomechanics,** ed R.C. Nelson and C.A. Morehouse, Baltimore: University Park Press, 289-305, 1974
8. Hosea, TM, CJ Gatt, KM Galli, NA Langrana, JP Zawadsky. Biomechanical analysis of the golfer's back. In A.J. Cochran (ED.), **Science and Golf: Proceedings of the First World Scientific Congress of Golf,** University of St Andrews, Scotland. London: E&FN Spon. 43-48, 1990
9. Jobe, FW, DR Moynes, DJ Antonelli. Rotator cuff function during a golf swing, **Am J Sports Med,** (14(5):388-392
10. Jobe, FW, J Perry, M Pink. Electromyographic shoulder activity in men and women professional golfers, **Am J Sports Med,** 17(6): 782-787
11. Jorgensen, T. On the dynamics of the swing of a golf club, **Am J Physics,** 38(5): 644-651, 1970
12. Lampsa, M A. Maximising distance of the golf drive: an optimal control study. **J Dynamic Systems, Meas. Control, Trans. ASME 97 (Series G),** December: 362-367, 1975
13. Maddalozzo, JGF. An anatomical and biomechanical analysis of the full golf swing. **Natl. Strength & Cond. Assoc. J.,** 9(4):6-8, 1987
14. Milburn, P D. Summation of segmental velocities in the golf swing,**Med Sci Sports Exerc.,** 14:60-64, 1982
15. Nagao, N, and Y Sawada. A kinematic analysis of the golf swing by means of fast motion picture in connection with wrist action. **J. Sports Med. Phys. Fit.,** 17:413-419, 1977

16. Neal, R J, B,Abernethy, MJ Moran, A W Parker. The influence of club length and shot distance on the temporal characteristics of the swings of expert and novice golfers. In A.J. Cochran (ED.), **Science and Golf: Proceedings of the First World Scientific Congress of Golf,** University of St Andrews, Scotland. London: E&FN Spon. 36-42, 1990

17. Neal, RJ, BD Wilson. 3D kinematics and kinetics of the golf swing. **Int. J. Sport Biomech.** 1(3):221-232, 1985

18. Pink, M, FW Jobe, J Perry. Electromyographic analysis of the shoulder during the golf swing **Int. J. Sport. Biomechn.** 1(3):221-232, 1985

19. Pink, M, J Perry, FW Jobe. Electromyographic analysis of the trunk in golfers, **Am J Sports Med,** 21(3):385-388

20. Rehling, C H. Analysis of techniques of the golf drive. **Res. Q, 26:**80-81. 1955

21. Richards, J, M Farrell, J Kent and R Kraft. Weight transfer patterns during the golf swing. **Res Q, 56(4):**361-365, 1985

22. Sanders, R H and P C Owens. Hub movement during the swing of elite and novice golfers. **Int. J. Sport Biomech.** 8:320-330, 1992

23. Slater-Hammel, A T. Action current study of contraction movement relationships in the golf stroke. **Res. Q, 19:**164-177, 1948

24. Vaughan, C L. A three dimensional analysis of the forces and torques applied by a golfer during the downswing. In **A. Morecki, K. Fidelus, K. Kedzior, and A. Wit (Eds.) Biomechanics VII-B,** University Park Press, Baltimore, 325-331, 1981

25. Wallace, E S, D Graham, E W Bleakley. Foot-to-ground pressure patterns during the golf drive: a case study involving a low handicap player and a high handicap player. In A.J. Cochran (ED.), **Science and Golf: Proceedings of the First World Scientific Congress of Golf,** University of St Andrews, Scotland. London: E&FN Spon. 25-29, 1990

26. Williams, A J, Jr. An obscure influence in the golf shot, **J. Dynamic Systems, Measurement and Control, Trans. ASME, Series G, (94),** December: 289-295, 1972

27. Williams, D. The dynamics of the golf swing, **Q.J. Mech. Appl. Math.,** 20:247-255, 1983

28. Williams, KR and PR Cavanagh. The mechanics of foot action during the golf swing and implications for shoe design. **Med. Sci. Sports Exerc.** 15(3):247-255, 1983

2 Usefulness of partial swings in the rehabilitation of a golfer

L.J. Lemak, G.S. Fleisig
American Sports Medicine Institute, Birmingham AL, USA
C.M. Welch
Orthopaedic Research Laboratory, West Palm Beach FL, USA
B. Marting
St. Joseph's Hospital, Pinehurst NC, USA
and J.E. Zvijac
Doctor's Hospital, Coral Gables FL, USA

Abstract
Before an injured golfer is ready to return to sport, he or she may
incorporate partial swings into his or her rehabilitation. No
scientific study has been conducted on partial swings previously; thus
the objective of this study was to quantify and compare the mechanics
of full and partial swings. The mechanics of 8 LPGA golfers were
digitized using a 3-dimensional motion analysis system. Results for the
full swing were similar to previously published 2-dimensional data. In
comparison to the full swing, the half swing showed a 2% to 31%
reduction in upper extremity range of motion and a 12% to 37% reduction
in acceleration. An understanding of full swing and partial swing
mechanics can lead to more efficacious rehabilitation programs.
Keywords: Golf Swing, Rehabilitation, Biomechanics

Introduction

During a golf swing, the upper extremities are required to go through
a large range of motion and achieve high velocities (Milburn, 1982).
In order to accomplish these tasks, large loads (i.e. forces and
torques) are applied at the elbow and shoulder joints. After injury to
an upper extremity, a golfer must rehabilitate in a logical progression
in order to return to previous level of activity. Typically, the
injured athlete's physician or therapist is concerned with the patient's
progress in reacquiring proper joint range of motion and strength.
Rehabilitation, usually progresses from basic one-joint exercises (e.g.
shoulder internal/external rotation exercises, forearm curls) to more
functional, multi-joint exercises (e.g. "partial" golf swings).
   In order to design partial golf swings into a rehabilitation program,
one must first understand the biomechanics of such activity. The
purpose of this study was to compare the biomechanics of partial golf
swings to full golf swings. When a golfer is asked to perform a "half
golf swing" during rehabilitation, does he or she reduce range of
motion, load exerted, or both? To help answer this question, elbow and
shoulder statics (range of motion) and dynamics (velocity, acceleration)
were quantified.

Methods

Eight right-handed members of the Ladies Professional Golf Association
(LPGA) were tested. All subjects were healthy and active at the time
of testing. The mean age was 29 yrs ± 5 yrs, the mean height was 1.70
m ± 0.03 m, and the mean mass was 63 kg ± 8 kg.
   During testing, each subject wore tight shorts, a sleeveless tank top
shirt, and golf spikes, with reflective markers placed on bony
landmarks. Markers were attached to the tip of the acromion, lateral

Science and Golf II: Proceedings of the World Scientific Congress of Golf. Edited by A.J.
Cochran and M.R. Farrally. Published in 1994 by E & FN Spon, London. ISBN 0 419 18790 1

humeral epicondyle, greater trochanter, lateral femoral epicondyle, lateral malleolus, and first metacarpophalangeal joint on each side of the body. Reflective tape was placed on each shoe near the distal end of the mid-toe. Markers were also attached about the top of each golf shaft, the bottom of the shaft, and on the mid-forehead region of a cap worn by each golfer. The golf ball used during data collection was covered with reflective tape in order that the ball itself could serve as a reflective marker.

After as many warm-up swings as desired, each golfer was analyzed during eighteen swings: six with her driver, six with her five-iron, and six with her pitching wedge. For the six swings with each club, the golfer took two swings of each "swing type": full-swing, 3/4-swing, and half-swing. Specific instruction on what a "3/4-swing" or "half-swing" meant was not provided to any golfer, so that she could make her own interpretation. The order of club and swing type were randomized to eliminate any data dependence on trial order.

A motion analysis system was used to determine the three dimensional locations of the markers. Four CCD cameras transmitted 200 images per second of information to a video processor. These images were digitized using Expert Vision 3D software (Motion Analysis Corporation). Testing of the system showed that computed three-dimensional locations of reflective balls had an average accuracy of 1.1 cm.

A computer program was written to calculate kinematics (i.e. angular displacements, velocities, and accelerations) for the club and upper body. Kinetic loads (i.e. forces and torques) could not be calculated since the dynamic equations were indeterminable. Specifically, forces and torques applied to the golf club could be calculated, but the portion applied by each hand - and therefore each arm - could not (Vaughan, 1982).

Figure 1 shows the angles that were calculated. For each arm the angle between the distal direction of the upper arm (as determined from the shoulder marker to the elbow marker) and the inferior direction of the spine (as the vector from the mid-point of the two shoulder markers to the mid-point of the two hip markers) was defined as "abduction." "Horizontal adduction/abduction" was defined as the angle between the distal direction of the arm and a vector between the two shoulder markers in a plane perpendicular to the spine. Notice that if for instance the arm was flexed 45°, the program would report 45° of abduction and 90° of horizontal adduction. Elbow flexion was calculated as the angle between the distal direction of the forearm (from elbow marker to the hand marker) and the distal direction of the upper arm. Rotation of the shoulders was calculated as the angle formed by a vector between the two shoulders and the direction of the target (from tee to hole) in the plane perpendicular to the spine. Club rotation was calculated as the angle between the distal vector of the club (from top of club shaft to bottom of club shaft) and the direction to the target.

The backswing phase was defined as the time from initial club motion until maximum club rotation. Downswing was the time from maximum club rotation until ball impact. Total swing was defined as the time from initiation of backswing until ball impact. The follow-through phase was defined as the portion of the swing after ball impact.

Angular velocity was calculated for rotation of the shoulders and for club rotation as the derivative of angular displacement. Angular acceleration for shoulder and elbow motion were calculated as the second derivative of angular displacement.

Descriptive statistics were calculated and all tests were accomplished using the general linear model (GLM) procedure from the SAS statistical analysis system, which took into account the design of the study. This procedure performed multiple linear regression and analysis of variance to identify the significant variables associated with swing type and club type. Duncan's multiple range procedure was used for pairwise comparisons.

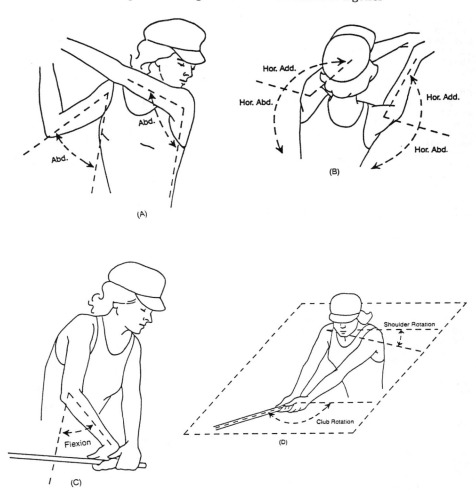

Results

Significant differences (P < 0.05) between all three swing types are shown in Table 1. For each swing type, means and standard deviations for all subjects and clubs are presented. Mean values for half-swings are also expressed as percentages of full-swing mean values. No statistically significant interaction was found between swing type and club.

Displacement, velocity, and acceleration driver data were similar to 2-D data reported by Milburn (1982). The backswing was significantly quicker for a half-swing than for a 3/4 or full-swing. At the peak of the backswing, horizontal adduction of the left arm decreased by 3 degrees from full-swing to half-swing, while all other shoulder and elbow range of motion parameters showed approximately 10 degrees of

Table 1. Significant differences between all three swing types

Variable	Full-swing Mean ± S.D.	3/4-swing Mean ± S.D.	Half-swing Mean ± S.D.	Half-swing % Full-swing	Significant Differences
Swing phases					
Backswing (sec)	0.99 ± 0.27	0.97 ± 0.26	0.92 ± 0.23	93	a,b
Total swing (sec)	1.29 ± 0.28	1.28 ± 0.26	1.22 ± 0.23	95	a,b
Backswing range of motion					
Maximum rotation of club (deg)	366 ± 11	349 ± 16	323 ± 34	88	a,b,c
Maximum rotation of shoulders (deg)	105 ± 10	98 ± 12	90 ± 13	86	a,b,c
Maximum abduction of right arm (deg)	39 ± 14	33 ± 13	27 ± 14	69	a,b,c
Maximum abduction of left arm (deg)	79 ± 14	75 ± 12	68 ± 17	86	a,b,c
Maximum horizontal abduction of right arm (deg)	51 ± 19	51 ± 19	42 ± 37	82	a,b
Maximum horizontal adduction of left arm (deg)	133 ± 5	131 ± 5	130 ± 8	98	b
Maximum flexion of right elbow (deg)	118 ± 8	115 ± 9	107 ± 13	91	a,b,c
Maximum flexion of left elbow (deg)	50 ± 13	45 ± 11	41 ± 6	82	a,b,c
Downswing angular velocity					
Maximum velocity of shoulders (deg/sec)	690 ± 60	660 ± 60	610 ± 56	88	a,b,c
Maximum club velocity (deg/sec)	2230 ± 220	2130 ± 170	1920 ± 250	86	a,b,c
Follow-through angular acceleration					
Maximum acceleration of left arm horizontal abduction (deg/sec²)	18,000 ± 13,000	17,000 ± 14,000	13,000 ± 13,000	72	a,b
Maximum deceleration of right elbow extension (deg/sec²)	17,000 ± 5,000	16,000 ± 5,000	15,000 ± 6,000	88	b
Maximum acceleration of flexion for left elbow (deg/sec²)	8,000 ± 2,000	7,000 ± 4,000	5,000 ± 2,000	63	a,b,c

a) Significant differences ($p < 0.05$) between half-swings and 3/4-swings
b) Significant differences ($p < 0.05$) between half-swings and full-swings
c) Significant differences ($P < 0.05$) between 3/4 swings and full-swings

decrease (Figure 2). Backswing rotation and downswing velocity of both the club and the shoulders were largest with the full-swing and smallest with the half-swing. Immediately after impact, maximum acceleration of left arm horizontal abduction and maximum deceleration of right elbow extension were achieved (Figure 3a). As the club was lifted during follow-through maximum acceleration of left elbow flexion was reached (Figure 3b). Accelerations and decelerations were largest during full-swings and smallest during half-swings.

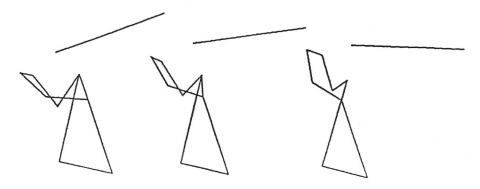

Figure 2. Digitized stick figure at peak of backswing for: (a) a half-swing; (b) a 3/4-swing; (c) a full-swing.

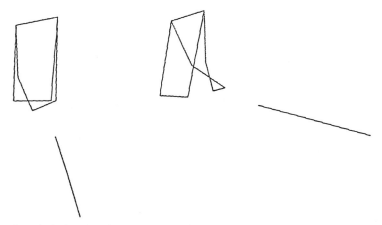

Figure 3. Digitized stick figure during follow-through for: (a) maximum acceleration of left arm horizontal abduction and deceleration of right elbow extension; and (b) maximum acceleration of left elbow flexion.

Discussion

In order to incorporate partial golf swings into a golf rehabilitation program, the relationship between reduction in range of motion and reduction in internal loads needs to be explored. As mentioned above, however, forces and torques could not be calculated with the current biomechanical model. Angular acceleration was felt to be an indicator of muscle torque since, according to Newton's Second Law of Motion, torque is the product of angular acceleration and moment of inertia. In comparing different swings, percent change in muscle torque is equal to percent change in angular acceleration if moment of inertia is the same for the different swings. This requires that there is no dependence on type of swing for: (1) the mass and mass distribution within the club and arms; (2) the distribution in load exerted by the two hands; and (3) the motion of the arms and club. The first assumption is easily acceptable. The assumption of consistent loading of the hands is unknown, but seems reasonable. The third assumption is, perhaps, the most difficult to accept since Table 1 showed that there were differences present.

Table 1 shows that acceleration of the left arm's horizontal abduction after impact decreased by 28% for the half-swing and deceleration of right elbow extension decreased by 12%. In general, 12% to 37% reductions were seen for acceleration parameters and 2% to 31% reductions were seen for range of motion parameters (Table 1). Standard deviation for maximum club rotation was noticeably larger for half-swings than for other swings, implying variability in interpretation by the subjects as to how far the club should be rotated back.

Another important factor is timing. Although backswing time was greatest for a full-swing and shortest for a half-swing, no difference between downswing times was observed (Table 1). This allows a golfer who incorporates partial swings in rehabilitation to practice proper downswing timing without using full range of motion and full acceleration.

Conclusions

A partial swing is an attractive rehabilitation modality for an injured golfer, as it is functionally similar to the activity desired (i.e. full-swing), but the range of motion and acceleration are slightly reduced. Using the data shown in this study, a partial swing can even be custom-designed into a rehabilitation program for a specific golf injury. For instance, if the right elbow of a golfer is being rehabilitated and has difficulty in achieving full flexion, progression from a half-swing to a full-swing may help in regaining motion. Or, for example, if a horizontal abductor muscle of the left shoulder (e.g. latissimus dorsi, posterior deltoid, rotator cuff) has been injured, a half-swing will enable the golfer to rehabilitate full horizontal adduction motion, without the need for full horizontal abduction dynamics (i.e. acceleration).

In this study, no guidance was given for achieving a partial swing in order to measure an athlete's natural interpretation. The data showed that attempts to perform a "half-swing" varied greatly, usually resulting in approximately "eight-tenths" of a full-swing. Clearer definitions and supervision could reduce variability and improve the usefulness of partial swings.

In conclusion this initial study has shown potential usefulness of partial swings for rehabilitation, however further work is needed. The effects of ability and gender should be investigated. Furthermore, determination of loads applied by each hand - such as data from Budney and Bellow (1990) - may enable joint forces and torques applied by each arm to be calculated.

References

Budney D.R., Bellow D.G., (1990) Evaluation of golf club control by grip pressure measurement, in **Science and Golf** (ed. A.J. Cochran), E & F.N. Spon, New York, pp. 30-42.

Milburn P.D. (1982) Summation of segmental velocities in the golf swing. **Medicine and Science in Sports and Exercise**, 14, 60-64.

Vaughan C.L. (1982) A three-dimensional analysis of the forces and torques applied by a golfer during the downswing, in **Biomechanics VII-B** (eds A. Morecki, K. Fidelus, K. Kedzior, and A. Wit), University Park Press, Baltimore, pp. 325-331.

3 Back pain in novice golfers, a one-year follow-up

G.A. Van Der Steenhoven, A. Burdorf and E.G.M. Tromp-Klaren
State University of Leiden, Leiden; Erasmus University, Rotterdam,
The Netherlands

Abstract
A one-year follow-up study on back pain was conducted among 196 men
taking up golf. The self-reported lifetime cumulative incidence of back
pain was 63%, 28% reported back pain in the month prior to answering
the questionnaire, and 13% reported current back pain. One year later,
a second survey was carried out. The incidence of first time back pain
during the 12 months follow-up was 8%, and the recurrence rate of back
pain was about 45%. Severe back pain in the past was a strong predictor
for recurrence of back pain among the novice golfers. Sportsmen were
also at risk for recurrence of back pain. Most likely, taking up golf
may aggravate pre-existing back pain because in golf, as in many other
sports, particular strenuous movements may induce spells of back pain.
Keywords: Novice Golfers, Back Pain, Incidence, Recurrence

1 Introduction

Golf is a fast growing sport in The Netherlands. The Dutch Golf
Federation (NGF) had 70,000 full members in 1992, and another 20,000
members are expected to join until the year 2000. The NGF recently
estimated that, at the moment, some 20,000 non-members are playing
golf. Since the number of new golf clubs is insufficient to accommodate
these people, it is predicted that non-membership will also grow
dramatically.

Golf is especially popular among men around the age of 40 with, at
least, a higher education. In the popular press it has been repeatedly
suggested that taking up golf may cause back disorders and that persons
without physically demanding jobs, such as managers and office clerks,
are particularly at risk.

In 1989, just after a new driving range was opened in a nearby
village, several men who had taken up golf as a sport sought medical
care for their low-back pain in a general practice and a practice for
Cesar remedial exercise training in Oegstgeest, The Netherlands. The
patients expressed the believe that their back complaints could be
attributed to taking up golf.

Although the body of scientific literature concerning golf injuries
is steadily growing, data supporting the association between the onset
of back pain and playing golf is almost absent. A cross-sectional
survey among amateur golfers showed that the back was the most common
site of injury. The majority of the complaints were attributed to
overpractice and poor swing mechanics (McCarroll et al. 1990). Another
survey among amateur golfers confirmed the occurrence of back injuries
associated with overuse, poor technique and poor physical condition
(Batt, 1992). However, both studies have some shortcomings that hamper
the interpretation of the evidence presented. Since back injuries are
prevalent in day-to-day life an appropriate reference group is needed
to establish whether the occurrence of back injuries may be caused by
playing golf.

Science and Golf II: Proceedings of the World Scientific Congress of Golf. Edited by A.J.
Cochran and M.R. Farrally. Published in 1994 by E & FN Spon, London. ISBN 0 419 18790 1

Preferably, a longitudinal study should be performed to assess the
occurrence of first time back pain among novice golfers without a
history of back complaints. The current study was undertaken with the
aims (i) to study risk factors for the first time occurrence of back
pain among novice golfers, and (ii) to evaluate the influence of taking
up golf on the recurrence of back pain episodes among subjects with a
history of back pain.

2 Subjects and methods

2.1 Subjects
The study population was formed with the aid of forty assistant golf
professionals working at golf clubs and driving ranges all over The
Netherlands. These professionals asked serious beginners to fill out a
questionnaire on back pain. Male novice golfers aged between 20 and 60
years were eligible to enter the population under study. During 1991
the baseline survey was conducted and 221 questionnaires were returned.
  After one year a second questionnaire was sent to each participant
in the baseline survey. Replies were received from 196 subjects,
resulting in a response rate of 89%. A non-response analysis showed
that in the baseline survey the non-responders to the follow-up survey
did not differ from the responders with regard to age, education, sport
activities and back pain history.

2.2 Methods
The questionnaire in the baseline survey consisted of three major
sections. The first section included individual characteristics such as
age, height, weight, education, occupation and basic postures at work.
The second section covered current sport activities including playing
golf. The third section requested information on occurrence and nature
of previous and current back problems and associated (temporary)
disability. The questions were formatted such as: "Have you ever
experienced a spell of back pain?". These questions were derived from a
questionnaire used in a large Dutch community-based study on back
disorders (Valkenburg et al., 1982). This study was also used to
construct an external reference group of males with comparable age and
education. Descriptive information on physical activity was also
available.
  The questionnaire in the follow-up survey focused on experienced
back problems in the past 12 months and frequency and duration of sport
activities during this period. Special emphasis was given to reasons
for quitting golf and for spells of back problems attributed to
specific causes in general life, occupation and sport, such as back
pain experienced while playing golf.

3   Results

Basic characteristics of the 196 novice golfers in the one-year follow-
up study are shown in table 1. The study population predominantly
consisted of middle-aged men with education at college or university
level. Not surprisingly, their occupations involved, for the best part
of the workday, a sedentary posture. Most subjects were actively
engaged in sports such as tennis/squash (35%), jogging (9%) and hockey
(6%). As is shown in table 1, 56 subjects were no longer involved in a
sport due to health problems. Most affected body parts were the lower
limbs including knees and ankles (54%), the back (30%) and the upper
limbs including wrist, elbow and shoulder (7%).

Table 1.   Characteristics of 196 male subjects taking up golf

Individual characteristics		
age (y)	38.8	± 9.9
height (cm)	183.1	± 7.1
weight (kg)	81.6	± 10.4
Educational level		
secondary school or less	71	36%
higher vocational school	75	38%
university education	50	26%
Occupation risk factors		
walking/standing for more than 2 hr/d	52	27%
walking/standing for more than 4 hr/d	25	13%
sitting for more than 2 hr/d	169	86%
sitting for more than 4 hr/d	120	61%
Leisure		
sporting regularly	134	68%
quit a sport due to health problems	56	29%
quit a sport due to back pain	17	9%

Table 2 presents the collected information on natural history and severity of back pain among the novice golfers. The lifetime cumulative incidence of back pain reported was 63%. Over 95% of the back pain was located in the lower back. On average, subjects with previous back pain experienced the first spell at an age of 27.4 (SD 9.5) years. Among the subjects with previous back pain the prevalence of back pain in the past month was 28% and the prevalence of current back pain 13%. Most of the subjects had experienced a spell of back pain more than once. The number of cases with a history of severe back pain was considerable; 27% reported several weeks bed rest due to severe back pain, 28% were absent from work due to their back problems, 6% were operated upon and 3% changed job because of back problems.

Table 2. Previous and current back pain among 196 subjects taking up golf

Lifetime cumulative incidence of back pain	124	63%
back pain more than once	102	(82%)
spell of back pain lasting > 3 months	27	(22%)
bed rest due to back pain	34	(27%)
back operated upon	7	(6%)
sick leave due to back pain	35	(28%)
change of job due to back pain	4	(3%)
Back pain in the past month	55	28%
Current back pain	25	13%

The lifetime cumulative incidence of back pain, back pain in the past month and current back pain, all were nearly constant with age and educational level. Occupational risk factors, such as prolonged standing and sedentary posture, were not associated with any of the health outcomes presented. Sportsmen showed an increased odds ratio of 2.1 (95% CI 1.1 to 4.0) for previous back pain.

Table 3 shows the result of the one-year follow-up of the subjects under study. The incidence of back pain in the past 12 months was estimated to be 8%. The recurrence rate of back pain was about 45%. Of the 62 subjects with back pain during the follow-up period 29 (48%) received medical treatment, predominantly physiotherapy. Forty-nine (79%) reported more than one spell of back pain and the prevalences of back pain in the past month and current back pain were similar to those in the baseline survey. Ten subjects were temporarily disabled and two subjects changed job due to their back pain. Six men attributed their back pain to golf and two actually stopped playing golf for this reason. Another 27 men stopped playing because of lack of leisure time or a preference for other sports.

Table 3. Prevalence of back pain in the 12 months during the follow-up of 196 novice golfers

Subjects without previous back pain	72	
onset of back pain	6	8%
absence of any back pain	66	92%
Subjects with a history of back pain	124	
recurrence of back pain	56	45%
absence of any back pain	68	55%

The number of incident cases was too small to conduct specific statistical analyses. The occurrence of back pain during the follow-up period showed no associations with age, education and occupational risk factors. No influence could be shown of warm-up, frequency of play, number of lessons, and quitting golf. Previous back pain proved to be a strong predictor of back pain during the one-year follow-up with a relative risk of 1.7 (95% CI 1.4 to 2.0).

Table 4 presents the predictors in the past and present for the recurrence of back pain among subjects who had previously experienced back pain.

Table 4. Univariate predictors for the recurrence of back pain in the 12 months after taking up golf among subjects with a history of back pain (N=124)

Predictor	Relative Risk	95% Confidence Interval
Conditions present before baseline survey		
previous back pain more than once	3.71**	1.33-10.32
spell of back pain lasting > 3 months	1.21**	1.00-1.47
sick leave due to back pain	1.27**	1.00-1.61
Conditions present at baseline survey		
current back pain	1.19*	0.99-1.42
back pain in the past month	1.31*	0.95-1.82
Conditions present during follow-up survey		
engaged regularly in other sport(s)	1.65*	0.96-2.81

** $p<0.05$
* $0.05<=p<0.10$

Various characteristics of the nature and occurrence of previous back pain were strong predictors for recurrence of back pain during the follow-up period of 12 months: two or more spells of back pain, at least one spell of back pain lasting more than three months, and sickness absence due to back pain. Complaints of back pain present in the baseline survey were moderate predictors for recurrent back pain. Subjects actively engaged in other sports were at higher risk for recurrent back pain than subjects only playing golf.

4 Discussion

For 12 months this study traced 196 male subjects who took up golf. The baseline survey focused on descriptive characteristics, and determined nature and occurrence of back pain in the past of the subjects under study. Back pain is a subjective phenomenon that is difficult to define. Therefore, the choice was made to apply a questionnaire on back pain that was used in a large Dutch community-based study (Valkenburg et al., 1982). This survey was also used as an external reference group. The same questions on back pain were part of the questionnaire used in the follow-up survey.

The finding of a lifetime cumulative incidence of back pain of 63% among the novice golfers is slightly higher than the rate of 56% found in the external reference group adjusted for age and education. The proportion of sportsmen in this reference group was substantially lower than in the population under study. This may explain why a clear association between sports and back pain was absent in this community based study.

Subjects currently involved in sport showed a higher lifetime incidence of back pain than non-sporting subjects. These sports (tennis/squash, jogging, hockey and others) can therefore be regarded as possible risk factors for back pain. The finding that 17 sportsmen changed sport due to back pain (see table 1) supports this suggestion. The risk of back pain was not influenced by duration of daily sitting and standing/walking at work. This is consistent with studies with comparable designs (Walsh et al. 1989).

In the follow-up survey the one-year incidence rate of first time back pain was 8%, which accords well with results from studies in a general population (Biering-Sorensen 1983, Valkenburg et al. 1982). The small number of incident cases in this study did not allow specific statistical analyses to determine risk factors for the onset of back pain. However, the result that the incidence rate is in accordance with rates expected from community-based studies suggests that golf is not a strong risk factor for the onset of first time back pain.

The one-year recurrence rate of back pain was 45%. Not surprisingly, the risk of occurrence of back pain during the one-year follow-up strongly depended on back pain experienced previously. The high significance of previous back complaints as a predictor of future symptoms has been demonstrated in several longitudinal studies (Biering-Sorensen 1983). Moreover, table 4 shows that the recurrence of back pain is strongly influenced by the frequency and nature of back pain. The more frequently and severely a subject experienced back pain in the past the more liable he will be to experience back pain in the year to come. Hence, subjects with pre-existing back pathology are at risk for future back problems. Age, education and occupational risk factors did not influence the risk of recurrence of back pain. Only sport was found to predict recurrence. This indicates that sport is a strenuous activity causing mechanical load on the back.

5 Conclusions

Since any association with duration and frequency of playing golf was absent, the results indicate that golf is probably not a strong independent risk factor for back pain. Most likely, taking up golf may aggravate pre-existing back pain because particular strenuous movements may occur when playing or practising golf (Hosea et al. 1990, Pink et al. 1993).

A warm-up did not prevent the recurrence of back pain in this study. This finding is difficult to interpret since by the nature of this study it was not possible to evaluate whether the warm-up was appropriate with regard to the particular muscular load on the back when playing golf.

The questionnaire used in the follow-up study did not distinguish between back pain of acute origin and back pain of more chronic nature. Hence, it is impossible to attribute the onset or recurrence of spells of back pain to specific causes such as particular movements during playing golf. When taking up golf, persons with a history of severe back pain are particularly at risk for recurrence of back pain.

6 References

Batt, M.E. (1992) A survey of golf injuries in amateur golfers. **Br. J. Sp. Med.** 26, 63-65.

Batt, M.E. (1993) Golfing injuries An overview. **Sp. Med.** 16, 64-71.

Biering-Sorensen, F. (1983) A prospective study of low back pain in a general population 1. Occurrence, recurrence and aetiology. **Scand. J. Rehab. Med.** 15, 71-79.

Hosea, T.M., Gatt, C.J., Galli, K.M., Langrana, N.A. and Zawadsky, J.P. (1990) Biomechanical analysis of the golfer's back, in **Science and Golf** (ed A.J. Cochran), E.& F.N. Spon/Chapman and Hall, London, pp 43-48.

McCarroll, J.R., Rettig, A.C. and Shelbourne, K.D. (1990) Injuries in the amateur golfer. **Phys. Sp. Med.** 18, 122-126.

Pink, M., Perry, J. and Jobe, W. (1993) Electromyographic analysis of the trunk in golfers. **Am. J. Sp. Med.**, 21,3, 385-388.

Valkenburg, H.A. and Haanen, H.C.M. (1982) The epidemiology of low back pain, in **Proceedings Symposium on Idiopathic Low Back Pain** (eds A.A. White III and S.L. Gordon), C.V. Mosby Company, St Louis, 1982, pp. 9-22.

Walsh, K., Varnes, N., Osmond, C., Styles, R. and Coggon, D. (1989) Occupational causes of low-back pain. **Scand. J. Work Environ. Health** 15, 54-59.

4 Discrete pressure profiles of the feet and weight transfer patterns during the golf swing

E.S. Wallace
University of Ulster, Jordanstown, Northern Ireland
P.N. Grimshaw
West London Institute, College of Brunel University, London, England
and R.L. Ashford
Belfast Institute of Further and Higher Education, Belfast, Northern Ireland

Abstract
Discrete foot pressures and movements of the body and club during the golf swing were studied using piezoelectric transducers and three-dimensional video techniques, with special consideration given to the load-bearing roles of the feet. Pressures at eleven specific foot locations were obtained for six male right-handed subjects as they played shots outdoors from a tee-box area with a driver club under two shoe type conditions: spiked soles and rubber moulded soles. Significant inter-subject variation existed in the onset times for both unloading and loading at specific foot locations, which along with peak pressure magnitude differences indicated different foot mechanics during the swing. However, there were some common findings across subjects. For all trials, the pressure at the left mid-heel location started to increase approximately midway through the backswing, with a subsequent modest increase sustained until some time after the top of the backswing. At this point in time a very rapid increase in pressure was initiated which culminated in a peak value before rapidly decreasing again. The modest increase indicated the first movement of the left foot in preparation for the downswing, while the rapid pressure changes represented the combined result of gravitational and body inertial effects. The longest drives yielded the highest peak pressures, which were found at the first metatarsal heads and occurred before the time of ball impact.In addition, the highest peak pressures were associated with the spiked shoe condition.
Keywords: Golf, Biomechanics, Foot Pressures.

1 Introduction

The golf swing can be broken down into four basic parts: address, backswing, downswing, and follow-through. One of the most widely researched aspects of the golf swing is the downswing, yet there continues to be much debate on the body movements responsible for its initiation. This focus of

Science and Golf II: Proceedings of the World Scientific Congress of Golf. Edited by A.J. Cochran and M.R. Farrally. Published in 1994 by E & FN Spon, London. ISBN 0 419 18790 1

attention on the downswing may be justified, since it is during this phase of the swing that the physical power of the body, or the potential energy developed from the preparation, is converted into the kinetic energy of the clubhead at impact.

Early work by King (1962) using observational analysis led to the conclusion that the downswing was initiated by the hands with the hips and lower limbs responding by moving sideways into the shot. However, Carlsoo (1967), using force plates, electromyography, and cinematographic analysis, clearly identified a turning force through the left foot before the backswing was completed. This led to the theory that the downswing in a right-handed golfer was in fact initiated in the left foot. Cooper et al. in 1974 quantified peak vertical forces and their distributions across the feet during the swing, and also provided data on rotational moments. Williams and Cavanagh (1983) suggested shoe design modifications based on their findings obtained from ground reaction force, centre of pressure and cinematographic analysis.

A major drawback of the research to date has been the application of laboratory-based findings to the actual game of golf. The artificial operating environment of the indoor golf station may affect the performance of the golfer, and the outcome of a shot is not known. The present study was conducted outdoors to overcome some of these limitations. Movements and pressures that occurred at the feet during the golf swing were examined to account for the initiation of the downswing, and to provide an insight into loading characteristics around the time of impact.

2 Methods

Six right-handed male golfers were used as subjects with club handicaps in the range of five to ten. Informed consent of the subjects was obtained in accordance with the policy statement of the American College of Sports Medicine. Each subject used his own driver, and wore two types of golf shoe: flat lasted utilising metal spikes (S), and spikeless utilising rubber moulded soles (M). Pre-fitted customised regenerated leather insoles each containing eight piezo -electric film transducers (10mmx10mm) were worn inside each shoe. The positioning of the transducers was previously determined by a podiatrist to coincide with the following plantar aspects (FL) of each foot: mid-heel (H), styloid process (A), the five metatarsal heads (1-5), and the interphalangeal joint of the first toe (T). The prefixes R and L for each of these positions are used throughout the text to indicate right and left foot locations respectively.

Ten golf shots were performed by each golfer for each shoe type after an appropriate warm-up period. The shots were made outdoors on a prepared tee-box area of turf which was

moist but firm. The result of each shot was assessed in
terms of ball trajectory and approximate landing distance was
noted. Foot pressures were obtained from the transducers by
means of the "Gaitscan" foot pressure measurement system
(Nevill and Pepper 1991) operating at 4000 Hz for a period of
10s incorporating the golf shot. Pressure data along with
input from a photo-electric beam triggered by ball movement
at impact were collected on-line by an IBM PC, and
subsequently analysed using Gaitscan analysis software.
      Three-dimensional video techniques were used to record
body movements and clubhead position using two JVC GYX1 gen-
locked cameras. A light bulb triggered by the photocell was
clearly observed in both camera views and was used to provide
event synchronisation, thus enabling the time of commencement
of the downswing using time code insertion to be accurately
determined (to 0.02s) from the time of ball contact.
Calibration of the filming volume was previously achieved by
the use of a Peak Performance 24-point calibration frame
incorporating 16 calibration points and 8 test points. Video
digitisation was performed using an XYZ Video Board and
coordinate digitisation using the Kine Analysis software
package for the Acorn Archimedes computer (Bartlett, 1990).
      Data reduction was subsequently carried out to yield
temporal and kinetic data for the single best shot, based on
shot outcome and data quality, from each set of trials for
the two test conditions for each subject. Temporal data were
comprised of the times for the commencement of the downswing
and the moment of ball impact, and were related to the
measured discrete foot pressures. The pressure conventions
used in this paper are described in terms of the force per
unit area (kPa) acting at the specific foot locations.
      Visual inspection of the pressure/time graphs yielded two
types of pressure changes during the swing. The first was a
gradually changing and generally irregular trace which
represented the application of pressure by the foot on the
shoe, and/or some weight-bearing role. Thus, for example, it
was possible to observe an increase in the mid-heel pressure
of the left foot while this part of the foot was off the
ground, which would result in its movement towards the
ground. The second pressure profile was more regular and
clearly observable with an obvious onset, followed by a rapid
increase, a peak value, a rapid decrease and an offset. This
pressure/time profile is referred to as load acceptance and
represents the combined effects of gravity acting on the body
and the inertial effects of the body plus club. Thus, higher
peak pressures were associated with greater weight-bearing
roles and the production of greater body forces.

3 Results

Overall, clear similarities were observed for each subject
across the two shoe conditions, but with a few notable

exceptions little inter-subject consistency was displayed.
During the swing the right heel (RH), right arch (RA), and
the fourth and fifth metatarsal heads (R4 and R5)
demonstrated an unloading from some maximal value for most
subjects with no subsequent increase in pressure observed
throughout the remainder of the swing (Table 1). In
contrast, the right and left foot locations shown at Table 2
each showed a marked increase in pressure from some minimal
value resulting in a clearly defined peak (Tables 3 and 4),
which was instantly followed by a rapid decline.

Closer inspection of Table 1 reveals the initiation of
unloading for these foot positions occurred before the top of
the backswing for the shots of subjects 1,3 and 6.
Interestingly, these were the longest and straightest drives.
Subject 2 displayed a peculiar pattern, in that after demonstrating the common initiation of unloading before the top of
the backswing, he uniquely proceeded to load the right foot
again approximately 0.08s before ball impact. This indicated
an incomplete transfer of weight on to the left foot.

Table 2 indicates that for most of the given locations the
onset of load acceptance occurs some time after the top of
the backswing. While this was noted for the left heel
location, there was nonetheless an earlier gradual increase
in pressure which commenced midway through the backswing.
Inspection of the times for the onset of loading at L1 and R1
show high intrasubject similarity for both shoe types.

Table 1. Onset of unloading at selected plantar locations
(FL) of the right foot in relation to the top of the
backswing

Foot location (FL) Subject number (S)	RH	RA [time (s)]	R5	R4
1M	−0.204	−0.120	−0.012	−0.024
1S	−0.304	−0.100	−0.064	−0.052
2M	−0.048	−0.292	−0.156	−0.140
2S	−0.056	−0.240	−0.220	−0.204
3M	NO	−0.132	−0.128	−0.128
3S	NO	−0.124	−0.064	−0.060
4M	NO	−0.096	+0.008	+0.044
4S	NO	−0.116	−0.008	+0.040
5M	−0.080	−0.032	−0.024	−0.020
5S	+0.096	+0.012	+0.016	+0.016
6M	−0.056	−0.172	−0.184	−0.168
6S	−0.096	−0.192	−0.214	−0.196

(key: "−" and "+" represent occurrence before and after the
top of the backswing respectively; "NO": not observed; and
"m" and "s": moulded and spiked soles respectively)

Table 2. Onset of loading at selected plantar locations (FL)
of the feet in relation to the top of the backswing

(FL) \ (S)	LH	LA	L5	L1 [time (s)]	R1	LT	RT
1M	+0.156	+0.204	+0.152	0.000	-0.012	-0.068	NO
1S	+0.112	+0.156	+0.212	-0.016	+0.008	-0.016	+0.008
2M	+0.260	+0.112	+0.128	NO	+0.096	NO	+0.120
2S	+0.228	+0.072	+0.104	+0.024	+0.164	-0.020	+0.120
3M	+0.012	+0.048	-0.012	+0.012	+0.028	-0.056	NO
3S	+0.048	+0.052	+0.044	+0.056	-0.036	-0.018	NO
4M	+0.080	+0.164	+0.076	+0.012	+0.096	0.000	+0.068
4S	+0.072	+0.156	+0.144	+0.132	+0.144	+0.020	+0.120
5M	+0.052	+0.072	+0.072	+0.096	+0.166	+0.064	+0.112
5S	+0.088	+0.084	+0.072	+0.108	+0.108	+0.088	+0.096
6M	NO	-0.096	+0.056	NO	+0.166	NO	+0.120
6S	NO	-0.032	-0.020	+0.060	+0.172	+0.068	+0.156

(key: as for Table 1)

The onset times for subject 3 are interesting in that they
all very close to the time of the top of the backswing. This
is accounted for by the observation that this subject lifted
this foot completely off the ground just prior to the top of
the backswing and promptly returned it flat to the ground
again. Subjects 3 and 5 each demonstrated an eversion action
of the subtalar joint with no heel lift, while subjects 1 and
2 each clearly demonstrated a high heel lift during the
backswing.

While the above results are important in the understanding
of the initiation of the downswing, the contribution of peak
pressures and their times of occurrence are highly
significant to a more comprehensive understanding of weight
transfer patterns (Tables 3 and 4). The highest peak
pressures tended to be associated with R1 and L1 for the
longer drives, but there is no obvious relationship between
their respective magnitudes. However, with only a few
exceptions, the peaks occurred before the moment of impact
with no differences observed between shoe types. These
findings clearly indicate the role of each foot in providing
a solid base of support during the critical period just prior
to and including the moment of impact. In addition, the peak
pressures at L1 and R1 are clearly associated with the spiked
shoe condition, with magnitudes sometimes in the order of
twice those for the moulded shoe condition. This finding
suggests the subjects were capable of generating much greater
force production during the downswing while wearing shoes
with spiked soles.

Table 3. Peak pressures at selected plantar locations (FL)
of the feet

(FL) (S)	LH	LA	L5	L1	R1	LT	RT
				[pressure (kPa)]			
1M	212.0	123.0	324.0	561.1	783.2	99.7	NO
1S	238.0	107.1	315.1	1092.1	860.7	113.3	NO
2M	242.3	152.4	337.3	195.4	652.7	294.6	646.9
2S	190.4	251.2	466.0	395.8	799.5	176.8	559.4
3M	315.8	164.7	315.1	80.1	648.6	23.5	17.5
3S	272.6	193.6	337.3	100.2	1240.1	34.4	22.5
4M	380.7	280.1	470.5	261.0	395.7	81.6	148.6
4S	307.2	424.1	550.4	400.8	228.4	95.2	183.6
5M	150.2	201.8	377.3	736.4	94.9	231.2	74.3
5S	51.9	107.1	563.7	866.7	126.5	231.2	153.0
6M	285.5	267.7	403.9	280.5	232.5	68.8	358.4
6S	302.9	350.1	399.5	335.6	65.3	40.8	305.9

(key: as for Table 1)

Table 4. Times of occurrence of peak pressures at selected
plantar locations (FL) of the feet in relation to the moment
of impact

(FL) (S)	LH	LA	L5	L1	R1	LT	RT
				[time (s)]			
1M	−0.060	+0.040	+0.068	−0.096	−0.012	−0.148	NO
1S	−0.048	+0.068	+0.212	−0.044	−0.032	−0.128	NO
2M	−0.004	+0.032	+0.032	−0.032	−0.048	−0.384	−0.032
2S	+0.020	+0.008	+0.024	−0.056	−0.016	−0.144	0.000
3M	−0.100	−0.076	−0.076	−0.132	−0.080	−0.104	−0.130
3S	−0.072	−0.048	−0.044	−0.100	−0.052	−0.108	−0.120
4M	+0.012	−0.016	−0.024	−0.120	+0.016	−0.132	−0.052
4S	+0.020	+0.008	−0.008	−0.092	−0.016	−0.120	−0.064
5M	+0.460	+0.400	+0.236	−0.060	+0.036	−0.120	−0.068
5S	−0.120	+0.564	+0.520	−0.052	−0.040	−0.096	−0.056
6M	−0.096	+0.108	+0.028	−0.240	+0.028	−0.140	−0.012
6S	−0.112	+0.076	+0.012	−0.240	−0.048	−0.232	−0.048

(key: "−" and "+" represent occurrence before and after the
moment of impact respectively; for others see Table 1)

4 Discussion

The apparent lack of overall similarities among these
subjects may be attributable to their different driving
abilities. A similar handicap does not imply similar driving
skill, since the game of golf has many facets which combine
to give a handicap rating. Furthermore, the sheer volume of
data collected during the golf swing necessitates data
reduction, which along with quantitative analysis inevitably
leads to the obscuring of important information.
  Nonetheless, there are significant implications for
performance associated with this study. The small increase
in pressure at the left heel prior to the completion of the
backswing lends support to the theory that the downswing is
initiated somewhere else in the body and not by the hands.
Further examination of the kinematic data should permit an
identification of these body parts and their relative
contributions. The occurrence of the onset of load
acceptance after the downswing has commenced also supports
the above theory, since under these circumstances the
inertial effects of the club will commence after the body has
begun to rotate. The high peak pressures at the first
metatarsal heads immediately prior to ball impact also
reflect the inertial effects of the club, with the
observation of the greater magnitudes while wearing spiked
shoes indicating the capacity for greater force generation by
the body under this condition.

The authors wish to acknowledge the financial and equipment support by
Titleist and Footjoy Worldwide, the Gaitscan equipment support from the
Department of Podiatry at the University of Brighton, and the guidance
on its operation and comments by Dr Matthew Pepper, University of Kent.

5 References

Bartlett, R. (1990) Kine Analysis, in **Proceedings of the
    Eighth International Symposium of the Society of
    Biomechanics in Sport**, Conex, Prague, pp 273-278.
Carlsoo, S. (1967) A kinetic analysis of the golf swing. **J.
    Sports Med. Phys. Fitness**, 7, 76-82.
Cooper, J.R. Bates, B.T. Bedi, J. and Scheuchenzuber, J.
    (1974) Kinematic and kinetic analysis of the golf swing,
    in **Biomechanics IV** (eds R.C. Nelson and C.A. Morehouse)
    University Park Press, Baltimore, pp 298-305.
King, L. (1962) **The Master Key to success in Golf**.
    Hodder and Stoughton Ltd., London.
Nevill, A.J.(1991) **A foot pressure measurement system
    utilising PVdF and Copolymer piezoelectric
    transducers**. University of Kent. PhD thesis.
Williams, K.R. and Cavanagh, P.R. (1983) The mechanics of
    foot action during the golf swing and implications for
    shoe design. **Med. Sci. Sports and Exerc.**, 15, 247-255.

5 Ground reaction forces and torques of professional and amateur golfers

S.W. Barrentine, G.S. Fleisig and H. Johnson
American Sports Medicine Institute, Birmingham, USA
and T.W. Woolley
Samford University, Birmingham, USA

Abstract
An understanding of forces and torques applied by the feet to the ground
during the golf swing is vital for achieving proper mechanics and
optimal performance. In this study, ground reaction forces and torques
for sixty male golfers of various abilities were recorded. A general
description was presented and was consistent with previously published
studies. Downswing time was similar for swings with a driver as with
a 5-iron, however greater downswing forces and torques at the feet were
generated with the driver. Different deceleration mechanics were used
for the two clubs. With the driver, the golfer's front foot applied
greater lateral force; with the 5-iron the golfer's front foot generated
greater outward torque. Differences were also seen between skill
levels. The low-handicap golfers achieved maximum torque with the rear
foot earlier in the downswing, which can be related to the greater club
velocity that was observed for the low-handicap golfer.
Keywords: Biomechanics, Golf, Feet, Force, Torque

1 Introduction

The golf swing is a complex movement which, to a large extent, is
influenced by the action of the feet. To better understand proper swing
mechanics, a number of researchers have studied the reaction between the
golfer and the ground. Studies by Carlsoo (1967) and Cooper et al.
(1974) provided an initial scientific description of ground reaction
forces and torques during the golf swing. More recent studies by
Williams and Cavanagh (1983), Richards et al. (1985), and Wallace et al.
(1990) have provided more information, including comparisons between
different skill levels. One potential limitation to all of these
studies was the number of subjects, which ranged from 1 to 20. In this
study, ground reaction forces and torques for 60 golfers of various
ability were quantified.

2 Methods

Sixty male golfers were used as subjects and divided into three skill
levels with twenty subjects in each group. The three skill levels were
PGA Tour Professionals and PGA Teaching Professionals; low-handicap (0 -
15); and high-handicap (16 +). The subjects had an average age of 39
yrs ± 13 yrs, an average mass of 86.65 kg ± 13.3 kg and an average
height of 1.82 m ± 0.05.
    Each subject performed swings with a driver and a 5-iron while
wearing flatlasted and goodyear-welted golf shoes. Twelve swings -
three trials for each condition (shoe,club) - were used in data
analysis. The order of shoe and club were randomized during testing.
Two force platforms covered with artificial grass were used to collect
ground reaction forces and torques (Figure 1). Data collected from the
force platforms were sampled at a frequency of 1000 hz with a 10.5 hz
low-pass filter. Force components and moments about three orthogonal
axes were collected from each force plate.

Science and Golf II: Proceedings of the World Scientific Congress of Golf. Edited by A.J.
Cochran and M.R. Farrally. Published in 1994 by E & FN Spon, London. ISBN 0 419 18790 1

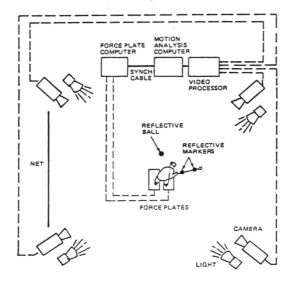

Figure 1.   Schematic of testing set-up.

A high speed motion analysis system was used to correlate the temporal aspects of club swing to the force platform data. The system utilized four electronically synchronized 200 hz CCD cameras to transmit pixel images of reflective markers, placed on the club shaft and the ball, into the video processor. Three dimensional locations of the markers were digitized utilizing the direct linear transformation method (Abdel-Aziz and Karara, 1971). The motion analysis system and force platforms were electronically synchronized within 0.01 sec.

For each subject, ground reaction forces and torques were normalized by bodyweight and height. A three factor (club, shoe, skill level) repeated measures analysis of variance and Bonferroni tests of simple effects were used, and differences for club and skill level were reported.

3   Results

Data from all subjects were summarized for both the driver and 5-iron (Table 1). Backswing was defined as the time from initial club movement away from the ball until the time of maximum backswing club rotation. Downswing was defined as the time from maximum backswing club rotation until separation of the ball from the clubface after contact. Total swing represented the time from initial club movement until ball separation from the clubface.

The foot closest to the target was defined as the front foot. Therefore, for a righthanded golfer, the left foot was the front foot, and the right foot was the rear foot. Anterior shear force represented the maximum force exerted horizontally along the surface of the force platform by the golfer's foot in the anterior (i.e. from heel to toe) direction. Posterior shear force was the maximum horizontal force exerted in the toe-to-heel direction. Lateral force was defined as the maximum horizontal force exerted by the golfer in the lateral (i.e. away from the body's mid-line) direction. Vertical force was a measurement

TABLE 1
Descriptive data for all subjects

Variable	Driver Mean ± SD	5-iron Mean ± SD
Swing Phases		
* Backswing (sec)	0.865 ± 0.17	0.819 ± 0.15
Downswing (sec)	0.297 ± 0.05	0.296 ± 0.05
* Total Swing (sec)	1.162 ± 0.19	1.115 ± 0.18
Anterior - Posterior Forces		
* Rear Foot Posterior Shear (N)	145.25 ± 23.6	128.52 ± 22.9
* time after peak (sec)	0.192 ± 0.06	0.200 ± 0.06
* Front Foot Anterior Shear (N)	185.79 ± 37.3	161.52 ± 35.5
time after peak (sec)	0.194 ± 0.05	0.198 ± 0.05
Anterior - Posterior COP Displacement		
Rear Foot (cm)	24.41 ± 5.44	23.50 ± 6.15
Front Foot (cm)	13.41 ± 3.99	12.47 ± 3.86
Lateral Forces		
Rear Foot Lateral Shear(N)	126.33 ± 31.9	127.49 ± 29.9
* time after peak (sec)	0.049 ± 0.13	0.079 ± 0.10
* Front Foot Lateral Shear (N)	133.27 ± 35.0	123.20 ± 29.3
* time after impact (sec)	0.012 ± 0.07	0.034 ± 0.07
Medial - Lateral COP Displacement		
Rear Foot (cm)	9.93 ± 6.40	9.65 ± 5.87
* Front Foot (cm)	6.78 ± 2.18	5.92 ± 1.96
Vertical Forces		
* Rear Foot Vertical (N)	703.20 ± 80.5	695.07 ± 81.7
time relative to peak (sec)	-0.267 ± 0.16	-0.259 ± 0.16
Front Foot Vertical (N)	950.55 ± 156.4	963.56 ± 135.9
* time after impact (sec)	0.010 ± 0.10	0.028 ± 0.08
Outward Torques		
* Rear Foot (N-m)	21.98 ± 9.73	20.77 ± 9.62
* time relative to peak (sec)	-0.088 ± 0.13	-0.110 ± 0.14
* Front Foot (N-m)	23.45 ± 7.13	24.16 ± 6.91
* time after impact (sec)	0.304 ± 0.17	0.269 ± 0.15

Based on average mass (kg) = 86.65 ± 13.3, height (m) = 1.82 ± 0.05
* Significant ($P < 0.05$) difference between driver and 5-iron

of the maximum force exerted downward by the golfer. Outward torque was defined as the rotational moment exerted by the golfer at the feet in a clockwise direction for the rear foot, (as seen from above) and in a counter-clockwise direction for the front foot.

Variables that were significantly different ($P < 0.05$) between skill level were identified. Mean values and standard deviations of these variables for golf swings using the driver are shown in Table 2. Similar patterns for these variables were seen for golf swings with the 5-iron, as well. Significant interactions ($P < 0.05$) between skill level and club were found for a number of variables (Table 3).

4 Discussion

4.1 General description
The general patterns of ground reaction forces and torques presented in Table 1 were similar to previously published data (Cooper, et.al). In order to understand these patterns, a description is provided based upon the driver data (Figure 2).

The swing was initiated with the club being moved away from the ball. The club reached its peak (end of backward movement) 0.87 sec after the first movement. As the club was moved away from the ball, most of the golfer's weight was shifted onto the rear foot, reaching a maximum

TABLE 2

Differences between skill levels - illustrated with driver data

Variable	PGA Mean ± SD	Low-Handicap Mean ± SD	High-Handicap Mean ± SD	Significant Differences
Swing Phases				
Downswing (sec)	0.281 ± 0.04	0.278 ± 0.04	0.331 ± 0.04	a,b
Total Swing(sec)	1.087 ± 0.12	1.124 ± 0.12	1.272 ± 0.25	a
COP Displacement				
Front Foot Anterior- Posterior Displacement (cm)	4.84 ± 1.76	5.30 ± 1.05	5.73 ± 1.82	a
Rear Foot Medial- Lateral Displacement (cm)	3.98 ± 2.32	4.63 ± 3.05	3.14 ± 1.79	b
Outward Torques				
Rear Foot Torque (N-m)	18.53 ± 4.62	17.00 ± 6.18	30.90 ± 10.81	a,b
Front Foot Torque (N-m)	26.27 ± 6.18	23.18 ± 6.18	20.09 ± 7.72	a
Timing				
Rear Foot Posterior Shear Force time after peak (sec)	0.164 ± 0.05	0.176 ± 0.05	0.235 ± 0.05	a,b
Front Foot Anterior Shear Force time after peak (sec)	0.176 ± 0.05	0.176 ± 0.04	0.231 ± 0.05	a,b
Front Foot Vertical Force time relative to Rear Foot Vertical Force (sec)	0.554 ± 0.18	1.384 ± 0.14	0.629 ± 0.18	b,c
Maximum club velocity time relative to peak (sec)	0.269 ± 0.04	0.262 ± 0.04	0.316 ± 0.04	a,b
Maximum club velocity time relative to impact (sec)	-0.012 ± 0.01	-0.016 ± 0.01	-0.014 ± 0.02	c
Club Speed				
Maximum club velocity (m/sec)	39.27 ± 2.70	37.62 ± 4.31	33.52 ± 4.55	a

Based on average mass (kg) = 86.65 ± 13.3, Height (m) = 1.82 ± 0.05

a) Significant differences (p < 0.05) between PGA and High-Handicap groups
b) Significant differences (p < 0.05) between Low and High-Handicap groups
c) Significant differences (p < 0.05) between PGA and Low-Handicap groups

TABLE 3

Variables which showed significant interaction (P < 0.05) between skill level and club

Swing Phases	Anterior - Posterior Forces
Backswing (sec)	Rear Foot Posterior Shear (N)
Total Swing (sec)	Timing
Club Speed	Rear Foot Posterior Shear time after peak (sec)
Maximum club velocity (m/sec)	Front Foot Lateral Shear time after peak (sec)
	Front Foot Torque (N-m)

vertical force of 700 N 0.27 sec before peak of backswing. Approximately 0.1 sec before peak of backswing, the rear foot applied a 22 N-m torque in the clockwise direction (as viewed from above). Because the spikes on the rear shoe locked into the ground, the reaction of this torque was to cause the golfer's body to rotate in the counter-clockwise direction.

Downswing lasted 0.3 sec. After 0.05 sec of the downswing, the rear foot applied a maximum force in the lateral direction. The maximum rear foot lateral force averaged 130 N. During the swing, the rear foot center of pressure moved 9.9 cm in the medial-lateral direction.

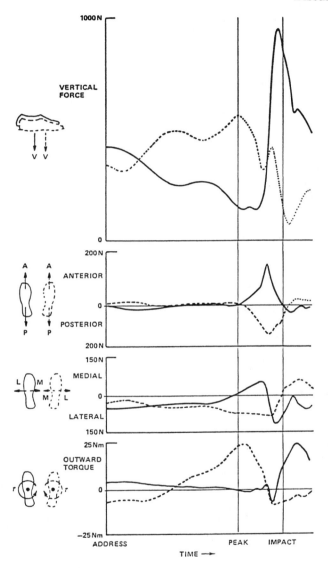

Figure 2.   **V**ertical force, **A**nterior/**P**osterior force, **M**edial/**L**ateral force, and outward **T**orque patterns for a typical golfer.   Solid lines represent lead foot data, and dotted lines represent rear foot data.

Next, both feet exerted a maximum force in the anterior-posterior (i.e. forward-backwards) direction. The rear foot pushed with 145 N in the posterior direction while the front foot pushed with 186 N in the anterior direction. This created a clockwise force couple that occurred 0.2 sec after peak of backswing. Because the spikes were locked into the ground, the reaction to this force couple caused the golfer's body to rotate in a counter-clockwise direction. The center of pressure moved 12 cm in the anterior-posterior direction for the rear shoe and 9.7 cm in the anterior-posterior direction for the front shoe.

Approximately 0.02 sec after separation of the ball from clubface, the front foot applied a maximum shear force in the lateral direction and a maximum force in the vertical direction. The 133 N lateral shear force exerted by the front foot helped stabilize the golfer and enabled the counter-clockwise velocities to be maximized. At this point, the golfer exerted a vertical force of 950 N, which is greater than total bodyweight. The front foot center of pressure moved 6.8 cm in the medial-lateral direction during the swing.

Three tenths of a second after impact, the front foot applied a maximum torque of 23 N-m. This torque was applied in the outward direction, helping decelerate the body's counter-clockwise rotation.

4.2 Differences between clubs

Although the backswing was significantly slower with a driver than with a 5-iron, downswing time was virtually identical for the two clubs (Table 1). In order to swing the driver with the same acceleration as the shorter 5-iron, the golfer applied greater foot forces and torques during the downswing. After ball impact, the golfer generated a greater front foot lateral shear force with the driver; in contrast, greater front foot torque was generated with the 5-iron.

4.3 Differences between skill levels

Table 2 shows that in comparison to the lesser-skilled subject, the higher-skilled golfer had greater acceleration during the downswing and his club achieved greater velocity, closer to the time of impact. It can be assumed that greater club velocity closer to the time of impact leads to greater ball distance. The low-handicap golfer achieved maximum posterior shear force earlier in the downswing with his rear foot and anterior shear force with his front foot compared to the high-handicap player. Subsequently, the high-handicap golfer generated greater rear foot torque and smaller front foot torque.

4.4 Interactions between club and skill level

For each variable listed in Table 3, there was an interaction between skill level and club used. For instance, the time from peak of backswing until the rear foot applied a maximum posterior shear force was shortest for the low-handicap golfers and longest for the high-handicap golfers (Table 2); how much shorter, however, depended on which club was used. Figure 3 shows that with the driver, the time of maximum rear foot posterior force occurred later in the downswing for the low-handicap group compared to the PGA group. Similarly, the high-handicap group achieved a maximum force later than the low-handicap group. With the 5-iron, the high-handicap group still achieved maximum force later in the downswing than either the low-handicap or the PGA group. However, negligible difference was seen between the low-handicap and PGA groups. Hence, the differences indicated in Tables 1 and 2 were statistically significant; but for the variables shown in Table 3, the differences were effected by both club and skill level.

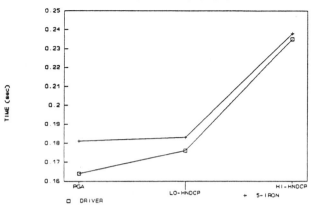

Figure 3   Example of interaction between club and skill level.

5   Conclusions

A general description of forces and torques applied by the feet to the ground was presented. Based upon the large number of subjects used in this study, statistically significant differences were found between different skill levels and between different clubs. Although every golfer cannot achieve the distance and consistency of professional golfers, an understanding of foot kinetics for highly-skilled golfers may help the individual golfer or instructor set goals for improvement.

6   References

Abdel-Aziz YI, Karara HM. Direct linear transformation: from compararator coordinates into object coordinated in close-range photogrammetry. (1971) *Proceedings from ASPUI symposium on close-range photogrammetry, Am Soc Photogrammetry*, 1-19.

Carlsoo, S. (1967) A kinetic analysis of the golf swing. **J. Sports Med. Phys. Fitness,** 7, 76-82.

Cooper, J.M. Bates, B.T. Bedi, J. and Scheuchenzuber, J. (1974) Kinematic and kinetic analysis of the golf swing, in **Biomechanics IV** (eds R.C. Nelson and C.A. Morehouse), University Park Press, Baltimore, pp. 298-305.

Richards, J. Farrell, M. Kent, J. and Kraft, R. (1985) Weight transfer patterns during the golf swing. **Res. Quarterly Exerc. Sport,** 56(4), 361-365.

Wallace, E.S. Graham, D. and Bleakley E.W. (1990) Foot-to-ground pressure patterns during the golf drive: a case study involving a low handicap player and a high handicap player, in **Science and Golf** (ed Cochran, A.J.), E. & F.N. Spon, London, pp. 25-29.

Williams, K.R. and Cavanagh, P.R. (1983) The mechanics of foot action during the golf swing and implications for shoe design. **Med. Sci. Sports Exerc.,** 15(3), 247-255.

7   Acknowledgement

This study was conducted by the American Sports Medicine Institute with financial support from Titleist and Foot-Joy Worldwide.

6 The biomechanics of the shoe–ground interaction in golf

G. Koenig, M. Tamres and R.W. Mann
Massachusetts Institute of Technology, Cambridge, Massachusetts

Abstract
The intent of this study was to analyze the kinematics and kinetics of the shoe-ground interaction in golf. The shoe-ground interaction was quantified as ground reaction forces and centers of pressure using the MIT TRACK system, an active marker system used in conjunction with a Kistler force plate. The system applies a stereophotogrammetric technique to measure the kinematics of human movement causing the kinetics generated at the force plate. The kinematic data was used to monitor shoe movement in order to quantify shoe kinematics in relation to ground reaction forces and the center of pressure migration. The experiment involved fourteen subjects, divided into three handicap groups (low: 0-7, mid: 8-14, high: 15+). Subjects wore conventional spiked shoes on an artificial turf platform, and struck golf balls into a golf cage using three different clubs (driver, 3-iron, 7-iron). A normalization routine was developed to characterize the data set of an individual, as well as to compare individuals and handicap groups. An algorithm was also developed to study data in the moving local reference frame of the shoe, in contrast to studying data in the conventional reference frame of the shoe at initiation of the swing. Results include differences between the left and right feet, as well as clear differences between handicap groups and individuals. The forces and centers of pressure for different clubs were shown to vary at specific phases of the swing, due primarily to inertial effects, but generally followed similar patterns. Also, the moving reference frame of the shoe demonstrated that the migrations of center of pressure on the shoes were more centralized to the shoe than with respect to the reference frame of the shoe at initiation. Furthermore, in contrast to common wisdom, statistical analysis revealed that the swings of low handicap players are not any more consistent than those of high handicap players.
Keywords: Golf, Center of pressure, Biomechanics, Vectograms.

1 Introduction

In recent years, sports biomechanics has expanded to include a multitude of fields, always with the goal of providing better understanding of the athlete's movements. Among such sports is golf, with the emphasis on enhanced performance. Cochran and Stobbs (1968) were among the first to apply scientific principles to the issues of golf. Subsequent research concentrated on developing models of the golfer's swing in providing key insight into the swing mechanics (Jorgensen 1970, and Neal and Wilson 1985). To a lesser degree, research has also been conducted to a limited degree on the foot-ground interactions of the golfer (Cooper et al. 1973, and Williams and Cavanagh 1983). Most recently extensive work has incorporated shoe movement, shoe-ground interaction, and the mechanics of the upper swing motion (Koenig 1993, and Tamres 1993). This paper presents a summary of this

Science and Golf II: Proceedings of the World Scientific Congress of Golf. Edited by A.J. Cochran and M.R. Farrally. Published in 1994 by E & FN Spon, London. ISBN 0 419 18790 1

comprehensive work, providing new insights and understanding of the golfer's actions related to shoe movement, ground reaction forces, and centers of pressure, together with some statistical analyses.

2 Methods

Fourteen male, right-handed subjects were analyzed in the Newman Laboratory for Biomechanics and Human Rehabilitation at the Massachusetts Institute of Technology, Cambridge, Massachusetts. The subjects ranged in skill level from a handicap of 1 to 18, and were divided into three groups (low: 0-7, mid: 8-14, high: 15+). Experiments were performed with each subject wearing spiked golf shoes and hitting golf balls off an artificial turf surface into a golf cage using one of three clubs (driver, 3-iron, 7-iron). Seven trials were conducted for each club and for each foot on the turf covered force plate.

Data was acquired using the MIT TRACK system, employing two Selspot II electro-optical cameras which monitor the positions of active markers attached to various body segments, clubs, and shoes. Simultaneously, a single Kistler force plate (9281A11) under the turf surface acquired the kinetics of the shoe-ground interaction. A sampling rate of 215 Hz was used and the data was smoothed using a Dohrman filter.

An algorithm was developed to analyze the ground reaction data in the continuously moving local reference frame of the shoe, as compared to the conventional initial stance reference frame. The shoe position and movement during the swing were measured using two arrays mounted directly on the shoe. Previous work by Williams and Cavanagh (1983) was limited to displaying the center of pressure data in an initial fixed stance reference frame. The moving frame approach represents the actual shoe movement during the swing, while the initial reference frame provides a global perspective of the shoe's motion.

In addition, an inter-subject and inter-group normalization routine was developed which permitted pooling data from individual subjects. The normalized data elucidated overall trends for the entire subject pool, as well as for the handicap groups. This routine took account of temporal effects, as well as representing the magnitudes of each data parameter, by identifying seven distinct kinematic locations of the swing as reference points[1]. Data defined by these key points, and corresponding to each period of time, compared each individual trial to the overall average time for each of these periods. Data related to each individual period was then scaled to fit the averaged time period, with inherent subject characteristics, such as body segment lengths and weight, incorporated within the data. The data was then averaged across the given data sets.

3 Results and discussion

The study of the shoe-ground interaction in the moving local frame of the shoe added to the understanding of the coupling of the golfer with the ground. As expected with an asymmetric activity, the two shoes exhibited distinctly different movement patterns. With respect to rotation, the left shoe, i.e. the lead shoe for a right-handed golfer, typically rotated up to a peak of 15 degrees towards the target during the backswing phase, returned to nearly its original orientation at the mid downswing, and then increased as the golfer completed the swing. This follow-through allowed the golfer further rotation, as well as relieving stresses on their musculoskeletal system. The less skilled players had excessive movement, rotating the shoe back and forth to a much greater extent. The right shoe remained well planted prior to the mid downswing. The shoe then lifted off the ground as

---

[1] Seven kinematic reference points: Initiation IN, Mid Backswing MB, Top of Backswing TB, Mid Downswing MD, Impact IM, Mid Follow-through MF, Top of Follow-through TF.

the swing proceeded towards impact. The better players kept their shoes in contact with the ground longer.

The center of pressure migration for the left shoe was of an elliptical shape (see Figure 1a). At initiation of the swing, the migration pattern began closer to the heel. As the club was raised during the backswing, the migration pattern traveled in the anterior direction as a result of the weight shift towards the right shoe and the rotation of the club around the body. This progression continued until the top of the backswing was reached and the club came to a brief rest. Overall, the migration during this phase was rather rapid. As the golfer proceeded through the downswing, the migration traveled in the opposite direction, returning towards the heel. The shifting of the weight back to the left shoe, as well as the swinging of the club out away from the body, caused the migration pattern to also proceed in the lateral direction. Before impact, the migration pattern returned towards the medial edge of the shoe while continuing towards the heel, due to the golfer compensating for the centripetal force produced by the club's inertia. The center of pressure migration returned near its point of origin as the golfer completed the swing. A slight looping characteristic was noted at the top of the backswing. The low handicap players did not demonstrate this feature which was found in both the mid and high handicap players. The low handicap players also kept their center of pressure migrations further towards their heels as well as more medial.

The moving frame demonstrated that the center of pressure migrations were more centralized to the shoe as compared to that for the reference frame fixed at initiation (see Figure 1b). The looping effect for the left shoe seen in the less skilled players was noted as well in the initial reference frame, demonstrating this to be an inherent feature of center of pressure migration and not a result of shoe movement.

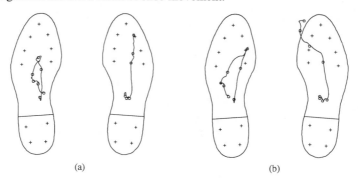

(a)   (b)

Figure 1: Center of pressure migration pattern for a typical golfer in the (a) moving reference frame, and (b) initial stance reference frame. Circles represent kinematic reference points.

The right shoe center of pressure migration pattern began at nearly the same corresponding point on the left shoe, demonstrating that the golfer's weight was nearly symmetrically distributed. The center of pressure migration progressed slightly posteriorly during the backswing. The right shoe remained well planted on the ground during the weight transfer, and the weight was kept towards the heel providing for a more stable posture. The downswing phase brought a rapid migration of the center of pressure towards the toe the shoe, which correlated with the rapid transfer of weight towards the other shoe as the body uncoiled and the club passed through impact. As the golfer approached and made impact with the ball, the right shoe rotated, raised and rolled. Considering the overall patterns, the better players kept their centers of pressure more towards their heels and the medial portion of their shoe. Furthermore, in the backswing phase their patterns progressed more towards their heels than the less skilled players. The less skilled players generated migration patterns that proceeded more laterally and rapidly in the anterior direction during the downswing phase.

In the initial stance reference frame, the migration patterns typically depart from the confines of the right shoe. In spite of difficulties encountered in the latter of portion of the swing, the data demonstrated a more centralized migration pattern than would have been expected.

The reaction forces produced between the golfer and the ground were analyzed with respect to the initial stance reference frame and divided into three components: vertical, mediolateral, and anteroposterior. These forces provide key information relating to movements of the larger masses of the golfer, i.e. upper leg segment, pelvis, and torso. The vertical force component provided information of the weight distribution exhibited during the swing (see Figure 2a). The golfers characteristically shifted their weight from an approximately 55:45 left-to-right foot ratio at initiation to a maximum 20:80 ratio at the mid backswing, and ending with a 35:65 ratio at the top of the backswing. As they progressed into their downswing, a rapid shift was evident back toward their left foot, reaching a peak around mid downswing as the golfers strove to produce their greatest thrust from their lower torso and pelvic motion. A local minimum in force for both feet was reached about the point of impact, indicating a lifting action by the golfers as they struck the ball. Comparing the skill level groups, high handicappers produced much less weight shift toward their right foot in the backswing, preferring to maintain a more even balance between their feet. However, while they did manage to achieve a similar percentage ratio between their two feet through most of the later portion of the downswing, the lesser skilled players were significantly out of phase, i.e. lagging in their timing sequence, compared to the better skilled players. Effects due to using different clubs proved to be minimal with respect to swing phase rates, but differences were noted in magnitudes of the weight shifts, attributed to club inertial effects and swing techniques.

The mediolateral forces characterize the side-to-side shoe-ground interaction (see Figure 2b). During the backswing, the golfers produced these forces to effectively shift their center of gravity translationally to the right (away from the target direction) and contribute to the rotation of the hips. Just prior to the top of the backswing, the forces produced by the left foot were redirected toward the target direction as the golfers prepared to shift their momentum forward. Around the mid point of the downswing, this force reached a maximum and the right foot began to redirect its lateral force, as the golfers subsequently braced themselves against the forward momentum generated by their upper body in swinging the club. In comparing the skill level groups, the higher handicap players tended to maintain greater lateral forces on both feet during their backswing, resulting in a sharply reduced hip rotation and weight transfer. Also, these lesser skilled players produced a significantly lower rate of decrease of the force on both feet during the latter portion of the downswing. Force profiles for the given clubs were overwhelmingly similar, the only differences due largely to inertial effects.

The front-to-back force action was specified by the anteroposterior forces (see Figure 2c). The actions of the golfers' feet showed a significant degree of symmetry due, by and large, to the inherent rotational movement which these forces produce in the golf swing. In the backswing, the forces initially reflect the clubhead movement straight back away from the target direction. Prior to the top of the backswing, where the clubhead is brought vertically upward by the hands, the forces are redirected in each foot allowing for a rotation about the golfer's trunk. As the mid downswing is approached, the golfer acts to reduce these lateral forces and effectively transfer the angular momentum segmentally to the clubhead. At the point of impact, the feet stabilize the counter-clockwise rotation produced in the downswing. Although similar patterns are exhibited by the different skill level groups, the better skilled players produced, on average, higher forces throughout the swing. Even more importantly, a the critical low momentum transition between the backswing and downswing, the lesse skilled players redirected their forces later than the better players. Comparison between th force profiles of the different clubs revealed golfers produced greater forces in executing th swing in proportion to the greater inertia of the driver.

While independent analysis of the force-time profiles of all three reaction forces provide essential information describing their specific actions, a better global understanding can b obtained by combining the center of pressure patterns and the resultant three-dimension: ground reaction force vectors, i.e. vectograms (see Figure 2d). These spatial depiction exhibit a general distribution pattern of the forces with respect to the shoe during the swin; provide relative magnitude comparisons between the shear and vertical forces, and highlig the key features inherent to the shoe's role in the golf swing.

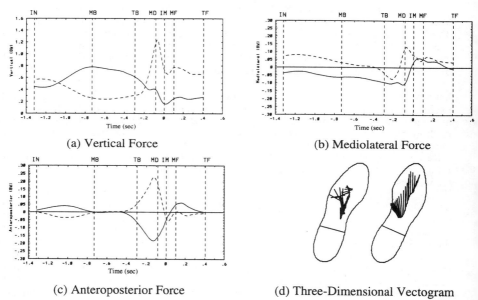

(a) Vertical Force

(b) Mediolateral Force

(c) Anteroposterior Force

(d) Three-Dimensional Vectogram

Figure 2: Normalized force profiles of the left (dashed line) and right foot (solid line) for a typical golfer.

Statistical analyses of the variability and repeatability revealed further insight to th golfers' actions. The findings were based on using percent uncertainty, which is defined a the sample standard deviation of the mean divided by the sample mean. For the groun reaction forces, analysis showed that no given handicap group was more consistent tha another in producing any of their force patterns, an example of which is shown in Figure 4 fo the vertical force component. A common trend among all golfers was increasing variability i their force production from initiation to the mid point of the downswing, followed by decrease during the impact phase, and a further increase in the follow-through. The rate c force production, as well as the force magnitudes produced by individuals, were shown to b very repeatable across all skill levels.

The timing sequences of the respective swing phases showed the largest range of varianc during the backswing and early downswing, as well as the latter portion of the follow-throug

However, percent uncertainty analysis revealed that all the phases of the swing were undertaken with similar consistency, ranging from 1.7 to 3.4%. This characteristic reflects the intricate timing pattern which golfers are able to maintain.

4 Conclusions

A brief synopsis of the conclusions of this investigation include:
• Expected differences between the two feet; showing the two sides of the body behave differently in the execution of the swing.
• Less skilled players make more shoe movement overall than the better players.
• Better players produced center of pressure migration patterns that are more circular. The center of pressure migration patterns for the better players are further towards the heel and medial edge of both shoes; appears to relate to stability and performance.
• General trends showed greatest activity in the ground reaction forces during the downswing, with the greatest rate changes occurring around the midpoint.
• Mediolateral and anteroposterior forces, which provide information on body rotation, showed clear differences among the skill level groups.
• Vertical force profiles showed that greater weight transfer, at a faster rate in the downswing, were characteristic of the low handicap golfer.
• Differences in the force-time profiles among the three clubs were largely due to club inertia and swing technique, with the driver generating greater forces during the downswing.
• Force-time profiles and swing phase timing were similar within an individual, and no statistical correlations were found between the level of skill and the degree of consistency for both individual and group profiles.

5 References

Cochran, A. J. and Stobbs, J. (1968) **The Search for the Perfect Swing.** J.B. Lippincott Company, New York, New York.

Cooper, J. M., Bates, B.T., Bedi, J. and Scheuchenzuber, J. (1973) Kinematic and kinetic analysis of the golf swing. **Biomechanics IV.** University Park, Pennsylvania, University Park Press. 298-305.

Jorgensen, T. J. (1970). On the Dynamics of the Golf Swing. **American Journal of Physics,** 38 (5), 644-651.

Koenig, G. C. (1993) **A Three-Dimensional Kinematic and Kinetic Analysis of the Golf Swing and Shoe-Ground Interaction**. Masters Thesis, Massachusetts Institute of Technology, Cambridge, MA.

Neal, R. J. and Wilson, B. D. (1985) 3D Kinematics and Kinetics of the Golf Swing. **International Journal of Sport Biomechanics**, 1, 221-232.

Richards, J., Farrell, M., Kent, J. and Kraft, R. (1985) Weight Transfer Patterns During the Golf Swing. **Research Quarterly for Exercise and Sport,** 56 (4), 361-365.

Tamres, M. P. (1993) **Shoe Movement and the Shoe-Ground Interaction in Golf.** Masters Thesis, Massachusetts Institute of Technology, Cambridge, MA.

Vaughan, C. L. (1981) A three-dimensional analysis of the forces and torques applied by a golfer during the downswing. **Biomechanics VII-B**, Baltimore: University Park Press, 325-331.

Williams, K.R. and Cavanagh, P. R. (1983) The mechanics of foot action during the golf swing and implications for shoe design. **Medicine and Science in Sports and Exercise,** 15 (3), 247-255.

7 A biomechanical analysis of the respiratory pattern during the golf swing

Kazuaki Kawashima
Biomechanics Laboratory, College of Agriculture and Veterinary
Medicine, Nihon University, Fujisawa, Japan
Shunichi Takeshita
Physical Education Laboratory, Kokusaigakuin Junior College of
Saitama, Omiya, Japan
Hirofumi Zaitsu
Kato International Design Inc., Tokyo, Japan
and Tetsuo Meshizuka
Graduate School, Cyukyo Women's University, Obu, Japan

Abstract
The purpose of this study was to investigate respiratory movement during a
golf shot. Eight males were tested using the 5 iron club for golf. The
subjects were four skilled golfers (handicap 7 ± 0.7) and four unskilled
golfers (handicap 29 ± 4) for this study. To analyze the point of the address,
top, ball impact, and finish during the swing, the swing phase of the VTR
tapes (60 fps) was used and Electromyographic (EMG) rectified activities of
four muscles, l.m.deltoideus(del), l.m.extensor carpi ulnaris (ecu) and, r.l.m.
obliquus externus abdominis (oea), and respiratory waves were recorded
during the golf swing. The EMG signals were amplified and rectified before
being measured with a digital oscilloscope. The results of this study
indicated the following conclusion: rectified and averaged EMG of oea (l),
and oea(r) before impact was less than the discharge in case of skilled
golfers than unskilled golfers ($p < .05$). Respiratory waves during golf
swing motions, appeared at the impact point or prior to impact. It was
noted that the skilled golfers had shallow breathing in swing motion, but
unskilled golfers had deep irregular breathing ($p < .05$).
Key words: Respiratory, EMG Rectified, Golf swing.

1 Introduction

It is very important to recognize the respiratory pattern in order to swing
timely and rhythmically during a golf performance. The golf swing needs to
change timing to strain or relax the muscles. So, respiratory pattern is
thought to have an effect on the golf swing. Shudel (1934) reported that the
respiratory pattern during the golf swing was similar to the pattern that
appeared when the breath was stopped after take a deep breath and
Masuda (1971) concluded that the product of the respiratory muscle could
be used to describe the efficiency of the swing technique, and best
performances would thus demonstrate the effectual respiratory muscle. A
Japanese lady professional golfer Okamoto (1982) has also mentioned that
she always swings unconsciously after some light breathing out. She

Science and Golf II: Proceedings of the World Scientific Congress of Golf. Edited by A.J.
Cochran and M.R. Farrally. Published in 1994 by E & FN Spon, London. ISBN 0 419 18790 1

recognized this from her experience. The research in relation to respiratory movement during the golf swing is hardly pursued at present. This study aims to investigate the respiratory pattern and the quality of a golf swing.

2 Method

The two groups of subjects for this study consisted of four skilled golfers (handicap of 7 ± 0.7) and four unskilled golfers (handicap of 29 $\pm$4) who were all right-handed persons. And all of them used a 5 iron for their shot. The respiratory waves during the swing were measured with a nostril-pickup and recorded through the amplifier. And electromyographic (EMG) activities of four muscles (l.m.deltoideus(l.m.del), l.m.extensor carpi ulnaris(l.m.ecu), and r.l.m.obliquus externus abdominis (r.l.m.oea)) were recorded. Then, those data were studied with a personal computer. So, to analyze the point of the address, top, impact, and finish, VTR camera was used, and especially impact was recorded with using laser-sensor.

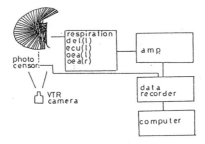

Figure 1. Diagrammatic illustration of experiment environment.

3 Results

Figure 2 shows respiratory waves and rectified EMG while comparing skilled golfer K with unskilled golfer Y. The results of this study would indicated the following conclusions: rectified and averaged EMG of l.m.del during take-back showed lesser discharge in the case of K than Y (p<.05). In the point of impact, EMG of l.m.del showed lesser discharge in the case of Y than K. And the discharge pattern of l.m.ecu showed lesser discharge in the case of Y than K. Moreover, it was found that there was a difference between K and Y at the point of discharge pattern of r.l.m.oea related to respiration when they started the take-back motion (p<.05). The difference was that the abdominal breathing of unskilled golfers was deep and irregular, and that of the skilled golfers was light. It was evidence that skilled golfers' respiratory waves indicated little curved lines and unskilled golfers' indicated big ones. Afterall, it was admitted that this difference of each of the respiratory waves was cuased by the difference of skill.

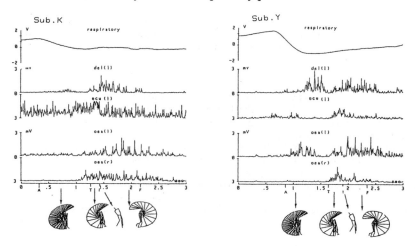

Figure 2. Typical set of computer showing the time course changes of respiratory waves and EMG rectified of l.m.(del), l.m.(ecu), and r.l.m.(oea) during the golf swing in the skilled golfer (subj.K) and unskilled golfer (subj.Y).

4 Discussion

It became obvious that there was a difference between skilled golfers' and unskilled golfers' respiratory functions by comparing both the pattern of respiration and the movement of muscles during the golf swing. The respiratory performance is done unconsciously and the disorder of respiration leads to the cause of a wrong swing. Such disorder can happen easily owing to the change of environment and tension, etc. And, breathing is influenced by a change of strength and condition of an exercise. In other words, the respiratory pattern indicates disorder because an excited state continues. As a results, the timing and rhythm of the swing become bad. Mechanisms of the respiratory pattern were described by different levels of golf skills in this experiment's result. As for the respiratory muscles at the initial motion in the swing, the form of the wave was different according to the skills. As it is observed from figure 2, EMG discharge of the skilled golfers was small. On the other hand, EMG discharge of the unskilled golfers was high. The skilled golfers led to make their shoulders relaxed during the swing. The unskilled golfers' movements were not smooth. As for m.obliquus externus abdominis in swing, a change was indicated by the levels of the skills. The skilled golfers suspended their respiration during the swing. On the other hand, the unskilled golfers inhaled.

As for the unskilled golfers in this experiment, their golf experiences were few.

The golfers usually increase respiration in order to expect a good result. At the same time, the golfers get excited and emotional while playing. Such excitment influences the medulla oblongata. A change happens to the respiratory movement with the cause. Because the skilled golfers have long term experiences, the efficient breathing method was learned. In terms of one good respiratory method in swing, a golfer is to inhale shallowly at the beginning and then unconsciously carry out respiration.

5 Conclusions

The results of this study indicated the following conclusions:
1.Respiratory movement of the skilled golfers was remarkbly shallow during the swing, compared with that of the unskilled golfers at the golf experiment ($p < .05$).
2.The respiratory muscles r.l (oea) of the skilled golfers recorded low amplitude of the EMG rectify prior to impact, compared with that of the unskilled golfers($p < .05$).

6.References

Masuda, M. (1971) A kinesiologic study of golf. **Bulletin of the physical Fitness Institute**. 21. 1-27.
Okamoto, A. (1982) Fascinating golf. **Nikann Golf of Japan**. p. 254.
Shudel, H. (1934) A study of the respiratory of golfers during the drive and the putt. **Res. Quart.**, 5. 62-71.

8 Spine and hip motion analysis during the golf swing

M. McTeigue
President, SportSense Inc., USA
S.R. Lamb
V-P Research and Development, Orthopedic Systems, Inc., USA
R. Mottram
Sports Physical Therapist, Palm Desert CA, USA
and F. Pirozzolo
Associate Professor of Neurology, Baylor College of Medicine, USA

Abstract
This study analyzed the three dimensional motion of a golfer's lumbar spine during the golf swing under actual shotmaking conditions. Fifty-one PGA Tour professional golfers, forty-six Senior PGA Tour professional golfers and thirty-four amateur golfers were tested. Measurements were made using a nonrestrictive, externally mounted, instrumented spatial linkage. Motion in the three orthogonal planes of rotation was measured and plotted on a time axis related to the events of a swing. Electronic sensors were used to supply event markers to the data at the appropriate points during the swing, including take-away, top of backswing and impact position. On average, the PGA Tour Players rotated their hips and upper bodies 55 degrees and 87 degrees respectively in 0.8 seconds at the top of the backswing, while amateurs rotated to 53 degrees and 87 degrees respectively in 0.9 seconds. Significant differences were found among the three groups in the forward bending angles, the side bending angles and the mean total swing time.
Keywords: Spine Rotation, Hip Rotation, Forward Bending, Side Bending, Swing Time, X-Factor.

1 Introduction

During the golf swing, a tremendous amount of complex motion is performed by a golfer's hips and lumbar spine. Torso motion plays a preeminent role in modern swing theory, yet disagreements abound regarding preferences for the sequence of hip and upper body rotations. The amount of rotation is usually summarized as 45 degrees for the hips and 90 degrees for the shoulders. The complex bending angles of the spine are simplified by the admonition to keep the spine angle constant relative to the ball (Bowden 1975, Hogan 1957, Nelson 1976, Leadbetter 1990).

Science and Golf II: Proceedings of the World Scientific Congress of Golf. Edited by A.J. Cochran and M.R. Farrally. Published in 1994 by E & FN Spon, London. ISBN 0 419 18790 1

The spine and hip rotations during a swing are very difficult to analyze with the human eye. Because of the limitations of most video equipment, the subtleties of these motions defy precise quantification. Studies have been performed under artificial laboratory conditions in order to utilize the sophisticated instruments necessary to make these measurements (Cochran, Stobbs 1968). Experts over the years have employed all these methods in search for the perfect swing, but all have been disappointed with the results (Wiren, 1990).

We conducted this study with a large number of players under real shotmaking conditions on practice ranges. A version of the CA6000 Spine Motion Analyzer (Orthopedic Systems, Inc., Hayward, CA), a sophisticated, portable computerized instrument, was used to record five parameters of motion: forward bending, side bending, upper body rotation, hip rotation and swing time (Dvorak, 1992). The motion parameters were plotted against time, which provided useful information about the velocity and accelerations of the torso rotation during the swing. We sought to shed light on common hypotheses about world-class golf swings, and to uncover key differences between the torso motions of "average" golfers and U.S. Tour players.

2 Methods

2.1 Population
Fifty-one PGA Tour Players, 46 Senior PGA Tour Players and 34 amateur players, all males, participated in this study. The Tour players were volunteers and were not selected on the basis of swing features, teacher affiliations or other potentially biasing sample characteristics. The stroke index (handicap) range for the amateurs golfers was between 5 and 36, with a mean of 17.5.

2.2 Protocol
Subjects were tested over a 24 month period using the Swing Motion Trainer (SportSense, Inc., Mountain View, CA). The Swing Motion Trainer (SMT), an adaptation of the CA6000, analyzes component motions of the golf swing in the field in real time. The data are collected with a proprietary measurement linkage consisting of a rate gyroscope and six precision potentiometers. It does not restrict the player's movements as it measures motion of the spine between the pelvis and the mid-thoracic spine. The linkage is connected by a cable to a DOS-based microcomputer with a data sampling rate of 100 samples per second. Data collected from the hardware is processed within the SMT software to provide rotational position and velocity.

With the SMT measurement linkage attached to the golfer's back, a neutral standing position was established and recorded. The zero position is defined as the position of the golfer's hips in relation to his upper body during the neutral standing calibration. All shots in the current study were made with a driver (No. 1 Wood). The golfers generally were not aware of which swings were recorded.

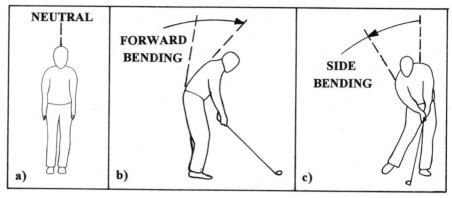

Figure 1. Orientation of the Bending Angles. a) Neutral b) Forward c) Side

2.3 Definition of measured parameters

The five major measured parameters shown in Figure 1. can be defined as follows:

1. Hip Rotation: This is the rotation in degrees of the golfer's hips toward (open) or away (closed) from the target. Hip Rotation in this context is actually rotation of the golfer's pelvis. By definition, hip rotation is zero in the address position.

2. Upper Body Rotation: This is the rotation in degrees of the golfer's torso, measured at the mid-thoracic spine, toward (open) or away (closed) from the target. This number is the sum of the Hip Rotation and the Differential Rotation. The Differential Rotation is the relative rotation of the golfer's upper body to hips, also known as the "X-Factor" (McLean, 1992, 1993).

3. Forward Bending: This is the flexion or extension in degrees of the golfer's lumbar spine measured from the pelvis to the mid-thoracic spine. Since the pelvis rotates during the swing, this motion at address and impact indicates bending toward the ball, while at top of the backswing, it indicates bending away from the target.

4. Side Bending: This is lateral flexion in degrees of the golfer's lumbar spine measured from the pelvis to the mid-thoracic spine. Due to pelvic rotation, this motion appears as leaning toward or away from the target at address and impact, and as leaning toward or away from the ball at the top of the backswing.

5. Total Swing Time: This parameter is the sum of the Backswing Time (from take-away to the top of the backswing) and the Downswing Time (from the top of the backswing to impact). The top of the backswing is defined as the largest (most closed) rotation of the golfer's upper body.

3 Results

The analog data from the measurement instrument were converted to digital data by the SMT and then exported into a spreadsheet for analysis. The data are presented at the appropriate event during the swing. Figure 1 shows a typical data curve set generated by the SMT for a complete swing.

The results of the analysis are separated into rotation of the hips and upper body, forward bending angles, side bending angles and the swing time. The data are presented using means and standard deviations and a 0.5 level of significance unless otherwise indicated. A summary of some of the measured data is shown below, grouped by rotation angles and bending angles.

3.1 Rotation of the Upper Body and Hips

3.1.1 Address

	Differential (Open)	
PGA Tour	5 +/- 1	SD: 3
Senior PGA Tour	5 +/- 1	SD: 1
Amateur	5 +/- 1	SD: 4

3.1.2 Top of Backswing (Closed)

	Upper Body		Hips	
PGA Tour	87 +/- 3	SD: 12	55 +/- 3	SD: 10
Senior PGA Tour	78 +/- 4	SD: 13	49 +/- 3	SD: 12
Amateur	87 +/- 4	SD: 13	53 +/- 4	SD: 11

3.1.3 Impact (Open)

	Upper Body		Hips	
PGA Tour	26 +/- 3	SD: 12	32 +/- 3	SD: 13
Senior PGA Tour	28 +/- 4	SD: 14	34 +/- 4	SD: 15
Amateur	27 +/- 3	SD: 9	35 +/- 3	SD: 9

3.2 Bending Angles

3.2.1 Address

	Forward		Side
PGA Tour	28 +/-2	SD: 8	6 +/-1 (right) SD: 4
Senior PGA Tour	23 +/-2	SD: 8	8 +/-1 (right) SD: 4
Amateur	25 +/-3	SD: 9	7 +/-1 (right) SD: 4

3.2.2 Top of Backswing

	Forward		Side	
PGA Tour	16 +/-3	SD: 10	3 +/-1 (left)	SD: 6
Senior PGA Tour	13 +/-2	SD: 8	4 +/-2 (left)	SD: 6
Amateur	10+/-3	SD: 10	16 +/-2(left)	SD: 7 **

3.2.3 Impact

	Forward		Side	
PGA Tour	19+/-2	SD: 9	31 +/-1 (right)	SD: 5
Senior PGA Tour	16 +/-2	SD: 8	28 +/-2 (right)	SD: 6
Amateur	16 +/-3	SD: 9	21 +/-2 (right)	SD: 5 **

3.3 Swing Time

The average swing times are shown below in seconds.

	Backswing	Downswing	Time to Impact
PGA Tour	.80	.29	1.09
Senior PGA Tour	.75	.28	1.03
Amateur	.91	.38	1.28 **

** Indicates significant difference from PGA Tour and the Senior PGA Tour data.

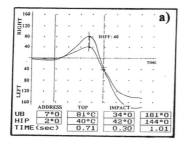
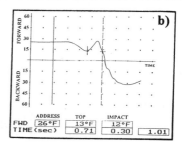
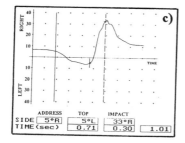
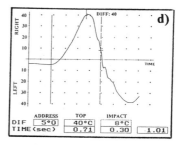

Figure 2.(a) Hip and Upper Body Rotation, (b) Forward Bending,
(c) Side Bending, (d) Differential Turn

4   Conclusions

The data collected and analyzed in this study provide precise new information about the golf swing. We use this information to analyze the Tour swings, compare Tour swing data to that of amateurs, consider some currently accepted notions about the golf swing and examine the implications of this new technology on teaching the swing.

4.1 Analysis of PGA Tour and Senior PGA Tour Swings

The similarities of the mean positions measured among the two groups are striking. It is tempting to recommend these averages as parameters to strive for, especially since the data of Tom Purtzer (shown in Fig. 2), who was named by his peers as having the best swing on Tour, most closely approximate the PGA Tour averages shown herein. However, we found considerable variance within each group.

With one possible exception, there seems to be no clear correlation among the Tour players between any specific torso motions or positions and excellence in driving distance or accuracy in hitting fairways and greens in regulation. The possible exception is that longer hitters on the PGA Tour tend to create a relatively higher percentage of their total backswing rotation from their differential turn than do shorter hitters (McLean 1992,1993). The 10 PGA Tour players in this study who ranked in the Top 50 in driving distance generated a mean of 42 percent of their turn from the differential turn, versus 35 percent for the rest of the group.

Nevertheless, there are numerous similarities among the swing of the Tour players measured. At least 70 percent, and in some cases 100 percent, of the Tour players measured share the following swing characteristics:

At address, right side bending is between 2 degrees and 10 degrees. The upper body is open 1 degree to 10 degrees, relative to the hips.

On the backswing, the upper body rotates first to initiate the take-away, and it rotates faster than the hips. The differential peaks at or very near the peak of upper body rotation. Side bending is 10 degrees or less at the top of the backswing.

On the downswing, the hips initiate the change of direction. The upper body rotates faster than the hips. Right side bending increases dramatically while forward bending increases, then decreases.

At impact, forward bending is less than at address. Right side bending is 23 degrees or more. The upper body and hips are open relative to their hip position at address. The differential is 10 degrees or less. The upper body decelerates slightly just prior to impact, and the hips decelerate substantially immediately after impact.

4.2 Comparisons Among PGA Tour, Senior PGA Tour, and Amateur Golfers

4.2.1 Rotation

Senior PGA Tour players achieved less total backswing rotation and fewer degrees traveled from the top of the backswing to impact than did the PGA Tour players or amateurs. This merits further investigation. Total backswing rotation and degrees traveled to impact by amateur and PGA Tour players were very similar, and cannot be considered a key difference between skill levels. This finding contradicts our general observation that many amateurs rotate their hips excessively in the backswing. In other cases, poor players occasionally demonstrate admirable rotation while exhibiting problems with bending angles, weight shift, arm/wrist action, grip pressure and/or swing plane. Nevertheless, PGA Tour players showed considerably less individual variation in degrees of rotation from swing to swing than amateur players, which helps to explain their superior consistency in shotmaking.

Moreover, amateurs rotate more slowly than Tour players on both the backswing and downswing. The Tour players' faster backswing motion may indicate a more efficient connection between the torso and arm motions. On the downswing, amateurs required an additional 31 percent more time (.09 seconds) to rotate the same distance to impact as PGA Tour players. The Tour players' faster rotation contributes to greater clubhead speed. Possible explanations for their faster rotation include 1) a faster change of direction (due to better arm-torso connection), 2) better retention of the wrist hinge, 3) more efficient swing path and 4) less hip slide on the downswing.

4.2.2 Bending Angles

The most notable difference between the PGA Tour players and amateurs occurs in side bending at the top of the backswing and at impact. The deeper left side bending shown by amateurs during the backswing results from sliding the hips away from the target and dropping the left shoulder toward the ground, possibly in an attempt to keep the head still over the ball. (See Figure 3.) In contrast, Tour

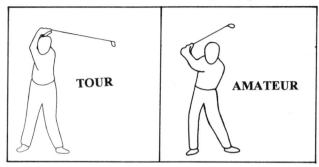

Figure 3. Bending Angles of Tour players and Amateur players.

players turn the hips without sliding and rotate the upper body on a more level backswing plane. On the downswing, amateurs typically achieve less right side bending than Tour players, probably because they slide the hips more towards the target, and their right shoulders move out instead of down to start the downswing.

4.3 Observations about Common Hypotheses Regarding the Golf Swing

4.3.1 The hips lead the downswing.
Approximately 70 percent of Tour players rotate their hips first in the downswing. Ten percent rotate hips and upper body together, and 20 percent rotate upper body first into the downswing.

4.3.2 The hips start down while the shoulders are still going back.
With a few exceptions, the data do not support this. Only 3 percent unwind hips noticeably while the upper body is still winding up. Sixty-nine percent show peak backswing rotation of the hips and upper body in very close proximity. Twenty percent begin unwinding hips as the upper body finishes the backswing. In many cases, the hips do pause briefly while the upper body completes its backswing rotation.

4.3.3 The address position approximates the impact position.
The data do not support this. On average, the upper body and hips are 20 degrees to 40 degrees more open at impact. The differential changes from a few degrees open to about 6 degrees closed. Right side bending is 20 to 25 degrees deeper and forward bending is about 8 degrees less at impact.

4.3.4 The shoulder turn remains level on the backswing and downswing, relative to the spine angle at address.
The data appear to confirm this notion on the backswing, but not on the downswing. At impact, the mean right side bending is 28 to 31 degrees, which indicates a much steeper shoulder plane in the downswing.

4.3.5 The spine angle remains constant during the swing.
This may be a useful image for two-dimensional viewing, but it is a vast oversimplification. (See Figs. 2b. and 2c.) Side and forward bending angles change dramatically during the swing. In fact, attempting to keep the spine angle constant appears to cause excessive left side bending and backward bending at the top of the backswing. Compared with the address position, the spine tilts more away from the target on the backswing and more towards the target line on the downswing.

4.4 Implications of Real Time Analysis and Feedback to Teaching the Golf Swing

The SMT quantifies swing motions precisely and reliably, in the field, without encumbering the player. It measures foot pressure, grip pressure and wrist action as well as torso motion. It enables rapid acquisition of data and provides meaningful, objective comparisons, which can answer enduring questions and foster broader consensus among instructors. This current study has identified fundamental torso motions shared by world-class golfers, documented significant differences between Tour players and amateurs, and shed new light on the complexity of spinal motion during the golf swing.

The ability to quantify motion in real time creates an additional opportunity: the power to provide precise instant feedback to players learning a new motions. Auditory "success" tones deliver immediate positive reinforcement to help students feel and repeat correct component motions of the swing. With precise analysis and instant feedback, students improve faster and retain the new skill better (Houser 1993, Pirozollo et. al. 1993).

The implications for instruction are exciting. The technology of measurement and feedback, combined with the guidance of informed instructors, enables the design and creation of the ideal swing for each individual.

5 References

Bowden, K. and Aultman, D.T. (1975) The methods of golf's masters. Coward, McCann and Geoghegan.

Cochran, A. and Stobbs, J. (1968) The search for a perfect swing. J.B. Lippincott Co, Philadelphia.

Dvorak, J., et. al. (1992) Age and gender related normal motion of the cervical spine. **Spine**, 17: 10S, L.B. Lippincott Co., Hagerstown, MD.

Hogan, B. (1957) Five lessons, the modern fundamentals of golf. A.S. Barnes and Company, New York.

Houser, D., (1993) The effects of augmented feedback related to weight transfer on the distance and accuracy of a five iron drive by experienced golfers. Masters Thesis, University of Virginia.

Leadbetter, D. (1990) The golf swing. The Stephen Greendress, Lexington, MA.

McLean, J., (1992) Widen the gap. **Golf Magazine**, December, 49-53.

McLean, J., (1993) X-Factor 2: closing the gap. **Golf Magazine**, August, 28-32.

Nelson, B. (1976) Shape your swing the modern way. **Golf Digest, Inc.**, Norwalk, CT.

Pirozzollo, F., (1993) Augmented kinematic feedback enhances learning of the golf swing. Submitted for publication.

Wiren, G., (1990) Laws, principles and preferences - a teaching model. **Science and Golf**, E. & F. Spon, London.

9 Centrifugal force and the planar golf swing

B. Lowe
FEI Expert Systems Research, Melbourne, Australia
and I.H. Fairweather
Department of Physical Education and Recreation, Victoria
University of Technology, Melbourne, Australia

Abstract
The familiar double-pendulum model of the golf swing was
applied to the downswing and follow-through swing planes of
low handicap golfers. Co-planar swings were predicted in
which downswing and follow-through clubhead displacements
follow the same plane. It was found that centrifugal forces
generated by the pendulum action are used by better players
to keep the clubhead on plane. Furthermore, centrifugal
force, rather than supination of the left wrist, provides
the mechanism to square the clubface at impact. The
clubhead was found to rotate about a central pivot.
Keywords: Golf Swing, Centrifugal Force, Double-Pendulum,
Planar.

1 Introduction

Although the concept of centrifugal force is central to the
popular double-pendulum interpretation of the golf swing
(Cochran and Stobbs, 1968; Daish, 1972), there is
disagreement concerning the role it plays in golf swing
mechanics. According to the double-pendulum model (Daish,
1972 p.30), centrifugal force explains how '...energy...in
the upper lever is gradually...fed outwards...into the
implement being wielded.'. Hay (1973) p.282, on the other
hand, argues 'Thus, since...centrifugal force...acts not on
the club but on the hands, it cannot possibly be
responsible for pulling the clubhead outward.'.
    According to Cochran (1993), centrifugal force '...is an
inertial force, and to that extent is fictitious in the
same way that all inertial forces are. But the effect is
quite real.'. Fowles (1985) p.122 claims that '...the
centrifugal force is the familiar force arising from
rotation about an axis. This force is always directed
outward and away from the axis of rotation and is
perpendicular to that axis.'. According to Daish (1972)
p.29 'The centrifugal pull on the hands...will be over 320
N for the clubhead of a driver whirling at 45 m s^{-1}.'. More

Science and Golf II: Proceedings of the World Scientific Congress of Golf. Edited by A.J.
Cochran and M.R. Farrally. Published in 1994 by E & FN Spon, London. ISBN 0 419 18790 1

recently, Milne and Davis (1992) have proposed that the shaft obtains an extra bending stiffness due to large centrifugal forces near impact. These claims suggest that a model of movement during the golf swing should include centrifugal force. Otherwise specific inertial effects will be inadequately explained.

Our pilot investigations indicate that the centre-fleeing effect of the forces generated during the swings of better players are responsible for a planar clubhead displacement. Furthermore, the downswings and follow-throughs of elite players are approximately co-planar when viewed along the X-axis, parallel with the target line. Despite a negative finding by Neal and Wilson (1985), various authors have argued for the planar swing concept, in particular, Budney and Bellow (1982). Not-withstanding these claims little formal support for the planar swing concept has been generated by 3D investigations using golfers. Literature reviews have failed to reveal studies, prior to this, which have compared the backswing, downswing and follow-through swing planes of good golfers.

The present study investigated evidence of centrifugal force in the swings of a group of low handicap golfers. To do so, an experimental, swivel headed club, was developed. The free hinge served to negate left wrist supination in correctly aligning the clubface at impact. This movement of the clubhead, according to Milne and Davis, (1992) involves a rotation through a right-angle about 50 ms before impact. It is proposed that the most parsimonious explanation for this 'squaring' of the clubface, should the rig be successfully implemented, would be the centre-fleeing effect of the clubhead undergoing rotation; its tendency, due to centrifugal force, to achieve a position distal to the hands throughout the swing.

The study also investigated the claim by Sanders and Owens (1992) that the pivot, or hub, is not located in a consistent position within the golfer throughout the swing. Their finding is at odds with our pilot investigations which found co-planarity in the downswings and follow-throughs of low handicap golfers. We propose this finding is most likely due to rotation of the clubhead about a central pivot, fixed within the golfer. The pivot, whilst maintaining the same relative position, could shift according to the movements of the golfer during the swing.

2 Method

2.1 Design of experimental rig
In order to test the model, an experimental club, similar in concept to that depicted in Cochran and Stobbs (1968)

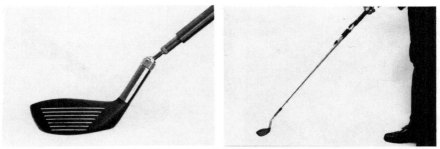

Fig.1a. The articulated golf club; fig.1b. at address.

p.146, was developed. A purpose built Lynson metal 5-wood was connected to a regular flex True Temper Lite shaft via a ball and socket joint with a 30° cone of mis-alignment, as shown in figure 1a. Figure 1b shows the club in the address position. The lipstick camera is not shown.

A linear displacement transducer (L.D.T.), attached to the long axis of the shaft, measured relative mass displacements along the shaft axis. The proximal end of the transducer was fixed to the shaft via a spring, whilst the distal end; free to move in the axis of the shaft, was fitted with a small mass. Radial displacement of the mass was outputted as an electrical signal proportional to the distance moved. The L.D.T. was calibrated in terms of the force required to distend the spring. Signals from the L.D.T. were acquired by computer with an acquisition rate of 1kHz over a period of 5 seconds. A microphone marked the time of impact.

A lipstick camera, mounted on the shaft near the L.D.T. and focussed on the clubhead, showed clubhead position and orientation relative to the shaft. Two S-VHS cameras were positioned to enable 3-D video analysis of swing plane geometry. PEAK 5.0 3-D software rotated the swing planes so that the downswing and follow-through swing planes, if possible, became co-planar (see sec.3 definition).

2.2 Subjects
Five subjects; one professional and four amateurs, participated in the study. Subjects 2 through 5; the amateurs, were off handicaps of three, four, one and zero respectively.

2.3 Experimental task
Subjects performed four medium paced swings with the experimental club and, subsequently, four slower swings at approximately half that pace. Subjects swung for rhythm and accuracy, and were requested to hit each ball straight out from the driving bay. Swings depicted in section 3 are the best swing identified by each subject and achieved realistic distance and accuracy.

Fig.2a. Subject 1 clubhead position at impact;
fig.2b. club suspended vertically.

3 Results

Figure 2a shows the clubhead at impact for subject 1; the
professional. The position and orientation assumed by the
clubhead appears to be the same as when the experimental
club is suspended vertically (figure 2b). This finding
suggests that the centre-fleeing effect maintained the
radial alignment of the clubhead centre of mass as the
clubhead was swung through the bottom of its arc.

Figure 3 shows the force-time profile of the medium and
slow swings of subject 1. It is evident from these
recordings that the apparent weight of the L.D.T. is
changing with time during both swings and that the faster
swing (dotted line) produced larger displacements/forces
than the slower swing (solid line). Data from the microphone
indicated that maximum force was produced at contact with
the ball. Video data confirmed that maximum clubhead
velocity also occurred at this time. The data for this
subject were typical of the force-time profile for the other
subjects.

Successful ball-striking appears to be mediated by the
planarity of the swing. Subject 3 (figure 4), who had a non-
planar swing, experienced great difficulty hitting the ball.
This swing was defined as non-planar as none of the clubhead
displacements formed a straight line when viewed along the
X-axis. The swing planes of the other subjects, when viewed
from a similar perspective, show near co-planarity, as
indicated by the degree to which the downswing and follow-
through swing planes were parallel. These subjects had
little difficulty striking the ball with the articulated
club and appear to have utilised the planar geometry of
their swings to achieve a successful ball-strike.

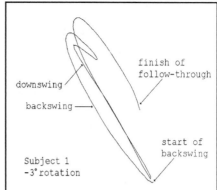

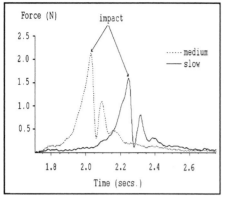

Fig.3. Force-time profile subject 1.

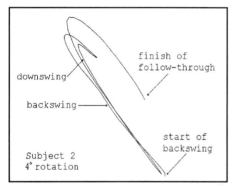

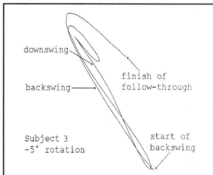

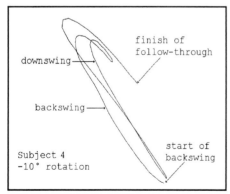

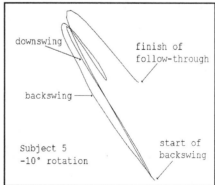

Fig.4. Clubhead swing planes subjects 1-5.

4 Discussion

The results of this study indicate that centrifugal forces were in operation when the experimental golfclub was swung, and that these centre-fleeing forces aligned the articulated clubhead in a position similar to when the club is suspended vertically.

The finding of primarily co-planar clubhead displacements in a group of low handicap golfers supports the view that centrifugal forces, generated by the pendulum action, were used by these players to ensure an effective ball-strike. In particular, support was found for the idea that better players primarily utilise centrifugal forces, rather than supination of the left wrist, to square the clubface, near impact. Successful wielding of the articulated golf club was consistent with the claim of Cochran and Stobbs, 1968 p.112 that 'One of the most interesting and important discoveries of the G.S.G.B. research programme is that, at impact, the clubhead behaves as though it were freely moving and not connected at all to the player.'.

Contrary to Sanders and Owens (1992), the golf club-head, at least for most of this group, was found to rotate about a central pivot. This claim is made as the the downswing and follow-through swing planes of the better players were co-planar. This finding does not preclude upper body movement during the swing; rather it suggests an internally consistent feature of an orthodox swing may be a co-planar clubhead displacement.

5 References

Budney, D. R. and Bellow, D.G. (1982) On the swing mechanics of a matched set of golf clubs. **Res. Quart. Exercise & Sport**, 53, 185-192.

Cochran, A. (1993) Personal communication.

Cochran, A. and Stobbs, J. (1968) **The Search for the Perfect Swing**. Heinemann.

Daish, C.B. (1972) **The Physics of Ball Games**. The English Universities Press Ltd, London.

Fowles, G.R. (1985) **Analytical Mechanics**. CBS College Publishing, PA.

Hay, J.G. (1973) **The Biomechanics of Sports Techniques**. Prentice Hall.

Milne, R.D. and Davis, J.P. (1992) The role of the shaft in the golf swing. **J. Biomech.**, 25, 975-983.

Neal, R.J. and Wilson, B.D. (1985) 3D kinematics and kinetics of the golf swing. **Int. J. Sport Biomechanics**, 1, 221-232.

Sanders, R.H. and Owens, P.C. (1992) Hub movement during the swing of elite and novice golfers. **Int. J. Sport Biomechanics**, 8, 320-330.

10 Categorisation of golf swings

M.A.J.Cooper and J.S.B. Mather
Department of Mechanical Engineering, University of Nottingham

Abstract
This paper discusses the methods of analysis needed to determine accurately the spatial pattern of the swing of a golfer. Results are presented using this analysis for golfers of differing ability. A categorisation appears simply from considering the results.
Keywords: Golf, swing, categorisation, velocity, photogrammetry.

1 Introduction

This paper describes the work to date in a study undertaken in the department of Mechanical Engineering at the University of Nottingham. The work is still ongoing as part of a Ph.D. thesis.

Much work done has been done in the past on the kinematic analysis of the golf swing. Initial work such as that by Jorgenson (1) and Williams (2) covered two dimensional analyses of the swing. Later contributors to the field such as Vaughan (3) extended the work to full three dimensional analysis of the motion. Almost the entire body of work however concerns the analysis of a single subject, usually a golf professional or a top amateur. Even where more than one subject has been studied, usually the results of only one subject have been presented. This is testament to the difficulty of this type of study. This paper presents initial results of a study which differs greatly from previous work. We aim to present three dimensional kinematic analysis of the swings of more than one subject, and moreover of subjects of differing abilities from professional to rank amateur, with the aim of comparing and contrasting these swings. We hope to show how these swings may be categorised according to certain characteristic kinematic behaviours and how this information might be used to improve club design.

2. Method

The basis of the work is photographic analysis of the swing, in particular the analysis of the position and orientation of the club at known time intervals in order to derive velocities and accelerations by differentiation. It was hoped at the start to produce an analysis system that was cheap to set up and use so that others in the field could also

Science and Golf II: Proceedings of the World Scientific Congress of Golf. Edited by A.J. Cochran and M.R. Farrally. Published in 1994 by E & FN Spon, London. ISBN 0 419 18790 1

benefit from the work. To this aim we decided to use 35mm SLR cameras with a stroboscopic flash system. In order to obtain 3 dimensional coordinates from two dimensional photographs, it is necessary to use two different views of the object under test. These can then be used to solve the collinearity condition, which states that a point on a photograph represents a line in space, so that if a point is imaged in two photographs then that point in the two photographs represents the intersection of two lines in space. Thus the pair of photographs can be used to find the position of any point imaged in both photographs. Initial work used two cameras arranged orthogonally. The analysis was based on simple perspective theory (Miller and Petak, 4). The system proved to be qualitatively useful in that different golfers could be distinguished by the results, but quantitatively very inaccurate, with positional resolution only in the order of tens of millimetres. After further research we decided to use a system based on the Direct Linear Transformation algorithm of Abdel-Aziz and Karara (5) as modified by Naftel and Boot (6) - the Iterative Linear Transformation algorithm. This method creates a set of linear equations for each point in each photograph which describe the position, orientation, and optical properties of each camera used and uses the collinearity condition with a least squares method to solve the equations for a set of known points in the photograph. Once solved these equations can be used to find coordinates of unknown points in the pair of photographs.

3 Biomechanics of the swing

As stated earlier, there have been many analyses of good golf swings and the biomechanics of the swing are fairly well described (see for example 7).
From photographic evidence in Cooper and Mather (7) it would seem in general that for many good swings, the head remains still, and the shoulders rotate about it, the left dipping under the chin, and the right moving behind the head. The arms take up a position with the club face perpendicular to the intended line of flight, and the arms close to the body ready to initiate a planar motion in the downswing. The hands then accelerate the club in the first 120° of rotation from where they move almost at constant velocity to impact. The left hip rotates virtually on a horizontal plane with the right dipping and turning to allow the right shoulder to drive down and through under the chin. After impact with the ball the momentum of the club carries the head on towards the target until the extended arms force the club around and over the shoulders. In this position the right leg must swivel and the knee joint bend until it comes into close proximity to the left leg. It is a modern trend that the knees remain bent at impact. Teaching of 40 years ago required that the left leg was straight at impact and the hips were parallel to the line of flight. Such a position required accurate timing in the swing and was abandoned in favour of a more consistent approach.
    The swing of most less able golfers is broadly similar. However in general, the wrists allow the club to flail outwards early in the swing. This is accompanied by a *horizontal* rotation of the shoulders about the torso axis which moves the club forwards away from the body and the intended swing plane. From this position the player has to make difficult and sizable adjustments to his movements in order to bring the club to impact with the ball. The motion is inwards and downwards and is confirmed by the force vectors. Impact is made on the ball with the club travelling across the line towards the

left hip, which has to pivot rapidly to make way for it. The natural follow through of the club does not materialise and the golfer has to apply large decelerations to the club to avoid injury. This open faced swing induces the sliced shot so often seen in poor golfers.

The amateur may be expected to differ significantly in the pattern and amplitude of forces that he generates from his swing (otherwise he would be able to reproduce the professional's swing!).

Essentially this means that the amateur, because of his poor timing and control, may generate larger forces than the professional, and from a biomechanical point of view, if his swing has the typical casting motion of the poor golfer, he generates his maximum forces at the time when his body is least able to control these forces. Thus, ironically, his poor swing pattern contributes to his poor swing pattern! It is our intention to investigate this, with a view to finding these forces and to find methods of controlling them so that the amateur's swing can be improved.

4 Method of analysis

Many photogrammetric analysis systems require the use of metric cameras (precision-made cameras with known optical properties) in order to obtain accurate positional data. These systems can give accuracies of up to 1 part in 100000 (8) but are unsuitable for our purposes because of their high cost - around £50000 for a pair of cameras. The ILT method allows the use of ordinary (non-metric) cameras, even down to the use of a basic Kodak instamatic if necessary! In our case a pair of 35mm Nikon SLR's costing £400 each were chosen. The ILT method requires the use of control points which must be imaged in the photograph and whose spatial coordinates must be known to the accuracy required for the derivation of the coordinates of the unknown points. A minimum of 6 points are needed for solution of the ILT equations, although more may be used with a least squares algorithm to give redundant information and improve accuracy. This means a rigid framework of accurately known points is required in the photograph. In our case, steel tubes bolted to the concrete floor of the lab provide the surfaces on which the control points are marked. Forty points are used which were tediously surveyed using a pair of theodolites, but if (as in our case) they are rigidly fixed, this only needs to be done once.

The control points surround the volume of the swing. A standard golf club, sprayed matt black and marked with its own control points, is used in the tests. These markings on the club define the position of a point on the shaft in three dimensions, and also the orientation of the shaft and the clubhead. The markings are positioned on the shaft at a point just below the end of the grip, which is slightly shortened. There are two markers on the shaft, 50mm apart, and one on a separate shaft extending from the uppermost marker at right angle to the club shaft, in the plane defined by the clubshaft and the clubface (see figure 1). The intersection of this second shaft and the centreline of the club shaft defines an origin for a local coordinate system. The strobes flash continuously and the camera shutters are operated by a laser switch system, the beam of which is broken on the backswing to trigger the delay which opens the camera shutters.

The negatives are digitised using a stereo plotter. This gives coordinates relative to the centre of the negative. In tests, using 30 of the control points to derive the other 10 gave an accuracy of the order of 0.2 mm over a distance of 3 metres.

The object space coordinates of the golf club are differentiated twice numerically to give velocities and accelerations. These are then resolved into the local coordinate directions defining the orientation of the club at that instant (see figure 1).

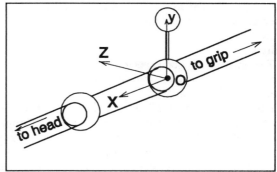

Figure 1

A smoothing cubic spline is then fitted to the data to give continuous velocity and acceleration against time curves. The rate of change of the local coordinate directions is used to derive the angular velocity of the club about the origin of the same local coordinate axes (Wittenburg, 9) and a smoothing cubic spline is fitted to these also (Lancaster and Salkausas, 10). Because the markers used to define the club orientation are close together, and attached to almost the thickest part of the shaft, it is assumed that the deflection of the shaft between the markers is negligible. Photographic evidence supports this assumption.

5 Results
Each subject generates 6 velocity/time and acceleration/time curves.

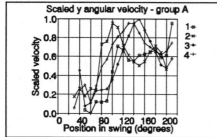

Figure 2

For comparison, we have chosen to consider only the y angular velocity. This is because this component is the major contributor to the clubhead velocity at impact. The results for our subjects are shown in the figures. The velocities have been scaled by dividing by the peak value for each curve so that the maximum velocity of each subject has a value of one in order that different subjects may be compared according to the pattern of their swing rather than the magnitude of it. The impact position is at 190 degrees on the horizontal scale.

We can see in the first group (figure 2) the typical amateur swing pattern - the hands start quickly, clubhead velocity peaks well before impact, and the swing is poor. The second group (figure 3) displays better characteristics, with more smoothness evident in the velocity profile. A third group (figure 4) shows only slight perturbations from the general trends of the curves while a fourth group (in fact only a single subject) shows an almost perfect velocity profile with peak velocity exactly at ball impact.

Purely from visual inspection, we can see that the grouped curves show marked

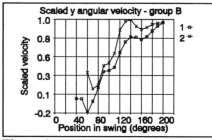

Figure 3

similarities to each other in terms of degree of smoothness, position of peaks, genral curve shape etc., while differing in these and other characteristics from other groups. Several independent observers have remarked upon this and they have generally grouped the subjects in the same manner.

It is intended to do a more mathematically rigorous grouping using cluster analysis as part of the ongoing work, but even by eye the results are acceptable. The groupings correlate well with the handicaps of the subjects, with group one being 25 and over, group two being 10 to 15, group three around 5, and the group four player is a club professional. We can see that similarly handicapped players obviously display similar swing patterns, and that there is a progression from poor to good. This perhaps gives weight to the theory that there is only one perfect swing, and that all golfers are trying to progress towards it!

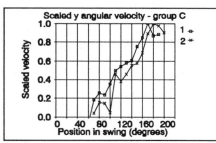

Figure 4

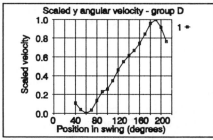

Figure 5

6 Conclusions

The preliminary study shows that the categorisation of golfers according to certain characteristics of their swings is a valid idea, and that these categories derived so far broadly coincide with playing ability. This and other previous work also suggests that the swing produced by a golfer is heavily influenced by his ability to control the club. The interaction between the forces applied to the club by the golfer, and the forces applied to the golfer by the club, heavily influence his ability to control the swing. It is plausible that the golfers in the poorer categories are unable to control the forces that their clubs subject them to using their current swing pattern. Also it is also plausible that they do not possess enough strength and/or degree of coordination to change their swing pattern because of the forces the golf club applies to their bodies. If true, it should thus be possible to use this data to design clubs to better suit each category of golfer found. This line of thought also suggests that current industry trends toward longer, larger headed clubs with lightweight shafts are exactly what the amateur does not need to improve his swing. The increased inertia of these clubs can only accentuate the poor swing of the amateur who is unable to control his present clubs by increasing the forces placed upon him. What would be needed is exactly the opposite - a reduction in the forces on the poor golfer enabling him to control his swing better and so progress to the next category of swing.

A second conclusion arises from the disparity in the swings of the categories. Clubs derived from robotic tests using ideal swings are hardly likely to be suitable for two and possibly three of the four categories that we have identified, as robot testing machine do not react at all to the forces applied to them by the club during the swing, whereas human beings certainly do.

7 References

1. Jorgensen, T., On the dynamics of the swing of a golf club. Am. J. Phys, **38** (5) p644. 1970

2. Williams, D. The dynamics of the golf swing. Quart. J. Mech. Appld. Math. XX (2), p247, 1967

3. Vaughan, C.L. A three dimensional analysis of the forces and torques applied by a golfer during the downswing. Proc 7th Int Cong Biomech. Univ Press Baltimore. p 325. 1981.

4. Miller, D.I., Petak,K., Three-dimensional cinematography, American Assoc. for Health, P.E., and Recreation, Kinesiology III, 1973, p 14-19

5. Abdel-Aziz, Y.I., Karara, H.M. Direct linear transformation from comparator co-ordinates into object space co-ordinates in close range photogrammetry. Proc. ASP/VI Symp. on Close Range Photogrammetry. Urbana, Illinois, 1971

6 Naftel, A.J., Boot, J.C., An iterative linear transformation algorithm for solution of the collinearity operators. Photogrammetric Engineering and Remote Sensing. **57** (7), 1991.

7 Mather J.S.B., Cooper, M.A.J. The response of club and golfer to the forces generated in the golf swing. Proc. 2nd Int Symp. on 3-D analysis of human movement. Poitiers. 1993.

8 American Society of Photogrammetry, Handbook of Photogrammetry,

9 Wittenburg, J., Dynamics of systems of rigid bodies, Teubner, Stuttgart, 1977. p29

10 Lancaster, P., Salkauskas, K., Curve and surface fitting, Academic press, 1986 p106 - 111

8 Acknowledgements

The authors wish to acknowledge the Wilson Sporting Goods Co of Chicago who sponsored part of this work, Dr. J.J. Webster of the Department of Mechanical Engineering of the University of Nottingham for his help on finite elements, Dr. Martin Smith of the Department of Civil Engineering for his help in photogrammetry and the use of surveying instrumentation, and to Mr. D. Vardy and Mr. A. Smith of the Department of Psychology for their help with experimental instrumentation and testing.

11 Dynamic model and computer simulation of a golf swing

S.M. Nesbit, J.S. Cole, T.A. Hartzell, K.A. Oglesby and A.F. Radich
Department of Mechanical Engineering, Lafayette College, Easton, PA, USA

Abstract
This paper discusses the development of a dynamic model and computer simulation of a golf swing. The simulation combines a variable model of a human with a parametric model of a golf club. The model is driven with data obtained from actual golf swings using a four camera motion analysis system. The model can be analyzed to study the biomechanics of a golfer including the kinematics and kinetics of his joints, the interactions between the golfer and his equipment, and how altering the dynamic parameters of a golf club effects both the golfer and his swing.
Keywords: Biomechanics, Dynamic Modeling, Computer Simulation, Kinematics, Kinetics

1 Introduction

The introduction of engineering science and computer technology into the golfing industry has caused an explosion of new high-tech products. Innovations include new methods of design and analysis, more accurate methods of testing, and the availability of exotic materials. With these new products have come a whole host of claims for performance enhancement.

It is difficult for a golfer to qualify and impossible to quantify the biomechanical effects that new equipment or changes to existing equipment has on his swing. Thus it becomes impossible to accurately study the effects of equipment on a golfer using the golfer alone. Therefore, to get an unbiased analytical perspective of a golfer's swing, a necessary step is to create a model that includes both the golfer and his equipment. For the model to be useful, it should allow for the wide variability in both the golfer and club configuration.

2 Computer Model

A computer model of a golf swing was developed to study the biomechanics of a golfer and the interactions between a golfer and his clubs during a swing. The computer model uses the software packages ANSYS (Swanson Analysis Systems, Inc., Ver 4.4) and ADAMS (Mechanical Dynamics, Inc., Ver 7.0) to model the golf club, ADAMS/ANDROID

Science and Golf II: Proceedings of the World Scientific Congress of Golf. Edited by A.J. Cochran and M.R. Farrally. Published in 1994 by E & FN Spon, London. ISBN 0 419 18790 1

(Mechanical Dynamics, Inc., Ver 1.0) to model the golfer, and ADAMS to solve the resulting model. Data to drive the model is obtained from a four camera motion analysis system (Motion Analysis Corp.). Coordination of the model components and the swing data is done with FORTRAN programs. The model is verified with the motion analysis system and force plates which are used to measure the vertical reaction forces between the golfer's feet and the ground. The resulting model simulates a golfer's swing and is analyzed to study the biomechanical effects of golf club changes on both the golfer and his swing.

2.1 Parametric Model of a Golf Club
The dynamic quantities of a golf club needed to create a parametric model include material properties, mass, mass center location, and inertia tensor of the shaft and club head plus the length, flexibility, and damping of the shaft. These quantities are relatively easy to determine for the shaft. Determination of mass properties for the club head is more difficult and is done using a combination of solid modeling and experimental techniques. Solid modeling using the finite element program ANSYS (Oglesby, 1992) was found to be an efficient method for determining these quantities for irons (Fig 1). The complex shape and non-homogeneity of woods and metal woods makes solid modeling difficult. Experimental techniques utilizing an inertia pendulum proved to be much better at determining the mass properties of these clubs (Johnson, 1993). The dynamic quantities are then entered into a FORTRAN program which creates an ADAMS model of the golf club (Fig 2).

2.2 ADAMS/ANDROID Model of a Golfer
The software package ADAMS/ANDROID is used to model the golfer. The "android" models a human as a complex three dimensional mechanism made up of fifteen rigid segments with mass and inertia properties (Fig 2). The segments are connected with fourteen spherical joints that can be constrained or driven by separate motions and/or forces. Android models are sized with population parameters that access GeBod data (ADAMS/ANDROID Users Manual) for representative segment geometry and mass properties. The ADAMS program performs the analysis of the model that the ADAMS/ANDROID module creates.

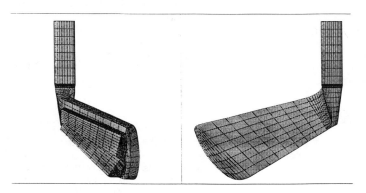

Figure 1 - Solid Model of an Iron Golf Club Head

Figure 2 - Complete Model Showing Android, Club, and Ground Surface

A golfer's swing, measured with a motion analysis system, can be used to drive the joints of the android. In this case, the joint kinematics are specified and the forces and torques at the golfers joints necessary to produce the swing can be calculated (kinematic analysis). A kinematic analysis allows for the study of how changing golf club parameters will affect the golfer by yielding changes in joint forces and torques. The outcome of the swing will not be altered.

If joint torques are used to drive the android, then the resulting joint motions can be determined (dynamic analysis). If the torques determined from a kinematic analysis are used to drive the android, then the original swing is recreated (assuming the club parameters have not been changed). A dynamic analysis allows for study of how changes in the golf club affect the outcome of the swing. This is noted in changes in joint positions, velocities, and accelerations. Unlike a human, the android will not adapt (unless instructed to) to new club configurations by altering joint forces and torques.

Thus if a change in a golf club parameter affects the android and/or the swing of the android, then it will affect the golfer in some way. A kinematic analysis gives an indication of how a golfer might feel different club configurations whereas a dynamic analysis indicates how the swing may be affected.

2.3 Motion Analysis System
To kinematically drive the model, actual golf swings are recorded and the data is used to drive the joints of the android. A four camera 180 hz motion analysis system tracks reflective markers that are strategically placed on the golfer. Marker paths are processed to yield joint motions.

Figure 3 - Recording Swing with Motion Analysis System

Marker placement is a major concern. Since a golf swing involves motion of all the major joints of the body, a large number of markers is required. However, it proved to be extremely difficult to track several markers through an entire golf swing - especially at the top of the back swing and follow through. Therefore, the important motions had to be identified, and the others ignored. The marker arrangement used allows for three dimensional motion tracking of the torso, hips, shoulders, and wrists. The elbows, knees, and ankles are restricted to two dimensional motion and the neck is held still relative to the ground (Fig 3).

2.4 Combining Components of the Model
The android, ADAMS club model, and ground surface are joined to make the complete model (Fig 2). First, the club is positioned relative to the global coordinate system using initial data from the motion analysis system. Next, the android and club are combined with the android oriented relative to the club. The android does not come with hands therefore it does not possess wrist joints. These are created by joining the club and android with spherical type joints placed at the ends of the lower arms. The linear degrees of freedom (DOF's) of the joint are rigid for one arm and flexible for the other because of the rigid nature of the android. The angular DOF's are either kinematically or dynamically driven to simulate the motions or torques of the wrist. Finally, the ground surface is added and positioned into place by sight. A spring-damper models the contact between the ground and the android's feet with the initial coefficients for this contact obtained from Scott (Scott, 1993).

The android is balanced by kinematically driving the angular DOF's of its lower torso segment relative to the global coordinate system. To avoid over constraining the model, the linear DOF's are set free. This balances the android but can cause one of the feet to lose contact with the ground if the joints are driven kinematically. The problem is solved with the force plates. Each remaining segment is driven relative to its adjacent distal segment.

2.5 Force Plates

Force plates were designed and built to measure the vertical reaction forces between the golfer's feet and the ground. The data is used for two purposes. First, it provides verification of the model since ground reaction forces are one of the outputs of the analysis (Fig 4). The force plate data is summed then compared to the results generated by the model. For a kinematic analysis, the summation is necessary because the stiffness of the model can cause one foot to lose contact with the ground.

This problem gave rise to the second use of the force plates. In order to get the android to keep both feet on the ground, it is necessary to dynamically drive the Beta rotation of one of the ankle joints to force the foot down. A torque control function is used that incorporates the force plate data for that foot (Eqn (1)).

$$T = \Sigma C_i (F_{meas} - F_{calc})^{P_i} + T_{weight} \tag{1}$$

The function constants (C_i and P_i) are adjusted and the solution iterated until the individual ground reaction forces from the analysis match the force plate data.

2.6 Solution of the Model

Once the android, club, and ground surface have been combined, the model is ready for solution by ADAMS. Both a kinematic and a dynamic analysis require a dynamic solution methodology because of the flexible shaft and spring-damper surface contact. The Wielenga's stiff integrator algorithm was found to be the most successful. The ability of ADAMS to solve the model depends heavily upon the values used for the torque control function constants, solution error tolerances, surface contact coefficients, and the initial position of the surface relative to the android's feet. These parameters can be adjusted to facilitate solution without compromising the analysis. Considerable smoothing of the marker path data is required to yield meaningful results.

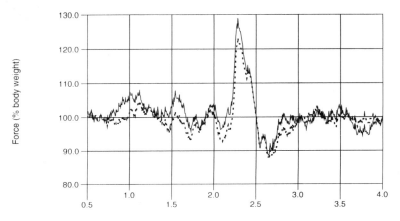

Figure 4 - Force Plate Data (dots) vs Analysis Results (line)

2.7 Uses of the Model

The model can be used to study the biomechanics of a golfer as well as quantify the effects of changing golf club parameters on both the golfer and his swing. Because the golfer is included in the model, it is possible to determine how club changes may affect different golfers in terms of body style, level of play, and swing characteristics. The analysis yields a wealth of information including the following:

- animation of the swing
- interactions between golfer, equipment and ground
- kinematics and kinetics of each joint
- kinematics of mass center of golfer
- position and orientation of club head
- shaft deflections

An example analysis performed using the model compared various 5-iron head configurations to determine if a golfer might feel any differences during a swing. The swing, shaft and club head mass were the same for each analysis. The differences were in the mass center locations and the inertia tensors of the club heads. The results (Fig 6) indicate that a golfer will feel the different mass distributions through the torque supplied down the long axis of the shaft. The figure also shows an animation of the swing used in the analysis (android removed from graphics for clarity).

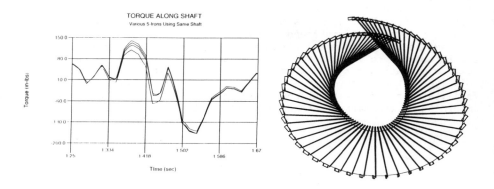

Fig 5 - Torque About the Long Axis of a Club for Various 5-Irons

3 References

Johnson, S.H. (1993) Experimental determination of inertia ellipsoids, (draft), in **Proceedings of the 1994 World Scientific Congress of Golf**.

Oglesby, K.A. Cole, J.S. and Nesbit, S.M. (1992) Parametric ANSYS model of golf clubs, in **1992 ANSYS Technical Conference** (eds D.E. Dietrich) Pittsburgh, PA, 3.3-3.5

Scott, S. and Winter, D. (1993) Biomechanical model of the human foot: kinematics and kinetics during the stance phase of walking. J.

12 A concise method of specifying the geometry and timing of golf swings

D.L. Linning
UK

Abstract
This paper provides a diagrammatic method for specifying the geometry
and timing of the actions of any golf swing, good or bad, and illustrates the procedures involved by applying them to one particular swing
within the family of effective swing styles.
Keywords: Golf Swing, Diagrammatic Specification, Geometry, Timing.

1 Method of Specification

Swing geometries are specified by diagrams which map swing paths of
knee-joints, hip-joints, shoulder-joints, hands, and clubhead.

Timing is specified by Phase Diagrams in which the durations and
sequences of swing actions are represented by individual horizontal
lines on a base of time.

2 Key Features of the Specified Representative Swing Style

The swing style specified aims at simplicity and effectiveness and is
based on a study of slow motion videos of tournament players plus some
geometrical and dynamical analysis (not included here) of relationships
between the various components of the body-arms-club system. However,
it is not claimed that this swing is better than other swings within
the family of effective swing styles.

Key features of the representative swing style include:

1 In the backswing the flows of muscular activation travel in parallel downwards through the body (that is, torso plus legs) and in-
wards through the arms. In the downswing the flows of activation
are reversed and travel in parallel upwards through the body and
outwards through the arms.
2 The head, or more precisely, the shoulders-centre is kept in or
near to its address location throughout the swing.
3 In the backswing the hips are pivoted round a still centre within a plane at right angles to the torso axis.
4 In the downswing and follow-through the forward pivot of the hips
is combined with a slide of the hip centre 45° left of target.
5 At impact the hips are about 45° open to the target and at completion they face the target with the right hip located where the
left hip was at address.

Science and Golf II: Proceedings of the World Scientific Congress of Golf. Edited by A.J.
Cochran and M.R. Farrally. Published in 1994 by E & FN Spon, London. ISBN 0 419 18790 1

6   During the backswing the right knee is braced to remain close to
its address location.
7   The gap between the knees stays constant through the backswing
and downswing, and into the follow-through.
8   The left arm is kept straight until well into the follow-through
and the elbows stay as close to each other as possible throughout.
9   During the downswing the wrists act as a hinge through which a
pure pull is transmitted to the club.
10 The clubhead stays within the same swing plane throughout backswing, downswing, and follow-through and this plane cuts the ground
on a line which passes through both the ball and the target. The
hands stay within a slightly steeper swing plane which cuts the
ground on a line parallel to but inside the clubhead intercept line.
This swing plane geometry is illustrated in Figure 1.

Figure 1. Hands and clubhead swing planes.

11 The downswing can be regarded as taking place in two phases. In
the Preparatory Phase only the legs and upper arms are working. In
the Power Phase all the components of the system make their optimum
contribution. The sketches in Figure 2 illustrate expert golfers at
the start of the Power Phase. Williams (1967) in his dynamical analysis of club motion treated the hands downswing path in two phases.

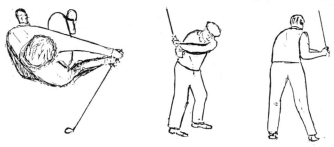

Figure 2. Expert golfers at the start of the Power Phase.

3   Knee Swing Paths

A plan view of the Knee Swing Paths is provided in Figure 3. The thick
-er lines indicate the Power Phase in all Swing Path Diagrams

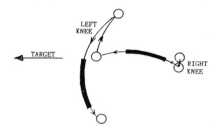

Figure 3. Knees Swing Path Diagram

Keeping the right knee braced close to its address location during the
backswing puts the knees in position to lead the downswing and also
ensures that the leg muscles which are going to initiate the downswing
are pre-tensioned. In effect, the right leg acts as a torsional buffer
which absorbs the angular momentum of the system as it decelerates to
rest at the top.

4   Hip-Joint Swing Paths

Figure 4 represents the Hip-Joint Swing Paths as viewed looking down
along the line of the torso axis at address. The diagrams indicate how
during the downswing and follow-through the hip pivot and hip-centre
movement combine to generate suitable Hip-Joint Swing Paths.

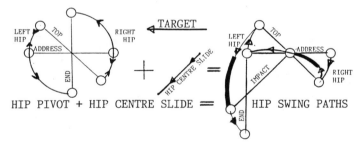

HIP PIVOT + HIP CENTRE SLIDE = HIP SWING PATHS

Figure 4. Hip-Joint Swing Path Diagram.

To keep the shoulders-centre near to its address location throughout
the swing the hips have to pivot in an inclined plane. The rocking
component of the hip movement which is implied is supplied by differential flexing of the legs.

5   Shoulder-Joint Swing Paths

In the backswing the shoulders turn in a plane at right angles to the
torso axis. In the downswing the shoulder-joint swing paths are much
steeper than in the backswing for a number of reasons:

1. There is twice as much hip turn in the downswing as in the backswing and consequently there is also twice as much rocking component.
2. The movement of the hip centre under a still shoulders-centre
during the downswing progressively increases the tilt angle of the
torso axis and consequently that of the shoulders.
3. The torso bows progressively in the second half of the downswing
and adds to the tilt angle of the shoulders.

Figure 5 illustrates the difference between the angles of shoulder
tilt at the top and in the follow-through.

Figure 5. Comparison of shoulder tilt at the top and in the
          follow -through.

Figure 6 represents the Shoulder-Joint Swing Paths as seen looking
towards the target, as in Figure 5. Figure 7 represents them as seen
looking down along the line of the torso axis at address.

Figure 6.   Figure 7.

The thicker lines indicate the movements of the shoulder-joints during
the Power Phase.
    At the instant of impact the shoulders are about 30° open to the
target and about 30° tilted to the horizontal.

6 The Timing of the Body Actions

The Phase Diagram in Figure 8 represents the sequences and durations
of the body actions. In a typical swing the backswing takes about
three times as long as the downswing and the follow-through takes
about twice as long. The whole swing lasts about 2 seconds.

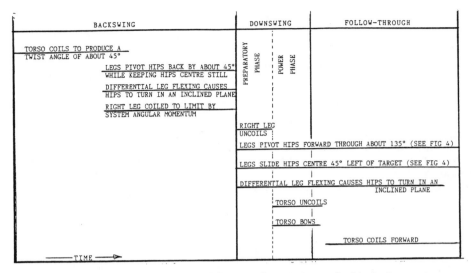

BACKSWING	DOWNSWING	FOLLOW-THROUGH

Figure 8. Phase Diagram specifying the timing of the body actions.

Although the individual independent actions are distinct the feeling should be of a flow or wave of activation travelling downwards through the body in the backswing and upwards through the body in the downswing.

7   Hands and Clubhead Swing Paths

The Hands and Clubhead Swing Paths are each contained within their respective swing planes, illustrated in Figure 1. Figure 9 represents the swing paths as viewed looking directly on to the Hands Swing Plane.

Figure 9. Hands and Clubhead Swing Path Diagrams

The reason why the downswing paths are inside the backswing paths is not because of a shift of the body towards the target. The shoulders centre must stay behind the ball till after impact. The main reason is that the strong leg pivot in the downswing turns the body more towards the target at corresponding left arm "clock" angles, taking the left shoulder-joint nearer to the target. Other associated reasons are the retention of the folded right arm and cocked wrists well into the downswing.

8 The Timing of the Arm Actions

It is convenient to deal with the wrist actions separately from those of the upper and lower arms. The actions available to the wrists are:

Cocking: The wrists move the hands in the plane of the palms.
Flexing: The wrists move the hands at right angles to the palms.
Rolling: Rolling is not actually an action of the wrists. It is a rotation of the wrists produced by coiling the forearms.

The main function of the wrists in the downswing is to act as a hinge through which a pure pull can be transmitted to the club. To orient the wrists so that they can act as a free hinge there must be a controlled rolling of the wrists through the swing. The Phase Diagram in Figure 10 represents the timing of the wrist actions.

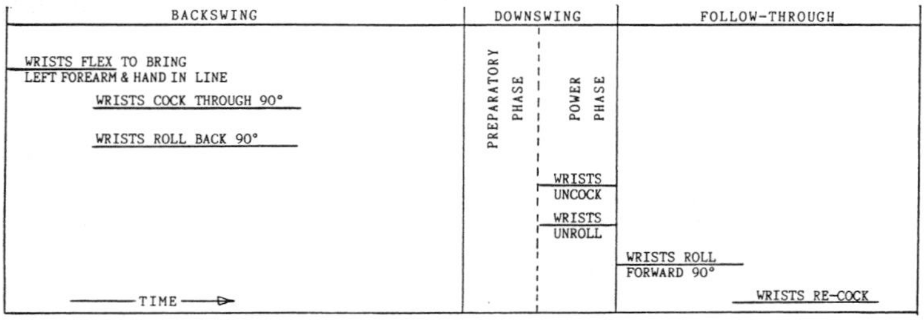

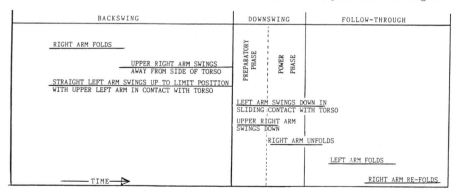

Figure 10. Phase Diagram for Wrist Actions

The wrists flex by a small amount early in the backswing to bring the back of the left hand into the plane containing the left forearm and do not flex again until after impact.

The swing path of the hands and the speed of the hands are determined by the actions of the body plus those of the upper and lower arms. The timing of the upper and lower arm actions is specified in Figure 11.

Figure 11. Phase Diagram for Upper and Lower Arm Actions

Delaying the start of the independent arm action in the backswing till the coiling torso has swung the left arm back to between 7 & 8 o'clock can help in generating a good well coiled configuration at the top.

Although the sequences of body and arm actions in the downswing are the reverse of those in the backswing, differences in timing produce critically different body-arm configurations at corresponding left arm positions, as is indicated in Figure 12.

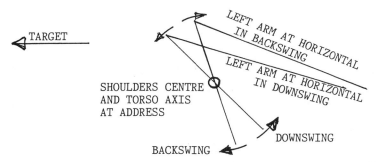

Figure 12. Configurations of shoulders and left arm as seen looking
        down along the line of the torso axis.

In the downswing the angle between the shoulders and the left arm is at its minimum value with the torso in close contact with the upper left arm. This situation is produced by a combination at the start of the downswing of a slightly delayed and slow independent arm action with a strong leg pivot, while keeping the hands within their swing plane. In the backswing the left arm makes a greater angle with the shoulder line, providing room for the straight left arm to be swung up into a good limit position at the top.

Allowing the straight left arm to lag against the torso in the downswing serves several purposes. It enables the turning body to use the left arm as a lever to transmit power. It allows the hips to be well open to the target through impact, thereby increasing the scope for leg action. It also provides a firm reference base for the left arm as it swings down and this can only help in grooving the hands downswing path.

9   Concluding Comments

The Concise Method of Specification provides an organised way of visualising the geometry and timing of the golf swing which can enhance the scope and accuracy of communication between golfers. It can also enhance communication between the conscious image and the subconscious control system.

The method identifies parameters which can be used to define swing geometry and timing. Measuring these would probably not be a simple matter but if it could be done it would be possible to build a set of Concise Specifications covering the range of effective and faulty swing styles. It would also be possible to confirm or refine the illustrative swing style specified in this paper.

10   References

Williams,D. The Dynamics of the Golf Swing. Quarterly Journal of
    Mechanics and Applied Mathematics, June 1967.

13 A study of the correlation between swing characteristics and club head velocity

R.L. Robinson
Coeur d'Alene, USA

Abstract
This paper presents the results of a study of the golf swings
of a group of touring professionals and amateurs of varying
skills. Their swings were recorded on a test set-up that
consisted of a three dimensional video graphics system, force
platforms supporting each foot, and a golf swing analyzer that
measured club head velocity at impact. Swing events were
selected for quantifying swing characteristics for each swing.
The swing characteristics exhibiting the most significant
correlation with club head velocity at impact for golfers
swinging the driver are identified and a comparison is made
between the mean values for the professionals and amateurs.
The results are summarized as to their relevance to the golfer
and teaching professional.
Keywords Event, Category, Characteristics, Club Head
Velocity, Stepwise Multiple Regression, Significant,
Correlation Coefficient, Predicts, Mean Value, Swing Keys.

1 Introduction

The study was done in conjunction with the development of a
weight shift measurement system utilizing a personal computer data acquisition system which can be synchronized with
video recordings of the golf swing. Rather than relying on
anecdotal insights into what swing characteristics to measure
and emphasize, the study was designed to yield information on
which measurable swing characteristics would make use of the
system productive for the swing instructor and student.

2 Methodology

The testing was done on a driving range where a set-up consisting of two force platforms and a swing analyzer was positioned under an open sided tent so that the golfers could
swing freely and the flight of the ball on the range could be
observed. Impact with the ball was sensed by a microphone.
The tent provided shade for the swing analyzer that requires

Science and Golf II: Proceedings of the World Scientific Congress of Golf. Edited by A.J.
Cochran and M.R. Farrally. Published in 1994 by E & FN Spon, London. ISBN 0 419 18790 1

an overhead collimated light source to operate. Four synchronized video cameras were arranged around the platform to
record the images required for the 3-D video data. The analog
data generated by the force platforms was recorded along with
the timing of impact. A line of markers on the range defined
the target line. The golfers were allowed to swing until they
were comfortable with the set-up and ready to have their
swings recorded. Their swings were then recorded and data
including ball flight, the readings from the swing analyzer,
and the measurements of the golfer's stance and ball position
for each swing were also recorded. Each participant was allowed to swing for record until a swing was obtained which
the golfer felt was representative of his game.

3 Analysis Approach

The analysis approach consisted of selecting a series of
clearly identifiable events occurring during the golf swing
and determining the values of the swing characteristics for
each event from the recorded data. The 22 point stick figures
obtained for the selected events are shown in Figures
1A,1B,1C, and 1D. Event 1 occurs at the point in the swing
just before the club head first begins to move away from the
ball at the beginning of the back swing. Event 2 occurs at the
point in the swing just before the club head begins to move on
the down swing. Event 3 occurs at the point in the down swing
when the left forearm is parallel to the ground. Event 4 occurs when the club head impacts the ball.

Fig. 1A. Event 1.   Fig. 1B. Event 2.   Fig. 1C. Event 3.   Fig. 1D. Event 4.

The swing characteristics evaluated at each event were
grouped into the following categories:

    1) Timing Between Events,

2) Reaction Forces on the Feet,
3) Relative Set-up and Swing Event Positions,
4) Linear Velocities,
5) Relative Angles,
6) Relative Angular Velocities.

The data was loaded into the matrix of a statistical analysis software program. A stepwise multiple regression analysis technique identifies the swing characteristics that best correlate with club head velocity at impact. The criteria for significance is the ratio of the regression mean square to the residual mean square consistent with a probability of 0.05 or less that the ratio would occur by chance sampling fluctuation. The driver swings of twenty amateurs with handicaps from 24 to 0 and ten touring professionals were selected for analysis.

4 Sample Data

Samples of vertical force vs. time data for each foot obtained during a driver swing are shown in Figures 2 and 3 which also show the stick figures and timing for the swing events. Note that the video frames cannot be synchronized exactly with impact with the ball and timing corrections were calculated to allow for interpolation between video frames so that a more accurate value of the analog data for each event could be obtained. The position and timing of the "Finish" of the swing is also shown but was not used as an event since it did not yield any significant characteristics in a preliminary analysis and was not always clearly identifiable.

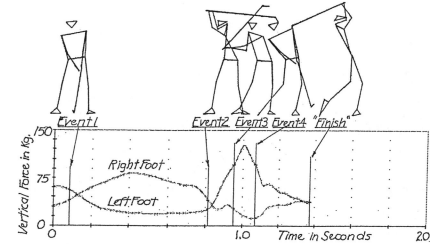

Figure 2. Vertical Force Data for a Selected Professional Golfer.

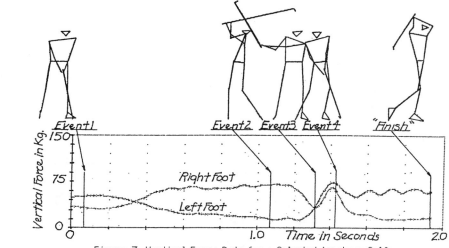

Figure 3. Vertical Force Data for a Selected Amateur Golfer.

5 Results of Analysis

The statistical description of the data obtained for club head velocity at impact for the 30 swings is presented in Table 1.

Table 1. Club Head Velocity at Impact in meters/second

Group	Mean	Std. Deviation	Minimum	Maximum
Amateur	41.8	3.5	35.8	48.7
Professional	48.3	1.8	45.1	51.0
Combined	43.9	4.3	35.8	51.0

Table 2 lists the most significant swing characteristics in their order of significance by category, the cumulative square (R-squared) of the correlation coefficient for each set of characteristics, the mean values of the characteristics for the amateurs and professionals, and the sign of the correlation coefficient for each characteristic. For example, for the category Timing Between Events, the time interval between Event 2 and Event 3 predicts 21.5% of the club head velocity at impact and when combined with the timing between Event 1 and Event 2, the two characteristics predict 31.9%. The sign of the correlation coefficient indicates that the shorter the time interval between Event 2 and Event 3, the greater the predicted club head velocity at impact. Note that the mean time interval between Event 2 and Event 3 is significantly shorter for the professionals. The single most significant

The single most significant swing characteristic identified in any category is the angle between the left forearm and the club or the wrist angle at Event 3 when the left forearm is parallel to the ground on the down swing. Refer to Figure 1C for clarity. Note the difference in this swing characteristic in the positions at Event 3 for the selected professional and amateur swings in Figures 2 and 3 respectively. This characteristic alone predicts 60% of the variation in velocity, more than the cumulative percentage of any of the other categories.

Table 2. Significant Swing Characteristics by Category

Category	Swing Characteristics in Order of Statistical Significance	R-Squared (cumulative by category)	Mean Values Amateur/Pro. (Units)	Sign of Coef.
Timing Between Events	1. Time Interval Event 2 to Event 3.	0.215	0.192/0.153 (seconds)	Neg.
	2. Time Interval Event 1 to Event 2.	0.319	0.872/0.887 (seconds)	Pos.
Reaction Forces on the Feet	1. Vertical Force on Right Foot - Event 1.	0.331	36.8/45 (Kg.)	Pos.
	2. Time Rate of Change of Vertical Force on Left Foot from Event 2 to Event 3.	0.477	119.4/157.9 (Kg./sec.)	Pos.
	3. Free Moment on Left Foot - Event 5 (Resisting Torque)	0.543	0.42/0.73 (Kg.-m.)	Pos.
Reaction Forces (Vertical Forces in % Body Weight)	1. Vertical Force on Right Foot - Event 1 in % of Body Weight.	0.204	42.1/50.9 (%)	Pos.
	2. Time Rate of Change of Vertical Force on the Left Foot from Event 2 to Event 3.	0.375	297/390 (%/sec.)	Pos.
	3. Free Moment on Left Foot - Event 5. (Resisting Torque)	0.453	0.42/0.73 (Kg.-m.)	Pos.
Relative Set-up and Swing Event Positions	1. Distance Along Target Line From Ball to Right Heel at Set-up.	0.265	0.33/0.41 (m.)	Pos.
	2. Shift in Center-of-Pressure on the Left Foot from Event 1 to Event 3(Heel-Toe).	0.388	-0.8/-0.9 (cm.)	Neg.
Linear Velocities	1. Linear Velocity of the Left Knee - Event 3.	0.235	1.05/1.37 (m/sec.)	Pos.
	2. Linear Velocity of the Left Knee - Event 2.	0.343	0.49/0.49 (m/sec.)	Pos.
Relative Angles	1. Angle Between the Left Forearm and Club - Event 3.	0.603	1.77/1.35 (radians)	Neg.
Relative Angular Velocities	1. Angular Velocity between the Left Arm and Shoulder - Event 4.	0.145	3.2/2.6 (radians/sec.)	Neg.
	2. Angular Velocity of the Hips - Event 3.	0.256	4.2/5.4 (radians/sec.)	Pos.

Table 3 lists the most significant swing characteristics identified in their order of significance when all categories are included in the analysis.

Table 3. Most Significant Swing Characteristics - Overall

Swing Characteristics in Order of Significance	R-squared (cumulative)	Mean Value Amateur/Pro. (Units)
X1 - Angle Between Left Forearm and the Club at Event 3.	0.603	1.77/1.35 (radians)
X2 - Time Interval From Event 3 to Event 4	0.746	0.112/0.108 (seconds)
X3 - Angular Velocity of the Shoulders at Event 4	0.812	7.93/9.44 (radians/sec.)
X4 - Angular Velocity of the Hips at Event 3	0.852	4.18/5.37 (radians/sec.)

The resulting regression equation with club head velocity as the dependent variable Y_i, and the most significant independent variables given in Table 3 may be defined as:

$$Y_i = -9.79\,X1 - 168.1\,X2 + 0.344\,X3 + 0.397\,X4 + 73.73 \text{ m/sec} \qquad (1)$$

6 Summary

For the golfer and the teaching professional, Table 2 amounts to a list of swing keys that relate to club head velocity at impact. For example, a rapid movement from the top of the back swing to a position halfway down on the down swing, coupled with a vigorous weight shift from right-to-left, promotes club head velocity at impact. These swing keys and others derived from Table 2, however, should be coupled with or contribute to minimization of the angle between the club and the left forearm well into the down swing, the most significant swing characteristic identified in the study. In theory, if the characteristics listed in Table 3 can be measured, 85% of the variation in club head velocity at impact may be predicted for a comparable group of golfers using Equation (1). When all the characteristics are analyzed together, besides the angle between the club and the left forearm and the timing of lower part of the down swing, the angular velocities of the shoulders at impact and the hips at the halfway point in the down swing are more significant than other swing characteristics identified in Table 2. The overall results differ from the results by category due to the interdependence of many of the swing characteristics.

The results of this study seem to fit with most of the popular swing ideas, but it was interesting to find no correlation between club head velocity at impact and the vertical force or weight on the left foot at impact, a swing characteristic often emphasized in golf instruction and swing measurement devices. Finally, the technology used in the study and the results of the study can be useful if they can be applied and interpreted by the golfer or teaching professional. This is often a difficult interface and one that the golf technology and science community need to address.

7 Acknowledgments

The author wishes to express his thanks to Henry-Griffitts Inc. and TI Apollo Ltd. for their sponsorship and support of this study. Special thanks are due to Dr. Richard Nelson and Tim Aro of the Penn State Biomechanics Lab. who were instrumental in setting up and implementing the study, and to Bruce Knoth of Advanced Mechanical Technology Inc., the staff at Peak Performance Technologies Inc., Dr. Jim Suttie, Nigel Rouse at the Country Club at Castle Pines for the use the driving range for our testing, and the amateurs and professionals that allowed us to test their golf swings.

14 Three-dimensional kinematic analysis of the golf swing

P.A. McLaughlin and R.J. Best
Biomechanics Unit, Centre for Rehabilitation, Exercise and Sports
Science and the Department of Physical Education and Recreation,
Victoria University of Technology, Melbourne, Australia

Abstract
Three groups of 10 golfers of differing handicap ranges
were videoed driving a golf ball for distance. 3-d motion
analysis techniques were used to measure kinematic data at
five points in the golf swing. Analysis of variance results
showed 11 parameters that were different among groups at
$p<0.001$. Some of these parameters were correlated allowing
further trimming of the list to; the vertical distance
between the clubhead and hands at the top of the backswing,
the position of the hips and knees at the middle of the
downswing, maximal clubhead velocity, trunk angle at
address and the angle between the left arm and the clubshaft at the middle of the downswing and this angle's angular velocity at ball contact. This study's data agreed
with previous literature that emphasised the delay of wrist
adduction or 'uncocking'. The major limitation in this
study was the relatively small sample size and frame rate.
Keywords: Golf, Biomechanics, 3-d kinematics, Statistics.

1 Introduction and Literature Review

Despite the huge amount of literature relating to the golf
swing, the application of scientific quantitative method to
this skill is scarce. Technological improvements since
Cochran and Stobbs' (1968) study has not seen a congruent
increase in the quantitative investigation of the skill.
  Cochran and Stobbs expounded a theory of the golf swing
as a double pendulum. Their report formed the theoretical
basis of the majority of the literature to follow. Milburn
(1982) and Neal and Wilson (1985) have all built upon the
foundations layed by Cochran and Stobbs (1968). Milburn
(1982) explored the double pendulum theory with his 2-d
motion analysis study of the downswing of 4 collegiate and
one low handicap golfer. Neal and Wilson (1985) further
advanced the area with a 3-d analysis of 4 professional and

Science and Golf II: Proceedings of the World Scientific Congress of Golf. Edited by A.J.
Cochran and M.R. Farrally. Published in 1994 by E & FN Spon, London. ISBN 0 419 18790 1

2 low handicap golfers. Neal and Wilson's technological advance was limited by a small sample size and the analysis of only a few parameters.

The objective of the authors' study was to use 3-d motion analysis techniques, a larger sample size and statistical techniques to analyse kinematic parameters of the golf swing and identify those parameters that distinguish between golfers of different ability.

2 Experimental Procedures

2.1 Sampling and Video Procedures
10 subjects from the Victorian Institute of Sport scholarship squad formed the low handicap (LH; AGU handicap <4) group. This group comprised outstanding young Victorian golfers (professionals and amateurs). Video was taken of the LH group as they hit a golf ball with a driver from an artificial surface and rubberised tee at the Moorabbin Driving Range. Two Panasonic S-VHS video cameras operating at 50 fields per second and a shutter setting of 0.001s were used to record the trials of all golfers. The placement of the cameras is illustrated in Fig. 1. Cameras were gen-locked and field synchronised. The horizontal field of view of each camera was approximately 5m. Videos were replayed and digitised on a National Panasonic D2020 Monitor with screen size of 0.4m x 0.3m. The Peak Performance Technologies (PEAK) 3-d calibration frame consisting of 24 spheres and accurately known geometry was videoed in the field of view of both cameras. This allowed reconstruction of the digitised points from the two camera views to 3-d coordinates using the direct linear transformation method of Abdel-Aziz and Karara (1971). The RMS error in digitising the calibration frame was 0.009 metres. The recommended procedures for 3-d motion analysis outlined by Bartlett et al. (1992) were used as a guide.

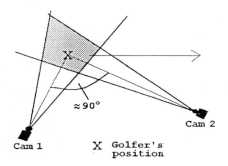

≈90°

Cam 2

Cam 1   X Golfer's position

Fig.1.   Camera set-up for both videoing sessions.

10 subjects in each of the middle handicap (MH; AGU handicap 9-18) and high handicap (HH; AGU handicap 19-27) groups comprised members, aged 21-60, of Medway Golf Club. Videoing was conducted on the 6th tee (220m par 3 hole), during a mid-week competition round. Videoing procedures were the same as those used in videoing of the LH group.

2.2 Data Capture
All swings were analysed using the PEAK Three-dimensional Motion Analysis System, Version 5. A spatial model was constructed consisting of 25 points; five on the club, one for the ball and 19 anatomical landmarks for the golfer. No joint centre markers were used. Dempster's (1955) body segment data were used to calculate the golfers' centre of mass (CM) position. The digitising rate was 50Hz. A Butterworth 4th order reverse digital filter was used to smooth the raw digitised data. An optimal cut-off frequency was calculated for each point in the spatial model using the method of Jackson (1979).

2.3 Statistical Analysis
26 kinematic parameters were measured at five instants in the golf swing (Fig. 2). The parameters were; the angle between a line joining the left shoulder and a point on the back of the left hand, and the clubshaft; right and left elbow angles; rotation of a line joining the hips relative to the address position; angle as above for shoulders and knees; angular velocities for each of the above angles; trunk angle to the forward horizontal; angle formed by the left shoulder, left hip and left knee; the angle between the clubshaft and the horizontal plane; the vertical displacement between the hands and the clubhead; change in vertical, lateral and forward displacement of the top of the head relative to the address position; change in vertical and forward displacement of the CM relative to the address position; x, y, z and resultant clubhead velocity; resultant velocity of a point on the back of the left hand. Six other parameters were calculated; swing time; backswing and downswing time; drive distance; maximal clubhead velocity; time when maximal clubhead velocity occurred.

One-way analysis of variance (ANOVA) was performed on each of the parameters to establish at what level that parameter varied among the three groups. With 136 parameters, a nominal significance level $p < 0.001$ was used as a cut-off. This reduced the chance of a type I statistical error, increased the chance of a type II error and reduced the statistical power. Avoidance of type I errors was deemed appropriate for this study since the data may be used by players and coaches. The Bonferroni post hoc test was used to locate significant differences. This test was appro—

priate considering the small sample size and equal group numbers.

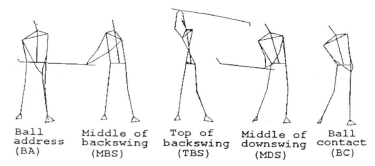

Ball   Middle of   Top of   Middle of   Ball
address   backswing   backswing   downswing   contact
(BA)   (MBS)   (TBS)   (MDS)   (BC)

Fig.2.   The five instants in the golf swing where
         kinematic parameters were measured.

3 Analysis of Results

11 parameters were found to be different at the p<0.001 level. These parameters are described in table 1. It should be noted that p<0.001 is a very conservative cut-off. 18 parameters were different across groups at p<0.005, 24 at p<0.01 and 47 parameters at p<0.1.

Table 1   Parameters different at the p<0.001 level.

Kinematic Parameter	LH&MH	LH&HH	MH&HH
Trunk angle at BA	*	*	
Vertical displacement between the club-head and hands at TBS	#	#	
Hip axis position at MDS	*	*	
Knee axis position at MDS	*	*	
Angle between the left arm and club-shaft at MDS	#	#	
Angular velocity at BC of the angle between left arm and clubshaft	*	*	*
Vertical clubhead velocity at MDS		#	#
Horizontal clubhead velocity at BC	*	*	
Resultant clubhead velocity at BC	*	*	
Maximal clubhead velocity	*	*	*
Drive distance	*	*	

*Lower handicap group has largest mean
#Higher handicap group has largest mean

Details of all mean, standard deviation, p value and effect size (ω^2) data are presented by McLaughlin (1994). To eliminate some parameters from the final list, a linear correlation matrix was calculated for the parameters in table 1. Not surprisingly, a high correlation was recorded between horizontal and resultant clubhead velocities at BC (0.996), and also with these parameters and maximal clubhead velocity (0.894 and 0.891 respectively). Knee and hip axes' rotations at MDS were also highly correlated (0.854). All correlation findings were confirmed by principal components analysis.

While the last five parameters in table 1 are not surprising, the first six parameters require more discussion. The angular velocity of the angle between the left arm and clubshaft was found to correlate highly with the resultant clubhead velocity at BC (0.869). The high p and correlation values recorded for these parameters support the double pendulum theory developed by Cochran and Stobbs (1968) and the importance of what they describe as wrist 'uncocking'. Using anatomical definitions, wrist 'uncocking' is wrist adduction (ulnar deviation) from an abducted (radially deviated) position. The importance of wrist adduction is further emphasised by the significant difference found for the angle between the left arm and the clubshaft at MDS. This finding supports Cochran and Stobbs' finding that delaying adduction to the last possible moment produces an effective golf swing; ie. the LH golfers had a greater degree of abduction at MDS compared to the other groups.

The data for trunk angle at BA showed that the LH group were in a more upright position than the other groups. This difference was about 7°. The LH group allowed the clubhead to drop below the level of the hands at TBS, whilst the other groups kept the clubhead in a position above the hands. Data for rotation of the hip and knee axes at MDS is an indication of the difference in timing of these rotatory movements among the groups. A significant difference was found to occur because the HH and MH groups recorded only a small amount of rotation in these axes. This data implied that the LH group utilised kinematic chain principles better than the other groups.

ω^2 data highlighted the need for higher subject numbers, especially within the non-elite groups. An example of this is shown in the ω^2 data for resultant clubhead velocity at BC. There is a significant difference only between the LH group and the other groups. ω^2 data showed that between LH and MH ω^2 was 1.3, between LH and HH ω^2 was 1.9 and between MH and HH ω^2 was 0.7. Cohen (1988) subjectively defines an $\omega^2 > 0.7$ as 'large' suggesting that this study's lack of significance may have been owing to a too small sample size.

4 Conclusions

The 3-d kinematic data presented in this study were used to find parameters that distinguish between golfers of varying ability. ANOVA results showed 11 parameters that were different among groups at $p<0.001$. Some of these parameters were correlated allowing further trimming of the list to; the vertical distance between the clubhead and hands at TBS, the position of the hips and knees at MDS, maximal clubhead velocity, trunk angle at BA, the angle between the left arm and the clubshaft at MDS and this angle's angular velocity at BC. This latter data agreed with previous literature that emphasised both the speed of wrist adduction and delaying the onset of wrist adduction. Limitations of the study included the low frame rate and sample size.

5 References

Abdel-Aziz, Y.I. and Karara, H.M. (1971) Direct linear transformation from comparator coordinates in object-space coordinates in close range photogrammetry. **Proc. ASP Symp.of Close-Range Photogrammetry**. Urbana, Il.

Bartlett, R.M., Challis, J.H. and Yeadon, M.R. (1992) Cinematography/video analysis., in **Biomechanical Analysis of Performance in Sport** (ed R.M. Bartlett), British Association of Sports Sciences, Leeds, pp. 8-23.

Cochran, A. and Stobbs, J. (1968) **The Search for the Perfect Swing**. Philadelphia, J.B. Lippincott Co.

Cohen, J. (1988) **Statistical Power Analysis for the Behavioral Sciences**. New York: Academic Press.

Dempster, W.T. (1955) Space requirements of the seated operator. **WADC Technical Report**, Wright Patterson Airforce Base, Ohio, pp. 55-159,.

Jackson, K.M. (1979) Fitting of mathematical functions to biomechanical data. **IEEE Transactions on Biomedical Engineering**, pp. 122-124.

McLaughlin, P.A. (1994) **Three-dimensional kinematic analysis of the golf swing**. Unpublished Master's Minor Thesis: Victoria University of Technology.

Milburn, P.D. (1982) Summation of segmental velocities in the golf swing. **Med. and Sci. in Exerc. and Sports**, 14, pp. 60-64.

Neal, R.J. and Wilson, B.D. (1985) 3D kinematics and kinetics of the golf swing. **Int. J. Sports Biomech.**, 1, pp. 221-232.

15 One move to better ball flight

K. Kanwar
Professional Golf Teacher, Willingdon Sports Club, Bombay, India
and R.V. Chowgule
Bombay Hospital Research & Medical Centre, Bombay, India

Abstract
The aim of this study was to find out whether one particular swing
change — widening of the on-plane backswing arc of the right arm during
takeaway — can produce significant improvements in distance, direction
and trajectory. Seventeen right-handed amateur golfers, 13 male and 4
female, of ages ranging from 10 to 62 years, and handicaps from -6 to
-20 participated in this study. They attended 3 consecutive one hour
sessions and used their 5 irons, off a tee. Subjects were divided into
two groups depending upon their swing Type — A or B, and specific
instructions were given to each group. The clearance angle, a measure
of the first wide position of the right arm as it passed the right side
of the body was noted, and compared with increase in distance. Results
for swing Type A showed an average distance increase of 8.5 yards and
accuracy increase of 0.8 yards. For swings of Type B, the average distance increase was 2.8 yards with an accuracy increase of 0.8 yards.
From the results of this short-term study it was concluded that the one
particular simple instruction imparted yielded an overall average distance increase of 6.16 yards with a marginal increase in accuracy of
0.76 yards.
Keywords : Widening Swing Arc, Swing Plane, Takeaway, Clearance Angle.

1 Introduction

Ever since the days of Harry Vardon, when golf instruction was first
imparted in a formal manner, the same swing fundamentals are being
taught to all golfers.

Instruction today incorporates club positions as required by the
Ball Flight Laws and body positions chosen from the Principles & Preferences of Wiren's (1990) Teaching Model. Additionally instructors
may or may not follow what the Centinela Hospital Research Centre's
study (Jobe & Moynes, 1986) shows about the big muscles producing power.
Specifically, that the left side, particularly the left hip pulls the
clubhead through impact, a fact which has been corroborated by
Williams (1969).

All this makes golf instruction simply too diverse and complex for
the average golfer desiring quick improvement, especially in distance,
and without much practise. Could there be one backswing change which
would simultaneously improve impact and follow all scientific findings?
The objective of this study is to prove that widening of the on-plane
backswing arc of the right arm during takeaway is one swing change,
which is in itself sufficient to improve ball-flight in every case.

Science and Golf II: Proceedings of the World Scientific Congress of Golf. Edited by A.J.
Cochran and M.R. Farrally. Published in 1994 by E & FN Spon, London. ISBN 0 419 18790 1

2   Materials and Methods

2.1   Subjects

Seventeen right-handed, amateur golfers, thirteen male and four female, of ages ranging from 10 to 62 years, and handicaps ranging from -6 to -20 participated in the study. Twenty was the cut-off handicap to ensure consistency of starting swing.

The swings of all subjects were broadly classified into two basic types. Swing Type A is one having mostly an arms pick-up during takeaway. Swing Type B is one with mostly body rotation (i.e. an early withdrawal of right shoulder, arm and hip away from target line) during takeaway. There were 10 cases of swing Type A and 7 of swing Type B.

2.2   Equipment

(a) The camera used was a National NV - M7EN at a shutter speed of 1/1000 second. It was placed at a distance of 15 feet from the ball. All swings were recorded from the face-on angle.
(b) Each subject used only his/her 5-iron off a tee.
(c) One set of 10 two-piece, 100-compression golf balls was used throughout the experiment.

2.3 Procedure

All subjects attended three consecutive one-hour sessions. During the first session, after a few warm-up shots, the golfer was asked to tee up the ball as close as possible to a wooden 2 X 4 board placed on the ground (Fig. 1). The board was aimed at the target and helped ensure consistent alignment. He/she then proceeded to hit a set of 10 shots which was recorded. To allow for human-error factors such as camera-shyness the subject could hit further recorded sets of 10, until satisfied that a set was typical of his/her existing ball-striking pattern. The criteria for selecting the best set of 10 required that at least 6/10 shots were good. The selected set comprised the 'before' results. Exclusion criteria for individual shots of a set were (a) complete mishits, such as shanked and badly topped shots, (b) any shots landing less than 50% of a subject's usual distance away and (c) shots more than 30 yards left or right of target. Such shots were omitted from all calculations.

Next, instruction was imparted depending upon the subject's basic swing type. A 12'' stake was placed on the target line 3 feet away from the ball. A subject of swing Type A was told to either keep the club-head moving low and wide until it passed the stake, or feel as if he/she was trying to hit the top of the stake (Fig. 1). Most importantly, he/she had to feel that the right arm, not just the left, moved away from the right side of the body. This prevented early elbow and/or wrist fold.

For Swings of Type B, the same stake described above was used. In addition, three lines were drawn on the ground. The body line along the toes, the right elbow line parallel to it, and the target line parallel to both the others (Fig.2).

The subject was asked to start the backswing with the arms-triangle, whilst keeping the right-shoulder and -elbow along their respective lines, and the clubhead along the target line, for as long during takeaway as possible.

Every subject was asked to make no intentional/extraneous movements of shoulders, hips, knees or ankles, during takeaway. The right shoulder was not to tense-up in trying to widen the arc. After take-away, the rest of the backswing to the top could continue as usual.

During the second and third sessions, the subject tried to implement the above instructions, for 30 - 45 minutes, under supervision. At the end of each session he/she was asked to hit one or two rounds of 10 shots, which were recorded. The best of the recorded sets requiring atleast 6/10 good shots was selected and comprised the 'after' results. Exclusion criteria for individual shots of a set were the same as before.

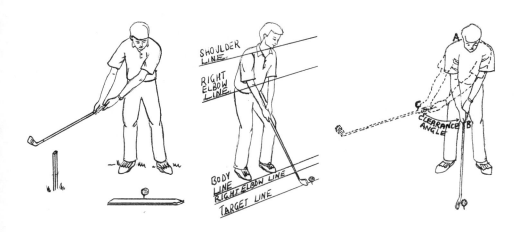

| Fig.1 Starting the recommended move | Fig.2 Body-, right elbow-, target-lines | Fig.3 Clearance angle |

2.4   Measurement of 'Clearance Angle'

The clearance angle measures the first wide position of the right-arm as it clears the right side of the body. 'Wide' means (a) before right elbow and/or wrist fold take place, or (b) before abrupt withdrawal away from the target line of the right arm and shoulder. This latter move manifests itself as the beginning of a 'reverse-pivot' with the chest not moving towards its desired position over the right leg. It is accompanied by an early disappearance of the right shoulder, when seen from the face-on angle.

To calculate clearance angle each recorded swing was replayed. The swing action was paused when the clubhead was grounded at address. A line (AB) was drawn on the video screen, through the right arm in its address position (Fig.3). The swing was then advanced frame by frame, to catch the player's first wide move away from the right side of the body. This position was used in all cases, although many swings continued to be wide well past this point. A second line (AC) was drawn through the right arm at the above point. (Fig.3). The angle between AB and AC was measured using a protractor. This angle was termed the 'clearance angle'.

3   Results

The subjects selected were divided into two Swing Types - A and B.
Tables 1 & 2 show their original mean distance (OMD), increase in
distance (ID) - (α), orginal mean clearance angle (OMCA), increase in
clearance angle (ICA) - ($\beta°$), correlation between increase in clearance
angle and increase in distance (αxβ), standard deviation of original
spray (SD-OS) and standard deviation of final spray (SD-FS). The
correlation monitors the variation of one parameter (α) relative to
another (β). Spray is the root-mean square deviation from target of
each set of 10 shots. Subjects are listed in descending order of
distance improvement.

Table 1. Swing Type A

Sr. No.	H'cap	OMD (yds.)	ID(α) (yds.)	OMCA (deg.)	ICA ($\beta°$)	Correlation (αxβ)	SD-OS (yds.)	SD-FS (yds.)
1	20	118.0	15.6	23.6	6.6	102.96	13.9	10.9
2	12	159.4	12.85	15.55	12.575	161.58	13.3	12.8
3	17	142.1	12.6	25.5	8.92	112.392	8.8	8.0
4	7	186.9	12.4	20.0	9.55	118.42	10.7	10.7
5	20	175.8	8.4	22.57	16.715	140.406	14.2	13.7
6	10	174.2	6.6	27.5	6.5	42.9	11.1	7.9
7	12	121.5	5.5	20.8	7.7	42.35	8.4	7.5
8	18	99.4	4.4	24.3	8.5	37.4	5.3	5.1
9	11	155.4	3.9	15.28	6.92	26.988	9.4	10.4
10	9	118.2	2.8	12.3	6.075	17.01	7.9	8.9
Average		145.0	8.5		9.0	80.24		0.8

Table 2. Swing Type B

Sr. No.	H'cap	OMD (yds.)	ID(α) (yds.)	OMCA (deg.)	ICA ($\beta°$)	Correlation (αxβ)	SD-OS (yds.)	SD-FS (yds.)
1	20	74.5	12.1	30.75	4.375	52.937	4.5	7.5
2	20	116.7	5.3	22.4	5.04	26.712	5.8	6.9
3	14	163.5	4.0	19.0	7.5	30.0	11.5	10.2
4	18	154.8	3.5	14.7	14.051	49.175	12.4	10.0
5	8	172.7	0.6	18.3	4.57	2.742	9.1	9.0
6	12	133.0	-1.6	26.6	4.4	-7.04	4.8	4.2
7	6	191.3	-4.2	20.0	5.125	-21.525	12.0	6.4
Average		143.7	2.8		6.4	19.0		0.8

4 Discussion

Great technological advances have taken place in equipment design and
golf ball manufacture. However, golf swing instruction is still mostly
imparted in terms of the tried and tested methods of famous golfers

rather than in terms of scientific validity. This study is aimed at proving that one simple yet scientifically valid instruction is sufficient to improve ball flight in every case.

The one simple instruction of widening the right arm backswing arc resulted in distance improvement in almost every case. There was an average distance improvement of 8.5 yards for swings of Type A and 2.8 yards for swings of Type B. This is a significant improvement for the average golfer because 5 - 10 yards represent a half to whole increase in the number of iron to be used. No distance improvement took place for subjects 6 and 7 of Swing Type B because they were still unable to keep the right shoulder and arm from withdrawing too early from the target line.

Observation made during the study showed that the right arm moving away from the right side of the body, forced the left arm to move too. This forced the entire left side (shoulder, hip, knee, ankle) to move, in a synchronised manner and about the central spine, producing correct pivot. This observation is substantiated by Leadbetter's (1990) definition of pivot which takes place when (a) the chest turns until it is over the right leg (b) the left shoulder is under the chin and turned well behind a vertical line drawn up from the left hip. A good pivot and weight-shift during the backswing should allow the left hip to pull the clubhead through impact more efficiently. This was found to be so, especially with subjects who showed marked improvement.

Distance improvement was impressive in spite of the short duration of the study. However, accuracy also improved marginally in 13/17 cases. In 4/17 cases (9 and 10 of Type A and 1 and 2 of Type B) accuracy reduced slightly. This reduction of approximately one yard in accuracy was not a particular sacrifice for the average golfer considering the size of most greens and the distance improvement made. Accuracy improvement took place because the subject was required to keep the clubhead low to the ground and square to the target line longer during takeaway. This bettered chances of the Ball Flight Laws (7) governing direction (club face angle, club path and centredness) being obeyed.

Although this study did not measure trajectory, it was seen to improve dramatically because the recommended backswing allowed a lower angle of attack in the through swing, as desired by the Ball Flight Laws (7).

There was an increase in mean clearance angle of 9.0° for swings of Type A and 6.4° for swings of Type B, with Type A swings continuing to remain wide well past this point. Maximum distance improvement took place with swings of Type A, because these swings already incorporate more elements of the recommended procedure, that is, arms starting takeaway and swing on plane. Type B did not show commensurate distance improvement because a too early shoulder rotation prevented proper weight-shift and an on-plane swing. Although many golf teachers such as Hebron (1984) require a shoulder turn to start the backswing, this study showed that shoulder turn should be the effect and not the cause of a correct backswing.

When the two different parameters clearance angle and distance, were correlated it was found that cases 6,7,8,9 and 10 of swing Type A and 2,3 and 4 of swing Type B represent the median, with an average correlation of 36.163. The first five cases of swing Type A (1,2,3,4 and 5) however, are in a league of their own with a correlation greater than 100. This can be attributed to the fact that the first five subjects continued to swing wide for at least another 15 degrees past the first clearance angle. They also exhibited the least amount of extraneous lateral/vertical body movements during takeaway.

It was noticed that widening of the swing arc eliminated relative movements of arm joints (wrist-cock, elbow fold, pronation-supination of forearms), during most of the backswing, so that the arms had less movements to reverse, while approaching the ball. This obviated the need for grip improvement changes, which many feel is a vital key to better impact.

5 Conclusion

A short-term study has been made of one particular swing change and its effect on distance and accuracy. The swing change made was to move the right arm as much away from the right side of the body as possible before it folded at elbow or wrist. It was found that this simple instruction yielded an average distance increase of 6.16 yards, with marginal increase in accuracy of 0.76 yards. Better and more consistent results would certainly follow for the average golfer continuing with this technique.

6 Acknowledgements

The authors wish to thank Dr. M.R. Press for all his help, particularly in data analysis.

7 References

Hebron, M. (1984) **See and feel the Inside move the Outside**, Rost Associates, NY, pp. 42.

Jobe, F.W. and Moynes, D.R. (1986) **30 Exercises for better Golf**, Champion Press, Inglewood, CA, pp. 15 - 17.

Leadbetter, D. (1990) **The Golf Swing**. The Stephen Green Press, USA, pp. 51 - 53.

Williams, D. (1969) **The Science of the Golf Swing**, Pelham Books Ltd. 52 Bedford Square, London, pp. 40 - 41.

Wiren, G. (1990) Laws, Principles and Preferences - A teaching model, **Proceedings of the first world scientific congress of golf**. (ed-A.J. Cochran), E & FN Spon, Boundary Row, London, pp. 3 - 13.

16 Common pre-swing and in-swing tendencies of amateur golfers

E. Alpenfels
Pinehurst Resort and Country Club, Pinehurst, USA

Abstract
This paper will offer an insight into the five most
common swing errors recorded of students attending an
instructional program for adult amateur golfers. Charts
are used to demonstrate the different handicap levels and
the most common swing errors along with pictures
demonstrating the correct and incorrect swing motion.
Keywords: Posture, Shoulder Turn, Stretch and Rotation,
Start to the Backswing, Stable Lower Body, Swing Plane.

1 Common Tendencies of Amateur Golfers

In this eight month study, handicap levels among the golfers
varied from beginners in the game of golf to scratch
handicap level. To learn more about the swing tendencies of
the different levels of play, each of the 945 students (625
males and 320 females) were asked their current handicap
level. They were observed hitting full swing shots and then
they were video taped. Both the student and instructor then
viewed the video tape and determined the swing errors being
made and their effect on the pre-set criteria of performance
which consisted of: (1) the club traveling on the
individual's swing plane, and (2) an effective turn of the
body. Records were kept, noting the swing changes that when
accomplished would allow the student to fit these criteria
of performance. Early analysis of the two to three swing
changes needed enabled each student to focus on the major
problem areas and learn how the overall swing shape was
effected by his or her initial swing errors. Such a focus
narrowed both instruction and practice to meet the
individual needs of the student. Throughout the process
both student and instructor evaluated the changes made to
the swing as to their effect on the criteria of performance.
Upon completion of the program the student and the
instructor re-evaluated the areas addressed and settled upon
the two to three most important swing changes to designed to
help the student fit the criteria of performance.

Science and Golf II: Proceedings of the World Scientific Congress of Golf. Edited by A.J.
Cochran and M.R. Farrally. Published in 1994 by E & FN Spon, London. ISBN 0 419 18790 1

The following charts offer a comprehensive summation of the most common swing errors addressed by students attending the instructional program. Percentages indicate what portion of each handicap group exhibited weakness in each area.

Table 1. Swing Tendencies of Male and Female Amateur Golfers

Swing Tip	Handicap					
	0-9	10-19	20-29	30+	?	Total
Posture	96%	91%	96%	88%	90%	94%
Shoulder Turn	51%	61%	73%	48%	71%	61%
Stretch and Rotate	38%	44%	56%	48%	77%	53%
Good Start	53%	52%	48%	32%	34%	41%
Stable Lower Body	20%	26%	24%	24%	20%	24%

? - Handicap unknown due to inconsistency in amount of play

Table 2. Swing Tendencies of Female Amateurs

Swing Tip	Handicap				
	10-19	20-29	30+	?	Total
Posture	62%	89%	94%	77%	87%
Shoulder Turn	48%	83%	45%	51%	53%
Stretch and Rotate	34%	57%	56%	68%	57%
Good Start	28%	33%	22%	14%	23%
Stable Lower Body	10%	17%	24%	14%	20%

? - Handicap unknown due to inconsistency in amount of play

Table 3. Swing Tendencies of Male Amateurs

Swing Tip	Handicap					
	0-9	10-19	20-29	30+	?	Total
Posture	96%	96%	98%	81%	99%	98%
Shoulder Turn	51%	63%	70%	52%	88%	65%
Stretch and Rotate	38%	46%	56%	39%	85%	51%
Good Start	53%	56%	52%	43%	50%	51%
Stable Lower Body	20%	29%	27%	24%	26%	26%

? - Handicap unknown due to inconsistency in amount of play

2 Common Swing Tendency Number One: Posture

Of the five most common swing errors of the amateur golfers
studied, only the first, **posture**, was considered a pre-swing
activity. Because all golfers are individuals and possess
individual physical characteristics, each had slightly
different address positions to the ball. Correct posture to
a golf ball included three basic elements (see Fig. 1).
First, there was a slight knee flex at address. Second, the
spine was as straight as the individual was able to create.
Last, the chin was up. This address position allowed the
golfer the greatest opportunity to turn without creating any
excess lifting or lateral motion of the body in the
backswing. One of the more typical errant postures taken by
golfers when addressing the ball had the spine curved and
the chin down (see Fig. 2).

Fig. 1   **Fig. 2**

As the statistics show (see Tables 1,2 and 3) a high
percentage of golfers, both male and female needed work to
some degree on their posture. These needed adjustments
ranged from extreme alterations to very simple changes. For
example, some needed a slight change of a ball position from
a forward position to one that was more centered with irons
and slightly forward of center with the woods. Others
required more drastic work on posture due to an extremely
curved spine at address that affected the initial direction
of the swing.

3 Common Swing Tendency Number Two: Shoulder Turn

The second most commonly addressed error for the amateur
golfers studied was the lack of a proper **shoulder turn** in
the backswing. A proper turn of the shoulders in the
backswing created a shoulder turn of ninety degrees at the
top of the backswing. This full turn positioned the left
shoulder behind the ball nearly over the right foot (see
Fig. 3). A full shoulder turn was crucial in allowing the
golf club to swing around the golfers body the necessary

amount. If, for example, one did not turn the shoulders
enough in the backswing (see Fig. 4), the shaft of the club
would not travel enough around the body. Such lack of turn
produced downswings that traveled too much from out-to-in or
too steeply through impact. Often, a lack of shoulder turn
in the backswing made it difficult for golfers to
effectively rotate the arms and body through impact. This
particular lack of rotation through impact often resulted in
an open clubface in the hitting area, producing slices.

Fig. 3   **Fig. 4**

4 Common Swing Tendency Number Three: Stretch and Rotation

The third most common area of swing changes addressed was in
the golfer's ability to stretch and rotate the arms through
impact. This **stretch and rotation** was crucial to producing
a consistently square clubface through the impact area. The
more common motion in the downswing was one in which the
golfer pulled the arms toward the body through impact (see
Fig. 5). Such narrowing of the arms eliminated the golfer's
ability to rotate through impact, thus affecting the
clubface position. A correct arm motion through impact had
the arms extending out towards the target with the right arm
rotating over the left arm (see Fig. 6). The amount of
stretch and rotation of the arms through impact was often
the result of the clubhead path through impact. If, for
example, the golfer had a downswing that was traveling too
much from out-to-in, the angle of approach to the ball would
tend to be too steep. This steepness in the downswing
forced the golfer to pull the arms into the body and open
the clubface in an effort to avoid the ground and shallow
out the steepness. In most cases the golfer's motion in
this area was a reaction and a compensation for what was
done in the backswing.

Fig. 5   **Fig. 6**

5 Common Swing Tendency Number Four: Start to the Backswing

The fourth most common area of swing changes addressed was
in the golfer's initial **start to the backswing.**   A correct
start to the swing combined two elements.   First, because
the golfer is positioned to the side of the ball, the club
had to swing in a circular motion around the body.   Second,
because the ball was on the ground the club had to be swung
at an angle to the ground.   The combination of these two
factors (the club swinging up and around the golfer's body)
was defined as the golfer's individual swing plane.   A key
to one producing a swing that travels on his or her own
individual swing plane was through a correct start to the
backswing.   A correct start to the backswing combined an up
and around motion that, if stopped at waist height, had the
shaft of the club parallel to the target line with the toe
of the club on the ball side of the shaft (see Fig. 7).   The
more common start to the backswing tended to swing the club
too inside (see Fig. 8).   This inside takeaway required the
clubhead and shaft at some point to be lifted to create the
missing angle in the backswing.   Frequently this resulted in
a compensation being made at the top of the backswing or in
the downswing.

Fig. 7   **Fig. 8**

6 Common Swing Tendency Number Five: Stable Lower Body

The fifth most common area of swing changes occurred in the use of the lower body in the backswing. The ability of the golfer to keep a **stable lower body** in the backswing had a direct effect where the club bottoms out (hits the ground) in the downswing. If, for example, the golfer had too much lower body motion in the backswing (see Fig. 9) the club sometimes bottomed out too far behind the ball. For some golfers this error resulted in heavy and even thin shots. A correct lower body motion in the backswing had the hips turning a slight amount with the knees remaining in their original flexed position and the space between them remaining consistent (see Fig. 10). The more common lower body motion in the backswing had the golfer moving his or her lower body to a point where the original address position was lost.

Fig. 9   **Fig. 10**

7 Instructor Observations

The study resulted in a clear indication of the five most common swing errors among the amateur golfers studied. From the student/instructor re-evaluations that took place throughout the process, it became apparent that these errors were often the result of intentional swing thoughts gathered from other golfers, articles in golf magazines, etc.
However these swing thoughts became overdone or misapplied the golfers studied in fact created their own swing errors.
As well, the strand of swing errors encountered tended to be constant regardless of handicap (see Tables 1,2 and 3).

17 Golf development in Australia

D. Wall
National Director of Coaching, Australian Golf Union, Melbourne, Australia

Abstract
This paper outlines some of the main reasons why golf development in
Australia is successful. Grass root and junior development is examined
through to elite development programmes. The role of organizations
such as Junior Golf Australia and the Australian Institute of Sport
Golf Programme is also outlined.
Keywords: Golf Development, Junior, Elite, Coaching, Competitions,
Sports Institutes, Training, Australia.

1 Introduction

Golf is Australia's most popular participant sport and a sport at which
we excel internationally. To achieve this prominence and success both
within and outside Australia a co-ordinated and effective golf
development system is in place. This system covers grass root through
to elite development and involves a variety of golf service
organizations. The system is also continually being evaluated and
improved and recent developments will see Australian Golf become even
stronger.

Outlined below are some of the main elements that make up the
Australian Golf Development System. These are discussed under the
following headings: Junior Development, Elite Development and Junior
Golf Australia.

2 Junior Development

Junior Development opportunities are provided for children aged 18
years and under. They are able to participate in golf activities,
competitions and programmes and are encouraged to further progress in
the sport.

2.1 Go-Go Golf
Go-Go Golf is a modified version of golf designed for children aged 9-
15 years. The Programme's aim is to introduce golf to children in a
safe, fun and educational environment while addressing their social,
emotional and physical needs. The emphasis is on fun and participation
with everyone being involved, despite skill level.

Science and Golf II: Proceedings of the World Scientific Congress of Golf. Edited by A.J.
Cochran and M.R. Farrally. Published in 1994 by E & FN Spon, London. ISBN 0 419 18790 1

To assist children learn Go-Go Golf and to add a further element of fun and excitement, four cartoon characters have been developed to help promote Go-Go Golf. These characters are Go-Go Goanna, Joanna Goanna, Bogey Roo and Turbo.

Go-Go Golf equipment has also been specifically designed for the programme. A modified 7-iron golf club has been developed by leading sporting manufacturer Spalding. These clubs are reduced in length, have slightly larger clubheads and more flexible shafts than "adult" clubs.

A P.V.C. vinyl golf ball is used which has similar flight characteristics to a real ball, however is much safer. The ball travels up to 100 metres and is ideal for use on school ovals or confined indoor spaces. Tennis balls are also used for some activities.

The key teaching resource is the Go-Go Golf Instructors Manual. This comprehensive manual covers a variety of information for the Instructor on Go-Go Golf, including: Safety, Fitness, The Golf Swing, Games and Activities, Instructional Units and other appropriate information.

Go-Go Golf was launched in February 1993 by Greg Norman. By the end of 1993 over 300 schools across Australia were involved in the programme. This figure exceeded our 1993 target and early signs for 1994 are also very promising.

2.2 Level 0 (Orientation) Course
One of the fundamentals underlying Go-Go Golf is that the programme can be delivered by school teachers, parents, high school students or other interested personnel who do not necessarily have any golf experience. To assist these people gain some basic skills in instructing golf the Level 0 Golf Course has been developed.

The Level 0 Course is a coaching orientation programme with the following general aims:
1 To prepare personnel to organize and conduct Go-Go Golf in schools and at clubs.
2 To ensure all Go-Go Golf Instructors understand the safety requirements of golf.
3 To train personnel to conduct a golf programme in a fun and learning environment.

The course is 6.5 hours in duration and covers the following information: safety and warm-up, organizational skills, golf skills, games and activities, rules, etiquette and resources. The Go-Go Golf Instructors Manual is the text for the course.

Upon completion of a course, participants receive a Level 0 Participation Certificate. By the end of 1993 over 250 people had completed the course.

2.3 Level One Golf Course
The Level One Golf Course has been developed to prepare personnel to co-ordinate junior golf programmes in schools and at clubs. The Course is targeted at school teachers, trainee teachers and amateur golfers. Successful candidates are referred to as 'Golf Co-ordinators'.

The Level One Course has been approved by the Australian Coaching Council as part of the National Coaching Accreditation Scheme. Level

One focuses on coaching while Level 0 only touches on this area. Additionally Level 0 is not a prerequisite for Level One. The Level One Course has the following general aims:
1 To prepare Golf Co-ordinators to introduce junior players to the technical and playing aspects of the game of golf.
2 To ensure a minimum standard of preparation for Golf Co-ordinators.
3 To provide an understanding of the general principles of coaching junior players.
4 To provide knowledge and understanding of the technical essentials for coaching the basic aspects of the game of golf to junior players.

The Course consists of 19 hours of lectures and demonstrations, 100% participation and completion of 25 hours of supervised practical coaching. Units covered in the course include: Role of the Coach, Developing the Athlete, Sport Safety, Golf Skills, Planning a Golf Programme, Psychology of Golf and so on.

The Level 0 and One Courses are co-ordinated by Junior Golf Australia and have the full support of amateur and professional golf organizations. They play an important role in helping establish golf in the school system and in developing a base of qualified personnel capable of conducting golf programmes.

2.4 Girls In Golf Programme
One of the main problems in Australian golf is in attracting and retaining young girls into the sport. To help address this problem a specific Girls in Golf Programme has been developed. Parts of this Programme have been adapted from the U.S.L.P.G.A.'s successful Girls in Golf Club while other elements have been developed in Australia. Activities and programmes are developed specifically for young girls so as to encourage them without intimidation from boys.

2.5 The CAPS Programme
The Challenge, Achievement and Pathways in Sport (CAPS) Programme is an Australian Government initiative which involves golf and various other sports in a leadership development programme for 14-20 year olds. CAPS is structured like the Duke of Edinburgh Award Scheme in that participants receive awards for service in various areas. Areas offered include: coaching, refereeing, administration, sports health, tournament organization and participation.

2.6 State Associations and Foundations
Much of the work is developing activities and programmes at the junior level is co-ordinated by State Associations and Junior Golf Foundations. For instance, Greg Norman (Queensland), Jack Newton (New South Wales) and Graham Marsh (Western Australia) have all established Junior Golf Foundations in their home States. These Foundations along with State Associations provide a range of services and activities and serve as a focal point for junior golf in their State.

These organizations conduct activities such as: golf championships, school development programmes, Level 0 and One Courses, junior development squads, training camps and so on. Importantly there is also national co-ordination through Junior Golf Australia (outlined below) for many of these activities.

2.7 Competitions

Young golfers in Australia are able to compete in a range of competitions at local, intrastate and interstate levels. There are also opportunities for international competition. Competitions within Australia include: age group championships, under 18 championships, individual and team school events, interstate team events and a variety of other competitions.

In addition there are generally no restrictions (other than handicap conditions) regarding juniors competing in open championships. Access to the various high level competitions plays a very important role in developing our golfers to the elite level. Once they have achieved a high standard our elite development programme will further assist them develop their skills.

2.8 Resources

A number of resources have also been produced to assist juniors develop their golf. These include: golf etiquette and fitness booklets; golf skill posters covering chipping, putting, driving and practice skills; golf skill videos; golf development and coaching manuals; and so on.

3 Elite Development

Elite Development programmes are generally offered to golfers aged 17 years and older. A variety of programmes and opportunities are available, dependent upon the skill level of the golfer.

3.1 Australian Institute of Sport Golf Programme

In 1992 the Australian Institute of Sport (A.I.S.) established a golf programme in Melbourne. The programme offers 6 male amateurs and 6 female amateurs, aged 17-19 years old, full-time residential scholarships based in Melbourne. There are also two non-residential scholarships for trainee professional golfers. All the golfers are selected based on an elite performance criteria, education and psychological profile and potential to succeed at the top international level.

The Programme utilizes Melbourne's famous sandbelt golf courses and is based at a driving range, close to Royal Melbourne Golf Club, which offers the following:
- A full-swing driving range with a 1600 square metre lazer levelled turf area.
- A doubled-sized sloping putting green.
- A short game facility specifically for chipping, pitching and bunker shots with 2 bunkers and multiple grass types and depths.
- An office and meeting room facility.

Golfers in the Programme are required to undertake a minimum of 47 hours per week which includes an education component. Benefits of the Programme include: accommodation and meals, access to sports science and sports medicine support, travel to competitions, coaching, equipment and vocational support and guidance.

In regard to sports science support, the golfers are profiled and specific programmes are developed in the following areas: biomechanics, physiology, psychology and nutrition. Leading Australian sports scientists work with the golfers under the direction of Head Coach, Mr. Ross Herbert.

The A.I.S. has only been in operation for two years, however, members have already achieved outstanding performance results. Scholarship holders have won numerous significant events and 5 of the 12 amateurs have represented Australia. It is generally agreed that these results have been achieved at a much earlier age that could have been expected if they weren't involved in the Programme.

The A.I.S. Golf Programme has not only helped the scholarship holders but has also assisted all Australian golf by providing elite programmes and standards that have been applied to other National and State programmes. The A.I.S. is acting as a "clearing house" for the identification, development and dissemination of elite training information. For instance, a National Skills Test (outlined below) has been developed as a talent identification and skill analysis test. Physiological testing protocols have been established that not only make golfers stronger but identify potential injuries before they happen. Sport psychology training modules have been developed and computer software style sheets are used by State associations in their talent development programmes.

3.2 State Sports Institutes

The A.I.S. Golf Programme has a national focus and provides opportunities for young golfers from across Australia to be involved in an elite residential programme. To assist athletes at State level, State Institutes of Sport have been established. By the end of 1993 golf is in the Victorian Institute of Sport (V.I.S.) and is likely to be introduced in Institutes in Queensland, New South Wales and South Australia.

The V.I.S. Golf Programme is non-residential and can therefore offer opportunities for a greater number of golfers. The Programme provides coaching, travel, sports science, elite performance support, education and vocational support. Both the A.I.S. and V.I.S. work closely together and co-ordinate may joint activities.

The V.I.S., under the direction of Head Coach Steve Bann, has also achieved some outstanding results in only a short period. Among the players the programme has assisted are: Robert Allenby, Richard Green, Jamie Taylor and Stuart Appleby.

3.3 National Skills Test

The A.I.S. and V.I.S. have developed a National Skills Test which is designed to assess golfers' ability in 10 skills. It can also be used as a talent identification measure (a copy of the National Skills Test is included as Appendix A.)

Golfers must perform 10 shots for each of the 10 different skills and record a score for each and the overall total out of 100. Activities include: 10 one and two metre putts; 10 5 irons within a 10 metre target at 150 metres; 10 wedges - 3 metre target - 70 metres; and so on.

The first objective is to evaluate a golfer's strengthes and weaknesses. It is also a means of measuring performance under pressure and of developing purposeful practice.

The National Skills Test is being used at local, State and National
levels and leading professionals are also undertaking the Test so that
standards can be established. For example a male tour player should
score 75-85% in the overall score. (A male golfer in the A.I.S.
Programme currently averages 76%).

3.4 Elite Training Camps

A series of Elite Training Camps aimed at 16-20 year old golfers are
conducted at national level. These camps utilize specialist coaches
and sports scientists and cover specific elite development information
such as: peaking for competition, nutrition and diet for travel and
competition, strength and conditioning for golf, specialist advanced
golf skills, psychological preparation and so on.

About 60 boys and girls attend the camps which are conducted over 5-
7 days. There are also slightly less advanced camps conducted at State
level which cover approximately 500 boys and girls. Preparation camps
are also used for Australian Teams.

3.5 National Squad

The Australian Golf Union has established a National Squad of
approximately 20 elite amateur golfers. These golfers, considered the
best in the country, are provided with opportunities to compete in
competitions, attend training camps and have access to physiogical and
psychological training protocols. The Australian Ladies' Golf Union
also has an Elite National Training Squad.

3.6 National Selection Trials

A series of National Selection Trials are held across Australia as a
means of selecting Australian Teams. These trials (one in each State)
are held in conjunction with major amateur titles. In addition to the
trials our leading amateurs are able to compete in numerous high level
competitions across Australia and in New Zealand.

4 Junior Golf Australia

One of the most important developments in Australian golf in recent
years has been the establishment of Junior Golf Australia (J.G.A.) in
1990. J.G.A. was established by the three national bodies responsible
for the development of golf in Australia, i.e. the Australian Golf
Union, the Australian Ladies' Golf Union and the Professional Golfers'
Association of Australia. J.G.A. is controlled by a Board with two
representatives from each body.

The establishment of J.G.A. arose from the need to co-ordinate the
overall development of junior golf through one central agency rather
than different organizations at State and National levels each pursuing
their own direction. J.G.A. prevents duplication of effort and coordinates resource (human, material, financial) development. J.G.A.'s
main aim is to co-ordinate the planning and development of National
Programmes, such as Go-Go Golf, Girls in Golf, Level 0 and Level One
courses and sponsorship and fundraising activities.

To help develop its' activities J.G.A. has appointed a National
Coaching Co-ordinator, a National Development Officer and has
established a Technical Committee. The Technical Committee consists of

representatives from all State and National golf development
organizations and is the main force in determining the direction and
priorities for J.G.A.   It also ensures all bodies are actively involved
in the planning and development of National Programmes.

5 Conclusion

The information outlined above is not a definitive list of all the
reasons why the Australian golf development system is successful.   To
achieve this would require a much more comprehensive analysis and
examine issues such as climate, affordability and availability of high
standard golf courses and facilities, impact of role models such as
Greg Norman and so on.

   Outlined above, however, are some of the main programmes, activities
and organizations responsible for golf development (see Figure 1).   The
overall Golf Development System is being addressed so that a broad base
of activities and programmes provide opportunities for young golfers to
develop to elite levels.

   It is also important that all golf organizations work together in
co-ordinating activities for the benefit of golf.   This approach,
occurring through Junior Golf Australia, will see golf stay ahead of
other sports in the highly competitive world of trying to secure
corporate and government funding.

   Golf in Australia, through all the activities outlined, has planted·
the seeds to produce many talented golfers and for many people to have
fun in our great game.

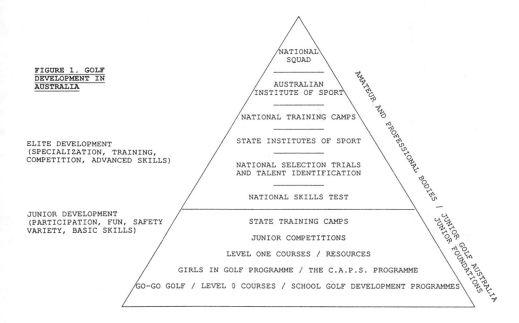

FIGURE 1. GOLF
DEVELOPMENT IN
AUSTRALIA

ELITE DEVELOPMENT
(SPECIALIZATION, TRAINING,
COMPETITION, ADVANCED SKILLS)

JUNIOR DEVELOPMENT
(PARTICIPATION, FUN, SAFETY
VARIETY, BASIC SKILLS)

NATIONAL SQUAD

AUSTRALIAN INSTITUTE OF SPORT

NATIONAL TRAINING CAMPS

STATE INSTITUTES OF SPORT

NATIONAL SELECTION TRIALS AND TALENT IDENTIFICATION

NATIONAL SKILLS TEST

STATE TRAINING CAMPS

JUNIOR COMPETITIONS

LEVEL ONE COURSES / RESOURCES

GIRLS IN GOLF PROGRAMME / THE C.A.P.S. PROGRAMME

GO-GO GOLF / LEVEL 0 COURSES / SCHOOL GOLF DEVELOPMENT PROGRAMMES

AMATEUR AND PROFESSIONAL BODIES / JUNIOR GOLF AUSTRALIA

JUNIOR GOLF FOUNDATIONS

Australian Institute of Sport

AUSTRALIAN INSTITUTE OF SPORT - GOLF - SKILLS TEST RECORD

Name: _____ Month of: _____

10 BALLS / SKILL	Date:	1	2	3	4	5	6	7	8	9	10	11	12	13	14	15	16	17	18	19	20	21	22	23	24	25	26	27	28	29	30	31	%
WEDGE	3 METRE TARGET AT 70 M.																																
9 IRON	5 METRE TARGET AT 100 M.																																
5 IRON	10 METRE TARGET AT 150 M																																
DRIVER	20 METRE TARGET AT 200 M (Landing point visually between target boundary)																																
PUTT	1 METRE DISTANCE (Surrounding hole)																																
PUTT	2 METRE DISTANCE (Surrounding hole)																																
PUTT	SPEED 10 METRE 5 uphill/5 downhill to 1M radius semi- circle. (Behind the hole)																																
	Sub Total																																
SHORT GAME — CHIP	(7 - 9) Iron 1 Metre Radius (10 Metres)																																
SHORT GAME — PITCH	Wedge - Sand Iron 1 Metre Radius(10 Metres)																																
SHORT GAME — BUNKER	1.5 Metre Radius (10 Metres)																																
	Sub Total																																
	Skills Test Total																																

Monthly Average %

Australian Sports Commission

18 Teaching methods and epistemic styles of golf instructors

R.J. Rancourt and R.Q. Searle
University of Ottawa, Ottawa, Canada

Abstract
Effective teaching is dependent, in part, upon the most
appropriate use of teaching methods within a particular
instructional environment. The research on golf
instruction has been to a large extent focussed on the
search for the "one best" method and the results have been
discouraging. Recently, some authors have suggested that
golf instructor traits should be examined in relation to
effective teaching methodology. It was the intention of
this study to identify teaching methods used by golf
instructors and to relate those methods to a set of traits
called knowledge accessing modes. The Golf Style
Indicator was administered to a sample of 145 golf
instructors to identify their knowledge accessing modes
and a Teaching Style Inventory was given to identify what
instructors considered to be their preferred approach to
teaching. Results indicated a definite tendency for golf
instructors to select teaching methods congruent with
their dominant knowledge accessing mode. The teaching
exemplars generated from this study will help develop the
observational tools necessary for golf instructors to
better match their teaching methods to the learner.
Keywords: Teaching Methods, Epistemic Orientation, Mode,
Rational, Empirical, Noetic.

1 Introduction

A general review of the teaching methodology research in
education reveals the existence of a plethora of methods.
Taken individually, each study on teaching methodology
presents a strong case for effective teaching. However,
when all the studies are taken together, the conclusions
are dramatically different. For example a 1974 study by
Avila Combs & Purkey states that "a review of all the
research available on good and poor teaching was unable to
discover any method of teaching which could be shown to be

Science and Golf II: Proceedings of the World Scientific Congress of Golf. Edited by A.J.
Cochran and M.R. Farrally. Published in 1994 by E & FN Spon, London. ISBN 0 419 18790 1

associated with either good or poor teaching."(p.4) More
recent reviewers commenting on the research involving
teaching methods have supported the 1974 study (Medley,
1982; Wittrock, 1986).

Concomitantly, the literature in the field of golf
instruction has produced a number of alternative methods
of teaching since Cochran's (1968) recommendation that
more research be done on didactics. In a review of some
100 research studies involving methods of golf
instruction, Kraft (1986) concluded that no one method
appeared to be more effective than any other. Confronted
with a no "one best" method of instruction, Cronbach &
Snow (1977) suggested that researchers might well begin
searching for some unknown instructor trait or cluster of
traits that may have been overlooked in the field of
didactics. Within the last ten years it has become more
evident that teaching effectiveness should be viewed as
being equally dependent on the instructor's style or
traits as it is on the use of appropriate methodology. And
that nothing will be effective if the philosophy or
psychological characteristics of the instructor does not
coincide with teaching methods (Rotella & Boutcher, 1990;
Rancourt & Dionne, 1982).

In fact, a recent investigation of the knowledge
accessing modes of eighty golf instructors,revealed a
difference in the manner in which they prefer to acquire
knowledge (Rancourt & Searle, 1990). This suggests that
they would select and use teaching methods most
appropriate to their own preferred style or traits.
However, there is no known empirical evidence in the
literature to verify the assumption that method selection
is related to the dominant knowledge accessing mode of the
instructor. Therefore, the purpose of this exploratory
study was to examine the preferred teaching methods of
golf instructors in relation to their preferred knowledge
accessing mode.

2   Methodology

2.1 Subjects
The initial sample comprised 170 male and 14 female golf
instructors who were members of the Canadian Professional
Golfers' Association (CPGA). When the criterion of
epistemic dominance was applied to the scores obtained on
the GSI to determine mode dominance, that is, when the
major mode has to exceed the associate mode by at least
five points to be considered dominant and stable, the
reconstituted sample of subjects became 145. Table 1
provides sample characteristics.

Table 1.   Frequency Distribution of Sample Characteristics

	AGE			YEARS TEACHING		
N	0-29	30-49	50+	1-4	5-14	15+
145	72	66	6	67	57	21

2.2 Instruments

The Golf Style Indicator [GSI],a twenty question forced-choice inventory was used to identify the knowledge accessing modes of golf instructors (Rancourt & Searle, 1990). The GSI is based on the Epistemic Orientation Model, (Rancourt, 1988). The model posits the existence of three distinct but interrelated information processing systems called Knowledge Accessing Modes. These three modes are interconnected and can be activated whenever a person's mental selective attending mechanism is engaged. At any one time one mode may override the other two and exclude them from most of the mental processing activity. When this happens, mode freezing is said to take place and the resulting mental architecture can be described as an epistemic mode dominance. The Epistemic Orientation Model labels the three knowledge accessing modes, the Rational Mode, the Empirical Mode and the Noetic Mode. Described in more detail elsewhere, (Rancourt & Noble, 1991; Rancourt, 1988; Rancourt, 1993), these knowledge accessing modes act as a guidance system which controls behaviour in the person-environment geography. The rational mode is defined as a deductive reasoning engine that requires logical, conceptual, lexical or verbal inputs. The Empirical Mode is an inductive reasoning engine that processes information emanating from the outside world and utilizes perceptual, sensory or motor inputs. The noetic mode is characterized as a random, intuitive reasoning engine that requires insight availability, subjective experiencing or proprioceptive inputs.

The Teaching Strategies Inventory [TSI], designed for this study, is a two-part questionnaire which was used to gather data describing the teaching behaviour and method preferences of golf instructors. The first part requests respondents to list key concepts or words (descriptors) that best describe their teaching. The descriptors are then assigned by a panel of experts to one of the three knowledge accessing modes. Descriptors not related to any particular mode are excluded. The second part of the TSI contains fourteen questions derived from literature pertaining to the teaching of golf. Each question provides exemplars of teaching approaches representative of the three knowledge accessing modes. Based on their

own teaching practices, subjects distribute six points
among the three choices to indicate the weighted value
they assign to each exemplar.

2.3 Procedures
Data were collected at three Canadian PGA approved events:
the 1993 Canadian Golf Instructors' Association
Assistants' Championship (n=46),the Ontario 1993 Fall
General Meeting and Seminar (n=103) and the Annual Fall
Clinic at Royal Oak (n=35). Subjects completed the GSI and
TSI. Debriefing followed the administration of the
inventories.

3   Results

The relative frequency distribution of the dominant
knowledge accessing modes of the sample indicates that
Noetic is the dominant mode of 46.9% of the instructors,
Rational is the dominant mode of 37.9% and Empirical is
the dominant mode of 15.2%.
    The portion of the TSI for which 145 subjects provided
concepts or key words that best describe their teaching
yielded a total of 639 descriptors. A panel of three
judges examined each descriptor and categorized it as
representative of either the Noetic, Empirical or Rational
mode.   The 241 descriptors that were not clearly related
to a particular mode were excluded.   The relative
frequency distribution of mode associated descriptors
revealed that 46% of the descriptors recorded by Noetic
dominant subjects were Noetic descriptors.   The remaining
descriptors were evenly distributed among the other two
modes.   Similarly 44% of the descriptors recorded by
Empirical dominant subjects were Empirical descriptors.
The remaining descriptors divided evenly between the
Rational and Noetic modes.   However, Rational dominant
subjects provided almost as many Noetic descriptors (35%)
as they did Rational descriptors (37%). This latter result
may be partially explained by the closeness of the
Rational and Noetic mode dominances in the sample.
    The descriptors within each mode category were then
grouped into synonymic clusters. For example, the
following descriptors: artistic, creative, expressive,
imaginative, insightful and original were subsumed under
the synonymic cluster labelled "creative".   The process
produced between 4 and 5 clusters for each mode category.
They can be found in Table 2. Overall, the results of
this portion of the TSI indicate that golf instructors
describe their teaching in terms more congruent with their
dominant mode than either their associate or minor mode.

Table 2. Synonymic Clusters and Dominant Instructor Mode

Noetic	Empirical	Rational
caring	analytical	logical
encouraging	practical	fundamental
creative	drill-practice	concepts
feel	technique	organized
rhythm	progressive	

An analysis of the section of the TSI requiring subjects to distribute numeric values among exemplars of different teaching approaches revealed that the Rational instructors preferred to: organize lesson content in a theory to practice format; provide short, sharp directions that focus on something visual; follow traditional and standard teaching approaches (P<.05); display physical and verbal expressions of reinforcement; use a tell then show approach(P<.05); communicate specific objectives of the lesson; prepare for teaching by reviewing content; explain principles and theory; have their own ideas about how golf should be taught. For the Empirical golf instructors, they preferred to: organize lesson content in small segmented steps; allow students to examine and analyze movements and recommend change; encourage learners to adopt standard swing mechanics and fundamentals(P<.05); focus on rewarding individuals for performance; let learners perform and then offer correction; provide only broad indicators of lesson objectives so they may adjust to students perceived needs; prepare for teaching by selecting appropriate technical aids; teach by analyzing and correcting. Finally, the Noetic golf instructors preferred to: organize lesson content according to individual learner needs; make use of metaphors and analogies; encourage students to discover and develop their natural swing(P<.05); encourage cooperation and group spirit; gain the confidence of students without directly communicating objectives; imagine themselves as the learner when preparing for teaching(P<.05); encourage discovery and development(P<.05); vary teaching approaches according to the situation(P<.05). The results of the second portion of the TSI also indicate a tendency for instructors to use teaching methods in consonance with their dominant mode.

This study contributes empirical evidence which links preferred teaching approach to the dominant knowledge accessing mode of the golf instructor. Cognizant of certain edumetric limitations of self-reporting techniques (Sax, 1980), future studies should focus on direct

observation of teaching behaviour. In addition to
providing data concerning actual teaching behaviours
relative to mode preference, direct observation would
allow the recording of time allocation to help quantify
the degree of emphasis among mode preferences.   Therefore,
instead of pursuing the illusive "one best" method of
teaching, golf instructors should focus on providing a
better instructional fit between themselves, their subject
matter and their learners through matching or mode flexing
behaviours.

References

Avila, D.L. Combs, A.W. and Purkey, W. (1974) **Helping
    Relationships: Basic Concepts for the Helping
    Professions**. Allyn & Bacon, Boston.
Cochran, A. and Stobbs, J. (1968) **The Search for the
    Perfect Swing**. J.B. Lippincott Co., New York.
Cronbach, L.J. and Snow, R.E. (1977) **Aptitudes and
    Instructional Methods**. Irvington, New York.
Kraft, R.E. (1986) **What Research Tells the Golf Instructor
    About the Golf Swing and Putting**. Eric: ED 316 513
Medley, D.M. (1982) Teacher Effectiveness,in
    Encyclopedia of Educational Research, (ed H.
    Mitzel).pp.1894-1903.
Rancourt, R. (1988) **KAMI: A consultant's Guide to Style
    Interpretation**. Impact Publications, Cumberland,
    Ontario.
Rancourt, R. (1993) Technology, Culture and Ways of
    Knowing. in **Universal Knowledge Tools and their
    Applications**,(ed K. Burkhart). Ryerson Polytechnical
    University Press, Toronto.
Rancourt, R. and Dionne, J.P. (1982) **A Study of the
    Teaching and Learning Styles in Ontario Schools**.
    Department of Education
Rancourt, R. and Noble, K.A. (1991) Administration and
    Intradisciplinary Conflict within Nursing. **Nursing
    Administration Quarterly**, 15, Summer, pp. 36-42.
Rancourt, R. and Searle, R. Q. (1990) Golfers Do It With
    Style: Epistemic Orientations of Golf Instructors and
    Students. in **Science and Golf**, (ed A.S. Cochran), E. &
    F.N. Spon, London, pp.105-110
Rotella, R. J. and Boutcher, S. H. (1990) A closer Look at
    the Role of the Mind in Golf. in **Science and Golf**, (ed
    A.J. Cochran), E. & F.N. Spon, London, pp.93-97.
Sax, G. (1980) **Principles of Educational and
    Psychological Measurement and Evaluation**,
    Wadsworth,Belmont, California. p.546.
Wittrock, M. (1986) **Handbook of Research on Teaching**.
  Macmillan Publishing Co., New York.

19 Possibilities available in teaching using videos and computers

P.A. Brostedt
Swedish Golf Academy AB, Stockholm, Sweden

Abstract
At Swedish Golf Academy video plays a major role in the learning situation.
Recent advances in desktopvideo has provided us with tools that has raised the
quality in our instructional material and given us new ways in providing the
student with videotaped feedback.
Keywords: Visual feedback, Examples, Equipment.

1 Introduction

Visual communication plays an important part in golfinstruction. Modern
technology is now providing the golfteacher with tools that earlier were only
found in sophisticated research set-ups, requiring expert knowledge to handle.
A distinction can be made between using that type of equipment, for research, i.
e. biomechanical analysis and used as a tool for visually communicating in the
actual teaching situation. To use such equipment on the lesson-tee places high
demands on speed, ease of use and low cost. It is fascinating that this
technology is now available to the golfteacher.

The video camera is now a very common tool in teaching, and modern
technology now makes it possible to bring live video into and out of the
computer. Once in the computer, it can be manipulated, edited and mixed with
graphics. This enables the teacher to show the student alternative ways of
doing something, more clearly than video can show, which in fact only shows
what the student is actually doing. The student can therefore be given more
information and help in answering important questions such as "What am I
doing, in relation to what the teacher is proposing?"

Science and Golf II: Proceedings of the World Scientific Congress of Golf. Edited by A.J.
Cochran and M.R. Farrally. Published in 1994 by E & FN Spon, London. ISBN 0 419 18790 1

2 Examples

All examples shown here, were produced using off-the shelf, mainstream, consumer-products widely available today. Focus is made on tools that can further enhance visual communication. What was earlier only possible to show with stills is now equally possible with moving pictures. Where the teacher earlier was restricted to giving a mental picture of something, he or she can now impose a mental film. Hardware and software for real time video input and output is available for both the Macintosh® and PC line of computers.

These pictures can be seen as examples of visual communication starting with the still picture where the teacher has drawn references and ending with the more complex film where the student is also shown what he or she is doing **in relation** to what the teacher is trying to communicate. The pictures on this page are printed and can as such only show still positions.

Adding reference lines to a still picture makes it easier for the student to pinpoint the information.

The student sees himself alongside the proposed alternative. With or without added references. This can be done with still pictures or moving film.

The student sees him/herself in relation to what the teacher is proposing. This can be done with still pictures or moving film.

3 Equipment

At the Swedish Golf Academy we have been using computers together with digital video since 1989. A regular videocamera has been used during lessons, but digital manipulation of the full motion recordings were not possible until 1993. We have also used a digital still videocamera, Canon RC-470, for capturing still pictures and swing sequences. It captures either stills or up to 50 frames in two and a half seconds, which is sufficient to capture a golf swing. A golf swing averages between one and a half to two seconds. This material is stored in the computer. Graphics, text comments and essential picture manipulation is added and the results are printed out on paper and handed to the student. Since 1993 we also supply it to the student recorded on videotape.

In 1993 we added new hardware that is able to digitize and play back full motion video. This enables us to use full motion video where we previously had to settle for stills.

Hardware used until 1993, allowing for still picture manipulation.

> Apple® Macintosh® II
> Apple® Macintosh® IIcx
> Digitizing card from Neotech®
> Video Explorer digitizing card from Intelligent Resources®
> Video cameras from Grundig® and Canon®
> Still video Canon® RC-470
> Still video player Canon® RV-311
> Apple® 13 inch monitors
> Apple® Laserwriter II
> TV monitors and videorecorders from Grundig®.

Hardware added 1993 enabling us to do the same things with full motion video as before with still pictures.

>Apple® Quadra® 700
>Radius® Video Vision Studio® (Digitizing and playing back full speed video)
>PLI® Mini Array 2 gigabyte

Hardware added 1994

>Apple® Quadra® 950

Software used.

>Adobe Photoshop®
>Adobe Premiere®
>Adobe Illustrator®
>Aldus Free Hand®
>Quark X-press®

20 Research based golf: from the laboratory to the course

D.J. Crews
Arizona State University, Tempe, Arizona, USA

Abstract
This paper presents a line of research examining the influence of attentional patterns on golf performance. The studies attempt to bring important attentional questions from the golf course into a controlled laboratory setting, and then to return to the course with answers that enhance performance. Beginning to elite skill level players were examined using behavioral, cognitive, and psychophysiological indicators of attention. It appears that consistent behavioral and cognitive patterns facilitate a consistent psychophysiological state conducive to best golf putting performance. These patterns can be trained using psychological skills training programs and EEG biofeedback. Fitness and age have also been found to influence attentional patterns suggesting that aerobic fitness may be important to maintain attention in golf and that psychophysiological patterns may need to change as one ages.
Keywords: Attention, Routines, EEG, Golf Putting, Arousal, Fitness, Age.

Introduction

Golf is a game that has been approached scientifically by researchers, coaches, players, and manufacturers of golf equipment. Interestingly, when searching the scientific journals for data based articles specific to golf, only a dearth of studies appear relative to the long history of the sport. It is possible that the research has not been submitted to the scrutiny of the scientific community, or that research of this caliber has not been conducted. In either case, there is a need for controlled, rigorous research in the sport of golf.

The purpose of this paper is not to convey all published research on the game of golf, but to present a line of research that has attempted to answer meaningful research questions examining the role of attention in the game of golf. The first step was to verify the existance of routines in the game of golf. Secondly, optimal attentional patterns were

Science and Golf II: Proceedings of the World Scientific Congress of Golf. Edited by A.J. Cochran and M.R. Farrally. Published in 1994 by E & FN Spon, London. ISBN 0 419 18790 1

defined, and lastly manipulation of attention was conducted to examine the influence on performance. Behavioral, cognitive, and psychophysiological techniques were used to define the attentional patterns and to manipulate these patterns during golf putting. The effects on performance were recorded as successful putts made and as total cm error from the hole. Similar attentional research has been conducted in other sports (i.e., archery, rifle shooting, basketball free-throw shooting); however, this paper will focus on golf and reference relevant research when appropriate.

A well-known psychophysiologist (Tecce, 1972, p. 100) defined attention as "a hypothetical process of an organism which facilitates the selection of relevant stimuli from the environment (internal or external) to the exclusion of other stimuli and results in a response to the relevant stimuli." Attention is an active directional process that guides our mental activities. Thus, in order to recall and execute the appropriate motor program for a successful golf shot, one must first select the relevant stimuli. Secondly, the sequence of selection, the time frame of attention, and the cues that program a **response** to the stimuli are critical for optimal performance. Researchers have examined behaviors, cognitions, and psychophysiological patterns to determine the optimal stimuli, sequence, time-frame, and cues to elicit the correct motor program (Boutcher & Zinsser, 1990; Crews & Boutcher, 1987; Crews & Landers, 1993; Molander & Backman, 1989; Schmid, 1989).

Figure 1 illustrates the time course for the influence of behaviors, cognitions,and psychophysiology prior to execution of a golf shot. Behaviors include the sequence of actions prior to the backswing, such as waggles and glances at the hole. Cognitions, or thoughts accompany these actions, and continue after the actions have been completed. For the experienced golfer, it is hopeful that the cognitions also stop prior to initiation of the stroke to allow the shot to be produced automatically. A switching mechanism, a thought or picture, is often used to turn off conscious thinking and to allow automatic shot execution. At this point, it is only possible to determine attentional patterns using psychophysiological techniques.

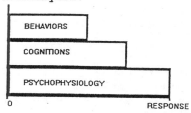

Fig. 1. The time course contribution of behavioral, cognitive, and psychophysiological indicators of attention prior to a response.

Electroencephalographic (EEG) measures convey the amount of activity in selected areas of the brain that may be important during golf. Electrocardiographic (ECG) measures are also indicators of attention, and patterns of acceleration or deceleration have been related to golf performance. Thus, measuring the activity patterns and defining the pattern associated with successful performance, allows for the identification of behavioral and cognitive strategies that facilitate the optimal psychophysiological state. Ultimately, it is the ability to create this psychophysiological state that is critical for optimal performance.

Behavioral/Cognitive Studies

The first study of attentional patterns in golf (Crews & Boutcher, 1987) was conducted to verify the existance of behavioral routines in the game of golf and to determine if routines are associated with better performance. Lady Professional Golf Association Tour Players (N = 12) were observed for 12 holes during a competition. Trained observers recorded and timed preshot routines for the full swing and the putt. Results indicated that these golfers were remarkably consistent with regard to time and behavioral actions, such as waggles and glances at the hole. Golfers were then divided into two groups based on rank from the previous year. The lower ranked players (more successful) evidenced significantly (p < .05) longer total routine times for the full swing (20.67 $\pm$ 5.42 s) and the putt (23.47 $\pm$ 4.07) than the higher ranked players (full swing = 14.38 $\pm$ 2.86 s; putt = 18.36 $\pm$ 3.63 s) with no significant differences in variability (i.e., standard deviation). It was speculated that the longer routine times of the successful players reflected more developed preparation strategies. It was not possible in this study to determine the cognitive strategies used by the two groups; however, consistent behavioral routines appeared to be necessary for successful performance.

Verification of the existence of routines among professional players and defining longer routines to be associated with better performers prompted the next question. If players develop a preshot attentional routine of appropriate length, would their performance improve? To answer this question, 12 collegiate golfers were randonly assigned to a routine or a no-routine group (Boutcher & Crews, 1987). An equal number of males and females were assigned to each group to control for possible gender effects. The players were pre- and posttested on an outdoor putting green, completing 18 putts, six each from distances of 4, 12, and 20 feet from the hole. The 6-week training program consisted of individually defining a putting routine for each player and then practicing that routine four times per week for approximately 20 min each session. Players practiced by

Table 1. Means and Standard Deviations for Pre- and Posttest
Preparation Time and Variable Error of Preparation Time for
the Golf Putt

Group	Pretest		Posttest	
	Time	Error	Time	Error
Exper. Females	4.18 ± .93	1.13 ± .29	6.41* ± 1.58	.81 ± .12
Exper. Males	5.11 ± .44	1.44 ± .31	6.81* ± 2.20	.83 ± .20
Control Females	5.72 ± 3.60	1.55 ± .98	4.50* ± 1.88	1.17 ± .73
Control Males	4.91 ± 1.26	1.08 ± .21	4.16* ± .83	.97 ± .09

* Significant differences ($p < .05$)

completing 12 putts in a cross pattern around the hole,
marking each ball to initiate use of the preshot routine.
     Results showed that the male and female routine groups
significantly increased time and decreased variability on the
putting task compared to controls (see Table 1). The female
routine group also improved putting performance with 1.67 more
successful putts and 6 cm less total error from the hole from
the pre- to the posttest. All other groups showed decrements
in performance from the pre- to the posttest. These results
suggest that golfers who use specific cognitions and a
consistent sequence of behaviors may enhance the ability to
achieve the optimal psychological state and may also improve
putting performance.
     If collegiate golfers potentially improve as a result of
using a preshot routine, it was questioned whether beginning
golfers who were taught to use a preshot routine, might also
benefit from these behaviors. A study of 30 undergraduate
students enrolled in beginning golf classes examined whether
the introduction of a preshot routine half-way through the
semester would improve golf swing or skill performance (Crews
& Boutcher, 1986). Subjects completed a full-swing pretest
examining ball trajectory, distance, direction, and total
points scored to a 50-yrd wide target divided into three
concentric circles. Performance was recorded subjectively by
an LPGA teacher who assessed the best five out of 10 shots on
a scale from 1-10, 50 maximal points. Objective performance

Table 2.   Means and Standard Deviations for Pre- and Posttest
Objective Performance Scores

Group	Pretest	Posttest
Exper. Females	8.33 ± 6.29	10.71 ± 3.60ab
Exper. Males	10.44 ± 5.94	17.33 ± 7.21a
Control Females	5.00 ± 4.04	8.29 ± 3.15
Control Males	14.38 ± 6.00	15.63 ± 7.48b

ab Significant difference ($p < .05$)

was based on the landing spot of the 10 balls on the target.
Subjects received three points for the inner circle, two
points for the middle circle, and one point for the outer
circle, 30 points maximum.

Results showed no differences for the subjective swing
assessment; however, the objective assessment revealed that
the males who received preshot routine training improved
significantly from the pre- to the posttest assessment
compared to the control males and to the experimental females
(see Table 2). A closer examination of the scores suggested
that the experimental males were more skilled before and after
training, perhaps suggesting that a given level of skill is
needed before introduction of a preshot routine will
facilitate performance. This seems logical since beginners
need to focus the majority of their attention on the
biomechanics of the skill and a routine may be distracting to
that focus.

Psychophysiological Studies

The use of consistent behaviors and cognitions prior to
execution of a golf shot appears to be related to successful
performance, but the question is "why?" Do these behaviors
and cognitions influence psychophysiological state? To answer
this question, it was first necessary to determine whether
better golfers have more consistent psychophysiological
patterns that accompany their consistent total routine time.
A study of 34 highly-skilled golfers was conducted to assess
the heart rate and respiration patterns of more and less
successful putters (Crews & Landers, 1989). While the golfers
had an average handicap of 3.64, putting skill was quite

variable. The five best putters made significantly ($\mathbf{F}$(1,8) = 135.3, $\mathbf{p}$ < .001) more of the 260, 12 ft putts (125 or more successful putts) than the five worst putters (50 or less successful putts). In addition, visual and auditory/ perceptual distraction were included in 180 of the 260 putts. The dominant heart rate (i.e., acceleration, deceleration) and respiration patterns (i.e., inhalation, exhalation) for the five best and the five worst golfers were defined and the percentage of trials using this pattern was determined.

Results indicated that successful putters displayed their dominant heart rate and respiration pattern 64% and 71% of the trials, respectively, while less successful putters showed percentages of 58% and 63% for heart rate and respiration, respectively. Thus, better performance also appears to be differentiated by more consistent psychophysiological patterns, suggesting that creating a consistent psychophysiological state may enhance performance.

Cardiac and electrocortical measures are both used as psychophysiological indicators of attention in sport (Boutcher & Zinsser, 1990; Crews & Landers, 1993; Molander & Backman, 1989; Schmid, 1989). Previous studies by Boutcher & Zinsser (1990) and Molander & Backman (1989) have defined cardiac deceleration as the psychophysiological pattern associated with best golf and archery performance, respectively. Schmid also found that delayed cardiac acceleration following the shot characterized elite performers compared with novice archers. The dominant cardiac pattern found among the 34 golfers in the previously mentioned study (Crews & Landers, 1989) was deceleration and Figure 2 shows that greater deceleration was found among better performers compared to worse performers in an incentive condition (Crews & Landers, 1994).

Electrocortical measures of attentional focus were also examined for the 34 teaching professional ($\mathbf{N}$ = 17) and amateur ($\mathbf{N}$ = 17) golfers. EEG activity was recorded from the right and left, motor and temporal cortices of the brain (Crews & Landers, 1993). Slow potential shift, 40 Hz EEG, and relative power spectrum were the three EEG measures recorded the final 3 s prior to initiation of 80, 12 ft putts. These measures represent readiness to respond, focused arousal, and general cortical activation, respectively. The three measures

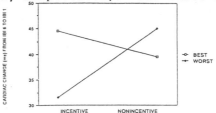

Fig. 2. Cardiac deceleration of the best and worst putters in conditions of incentive and nonincentive.

suggested decreased left hemisphere activity and greater readiness to respond as the player prepared to putt. During the last second preceding the putt, increased right hemisphere alpha activity correlated (r = -0.51, p < .001) with and predicted (25%) less error. Alpha activity represents a more relaxed psychophysiological state, facilitating attentional focus as opposed to beta activity, a state of active processing.

A comparison of the relative power measures of the five best and the five worst performers revealed several significant differences. As seen in Figure 3, two right and two left hemisphere measures from four frequency bands showed that the best five performers were consistently decreasing cortical activity over time, while the worst performers increased cortical activity as they approached stroke initiation (see Figure 3). These two groups of subjects also reported using different cognitive strategies to initiate the stroke. The cues used by the best performers were primarily target and feel cues, while the worst performers reported using primarily biomechanical cues. It appeared that the worst performers were still attempting to direct, or consciously send information to the muscles to produce the stroke, while the best performers were in a cognitive state to receive sensory information from the target or muscles. Best performers showed reduced active processing (i.e., beta activity) over time, perhaps reflecting this psycho-physiological state of heightened sensory awareness.

Results of this study identify three EEG patterns used during golf putting and indicate that greater right hemisphere alpha activity is optimal the final second before the stroke. The next logical study would need to determine whether training golfers to produce one of these three EEG patterns would improve performance. Biofeedback training of the slow potential shift measure in the left hemisphere of the brain was compared with conditions of visualization/imagery, relaxation, and control reading (Crews, Martin, Hart, & Piparo, 1991). Slow potential shift was selected because biofeedback of this measure had been associated with better archery performance (Landers et al., 1991).

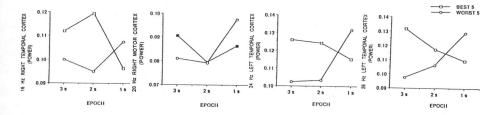

Fig. 3.   EEG patterns of the best and worst putters the final 3 s of preparation.

Moderate level golfers (N = 20, 8-20 handicap) completed 40, 12 ft putts before and after each of the four experimental conditions. Manipulation checks (i.e., slow shift change, heart rate, self-report anxiety) indicated the effectiveness of the treatments. The number of successful putts increased following the EEG biofeedback (+2.6) and visualization/imagery (+2.6) conditions compared to the relaxation condition(-1.6). Interestingly, relaxation actually produced a decrement in performance; however, these subjects were not overaroused prior to testing. Biofeedback training of a specific psychophysiological pattern improved golf putting performance, but not significantly better than visualization/imagery. It is possible that both EEG biofeedback and visualization/ imagery are producing the correct psychophysiological state for successful performance. It may be possible to train the correct psychophysiological state using a cognitive strategy (i.e., visualization/imagery), while others may require EEG biofeedback training, a direct psychophysiological indicator.

Fitness and Age Factors

An examination of factors that my influence attentional focus in golf prompted the design of the last two studies. The first of these factors was fitness level. The aerobic demands of golf are certainly not great, about 5 kcal/hour(McArdle, Katch, & Katch, 1991); however, it may be necessary to be in good aerobic condition to maintain attentional focus the final holes of a round when fatigue may develop.

To determine the influence of fitness level on golf putting performance, high (N = 10) and low (N = 10) fit golfers were tested prior to and following a 20 min walk at 80% of their maximal aerobic capacity (Piparo, Crews, & Hart, 1991). Subjects completed 20, 12 ft putts and performance was recorded as the number of successful putts and as cm error from the hole. Interestingly, the high fit golfers improved putting performance (pre = 21 cm, post = 20 cm; pre = 6.0 putts made, post = 9.7 putts made) following the strenuous walk, while the low fit golfers showed greater total error (pre = 19 cm, post = 26 cm) and a lower number of successful putts (pre = 9.2, post = 7.8). It is known that a certain level of physiological arousal is optimal for best performance, but it appears that low fit golfers may have been distracted by physiological cues of fatigue (i.e., heavy breathing, increased heart rate) and this elicited a decrement in performance.

Lastly, age is a factor that may influence the ability to attend to relevant cues. Molander and Backman (1989, 1991) have shown an inverse psychophysiological pattern (i.e., heart rate acceleration vs. deceleration) among older elite putters compared to younger players. They suggested that perhaps different attentional strategies are needed by older players to maintain successful performance.

In addition, EEG patterns also change with age. Alpha activity (8-12 Hz) in the right hemisphere increases in amplitude and the dominant frequency becomes slower in both hemispheres. The persistence and incidence of beta activity increases with age until the very old stage (i.e., 80 yrs). Interestingly, beta activity disappears in the very old. The optimal psychophysiological pattern that occurs in young adults preparing to putt has been characterized by increased right hemisphere alpha (or reduced activity), and by reduced left hemisphere activity over time (Crews & Landers, 1993). Thus, aging could facilitate the development of alpha activity, but would interfere with the ability to reduce beta activity until a very old age.

A pilot study examining the EEG patterns of four older subjects (ages 40-69 yrs) who completed 20, 12 ft putts, revealed a significant ($F(2,2) = 27.29$, $p < .04$) Hemisphere x Time interaction (Crews, 1992). The right hemisphere showed a decrease in cortical activity the final 3 s before the putt while the left hemisphere increased slightly. This finding is consistent with the pattern of the younger adults for the right hemisphere, but opposite for the left hemishpere. Examining the four frequency bands (theta, alpha, beta, beta II) of the best four and the worst four trials of these subjects, the only significant ($F(2,2) = 7.30$, $p < .03$) differences occurred in the beta II band. Best trials were characterized by increased activity over time, while the worst trials showed reduced activity in both the right and left hemispheres (see Figure 4).

Age produces higher base levels of beta activity than found among younger subjects, but it also appears that increasing beta activity during shot preparation is important for successful performance. This is contrary to the pattern of younger players. Similar to the findings of Molander and Backman (1989), psychophysiological state may differ for older individuals, and may need to change, due to general aging effects, to maintain successful performance.

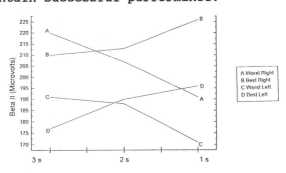

Fig. 4. Beta II activity for the best and worst trials of four aged golfers.

Conclusions

In summary, behavioral, cognitive, and psychophysiological indicators of attentional focus suggest that consistent behavioral routines are necessary, that appropriate attentional cues facilitate performance, and that obtaining a specific psychophysiological pattern elicits successful putting in golf. It is also apparent that aerobic fitness can facilitate performance on a nonaerobic task (i.e., putting), perhaps through enhanced attentional focus. Lastly, age may produce psychophysiological patterns that differ from younger individuals, particularly in the left hemisphere, and this may be necessary for optimal performance.

It is also apparent from the results of these studies that the behavioral, cognitive, and psychophysiological patterns necessary for best performance can be learned by players above a beginning skill level. These techniques are learned through psychological skills training programs and through the use of biofeedback training. As the player becomes more advanced in skill, it may be necessary to use a more complex attentional training technique. For example, intermediate level players probably exhibit a relatively consistent behavioral routine; however, their cognitive strategies may not be consistently established. In turn, a professional player who displays a consistent behavioral and cognitive routine may need to use biofeedback training to be able to consistently feel and create the optimal psychophysiological state for successful performance. Ultimately, it is creating this psychophysiological state, the final second prior to execution of the shot, that elicits best performance. This state appears to be characterized by increased sensory awareness and reduced processing output.

This paper attempted to convey information to the researcher, teacher, coach, and player of golf from a scientific perspective. A specific aspect of the game, attentional focus, was examined using a multidisciplinary (i.e., psychological, physiological) and multiple measure approach. Players of all skill levels were examined and answers to questions were validated through experimental manipulation. An attempt was made to apply study results to the teaching and learning of the game of golf. Hopefully all golfers will come to appreciate the importance of scientific inquiry to enhance the field of knowledge in this complex game.

References

Boutcher, S.H., and Crews, D.J. (1987) The effect of a preshot attentional routine on a well-learned skill. **Int. J. Sport Psych.**, 18, 30-39.

Boutcher, S.H. and Zinsser, N.W. (1990) Cardiac deceleration of elite and beginning golfers during putting. **J. Sport Exerc. Psych.**, 12, 37-47.

Crews, D.J. (1992, May) The influence of age on attentional patterns in golf putting. Paper presented at the **American College of Sports Medicine**, Dallas, TX.

Crews, D.J., and Boutcher, S.H. (1986) An exploratory observational behavior analysis of professional golfers during competition. **J. Sport Beh.**, 9, 51-58.

Crews, D.J., and Boutcher, S.H. (1986) Effects of structured preshot behaviors on beginning golf performance. **Percept.Motor Skills**, 62, 291-294.

Crews, D.J. and Landers, D.M. (1994) Cardiac pattern response to incentive and to visual and auditory perturbation of an automatically produced sport skill. Manuscript submitted for publication.

Crews, D.J. and Landers, D.M. (1993) Electroencephalographic measures of attentional patterns prior to the golf putt. **Med. Sci. Sports Exerc.**, 25, 116-126.

Crews, D.J., Martin, J., Hart, E.A., and Piparo, A.J. (1991, June) The effects of EEG biofeedback, relaxation, and imagery training on golf putting performance. Paper presented at the **North American Society of Sport and Physical Activity**, Asilomar, CA.

Crews, D.J. and Landers, D.M. (1989) Heart rate and respiration pattern in the golf putt. **Med. Sci. Sports Exerc.**, 21, p. S60.

Landers, D.M., Petruzzello, S.J., Salazar, W., Crews, D.J., Kubitz, K.A., Gannon, T.L., and Han, M. (1991) The influence of electrocortical biofeedback on performance in pre-elite archers. **Med. Sci. Sports Exerc.**, 23, 123-129.

McArdle, W.D., Katch, F.I., and Katch, V.L. (1991) **Exercise Physiology: Exercise, Nutrition, and Human Performance.** Malvern, PA: Lea & Febiger, p. 806.

Molander, B. and Backman, L. (1989) Age differences in heart rate patterns during concentration in a precision sport: Implication for attentional functioning. **J. Gerontology: Psychol. Sci.**, 44, 80-87.

Piparo, A.J., Crews, D.J., and Hart, E.A. (1991, March) Level of fitness and performance of a precision task. Paper presented at the **Sport Exerc. Psych. Symposium**, College Park, MD.

Schmid, W.D. (1989) Heart rate patterns of archers while shooting. **Fiziologiya Cheloveka**, 15, 64-68.

21 Contributions of psychological, psychomotor, and shot-making skills to prowess at golf

P.R. Thomas
Faculty of Education, Griffith University, Queensland 4111,
Australia
and R. Over
Department of Psychology, La Trobe University, Victoria 3083,
Australia

Abstract
Relationships between levels of molar performance (golf handicap) and components such as shot-making, psychological, and psychomotor skills are examined for a sample of male amateur golfers. Although molar performance was most closely associated with shot-making skills (length of drive from the tee, putts per round, and likelihood of reaching the green in regulation strokes), further contributions came from psychological skills and tactics (such as mental preparation and striving for maximum distance) and psychomotor skills (such as automaticity). The implications of these results for understanding previous research findings and effecting improvement in golf performance are considered.
Keywords: Psychological Skills, Psychomotor Skills, Shot-making Skills, Golf.

1 Introduction

Schulz and Curnow (1988) argued that sports can be distinguished in relation to the extent each relies on skills such as reaction time, speed of limb movement, flexibility, explosive strength, gross body coordination, control precision, rate control, arm-hand steadiness, aiming, and stamina. Golf is a sport that places low demands on reaction time, speed of limb movement, extent flexibility, dynamic flexibility, dynamic strength, and stamina, but requires a high level of control precision, multilimb coordination, rate control (timing), arm-hand steadiness, aiming, explosive strength, fine body coordination, and gross body coordination. The 2 hands control a long lever (the golf club) through a side-arm pattern of movement in order to strike the stationary golf ball. Broer and Zernicke (1979) differentiated the "driving" stroke and the putting stroke, but noted that the same mechanical factors are involved in both. In execution of the "driving" stroke, a golfer can control the vertical angle of projection without much change in swinging action by choosing the appropriate golf club. Whether the golf ball comes to rest where the golfer intended will depend, among other factors, on whether the player applied appropriate force through the center of gravity of the ball in the desired direction.

Specific shot-making skills such as driving from the tee, hitting from the fairway to the green, exploding from sand bunkers, and putting on the green are needed in order to complete a round of golf in the fewest strokes possible. Davidson and Templin (1986) used statistics from the 1983 Professional Golfers' Association (PGA) tour to establish the extent to which these shot-making skills predicted a player's average score per round over the season. They demonstrated through regression analysis that the golfers with lowest average scores were those who reached the green most often in regulation shots (beta of -.95), took fewest putts per round (beta of .78), and had greatest length from the tee (beta of -.11). Prowess on these three aspects of shot-making predicted 86% of variance in shots per round; a player's ability to finish a hole in 2 shots or less out of a

Science and Golf II: Proceedings of the World Scientific Congress of Golf. Edited by A.J. Cochran and M.R. Farrally. Published in 1994 by E & FN Spon, London. ISBN 0 419 18790 1

greenside bunker did not account for additional variance. In a similar analysis based on statistics from the 1987 PGA tour, Nix and Koslow (1991) found that 87% of variance in average score per round over the season was associated with (in order of relative contribution) a lower number of putts per round, reaching greens in the regulation number of shots, length of drive from the tee, and holing within 2 shots from a greenside bunker.

Since success at golf is correlated with processes such as mental preparation, concentration, automaticity, commitment, and control over thoughts and feelings (see Cohn, 1991; McCaffrey & Orlick, 1989; Thomas & Over, 1994), molar performance needs to be considered with reference to psychological and psychomotor skills as well as shot-making skills. It may be that psychological and psychomotor skills are correlated with aspects of shot-making such as putting, reaching the green in regulation, length of drive, and sand saves, and therefore do not account for variance in molar level of performance (shots per round) over and above the contribution that comes from shot-making. Alternatively, psychological skills may predict additional variance in shots taken per round, or even prove to be more powerful predictors of molar performance than shot-making skills.

The present study examines relationships between psychological skills, shot-making skills, and molar level of performance within a sample of club players. The *Golf Performance Survey* developed by Thomas and Over (1994) is a self-report measure covering nine psychological and psychomotor skills and level of involvement in golf: negative emotions and cognitions, mental preparation, conservative approach, concentration, striving for maximum distance, automaticity, putting skill, seeking improvement, and commitment. Thomas and Over found that more skilled players (those with lower golf handicaps) demonstrate significantly greater mental preparation, concentration, automaticity, and commitment than less skilled players (those with higher golf handicaps). Further, more skilled golfers are less prone to negative emotions and cognitions. As well as completing the *Golf Performance Survey*, the participants in the present study provided information on the aspects of shot-making (length of drive, putts per round, reaching greens in regulation, sand saves) that Davidson and Templin (1986) and Nix and Koslow (1991) identified as predictors of shots taken per round by professional golfers. The measure of molar performance in the present study was a player's golf handicap, a measure that reflects average shots per round.

2 Method

2.1 Subjects
All men who played a round of competitive golf at the Pacific Golf Club in Brisbane, Australia on 24-25 August 1991 were asked as they were leaving the last green if they would complete a questionnaire in privacy, and then return the questionnaire to the investigators by reply-paid post. Only 4 players declined to participate. Of the 400 questionnaires that were distributed, 172 were returned fully completed (a response rate of 43%). Respondents ranged in age between 13 years and 74 years (M = 46.8 years, SD = 13.4), and golf handicaps as determined by the Australian Golf Union ranged from 5 to 27 (M = 15.6, SD = 5.3).

2.2 Instrument
The questionnaire (the *Golf Performance Survey*) sought details such as age, height, weight, years of playing golf, and rounds played per month, as well as indicators of performance including golf handicap, average length of drive, average number of putts per round, ability to complete a hole within 2 shots from a greenside bunker, and the probabilities of hitting par 3 greens with the tee shot, par 4 greens in two shots or less, and par 5 greens in three shots or less. The overall greens in regulation rating was

determined by weighting these probabilities according to the course configuration (4 par 3 holes, 10 par 4 holes, and 4 par 5 holes).

Respondents also rated 95 items covering psychological and psychomotor skills involved in golf (e.g., "I am competitive when playing golf") on a 5-point scale ranging from "strongly disagree" to "strongly agree". These ratings were scored to obtain measures for each player on five psychological skills: negative emotions and cognitions, mental preparation, conservative approach, concentration, and striving for maximum distance; three psychomotor skills: automaticity, putting skill, and seeking improvement; and the level of involvement in golf: commitment (see Thomas & Over, 1994).

3 Results

Golfers on the 1987 PGA tour drove an average of 240.1 metres, averaged 29.6 putts per round, reached 67.3% of greens in regulation shots, and holed from a greenside bunker in 2 shots or less on 49.1% of attempts (Nix & Koslow, 1991). The golfers in the present study reported driving an average of 207.8 metres (SD 24.8) from the tee, taking 36.0 putts (SD 3.8) per round, reaching 51.0% (SD 20.0) of greens in regulation strokes, and holing from a greenside bunker in 2 shots or less on 34.9% (SD 23.2) of attempts. Table 1 shows correlations between these shot-making skills and molar performance (a player's golf handicap). All correlations are significant, p < .01.

Table 1.   Correlations between shot-making skill measures and golf handicap

	Handicap	Drives	Putts	Greens in regulation	Sand saves
Handicap	1.00	-.59	.50	-.59	-.34
Drives		1.00	-.36	.46	.28
Putts			1.00	-.26	-.33
Greens in regulation				1.00	.50
Sand saves					1.00

Following Davidson and Templin (1986) and Nix and Koslow (1991), stepwise multiple regression analysis was undertaken to establish the relationship between molar performance levels and skills at shot-making. Golf handicap was the criterion measure, while length of drive, putts per round, probability of reaching greens in regulation shots, and rated likelihood of holing in 2 shots or less from a greenside bunker were the predictor variables. The four shot-making skills were associated with 55.2% of variance in level of molar performance. Beta values were -.34 for greens in regulation shots, -.33 for length of drive from the tee, .30 for putts per round, and .04 for likelihood of holing in 2 shots or less from a greenside bunker.

Table 2 shows correlations between the four shot-making measures employed in the study and scores on the nine subscales of the *Golf Performance Survey*. Although many of the correlations reach statistical significance, they generally are low to moderate in magnitude. The question next addressed is whether skills measured by the *Golf Performance Survey* contribute to prowess at golf (indexed by handicap) additionally to or independently of shot-making skills. In the hierarchical regression analysis undertaken for this purpose, the four shot-making skills comprising the initial block of predictors were entered in a single step in order of decreasing tolerance. The three psychomotor skills were entered in the next block to determine whether self-ratings on these subscales added

Table 2. Correlations between shot-making measures and the psychological and psychomotor skills and involvement level assessed by the *Golf Performance Survey*

Psychological and psychomotor skills	Shot-making skills			
	Drive (metres)	Putts per round	Greens in regulation	Sand saves
Negative Emotions/Cognitions	.16*	.21**	-.20**	-.04
Mental Preparation	.18*	-.22**	.35**	.34**
Conservative Approach	-.31**	.13	-.19*	.08
Concentration	.06	-.11	.13	.05
Striving for Maximum Distance	.35**	-.01	.14	.09
Automaticity	.19*	-.20**	.46**	.21**
Putting Skill	-.14	-.39**	.10	.32**
Seeking Improvement	.27**	-.03	.00	.11
Commitment	.24**	-.21**	.17*	.32**

* p<.05   ** p<.01

significantly to the variance in golf prowess accounted for by the differences in shot-making skills. Then followed the subscale measuring golf involvement, and finally a block of five psychological skills and tactics subscales. Thus the model provided a very conservative test of the contribution of psychological skills to prowess at golf by assessing their influence only after statistically accounting for the effects of all other predictor variables.

Table 3 confirms the significant relationship between golf prowess and shot-making skills previously revealed by stepwise regression, $F_{(4,155)} = 48.02$, $p < .001$. The beta coefficients shown in Table 3 were computed at the final step of the analysis after all predictor variables were entered into the regression equation. At the initial step, the respective coefficients were -.36 for greens in regulation, -.33 for length of drive, .31 for putts per round, and .04 for sand saves. When self-ratings on psychomotor skills were added to the data on shot-making skills, the proportion of sample variance in golf prowess that could be accounted for increased significantly from 55.3% to 60.6%, $F_{(3,152)} = 5.00$ $p < .01$. It is clear from the beta coefficients that automaticity in the golf swing is responsible for much of this significant increase. Adding data on level of involvement in golf at this stage of the analysis did not significantly improve the prediction of golf prowess, $F_{(1,151)} = 1.50$, $p > .05$. However, when data on psychological skills and tactics were considered in the final step, the proportion of sample variance in golf prowess that could be explained increased significantly from 60.6% to 66.5%, $F_{(5,146)} = 5.11$, $p < .001$.

Whereas there was a significant negative correlation between mental preparation and golf prowess as indexed by handicap ($r = -.24$, $p < .01$), the beta weight for the mental preparation subscale was significantly positive ($\beta = .14$, $p < .05$). This pattern signals the presence of a suppressor variable. Following the recommendations of Tabachnick and Fidell (1989), changes in the beta coefficient for mental preparation were monitored as each of the predictor variables was systematically omitted from the regression equation. These procedures revealed that responses to the automaticity subscale were suppressing irrelevant variance and thus enhancing the importance of mental preparation in the prediction of golf prowess.

Table 3.   Hierarchical regression analysis of golf prowess (handicap) on shot-making, psychomotor skills, level of involvement, and psychological skills

Step	Variables	Multiple R	R^2	F_{inc}	Beta Coefficient
1	Sand saves				-.04
2	Length of drive				-.36 ***
3	Putts per round				.27 ***
4	Greens in regulation				-.27 ***
	Shot-making skills	.744	.553	48.02 ***	
5	Seeking improvement				-.06
6	Automaticity				-.20 ***
7	Putting Skill				.08
	Psychomotor skills	.778	.606	5.00 **	
8	Commitment				-.08
	Level of involvement	.779	.606	1.50	
9	Concentration				-.09
10	Striving for maximum distance				.19 ***
11	Conservative approach				.08
12	Mental preparation				.14 *
13	Negative emotions and cognitions				.06
	Psychological skills	.815	.665	5.11 ***	

* p < .05   ** p < .01   *** p < .001

4   Discussion

The results of this research show that the shot-making skills associated with prowess in amateur golf are very similar to those associated with success in professional golf. All four shot-making skills were significantly correlated with handicap, just as they were with scoring average on the US PGA tour (Davidson & Templin, 1986). The regression analyses indicate that length of drive, proportion of greens reached in regulation shots, and number of putts per round all made significant and approximately equal contributions to the amateur golfer's level of performance. However, these analyses also confirm earlier findings that skill in playing bunker shots contributes little to the prediction of molar performance that cannot be accounted for by the other three skills. Putting skill may account for much of the variance in performance associated with getting the ball to the hole from a greenside bunker.

Davidson and Templin (1986) acknowledged that sociopsychological factors (motivation, temperament, "peace of mind") may explain some of the variance in golf achievement, but they were unable to consider the contribution of such factors. In this study of amateur golfers there clearly were significant correlations between each of the four shot-making skills and many of the psychological and psychomotor skills measured by the *Golf Performance Survey* . These related psychological skills may have accounted for some of the large percentage of variance in success on the tour attributed in previous research to shot-making skills.

After differences in shot-making skills were taken into account, the skills measured by the *Golf Performance Survey* made significant contributions to the prediction of prowess in amateur golfers. Automaticity, the act of swinging the club consistently with little conscious effort to guide movement, is clearly an important component in the execution of psychomotor skill accounting for substantial variation in golf performance. The club golfer's level of commitment had little additional impact on performance once differences in shot-making skills and psychomotor automaticity were considered. But the remaining psychological skills significantly improved the prediction of prowess, although their contributions were often complex. Striving for maximum distance is a tactic associated with high handicap golfers and young players (Thomas & Over, 1994). On the other hand, mental preparation is characteristic of more skilled performers. The complex relationships revealed in this study between automaticity, mental preparation, and performance level offer some empirical support for the notion of "paralysis by analysis".

It is often claimed that up to 90% of success in sports is due to mental factors, particularly at the higher levels of competition (Williams & Krane, 1993). Some elite golfers publicly endorse such a view. Jack Nicklaus (1976) wrote, 'I feel that hitting specific shots - playing the ball to a certain place in a certain way - is 50 percent mental picture, 40 percent setup, and 10 percent swing' (p.77). The full extent of the contribution made by mental factors is revealed in Nicklaus' elaboration of the importance of setup, 'This includes picturing the shot, aiming and aligning the clubface and your body relative to your target, placing the ball relative to your intended swing arc, assuming your over-all address posture, and mentally and physically conditioning yourself just before pulling the trigger' (p.79). Although the results of the present study do not support the view that mental factors account for such a high percentage of variance in golf performance, they clearly do make a significant contribution in their own right. Those players able to effect improvement in their psychological skills can justifiably look forward to better performance and a reduction in their golf handicap.

5   References

Broer, M.R., & Zernicke, R.F. (1979) **Efficiency of Human Movement.** Saunders, Philadelphia.

Cohn, P.J. (1991) An exploratory study on peak performance in golf. **The Sport Psychologist,** 5, 1-14.

Davidson, J.D., & Templin, T.J. (1986) Determinants of success among professional golfers. **Research Quarterly for Exercise and Sport,** 57, 60-67.

McCaffrey, N., & Orlick, T. (1989) Mental factors related to excellence among top professional golfers. **International Journal of Sport Psychology,** 20, 256-278.

Nicklaus, J. (1976) **Golf My Way.** Pan Books, London.

Nix, C.L., & Koslow, R. (1991) Physical skill factors contributing to success on the professional golf tour. **Perceptual and Motor Skills,** 72, 1272-1274 .

Schulz, R., & Curnow, C. (1988) Peak performance and age among superathletes: Track and field, swimming, baseball, tennis, and golf. **Journal of Gerontology: Psychological Sciences,** 43, 113-120.

Thomas, P.R., & Over, R. (1994) Psychological and psychomotor skills associated with performance in golf. **The Sport Psychologist,** 8 (1).

Williams, J.M., & Krane, V. (1993) Psychological characteristics of peak performance, in **Applied Sport Psychology** (2nd ed) (ed J.M. Williams), Mayfield, Palo Alto CA, pp. 137-147.

22 Factors affecting the salience of outcome, performance and process goals in golf

K. Kingston and L. Hardy
Division of Health and Human Performance, University of Wales, Bangor, UK

Abstract

This paper focuses upon the appropriateness in relation to golf performance of different types of goal which, it is suggested, differ according to their primary focus. Contrary to trends suggested elsewhere, for example in the goal orientations literature (Burton, 1992; Duda, 1992), it is argued that outcome goals should not be denigrated to the extent that golfers are encouraged to totally ignore them. Rather, the suggestion is made that certain types of goal may be more salient than others to the golfer at different stages during golf performance. This suggestion is based on the available empirical evidence regarding the relative effects of different types of goal upon the cognitive processes that are thought to underly golf performance.
Keywords: Golf, Goals, Attention, Pre-performance Routines, Automaticity.

1 Introduction

Despite the obvious importance of psychological factors in golf, few researchers have rigorously examined the psychological processes that might underly and support golf performance. Notable exceptions to this statement include Boutcher and Crew's (1987) work on pre-shot routines, Kirschenbaum's work on self-regulation (see, for example, Johnston-O'Connor & Kirschenbaum, 1986), and Masters' (1992) work on automaticity. However, previous research has not considered the use of goal-setting strategies within golf. The present paper first reviews some of the more relevant literature on goal-setting. It then presents a reasoned argument for the use of a number of different types of goal during preparation for, and performance at, major golf competitions.

One of the most widely accepted definitions for a goal is that generated by Locke, Shaw, Saari and Latham (1981); namely, "a specific standard of proficiency on a task, usually [to be achieved] within a specified time limit" (Locke et al., 1981, p. 145). Furthermore, Locke et al. (1981) also presented comprehensive review of goal setting and its influence on task performance in organisational and industrial settings. This review identified four mechanisms via which goal setting appeared to improve performance.

   i)   Directing attention and action;
   ii) Mobilising and regulating effort expended on a particular task;
   iii) Prolonging effort until the goal is reached;
   iv) Motivating individuals to develop alternative strategies in their attempts to reach the goal.

Science and Golf II: Proceedings of the World Scientific Congress of Golf. Edited by A.J. Cochran and M.R. Farrally. Published in 1994 by E & FN Spon, London. ISBN 0 419 18790 1

2 Goal setting in sport - Does it transfer?

It has been suggested that tasks performed in industrial and organisational settings (where the majority of early research was carried out) have much in common with sports activities. Consequently, there is every reason to believe that goal setting will work equally well in the realm of sports as it does in work settings. Early research into the effects of goal setting upon sports performance can be regarded as somewhat encouraging (Beggs, 1990). For example, Locke and Latham (1985) concluded that when specific, challenging goals were given in a psychomotor task, subjects performed better than when simply asked to "do their best". Furthermore, specific goals have been found to lead to higher performance than a goal free condition (Beggs, 1990). More recent examples of support for these contentions are provided in the works of Burton (1983), and Hall, Weinberg and Jackson (1987). Despite the body of literature which supports the transferability of industrial/organisational findings on goal setting to sport (e.g. Burton, 1983; Locke and Latham, 1985; Hall and Byrne, 1988), a number of studies have brought this notion into question. The reasons cited for the lack of effects in some sport studies include; "no goal" groups setting covert goals; competition between control subjects; and unknown environmental influences. Tubbs (1986) carried out a meta-analysis on some of the literature on goal setting, and concluded that the findings obtained in controlled laboratory settings may not accurately reflect goal setting effects found in more realistic environments. Laboratories cannot duplicate the levels of ego involvement and success/failure histories that can so profoundly influence behaviour in real sports contexts (Burton, 1989). Studies therefore need to address both situational factors as well as personality differences in attempting to obtain meaningful results.

3 The problem with outcome goals

The competitive ethic "winning is everything" has, according to Burton (1989), become the creed of modern sport, and sports psychologists have questioned whether this attitude to winning was actually more harmful than beneficial in its effects on performance (c.f. Burton, 1989). "Winning" or "to win" are perhaps the most notorious of outcome goals, where evaluations of success are based entirely on social comparison processes, i.e. comparing one's performance with the performance of other competitors. Outcome goals can, according to Burton, (1983) be defined as "standards of performance that focus on the results of a contest between opponents or teams". The danger with outcome goals which are based on social comparison processes is that they lack the control and flexibility necessary to ensure consistent success and the acceptance of credit for that success. It has been found that failure to achieve outcome goals may lead to a reduction in confidence, an increase in anxiety, decreased effort and an overall deterioration of performance (Hall and Byrne, 1988). Even though athletes may perform to their best, they may still not achieve outcome goals. Continued failures may well confirm a perceived low ability level, and thus further reduce self confidence. As Burton (1988) points out, when expectations of success decrease, cognitive anxiety increases, self-confidence decreases and both of these factors significantly impair performance.

4 Performance oriented goals

One suggested solution for overcoming the problems associated with outcome goals is to encourage athletes to view success in terms of surpassing personal performance standards rather than exceeding the performance of others, i.e. get them to set performance goals instead of outcome goals. Simply put, performance goals focus on improvement relative to one's own past performances. According to Burton (1989), performance goals are more controllable and flexible than outcome goals, and as such allow athletes of all abilities to raise or lower their goals in order to keep them both challenging and realistic, thus ensuring high motivation, low anxiety, and consistent success. Burton's (1989) study on collegiate swimmers was designed to evaluate whether a goal setting training programme which taught athletes to set appropriate performance, rather than outcome, goals would influence perceived stress and performance. His results indicated that, despite numerous limiting factors, the goal setting training programme not only enhanced perceived ability and competitive cognitions, but also actually improved performance. Furthermore, although causal relationships were impossible to confirm, Burton reasoned that goals would dictate how an individual defined success and failure, and how readily this failure or success would be internalised as indicative of ability. These factors, he suggested, should prominently influence both perceived stress and performance. Further support for the denigration of outcome goals has come from the goal orientations literature, e.g. Duda (1992). Indeed, Albinson and Bull (1988), suggest that a "common error is the setting of 'a goal' which is an outcome of performance...." (c.f. also Brawley, Carron and Widmeyer, 1992).

Whilst the empirical research clearly supports the use of performance oriented goals, Beggs (1990), went so far as to suggest that all goal-setting is something of a "double-edged sword". Consequently, he surmised that even performance goals may elicit negative effects similar to those normally associated with outcome goals, since they satisfy all of Locke and Latham's (1985) criteria for generating stress; they are important, require action, and may not always be reached.

5 Process oriented goals

Given the arguments outlined above, and considering the wealth of literature suggesting that degree of control is an important quality of effective goals, it would seem appropriate to encourage performers to set goals that will enable them to achieve consistent success, as well as to alleviate the negative stress related effects that, according to Beggs (1990), may be associated with outcome and performance oriented goals. Process goals may be the key. Hardy and Nelson (1988) defined process goals as those which focus upon particular elements of the task, rather than upon attaining or surpassing overall performance standards. If attained, Hardy and Nelson argued that such process goals should lead to the achievement of desired overall performance standards. Focusing on specific aspects of technique (a typical example of a process oriented goal) has been identified as an effective strategy in enhancing performance. More clear-cut support for the use of process oriented goals has come from studies by Kingston, Hardy and Markland (1992), with university hockey players, and by Kingston and Hardy (in press), using mental training with club golfers. The results from this second study clearly supported the use of goal-setting for the enhancement of golf performance, whilst further identifying specific benefits associated with process oriented goals over and above those gained from performance oriented goals. More specifically, Kingston and Hardy found that subjects trained in the use of process oriented goals were able to concentrate better, had increased self-efficacy (situationally specific self-confidence), were more able to control their negative expectations about performance, and probably most importantly were able to realise significant reductions in their handicaps (on average 0.8 over 5 months).

6 Performance routines using holistic process goals

Whilst the primary focus of Kingston and Hardy's (in press) study was to determine the relative efficacy of process oriented goals over performance oriented goals and a control condition, it must be acknowledged that consciously focusing on specific parts of the process could lead to a breakdown in "chunking" and automaticity, with consequent decrements in performance (Masters, 1992). Subjects were therefore instructed in the construction of pre-performance routines that were based on holistic process goals, e.g. "smooth", "slow", "tempo". An example of a typical routine as used by professional golfers is:

- Shot analysis (choice of club)
- Setting (establishing optimal physiological arousal level)
- Imagery (visualise the path and the outcome of the shot)
- Kinaesthetic coupling (establishing the feel of the shot)
- Set-up (the address position)
- Waggle (small movements of the club)
- Swing thought (e.g. think "tempo")

It has been suggested that these routines will tend to improve performance in closed skill sports such as golf by influencing how the performer thinks and behaves in three major ways (Boutcher and Crews, 1987). Firstly, by focusing thoughts on a series of well-rehearsed cues, there is less likelihood of the performer concentrating on negative or superfluous information that might otherwise distract attention. Secondly, these routines may provide a mechanism to achieve appropriate activation sets; that is, lower physiological arousal levels generated by stress, whilst also serving to increase concentrational abilities when situations are monotonous or unstimulating. Finally, since the routines themselves become automated with practice, so they may help performers to get into a state of automatic processing prior to performing. Clearly, different golfers may require different components in their pre-performance routines, but the basic principle remains the same; the routine establishes a rhythm and attentional focus plan that simultaneously prepares the body and the mind for the ensuing skill.

7 An appropriate combination?

In highlighting studies which have demonstrated the points we are trying to make, it becomes apparent that there is a need to consider the influence that different types of goals have upon the golfer at different stages of performance (practice and competition), and perhaps more importantly how such goals interact to enable the golfer to realise his or her potential.

Whilst the lack of research examining the ways in which different types of goals can be used in conjunction with each other does not enable firm conclusions to be drawn, the available evidence does allow us to provide a rationale for the use of different types of goals at different stages of performance. For example, several weeks prior to a competition the performer may make explicit a desire to win that competition, i.e. set an outcome goal. This goal may provide the performer with the motivation to expend appropriate resources in order to accomplish the objective he has set. Furthermore, whilst many researchers have denigrated outcome goals to the extent that they should be totally ignored e.g. Burton (1989), and Duda (1992), it can also be argued that they provide the necessary incentives for performers to develop those strategies which will lead to the realisation of their outcome goals. In preparation for a competition performers are likely, (assuming they are serious about their outcome goals) to embark on some sort of practice regimen. For golf, this practice may involve spending considerable time at a driving range or on the practice ground. The use of performance goals (e.g. pitching onto the practice green 8 out of 10 times), which have been found to aid self-confidence (Burton, 1989), as well as process goals (e.g. "one piece take away") which aid concentration and the allocation of attentional resources (Kingston and Hardy, in press), will ensure more effective practice. This is clearly important, because practice is where the foundation for effective performance is laid.

Outcome, performance, and process goals can therefore all be used as strategies to ensure more adequate preparation for competition. However, whilst practice can undoubtedly lead to increased confidence, it cannot completely eradicate the stress associated with the competitive environment. The performer should therefore approach this environment with a set of goals designed to maximise the effectiveness of performance. When performers are anxious, goals which were previously accepted and attained in training may be rejected as unrealistic (Hardy, Maiden and Sherry, 1986). The performer should therefore ensure that the performance goals for competition reflect the additional situational stressors which exist, as these may lower performance capabilities (Burton, 1989), e.g. just because a golfer shoots 76 in practice does not mean that the same score will be realistic in serious competition. Performance goals such as these have been found, amongst other things to direct attention away from the worries about winning, and to aid performance (Burton, 1989). However, given the misgivings of Beggs (1990), and studies which have identified specific benefits associated with process oriented goals, it is reasonable to suggest that the performer should use process oriented goals which focus on holistic aspects of technique during skill execution. As mentioned previously, such goals may aid concentration and the allocation of attentional resources, as well as increasing self-efficacy (Hardy and Nelson, 1988; Kingston and Hardy, 1993). It should follow that if the performer is focusing on a series of well-rehearsed cues, there is less likelihood of him or her concentrating on negative or superfluous information that might otherwise distract attention. Such distractions may be associated with outcome or performance goals that have been set.

8 Conclusion

Many sport psychologists have been fighting against the "winning is everything" mentality and have attempted to re-focus performers' goals totally toward self-improvement and task mastery. It may be, however, that it is the combination of the different goal types, and their implementation at different stages within the framework of preparation and execution of skills that is the key. Afterall, it seems unlikely that one could win (say) the British Open without wanting to beat other players! What is important is that we do not become so preoccupied with winning that it interferes with those things that we need to do in order to realise that objective.

9 References

Albinson, J.G. and Bull, S.J. (1988) **A Mental Game Plan**, Ontario: Spodym Publishers.

Beggs, A. (1990) Goal setting in sport, in **Stress and Performance in Sport** (eds G. Jones and L. Hardy), Chichester: John Wiley, pp. 135-170.

Boutcher, S. and Crews, D. (1987) The effect of a preshot routine on a well-learned skill. **International Journal of Sport Psychology**, 18, 30-39.

Brawley, L.R., Carron, A.V., and Widmeyer, W.N. (1992) The nature of Group Goals in Sport Teams: A Phenomenological Analysis. **The Sport Psychologist**, 6, 323-333.

Burton, D. (1983) Evaluation of goal setting trainingon selected cognitions and performance of collegiate swimmers. **Unpublished Doctoral dissertation**, University of Illinois.

Burton, D. (1988) Do anxious swimmers swim slower? Reexamining the elusive anxiety-performance relationship. **Journal of Sport and Exercise Psychology**, 10, 45-61.

Burton, D. (1989) Winning isn't everything: Examining the impact of performance goals on collegiate swimmers' cognitions and performance. **The Sports Psychologist**, 3, 105-132.

Burton, D. (1992) The Jekyll/Hyde Nature of Goals: Reconceptualising Goal Setting in Sport, in **Advances in Sport Psychology** (Ed. T. Horne), Champaign, IL; Human Kinetics, pp. 267-297.

Duda, J. (1992) Motivation in Sport Settings; A Goal Perspective Approach, in **Motivation in Sport and Exercise** (Ed. G. Roberts), Champaign, IL; Human Kinetics, (pp. 57-91).

Hall, H.K. and Byrne, T.J. (1988) Goal setting in Sport: Clarifying Recent Anomalies. **Journal of Sport and Exercise Psychology**, 10,184-198.

Hall, H.K., Weinberg, R.S. and Jackson, A. (1987) Effects of goal specificity, goal difficulty, and and information feedback on endurance performance. **Journal of Sport Psychology**, 9, 43-54.

Hardy, L., Maiden, D.S. and Sherry, K. (1986) Goal setting and performance anxiety. **Journal of Sports Sciences**, 4, 233-234.

Hardy, L. and Nelson, D. (1988) Self control training in sport and work. **Ergonomics**, 31,1573-1585.

Johnston-O'Connor, E.J. and Kirschenbaum, D.S. (1986) Something succeeds like success: Positive self-monitoring for unskilled golfers. **Cognitive Therapy and Research**, 10, 123-126.

Kingston, K. and Hardy, L. (in press) When are some goals more beneficial than others. **Journal of Sports Sciences**, to appear.

Kingston, K., Hardy, L. and Markland, D. (1992) Study to compare the effect of two different goal orientations on a number of situationally relevant performance subcomponents. **Journal of Sports Sciences**, 10, 610-611.

Locke, E.A. and Latham, G.P. (1985) The application of goal setting to.sports. **Journal of Sports Psychology**, 7, 205-222

Locke, E.A., Shaw, K.N., Saari, L.M. and Latham, G.P. (1981) Goal setting and task performance: 1969-1980. **Psychological Bulletin**, 90, 125-152.

Masters, R.S.W. (1992) Knowledge, knerves and know-how: The role of explicit versus implicit knowledge in the breakdown of complex motor skill under pressure. **British Journal of Psychology**, 83, 343-358.

Tubbs, M.E. (1986) Goal setting: A meta-analytic examination of the empirical evidence, **Journal of Applied Psychology**, 71, 474-483.

23 The self-regulatory challenges of golf

D.S. Kirschenbaum
Center for Behavioral Medicine, Chicago, USA

Abstract
Golf is quite probably the ultimate self-regulatory challenge in all
of sports. This paper reviews conceptualizations and research on
self-regulation and applies them to golf. More specifically, the
paper considers five phases of self-regulation (problem
identification, commitment, execution, environmental management, and
generalization) and qualifiers of this general model of self-
regulation (affect, task difficulty, expectations, attributions, and
dispositions). Methods to increase mastery of the self-regulatory
challenges of golf that have been tested and proposed are also
discussed.
Keywords: Sport Psychology, Self-regulation, Golf Psychology.

Concepts and research findings pertaining to self-regulation may help
golfers decrease their frustration, increase their enjoyment, and
lower their scores (Kirschenbaum and Bale, 1980). Self-regulation
refers to those processes that enable people to guide their behaviors
in pursuit of goals over time and across changing circumstances - in
the relative absence of immediate external control (Kanfer and Karoly,
1972; Karoly, 1993). Self-regulatory processes include goal-setting,
planning, self-observation and self-monitoring, problem identification
and problem solving, self-reinforcement, and related cognitions and
behaviors. Since self-regulation does not occur in a vacuum, self-
regulation involves a variety of complex interactions between
cognitions, (e.g., planning, goal-setting), affect (emotional states),
physiology (e.g., physical fitness), and environmental constraints.
   Researchers and theorists organized these complex interactions by
describing them as sequences of activities or phases (e.g., Kanfer and
Karoly, 1972). Kirschenbaum (1984) suggested that the following five
phases most appropriately summarize self-regulation: problem
identification, commitment, execution, environmental management, and
generalization. Recent research and theorizing also suggest that
self-regulation is further complicated or qualified by a variety of
factors, some of which Karoly (1993) referred to as "metaskills."
Such metaskills include the hierarchial structure of goals, affect,
memory, imagery ability, understanding of task components, task
mastery, among other factors (see Carver and Scheier, 1990). In the
present paper, the self-regulatory challenges of golf will be
described within each of the five phases of self-regulation (from
problem identification to generalization) and the impact of some of

Science and Golf II: Proceedings of the World Scientific Congress of Golf. Edited by A.J.
Cochran and M.R. Farrally. Published in 1994 by E & FN Spon, London. ISBN 0 419 18790 1

the key qualifiers of the usual self-regulatory processes will also be described.

1 Problem Identification

Many behaviors in sport consist of essentially automatic chains of responses. For example, most golfers may not be able to identify their pre-shot routines. Golfers who perform at elite levels may ignore certain aspects of their games that they think are "excellent." How many low handicappers think they are "great chippers" or "great short iron players?" These perceptions may lead to failures to identify problems that could benefit from a more systematic analysis.

For example, very few golfers are aware of the importance for golf performance of excellent physical conditioning (e.g., Crews et al., 1984). Good physical fitness enables well-conditioned golfers to maintain high levels of alertness and muscle tone - even during the final holes of their rounds.

Cognitive and social psychological research shows that people often discredit, minimize, distort, and ignore negative information about themselves (Karoly, 1993; Taylor, 1991). Because of this, most golfers probably ignore critical aspects of their performances that may contribute to higher scores. Ignoring or distorting this information may culminate in failure to identify problems in physical preparation (including sufficiency of practice time, especially for putting), psychological preparation and skills, and mechanical aspects of the swing. Working regularly with teachers (e.g., teaching professionals; sport psychologists) may decrease these tendencies to ignore or distort critical problems that affect performance.

2 Commitment

In the problem identification phase, people search for understanding about what to change in their lives. There would be no purpose to this search without the assumption that change is possible. Once viewing change as a possibility, the athlete must decide to seek that change, thereby promising (committing) to change. Many factors affect whether someone makes a commitment. Among the more important ones for golfers may pertain to the nature of their plans for change (Kirschenbaum, 1984). Many golfers express desires to change without creating a plan that has a reasonable chance of helping them reach those goals. Golfers tend to search for the quick fix (e.g., the new oversized "moon rock" club), as do most people when they attempt to solve difficult problems. A much more effective plan might involve a series of lessons and scheduling more practice time every week.

In addition to defining and elaborating plans, a procedure called "decisional counseling" has demonstrated success at improving commitment and behavior change (see Janis and Mann, 1977). Decisional counseling includes analysis of the rational basis for a particular goal or plan. It also includes confronting irrational ideas and constructing a decision balance sheet. A balance sheet is a list of all of the advantages and disadvantages of a particular goal or plan. Golfers could use this approach to list advantages and disadvantages of increasing their practice times or obtaining professional lessons. It seems likely that if golfers were to complete such a balance sheet, with the support and advice of a professional consultant (i.e., a sport psychologist), they would be more likely to solidify their commitments and increase the probability of changing requisite behaviors (cf. Janis and Mann, 1977).

3 Execution

Once the self-regulatory problem is identified and the commitment is formed to modify it, the individual must begin to change actual thoughts and behaviors in order to achieve the desired outcomes. Self-regulatory theorists have proposed that this complex process can best be viewed as a cybernetic model in which a negative feedback loop serves as the basic unit of functioning (Carver and Scheier, 1990; Kanfer and Karoly, 1972). Cybernetic models are information processing units or means of organizing how people receive and use information. This unit is "negative" with regard to self-regulation because its purpose is to negate, or reduce, behaviors that deviate from goals.

Let us consider the execution phase of self-regulation in a cybernetic model by using an example of an avid golfer who decides to improve his performance from a current handicap of 14 to a handicap of 9.9 over the next two years:

a. Problem Identification - Inconsistency in performance and scores that are unacceptably high.

b. Commitment - To practice and get some lessons in order to reduce current handicap.

c. Execution - i. **Self-monitoring:** I will keep track of my scores and the elements of those scores (putting, greens and regulation, tee shots in fairway, etc.); also I'll keep a log of my practice time divided into putting, non-putting. ii. **Self-evaluation** - After two weeks of self-monitoring, I realize that I am averaging 39 puts per round (which I consider much too high) and that I am hitting an inadequate number of fairways and greens. I also note that my practice time is far too little, especially on putting.

d. Feedback (information and reinforcement): I am dissatisfied with this level of performance and will take steps to improve it (e.g., set aside Tuesday afternoon for regular practicing with Bob; begin a series of lessons).

This example reveals several aspects of the execution phase of self-regulation. In order to self-regulate, people generally must self-monitor, self-evaluate and then provide systematic feedback to themselves. In addition to these elements of self-regulation, the example shows that goals must be set (usually during a commitment phase) in order to allow for self-evaluation and feedback to occur. If these goals are relatively vague, as they were in this example, the other elements in the cybernetic self-regulatory system failed to function effectively. Thus, in the present example some rather vague commitments to modify existing patterns followed the evaluation phase. It would have been more helpful for this golfer to establish a more specific plan that indicated, for example, the number of hours per week of practice that was desired.

Kirschenbaum and Bale (1980) developed a five-component self-regulation training program for golfers to help them clarify their plans and improve on-course self-regulation. Their "Brain Power Golf" program included training in deep muscle relaxation, planning, imagery, positive self-monitoring (keeping records of only good shots after each hole) and positive self-statements (e.g., reminding themselves, as needed, to: "play at your own pace;" "you've made this shot before;" "trust your practicing - you're ready for this challenge.")   Evaluations of Brain Power Golf included two quasi-experimental studies with university-level golfers (0 to 3 handicaps). Both of those studies, in addition to correlational and program evaluation data, supported the efficacy of the approach (Kirschenbaum and Bale, 1980).   Moreover, additional experimental investigations of related approaches (see Kirschenbaum, 1984; Whelan, Mahoney, and Meyers, 1991) clearly suggest that components of this kind of self-regulatory training can produce significant improvements in performance.

4   Environmental Management

Achievement of self-regulated goals usually requires management of the limitations imposed by physical and social environments. For golfers, obvious limitations include the availability of practice facilities and high quality instruction, time, money, and support/acceptance of family members.

5   Generalization

People often fail to maintain self-regulated behavior change over time and across situations. The nature of this "self-regulatory failure" suggests that "obsessive-compulsive self-regulation" often seems warranted (Kirschenbaum and Tomarken, 1982). That is, people maintain behavior better when they self-monitor and engage in other methods of self-regulation vigilantly and intensely. In fact, athletes often develop an obsessive-compulsive style of involvement in their sports. Studies with gymnasts, golfers, wrestlers, and divers (see Kirschenbaum and Wittrock, 1984; and Whelan et al., 1991, for reviews) indicate that a variety of ritualistic behaviors and thoughts are associated with favorable and well-maintained performance outcomes. Kirschenbaum and Bale (1980), for example, showed that better golf scores were obtained by university-level golfers who endorsed items on an attentional style questionnaire that were labeled "obsessive."
    Some research with golfers also suggests that positive self-monitoring (systematically attending to favorable outcomes) supports this attentional style (Johnston-O'Connor and Kirschenbaum, 1986; Kirschenbaum and Bale, 1980).

6   Qualifiers: Affect, Task Difficulty, Expectations, Attributions and Dispositions

The preceding perspective on self-regulation does not incorporate a variety of factors that can have substantial impacts on performance. Affect (mood), task difficulty (and perceived task difficulty or mastery), expectations, attributions, and dispositional styles are among these potentially critical factors.
    Affect. Prapavessis and Grove (1991) conducted a study that compared Morgan's Mental Health Model and Hanin's Zone of Optimal Function (ZOF) model to describe the relationship between affect and sport performance. Morgan's Mental Health Model indicates that the "iceberg profile" (relatively low levels of anxiety or tension

combined with relatively high levels of vigor prior to competition)
should predict more effective performance. This conceptualization was
derived from studies comparing groups of athletes (successful versus
unsuccessful groups across sports). In contrast, Hanin's ZOF model
suggests that individual athletes have an optimal level of arousal;
best performances may be predicted by high levels of arousal for some
athletes, whereas others may perform much better when deeply relaxed
or moderately aroused. The latter ZOF conceptualization conforms more
closely to the recommendations made by a host of reviewers who
examined the relationship between affect and performance in recent
years. It was also clearly supported by research conducted by
Prapavessis and Grove (1991) in a careful analysis of target shooters
tested over an entire competitive season. Many golfers may benefit
from using methods that help them modify their arousal levels to
optimal states prior to and during competition. For most golfers,
this arousal state would probably be a rather positive one without a
great deal of tension or anxiety. However, some notable exceptions
are rather apparent when one observes professional golfers perform
(for example, compare the apparent affective states of Paul Azinger to
Nick Faldo). Consistent use of pre-shot routines may help golfers
with such ZOF affect modulation (Boutcher and Crews, 1987).

  Task Difficulty. Actual difficulty levels of tasks and
perceptions of task difficulty can dramatically affect sport
performance (Kirschenbaum and Tomarken, 1982; Jackson and Roberts,
1992). Analysis of self-regulatory behaviors shows, in particular,
that when tasks are difficult or when self-monitoring occurs in a
negative fashion, a variety of subsequent negative self-evaluative
reactions can occur and behavioral withdrawal from the task itself may
ensue (Carver and Scheier,1981; Kirschenbaum and Tomarken, 1982).
Golf is an inherently difficult task. It is also a game that one can
perceive as difficult at all levels of proficiency. Research by Simek
and O'Brien (1981) demonstrates this point rather nicely. Novice
golfers either received eight instructional lessons in a traditional
teaching approach or they receive an experimental treatment that
encourages mastery of the easiest elements of golfing performance,
(e.g., short putts) before proceeding gradually to more difficult
elements of performance (e.g., longer putts, then chips, then pitches,
etc.). The mastery-oriented approach probably affected perceptions of
task difficulty in a favorable way (see Jackson and Roberts, 1992) and
actually led to significant improvements in scoring and shot-making
(Simek and O'Brien, 1981). In a similar vein, positive self-
monitoring has led to perceptions of the task as being easier and golf
as being a more enjoyable sport compared to neutral and negative self-
monitoring (Johnston-O'Connor and Kirschenbaum, 1986).

  Expectations, attributions, and dispositions. Professional
golfers have consistently emphasized the importance for average
golfers of modifying expectations for their scores on each hole from
par to bogey or beyond, depending on their actual ability levels
(Kirschenbaum and Bale, 1980). These more moderate expectations
should lead to more positive affect and better sustained involvement
in golf (Carver and Scheier, 1990). In a similar vein, when golfers
attribute their successes to their own efforts, they should accelerate
systematic attempts at improving their games. Dispositions (or
traits) pertaining to seeking and using information about one's self
have also been shown to affect skillful performance (Baumeister,
1984). Thus, more obsessive-compulsive styles of attentional focusing
may contribute to success (Kirschenbaum and Bale, 1980); in part by

decreasing choking under pressure (Baumeister, 1984).   While the
relationships between attributions, expectations, and dispositional
styles in golf remain to be specified, these factors and others (e.g.
affect, task difficulty) clearly qualify the degree to which extant
self-regulatory models help describe and explain the challenges of
golf.

7   References

Baumeister, R.F. (1984) Choking under pressure: Self-consciousness
      and paradoxical effects of incentives on skillful performance.
      J. Pers. and Soc. Psych., 46, 610-620.
Boutcher, S.H. and Crews, D.J. (1987) The effect of a preshot
      attentional routine-learned skill. **Int. J. Sp. Psy.**, 18, 30-39.
Carver, C.S. and Scheier, M.F. (1990) Origins and functions of
      positive and negative affect: A control-process view. **Psych.
      Rev.**, 97, 19-35.
Crews, D., Thomas, G., Shirreffs, J.H. and Helfrich, H.M. (1984) A
      physiological profile of Ladies Professional Golf Association
      toward players. **Phys. Sp. Med.**, 12, 69-74.
Jackson, S.A. and Roberts, G.C. (1992) Positive performance states of
      athletes: Toward a conceptual understanding of peak
      performance. **The Sport Psych.**, 6, 156-171.
Janis, I.L. and Mann, L. (1977) **Decision Making.** The Free Press, New
      York.
Johnston-O'Connor, E.J. and Kirschenbaum, D.S. (1986) Something
      succeeds like success: Positive self-monitoring for unskilled
      golfers. **Cog. Ther. Res.**, 10, 123-136.
Kanfer, F.H., and Karoly, P. (1972) Self-control: A behavioristic
      excursion into the lion's den. **Beh. Ther.**, 3, 398-416.
Karoly, P. (1993) Mechanisms of self-regulation: A systems view.
      Ann. Rev. of Psych., 44, 23-52.
Kirschenbaum, D.S. (1984). Self-regulation and sport psychology:
      Nurturing an emerging symbiosis. **J. Sport Psych.**, 6, 159-183.
Kirschenbaum, D.S. and Bale, R.M. (1980). Cognitive-behavioral skills
      in golf: Brain power golf, in **Psychology in Sports: Methods
      and Application** (ed. R.M. Suinn). Burgess, Minneapolis, pp.
      334-343.
Kirschenbaum, D.S. and Tomarken, A.J. (1982) On facing the
      generalization problem: Study of self-regulatory failure, in
      Advances in Cognitive-Behavioral Research and Therapy (Vol. 1),
      (ed. P.C. Kendall), Academic Press, New York, pp. 121-200.
Prapavessis, H. and Grove, J.R. (1991) Precompetitive emotions and
      shooting performance: The Mental Health and Zone of Optimal
      Function model. **The Sport Psy.**, 5, 223-234.
Simek, T.C. and O'Brien, R.M. (1981) **Total Golf: A Behavioral
      Approach to Lowering Your Score and Getting More Out of Your
      Game.** Doubleday, New York.
Taylor, S.E. (1991) Asymmetrical effects of positive and negative
      events: The mobilization-minimization hypothesis. **Psych. Bul.**,
      110, 67-85.
Whelan, J.P., Mahoney, M.J., and Meyers, A.W. (1991). Performance
      enhancement in sport: A cognitive behavioral domain. **Beh.
      Ther.**, 22, 307-327.

24 Promotion of the flow state in golf: a goal perspective analysis

J.L. Duda
Purdue University, West Lafayette, Indiana, USA

Abstract
Every golfer is interested in having more flow or optimal experiences in his or her golf game. It is suggested that golfers will witness a higher frequency and intensity of flow states if they adopt a task-involved (success equals hard work and improvement) in contrast to an ego-involved (success is demonstrating superior ability) goal perspective. With respect to the psychological antecedents of flow, research is reviewed which indicates that a task-involved approach should result in higher perceived competence, a preference for optimally challenging tasks, perceptions of personal control, more focused attention, and greater intrinsic enjoyment. Suggestions for fostering task involvement are provided.
Keywords: Flow, Motivation, Goal Orientations, Perceived Competence

1 Introduction

One of the most wonderful experiences for golfers is when they are in "flow" on the golf course. These are those occasions when the golfer feels like there is a "merging of action and awareness" in his or her game (Csikszentmihalyi, 1975). Studies of the flow state in sport have found this experience to result in heightened motivation and be linked to positive and often peak athletic performance (Jackson and Roberts, 1992).

Research by Csikszentmihalyi (1975, 1990) has indicated that flow is marked by several characteristics including focused attention, a sense of control and competence, and intrinsic enjoyment. This work has also shown that flow states are more likely to occur when individuals perceive a balance between above average skills and task demands. In other words, people are more likely to get into flow if they believe that they possess the skills required to successfully perform an optimally challenging task.

Science and Golf II: Proceedings of the World Scientific Congress of Golf. Edited by A.J. Cochran and M.R. Farrally. Published in 1994 by E & FN Spon, London. ISBN 0 419 18790 1

What is considered an optimally challenging task will vary as a function of the ability level of the golfer. An optimal challenge is one in which the golfer needs to extend himself or herself and give a best effort. If a task is deemed to be too difficult, anxiety will result. When what we need to do is viewed as not demanding enough, the golfer is likely to become bored.

The major focus of this paper is to review research suggesting that there is an interdependence between the goals that athletes emphasize and the psychological dimensions with have been found to underlie the flow state. It will be argued that golfers will experience flow more frequently and intensely if they adopt a task-involved (rather than ego-involved) goal perspective. A second purpose is to highlight how those involved in coaching and teaching golf can set the motivational stage for greater task involvement and subsequently more flow.

2 Goal Perspectives and Their Motivational Correlates

A golfer's goal perspective relates to how he or she defines success and judges one's level of competence while playing the game (Nicholls, 1989). Two predominant goal perspectives are operating in sport settings, namely task and ego involvement (Duda, 1992, 1993). When emphasizing task-involved goals, the golfer equates success and the demonstration of ability to personal improvement, trying hard, and meeting the demands of the task at hand. If ego-involved, however, subjective success and judgments about the golfer's competence are tied to showing that he or she is superior to others. When ego involvement prevails, a golfer will also feel successful and able if he or she performed as well as others with less effort.

Research has shown that the goal perspective assumed in sport corresponds to how a participant will cognitively and emotionally respond to the activity. Moreover, individual differences in goal perspectives have been found to predict athletes' views about and values within sport. In relation to factors which are fundamental to the prevalence and existence of flow, sport studies have examined the relationship of goal perspectives to perceptions of competence, the preference for challenging tasks, perceptions of personal control, intrinsic enjoyment and attentional focus.

2.1 Perceived Competence
Critical to the occurrence of flow is the belief that one possesses adequate competence to meet what he or she is trying to do or accomplish in a sport outing. For example, specific to golf, Catley and Duda (1994) examined the pre-performance psychological factors which predicted the frequency and intensity of flow experienced. Over one hundred recreational golfers (120 males and 38 females), who varied in

skill, completed short questionnaires before and immediately after a round of 9 holes. Pre-round perceived confidence emerged as a positive and the most significant predictor of flow. This result held even when actual golf ability (i.e., average score) was controlled for in the analyses.

It is predicted that people are more likely to view themselves as capable (and, thus, express positive performance expectations) when they are task-involved. This is because perceptions of high competence result from exerting effort and personal improvement.   Perceiving oneself to have sufficient competence is expected to be less common when individuals are strongly ego-involved. As a person needs to outplay others to meet his or her ego-involved goals, there is a greater chance of feeling incompetent.

These predictions have been supported in the physical domain. A series of experiments have shown that people are likely to doubt their competence even more if they are highly ego-involved and approach the task with initially low perceived ability (Duda, in press). Similar findings emerge when ego-involved individuals face losing. Perceptions of competence have been found to be more resilient among those who are predominantly task-involved.

2.2 Preference for Challenging Tasks
The flow state is unlikely if a golfer is afraid of challenges which can bring out the best in him or her and require concentration, effort and the maximizing of one's present skills. Setting the demands of a round of golf below or considerably above one's level of ability will probably not result in flow (Csikszentmihalyi, 1990).

Goal perspective theory (Nicholls, 1989) suggests that there is a correspondence between a person's goal perspective and their selection of tasks which vary in difficulty. A task-involved golfer, regardless of his or her level of perceived ability, is expected to strive for optimally challenging goals. This pattern of task choice is predicted because task-involved individuals are concerned with performing the task as well as possible, not with how they appear or do in comparison to others. If strongly ego-involved and questions about one's ability exist though, a golfer would most likely choose a task which is much too easy or one that is far too difficult. By so doing, this golfer would avoid demonstrating inferior competence in the sport. Such a person would also not witness maximal skill development if he or she works toward a goal in which success is practically guaranteed or impossible to reach. Recent research involving sport-related tasks has provided evidence for these proposed interrelationships between goal perspective and the preference for challenging tasks (Duda, in press).

2.3 Personal Control

Perceiving that the causes of one's performance and what occurs in the experience itself are internal is endemic to the flow state (Csikszentmihalyi, 1975, 1990). When a golfer feels in control of his or her game, the individual believes that the major precursors of accomplishment in the sport are self-determined. That is, there is a sense that he or she, not someone or something else which is beyond the realm of direct influence, is primarily responsible for what happens.

Individual differences in goal perspectives have been found to relate to divergent views about the determinants of sport success (Duda, 1993, in press). Specifically, a preference for task-involved goals is associated with the beliefs that hard work and the desire to learn and improve lead to sport success. Such perceived causes of achievement are within a person's own control. In contrast, a pronounced ego-involved goal perspective has been linked to the view that the possession of natural talent, external factors (such as having the right clothes and equipment) and deceptive tactics will get one ahead in sport. These explanations for sport success are external to the individual and/or less controllable.

2.4 Intrinsic Enjoyment

Since it is inherently enjoyable and intrinsically satisfying, the flow state is self-rewarding. Further, flow is more likely to occur when people are motivated to do the activity for its own sake rather than some external gain (Csikszentmihalyi, 1990).

Differences in goal perspectives are presumed to relate to the probability of having fun while participating in sport. Previous work has revealed a consistent and positive association between the preference for task-involved goals and reported enjoyment of the activity (Duda, 1993). This positive relationship has emerged regardless of the participant's perceived competence and the outcome of the competition.

Which goal perspective is emphasized by a golfer should also have implications for that individual's degree of intrinsic motivation. Research has shown that a task orientation is coupled with more intrinsic motives for athletic participation (e.g., becoming involved to develop one's skills; Duda, in press) and views concerning the overall purposes of sport (e.g., the view that sport should teach us the value of trying hard; Duda, 1989). On the other hand, an ego orientation relates to extrinsic reasons for participation (e.g., becoming involved to gain social recognition) and beliefs about the important functions of athletic involvement (e.g., the belief that sport should enhance popularity).

2.5 Focused Attention

Csikszentmihlayi's (1975, 1990) work indicates that people are focused exclusively on task-relevant cues when they are in flow. Whether this state of deep concentration will occur should be dependent on the goal perspective adopted by the athlete.

When task-involved, golfers are more likely to be concentrating on the task at hand. That is, they are more concerned about the performance process and whether they are giving their best effort at any one point of time. When ego-involved, golfers are more likely to be thinking ahead to a possible future outcome as well as the ramifications of that outcome. The performance is a means to an end in this instance and such an outlook would probably interfere with optimal attentional focus.

Sport research has been consonant with these hypotheses (Duda, 1993). In a study of students involved in a class tennis tournament for example, those who were strongly ego-oriented and expected to lose reported greater performance-related worry. In another investigation of young elite athletes, a preference for ego-involved goals corresponded to higher reported concentration disruption while competing.

3 Creating a Task-Involving Environment in Golf

The personal goals that golfers emphasize are strongly impacted by the motivational climate which is perceived to surround their golf. Whether a golfer will be task- or ego-involved while playing is related to whether his or her significant others (such as coaches, teaching professionals, parents, playing partners) create a task- or ego-involving atmosphere for him or her. The sport literature has identified the salient features of these two distinct environments (Duda, in press). When the situational goal structure is highly ego-involving, the focus of all involved is on the competitive outcome. Social reinforcements are received by the golfer when he or she beats other competitors. In terms of the reactions to performance, an environment is created which reeks of negative evaluation. Consequently, the golfer lives in fear of making mistakes.

In a task-involving situation, every golfer feels like he or she has something to contribute to and get from the game. Accolades are not reserved for the talented golfers only. Most critically, significant others ensure that the golfer realizes that mistakes are part of learning and skill progression.

Given the arguments presented above, it should be apparent that a task-involving climate is flow-conducive. Thus, if we restructure the social context of golf so that it promotes task involvement, golfers should experience peak performance more often, love the game, and want to continue involvement in this sport.

4 References

Catley, D. and Duda, J.L. (1994) **Psychological antecedents of the frequency and intensity of flow in golfers**. Manuscript under review.

Csikszentmihalyi, M. (1975) **Beyond boredom and anxiety**. Jossey-Bass, San Francisco.

Csikszentmihalyi, M. (1990) **Flow: The psychology of optimal experience**. Harper Row, New York.

Duda, J.L. (1989) The relationship between task and ego orientation and the perceived purpose of sport among male and female high school athletes. **J. Sport Exer. Psych., 11**, 318-335.

Duda, J.L. (1992) Sport and exercise motivation: A goal perspective analysis, in **Motivation in sport and exercise** (ed G.C. Roberts), Human Kinetics Publishers, Champaign, IL, pp. 57-91.

Duda, J.L. (1993) Goals: A social cognitive approach to the study of motivation in sport, **Handbook on Research in Sport Psychology** (eds R.N. Singer, M. Murphey and L.K. Tennant), Macmillan, NY, pp. 421-436.

Duda, J.L. (in press) A goal perspective approach to meaning and motivation in sport, **International Perspectives on Sport Psychology** (ed S. Serpa), Benchmark, Indianapolis, IN.

Jackson, S.A. and Roberts, G.C. (1992) Positive performance states of athletes: Toward a conceptual understanding of peak performance. **The Sport Psych., 6**, 156-171.

Nicholls, J.G. (1989) **The competitive ethos and democratic education**. Harvard University Press, Cambridge, MASS.

25 Mental preparation for golf: achieving optimal performance

S. Murphy
United States Olympic Committee, Colorado Springs, USA

Abstract
Three approaches to understanding the mental factors associated with excellence
in golf are examined and commonalities are identified. A performance
management model is presented which suggests that a golfer can use a variety of
mental strategies to create the optimal internal conditions for playing the game.
The critical aspect of the model is focusing attention during the performance
phase. The paper concludes with some practical suggestions for creating the
right conditions to allow peak performance to occur.
Keywords: Peak performance, Mental Strategies, Flow, Performance
management, Sport psychology.

1 Introduction

Golfing, 1.n. A pastime that gives people cooped up in the office all week a
chance to lie and cheat outdoors (From Beard & McKie, 1987).

What is it about golf that has produced so many volumes of prose, poetry and
analysis about the game? Surely part of the mysterious attraction of the game is
that the mind has such vast quantities of time to ponder the progress of
competition during a round. If we play a round in 4 hours, hit 90 shots in that
time, and take about 20 seconds to play each shot, then we "play golf" for only
about 30 minutes, and have the remaining three and a half hours, or 210
minutes, or 12,600 seconds, to think about how the game is going. When the
mind is allowed to wander in such a manner, usually in beautiful and scenic
settings, with good friends, and while playing such a frustrating and difficult
game, is it any wonder that a whole mythos has been created about the magic of
golf?

My personal experience for the last decade has revolved around helping elite
athletes struggle with the issues of how to mentally approach their sport in order
to achieve excellent performance. What is the right attitude, how do you play
your best under pressure, how do you learn to concentrate, how can you get
everything just right so that you can perform optimally? The lessons I have
learned from them, and from constant interactions with other sport psychologists
who are dealing with the same concerns, can be applied to the game of golf.
Despite its mystery and allure, the mental challenges posed by golf are not
unique, and the psychological lessons we have learned from elite athletes in other
sports can help us do our best at golf. I am convinced that if you can learn to

Science and Golf II: Proceedings of the World Scientific Congress of Golf. Edited by A.J.
Cochran and M.R. Farrally. Published in 1994 by E & FN Spon, London. ISBN 0 419 18790 1

make those 12,600 seconds of non-playing time work for you, rather than against you, then you can consistently enjoy playing golf to the best of your abilities.

First I will examine three approaches to understanding the mental factors related to golf excellence.

2 Mastering the mental game in golf

Golfing, 2.n. the art of using a flawed swing, a poor stance and a weak grip to hit a small ball badly towards the wrong hole (Beard & McKie, 1987).

2.1 Peak performance in golf

A promising research avenue in recent years has been the study of the experiential qualities which define superior performance in sport. Patrick Cohn (1991) used an open-ended qualitative interview technique to examine the shared characteristics of peak performance in 19 elite golfers and found the following qualities shared by at least 80% of his sample:

- Temporary
- Narrow focus of attention
- Automatic and effortless performance
- Immersed in the present
- Feeling of control
- Self-confident
- Absence of fear
- Relaxed
- Fun or enjoyment

These characteristics are similar to those reported in other studies of peak performance in sport and suggest that during very superior performance, the athlete is in a state identified by Csikszentmihalyi as "flow". Csikszentmihalyi (1990) argues that flow occurs when the skill level of the performer is exactly equal to the challenge presented by the performance task. His research indicates that the common quality of the flow state is enjoyment, and he has identified the following characteristics of flow:

- A challenging activity that requires skills
- The merging of action and awareness
- Clear goals and feedback
- Concentration on the task at hand
- The paradox of control (no worry about losing control)
- The loss of self-consciousness
- The transformation of time

We can see that golf and other sports are, by their very structure, conducive to the flow state. Golf is a challenging activity, it requires great skill and practice, the goals are clear and the feedback is immediate. During the peak performances studied by Cohn, the feelings described are very similar to the flow qualities identified by Csikszentmihalyi across hundreds of different activities. The central element which determines whether flow is experienced is not the task itself, nor even the skill level of the performer, for Csikszentmihalyi has found that flow can occur even when a person's skill level is low. The critical factor is the attentional focus of the individual. If the attention is completely on the task at hand, if there is no excess attention left over to engage in worry or doubt, and if self-awareness becomes lost as attention is absorbed in the activity, flow is likely to occur. In his theory, Csikszentmihalyi identifies attention as a form of psychic energy, and notes that no work can be done without it, and that in doing work it is dissipated.

When superior performance in golf is examined from this perspective, the question arises as to what prevents the player from experiencing flow whenever she/he steps on the course? We have seen that golf is designed to encourage flow, and that the critical factor which determines flow, attention, is under an individual's control. Yet in my thousands of consultations with athletes it is much more common to encounter the athlete who is struggling to regain enjoyment, satisfaction and high level performance than it is to work with the athlete who can seemingly enter the flow state at will. For an experiential examination of the mental factors associated with greatness at golf, let me now turn to the thoughts of one of the greatest golfers who has ever played the game.

2.2 Lessons from experience: The Nicklaus approach

In a recent article in "Golf" magazine, Jack Nicklaus (1993) identified the thought characteristics which he feels have helped him become the most successful golfer of this century. Analysis of these suggestions provides insight into the factors which make the game difficult and can prevent flow. Nicklaus' suggestions are:

- Think and play score, not swing
  - Keep swing thoughts simple
  - Analyze what the cost of a mistake will be
- Manage your misses better
- Relate strategy to pain potential
- Don't try to force good shots (patience)
- Don't over-concentrate (pacing)
- Go to the movies (imagery)
- Give the game your best effort - always

As I was pondering this list, the one suggestion that seemed to jar with the flow state model of peak performance was Nicklaus' dictum to "Think and play score, not swing". At first glance, this advice seems to contradict the often stated suggestion that athletes should not focus on the external result, or outcome, of performance, but rather on the process of performance. However, upon closer examination, it appears that the thrust of Nicklaus' argument is to encourage golfers to think as simply as possible under pressure, not to worry about a number of technical swing thoughts. "Boil down your swing thoughts or keys to the simplest two or three that have worked best for you in the past" (1993, p.45). Nicklaus' advice is thus very congruent with allocating attention to the factors identified by Csikzentmihalyi as critical for flow - clear goals and feedback (the score), and concentration on the task at hand (hitting the ball, not worrying about technical swing thoughts). Indeed, when Nicklaus' suggestions relating to the actual strategy of playing golf are removed, his other suggestions all relate to achieving excellent performance through attainment of a flow-like state.

2.3 The inner game of golf

One of the best-selling and most influential books on the mental side of golf is "The inner game of golf" by Timothy Gallwey (1979), one of a series of "inner game" books. Gallwey's most important distinction is between two modes of awareness which are common in sport, what he calls Self 1 versus Self 2. Gallwey identifies Self 2 with the body, and argues that in sport, Self 2 control of action will always result in superior performance to Self 1 control. Self 1, on the other hand, is the self-verbalizing, critical and analytical form of awareness, which Gallwey summarizes as interference. His equation for our quality of performance relative to our potential is:

Performance = Potential (Self 2) - Interference (Self 1)

The essence of the inner game is to enjoy golf and let Self 2 perform optimally, in the absence of the self-doubt expressed by Self 1. Gallwey argues that golf (and any human activity) actually involves three kinds of benefits, though most golfers concentrate on only one. The first benefit is produced by performance, the external results or the reward of the score. The second source of satisfaction is produced by learning, mastering new skills. And the third benefit is produced by experience, the joy of actually playing. All players, from Nicklaus to a beginner, can derive satisfaction from all three aspects of what Gallwey calls "The Performance Triangle". Gallwey stresses that every player should answer the question, "Why do you play the game?". It might be a good exercise for you to try right now.

3 Creating the flow state: The performance management approach

Whiff, n. a stroke that completely missed the ball. The more prevalent term for this type of shot is "warm-up swing" (Beard & McKie, 1987).

3.1 The performance management model

Earlier I asked the question, "What prevents golfers from playing the game in a flow state?" The question may also be asked in a somewhat different manner, "Can a golfer learn strategies to help ensure a flow experience?" Over the last decade, sport psychologists have studied closely the mental factors associated with sports excellence. From their research and applied practice experience, sport psychologists has distilled a cluster of psychological techniques and approaches to achieving optimal sports performance. A variety of books have been written on this subject (Bennet & Pravitz, 1987; Lochr & Kahn, 1987; Nideffer, 1985; Orlick, 1990; Porter & Foster, 1986; and Williams, 1986), but the approaches they describe have much in common.

PRACTICE ⟶ PREPARATION ⟶ PERFORMANCE ⟶ ANALYSIS

goal setting	imagery	attentional control	self-talk
	relaxation	automaticity	emotional control
	activation		

Figure 1. The Performance Management Model

From an examination of this literature, and after empirical research on the psychological factors associated with excellent performance, my colleagues Lew Hardy, Pat Thomas, Jeff Bond and I have identified eight mental strategies which we believe to be associated with the optimal management of performance (see Figure 1).

The hypothesis we are examining in our present research is that an individual will consistently produce better performance when she/he incorporates these strategies into performance, and that better performers will use more of these strategies or use some of them more often than less skilled performers. This concept is fundamental to what has become known in the literature as "psychological skills training", or PST (Vealey, 1988). Our questionnaire to measure these strategies is in the beta testing stage (Murphy, Thomas, Hardy, & Bond, 1993).

A critical distinction we have made in our research is that mental strategies are relevant not only to competition performance, but also to practice and training, to performance preparation, and to post-performance analysis.

The eight strategies we have identified relate to various time phases of competition. The time phase most theorists have focused upon is the performance phase itself. All three approaches described earlier emphasize that when playing sport, peak performance is most likely achieved when the athlete is in a state of flow, his attention completely absorbed in the task at hand. Thus in the performance management model described in Figure 1, attentional control and automaticity are the two key factors identified with the actual performance phase. Attention is the key. If it is allocated in the wrong places, performance will suffer. If it is allocated fully to the task at hand, a feeling of automaticity will likely be the result.

When the central factor of attentional control is identified in this way, it can be seen that the other performance management strategies support an approach based on optimal attentional focus. A skilled golfer must first learn the skills necessary to play the game (the practice phase), must then get ready for competition (the preparation phase), must compete (the performance phase), and finally must identify and learn from mistakes and successes (the analysis phase). Each of the mental strategies identified in Figure 1 is critical for successful completion of each of these phases of performance.

4 Summary

Putter. n. a specialized club used on the green. The putter differs from all other clubs in the bag in that it *always* produces shots that roll forward a few feet and stop (Beard & McKie, 1987).

In summary, the performance management approach to optimal performance suggests that the individual has control over the factors which create the internal environment in which the game is played. Golfers have no control over the external factors of the game (the weather, the course conditions, the level of play of opponents) and yet many golfers expend a great deal of psychic energy worrying about these external elements. All the approaches examined in this paper suggest that this energy will be expended much more profitably in creating an optimal internal environment for the play of the game. I will close with some practical suggestions derived from the preceding analysis which should help in the creation of such an internal environment.

• **Set clear goals for every round.** Although Nicklaus emphasizes score, other goals should be experimented with, particularly those in the areas of experience and learning.

• **Stay focused on your goals.** In golf, it is too easy to give up on a goal after one bad hole, when a certain score now seems unattainable. Create goals within the round if this problem threatens your focus on the game. Also, leave distractions behind. How can you attain flow if your cellular phone is still in your bag?

• **Develop a mental routine in preparation for every shot.** Those 12,600 seconds of non-playing time are the enemy of flow. After a shot, there are many opportunities for the golfer to lose sight of her goals. A mental routine helps focus attention back on the game.

• **Remember that golf is a game.** Golf makes the flow state possible because it is a game, meant to be enjoyed and to give fun. But the lessons learned from achieving flow on the course are lessons that can be applied in all aspects of life to achieve a more rich, satisfying and harmonious existence. Perhaps that is the secret to the mystery and allure of golf.

5 References

Driving range, n. a place where golfers go to get all their good shots out of their systems (Beard & McKie, 1987).

Beard, H. & McKie, R. (1987). A duffer's dictionary. Workman Publishing, NY.
Bennet, J.D., & Pravitz, J.E. (1987). profiles of a winner: Advanced mental training for athletes. Sport Science International, Ithaca, NY.
Cohn, P.J. (1991). An exploratory study of peak performance in golf. The Sport Psychologist, 5, 1-14.
Csikszentmihalyi, M. (1990). Flow: The psychology of optimal experience. Harper & Row, NY.
Gallwey, W.T. (1979). The inner game of golf. Random House, NY.
Loehr, J.E., & Kahn, E.J. (1987). Athletic excellence: Mental toughness training for sport. Forum Publishing, Denver, CO.
Nicklaus, J. (1993). My strongest weapon. Golf magazine, 44-49, December.
Nideffer, R.M. (1985). Athlete's guide to mental training. Wyden Books, NY.
Orlick, T. (1990). In pursuit of excellence (2nd ed.). Human Kinetics, Champaign, IL.
Orlick, T., & Partington, J. (1988). Mental links to excellence. The Sport Psychologist, 2, 105-130.
Porter, K., & Foster, J. (1986). The mental athlete: Inner training for peak performance. William C. Brown, Dubuque, IA.
Vealey, R.S. (1988). Future directions in psychological skills training. The Sport Psychologist, 2, 318-336.
Williams, J. (1986). Applied sport psychology: Personal growth to peak performance. Mayfield, Palo Alto, CA.

26 Visual performance differences among professional, amateur, and senior amateur golfers

B. Coffey, A.W. Reichow, T. Johnson
Pacific University College of Optometry, Forest Grove, Oregon, USA
and S. Yamane
VISTAKON, Inc., Jacksonville, Florida, USA

Abstract
This study compared the visual performance characteristics of three groups of golfers: PGA Tour Players, amateurs, and senior amateurs. Several visual abilities related to the visual task demands of golf were measured and subjected to comparative statistical analysis. Visual performance was found to be related to both golf expertise and age. The PGA Tour Players demonstrated better visual acuity (clarity of eyesight), contrast sensitivity (ability to see subtle visual contours), and stereopsis (one aspect of depth perception). On these measures, the senior, high-handicap golfers generally demonstrated the poorest performance. No differences between the groups were found for fixation disparity (visual alignment error), nor for incidence of mixed eye-hand preference. These results have application in development programs for junior golfers and in enhancement programs for golfers who have experienced age-related visual changes.
Keywords: Golf, Vision, Visual Performance, Visual Acuity, Contrast Sensitivity, Stereopsis, Fixation Disparity, Eye-Hand Preference.

1 Introduction

Success in nearly all sports is highly dependent upon the accurate processing of visual information. Golf, unlike sports that are dynamic and reactive, allows the athlete ample time to gather visual information about the target and the area surrounding the target. If the visual information provided by multiple assessments of the target situation is consistent and accurate, the golfer feels confident about the shot. If the visual information is variable or inconsistent, the golfer may experience uncertainty and a decrease in confidence when approaching the ball.

We have previously reported that instability in two-eyed visual alignment (unstable fixation disparity) is related to inconsistency in putting alignment, and that golfers who have unstable putting alignment tend to have larger amounts of error in the putt endpoint (Coffey, et al., 1990). The results of that study suggested that individuals with esophoria, a condition in which the eyes tend to aim closer than the true target location, were more likely to experience inconsistent visual information regarding target location. Head and eye position have been shown to affect measures of visual alignment. The visual alignment tendency shifts toward esophoria when the head or eyes are moved away from the primary position of gaze and into the non-primary head/eye positions common in golf putting (Coffey, et al., 1991). Also, the physiological stress response has an indirect influence on the visual alignment system and can cause a shift toward esophoria for susceptible individuals (Birnbaum, 1993).

Science and Golf II: Proceedings of the World Scientific Congress of Golf. Edited by A.J. Cochran and M.R. Farrally. Published in 1994 by E & FN Spon, London. ISBN 0 419 18790 1

Golfers in the age range 35-50 years experience normal age-related changes in the visual system that can influence the accuracy and stability of visual target information. These changes, termed presbyopia, primarily affect the focusing system and eventually lead to the loss of visual clarity when viewing close objects, necessitating the use of some optical means to compensate the condition. In the early stages of the development of presbyopia, it is common for golfers to notice inconsistency in judging target location due to changes in the neurological relationship between the focusing and aiming processes of the visual system.

The studies discussed above indicate several sources of potentially inconsistent visual information regarding target location in golf. Since the eyes lead the body in virtually all sport-related tasks, visual inconsistency should be considered a potential source of performance inconsistency for the golfer who has mastered the many motor skills of golf. The purpose of the current study was to examine several measurable visual skills in samples of PGA Tour Players, amateur golfers, and senior amateur golfers, and to determine whether differences in visual function exist between these groups. If differences do exist, this information may be helpful in development programs for young golfers, and in the enhancement of visual function for experienced golfers who do not feel they have achieved their competitive potential.

2 Methods

2.1 Subjects

The subjects used in the study consisted of three basic groups: 31 PGA Tour Players, 48 young amateurs, and 29 senior amateurs. All subjects were men. The two amateur groups were subdivided based upon handicap index to yield the following groups used in comparative analysis (group abbreviations are used in later text):

	n	Age (yrs)	Handicap Index
PGA Tour Players (PRO)	31	35.3 ±5.8	NA
Young Amateur, low handicap (YL)	33	36.8 ±10.3	3.9
Young Amateur, high handicap (YH)	15	44.5 ±5.7	16.5
Senior Amateur, low handicap (SL)	14	56.7 ±6.0	5.4
Senior Amateur, high handicap (SH)	15	63.9 ±8.7	15.6

The PGA Tour Players were evaluated during The 1993 Players Championship at Sawgrass in Pointe Vedra, Florida. The amateur golfers were recruited from three private golf clubs in Portland, Oregon. All subjects were provided with a computer-generated summary of their evaluation results.

All visual testing was conducted while the golfers wore their habitual ophthalmic lenses (spectacles or contact lenses) that were routinely used on the golf course. It is noteworthy that the incidence of ophthalmic lens usage was much higher among the amateurs than the PRO's (74% vs 19%), and that the PRO's who did require prescription lenses were more likely than the amateurs to wear contact lenses (83% vs 52%).

2.2 Procedures

Measurements of several visual abilities were carried out for all subjects. Four of those abilities are discussed in this report: **Visual acuity**, the ability to resolve detail in a high contrast target; **contrast sensitivity**, the ability to resolve detail under reduced contrast conditions; **stereopsis**, an important aspect of depth perception that requires simultaneous two-eyed processing of subtle visual information; and **fixation disparity**, a slight misalignment of the two-eyed aiming system that may be measured for either lateral or vertical alignment of the eyes. All testing was conducted in accordance with the revised testing protocols of the Pacific Sports Visual Performance Profile (Coffey & Reichow, 1990).

2.21 Visual acuity was measured using the Mentor BVAT device, a system that uses a high resolution video monitor to present various types of visual stimuli. Targets were high contrast Landolt rings (C's oriented with the opening of the C either upward, downward, to the right, or to the left) of decreasing size. Acuity was measured for each eye alone and for both eyes together. Smaller Snellen denominators indicate better visual acuity in the plotted data (See Figure 1).

2.22 Contrast sensitivity was measured at four different spatial frequencies using the Vector Vision system. The subject must discriminate between a series of two test patches, one of which contains subtle visual detail. The test is a two-alternative forced choice at four spatial frequencies with eight repeated trials of decreasing contrast at each spatial frequency. Higher total scores indicate better contrast sensitivity (See Figure 2).

2.23 Stereopsis was measured using the Mentor BVAT device coupled with high-frequency liquid crystal goggles that enable the presentation of slightly different visual targets to each eye. The subject's task was to determine which of four circle targets was three dimensional and seemed to be floating in front of the BVAT video monitor. Subjects were timed to determine their response speed to a series of stereopsis targets that became progressively more challenging. Six levels of stereopsis were measured using a timed four-alternative forced choice procedure. Data were acquired for speed of stereopsis discrimination and also for the proportion of each subject group that was able to correctly identify the stereopsis stimulus at each level tested.

2.24 Fixation disparity (visual alignment error) was measured using the same set-up as that described for stereopsis, but with stimuli which enabled the measurement of any subtle two-eyed aiming error (horizontal or vertical) that was present for each subject.

2.3   Data analysis
The data for each subject were entered into a computer database and subjected to statistical evaluation using analysis of variance (ANOVA) and chi square procedures. Post hoc comparisons for significant ANOVA's were made using Fisher's PLSD method. All data for all subjects were analyzed except in one case: Subjects who were unable to identify any of the stereopsis stimuli within 30 seconds after presentation were not included for analysis in that stimulus condition.

3   Results

Visual acuity differed ($p < 0.0001$)between the groups for the right eye, left eye, and both eyes together with the PRO group demonstrating better visual acuity than any other group in all post hoc comparisons (Fisher's $p < 0.05$) The mean visual acuity measurement taken with both eyes open for the PRO group was 6/3.45 (20/11.5) compared to 6/5.64 (20/18.8) for the SH group. The functional relationship between the five groups was similar for each measurement condition. See Figure 1.

Contrast sensitivity scores were summed over the four spatial frequencies tested. The total contrast sensitivity scores differed ($p < 0.0001$) between the groups with the PRO group demonstrating significantly better performance (Fisher's $p < 0.05$) than any other group except the YH group (see Figure 2).

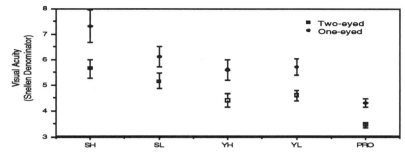

Figure 1. One-eyed and two-eyed visual acuity data by group.
Error bars represent ±1 std. error

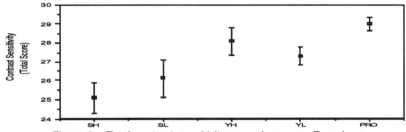

Figure 2.   Total contrast sensitivity score by group. Error bars
represent ±1 std. error

Stereopsis results revealed differences in speed between groups ($p<0.002$) only
for the two most obvious stereopsis stimuli. For these stimuli, the PRO group was
able to discern the targets significantly faster than the senior groups (Fisher's $p<0.05$).
This difference in speed of stereopsis was not present for the more challenging levels of
stereopsis stimuli. Chi square analysis of the proportion of each subject group that was
able to discern the stereopsis stimuli within 30 seconds revealed no differences between
groups for the three least challenging stimuli. However, significantly more members of
the PRO group were able to see the stereopsis stimulus in the three most challenging
test conditions ($p<0.01$). As an example, the proportions of each group able to
correctly identify the penultimate (30 sec arc) stereopsis stimulus were: PRO - 94%;
YL - 68%; YH - 67%; SL - 57%; SH - 40%. The speed of stereopsis group data for
the least challenging, most obvious stereopsis stimulus are depicted in Figure 3.

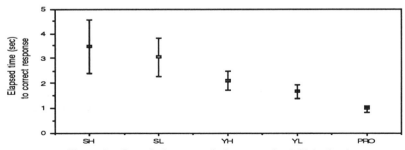

Figure 3. Speed of stereopsis by group for initial stimulus
(240 sec arc).   Error bars represent ±1 std. error.

Fixation disparity data showed no differences between the groups for either the lateral or vertical measurements (p>0.05).

4   Discussion

4.1   Visual sensitivity

The visual acuity and contrast sensitivity data indicate the presence of better visual sensitivity to detail among the PRO golfers. The relationship of each group's performance on these measures is generally consistent and suggests the presence of effects related to both golf expertise and to age: In general the PRO's demonstrated the best visual acuity and contrast sensitivity scores, followed by the amateurs, then by the senior amateurs, typically with the SH group showing the poorest performance on the measures. Since these measures can be directly affected by wear of an inappropriate lens prescription, we evaluated whether the groups differed in terms of the time elapsed since the last visit to their eye care practitioners. There was no significant difference between the groups on this variable, and the SH group had the most recent average time, 10.5 months, since the last vision exam. The PRO, SL, and YL groups each averaged 26 months since the last vision exam; the YH group averaged 20 months.

The visual sensitivity data imply that better golfers tend to have better ability to see visual detail, and that this ability tends to decline with advancing age. It has been well-documented (Gil, et al., 1986; Ricci & Collins, 1988) that both visual acuity and contrast sensitivity can be enhanced using appropriate techniques, and these procedures may be of value to both the junior golfer (for development of excellent visual sensitivity) and to the senior golfer (for maintenance of excellent visual sensitivity).

4.2   Stereopsis

Stereopsis is an important aspect of depth perception and enables us to make precise visual judgments regarding distance between ourselves and objects. The method used to measure stereopsis in this study enabled assessment of both **sensitivity** and **speed** of stereopsis. For the two easiest stereopsis targets, speed was a useful discriminator between the groups. The pattern of relationship between the groups was similar to that discussed for visual sensitivity: The PRO group had the fastest stereopsis times followed, in order, by the YL, YH, SL, and SH groups. This speed relationship disappeared for the four most challenging levels of stereopsis testing. The speed difference, however, was replaced by a different phenomenon for the three finest stereopsis stimuli. While nearly all the golfers in each group could discern the two most obvious stereopsis stimuli, the proportion of each group that could discern the more challenging stimuli steadily dropped off and became significantly different between groups for the final three stimulus levels. The reduced stereopsis performance by the seniors may be linked to the previously discussed reductions in visual sensitivity. Reduced visual acuity, for example, is often a cause of reduced performance on tests of binocularity such as stereopsis. Overall, the data suggest that limitations in stereopsis or in visual sensitivity may be a contributing factor for the inconsistent golfer or for the golfer who plays below potential.

4.3   Fixation disparity (visual alignment error)

Magnitude of lateral and vertical fixation disparity did not differ between any of the groups. Incidence of unstable fixation disparity also did not differ between the groups, ranging from a high of 47% in the SH group to a low of 32% for the PRO's.

4.4   Mixed eye-hand preference

Because of the amount of golf lore surrounding the topic, we evaluated the data for any differences between groups in the incidence of mixed eye-hand preference (or crossed dominance) in which the preferred eye and hand differ (e.g., right-handed golfer with preferred left eye). Many golfers and golf instructors believe that the golfer with mixed preference has a slight advantage in that the preferred eye is positioned to better see the golf course and is not blocked by the nose, especially during putting. The five groups studied did not differ in the incidence of mixed preference (p>0.05), ranging from a low incidence of 17% in the PRO group to a high incidence of 47% in the YH group. It is interesting to note, perhaps, that approximately 10% of all the golfers studied did not demonstrate a consistent eye preference. The data from the golfers evaluated in this study do not support the notion that crossed eye-hand preference is a significant advantage in golf.

4.5   Summary conclusions

Taken together, the results of this study demonstrate several differences in visual performance between PGA Tour players, amateurs, and senior amateurs. The data suggest that these differences are related to both golf expertise and to age. The visual factors measured in this study are all developmental in nature; i.e., each is learned to some extent and may be developed to different levels for different individuals. The presence of superior visual performance among the PRO's may be due to the years of practice and significant benefits associated with the development of consistent and accurate visual function. The amateur golfers do not have the same level of motivation for development of their potential and, hence, may not achieve the same level of visual performance. The data could also be interpreted to support the hypothesis that the golfers who qualify to play the PGA Tour are those who have superior visual function inherently, and that those golfers who do not have these talents are less likely to play professionally. The resolution of this rendition of the nature/nurture question must await longitudinal studies of the visual performance of junior golfers.

5   References

Birnbaum MH. (1993) **Optometric Management of Nearpoint Vision Disorders,** Butterworth-Heinemann, Stoneham, Massachusetts.

Coffey B, Reichow AW. (1990) Optometric evaluation of the elite athlete: the Pacific Sports Visual Performance Profile. **Problems in Optometry,** 1(2), 32-58.

Coffey B, Mathison T, Viker M, Reichow AW, Hogan C, Pelz D. (1990) Visual alignment considerations in golf putting consistency, in **Science and Golf** (ed. A.J. Cochran) E.&F.N. Spon, London.

Coffey B, Reichow AW, Colburn PB, Clark DL. (1991) Influence of ocular gaze and head position on 4m heterophoria and fixation disparity. **Optometry and Vision Science, 68,** 893-898.

Gil KM, Collins FL, Odom JV. (1986) The effects of behavioral vision training on multiple aspects of visual functioning in myopic adults. **Journal of Behavioral Medicine, 9,** 373-387.

Ricci JA, Collins FL. (1988) Visual acuity improvement following fading and feedback training - III: effects on acuity for stimuli in the natural environment. **Behavioral Research and Therapy, 26,** 475-480.

6 Acknowledgment

The authors wish to acknowledge the vision and generous support of VISTAKON, Inc. in the completion of this research. Mr. Lance Mintle is acknowledged for his assistance with data acquisition and preparation of figures.

27 Toward putting performance enhancement: a methodology using quantitative feedback

P.H. Beauchamp
Department of Physical Education, Université de Montréal, Montreal,
Canada
L.M. Landsberger
Department of Electrical and Computer Engineering, Concordia
University, Montreal, Canada
W.R. Halliwell
Department of Physical Education, Université de Montréal, Montreal,
Canada
R. Koestner
Department of Psychology, McGill University, Montreal, Canada
and M.E. Ford
Graduate School of Education, George Mason University, Fairfax,
VA, USA

Abstract
The purpose of this paper is to outline a putting performance feedback system for use
by golfers, teachers, coaches, and sport psychologists for performance enhancement.
The methodology is implemented using Landsberger's stroke-by-stroke quantitative
assessment tool. Putts are conceptualized as short, makeable, or long. Suggestions are
made for performance enhancement by coaches and applied sport psychologists.
Keywords: Performance Enhancement, Quantitative Feedback, Putting, Methodology

1 Introduction

Sport psychologists currently utilize numerous techniques and interventions intended
to enhance performance of golfers in competition (Boutcher & Crews, 1987; Bunker
& Owens, 1985; Cohn, Rotella, & Lloyd, 1990; Crews & Boutcher, 1986;
Kirschenbaum & Bale, 1980; Rotella & Bunker, 1981). Quantitative performance
feedback is the method most widely used by coaches for performance enhancement,
since objective numerical or statistical feedback can help correct misperceptions and
may motivate more effective practice strategies. However, current research on golf
putting performance has generally used a *global* indicator (total putts per round) to
measure putting proficiency. This is problematic because, from a coaching perspective, such a global indicator cannot pinpoint specific areas of strength and weakness.
Therefore, this paper proposes to use a *stroke-by-stroke* performance feedback system
based on Landsberger's (1994) Golf Stroke Value Scale (GSVS) applied to putting,
by which the value of *each putt* can be measured against certain standards.

2 Why Quantitative Putting Performance Feedback?

From the perspective of the coach or sport psychologist, effective feedback for the
purpose of performance enhancement requires the identification of specific and
measurable behaviors in the golfer's performance. Without the ability to detect
specific areas which need improvement, progress is usually quite limited. For
example, the coach must be able to offer objective observations such as "the weakest
part of your game is your short putts and the strongest part of your game is your long
putts," or "when you putt from 30 feet, your stroke is smooth, but when you putt
from 5 feet, your stroke loses its rhythm." Consequently, the job of the coach
demands a tool to objectively measure the value of each stroke, and to analyze these
strokes according to meaningful categories.

Science and Golf II: Proceedings of the World Scientific Congress of Golf. Edited by A.J.
Cochran and M.R. Farrally. Published in 1994 by E & FN Spon, London. ISBN 0 419 18790 1

The GSVS provides such a system. By developing definitions for different stroke types such as "short", "makeable" and "long" putts, the system can accurately identify not only the number of putts in each category, but also the golfer's strengths and weaknesses by category. This will give the coach, sport psychologist, teacher and golfer a plan by which to focus attention on specific areas for improvement.

3 Overview of the Golf Stroke Value Scale Applied to Putting

3.1 General

While the Golf Stroke Value Scale (GSVS) can be useful for analysis of the entire game from tee shots to the hole, it can be especially appropriate for use in the study of putting. If one's intent is to study only putting, a simple version of the GSVS can be used, requiring as input for each stroke only the distance to the hole before the stroke is taken (Xi -- "x-initial") and the distance to the hole after the stroke is taken (Xr -- "x-remaining"). In its simplest form (neglecting any correction factor for especially severe slopes or breaks), all the golfer or coach would do is record the distance to the hole before each putt during a round or practice session, input the numbers into the GSVS computer program, and read the calculated summary.

The GSVS is a quantitative system to measure the value of single golf strokes. A total stroke value (V_T) can be assigned to each distance from the hole. V_T represents an estimate of the number of strokes needed, on average, to get into the hole. Table 1 presents examples of V_T from various distances. Then the stroke value (V) for an individual stroke, can be computed by the difference between V_T at Xi and V_T at Xr, or $V = [V_T(Xi) - V_T(Xr)]$. For example, for a scratch player, a stroke that begins at Xi = 30 feet from the hole and comes to rest at Xr = 2 feet from the hole has V = 2.00 - 1.08 = 0.92. Further, since players of different abilities will take different numbers of strokes from the same distance, the stroke values are adjusted, indicative of putting ability scaled by handicap. Most golfers' performances deviate in some way from these standards and thus the listings in Table 1 are not intended to precisely represent data for actual golfers. Rather, the system is intended to provide a mathematical framework by which performance can be analyzed in an integrated way.

Table 1:   Total stroke values to the hole (and equivalents) from various distances

Xi	V_T(scratch)		V_{Tadj}(~11-H'cap)		V_{Tadj}(~26-H'cap)	
in cup	0.00		0.00		0.00	
≤ 1 ft	1.00	|	1.00	|	1.00	|
2 ft	1.08	Short	1.19	Short	1.33	Short
3 ft	1.22	|	1.35	|	1.50	|
4 ft	1.32	|	1.46	|	1.66	|
5 ft	1.39	|	1.55	|	1.77	Makeable
6 ft	1.46	|	1.62	Makeable	1.86	|
8 ft	1.55	|	1.74	|	1.99	|
10 ft	1.63	Makeable	1.83	|	2.10	|
12 ft	1.70	|	1.90	|	2.18	|
15 ft	1.76	|	1.98	|	2.29	|
20 ft	1.86	|	2.10	|	2.43	Long
30 ft	2.00	|	2.27	Long	2.61	|
40 ft	2.10	Long	2.38	|	2.77	|
55 ft	2.20	|	2.50	|	2.91	|

Note that any putt into the hole must be worth at least one stroke, because the average number of strokes taken from any location not already in the hole can never be less than 1. Moreover, there is a zone immediately around the cup within which the probability of missing is very low, within which the golfer expects to make essentially all putts, and within which distance realistically does not matter. Therefore, GSVS deems $V_T = 1.00$ inside a certain radius where the probability of missing is below 0.005.

3.2 Putt Types: "Short," "Makeable" and "Long"

Golfers generally have some qualitative standards in mind when they routinely describe putts by adjectives such as these. The GSVS provides a framework for definition of quantitative categories corresponding to these ideas. Distinctions can be made between different putt types based on distance to the hole. As seen in Table 1, these can be adjusted depending on handicap or putting skill. A reasoned set of definitions follows.

Starting near to the hole, a radius can be defined at which the golfer sinks 50% of his or her putts. "Short" putts are from inside this radius (X_{short}). From this distance, the golfer will 1-putt 50% and 2-putt 50% (the slight possibility of 3-putts from this distance is ignored). Therefore X_{short} corresponds to the distance at which $V_T = 1.5$ (for example, about 6.8 ft. for the scratch golfer in Table 1). Since we sink a half of the putts from X_{short}, it can be reasoned that it only requires our median performance to sink such putts. No wonder we *feel* that we should sink all such "short" putts from inside this radius, since our median ability is at least equal to the task. To sink these, we feel that we don't need to do anything out of the ordinary. When we miss one, we feel certain that we have made an error, because it was "...not one of my better efforts."

Next, "makeable" putts can be defined as putts long enough that the golfer needs a better than median performance to sink it, but short enough that considerable luck is not necessarily required. The outer limit of this region, less easily defined, has been chosen to be at $V_T = 1.84$. At this breakpoint (X_{long}), the golfer expects to sink about 1/6 of putts. This category of putts starts outside X_{short}, and we do not feel such intense disappointment if we miss them, since we can, at least subconsciously, understand that it would have taken a better than ordinary effort to sink it. For the scratch golfer in Table 1, "makeable" putts are from between $X_{short} = 6.8$ feet and $X_{long} = 18.7$ feet.

Finally, "long" putts are those from outside the X_{long} radius. While Pelz (1989) correctly argues that luck factors are important to sink even short putts, clearly the luck involved increases as the distance increases. In the "long" region, this system proposes that, in order for the putt to be sunk, a high-quality stroke is needed, and luck must be both dominant and acting in our favor.

The GSVS and the above definitions provide a ready framework for analysis of individual performances according to either external or personalized standards.

4 Putting Performance Feedback Using the Golf Stroke Value Scale

4.1 Putting Performance Feedback: How Should It Be Presented?

There are a variety of ways in which objective performance feedback may enhance *or diminish* performance. For instance, golfers, like other athletes, often have distorted perceptions of their own putting ability. In this case, objective feedback on performance can correct misconceptions, and may motivate corrective practice. On the other hand, consider the first column of Table 1. While this scale provides the required objectivity and meaningful categories for scratch golfers, failure to meet these standards may lead to negative consequences for one's feelings of competence, with subsequent tension and anxiety. There is much more to performance feedback than a system of numbers. A coach or sport psychologist must recognize that performance feedback has not only instructional but motivational effects.

From the perspective of applied sport psychology, there are two major goal perspectives in achievement contexts such as sport: ego-involvement and task-involvement (Nicholls, 1992). Ego orientation has generally been related to lack of effort, and a belief that success is largely determined by ability. Task orientation has generally been related to intrinsic interest, enjoyment and cooperation and a belief that effort leads to success (Duda, 1993). The ego-involved golfer focuses foremost on the outcome in comparison with peers, while the task-involved golfer focuses on the process of personal improvement in the task, rather than on the final outcome of the activity. These differences in styles of internal regulation are generally interpreted as reflecting different achievement goals (Nicholls 1992). In summary, setting personal performance goals (task focus) has been shown to be more effective for performance than setting outcome goals (ego focus).

In particular, promising concepts such as Keogh & Smith's (1985) perform-ance standard system ("Personal Par") can be implemented as an alternative to the usual scratch standard (par). Their book, written out of concern for the detrimental aspects of performance anxiety, advocates explicit techniques to enhance performance by strategies readily characterizeable as task-oriented. For example, they suggest rea-djusting one's standards according to one's personal ability, thus deriving an individ-ualized personal par for each hole. The two rightmost columns of Table 1 implement just such a system. By using such personalized performance goals, emphasizing a task focus, a coach can create a climate potentially more conducive to success.

4.2 Comparison of Two Feedback Styles

Table 2 presents examples of two different styles of performance feedback. The com-parison to the Scratch Standard typifies the feedback environment in which golfers normally function. The strokes are evaluated with respect to the external standards set for scratch golfers. On the other hand, the comparison to the Personal Par Standard departs from the usual focus on external standards. Instead, the golfer receives feedback on the value of each stroke *relative to his or her personal average*. The numerical stroke values are calculated such that the *average* stroke has value $V=1$. Thus, while the scratch golfer would be expected to take a total of about 17 putts, the Total Stroke Value in the Personal Par case is the same as the number of strokes taken (19). Moreover, more than half of the strokes will be seen as satisfactory or better according to the Legend, and the golfer has the opportunity to clearly identify a not-overwhelming number of strokes which "Need Improvement."

By contrast, the comparison to Scratch sets objective, but often daunting standards which the golfer may feel pressure to meet. This tends to influence the golfer to become ego-involved, with accompanying anxiety. The Legend is hierarchically scaled, such that only one's outstanding strokes have the possibility of meeting the Scratch Standard (very short putts sunk can also meet these high standards, but only because no matter how short the putt, 1 stroke is the minimum that even the pro can take).

Another very important distinction that relates specifically to putting regards a golfer's expectations for the result of putts from given distances. As defined in Sect-ion 3 above, the putting classifications of "short," "makeable" and "long" give diffe-rent expectations for sinking the putt. For example, if one uses the Scratch Standard, one expects to make over 50% of 6-footers. This can lead weaker putters to face immense frustration when they don't make near 50% of these so-called "short" putts.

By contrast, in the "Personal Par" columns, the breakpoints are scaled to the

Table 2. Nine Hole Summary Comparison of Two Performance Feedback Styles

Feedback According To:			**Scratch Standard**		**Personal Par Standard**	
Hole #	Stroke #	Distance to Hole (ft)	Putt Type	Stroke Value	Putt Type	Stroke Value
1	1	20	Long	.47	Long	.55
	2	5	Short	1.39	Makeable	1.55
2	1	10	Makeable	.41	Makeable	.48
	2	3	Short	1.22	Short	1.35
3	1	40	Long	.64	Long	.75
	2	6	Short	.46	Makeable	.62
	3	1	Short	1.00	Short	1.00
4	1	10	Makeable	.63	Makeable	.82
	2	1	Short	1.00	Short	1.00
5	1	15	Makeable	1.76	Long	1.98
6	1	55	Long	1.12	Long	1.31
	2	2	Short	1.08	Short	1.19
7	1	30	Long	.45	Long	.52
	2	8	Makeable	.23	Makeable	.27
	3	4	Short	1.32	Short	1.46
8	1	12	Makeable	.62	Long	.71
	2	2	Short	1.08	Short	1.19
9	1	30	Long	1.00	Long	1.26
	2	1	Short	1.00	Short	1.00
Totals:		19 Putts	9 Short 5 Mkbl. 5 Long	16.87	7 Short 5 Mkbl. 7 Long	19.00

Ranges for Each Putt Type:

	Scratch Standard	Personal Par Standard
Short Putt	inside 6.8 ft.	inside 4.5 ft.
Makeable Putt	6.8 ft. - 18.7 ft.	4.5 ft. - 10.5 ft.
Long Putt	outside 18.7 ft.	outside 10.5 ft.

Legends:

	Scratch Standard	**Personal Par Standard**
	over 1.06 Meets Pro Standard	over 1.25 Excellent
	1.00 - 1.06 Meets Scratch Standard	1.05 - 1.25 Good
	.90 - .99 0 - 7 Handicap	.90 - 1.04 Satisfactory
	.80 - .89 8 - 15 Handicap	below .90 Needs Improvement
	.70 - .79 16 - 27 Handicap	
	.60 - .69 28 - 41 Handicap	
	below .60 over 41 Handicap	

Summaries: Overall Equivalent Handicap: -11.
Scratch Standard:
In your Short putts, you averaged   1.09 strokes, equivalent to about a +6 H'cap.
In your Makeable putts, you averaged 0.73 strokes, equivalent to about a -27 H'cap.
In your Long putts, you averaged   0.74 strokes, equivalent to about a -23 H'cap.
Personal Par Standard:
In your Short putts, you gained   1.19 personal strokes, for a   1.17 average.
In your Makeable putts, you lost   1.26 personal strokes, for a   0.75 average.
In your Long putts, you gained   0.08 personal strokes, for a   1.01 average.

golfer's personal performance on this particular set of holes (or alternatively, can be scaled to his or her actual handicap), establishing a much friendlier standard. As a result the golfer is much more likely to focus his or her attention on the actual execution of the stroke. The 6-footers are seen as "makeable" opportunities, to be executed with full focus and commitment, rather than "short" opportunities to fail.

The bottom of Table 2 presents summaries according to the two feedback styles. When the putts are compared to the Scratch Standard, equivalent handicaps for each category are the most meaningful summary. However, when the putts are compared to the Personal Par Standard, the summary is correspondingly self-referential, measuring strength and weakness according to "personal strokes" gained or lost.

5 Conclusions

This paper has outlined a putting performance feedback system toward performance enhancement. Teachers, coaches, and sport psychologists using the stroke-by-stroke quantitative feedback system (GSVS) can accurately provide objective assessment of a golfer's strengths and weaknesses in putting skill. This, in turn, has formed a concrete methodology for presenting two different styles of quantitative feedback, with suggested potential advantages of using a task-oriented ("personal par") approach.

Finally, to aid golfers' quest for excellence, further application of this methodology can include investigation of correlations between detailed performance data and non-performance variables that may be associated with golf performance.

6 References

Boutcher, S.H., & Crews, D.J. (1987). The effect of a preshot routine on a well-learned skill. **International Journal of Sport Psychology, 18**, 30-39.

Bunker, L.K., & Owens, N.D. (1985). **Golf: Better practice for better play**. West Point, NY: Leisure Press.

Cohn, P.J., Rotella, R.J., & Lloyd, J.W. (1990). Effects of a cognitive-behavioral intervention on the preshot routine and performance in golf. **The Sport Psychologist, 4,** 33-47.

Crews, D.J., & Boutcher, S.H. (1986). The effects of structured preshot behaviors on beginning golf performance. **Perceptual and Motor Skills, 62,** 291-294.

Duda, J.L. (1993). Goals: A social cognitive approach to the study of achievement motivation in sport. In R.N. Singer, M. Murphy, & L.K. Tennant (Eds.), **Handbook of research on sport psychology** (pp.421-466). NY: Macmillan.

Keogh, B.K., & Smith, E.S. (1985). **Personal par**. Champaign, Il: Human Kinetics.

Kirschenbaum, D., & Bale, R. (1980). Cognitive-behavioral skills in golf: Brain power golf. In R. Suinn (Ed.), **Psychology in sports: Methods and applications** (pp. 334-343). New York: Burgess Publishing Co..

Landsberger, L.M. (1994). A unified golf stroke value scale for quantitative stroke by-stroke assessment. In **World scientific congress of golf 1994**. London, England: E. & F.N. Spon, Chapman and Hall.

Nicholls, J.G. (1992). The general and the specific in the development and expression of achievement motivation. In G. Roberts (Ed.), **Motivation in sport and exercise** (pp.31-56). Champaign, Il: Human Kinetics.

Pelz, D. (1989). **Putt like the pros**. New York: Harper & Row.

Rotella, R.J., & Bunker, L.K. (1981). **Mind mastery for winning golf.** Englewood Cliffs, NJ: Prentice-Hall.

28 A study of golfers' abilities to read greens

D. Pelz
Independent Golf Research Corporation, Austin, Texas, USA

Abstract
An interesting phenomenon has been discovered to exist in golf, in that golfers consistently and substantially underestimate the amount putts break, sometimes by a factor of 3 to 5. A detailed study of 313 golfers shows that for men, women, pros and amateurs, the inability to predict the correct amount of break in putts is accompanied by sub-conscious compensations, set-up alignment and in-stroke compensations during the stroke itself. Most golfers tend to stand in what may be the wrong position to read their putts, and the method of plumb-bobbing proved to make no difference whatsoever. After repeatedly putting the poorly read putts, and watching their balls roll to the hole, golfers did not recognize either the amount of break they actually played, or the amount they should have played. The golfers learned very little from the experience of watching their own putts, which substantiates why this problem can exist today.
Keywords: Greens, Putting, Reading Greens, Underestimate, Borrow, Plumb-bob

1 Introduction

I teach a significant amount of golf, spending approximately 25% of my working days helping golfers discover and correct weaknesses in their 'short games' and improving their abilities to score. Approximately one half of my teaching focuses on golfers' putting and in this work, with all skill levels from PGA Tour players, through handicaps of all values, I have discovered a consistent, recurring problem. The problem is, most players consistently underestimate the amount of break (borrow) they need to allow for, to efficiently roll their putts into the hole.

Poor green reading is so prevalent and severe in my schools, that I associate at least part of most players' putting difficulties with it. Because of this severity, I have conducted a study of golfers' green reading abilities, which is the subject of this report.

My study consisted of measuring 1) golfers' ability to estimate the amount their putts will curve or break on the way to the hole (their ability to read the green), and 2) what they learn from their putting, following this estimation. This testing included 179 amateur players reading and putting to 40 different holes (423 individual player-hole samples), 128 PGA club professionals putting to 4 different holes (258 samples), and 6 PGA Tour professionals putting to 20 different holes (54 samples). 23% of the amateurs, and 10% of professionals were female. Measurements were

Science and Golf II: Proceedings of the World Scientific Congress of Golf. Edited by A.J. Cochran and M.R. Farrally. Published in 1994 by E & FN Spon, London. ISBN 0 419 18790 1

obtained on a variety of flat to severely sloping greens of both bent and bermuda grasses, with green speeds ranging from Stimpmeter 2.3 meters (m) to 3.2m. All test putt lengths were between 3 and 4.5 m.

2 The optimum speed for putts to roll

To fully understand the green reading portion of the test, one must first be aware of an unrelated test performed previously, Pelz (1989). In this earlier test, it was determined that for any putt, there is both an optimum speed the ball should roll as it approaches the hole, and an optimum direction along which the roll should be started, to optimize chances of holing the putt. These results were obtained using a device called the 'True Roller', an inclined ramp down which balls roll in precisely controlled directions at precisely controlled speeds.

Results of True Roller tests show that for putts approaching the hole just fast enough to hold their line through the footprints and imperfections of the green, yet slow enough to not lip-out of the hole too often, a maximum percentage of holed putts can be achieved (thus an optimum speed and initial direction exist for every putt). Putts rolling slower than the optimum speed will be deflected from hole contact more frequently due to footprints, spike marks, etc., and putts rolling faster upon arrival at the hole, will lip-out more often. Likewise, putts started to the left or right of the optimum starting line for the optimum speed, will hit the hole less frequently and result in a lower percentage holed.

While True Roller testing could be a discussion in and of itself, the point here is that the optimum putt speed has been determined to be a rolling speed (upon arrival at the hole), sufficient to carry the ball 43 centimeters (cm) past the hole (if the cup were to be covered over with a smooth, low friction surface). Although this exact optimum speed (or roll past distance) of a ball varies slightly (depending on the up or downhill nature of the area around the cup, type of grass, speed and condition of the putting surface), the value of 43 cm has proven to be the best average value over a large number of tests and conditions.

3 The green reading test

The concepts of optimum speed, maximum holed percentage and 43 cm past were explained prior to testing. Most golfers were aware that speed controls the amount putts will break, and readily accepted that there is always a 'best' speed, to optimize chances of making a putt. Participants were told to describe their estimated putt break, in terms of where they perceive the optimum starting line direction (aim line) to be relative to the cup, assuming the putt would be rolled at optimum speed.

Next all ball (tee) positions and corresponding holes (usually four or more) were identified, and golfers cautioned to report their estimates of break in private to eliminate any player influencing another. To avoid misunderstandings, examples were shown of what approximate breaks of 10 cm (width of hole), 4 cm (width of ball), 30 cm and 1 m look like. Finally, golfers were reminded to read each putt assuming they would roll their putts at optimum speed, to achieve the highest holed percentage possible.

After reading all putts, golfers were instructed to putt to each hole 6 to 12 times, and to watch and learn how much the putts actually broke. They were again requested to privately report their final read of the true break. During their putting period, observations of actual putter alignment were made from behind (by viewing putters through a clear plastic template onto which a perpendicular set of lines had been etched. By placing one line along the golfers' putterface, the perpendicular line pointed along the actual aim direction of the putter, which could be seen to within an accuracy of +/- 5 cm). The initial starting lines of putts were also measured using this device. On two occasions (54 samples) actual putter alignment was measured by means of a laser beam reflected from the putter (without golfer interference), to an accuracy of +/- .3 cm.

At the conclusion of putting, the true break of each putt was measured by rolling balls at the optimum speed from a True Roller.

4 Green reading terminology and definitions

Ball-hole line	Line BH passing through ball (B) and hole (H)
Aim line	Line BA through ball (B) and point A (toward which an optimum speed putt would start, for maximum holed percentage)
Break	Distance AH, between ball-hole line and aim line, measured along a line perpendicular to ball-hole line
Initial read	Golfer's estimate of break verbalized prior to actually putting
Final read	Golfer's estimate of break verbalized after watching his/her own putts roll at least 6 times
Putter aim	Direction along which golfer aims his/her putter prior to striking putts
Initial putt line	Initial direction putt rolls, immediately after putter impact
Below the hole	Area on low side of hole, through which putts roll that are rolled with too little break, too slowly, or both
Above the hole	Area on high side of hole, through which putts roll with too much break, faster than optimum speed, or both

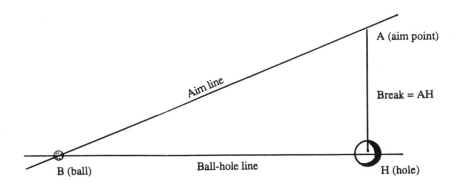

Fig.1. Measurement of break

5 Results

(a) Golfers generally read putts while standing on, and looking along both sides of the ball-hole line, looking intently at the green from the ball to the hole and vice-versa.

(b) 28% of the golfers tested plumb-bobbed their putts. Plumb-bob users hung their putters in front of their bodies, closed one eye, and looked past the shaft toward the hole before making their break estimate.

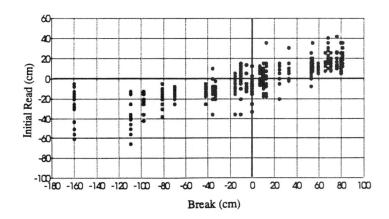

Fig.2. Initial read vs break

(c) All golfers underestimated the break for all putts which broke more than 15 cm. As Fig. 2 shows, the initial read of break averaged only 25% (+/- 10%) of the true break. The most frequent read was even farther from reality, being 21% of true break. The severe underestimation of the break occurred on both left-to-right (negative values) and right-to-left (positive values) breaking putts.

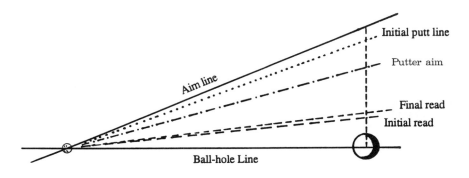

Fig.3. Golfers' performance

(d) Golfers aligned their putters not where they read the break, but along a line at 60-75% of the true break location (they were not consciously aware of this alignment difference and many did not believe this difference, when told afterward), as shown in Fig. 3. They then used in-stroke compensations to start their putts along a line at 80-95% of the true break direction (right handed players pulled left to right breaking putts, and pushed right to left breaking putts).

(e) Golfers in this test holed less than 5% of putts which broke more than 15 cm, compared to 15% of putts breaking less than 5 cm of the same length. More than 84% of all putts breaking more than 15 cm missed below the hole, and less than 9% missed above the hole. Virtually all putts missed above the hole, rolled more than 43 cm past the hole.

(f) After putting and watching a minimum of 6 putts roll to the hole (sometimes up to 25 putts), golfers reported a final break read at an average of 29% (+/- 10%) of the true break value (Fig. 4). Again the most frequent read was significantly farther from reality, at 25% of true break. More than 7% of the golfers amended their final read in the wrong direction from their initial read, as compared to the true break (i.e. the final read was farther from reality than their initial read had been). This happened, even though intellectually they understood the physics of speed and break, during later questioning.

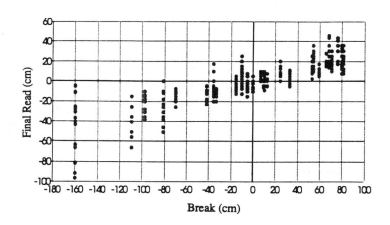

Fig.4. Final read vs break

(g) Of all golfers tested, only one did not stand along the ball-hole line during his green-reading deliberations.

(h) Use of the plumb-bob technique did not have a significant effect on a golfer's green reading ability or accuracy, as was also the case with the sex of the golfer, the amateur golfer's handicap and age.

(i) Club professionals read the breaks 2% closer to reality than the amateurs, with tour professionals coming 3% closer still. These percentages held true for both the initial and final read accuracies (i.e. the professionals failed, as did the amateurs, to recognize the true breaks even after watching their own putts roll to a stop).

6 Conclusions

Golfers severely underestimate the break they read prior to putting. This underestimation is consistently large, most often by a factor of 3 to 5. They then, apparently subconsciously, compensate with both their set-up alignment and in-stroke manipulations, to achieve a 'reasonably' rolled putt although most putts are missed 'below' the hole. I believe for most golfers green reading inaccuracies are a major contributor to the difficulty of developing a successful putting game.

When shown their data, golfers are generally disbelieving, and seem to want their putts to break only a small amount. They must be shown by actual demonstrations with a True Roller, before they will believe the reality of how much putts truly break.

Golfers generally stand in what I now believe to be the wrong place, along the ball-hole line, to read putts. A better position from which to see the true break and imagine a ball starting along the aim line and breaking into the cup at the perfect speed, is probably from somewhere behind the ball on the aim line.

Because of their poor read of the break, and poor putter alignment below the true aim line, golfers must either pull or push breaking putts, or roll them faster than optimum speed, to have any chance of making them. Their low holed percentage of these breaking putts indicates they are not successfully accomplishing these compensations.

From these test results, I speculate that golfers can putt better if they learn to read greens more accurately. I believe a major improvement in putting should be obtained by golfers who learn in the future, to read greens accurately and then use one single non-compensating stroke for all putts.

6 References

Pelz, D. (1989) **Putt Like the Pros**. Harper & Row, New York, NY.

29 How to lower your putting score without improving

B. Hoadley
Middletown, New Jersey, USA

Abstract
While playing golf, after you have mercifully reached the green,
you have to decide where to target your putts. You might say that
it is obvious - target the hole. But then the probability of being
short is about 0.5. The conventional wisdom is to target beyond
the hole, so that you won't be short. The pundits use expressions
like, "never up never in." But how far beyond the hole? Here the
advice gets diverse and qualitative. Dave Pelz (1989) says 17"
for all putts. My pro says, "for long putts target a two-foot circle around the hole and for short putts target about one foot
beyond the hole." The purpose of this research is to provide more
specific quantitative advice. An approximate solution is to target a distance beyond the hole given by the formula:
[Two feet]*[Probability of sinking the putt].This solution
applies to any putt. The dependence on putting ability and the
difficulty of the putt is captured by the probability of sinking
the putt. This tactic saves about 1 putt per round over conventional wisdom. The solution is derived from a Markov decision
model of the putting process.
Keywords: Dynamic Programming, Markov Decision Model, Optimization, Probability, Putting, Simulation, Statistics, Tactics.

1 Introduction

The problem addressed in this paper is introduced in the
abstract. To attack the problem, I need a model of a single putt.
Associated with a putt, is the position on the green that the ball
would stop if there were no hole. I call this the *stopping position*. Of course, if the putt is sunk, then the ball never gets to
the stopping position, because it falls in the hole. The stopping
position is modeled as a random position on the green. The probability distribution of the stopping position depends on (i)the
difficulty of the putt, (ii)the skill of the putter, and (iii)the
target selected by the putter. The target selected by the putter
is the expected value of the random stopping position. The question addressed in this paper is: what is the optimal target for
each putt?

I assume in this paper that the green is flat. The advice
derived from the flat green assumption is useful for most non-
flat green scenarios. However, there are exceptions. For example,
suppose the hole is at the edge of a cliff. Then you would aim
short of the hole until the probability of sinking the putt was

Science and Golf II: Proceedings of the World Scientific Congress of Golf. Edited by A.J.
Cochran and M.R. Farrally. Published in 1994 by E & FN Spon, London. ISBN 0 419 18790 1

near 1. Another example is where one side of the hole is flat but
the other side is very curved. Then you might target the flat
area.

The next idea that I use in my model is the *footprint of success*. If the stopping position of a putt is in the footprint of
success, then the putt sinks. It is an oblong area about 4 feet
long on the far side of the hole and includes the hole. It is
defined precisely in Section 3.

The sequence of events during putting is as follows: (i)select
a target and putt, thereby generating a random stopping position;
(ii)if the stopping position is in the footprint of success, then
you are done putting, otherwise repeat steps (i) and (ii).

The first step in finding the optimal target is to note some
limiting cases. If the probability of sinking the putt is near
zero, then the optimal target distance beyond the hole is near
zero. If you are not going to sink the putt, then you should minimize the expected distance for the next putt. To do this, you
target the hole itself.

If the probability of sinking the putt is near one, then you
should pick a target that maximizes the probability of sinking
the putt. So the target should be in the middle of the footprint
of success, which is about two feet beyond the hole.

So as the probability of sinking the putt goes from 0 to 1, the
optimal target goes from 0' beyond the hole to 2' beyond the hole.
Therefore, I assume that the optimal target beyond the hole is a
monotonically increasing function of the probability of sinking
the putt. This function starts at 0' and goes to 2'.

I then consider a two dimensional tactic space defined by the
parameters x and y of a beta cumulative distribution function,
$B(p|x,y)$. This is a monotonic function of p, which goes from 0 to
1. p is the probability of sinking the putt, and the tactic is to
target the putt for (Two feet)$*B(p|x,y)$. I then show via simula-
tion and sequential search that $x=1,y=1$ (i.e., $B(p|x,y)=p$) is
nearly optimal.

2 Random model of putting

To model a single putt I use a polar coordinate system centered at
the ball. Figure 1 shows the position of the ball and hole in
polar coordinates. The coordinates of the ball are $(0,0)$. The
first coordinate is the 0 angle and the second coordinate is the
0 radius. The coordinates of the hole are $(0,s)$. So the distance
between the ball and the hole is s.

The stopping position of the ball is the random position (A,R).
A is the random angle of the putt and R is the random radius of
the putt.

I define the target of the putt to be the expected value of
(A,R), namely $(E[A],E[R])$, where $E[.]$ is the expectation operator.

I assume that A and R are statistically independent with Normal
(sometimes called Gaussian) probability distributions. It is
clear that the target angle should be 0, so $E[A]=0$. The standard
deviation of A is denoted α. The mean and standard deviation of R
are denoted μ and σ respectively.

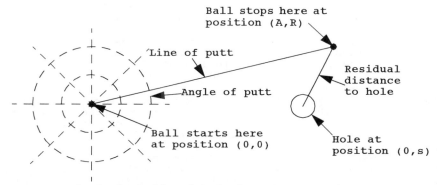

Fig.1.The ball and hole in polar coordinates.

It is clear that as μ get larger so does σ. A quick and dirty empirical study on a putting green suggested the relationship σ=kμ, where k is a constant. The same study suggested that α does not depend on μ.

In a putting situation, to select a target, you just select μ, which will depend on s. The parameters (α,k) quantify the ability of the putter and the difficulty of the putt.

Note the assumption that the ability of the putter is given. I will show how to reduce the expected number of putts without improving the ability - hence, the title of the paper.

3 Probability of sinking a putt

Figure 2 shows the footprint of putting success (cross hatched area along with the hole). If the stopping position (A,R) is in the footprint, then the putt is sunk. The footprint is defined in terms of s=[distance to the hole], b=[footprint distance beyond the hole], and d=[radius of the hole].From empirical studies I found that b=4'. The radius of the hole is d=2".

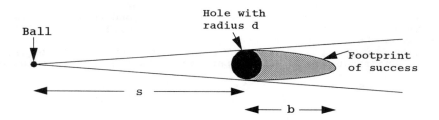

Fig.2.Footprint of putting success.

As an approximation, the conditions for putting success are

$$-\text{atan}(d/s) < A < \text{atan}(d/s)$$

$$s < R < s + \left[1 - \left|\frac{A}{\text{atan}(d/s)}\right|^2\right]b \tag{1}$$

The function atan is sometimes called arc tan.

The right hand side of equation 2 is an approximate model of the curvature of the footprint. The left hand side of equation 2 ignores the front half of the hole, so it is also an approximation.

The probability of sinking the putt can be expressed as the integral of the joint probability density of (A,R) over the footprint of success. This integral is

$$\int_{-t}^{t} \int_{s}^{(s+g)} q(a,r) \; dr \; da \,, \tag{2}$$

where t=atan(d/s), $g = \left[1 - \left|\frac{a}{\text{atan}(d/s)}\right|^2\right]b$, and q(a,r) is the Gaussian probability density of (A,R).

4 Residual distance of a missed putt

Figure 3 shows the geometry needed to compute the residual distance to the hole if a putt is missed. In the figure, the residual is labeled e.

The equations needed to solve for e are:

$$e^2 = w^2 + h^2 \tag{3}$$

$$\sin(A) = h/R \tag{4}$$

$$\cos(A) = (s+w)/R. \tag{5}$$

Simple algebra yields

$$e = \{[R \cdot \cos(A) - s]^2 + [R \cdot \sin(A)]^2\}^{1/2}. \tag{6}$$

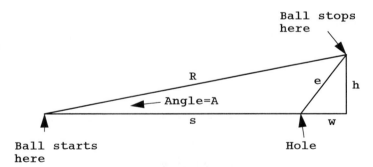

Fig.3. Residual distance of a putt.

5 Putting tactics

In the introductory Section 1, I argued that the target for the putt should be of the form
$$\mu = s + (2').B(p),\tag{7}$$
where B(.) is a monotonically increasing function, with B(0)=0 and B(1)=1. This can be proved rigorously using dynamic programming and Markov decision theory. Space does not permit that here.

To find an approximation to the optimal B(.), I consider a two parameter family of such functions based on the cumulative beta distribution.

The generic member of the class is

$$B(p|x,y) = \int_0^p \frac{\Gamma(x+y)}{\Gamma(x)\Gamma(y)} v^{x-1}(1-v)^{y-1}\ dv.\tag{8}$$

This is a fairly general class of functions with lots of different shapes - convex, concave, s-shaped, and backwards s-shaped.

The parameters x and y are now the variables to be optimized.

6 Optimization methodology

The optimization methodology proceeds as follows:

Step 1. Pick an initial position on the green for which the probability of sinking the putt is near 0.

Step 2. Guess at the optimal values of x and y to define putting tactics.

Step 3. Estimate via simulation the expected number of putts (see Section 7) needed to hole out.

Step 4. Pick nearby values of x and y and repeat Step 3. This could be done using response surface methodology, but I did not.

Step 5. Continue to sequentially search for better and better values of x and y based on the sequence of values generated by Step 3.

Step 6. Stop when there is enough data to fit a parametric response surface. Then find the minimum of the surface to get an approximate optimal putting tactic.

7 Expected number of putts

For a given initial position on the green and a given putting tactic, the expected number of putts needed to hole out is estimated via repeated Monte Carlo simulation of a single sojourn on the green.

The simulation of a single putting sojourn goes as follows: The initial position of the ball and the putting tactic (x,y) are given.

Step 1. Target the first putt according to equations 8 and 9.

Step 2. Compute the probability p of sinking the putt using equation 3 and numerical integration.

Step 3. Pick a random number U between 0 and 1. If U < p,
then the putt is sunk and you record the number of
putts taken. Otherwise, continue.

Step 4. Compute the residual distance to the hole using
equation 7.

Step 5. Redo Steps 2-4 until you hole out.

8 Simulation results

Consider an example where the distance (s) to the hole starts out
at 60', the standard deviation (α) of the putting angle (A) is
1.44, and the standard deviation (σ) of the putting radius (R) is
(0.22)(s); i.e., k=0.22.

The parameters (α,k)=(1.44,0.22) were chosen by fitting my
theoretical putting model to the lower curve on p.38 of Pelz
(1989). This curve gives the probability of sinking a putt as a
function of distance. The lower curve is for the worst putters on
the PGA tour. My fit to Pelz's empirical curve is very good, which
lends credibility to my model. Space does not permit a demonstration of this.

Following the steps described in Section 7, I simulated many
tactics of the form (x,y). For every pair (x,y), the simulation
produced an estimated expected number of putts along with its
standard deviation. Different numbers of iterations were used for
the various runs. For example, for (x,y)=(3,1), the number of
iterations was 10,000, and the expected number of putts was 2.781
with standard deviation 0.0067.

An empirical plot of these results suggested that (x,y) be
transformed before attempting to fit a simple quadratic response
surface. The transformation selected was

$$u=x/(x+y) \tag{9}$$
$$v=[LN(x+y)]/15. \tag{10}$$

The fitted response surface is

$$E[\#Putts]= 3.1+(0.74)u+(1.1)v-(1.3)uv+(0.73)u^2-(1.1)v^2. \tag{11}$$

The minimum of the fitted response surface is 2.753 putts,
which occurs at (u,v)=(0.529,-0.015) or (x,y)=(0.421,0.375).

So the optimal tactic is to target the putt
(2)*B(p|0.421,0.375) feet beyond the hole, where p=Pr{Sink Putt}.

Figure 4 shows a plot of B(p|0.421,0.375).As you can see, this
function is fairly close to B(p|1,1)=p. In fact, (x,y)=(1,1) cor-
responds to (u,v)=(0.5,0.046). Plugging this value into equation
12 yields E[#Putts]=2.755, which is only slightly larger than
2.753.

9 Comparison with other tactics

It is of interest to compare my optimal tactic with other proposed
tactics. For example, Pelz (1989) on p.127 says to target 17"
beyond the hole for all putts. A simulation of Pelz's tactic with
5,000 iterations yielded an estimated expected number of putts of
2.81 with a standard deviation of 0.01. So my optimal tactic is
0.06 putts per hole better (for putting situations, which start
at 60' from the hole). That is (0.06)*(18)=1.08 putts per round.

Of course, to get a more personalized result, you should average over your starting positions.

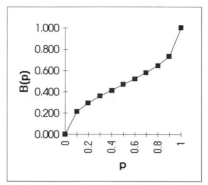

Fig.4.The function B(p|0.421,0.375).

    As a final benchmark, consider the tactic of always targeting the hole itself - not beyond the hole. A simulation of 10,000 iterations yielded a result of 3.059 putts per hole with a standard deviation of 0.0086. So targeting the hole itself costs you 0.3 putts per 60' hole.

10 References

Pelz, Dave with Mastroni, Nick (1989) *Putt Like the Pros*. Harper-Collins Publications, New York, NY.

30 Comparing players in professional golf

P.D. Larkey
Carnegie Mellon University, Pittsburgh, Pennsylvania, USA

Abstract

Ranking professional golfers is a special case of the following general rating problem: Rate each player's performance relative to that of the other N-1 players when N players have participated in varying subsets of M tournaments and there is no useful exogenous information about the relative skills of players or about the relative difficulty of the tournaments. This paper describes an algorithmic approach to solving this problem and presents some player rankings that result from applying the algorithm.
Keywords: Golf Statistics, Golf History, Performance Ratings, Performance Measures

1 The Problem of Comparisons

The first difficulty in comparing professional golfers fairly is that there is an insufficient basis in common events to support the comparisons. Players, even two players on the same tour in the same year, are apt to have a limited number of common events as a basis for fair comparisons; Faldo and Langer or Price and Norman usually play in ten to fifteen common events and a like number of "uncommon" events, events in which only one of the pair participates. For comparing many players across tours and years, there is apt to be little or no basis for fair comparisons in common events; Faldo, Langer, Price and Norman may all appear in only the Majors and a handful of other events such as the Memorial and the Player's Championship. The most ambitious comparison, an all-time comparison including the likes of Vardon, Taylor, Braid, Jones, Hagen, Sarazen, Nelson, Snead, Hogan, Palmer, Nicklaus, Watson, Faldo, Langer, Price and Norman, has no possible basis in common events.

Comparing the performances of professional golfers, then, requires the use of uncommon events, events that often vary significantly in scoring conditions, purses, and field quality. The analysis is unusually difficult because there is no directly observable, uncontaminated dependent variable on player performance that can be used to understand the factors that affect performance. We cannot know the quality of a player's performances until we understand the difficulty of the contexts in which the performances occur; but we cannot know the difficulty of the contexts--the quality of the competition -- until we know the relative quality of individual players. Solo third at The Open or the Masters is surely a more significant accomplishment than solo third in the German Open or the Hardee's Classic. But how much more? Ultimately, the relative significance turns on the relative quality of the competition.

The second main difficulty in doing fair comparisons is choosing a base measure of performance. Candidate measures include money won, stroke average, total strokes, and various measures of rank (e.g., # of top ten finishes). Each of these candidates is flawed. Money won is grossly misleading in intertemporal comparisons because both the value of money and the amount of money available to win have changed significantly over time. Money won is also misleading in contemporaneous analyses of performance because purse sizes and the significance of the events are imperfectly correlated. Stroke measures are treacherous because there are so many factors that have a profound influence on scoring difficulty; high winds, wind from an unusual direction, soft fairways and hard greens, the speed or grain of the greens, and a few nasty pin placements are some of the many factors that might inflate the scores of any field on a given day. Scores have meaning only relative to the performance of a field of known

Science and Golf II: Proceedings of the World Scientific Congress of Golf. Edited by A.J. Cochran and M.R. Farrally. Published in 1994 by E & FN Spon, London. ISBN 0 419 18790 1

quality on a given course and day. The ranking measures such as Top Ten Finishes, while they get a lot of media play, do not deserve much comment here because they only have relative meaning and reduce interval scale measures to a much less informative ordinal scale [see Larkey (1991b)].

2 A Method for Fair Comparisons

The method proposed for comparing professional golfers consists of two parts: a measure of accomplishment for specific players in specific events and an algorithm for simultaneously determining the quality of tournament fields and individual player quality.

2.1 The Measure of Accomplishment

Quality Points (QPS) are a measure of a professional golfer's performance based on how well he did relative to how well he might have done. The best he might have done is win which is worth the winner's share of the purse (usually 18 percent of the total) and 1.0 **QPS**. The worst he can do is finish out of the money which is worth 0 **QPS**. Second place to seventieth places are paid according to the PGA TOUR's nonlinear purse distribution scheme (.108 of the total purse for second, .068 for third,...., and .00232 for seventieth). For **QPS**, second place is .108/.18 percent or .6 of the best the player might have done; second place receives .6 **QPS** and so on down the line. The statistic is reported in two basic forms, **Total Quality Points (TQP)** and **Quality Points per Tournament (QPT)** Symbolically, the computations are:

$$\text{TQP}_{i,T} = \sum_{t=1}^{T} \frac{won_{i,t}}{max_t} \tag{1}$$

Where,

$\text{TQP}_{i,T}$ = Quality Points for the $_i$th player in the set of T tournaments
max_t = Winner's Share, tournament$_t$.
$won_{i,t}$ = Amount won by player$_i$ in tournament$_t$.

QPT is simply **TQP** divided by the number of events entered. **QPT** can be interpreted as the average place finish in some set of tournaments (all tournaments in a year, all Master's since 1934, etc.) where a **QPT** of 1.0 would signify that the player won all events entered and a **QPT** of 0 would indicate a player failed to cash anywhere. A **QPT** of .378 is equivalent to finishing third place on average and .267 is fourth place on average. **TQP** is most useful for understanding the cumulative accomplishments of players; each **TQP** is equivalent to a win in unweighted comparisons. For comparisons, **TQP** favors players who have played in the most tournaments. **QPT** without some restriction on the number of events to be eligible for the comparison, conversely, favors those players with a few good performances.

  QPS offer several advantages over alternative measures: 1) amateurs can be ranked with professionals by simply imputing the money they would have won and computing their quality point measures; 2) for intertemporal comparisons the measures solve the problems of changing values in currency; 3) for both intertemporal and contemporaneous comparisons, the **QPS** handle the difficulties of changes in the schemes for distributing prizes and of changing purse sizes; 4) the measures can easily handle medal play, match play, and Stableford Scoring events such as the International on the PGA TOUR; and 5) the measures have fairly natural interpretations by reflecting the incentives in proportion to the monetary incentives confronting players.

The **QPS** measures by themselves enable systematic comparisons that have not heretofore been possible when it is reasonable to assume that tournaments are equivalently difficult. For example, Table 1 shows the top twenty players ranked by **QPT** who played in five or more U.S. Opens since 1916.

Table 1. U.S. Open From 1916 to 1993

RANK	PLAYER	QPT	TQP	$$	STRK AVG	EVENTS	ROUNDS
1	BOBBY JONES	.53	6.40	0	73.85	12	48
2	BEN HOGAN	.41	8.25	33,551	71.83	20	80
3	BYRON NELSON	.32	2.88	3,359	73.42	9	36
4	HARRY COOPER	.25	3.30	3,674	74.33	13	52
5	BOBBY LOCKE	.25	1.75	5,060	72.46	7	26
6	WIFFY COX	.23	1.86	1,870	75.16	8	32
7	JACK NICKLAUS	.23	8.53	330,870	72.39	37	136
8	WALTER HAGEN	.23	4.36	3,104	75.13	19	76
9	RALPH GULDAHL	.23	3.60	4,052	74.30	16	64
10	CLARENCE CLARK	.22	1.09	1,171	74.05	5	20
11	CRAIG WOOD	.20	3.27	3,654	74.90	16	62
12	PAYNE STEWART	.20	2.04	457,342	71.59	10	34
13	GENE SARAZEN	.20	6.22	5,591	75.07	31	115
14	LLOYD MANGRUM	.20	3.16	9,415	73.08	16	62
15	CURTIS STRANGE	.20	2.94	499,736	72.00	15	54
16	CLAYTON HEAFNER	.19	1.32	3,666	73.40	7	25
17	HALE IRWIN	.18	4.41	427,303	72.78	24	92
18	LEO DIEGEL	.18	2.72	2,120	75.45	15	60
19	TOM WATSON	.18	3.79	314,586	72.03	21	74
20	CARY MIDDLECOFF	.18	2.84	13,795	73.55	16	53

Note the different rankings that would result from using **TQP** or money. So much for the *Career Earnings* as a measure of career accomplishment!

Consider another ambitious ranking example. Table 2 ranks players by **TQP** in all Major Championships since 1960. Jack Nicklaus has amassed more than twice the **QPS** of anyone else and has averaged between third and fourth place in 132 Majors. Nick Faldo has won more money, at least in nominal dollars.

Table 2. All Major Championships Since 1960

RANK	PLAYER	TQP	QPT	$$	STRK AVG	EVENTS	ROUNDS
1	JACK NICKLAUS	41.69	0.31	1,577,724	70.11	132	497
2	GARY PLAYER	19.14	0.17	583,184	71.85	116	421
3	TOM WATSON	18.51	0.23	1,428,245	70.38	81	301
4	ARNOLD PALMER	17.49	0.16	348,929	73.29	114	385
5	RAY FLOYD	14.10	0.13	1,225,522	71.84	107	392
6	LEE TREVINO	13.58	0.16	730,256	72.01	86	312
7	NICK FALDO	11.94	0.25	1,921,324	70.47	47	184
8	SEVE BALLESTEROS	11.38	0.18	1,107,332	71.45	63	225
9	BEN CRENSHAW	10.70	0.14	915,508	71.86	78	279
10	HALE IRWIN	9.7	0.13	810,470	71.86	74	282

2.2 The Quality Determination Algorithm

Ranking golfers requires simultaneously knowing the quality of the players and the quality of the tournament. The approach is: (1) compute **QPT** for each player in the set assuming that all tournaments are equally difficult; (2) use the **QPT** from (1) to estimate the strength of each tournament field as the proportion of the best forty players participating in terms of **QPT**; (3) use the estimates of tournament field strength as weights to reestimate **QPT**; (4) use the reestimated **QPT**s to reestimate tournament field strength; and so on to convergence. Symbolically,

$i \in \{1, 2, ..., N\}$ is an index of the players
$j \in \{1, 2, ..., M\}$ is an index of the tournaments

p_{ij} = performance in quality points for player i in tournament j.
n_i = number of tournaments for player i.
m_j = number of players in tournament j.

q_i^k = Adjusted QPT of player i at k^{th} stage of algorithm.
d_j^k = Difficulty of tournament j at k^{th} stage of algorithm.

For all i, initialize q_i^0 as standard QPT, i.e.,

$$q_i^0 = \frac{\sum_j p_{ij}}{n_i}, i = 1, 2, ..., N$$

Repeat until ratings converge

$$d_j^k = \frac{\sum_i \frac{p_{ij}}{q_i^{k-1}}}{m_j}, \quad j = 1, 2, ..., M$$

$$q_i^k = \frac{\sum\limits_j \frac{p_{ij}}{d_j^k}}{n_i}, \quad i = 1, 2, ..., N$$

The algorithm has been applied to equivalent problems such as the on-time performance of U.S. airlines (Caulkins et al, 1993) and to student academic performance (Larkey and Caulkins) as well as to professional golf (Larkey, 1991a & 1991d). Many of the technical characteristics of the algorithm are explored in Yuan et al (1992) and Caulkins et al (1993). Uniqueness is proven. Convergence has not yet been proven but the algorithm has always converged quickly on the variety of data sets to which it has been applied.

The best way to evaluate the algorithm is in terms of its results. Does it yield plausible rankings of tournaments and players? Table 3 shows the values for the strongest and weakest tournaments on the PGA TOUR plus the British Open in 1993. The ordering should be intuitively plausible for most knowledgeable observers of professional golf. While we can quibble about the finer points such as whether or not we should use a procedure that looks at fifty players or full fields rather than 40 which would move some events, particularly the Players' Championship, up in the rankings, we should never forget that the PGA TOUR's current procedure weighs every tournament at 1.0 except for the British Open which it weighs at 0. A dollar earned at the BC Open may spend the same as a dollar from the PGA Championship but this does not imply that they were comparably difficult to acquire.

Table 3. Tournament Field Strength for 1993

RANK	EVENT	FIELD STRENGTH
1	BRITISH OPEN	.980
2	PGA	.970
3	USOPEN	.955
4	PLAYERS	.930
5	MASTERS	.918
6	NESTLE	.850
7	DORAL	.813
8	MEMORIAL	.801
9	COLONIAL	.774
10	HERITAGE	.767
11	TOUR CHAMPIONSHIP	.745
12	WORLD SERIES	.721
......	....	....
41	SOUTHERN	.399
42	BUSCH	.371
43	BC OPEN	.349
44	GUARANTY	.120

Table 4 shows the top ten players on the PGA TOUR plus the British Open in 1993. Greg Norman had a much better year than the post-season awards and conversation would seem to indicate.

Table 4. PGA TOUR plus British Open in 1993

RANK	PLAYER	QPT	TQP	$$	STRK AVG	EVENTS	ROUNDS
1	BERNHARD LANGER	**.43**	2.98	730,117	68.30	7	24
2	GREG NORMAN	.42	**6.68**	1,513,653	**67.55**	16	58
3	NICK PRICE	.34	6.38	**1,529,633**	68.60	19	73
4	PAUL AZINGER	.26	6.40	1,464,654	69.88	25	85
5	NICK FALDO	.25	1.76	312,086	69.64	7	27
6	TOM KITE	.22	4.52	911,241	69.51	21	72
7	DAVID FROST	.21	4.86	1,043,653	69.40	23	77
8	FRED COUPLES	.21	4.11	835,849	69.63	20	75
9	VIJAY SINGH	.20	3.06	664,029	69.83	15	53
10	PAYNE STEWART	.18	4.84	1,015,984	69.43	27	100

3 Conclusion

The ways in which the PGA TOUR ranks professional golfers for the purpose of awards, eligibility, and exemptions are, without exception, conceptually flawed. This paper has sketched a superior alternative. The PGA TOUR should adopt something like it for important decisions on performance awards, for maintaining the historical records on career accomplishments, and for determining exemptions for both the regular and senior tours.

4 References

Jonathan Caulkins, J., Barnett, A., Larkey, P.D., Yuan, Y., and Goranson, J. (1993) The On-Time Machines: Some Analyses of Airline Punctuality. **Operations Research**, Vol. 41, No 4, July-August.

Larkey, P.D. (1992) All the Numbers Back Up the Bear; a Cross-Generational Analysis. **Golf World**, April 3.

Larkey, P.D. (1991a) How to Measure Strength of Field, **Golf World**, March 29.

Larkey, P.D. (1991b) Taking the Measure of Top Ten Finishes, **Golf World**, February 1.

Larkey, P.D. (1991c) A Distinction That Money Can't Buy, **Golf World**, January 25.

Larkey, P.D. (1991d) A Better Way To Find the Top Scorer, **Golf World**, January 11.

Larkey, P.D. (1990) A Batting Average For Tour Golfers, **Golf World**, December 14.

Larkey, P.D. and Jonathan Caulkins (1992) Incentives to Fail, H. John Heinz III School of Public Policy and Management Working Paper, Carnegie Mellon University, December.

Yuan, Y., Caulkins, J., and Larkey, P.D. (1992) Adjusting Ratings for Tournament Difficulty: The Case of Rating Airlines' On-Time Performance, H. John Heinz III School of Public Policy and Management Working Paper 92-25, May.

31 An analysis of 1992 performance statistics for players on the US PGA, Senior PGA and LPGA tours

F. Wiseman, S. Chatterjee, D. Wiseman and N.S. Chatterjee
Northeastern University, Boston, MA USA

Abstract
This study analyzed and compared performance statistics for golfers on three professional tours, the US PGA, the Senior PGA (SPGA), and the Ladies PGA (LPGA). A large percentage of the variability that existed in overall performance as measured by a player's average score on the SPGA and LPGA tours could be statistically explained by just two measures, putting performance and greens in regulation. However, for the US PGA, the estimated predictive model did not do as well despite the fact that two additional performance statistics, driving distance and driving accuracy, were also found to be significantly correlated with average score.
Keywords: Golf, Performance Statistics, Regression Analysis, US PGA, Senior PGA, LPGA

1 Introduction

Numerous attempts have been made by those interested in professional golf statistics to determine the nature and extent of the relationships that exist between various aspects of a golfer's game and the golfer's overall record of performance. Past attempts have focused primarily on the US PGA and the European PGA tours.

Surprisingly, the results to-date have been inconclusive. For example, Hale and Hale (1990) found few significant correlations between five commonly reported statistics [driving distance (DD), driving accuracy (DA), greens in regulation (GIR), sand saves (SS), and putting performance (PP)] and overall performance for the top 20 golfers on the European tour between 1984-1988. Similarly, Jones (1990) reported weak correlations among a set of performance statistics for players on the 1988 US PGA tour. In both of these analyses, money earned was used as the overall performance measure. However, when Rotella and Boutcher (1990) used average score (AS) as the dependent measure, significantly higher correlations were obtained, especially between AS and GIR, for players on the 1987 US PGA tour.

The purpose of the present study is to update the results of previous analyses and to extend them to include players on both the SPGA and the LPGA tours.

Science and Golf II: Proceedings of the World Scientific Congress of Golf. Edited by A.J. Cochran and M.R. Farrally. Published in 1994 by E & FN Spon, London. ISBN 0 419 18790 1

2 Research design

Performance statistics for 1992 were obtained for players on the three US professional tours (**Golf Almanac, 1993**). The overall performance measure used was average score and four performance statistics (DD, DA, GIR, and PP) were investigated. A fifth measure, sand saves, was not used because performance data on this factor were not available for a substantial number of golfers in each of the tours. The specific operational definitions of the four performance statistics reported by each tour were:

Driving distance (DD) -- The average distance driven on two tee shots per tournament on a predetermined par 4 or par 5 hole.
Driving accuracy (DA) -- The percentage of fairways hit on par 4 or par 5 holes.
Greens in regulation (GIR) -- The percentage of greens that were reached in regulation.
Putting performance (PP) -- For the PGA and the SPGA, the average number of putts per hole on greens reached in regulation. For the LPGA, the average number of putts per 18 holes.

Also considered for the US PGA and SPGA tours were the relationships that existed between AS and a golfer's age, height, and weight. For the LPGA tour, data were only reported for age and height.

The initial stage of each tour's analysis consisted of an examination of the bivariate correlation coefficients. This was followed by the estimation of a predictive and explanatory model which was obtained using multiple regression analysis. In total, data were available for 113 US PGA, 44 SPGA, and 50 LPGA tour players.

3 Results

The average values of each of the performance statistics are presented in Table 1. US PGA tour players outhit players on the SPGA and LPGA tours by an average of 5 and 33 yards, respectively. However, in terms of accuracy, there was virtually no difference as approximately 70% of all the tee shots in each of the three tours landed on the fairway. Players on the US PGA and SPGA tours were more likely to reach the green in regulation compared to those on the LPGA tour. There was little difference in terms of putting performance between members of the US PGA and SPGA. Comparisons with the LPGA could not be made due to a different operational definition for this measure.

As far as the overall performance measure, US PGA players had the lowest average score, followed by SPGA and LPGA tour players. The variability in the average scores was considerably smaller among US PGA players, especially in comparison to SPGA players.

Table 1. Average performance measures for the three tours during 1992

	Performance statistics				Average Score		
Tour	DD (yds)	DA	GIR	PP*	Mean	Variance	n
US PGA	261	70%	68%	1.779	70.9	.38	113
SPGA	256	69%	69%	1.798	71.3	.83	44
LPGA	228	69%	65%	30.411	72.2	.48	50

*See operational definitions for this statistic.

3.1 Correlation analysis

Presented in Figure 1 are the scatterplots and the accompanying correlation coefficients between all pairwise sets of statistics for each of the three tours. (Correlations that are significant at the .01 and .05 levels are noted by the superscripts a and b, respectively).

Each point on a particular scatterplot represents the performance of an individual golfer during 1992. When there is a strong correlation between two statistics, most of the points fall close to a straight line. If the slope of this line is positive (negative), the correlation will be positive (negative). If the points on the scatterplot appear to be randomly located, the correlation coefficient will be close to zero.

From a visual inspection of the scatterplots, it is clear that GIR is the measure that is most highly correlated with AS. The correlations are substantially higher for the SPGA and LPGA tours than they are for the US PGA tour. The second most highly correlated measure with AS is putting performance. The correlation is strong for both the SPGA and US PGA tours, but not as strong for the LPGA tour. This latter result is apparently due to a different operational definition. The scatterplots also indicate the relationships that exist among all the performance statistics. For example, they illustrate that there is a strong negative correlation between DD and DA and a strong positive correlation between DD and GIR in all three tours. Further, for both the US PGA and SPGA, there is a significant positive correlation between DA and GIR.

There was but one significant correlation between the three demographic characteristics and AS. This occurred for the SPGA tour where a negative correlation existed between weight and AS ($r=-.3$). That is, the "heavy" (perhaps, overweight) players on the Senior tour did not do as well as those who did not weigh as much. Due to the relatively poor explanatory and predictive power of age, height, and weight (especially in comparison to the performance statistics), they were not included in the regression analyses.

3.2 Multiple regression analyses

The results of the regression analyses are given in Table 2. As indicated, the findings for the LPGA and SPGA tours were similar as only GIR and PP were significant explainers and predictors of AS. Further, taken together, these two measures statistically explained 93% of the variability in AS for players on the SPGA tour and 88% for players on the LPGA tour. This amount of explained variation is considerably larger than what has been previously reported for either US PGA or European PGA tours.

Table 2. Regression results for the 1992 US PGA, SPGA, and LPGA tours

| Measure | Standardized Regression (Beta) Coefficients | | | | | |
| | US PGA | | SPGA | | LPGA | |
	Beta	t	Beta	t	Beta	t
GIR	-.44	-6.2[a]	-.66	-15.0[a]	-1.03	-18.5[a]
PP	.59	10.6[a]	.49	11.0[a]	.70	12.0[a]
DA	-.22	-2.8[a]				
DD	-.18	-2.5[b]				
R^2	.67[a]		.93[a]		.88[a]	
n	113		43		50	

[a]Significant at the .01 level.
[b]Significant at the .05 level.

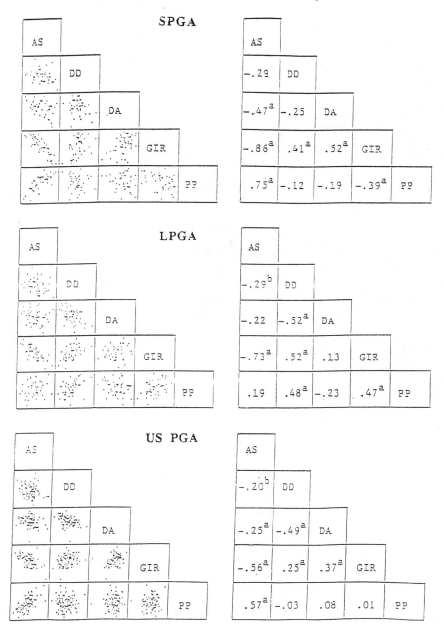

Figure 1. Scatterplots and correlation matrices for each tour

The predictive strength of PP and GIR is further evidenced by an examination of the scatterplots which are highlighted in Figure 2. The five golfers (Trevino, Hill, Archer, Rodriquez, and Stockton) represented in the upper left hand portion of the scatterplot for the SPGA and enclosed within the circles were among the top performing golfers with respect to both PP and GIR. They also happened to be the five golfers who had the lowest overall average scores during the 1992 SPGA season. Similarly, for the LPGA, the five golfers (Mallon, Lopez, Mochrie, Sheehan, and Burton) who fell above the straight line on their scatterplot were also the five golfers who had the lowest average scores on the 1992 LPGA tour.

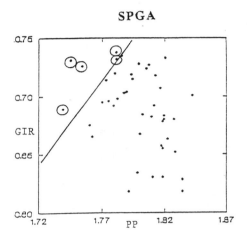

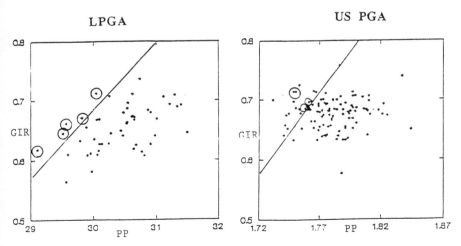

Figure 2. Location of the lowest average scorers on the scatterplot of GIR and PP for each of the tours

A smaller percentage of the variability in AS was explained (R^2=.67) by the four performance statistics for golfers on the US PGA tour. This result was obtained despite the fact that all four statistics were found to be statistically significant. Such a finding suggests that there may be additional factors (for example, sand saves) that affected AS that were not included in the regression model.

A second possible reason for the substantial decline in R^2 compared to the SPGA and LPGA tours was the relatively small amount of variability that existed in the AS of US PGA players. As indicated in Table 1, the variance in AS for the US PGA players was less than half the variance in AS for SPGA players. Given such a small amount of variability in the dependent variable (AS), the regression model was unable to explain more than two-thirds of the variability that existed.

The corresponding scatterplot for the US PGA in Figure 2 shows that the top five golfers (Couples, Price, Floyd, Kite, and Azinger) all performed above average in terms of both PP and GIR. However, there were a number of other players on the US PGA tour who had similar PP and GIR statistics, but who did not do as well in terms of average score.

4 Conclusions

The regression results demonstrated that two performance statistics, greens in regulation and putting performance, were able to satisfactorily explain a substantial percentage of the variation in average scores for players on both the SPGA and LPGA tours. However, these two statistics, together with driving distance and driving accuracy, were unable to explain approximately one-third of the variability in AS for players on the US PGA tour. This result could be due to either the regression model's omission of one or more key factors or the relatively small amount of variability that existed in the average scores among the US PGA tour players who were included in the analysis.

5 References

Golf Almanac (1993), Publications International, Ltd., Lincolnwood, Illinois.
Jones, R.E. (1990) A correlation analysis of the Professional Golf Association (PGA) statistical rankings for 1988, in Science and Golf (ed by A. J. Cochran), E. & F. N. Spon, Chapman and Hall, London, pp. 165-167.
Hale, T. and Hale, G.T. (1990) Lies, damned lies and statistics in golf, in Science and Golf (ed A. J. Cochran) E. & F.N. Spon, Chapman and Hall, London, pp. 159-164.
Rotella, R.J. and Boutcher S. H. (1990) A closer look at the role of mind in golf, in Science and Golf (ed A. J. Cochran), E. & F.N. Spon, Chapman and Hall, London, pp. 93-97.

32 The Ryder Cup: an analysis of relative performance 1980–1993

T. Hale, V. Harper and J. Herb
Centre for Sports Science, West Sussex Institute, Chichester, UK,
PGA European Tour, Wentworth, Surrey, UK and PGA Tour, Ponte
Vedra Beach, Florida 32082, USA

Abstract
Performance statistics and stroke averages for the American and European PGA Tours over the 1980 - 1993 period have been analysed in an attempt to explain recent results in the Ryder Cup matches. Within Tour improvements ($P<0.05$) have been found in four out of the five performance categories for both groups; Greens in Regulation (GIR) for the Americans and Driving Accuracy (DA) for the Europeans were the exceptions. Between Tour analysis showed that in 1985 the American Tour golfers were better in all categories except bunker play (Sand Saves - SS), but by 1993 they were superior in (DA) and putting (PPR) only and the Europeans were significantly better out of bunkers. The ultimate indicator, the average number of strokes each round (SPR), revealed significant ($P<0.001$) within Tour improvements for both groups since 1980; between Tour analysis showed the Americans were superior in 1980 and 1993 ($P<0.001$). Analysis of the SPR for the actual Ryder Cup teams showed a significant drop in this indicator by the American teams of 1983 and 1985. However, there were no significant differences between the two sides in 1983, 1985 and 1987 during which time the Europeans won twice. Since 1989 the Americans have established over 0.5 SPR advantage ($P<0.05$) in the last three matches; they have tied one and won the other two.
Keywords: Ryder Cup Teams, Performance Statistics, Average Strokes per Round

1 Introduction

The Ryder Cup, a team competition between the professional golfers of Great Britain and the United States, was inaugurated in 1927 and has been played every two years since that time with the exception of the ten years spanning the Second World War. Thirty matches have been played with the USA demonstrating considerable overall superiority with 25 victories, 2 ties and only 5 losses. In 1979 the rules governing player eligibility were changed to allow the Great Britain team to be strengthened by the inclusion of players from Continental Europe, a move that reflected the growth of the PGA European Tour. Since that time, the teams have become much more evenly matched with the European team being in possession of the trophy for six of the last ten years and gaining their first victory on American soil. This change of fortune led to considerable concern amongst the supporters of American golf particularly and various suggestions have been advanced for the improved performance by the European teams; this paper sets out to examine the validity of some of those suggestions.

Science and Golf II: Proceedings of the World Scientific Congress of Golf. Edited by A.J. Cochran and M.R. Farrally. Published in 1994 by E & FN Spon, London. ISBN 0 419 18790 1

The most widely canvassed explanation is that the American golfers were in decline. It is argued that the introduction of the all-exempt American PGA Tour and the increased prize money now available, has allowed a growing number of merely competent golfers to earn a comfortable living by regularly finishing in the top twenty in the majority of tournaments. Further evidence that is cited to support the argument of an American decline is the recent lack of success of American golfers in two major championships - the Masters and The Open Championship. The evidence is reinforced by the greater success of European golfers in these two tournaments over the past ten years.

This paper sets out to test the hypotheses that either the USA golfers are becoming poorer golfers, or that the Europeans are improving or that other factors, such as team selection or team captaincy, are at play. Analysis of the performance statistics of players on the respective Tours is one way to examine the issue to see if there are any changes in performance that support such conjectures.

2 Methods

Performance statistics were obtained from the two PGA Tours. The USA statistics were first collected in 1980, followed by the Europeans in 1984. The data were analysed in three ways. Firstly, the SPR (called scoring leaders in the USA) of the top 20 golfers from each Tour for 1980 were used as a base line since this was not a Ryder Cup year and this comparison would give a general picture of the relative performances of each Tour. Secondly, performance statistics - driving distance (DD), driving accuracy (DA), greens in regulation (GIR), sand saves (SS) and putts per round (PPR) - of the top 40 golfers on each Tour in 1985 and 1993 were compared to see if a particular aspect of the game distinguished the two sets of players. European performance statistics did not become available before the 1985 competition. Finally, the mean SPR of each Ryder Cup team were compared for all of the competitions since 1981. Student's t-test for independent samples was used in all cases with the critical level of probability being set at 5%. The Levene Test for Homogeneity of Variances was applied to all comparisons. Where variances were not equal " a more conservative formula," (Munro & Page1993) - the "Separate" t-test - was used.

3 Results

All data given in the tables are means ($\pm$ SE). Table 1. below shows the average number of strokes per round for the leading players on each Tour since the time the Great Britain team was strengthened by the inclusion of European members of the Tour.

Although there have been fluctuations in this measure over the 13 years surveyed the general trend has been one of steady improvement with leading players on both Tours showing small but statistically significant reductions in SPR (P< 0.001 in each case). The differences between the Tours were also statistically significant in 1980 and remained so in 1993 (P<0.001 in each case). The only time the SPR of the leading Europeans was lower than their American counterparts was in 1983 and even then the difference was too small to be statistically significant.

Table 1 Mean (± SE) SPR of the top 20 golfers on the USA and European Tours 1980 - 1993

YEAR	USA		GB & EUROPE	
1980	70.87	± 0.09	71.66	± 0.01
1981	70.82	0.08	71.47	0.15
1983	70.86	0.04	70.70	0.12
1985	70.83	0.06	70.96	0.14
1987	70.51	0.04	Not available	
1989	69.98	0.05	70.59	0.10
1991	70.09	0.05	70.87	0.13
1993	69.89	0.09	70.99	0.14

Performance statistics have been collected by the Americans since 1980 and the Europeans since 1984. These data were analysed because it was felt that they may isolate particular components of the game that might help to explain the overall differences between the two Tours. The next table shows the changes in performance in each statistic between 1985 and 1993.

Table 2. Performance statistics of the top 40 golfers on each Tour in 1985 and 1993 (means ± SE)

Statistic	USA 1985		USA 1993		EUROPE 1985		EUROPE 1993	
Driving distance (yds)	269.0	± 0.6	271.4	± 0.74	254.2	± 0.79	272.5	± 0.82
Driving accuracy (%)	71.6	0.5	75.5	0.35	69.2	0.75	70.4	0.49
Greens in regulation (%)	68.4	0.23	69	0.23	67.3	0.39	70.4	0.49
Sand saves (%)	54.6	0.43	59.5	0.41	53.8	1.42	62.3	1.16
Putts per round (shots)	29.2	0.04	28.8	0.04	30.3	0.08	29.3	0.1

There have been significant improvements in American performance in DD (P<0.05), DA (P<0.001), SS (P<0.001) and PPR (P<0.001) over the eight year period but not in accuracy of reaching the greens in regulation (GIR). There have also been statistically significant improvements (P<0.001) in all categories except DA for the Europeans over the same period. In 1985 the Americans were better than their European counterparts in all aspects of the game except recovery from greenside bunkers (SS) where there was no difference between the groups. By 1993 the Europeans were better at bunker shots (P<0.001) but the Americans were still superior in DA and PPR (P<0.001).

The data reported thus far give an indication of the general differences between the two Tours. In both cases the data include performances by golfers who would not be eligible for inclusion in either Ryder Cup team because of their nationality. It may be more illuminating therefore to consider the SPRs of the actual teams that played in each competition since the introduction of the wider selection of European golfers in 1980.

Both Tours have seen a significant lowering in SPR over the 12 years since 1981 (P<0.05). However, the American teams have gone into the matches with significantly lower scores per round (P<0.05) on all but three occasions. The greatest difference between the teams occurred in 1981, and over the last three meetings the Americans have had the advantage with differences being significant at the 5% level in each case. In period from 1983 to 1987 there were no significant differences between the teams.

Table 3. Mean ($\pm$ SE) SPR of USA and European Ryder Cup teams since 1981

Year	USA		EUROPE	
1981	70.69 $\pm$	0.14	71.63 $\pm$	0.18
1983	71.11	0.14	70.73	0.23
1985	71.08	0.13	70.89	0.27
1987	70.69	0.1	70.46	0.21
1989	70.06	0.16	70.56	0.15
1991	70.24	0.12	70.96	0.23
1993	70.21	0.16	70.94	0.21

4 Discussion

The general assertion that the American golfers have been in decline since 1980 is not supported by the data. There have been significant improvements (P<0.05) in each of the performance statistics categories except GIR and in the key indicator - SPR. Bunker play (SS) has improved by some 5% but DD has increased by only 2 yds, DA by about 5% and GIR figures have barely changed. PPR has improved by just less than 0.5 of a stroke per round, but over the course of a four round tournament this may make a difference to an individual's final position and thus affect the points gained towards selection for the Ryder Cup team. Improved PPR may also go some way towards explaining the reduction of the mean SPR by almost 1 shot - 70.87 in 1980 to 69.89 by 1993.

The hypothesis that the Europeans have improved is supported by these analyses. In the period when the European golfers held the trophy for six consecutive years DD had improved by almost 20 yds, GIR rose by 5%, SS improved by over 8% and an average of 1 SPR was gained by better putting. Indeed, by 1993 the Europeans were hitting the drives fractionally further than the Americans (273 - 271 yds), reaching more greens in regulation (70.42 - 69.03%) and were better from the bunkers (62.23 - 59.46%) but only the last named was statistically significant. The rate of improvement has been greater than the Americans, but it must be remembered that the Europeans were starting from a lower base line. Nevertheless, they were still poorer at hitting fairways (70.43 - 75.48%) and in putting (28.71 - 29.25) in 1993. Even taking the improvement in average stroke per round over the past 13 years (71.66 - 70.99) made by the Europeans into account, it is the key area of putting which may go some way towards explaining the difference which still exists between the two Tours in 1993 - 69.89 strokes per round compared to the European figure of 70.99 (P<0.05). Thus the

Europeans may need to improve this department of their game if they are to regain the initiative.

However, with the possible exception of the increased DD by the Europeans, the improvements in performance recorded for both Tours are often quite small and it is difficult to determine their importance for testing the hypotheses outlined earlier. Indeed, on the basis of the analyses of the relative standards within and between the two groups, it is difficult to see how the Europeans have managed to compete any more successfully in the last 13 years than Great Britain was able to do previously. It is possible that the applicability of performance statistics gathered during medal play to match play situations may not be entirely justified. It has been shown previously that a reductionist approach to golf, whilst interesting in producing descriptive data, is largely ineffectual in predicting outcomes (Hale & Hale 1990). It is equally possible that the quite different demands of the match-play formula allow the top golfers of each Tour to play very differently as specific situations demand. For example, a hole halved in 5 strokes is regarded very differently from a shot dropped to par in a medal competition. Also, strategies adopted for the team matches, particularly the four-ball-better-ball kind, permit much more attacking play by one member of the team than would be prudent in stroke play situations.

However, if the mean SPRs for the 12 members of the respective teams are examined a different picture emerges. In 1981 the USA won the match by 17 games to 8 with 3 halved. The mean SPR of the winning team - 70.69 - was almost a stroke better than the Europeans - 71.63; this difference was statistically significant (P<0.001). By the time the next match was played the USA team's stroke average was not only poorer than 1981 - 71.11 compared to 70.69, but it was also poorer than the Europeans at 70.73 strokes, although neither difference was significant (P>0.05). The result of this 1983 match was a victory to the USA by 12 games to 11 with 5 halved. European superiority in SPR was maintained over the next two matches with the Europeans having a small, but not significant edge over the American teams. In both cases the Europeans won the matches - 15 - 10 with 3 halved in 1985 at the Belfry, and even more remarkably 13 - 11 with 4 halved at the Muirfield course in Ohio in 1987. By 1989 the Americans had regained their superiority in SPR and have had a significant edge (P<0.05) over the Europeans in the last three matches. The 1989 match at the Belfry finished in a tie with Europeans retaining the Cup. The European performance at Kiawah Island was surprising in that the difference in stroke averages was almost three-quarters of a stroke (70.24 - 70.96) yet the match was only resolved on the final green of the final game. In the most recent encounter the difference between the sides was the widest since 1981 (70.21 - 70.94) with the USA retaining the trophy by two clear points. The analysis of the mean SPR of the respective teams suggests that this may be the single most useful predictor of the outcome of the matches. Consideration of this issue may lead to different selection procedures.

5 References

Hale, T. and Hale, G.T. (1990) Lies, damned lies and statistics in golf, in **1st World Scientific Congress of Golf** (ed A. Cochran), E & F.N. Spon, London, pp. 151-155.
Munro, B.H. & Page, E.B. (1993) **Statistical Methods for Health Care Research.** J. B. Lippincott Company, Philadelphia

33 The ageing of a great player; Tom Watson's play in the US Open from 1980–1993

L.J. Riccio
Golf Analyzer, New York, USA

Abstract
A statistical, longitudinal analysis of an expert golfer is presented to determine which parts of play most significantly affect a golfer's decline in competitiveness due to age. Detailed stroke-by-stroke data were collected for Tom Watson's play in the US Open for 14 consecutive years. Findings indicate that a decline in tee-to-green play has been far more instrumental to his weakened competitiveness than a decline in putting.
Keywords: Statistics, Tom Watson, Greens-in-Regulation, Putting

1 Introduction

Athletes in all sports reach a peak and then go through a period of decline. Golfers are no exception. A few are blessed with a long peak (Nicklaus), others retire at their peak (Bobby Jones), and others peak, decline and then have a come back (Johnny Miller). But as they age, all face a decline in their skills.

What happens to the play of a great golfer as he ages? Which skills most affect that decline? Is it putting that goes first and affects the decline most as the experts have long claimed for such greats as Palmer and Watson?

In an effort to find an answer to these questions one would need a detailed record of the play of a great golfer covering a long period of time in events which were important to the golfer. The PGA Tour statistics program provides good but not detailed data (e.g. no real measure of iron play, chipping, pitching or true putting skills). [PGA Tour] Their statistics program is too simplistic when compared to other major league sports and is not capable of supporting the kind of analysis needed to discern key and subtle differences in golfer's play whose good rounds are 69 and bad ones are 72. No other formal data set exists for great golfers.

2 The Data Set

In 1980, the author began collecting stroke by stroke data on the play of Tom Watson and others at the US Open. [Riccio, 1981] As a result of 14 years of observation, using a specially designed scorecard, [Riccio, 1987] the data set now contains detailed information on every one of Tom Watson's 3719 strokes in the US Open from 1980

Science and Golf II: Proceedings of the World Scientific Congress of Golf. Edited by A.J. Cochran and M.R. Farrally. Published in 1994 by E & FN Spon, London. ISBN 0 419 18790 1

through 1993. Each tee-to-green stroke had the type of stroke, the club used, how it was hit, and the resulting location dutifully recorded. Every putt had its length registered.

Since it is well known that Tom Watson considers winning the US Open one of his highest quests in golf, there is no question that the data represents his play when he most truly cares. It should be noted that his record in the championship, although not near that of Jones, Hogan, or Nicklaus, has to be classified as outstanding. [Johnson, 1991] In his 20 Opens, he won once, finished second twice, third once, and in all has had ten top ten finishes. His best stretch was the ten years from 1974 to 1983 in which he had eight top ten finishes.

The fourteen years from 1980 to 1993 span a period of Watson's play from the middle of his peak through his "era of decline." As such, this data set is useful for examining the questions posed at the beginning of this paper.

3 The Putting Myth

It should be pointed out at the outset that to most pundits the answer in Tom Watson's case is obvious. They say it's his putting. [Strvinsky, 1990] The notion that Watson's putting was always good in his early days and always the cause for his weaker play in his later years is considered gospel. This consensus is not based on a scientific analysis but instead on a collectively reinforced speculation repeated enough times that it has become the truth. There's no denying that at times Watson does not look as confident on the putting greens as people seem to remember he used to look. But they also don't remember him missing several short putts early in his Sunday round at the 1974 US Open at Winged Foot, which cost him the championship; or the missed putts coming down the stretch at the 1978 PGA at Oakmont or at the 1979 Masters, both of which he could have won, or the four footer he missed at the 71st hole at the 1983 Open at Oakmont, which would have forced a playoff.

It is not unusual to rely on the putting excuse. Professionals and amateurs do it all the time themselves. Ask almost any golfer how they played on almost any given day and they will tell you they shot such-and-such but "it could have been better if I only made a few putts". They rarely say they would have scored better if they hit a few more fairways or hit a few more greens with their irons. Since putting is the final stroke, it is the last thing you remember. It "determines" your score. It is also one of the few parts of the game golfers keep special count of.

As such, golfers at all levels place a high emphasis on the importance of putting. However, studies indicate that if a professional did the putting for a golfer who scores 85, his score would almost never go below 80. At most, he may pick up 2 to 4 strokes, most likely 1 to 3. [Riccio, 1990] On the other hand, an experiment was held having a 90-shooter play off the tee shot of the professional, and an "easy" 82 was recorded. [Andrews, 1991]

4 Analyzing Watson's Play - Inspection

The fourteen year period covered by the data (Table 1) can be divided into a five year period of peak play (1980 to 1984 with 3 top ten finishes) and a nine year period of decline (1985 to 1993 with only 2 top ten finishes). Some things stand out from simple inspection:

Watson's record in the peak period was clearly better than the period of decline. His average finishing position was 8th in the peak period; it was 44th in the period of decline. There wasn't a poor outing in the peak period. In the period of decline he had only two championships in which he truly contended and had four poor outings. If not for the second place finish in 1987 and fifth place finish in 1993, his performance in this period was undistinguished.

Watson's overall putting, as measured by a special statistic accounting for the length of the first putt on each green, deteriorated but was not consistently worse in the period of decline than in the peak. Although he lost, on average, about nine-tenths of a stroke per round on the putting greens from peak to decline, he putted better in six of the decline period Opens than he did in 1980 when he finished a strong third.

Watson's tee-to-green play weakened substantially from peak to decline. He averaged 1.3 fewer greens-in-regulation (GIR) per round in the decline period. In the period of decline he bettered 10.5 GIRs per round in only three of those nine Opens; 10.5 GIRs was the worst he did in the peak period. He also averaged 0.6 fewer birdie opportunities (putts of 15 feet or less for birdie) per round indicating not only a weakened ability to get the ball on the green, but also a lower ability to get the ball close enough to have a realistic chance of making putts.

Table 1. Selected Performance Statistics By Year

year	finish	score	pctfair	gir	pctgff	birdops	updnchip	putts	putts3	proputts
1980	3	69.00	75.0	14.0	73.9	6.3	75.0	31.0	0.5	0.5
1981	23	71.25	63.2	11.0	60.6	4.8	61.1	29.5	0.3	-1.1
1982	1	70.50	67.9	11.3	56.1	4.5	86.7	26.8	0.3	-2.3
1983	2	70.25	60.7	12.5	70.0	4.0	73.3	29.5	0.3	-1.5
1984	11	71.75	60.7	10.5	58.1	4.5	85.7	30.3	0.8	0.4
1985	100	73.50	50.0	10.5	71.4	2.5	80.0	32.0	1.0	0.8
1986	24	72.25	64.3	10.3	57.8	3.8	80.0	30.0	0.5	0.1
1987	2	69.50	60.7	12.5	76.2	4.3	58.3	30.0	1.0	-0.2
1988	36	72.25	75.0	11.8	60.9	5.0	64.7	30.3	1.0	1.5
1989	46	72.75	62.5	9.3	68.2	3.5	77.8	29.5	0.5	-0.4
1990	104	74.50	75.0	9.5	52.2	4.0	71.4	30.0	1.0	0.0
1991	16	72.75	73.2	9.8	60.0	3.5	93.3	28.0	0.3	-1.1
1992	67	74.00	67.9	9.5	36.8	6.0	58.3	28.5	0.0	0.6
1993	5	69.50	55.4	11.8	69.2	5.3	87.5	28.8	0.5	-0.3

Definitions:

finish:	Final position in championship
score:	Average per round score
pctfair:	Percentage tee strokes in fairway on par 4s and 5s
gir:	Greens in regulation per round
pctgff:	Percentage greens hit with iron club from fairway or par 3 tee
birdops:	Number of holes per round putting for birdie from 15' or less
updnchip:	Percentage up and down after a chip
putts:	Average putts per round
3putts:	Number of 3 putt greens per round
proputts:	Putting strokes per round better (if negative) or worse (if positive) than average professional given length of first putt on each green

These results provide a good overview but do not provide conclusive evidence of the specific problem. Averages can be misleading - would you ford a stream that was on average four feet deep? All of the major statistics were generally better in the peak than in the decline period, but not always. Good putting did not guarantee a good finish, nor did poor putting guarantee a poor finish.

In 1980, he finished third when he played great from tee-to-green (actually better than the winner Nicklaus), but he putted worse than he did in six of the nine decline period Opens. On Sunday of that championship, he had 7 birdie putts of 15 feet or less (5 less than 10 feet) on the back nine, but made only two. Remember, those were the days he was supposedly a great putter. On the other hand, in 1989 he putted better than two of the five peak period Opens but finished 46th because he had his worst tee-to-green Open of this whole study period.

Clearly, the question requires more sophisticated analysis. The interaction of all the different parts of Watson's play is more complicated than simple inspection can uncover. That is precisely for which the field of statistics was invented.

5 Correlation Matrix and Regressions

The correlation matrix revealed considerably more. The highlights are the following:

The factor best correlated to SCORE was Greens-in-Regulation (.87). Next best was iron accuracy (.64) and birdie opportunities (.40). Putting as measured by the length-of-first-putt adjuster (PROPUTTS) was the best correlated of the putting measures (.32), a good correlation but low compared to the others mentioned. TOTAL PUTTS was virtually uncorrelated (.08).

The factor best correlated to FINISHING POSITION was GIRs (.61). Putting as measured by PROPUTTS was next best at 0.45. Iron play was well related (.36) as was birdie opportunities (.35).

Not surprisingly, but important to mention for statistical purposes, SCORE was highly correlated to FINISHING POSITION (.85).

FINISHING POSITION (.34) and SCORE (.45) were positively related to YEAR indicating a general, but not wholesale, decline over time. GIRs was the most strongly correlated to YEAR (.53). Putting was not only not strongly related but also mixed, indicating that GIRs are a much more significant factor than putting. PROPUTTS was mildly related positively (.25) indicating a decline, but TOTAL PUTTS was negatively relating (-.25). The negative relationship is probably indicative of a very strong chipping and bunker game - as more greens are missed there are more one-putt, up-and-down situations. TOTAL PUTTS was positively related to GIRSs (.44), but PROPUTTS was not (-.05) indicating PROPUTTS is a purer measure of putting.

Of the factors that could logically affect GIRs, iron play was the best correlated (.63). Fairway accuracy measures were virtually uncorrelated. Interestingly, when these same analyses were first done with data only from the l980's decade, fairway accuracy was strongly related (.68) and iron play next best (.48). His fairway accuracy in the four years of the '90's was not only better than the last five years of the '80's, it was actually better than in the peak years. It was his iron play that weakened badly in the '90's.

The factor best related to birdie opportunities was fairway accuracy (.4l) indicating as everyone knows most birdies are set up by a good tee shot. Conversely, a bad tee shot most often takes away the possibility of a birdie.

The confidence levels for the key correlations were high. All GIR correlations were significant at the 95+ confidence level. The lower correlations were significant for the most part at the 90% level.

Clearly, tee-to-green play dominates in this analysis. Following the review of the correlation matrix, multi-variate and stepwise regressions were performed on the data. In the stepwise regression to "predict" SCORE, GIRs was entered first accounting for 74% of the variation, reinforcing the premise that GIRs is the most important factor. Next into the regression was PROPUTTS increasing explained variance to 85%.

Predicting FINISHING POSITION proved to be more difficult but not impossible. You would expect that since FINISHING POSITION is dependent on the play of others, not just on your play. Even with this fact, the combination of GIRs and PROPUTTS was able to explain 56% of the variance, not bad by social science standards.

6 Conclusions

Although the argument can be made that Watson's putting has weakened in the last several years, it cannot be argued that putting is the dominant, let alone, the only factor that has led to his period of decline. The models clearly show that although his putting has weakened, his tee-to-green play dominated in determining his score and finishing position. The models were strong and the results significant. The arguments that putting is the sole reason must be relegated to myth. In stating the importance of the two parts of play, this and other research indicates that tee-to-green play separates the leaders from the also-rans, and then putting affects the order of the leader board.

Studies of golfers of a wide range of abilities indicate that GIRs or specific aspects of tee-to-green play are the defining qualities that separate golfers. [Riccio, 1990, Cochran and Stobbs, 1968]   Therefore, it is not surprising that GIRs would be significant in the difference between a golfer's best play and his worst play. Nicklaus attributes his reduced competitiveness to a reduction in green-hitting ability [Golf Digest, 1991] and Arnold Palmer - another golfer with the putting myth label - confirmed another work of this author that tee-to-green play was the problem of his reduced competitiveness. [Dennis, 1982] I believe further studies will only strengthen this finding.

7 References

Andrews, P. (May 1991) "What Could You Do Off A Pro's Tee Ball?", Golf Digest, Trumbull, CT. USA

Cochran, A.J. and Stobbs, J. (1968) The Search for the Perfect Swing, The Booklegger, Grass Valley, CA. USA

Dennis, L. (Feb. 1982) "Arnie Sounds Off," Golf Digest, Trumbull, CT. USA

Golf Digest (Oct. 1991) "An Interview with Jack Nicklaus," Trumbull, CT. USA

Johnson, S. (June 1991) "The Best Open Players in the Steel-Shaft Era," Golf Illustrated, New York, NY USA

PGA Tour Statistics, PGA Tour, Inc., Ponte Verde, FL. USA

Riccio, L.J. (June 1981) "How Jack Won the 1980 US Open," Golf Magazine, New York, NY USA

Riccio, L.J. (1987) Golf Analyzer, New York, NY USA

Riccio, L.J. (1990) "A Statistical Analysis of the Average Golfer," Science and Golf, Chapman and Hall Co., New York, NY USA

Strvinsky, John (March 25, 1990) "The Man with the Golden Arm," New York Times Sunday Magazine, New York, NY USA

34 A unified golf stroke value scale for quantitative stroke-by-stroke assessment

L.M. Landsberger
Department of Electrical and Computer Engineering,
Concordia University, Montreal, Canada

Abstract
This paper introduces a unified quantitative system of value for single golf strokes. The system uses as input the pre- and post-stroke distance to the hole, and green attainment, along with more subjective factors such as lie, obstacles, wind and slope. By quantification of two different types of standards for long and short strokes, an integrated scale is developed, relatively consistent with established course rating systems, by which all strokes can be compared. This also provides a framework for calculation of effective handicaps for different stroke types, and development of personalized performance standards.
Keywords: Stroke Value, Standards, Statistics, Quantitative Analysis, Handicap.

1 Introduction

At present, the finest-scaled objective measure of golf performance is the number of strokes that a player takes on a given hole. While accurate and indisputable, this number is often quite unsatisfying, since the clearest basic building block of a golf round is the episode of a *single stroke*. The objective of this paper is to present a quantitative system of logic for integrated objective evaluation of a *single golf stroke*, so that its *value* toward the final score for the hole can be compared to that of other single strokes.

This system bases its judgement on the factual result of the stroke. Given where your ball started before the stroke, and where it came to rest after the stroke, what was the stroke worth, compared to a "Course Rating" (CR) standard, or compared to your "personal average" standard? While there often is the necessity for subjective judgements of wind, slope, lie and obstacles, this system provides a useful, integrated framework for comparison of the value of each stroke to the value of any other stroke.

For example, consider a relatively straightforward and flat 400-yard par-4 (a male golfer in this example) with a not-too-severe green on a windless day. The golfer hits a 200-yard tee shot, and a fairway stroke that finishes wide of the green 60 feet from the hole. Then he chips to 15 feet, putts to a foot and a half, and makes the short putt. On the scorecard it is a 5 (bogey). But last week he made his 5 by 3-putting from 10 feet! How is he to distinguish between these drastically different scenarios, with dramatically different consequences on his mental state? The serious golfer, with an eye to game-improvement, can greatly benefit from objective stroke-by-stroke record-keeping. The system described in this paper provides a tool for such fine discrimination on a quantitative scale. Then, if any of the two scenarios described above were more common than the others, such record-keeping could recognize strengths and suggest effective practice strategies to improve on weaknesses. This system, inspired by Cochran & Stobbs' (1968) (C&S) book chapters on "Analysing a Tournament", provides a vehicle to capture and record in a quantitative, objective way some of the richness of information that is lost in

Science and Golf II: Proceedings of the World Scientific Congress of Golf. Edited by A.J. Cochran and M.R. Farrally. Published in 1994 by E & FN Spon, London. ISBN 0 419 18790 1

the usual hole-by-hole performance measures.

While other quantitative systems of stroke-by-stroke evaluation exist, notably the commendably detailed statistical approach of P.J. Sanders (1992), including "Lost-Saved Analysis" for different stroke types, developed around the same time as this one, such systems generally rely on more complex data collection and a large set of heuristics to cover all possible golfing situations. This paper presents a value scale based on a single integrated scheme by which all strokes can be compared, and which is flexible enough to provide useful judgements for golfers of any skill level (Landsberger, 1991, 1992). Some heuristics are still required to handle a breadth of detailed cases, but the integrated mathematics allows rapid quantitative adjustment for a wide variety of conditions, including golfers' differing abilities and golf courses' differing conditions and difficulty.

The algorithms have been implemented in a computer spreadsheet program, with options to compare any stroke to a CR standard, or to a particular handicap standard, for women or men, and/or adjusted to particular distance ability. For example this system could provide integrated quantitative measures for the "Personal Par" system of Keogh & Smith (1985). Many types of modifications and many different levels of detail are relatively easily available within this framework.

While the forum of this article is too limited for comprehensive detail of the algorithms and implementation, a conceptual and simplified version follows.

2 Overview of System Fundamentals

The system rests on a combination of (a) a rudimentary version of the course rating schemes in effect from golf's governing bodies (the R&A, the USGA), and (b) an analysis of the short game based on a probabilistic estimate of how many strokes, on average, it takes a golfer to get his or her ball into the hole from a given distance on or near the green ("How many from how far?" in C&S.)

In general, golf's governing course rating systems in effect today can be understood in a simple manner as allowing (par minus 2) strokes to get on (or near to) the green, and allowing 2 strokes on (or near) the green. Then the par of a particular hole is given by the integer nearest to the "fractional par" determined by a formula:

$$p = Yx + S \tag{1}$$

where p is the fractional par, Y is the per-yard value for long strokes, S is the short-game strokes allowance, and x is the total distance of the hole in yards. (See "Standard Scratch Score" in C&S.) For the British system, $Y=0.0044$, $s=2.35$, and for the USA system, $Y=0.00455$, $S=2.27$ are calculated. For example, according to C&S, in Britain a 500-yd hole has $p = 4.55$. When rounded to the nearest integer, this is a par-5 hole. The distance breakpoint between a par-4 and par-5 holes is found by setting $p = 4.5$, and solving for x $= 488$ yds. This breakpoint is usually applied loosely, depending on other factors such as slopes or placement of hazards.

The system proposed in this paper is consistent with the above in that a constant value is assigned to each yard covered outside of a certain radius (R) near (off) the green.

$$V = (Xi - Xr)/(C1/K1) \tag{2}$$

where V is the stroke value for the distance covered, Xi is the distance to the hole before the stroke ("x-initial"), Xr is the distance remaining to the hole after the stroke ("x-remaining"), K1 is a constant depending on the performance standard used (CR/personal) or the golfer's distance ability, and C1 includes the effect of correction factors for wind, slope, lie and obstacles. Therefore (C1/K1) is equivalent to the parameter Y in Eq. 1 above.

Inside the radius R (calculated to be about 30 yds. from the hole), however, stroke value is assigned according to the formula:

$$V = (C2)(\log[Q]) \tag{3}$$

where the short-game stroke quality is $Q = (Xi/Xr)(K2)$, K2 includes the effect of short-game correction factors (green attainment, lie or obstacles such as bunkers or severe slopes), and C2 is a constant depending on the performance standard or distance ability. Note that inside R the value of each yard covered is not constant and depends strongly on how close the ball is to the hole. As such, traversing the last yard to the hole is worth much more than traversing a yard 15 yds. away. This is related to C&S' concept of evaluating a stroke by "How close from how far?". The transition radius R is chosen such that the stroke value remaining to the hole from R is near to the parameter S in Eq. 1. It has been adjusted to 2.475 in order to more accurately fit the model to the available data.

The performance standard for distance is based on the concept of a "Comfortable Long-Shot Distance" (CLSD). This is the distance that a golfer would expect to reliably hit a 4- or 5-wood under normal conditions, for example CLSD = ~225 yds for the male CR golfer, or ~180 yds for the female CR golfer. The performance standards are set such that long shots finishing far from the hole that gain this distance are given V=1.0. This allows the performance standard for distance to be decoupled from the performance standard for the short game. Inside R, the performance standards can be the same for men and women, and are determined only by the handicap standard selected or computed.

Analysis of data presented in the sections on "Putting" and "Short Approaches" in C&S' original study is consistent with professionals having short-game ability corresponding to stroke quality of $Q = \sim20$. For example, this means that from on the green a distance of $Xi = 30$ ft. to the hole, they tend to putt the ball to a distance of $Xr = 1.5$ ft., or 20 times closer to the hole ($Q = Xi/Xr = 20$). Since the scores in C&S' data set averaged out to the course rating, their data can be taken to be representative of the CR golfer. Accordingly, the constants for a CR golfer are adjusted such that a stroke having $Q = 20$ is assigned a value V=1.0. Note that this putt *has been assigned the same value* as that of the 225-yd. stroke in the previous paragraph. By using the two different types of standards for long and short strokes, quantitative comparison between all different strokes will be possible.

Analysis of C&S data also showed approximately that for the professionals in their study Xi/Xr was on average about 1.5 times better if the golfer's stroke began and ended on the green than if the stroke began off the green and ended on the green. In other words their accuracy appeared to be ~1.5 times better putting than chipping. While no other extensive quantitative data was available for this, the factor of 1.5 has seemed to be reasonably accurate in the use of the system so far. Therefore, if the stroke described in the previous paragraph began 30 ft. from the hole *off* the green in a good lie with no major obstacles and again ended at $Xr = 1.5$ ft., the factor K2 would equal 1.5, and therefore Q would equal 30 and V would be *greater* than 1.0. The exact value of 1.5 is not critical and can be modified, or made to vary with handicap, etc. as more relevant data becomes available.

Further, C&S were able to compute average strokes needed to get into the hole from different distances on the green. Let us call this V_T (total stroke value). For example, C&S found that the professionals took an average of $V_T = 1.62$ putts to get down from 9-12 feet, and $V_T = 2.15$ putts to get down from 42-48 feet. These average numbers of strokes taken to get down from varying distances on the green provide standards for stroke values for putts. This is the source of the concept of stroke value described herein. Therefore, a stroke which begins on the green at $Xi = 30$ feet ($V_T = \sim2.0$) and ends at $Xr = 4$ feet ($V_T = 1.32$) has stroke value $V = (2.0 - 1.32) = 0.68$.

This concept is extended to the region farther away from the hole and outside R as well. The second column of Table 1 gives examples of V_T from various distances to the hole calculated to approximate the male CR golfer in the British system (CLSD = 228). (The analogous numbers for the USA-based CR golfer are very close, though slightly different.) Then the stroke value V for any individual stroke can be computed by the difference between the V_T at Xi, and V_T at Xr, $[V_T(Xi) - V_T(Xr)]$. For example, a stroke that begins a distance of 300 yds from the hole in a good lie on the fairway, that is relatively unaffected by a gentle crosswind over flat ground, and that comes to rest in another good lie on the fairway 110 yds from the hole has V = 3.67 - 2.84 = 0.83.

Note that any putt into the hole must be worth at least 1 stroke, because, from *any* location not already in the cup, one can never take less than 1 stroke to get into the hole, and thus the average number of strokes taken from such a location can never be <1.

3 Features and Discussion

3.1 Model Fit to Some Data
As described above, the model is designed to closely approximate the currently operative course rating systems for long-distance strokes. Table 1 includes a comparison to the C&S Standard Scratch Score for par-3 holes or longer, with satisfactory agreement.

Next, Figure 1 graphs comparisons of the model for putting with data from C&S, Diaz (1989), Pelz (1989), and Sanders (1992). Again, the analytical curve provides a good fit to the data.

3.2 Handicaps and Adjustments for Distance Ability
There are many different types of golfers: women, men, scratch, beginner etc.. Even at a single handicap, there are many types, e.g. "long & wrong", "short & steady", good putters, bad putters. This scale gives a mathematical framework to understand the variations.

One fundamental difference among golfers is our basic distance ability, reflected in the CLSD. The simplest adjustment to the system is to derive a "personal par" for each golfer based on distance ability. Table 1 shows such adjusted V_{Tadj} for several different types of golfers: (a) one whose short game and consistency are comparable to a CR

Table 1:   Total stroke values to the hole (and equivalents) from various distances

Xi	V_T(CR)	p (C&S)	V_{Tadj}(a)	V_{Tadj}(b)	V_{Tadj}(c)
1.5 ft	1.00	-	1.00	1.11	1.11
4 ft	1.32	-	1.32	1.70	1.70
6 ft	1.46	-	1.46	1.88	1.88
10 ft	1.63	-	1.63	2.10	2.10
15 ft	1.76	-	1.76	2.26	2.26
30 ft on grn	2.00	-	2.00	2.57	2.57
60 ft off grn	2.37	-	2.37	3.05	3.05
50 yds	2.58	2.57	2.60	3.31	3.28
110 yds	2.84	2.83	2.94	3.65	3.55
150 yds	3.01	3.01	3.17	3.87	3.72
200 yds	3.23	3.23	3.45	4.16	3.94
250 yds	3.45	3.45	3.73	4.44	4.16
300 yds	3.67	3.67	4.01	4.72	4.38
400 yds	4.11	4.11	4.58	5.28	4.82
500 yds	4.55	4.55	5.14	5.85	5.26
605 yds	5.00	5.01	5.73	6.44	5.72

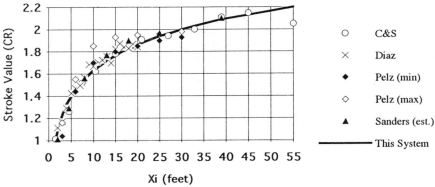

Figure 1. Comparison of analytical curve to existing data sets.

player, except that the CLSD is taken as 177 yds. instead of 225 yds., representative of an average male 18-handicap's *effective* CLSD; (b) one whose peak skills are comparable to a male CR player, but whose overall lack of consistency yields an 18-handicap; (c) one whose long strokes are comparable to a male CR player, but whose chipping and putting are comparable to the level of an 18-handicap. Here, V_{Tadj} is scaled to the "personal par" stroke value, where $V_{adj} = 1.0$ corresponds to the *particular player's average* stroke. Such results can be used to find a personalized fractional par for each hole or course, and can form the basis for more personalized adjustments based on particulars such as hazard placement and severity.

Conversely, a profile of a golfer's abilities can also be readily generated using input data from a number of holes or rounds. Table 2 shows a sample of a simplified integrated profile for 9 holes by a low-handicap player. The stroke type "OtherShort" includes sand and trouble shots. Such a summary can provide the golfer with valuable information on which to base post-round analysis or practice strategy. In this particular 9 holes, the golfer drove well, did not miss any putts under 6 ft., and generally hit long strokes well, including hitting a par-5 green in two. There were two 3-putt greens, and clearly the golfer had trouble with long and intermediate-distance putts. It remains for the golfer to answer whether such putts are a common problem and need long-term practice, or whether this was merely a question of some transient phenomena like an unfamiliar golf course with unfamiliar green speed.

3.3 Other Caveats and Extensions

The simplest workable version of the system requires as input for each stroke only Xi, Xr and whether the ball crossed off-to-on the green or on-to-off the green. Oversimplified, this misses much. In the full computer implementation of the system, several additional *subjective* pieces of input data are required for each stroke. The effect of wind and slopes can be estimated for long strokes, based on the estimated effect of wind velocities and altitude differentials on the distance covered by the stroke. For example, into a 25 mph (C&S) headwind, the CR golfer needs only produce about 165 yds to achieve $V = 1.0$. Note that the V_T for the hole must be increased accordingly. Also, the effect of a compromised lie or flight path can similarly be described by a correction factor. This factor describes the effect of the resulting lie on the *next* stroke, by estimating the best result that the golfer can reliably expect to achieve from the compromised lie. It is formulated such that V_T for the hole remains constant, while the value lost to the offending stroke is transferred to *enhance* the value of the next stroke. Lies which make the next stroke unusually easy are readily accomodated as well.

While this paper presents only a simplified analysis, the computation of the average stroke value for the attainment of a given score is problematic due to the possibility for widely varying distributions of stroke values, and due to arguments that there are aspects of golf courses which make the effective total V_T *different for players of different handicaps*, notably the fundamental assumptions of the Slope Rating System in the USA, and assumptions regarding lost stroke value in putts.

Table 2:   Stroke Values and Effective Handicaps derived from data for 9 holes

Stroke Type	Strks. Taken	Total CR Strk. Value	Average Strk. Value	Value Gain vs. CR	Effective Handicap
Tee Drivers	7	7.37	1.05	+0.37	+3.6
Other Woods	3	2.81	0.94	-0.19	4.8
Long Irons	3	2.66	0.89	-0.34	9.2
Short Irons	4	3.41	0.85	-0.59	12.6
Pitch/Chip	3	2.81	0.94	-0.19	4.8
Other Short	1	0.75	0.75	-0.25	24.5
Long Putts	5	3.72	0.74	-1.28	24.9
Makeable Putts	3	1.90	0.63	-1.10	41.4
Short Putts	10	10.68	1.07	+0.68	+4.6
Overall	39	36.11	0.93	-2.89	5.8

4 In Conclusion

A richness of new detail and insight is available. For example, one can mathematically investigate and understand golf adages like "It's not how good your good strokes are, but how good your bad strokes are". For the bogey golfer, it is much easier to make two strokes of V=0.78 than it is to follow a stroke of V=0.4 with a professional-quality stroke of V=1.16. Table 1 can provide many insights. A 4-footer is quite valuable, more so than a 250-yd drive, if your effective CLSD is above 190 yds. If birdie was made on a 150-yd par-3 by a 10-ft putt, which stroke was more valuable, the tee stroke or the putt?

This system provides a powerful tool for quantitative golf analysis on a stroke-by-stroke basis. The integrated mathematics gives a framework for comparison of all different types of strokes, relative to absolute or personalized standards. There are many realms that could benefit from use of such a system, including course rating, golf instruction, sports psychology, even media analysis.

5 References

Cochran, A. & Stobbs, J. (1968). **The Search for the Perfect Golf Swing**, Grass Valley, CA: The Booklegger.

Diaz, J. (1989). Perils of Putting. **Sports Illustrated Magazine** Vol. 70 No. 14, p.76-79, April 3, 1989, USA.

Keogh, B.K. & Smith, E.S. (1985). **Personal Par**. Champaign, Il.: Human Kinetics.

Landsberger, L.M. Golf shot values, (1991), The value and quality of your golf strokes, (1992), Realistic expectations for golf strokes, (1992), Unpublished documents, Montreal.

Pelz, D. (1989). **Putt Like the Pros**, New York: Harper & Row.

Sanders, P.J. (1992). Golf performance analysis system. **Golf Research Associates LP**, Stamford, CT: USA.

35 The search for the perfect handicap

F.J. Scheid
USGA Handicap Research Team, Far Hills, NJ, USA

Abstract
Golfers come in many shapes and sizes, the sizes of their scores and
shapes of their score profiles, which suggests that to be accurate handicaps ought to reflect both these features. Fictitious players can easily be
imagined for whom any current handicapping system is inefficient. (One
who shoots only birdies and double bogeys might fit this description.)
But using shape as well as size means a "two-dimensional" system, a
normal model being the principal contender. The idea is stimulating but
would involve a quantum leap in system complexity. Would the gain be
worth it? The following sections describe a first effort to answer the
question and, more generally, to search (futilely) for the perfect handicap.
Keywords: Handicap Accuracy, Normal Model.

1   The method used

There are several popular types of competition and experience shows that
what is needed for equity in one may not be fair in others. For a few of
these types a serious (heroic) effort was first made to estimate the
strokes truly needed for equity. Then a broad variety of handicap systems were tested to see how well they could predict this need.

As a preview, if score distributions were symmetric the mean would be
a perfect predictor for individual match play. Give enough strokes to
equalize means and, as Fig. 1 shows, fair play has been realized. If net
scores a and b are shot one day then the symmetric pair a' and b' will be
shot on another, and with equal probability. It is too bad that A's very
best round can still lose, but his (her) very worst round can still win.
Things are about as fair as a cruel world allows. But symmetry cannot
be counted on, so there is work to be done.

In all about 50 handicap types were tested for accuracy. Included
were the present USGA handicap, some approximations to the UK handicap such as the second (2), third (3) and fourth (4) best differentials

Science and Golf II: Proceedings of the World Scientific Congress of Golf. Edited by A.J.
Cochran and M.R. Farrally. Published in 1994 by E & FN Spon, London. ISBN 0 419 18790 1

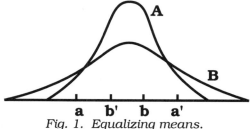
Fig. 1. Equalizing means.

(scores minus course rating), a host of averages such as the best five (1-5), best ten (1-10), middle ten (6-15), slight trim (2-19), best and worst (1,20) and so on, only a few of which have found mention in the history of the subject. Also included were systems counting points instead of strokes such as 1 for bogey, 2 for par, etc. (PT1234) or the simpler (PT12) offering 1 for par and 2 for birdie. Stableford methods and the Swedish system of handicapping are of this type. Also systems based on the twelve best (B12) and fifteen best (B15) holes per round, judged relative to par, averaged and then adjusted to an eighteen hole basis. A normal model was represented by the mean minus multiples of sigma. Even a few exotic measures such as spread (SPRD = worst minus best), average worst half (11-20) and average birdies per round were included, not because of suspected merit but for their entertainment value, the testing process to serve as impartial judge.

2   Individual match play

Given two individuals how can true need for this type of play be measured, the difference in means, medians or whatever? Eventually, with twenty rounds of hole by hole scores available for thousands of players at many clubs, it was decided to use simulated play, matching each round of one player against each of the other. This does involve an assumption that rounds are independent, which reference (1) showed to be not quite true. But (1) also reported correlations of only .02 and made this choice the most promising.

Accordingly, at each of several clubs fifty pairs of golfers were selected using current USGA handicaps to assure a variety of ability differences. An initial number of strokes was then offered, 400 matches "played" and adjustments made until each player had close to 200 wins. The final stroke offering (interpolating as needed) was then adopted as the true need between each pair. About 80,000 matches were simulated at each club. The output was a list of player IDs and strokes needed, beginning as follows.

Club	Players	Strokes needed
01	01 02	2.1
01	02 05	0.9

Regressions were then run to see how well each type of handicap could (if used optimally) predict the strokes needed, the rms error of the fit serving as indicator. This was done at eighteen clubs and the 18x50 errors tabulated. (A preliminary effort using Fourier methods had shown that quadratic or higher degree terms would bring miniscule improvement.) Informal inspection of the matrix showed consistent differences between the handicap types and a Friedman test placed significance at well under the one percent level. The full table is not reproduced here but Table 1 offers a selection of median errors, enough to reveal a message which is both believable and in hindsight predictable.

An accurate handicap system for match play must use a central measure of ability, like the mean. (In this test the normal model was best represented by the mean.) A Wilcoxon test showed error differences of .1 to be significant and this step is minimal in the table.

3   Large field net events

An intuitive argument is helpful. In a field of 100 players it can be argued roughly that one of them is likely to play in the top hundredth of his score profile and so doing ought to be a winner, leading to the suggestion that fair play calls for equalizing the percentile 1 scores of all competitors (not equalizing their means). The weaker player's scores need now be shifted leftward only by the amount shown in Fig. 2.

The argument that fairness means equal chance to win is vulnerable. As the figure shows, more good golfers than bad will finish well, while the bottom of the order will be heavy with hookers and slicers. Even so let us see how the handicap types respond to the percentile 1 criterion.

Table 1. Median errors, individual match play

Error	Types
.4	MEAN, (2-19), (3-18), (4-17), (8,13)
.5	(1-15), MEDIAN, (6-15), (10-11), B15, (8)
.7	PT1234, B12
.8	USGA
1.0	(2), (1-5)
>	(1), (3), SPRD, PT12, (11-20), BIRDIES

Fig. 2. Equalizing percentile 1 scores.

It is no easy thing to estimate this extreme level of individual play.
The idea of pooling golfers with the same handicap until a hundred
scores were in hand was tried but led to chaotic results in the sense that
similar handicap types showed quite different errors (a sort of sensitivity
to initial conditions). Eventually the slight correlation between rounds
was accepted as unavoidable and simulations again got the nod. The
record of each player was extended to a hundred rounds by selecting
hole by hole scores randomly from the 20 actual rounds in hand. The
best of the hundred was then adopted as his (her) personal percentile 1.

These percentiles were then regressed against each handicap type in
its turn, with rms errors again used as measures of accuracy. A selection of median errors across the eighteen clubs is provided in Table 2.
An error difference of .2 proved significant and this is the step used in
the table. One notices that handicaps which emphasize the best part of a
player's game now top the list with the one best of twenty leading the
way. Intuition approves of this, though a few central measures of ability
are not far behind. One is also sure to notice that the normal model, with
NORM now representing mean minus 2.326 sigmas, is in a virtual tie for
the honor. (As the mean it was also in first place for individual match
play.) Notice too that the errors are much larger than for match play,
indicating that large field events are harder to handicap.

Table 2. Median errors to equalize percentile 1 scores

Error	Types
1.2	(1), (1-5), NORM
1.4	(2), (3), (4), USGA, (1-15), (2-19)
	MEAN, PT1234, B12, B15, (2-17)
>	PT12, MEDIAN, SPRD, (11-20), BIRDIES

4   Team play

For better-ball match play a target score was determined by using many pairs of scratch players, whose mean proved to be -4.0. Handicap types were regressed against this target score. Selected results are given in Table 3. To see if the test was sensitive to the target score it was replaced by 0, with no noticeable effect on errors. Type (B15) which selects the best fifteen holes per round was a surprise leader. Better-ball stroke play and best ball teams of four were also tested. Tables 4 and 5 give the results. For all three forms of competition the normal model appears among the more accurate handicap types, as MEAN in match play and as NORM equals mean minus one sigma in the others.

5   Conclusions

There are several. Foremost among them, and hardly astonishing, there is no perfect handicap. The variety of forms of competition and the variety of shapes and sizes assumed by golfers' score profiles makes so noble a goal unattainable. Also, the current official handicap systems do about as well as any.   Large field events bring the largest errors, but in these

Table 3. Better ball, match play

Error	Type
.5	(B15)
.7	(2-19), MEAN, (B12), (3-18), USGA
	(3-18), (6-15), MEDIAN
.9	PT1234
>	PT12, (1), (2), (1-5), SPRD, BIRDIES

Table 4. Better-ball, stroke play

Error	Type
1.6	(1)
1.8	(1-5), NORM, (2)
2.0	USGA, (3), (4), (1-15)
>	MEAN, (6-15), PT1234, B15, B12
	MEDIAN, P12, SPRD, (11-20), BIRDIES

Table 5. Best ball of four

Error	Type
2.0	B9, B12, USGA, NORM, (1-5)
2.2	B15, MEAN, PT1234
2.4	MEDIAN, (2), (1)
>	PT12, SPRD, (11-20), BIRDIES

high profile events current systems stand near the top. And last, the normal model, principal contender for a two-dimensional system, fairs well but does not bring truly dramatic improvement. Perhaps there may still be use for such a system for players with extravagant profiles but taking golfers by and large the added complexity would appear to offer little return.

6 References

McCullough, J. (1992)   The Application of the normal probability distribution function model to the analysis of the scores of professional golfers. **Anglia Polytechnic University.**

Scheid, F.J. (1990)   On the normality and independence of golf scores with various applications, in **Proceedings of the First Scientific Congress of Golf** (ed. A.J. Cochran), E.& F.N. Spon, Chapman and Hall, London, pp.147-152.

36 Outlier identification procedure for reduction of handicaps

D.L. Knuth, F.J. Scheid and F.P. Engel
USGA Handicap Research Team, Far Hills, NJ, USA

Abstract
The USGA Handicap Research Team developed a procedure to identify exceptionally low net tournament scores below a threshold of acceptability. The procedure was implemented in the USGA Handicap System in 1991 to automatically reduce the USGA Handicap Index of any player who has returned two or more exceptional net tournament scores (from special competitions designated by the golf club). This Formula was developed using combinatorial theory, the normal model and sampling theory and tested using empirical data. Tournament scores are tracked for a calendar year and two exceptional tournament scores will be applied to re-compute a lower USGA Handicap Index, overriding the usual USGA Handicap Formula which uses the best 10 of the latest 20 scores.

The process has resulted in lowering the handicaps of one-half of one percent of the 3.4 million American golfers with USGA Handicap Indexes. Reports from golf clubs indicate that those players being reduced are often the same players who previously were dominating handicap competitions. The procedure continues to evolve based on research and data analysis.
Keywords: Exceptional Tournament Score, Handicap, Reduction of Handicap, Net Competition.

1 Introduction
The United States Golf Association Handicap Research Team (HRT) has studied the reliability and accuracy of the USGA Handicap System since 1979. Through the introduction of the USGA Course Rating System and the USGA Slope System in 1983, USGA Handicaps have become portable from course-to-course. A remaining problem affecting the reliability of handicaps was that a very small number of golfers would repeatedly score so well in major handicap competitions that it would diminish the enjoyment of the game for the entire field of players. Some of these exceptional performers have been labeled "sandbaggers" or "mug hunters," but many times honest golfers naturally play better than normal in major competitions.

The HRT undertook a study to determine methods of identifying outlying low scores. These scores were defined by establishing low occurrence rates (1/200) to identify exceptionally low scores and to adjust the handicaps of identified golfers

Science and Golf II: Proceedings of the World Scientific Congress of Golf. Edited by A.J. Cochran and M.R. Farrally. Published in 1994 by E & FN Spon, London. ISBN 0 419 18790 1

downward to a probably level based on these scores.

The study eventually led to a procedure that was tested widely and then implemented throughout the United States in 1991. This procedure has reduced the handicaps of approximately 16,000 golfers of the 3,400,000 golfers nationwide (0.47%).

2 Defining the Golfer and Equitable Net Competitions

USGA research in 1974 by T. Bogevold studied the relationship between handicap level and the odds of scoring low net scores. F.J. Scheid in 1979 conducted research into methods to compare more than 100 handicap systems under various forms of competitions. Research using more than 100,000 scores indicated that golfers' scores could be approximated by the normal model, but that the variability of scores, as measured by the standard deviation, varies widely between golfers and that scores are not symmetrically distributed. Poor scores range farther from the mean than good scores and this is generally more pronounced in less skilled golfers than highly skilled golfers. Partly because of the lack of symmetry, the USGA Handicap System Formula is based on a player's better-half scoring average so that potential ability is the basis of the handicap rather than the player's average performance. Net competitions with many competitors have been termed Large Field Net Events (LFNE) and are difficult to handicap equitably even if all player's distributions were identical, which they are not. In a field of 100 players, for example, it can be argued that only one will probably play in the top one hundredth of his score distribution, and in doing so ought to be the winner. This suggests that fair play in LFNE's calls for equalizing the percentile one scores of the competitors, which is not the basis for how players are handicapped. The USGA Handicap Formula came out in Scheid's research as nearly the best formula and was exceeded only slightly by the normal model (The HRT uses mean - 2.326 sigma). In both cases, the median RMS errors were slightly greater than 1.2 stroke. It was concluded that the cause of the error is the fact that the tails of a distribution are hard to define with precision which makes it difficult to arrange fair play in LFNE's. However, the USGA System does better than any other overall when considering that it also does quite well in other forms of play, such as head-to-head match play. Research also indicated that a "Bonus for Excellence" is built into the USGA Handicap System by use of the 96% multiplier and that the multiplier would have to be 113% to make all levels of players equal in individual match play and 101% to equalize net scores in LFNE's to finish in percentile one.

Using a field of 100 golfers playing 36 holes, American players' distribution of handicaps and chances of winning in LFNE's is as follows:

Table 1. Probability of Winning LFNE Based on Handicap

Group	Handicaps	% of USA Men	Probability of Winning
A	10 and under	23.1	.38
B	11 to 15	26.9	.25
C	16 to 20	22.8	.18
D	21 and over	27.1	.19

Using a new data base from 20,000 golfers from 300 clubs in Massachusetts, in 1980 Scheid found an average RMS error of 1.4 stroke in LFNE's and this result was only one-tenth stroke worse than the normal model, which finished best. The problem of producing equity in LFNE's is further complicated by Scheid's finding that a player's individual scoring variability can make a difference in performance of four strokes. Based on 1985 research, a player with a standard deviation of 5 may be getting two strokes too many, while a steady player with Sigma of two may need two more strokes.

3 Identifying Unusual Sequences of Good Scores

F.P. Engel used Bogevold's data in 1983 to determine the likelihood of a player's recording a low sum of negative differentials (net score lower than the Course Rating) using combinatorial theory based on number of rounds played. By grouping the scores by sum of the ones that beat the Course Rating, a well defined linear order to the outcomes was used to identify unusually strong performances. The result was a series of tables based on handicap level and number of rounds. For example, players in the handicap range of 14 to 22 in six rounds will have a one in 121 chance that the sum of his negative differentials is equal to or greater than -8.

The HRT was concerned with how to relate the seemingly many ways that a player could arrive at a low net sum. For example, one score of -8 would have the same sum as two -4's or four -2's. Since the principle of the USGA Handicap System is and has been to reduce the handicap of a player who <u>consistently</u> scores much better in competitions than in informal games, in 1984 the HRT proposed to consider reducing only golfers with at least two exceptional tournament scores. Engel developed new tables based on the following logic:

$$P(\hat{x}_1{=}x,\hat{x}_2{=}y) = \sum_{\substack{i=1 \\ j=1 \\ i \neq j}}^{\substack{20 \\ 20}} P(x_i{=}x)P(x_j{=}y)\cdot P(x_1,i,\ldots,j,x_{20}{\geq}y)$$

where $\hat{x}_1$ and $\hat{x}_2$ are the lowest two scores
for USGA Handicap purposes this simplifies to:

$$P(\hat{x}_1{=}x,\hat{x}_2{=}y) = \binom{20}{2} P(x_1{=}x)P(x_2{=}y)P(x_3{\geq}y)^{18}$$
$$= 190\cdot P(x_1{=}x)P(x_2{=}y)P(x_3{\geq}y)^{18}$$

The values in these tables only include pairs of best negative differentials and determines how many strokes a golfer's handicap should be reduced to allow his best two differential likelihood to be an acceptable "rarity." As an example, consider the golfer whose best two differentials of his last 20 scores were -6 and -8 and the player has a handicap of 15. This event would have a 1 in 7,249 chance. If a threshold of 1 in 258 was established as the limit of reasonability, this player should have his handicap lowered three strokes (three diagonal steps to the left in Table 2).

Table 2. Probability of Two Best Scores Beating Handicap

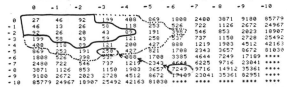

	0	-1	-2	-3	-4	-5	-6	-7	-8	-9	-10
0	27	46	92	199	408	869	1808	2480	3871	9180	85779
-1	46	13	26	58	118	253	526	722	1126	2672	24967
-2	92	26	20	43	89	191	338	546	853	2023	18907
-3	199	58	43	59	121	258	437	737	1150	2728	25492
-4	408	118	89	121	200	427	888	1219	1903	4512	42163
-5	869	253	191	258	427	821	1708	2343	3657	8672	81030
-6	1808	526	338	437	888	1708	3385	4644	7249	17189	****
-7	2480	722	546	737	1219	2343	4644	6225	9716	23041	****
-8	3871	1126	853	1150	1903	3657	7249	9716	14912	35361	****
-9	9180	2672	2023	2728	4512	8672	17189	23041	35361	82951	****
-10	85779	24967	18907	25492	42163	81030	****	****	****	****	****

Tables were produced for five different levels of players. Generally, the odds decrease as handicaps increase because of the increasing variability of scores of higher handicap players.

4 Adopting the Outlier Identification for Tournament Scores

Engel refined his tables in 1985 for use with tournament score identification. Unlike, the CONGU (Council of National Golf Unions) system, the USGA Handicap System uses all scores, whether made in casual rounds or in competitions. "Tournament scores" are special rounds resulting with winners as determined by the Committee and announced in advance.

In converting the outlier identification procedure to one which identifies only tournament scores as the outliers, the handicap adjustment procedure is complicated by the fact that the adjustment is a function of the actual sequence of tournament score differentials and not just a function of the sum of the negative differentials.

Scheid studied net differentials in 1989 by using the normal model and different sets of mean and standard deviation as the basis for scoring performance. His conclusion was that the more reliable mechanism for identification and reduction would be to average a player's two best tournament scores and factoring in the number of tournament scores reported. Having studied combinatorial and the normal model methods of determining outlier scores, Scheid approached the problem using sampling theory with a sample of 20,000 golfers. His tables agreed closely with Engel's earlier work. He also concluded that to base the acceptance level on a probability of 1/200 makes no sense unless long-term tournament score performance records are maintained, because controls are not being enforced well if players are allowed to score "once-in-a-lifetime" tournament scores every twenty rounds. Lowering the acceptance level (error) to say one in 50 instead of one in 200 would penalize many honest players.

5 First Reduction Procedure Introduced to American Clubs

In 1988, the USGA approved including in the Handicap Manual a guideline for golf clubs to mathematically determine handicap reductions. This procedure appeared in the 1989 USGA Handicap System Manual. The first process read as follows:

"Generally, if there are two or more scores among either the player's last 20 scores or any scores made in the current season, and the handicap differentials of the two best tournament scores are at least three strokes better than his USGA Handicap Index, the Committee would be justified in reducing the player's USGA Handicap Index to a value equal to the second-best tournament differential plus three. Example: The USGA Course Rating is 70.6, the Slope Rating is 130 and the player's USGA Handicap Index is 17.6. The player's best two scores in competition are an 82 and 83. The second-best tournament differential is 10.8 (83-70.6 x 113/130 = 10.8). Since this differential is more than three strokes better than 17.6, the Committee would be justified in lowering the player's USGA Handicap Index to 13.8 (10.8+3=13.8)."

This procedure was quickly adopted by major handicap services and was provided as a tournament score tracking service. Golf clubs would identify tournament scores with a "T" next to such scores and the handicap service companies would provide recommended handicap reductions for exceptional players based on the above formula.

Based on Scheid's research, Engel recomputed his probability tables in 1990 to use the average of the best two tournament scores.

6 Automatic Reduction of Handicap Based on T-Scores

By 1990, the number of golfers identified for handicap reduction was in the thousands, but only a small percentage of clubs had taken action to reduce the handicaps of such players. Surveys by state golf associations indicated a desire of the clubs to take action, but a reticence on the club's part to do so. Many clubs asked the USGA to make the reduction procedure automatic and a part of the USGA Handicap Formula.

At a four-day meeting of the HRT in September, 1990, the Committee combined the most recent works of Scheid and Engel to develop a simplified table that would ultimately lead to an automatic procedure that would be included in the 1991 USGA Handicap System Manual for implementation by all golf associations and golf clubs and their computation services by January 1, 1992.

The procedure now in effect can be summarized as follows:

a. Save tournament scores contained within the player's last 20 scores or any made within the current calendar year.

b. If a player has two or more eligible tournament scores (see Section 7a) and at least two tournament score differentials are at least three strokes better than the player's current Handicap Index, proceed to c.

c. Average the two lowest tournament score differentials.

d. Add the result to the following performance limit based on number of T-Scores and round to a tenth:

Number of eligible T-Scores	Performance Limit
2	3.0
3	3.5
4	4.0
5	4.3
6-9*	4.5
10-19*	5.0
20-29*	5.5
30-39*	6.0
40 or more*	6.5

*table extension effective January 1, 1995

e. If the resulting value is at least 1.0 less than the original Handicap Index, the result becomes the player's new USGA Handicap Index unless overridden by the club Handicap Committee.

7 Example

a. A player has a USGA Handicap Index of 17.6, three eligible tournament scores and his lowest two are 82 and 83 scored on a course with a Course Rating of 70.6 and a Slope Rating of 130.

b. Tournament score differentials are:

$$(82-70.6) \cdot \frac{113}{130} = 9.9$$

$$(83-70.6) \cdot \frac{113}{130} = 10.8$$

10.8 is 6.8 less than the 17.6 Index

c. Average of the best two = 10.35

d. Performance limit for 3 T-Scores is 3.5, 3.5+10.35 = 13.85, round to 13.9

e. New USGA Handicap Index is 13.9 instead of 17.6.

8 Concluding Remarks

The support for this procedure has been overwhelming. 92% of 7,200 golf clubs surveyed have responded that the procedure is a good change to the Handicap System and that it identifies the right golfers. The HRT continues to refine the procedure with emphasis on using T-Scores from a moving twelve month window and seeking ways to keep from reducing declining players whose early year tournaments are much better than their current performance. The result of combining the different handicap tables has caused the error to be approximately one in 200 for higher handicap players, one in 300 for average players and one in 400 for low handicap players. Many clubs would like to see the performance limit values reduced so that reductions are greater with an error level of approximately one in 100.

9 References

Bogevold, T. (1974) **Computer Assisted Handicap Survey**, USGA

Engel, F.P. (1983) **Identifying Unusual Sequences of Good Scores**, USGA

Engel, F.P. (1984) **Handicap Adjustments Under Section 8-3**, USGA

Engel, F.P. (1985) **Arresting the Sandbagger via T-Scores**, USGA

Engel, F.P. (1990) **Best Two T-Scores Analysis**, USGA

Scheid, F.J. (1979) **The Search for the Perfect Handicap**, USGA

Scheid, F.J. (1979) **Golf Competitions Between Individuals**, USGA

Scheid, F.J. (1980) **The Search for the Perfect Handicap, Part II**, USGA

Scheid, F.J. (1985) **A Note on Handicapping Error and Sigma**, USGA

Scheid, F.J. (1989) **Average of Two Best T-Scores**, USGA

Scheid, F.J. (1989) **T-Scores Follow-Up**, USGA

Part Two
The Equipment

37 The state of the game, equipment and science

F.W. Thomas
Technical Director, United States Golf Association, Far Hills, NJ, USA

Abstract
The game of golf has a long history, and today it is enjoyed by an ever increasing number of golfers around the world.

The governing bodies of the game, The United States Golf Association (USGA) and the Royal and Ancient Golf Club of St. Andrews (R&A), promulgate and interpret the rules. The object is to preserve and protect the traditions of the game and the challenge it presents.

Equipment design has evolved over time, and progress has been made based on trial and error, rather than the application of scientific principles. This is changing, and science is starting to take its place in the industry. Competition for part of the $5 billion market requires that products with superior performance properties be produced. Hype, without sound data to support it, has sufficed in the past, spurred on by a natural phenomenon, which results in an initial but short lived improvement in performance with each new piece of equipment.

The stories of improved performance are of great concern to many who care about the future of the game. Some have suggested that more rigid performance standards should be adopted.

A review of performance statistics over the last 25 years, and scoring over the last 50 years, does not seem to indicate an improvement beyond reason.
Keywords: The Game of Golf, Rules, Golf Market, Science in Golf Equipment Design, U.S. PGA Tour Statistics, USGA/R&A.

1   Introduction

The views expressed herein are those of the author, borne of 20 years experience in setting standards, ruling on golf clubs, considerable effort trying to understand the science of it all and a lifelong love and fascination of this most challenging of games.

The game of golf has been played in one form or another for more than 400 years. The rules have not changed significantly since they were formally documented in 1774 (220 years ago). In spite of Peter Guthrie Tait's work and publications over 100 years ago, club design, and until recently, ball design, has not had a scientific base, but rather followed a path of trial and error. Science is now taking its place in the game, and this will result in a better understanding of why clubs and balls perform the way they do, rather than in discovering a dramatically different club or ball design, or a swing technique, which will alter the game

Science and Golf II: Proceedings of the World Scientific Congress of Golf. Edited by A.J. Cochran and M.R. Farrally. Published in 1994 by E & FN Spon, London. ISBN 0 419 18790 1

forever.

The game of golf is, however, an activity from which people derive a great deal of satisfaction. Although the real numbers are hard to establish, by the most conservative estimates golf is played and enjoyed by approximately 35 million people around the world, and this number is growing, as is the industry.

Manufacturers are supplying a demand driven mostly by our insatiable urge to get a little more out of equipment than we are prepared to work for. Our wishes seem to be granted by each new piece of equipment we decide to purchase, as this seems to carry with it a presently unexplained phenomenon, which temporarily separates our minds from interfering with our natural swing movements, exposing our real potential for a brief period of time. From the golfer's standpoint, our inability to understand or quantify the effect or control that the mind has over our performance makes us vulnerable and gullible to those who sell hope. In this regard we are slow learners, as we seem to come back for more over and over again. We rationalize that this improvement is due to the only thing which is different, i.e., our new piece of equipment. It is from this form of logic that fads and fears are born. Fads, in that manufacturers derive a false sense of achievement from initial success stories, and the hype follows. The excitement then slowly fades, when reality sets in, and the golfer's mind eventually finds its rightful place of interfering with his swing, resulting in a return to prior performance levels. The "magic" is gone, but the quest to find it elsewhere goes on. It seems to be true that the seeking and anticipation is more exciting than the actual finding.

It is also a part of the game, that those who are the most caring, express concern that the game is being spoiled by new equipment. Such concerns have been expressed for more than 100 years, and we can anticipate they will be expressed 100 years from now. Small changes have occurred in the game; golfers have improved, as have golf courses.

Real improvements in equipment have happened, even by design, but none of these improvements have had a measurable effect on performance; and many have probably enhanced the enjoyment of the game.

The most highly skilled have turned their avocation into a full-time profession, due in part, to the dramatic growth in the financial incentives. But even at the highest level of competition there is little evidence to show that the game has been detrimentally affected by improvements in course maintenance, teaching and training techniques or new equipment.

Science will show that new designs can improve performance minimally, and statistics seem to indicate that this is nowhere near the magnitude that some fear, or others would like.

2   The Game

The game of golf is one of a few activities which allows us to satisfy a subconscious urge to evaluate ourselves. There is this need in man periodically, on a very personal level, to take stock of himself and truthfully compare what he finds to a basic set of self established values. Thus, only he can be the judge of his success or failure. Golf exposes many of our strengths and weaknesses to our playing companions, but much more so to ourselves. We are both humbled and strengthened by our participation and derive an inner warmth from achieving our goals, seldom experienced elsewhere. Without this very personal challenge that golf presents, the game would be without real substance.

3   Governing Bodies

The United States Golf Association (USGA) and Royal & Ancient Golf Club of St. Andrews (R&A) promulgate, and interpret the rules of the game. They also conduct major national and international competitions and enforce the amateur status code. The strength of these governing bodies lies in their ability to persuade golfers that what they stand for and do is good for the game of golf. Golfers have an intuitive understanding of a need for rules which will protect the traditions of the game and preserve the challenge it offers. This is the invisible bond between golfers and the rules making bodies. Golfers will support and abide by the rules if they make good sense.

It is understood by the administrators of the game, as it is by the participants, that a golfer's *needs* and *wants* differ fairly dramatically at times.

"Sure I *want* a club that is guaranteed to drive the ball 250 yards straight down the middle of the fairway." After a moment of reflection, however, it becomes obvious that we don't *need* this club. When the golfer comes to this conclusion, he is probably as close to a philosophical understanding of what the game is all about, as he will ever be. The governing bodies must, however, be forever vigilant and able to distinguish between the needs and the wants. In this regard, the Rules are designed to preserve and protect the game and what it has to offer. Most golfers and manufacturers understand and respect this but may not always like it.

4   Equipment Rules

The playing rules were formally drawn up in 1774 and Equipment rules first appeared in the Appendix of the Rule Book in the 1920's. Prior to this there was little concern about innovations in club design, which would potentially have a detrimental effect on the skill required to play the game. Most concerns were about the ball. It was surmised that little could be done to the club, thus, an all encompassing and vague clause was introduced, which stated that "clubs shall be of the traditional and customary form and make and shall contain no contrivances such as springs." With slight modification and a very liberal interpretation of the words "traditional and customary," this clause might suffice today.

From the turn of this century, many caring golfers have expressed their concern about improved ball performances, specifically, as it relates to distance. In 1907 it was feared by some that the average drive would soon be 300 yards and that every golf course would need to be lengthened and redesigned. A cartoon, describing a new course design concept to cope with this potential problem, which shows bunkers and greens on wheels, was published in 1912.

The size and weight of the golf ball took some time to settle on. The number "1.62" was chosen. This was used for both size (in inches) and weight (in ounces). The USGA moved to a larger size in 1932 making it a minimum of 1.68", holding the maximum weight at 1.62 ounces. This became the international standard size and weight in 1990. It was not until 1942 that a standard, limiting the coefficient of restitution of balls, was adopted by the USGA.

In 1976 an Overall Distance Standard (O.D.S.) was adopted, after it was recognized that controlling weight, size and coefficient of restitution were insufficient to control the distance a ball would fly. The O.D.S. did not isolate any of the properties contributing to overall performance but lumped them all into a crude, but relatively effective test.

The ball was at last under control, and a method of measuring overall performance was in hand. This gave some comfort to those who believed that under average launch conditions, without these standards, it is possible that the ball may go 400 yards or more.

In general, golf club rules have their roots in a general understanding that we should retain some traditional values of the game. From a performance point of view, fear of the unknown has probably had the most influence over the introduction of the club specifications.

It is the concern of the rules makers that new equipment not covered by existing specifications is going to spoil the game, which has influenced the dramatic increase in research funds aimed at a thorough scientific investigation of golf. The current object of that investigation is to analyze and model the interaction between man, the club and the ball, as well as its flight path.

This does not mean that the rules designed to maintain some of the traditional values of the game will be abandoned, but rather that the governing bodies will better understand how and why equipment performs the way it does. Thus, they will be in a position to anticipate problems, and also able to more effectively and rapidly evaluate new ideas, when introduced.

5   State of Equipment Design

Golf club design with few exceptions, is still an art form without any real scientific basis. Ball design has, however, been influenced by science. The introduction of new materials and processes has brought *production* into the "high tech" world, but club design, based on science, is lagging. This is not to say that today's equipment is not good in doing what it is supposed to do, but rather that it did not get there through science. However, we now have the tools to evaluate existing designs and determine properties not previously understood or measurable, such as exact location of c.g., inertia ellipsoids, acceleration, impact and aerodynamic forces, and various other dynamic properties.

Computers to aid in design and manufacturing have taken their place in research & development departments, but more to assist in the manufacturing process, than to adapt scientific principles to the design of equipment. This is now changing.

6   Hype & Marketing?

It is very common that extraordinary performances are credited to new equipment by the golfer, his golfing companions, and the manufacturer "The Placebo Effect". The manufacturer would like to believe that the new design actually works, and the golfer would like to believe the manufacturer's claims. This synergistic form of wishful thinking results in a temporary dislocation of the golfer's mind from interfering with his body. He is on the fringes of the world of "make believe," and the results are extraordinary. The golfer swings better, and the manufacturer takes heart (considerably more than he should) from this extraordinary performance. This then snowballs, sending the manufacturer's marketing division into a "hype frenzy." The elders of the game understandably express concern and call for something to be done to curb this new innovation. At the same time, they seem anxious to get their hands on the particular piece of equipment in question. This cyclical phenomenon is as predictable as winter following summer, and almost as common.

7   Improvements in Performance

Yes, real improvements have been made and competitive scores at the highest skill levels are decreasing, and the average score of the field is decreasing faster than winning scores -- all for many reasons. The question is, is this rate of improvement explainable and acceptable?

In every athletic activity in which man is involved, he is getting better. It is the nature of competition to be the best. To unseat the best calls for greater skills and greater dedication. In today's world, where the financial incentives continue to grow, it only adds to the dedication to excel. A better understanding and analysis of successful swing techniques by teachers, and control of mental attitudes by sports psychologists will continue to produce athletes with improved skills and better performances. This rate of improvement is decreasing, however. There is, as some have theorized, a limit to our physical abilities, and we are slowly approaching this limit in many athletic activities. We cannot believe that golf is immune to both a natural rate of improvement and some limit in performance.

At something less than the highest levels of competition (99.9% of us), many of the same tangible incentives to improve don't exist. It is only the competitive nature in man that provides the drive to get better, and in golf, that competition is probably more with ourselves than with others. Some data does exist that indicates that the weekend golfer is not improving in his abilities.

The reasons for our extraordinary but fleeting exhibits of brilliance in performance, be it a single shot or an entire round, are real, but difficult to explain. We are inclined to remember and build on these, crediting our new equipment for this improvement. We forget the bad times that follow, which often result in that piece of equipment finding a place deep in our closet. This equipment, when it is discovered years later, again performs the way it did when it was new. It seems to have generated what it had lost while in seclusion.

8   Science and Golf

Science has at last entered every aspect of the game of golf. This is, in the most part, due to competition in the marketplace, and thus, the need to produce something that *really is* better. Also, men of science are among those who have taken to the game. From the rules making point of view, it has become evident that a rule which permits only clubs of the "traditional and customary form and make," is extremely important to retain, but may not be sufficient anymore, and that *as science enters the game, so must science be used to protect it*.

The research conducted by the USGA and R&A in Far Hills, New Jersey, will hopefully result in a much clearer understanding of what happens when a club collides with a ball, as well as understanding how the club head manages to arrive at the point just before collision. Not only is it necessary to understand and measure the forces involved in this complex collision, dictated by properties and conditions of the two colliding bodies, but also the results of this collision and to understand and measure the forces acting on the ball while it is in flight.

During the course of these Congress meetings, the research efforts being made to understand the game through the development of reliable models will be presented from various people representing the rules makers, the industry, and the academic world. It is not the intent of the guardians of the game to stifle innovation through their scientific investigation, but rather to preserve and protect the enjoyment for those who participate.

A better understanding of what goes on is not anticipated to result in significantly enhanced performance properties of equipment, as trial and error has taken care of most of this over the last four centuries. Most advances are expected to be made in fitting, and thus, customizing of equipment.

9   State of the Game

By most every count, the game is in good shape. There are more participants than ever before, and the growth rate is increasing. In the United States alone, it is estimated that approximately 505 million rounds of golf were played in 1993. Sales of clubs are, however, lower than expected in most cases, based on the state of the world economy. Ball sales seem to have a continually increasing growth rate. Sales of all other golf related products also seem to be improving.

World wide sales of equipment (balls, clubs, shoes and gloves) were approximately $5 billion in 1993 with ball sales being $1.3 billion and clubs, $2.6 billion. The bottom line is that the game continues to be enjoyed by a growing population. One may conclude, therefore, that something is going right.

10   Concern About Golf's Future

It is of utmost importance to be concerned about the future of all good things, and golf is a good thing.

The game is not static. If equipment, both in material and design, had been frozen three quarters of a century ago, the game would most probably not be where it is today; and certainly not as many people would be enjoying it. Variety in equipment is good, but controlled evolution is probably what is needed. Being overly liberal and catering to the wants of golfers or commercial interests is as detrimental to the future of the game, as is being overly restrictive.

It is in the very nature of those who really care to ask others around them to share in their concern. The response is not to ignore this, but rather to treat it as one would any concern, i.e., identify and define the problem and find a solution. Trying to define the problem may, in itself, determine whether or not we really have a problem.

The specific concerns expressed revolve around the distance balls are now going and how straight they fly, and also how new club designs are making the game easier. In trying to quantify the effect of these claimed improvements, we should isolate the natural improvements in skill from those due to changes in equipment, if this is at all possible. We also need to establish some criteria, against which to judge what is an acceptable change.

This writing is not going to address what changes are acceptable, but will present some information which will place the extent of the problem into the proper perspective.

11   Performance Statistics

The following graphs represent performance data from the US PGA Tour over the last 25 years. They are entitled, Distance, Accuracy, Greens in Regulation, and Putting. During a period from 1969 to 1980 the data was not collected. Scoring data has been presented for each year for a 25 and 50 year period. The first four graphs, Figures 1 - 4, represent the year's average performance for the golfer who has performed best, as well as the golfer in 5th, 15th and 25th place. Scoring graphs, Figures 5 - 7, will show the average of a particular golfer in 1st, 5th, 15th, and 25th place, and the average of the winning scores, the 5th and 25th place scores.

The data has been recorded from at least 40 tournaments each year; many are played at the same sites year after year. Weather and course conditions do change, but the course length has generally remained the same, at approximately 6,900 yards.

Driving Distance (1968 - 1993)

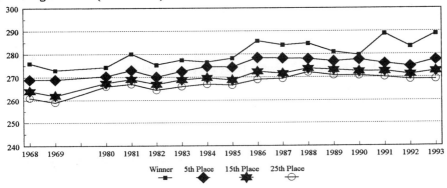

Fig. 1. Distance
This graph represents the individual golfer's yearly average driving distance. 1st, 5th, 15th and 25th places have been plotted for each year, excluding the years 1970 - 1979. There are two measurements made for each round of 18 holes. Total Distances are recorded, whether the ball comes to rest in the rough or fairway.

Driving Accuracy (1968 - 1993)

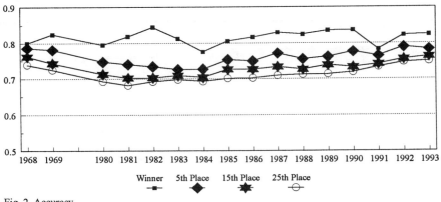

Fig. 2. Accuracy
This graph represents the individual golfer's yearly average percentage of the number of drives hit in the fairway. 1st, 5th, 15th and 25th places have been plotted. (Data from 1970 - 1979, not available.)

Greens in Regulation (1968 - 1993)

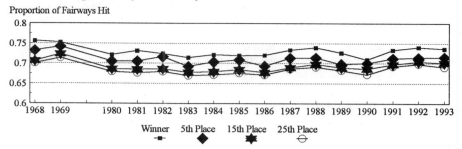

Fig. 3. Greens in Regulation
This graph represents the individual golfer's yearly average of the number of greens hit in regulation. 1st, 5th, 15th and 25th places have been plotted. (Data from 1970 - 1979, not available.)

Putting - putts per round (1968 - 1993)

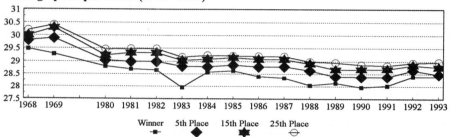

Fig. 4. Putting
This graph represents the individual golfer's yearly average number of putts per round. 1st, 5th, 15th and 25th places have been plotted. (Data from 1970 - 1979, not available.)

Score (1968 - 1993)

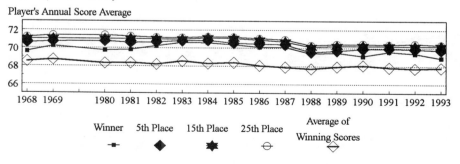

Fig. 5. Scoring
This graph respresents the individual golfer's yearly average scores per round. 1st, 5th, 15th and 25th places have been plotted as well as the average of the winning scores for each year. (Data from 1970 - 1979, not available.)

Scoring Average vs. Winning Score (1937 - 1993)

Fig. 6. Scoring Average vs. Average of Winning Scores
This graph represents a comparison between the best individual golfer's yearly average and the average of winning scores for the years 1940 - 1993.

Scoring Averages (1940 - 1993)

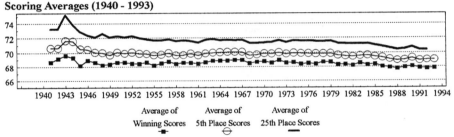

Fig. 7. Scoring Averages
This graph represents the annual average of winning scores, the 5th and 25th place scores, per round.

From a review of the data presented, we find that the driving distance for the best and longest, since 1968, has increased no more than 12 yards. (It should be noted that each year since 1986, the winner of this statistic and others is paid $25,000.) There seems to be no improvement in Accuracy or Greens in Regulation, but Putting has improved approximately one stroke over the 25 year period from 1968 - 1993. A review of scoring over the same period shows an improvement of an amount approximately equivalent to the improvement in putting. The field is getting better, and understandably so. Even though data has been gathered from more than 60 different sites at 40 tournaments each year, and the weather conditions have varied, the numbers seem to be valid.

A regression of the scoring data shows that over the last 25 years, the average winning score is improving at 1 stroke per round per 21 years; the 5th place at 1 stroke per round at 17.5 years; and, the 25th place at 1 stroke per round per 14.5 years. From this we can deduce that the field is getting stronger. If we compare this rate of improvement to most every other athletic activity over a similar period of time we may ask ourselves the question; Why is the rate of improvement not greater than it is?

A review of the data presented does not seem to indicate that there is a great need for concern.

12 Summation

Science is entering golf, and the game can only benefit from this. The consumer will be better informed, the manufacturer will feel more comfortable about his claims, and the rules makers will gain comfort from knowing that they have left no stone unturned to understand and protect the game. Revolutionary new ideas resulting in equipment that will dramatically outperform existing equipment are not expected. Improvements in matching sets and in turn matching these to golfers and optimizing the performance for specific individuals is expected to be a result of the introduction of science.

The game is in good shape; more people are playing and enjoying it, and science is taking its rightful place. We must, however, leave a little room for "magic."

References

Benson, H. (1984) **Beyond the Relaxation Response**, Times Books, New York, NY.

Gould, Stephen Jay (August, 1986) Entropic Homogeneity Isn't Why No One Hits .400 Any More, **Discover Magazine**, pp. 60 - 66.

McKirdy, A.S. (1990) Professor P.G. Tait and the Physics of Golf, First World Scientific Congress of Golf, **Science and Golf**, E & FN Spon.

Record Book of USGA Championships and International Events (1993), Far Hills, NJ

The Rules of Golf (1994), as approved by The United States Golf Association and The Royal and Ancient Golf Club of St. Andrews, Scotland.

US PGA Tour Statistics

38 Golf shafts – a technical perspective

G.P. Horwood
TI Apollo Limited, West Midlands, UK

Abstract
This paper discusses the importance of various golf shaft
characteristics and attempts to differentiate the
technical facts from the marketing hype. It concludes
that with the present understanding of the biomechanics
of the golf swing and the linkage between the golfer and
his equipment, the shaft designer should aim to provide
the widest envelope of characteristics in his product
range along with unambiguous data about these
characteristics to allow the club maker to make informed
choices. This leads on to a discussion of the
significance of new materials in the future development
of golf shafts.
Keywords: Golf Shafts, Swing, Bending Stiffness,
Torsional Stiffness, Bend Point, Weight, Materials.

Possibly more has been written about golf shafts than any
other sporting component of comparable simplicity.
Articles appear regularly in golf magazines on how choice
of shafts for your clubs can affect your golf game.
Shaft manufacturers and independent test laboratories
alike claim to have scientifically proved that one shaft
will hit balls further than another and the most
sophisticated analysis of ball dispersion patterns has
been used to prove that shot accuracy can be improved by
use of a particular shaft.

Are these claims justified or just examples of
advertising hype? What can be said about golf shafts
which will stand up to proper technical examination? A
good starting point is to look at the dynamics of the
swing which may provide some clues.

The trace shown in Fig. 1 is taken from strain gauges
attached to a shaft from which the bending and stress
levels in the plane of the swing can be deduced. This
trace is typical regardless of shaft design or golfer
ability. Note that over half the time covered by the
trace, 2 seconds in total, is taken up by the back swing,
that very violent vibrations occur in the shaft after
impact with the ball and that this impact is an event
which lasts a very brief moment indeed. In fact, for a

Science and Golf II: Proceedings of the World Scientific Congress of Golf. Edited by A.J.
Cochran and M.R. Farrally. Published in 1994 by E & FN Spon, London. ISBN 0 419 18790 1

typical driver, the contact between head and ball lasts
for around .0005 seconds (half a millisecond).

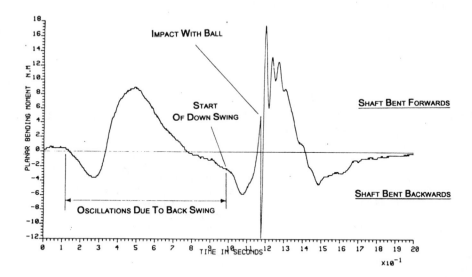

FIG 1 SHAFT BENDING IN A TYPICAL SWING

It can take up to 1 msec for the shock wave to travel
up a steel shaft (longer for some other materials) and
perhaps 20 times longer before the signal has been
processed by the golfer's brain. By this time the ball
is some distance from the club head travelling down the
fairway.

It is obvious that the golfer cannot use information
about the impact to influence the flight of the ball. We
may talk of the feel of a golf shaft but if we take this
word literally it seems that feel is largely
characterised by events which happen after impact. Its
importance is probably more psychological than anything
else, affecting the confidence that the golfer has in his
equipment and conditioning his attitude to his next shot.

Notice that during the down swing the shaft goes from
a bent backwards position to a bent forward position at
the moment of impact with the ball. Generally this
motion is referred to as the recovery of the shaft and
claims have been made about how different shafts,
particularly those made from certain materials, have a
faster recovery than others and can add to club head
speed. Perhaps this is how the term kick point came into

being, the notion that the shaft recovers and "kicks" the ball providing extra distance. This belief is spurious. The recovery is determined by the timing of the swing and is largely a function of the centrifugal and inertia forces, shown in Fig. 2, acting on the shaft from the head and the golfer's hand action.

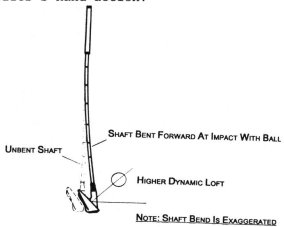

UNBENT SHAFT

SHAFT BENT FORWARD AT IMPACT WITH BALL

HIGHER DYNAMIC LOFT

NOTE: SHAFT BEND IS EXAGGERATED

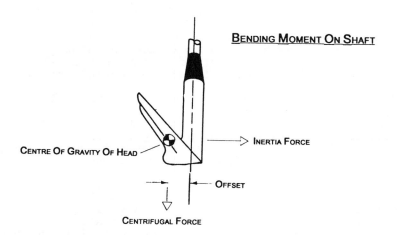

BENDING MOMENT ON SHAFT

CENTRE OF GRAVITY OF HEAD

INERTIA FORCE

OFFSET

CENTRIFUGAL FORCE

FIG 2 SHAFT BENDING IN THE PLANE OF THE SWING

The bending stiffness of the shaft must define the magnitude of the movement from bent back to bent forward but the time for the recovery should be independent of the material from which the shaft is made.

The trace shown in Fig. 1 was actually recorded with a driver using an S flex shaft. A club head speed of approximately 95 mile/h (42.5m/s)was recorded at impact with the ball. The recovery time of the shaft can be measured as 0.1s and the bending displacement from bent back to bent forward was estimated at approximately 5" (12.7cm). A simple calculation indicates that the average head speed for this recovery to occur in this time is 2.8 mile/h (1.25m/s) with a probable maximum speed of around 4.5 mile/h (2.01m/s). While this maximum speed is some 5% of the recorded club head speed at impact, it is unlikely in this case that this recovery component usefully increased the head speed from the overall swing. At the point of impact with the ball the shaft was bent forward and any head speed from shaft recovery is certainly past its maximum and reducing towards zero.

The bending stiffness of the shaft is undoubtedly an important parameter. A more flexible shaft will bend more due to the inertia forces acting on it and the consequences of different timing in the swing will therefore be greater. The more bent forward the shaft is at the moment of impact the more will be the dynamic loft imparted to the head which should lead to a higher ball trajectory.

The above concerns bending in the plane of the swing but the shaft will also bend in the perpendicular plane again due to the centripetal force from the head. The significance of this bending is easily demonstrated.

Fig. 3 is based on observations from testing a club on an Iron Byron swing machine and shows how the address position of the head must be offset to ensure the ball makes contact with the centre of the head during the swing.

This bending of the shaft is a handicap to the golfer making the best contact between head and ball. Some flexibility in the shaft in the plane of the swing may be an advantage but high stiffness in the perpendicular plane is also desirable. This was achieved in some early steel shaft designs which used elliptical cross sections. Unfortunately such shafts are now banned by the Rules of Golf. The non symmetrical section directly conflicts with Rule 4-1 (b) which states that shafts shall have the same bending and twisting properties in any direction.

As described earlier, the fact that the shaft is bent forward at the moment of impact with the ball will impart a dynamic loft to the head. However as shown in Fig. 4 if the distribution of bending stiffness along the length of the shaft can be varied then the magnitude of the dynamic loft can be changed. A shaft which is more flexible towards the tip should provide more dynamic loft to the head than a shaft with a relatively stiffer tip but the same overall bending stiffness.

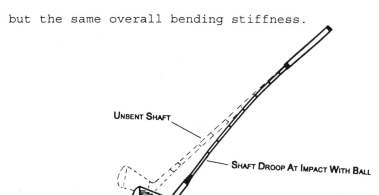

UNBENT SHAFT

SHAFT DROOP AT IMPACT WITH BALL

NOTE : SHAFT BEND IS EXAGGERATED

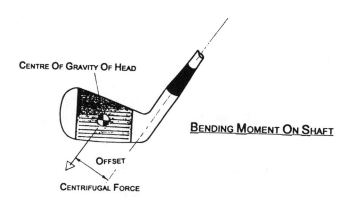

CENTRE OF GRAVITY OF HEAD

BENDING MOMENT ON SHAFT

OFFSET

CENTRIFUGAL FORCE

FIG 3 SHAFT BENDING IN A PLANE PERPENDICULAR TO THE SWING

The significance of this depends on how much the bending stiffness distribution can be varied in practice. Some of the claims made are questionable but the effect is real.

Most existing measurements for kick point are rather incomplete attempts to quantify this bending stiffness distribution. Clearly therefore bend point or flex point are preferred terms to the commonly used kick point. A shaft with a low bend point is more tip flexible and will increase dynamic loft if all other parameters of the swing are unchanged.

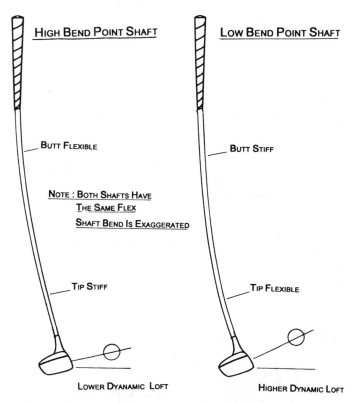

HIGH BEND POINT SHAFT   LOW BEND POINT SHAFT

BUTT FLEXIBLE   BUTT STIFF

NOTE : BOTH SHAFTS HAVE
THE SAME FLEX

SHAFT BEND IS EXAGGERATED

TIP STIFF   TIP FLEXIBLE

LOWER DYANAMIC LOFT   HIGHER DYNAMIC LOFT

FIG 4 EFFECT OF BENDING STIFFNESS DISTRIBUTION ON DYNAMIC LOFT

Since graphite (carbon fibre - epoxy resin composite) shafts were introduced there has been much discussion about the "torque" of golf shafts. Torque as used here is golf terminology and technically an incorrect term for how much a shaft will twist under an applied torsional loading. We should refer to the torsional stiffness of a shaft being high and not that it is a "low torque" design.

As well as bending the shaft forward at the moment of impact with the ball the inertia forces also introduce a torsional load which twists the shaft affecting head alignment. Depending on the torsional stiffness and the bend in the shaft, Fig. 5 shows that the head will always be closed to some extent. A high torsional stiffness as provided by steel shafts should therefore be an advantage in making square contact between the head and ball.

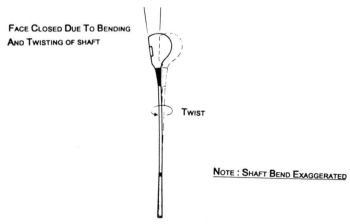

FACE CLOSED DUE TO BENDING AND TWISTING OF SHAFT

TWIST

NOTE : SHAFT BEND EXAGGERATED

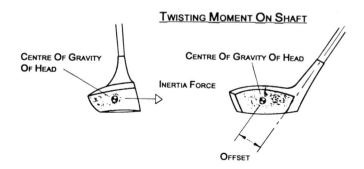

TWISTING MOMENT ON SHAFT

CENTRE OF GRAVITY OF HEAD

CENTRE OF GRAVITY OF HEAD

INERTIA FORCE

OFFSET

FIG 5 EFFECT OF TORSIONAL STIFFNESS ON HEAD ALIGNMENT

In practice however it appears that a fairly wide range of stiffness can be accommodated by players without a serious effect on shot accuracy. The focus on the torsional stiffness of graphite shafts may not be unconnected with the relatively high cost of achieving "low torque" as more expensive high modulus carbon fibre must be used in the shaft construction.

It is interesting to note that much of the motion and bending of the shaft discussed above is brought about by the offset position of the centre of gravity of the head from the longitudinal axis of the shaft. If this offset were eliminated the challenge of making the best contact between head and ball would be much simplified. Unfortunately once again this contravenes the Rules of Golf. Rule 4.1(b) states that the shaft shall be attached to the club head at the heel.

So far the discussed characteristics of the shaft have been more concerned with ball trajectory and shot accuracy than distance. Assuming that good contact is made with the ball, simple physics shows that for a given head weight club head speed will govern distance. While the overall timing of the swing is of great importance it might seem obvious that longer shafts should also achieve greater speed. However, simple mechanical analysis shows this to be largely illusory, added to which it also makes accurate club head contact with the ball more difficult.

Perhaps a more sound approach is to use lighter shafts leading to overall lighter clubs but with the same head weight which again the golfer may be able to swing faster. Although this merits more research, what experimental evidence exists suggests that the swing speed achieved by an individual golfer is quite insensitive to club weight variation introduced by the extremes of shaft weight available today.

The reader by now may be thinking that the shafts in his clubs really are unimportant. This is certainly not the case. While the shaft designer cannot answer the most common request to provide "the best golf shaft in the world" giving maximum distance and accuracy, there is little doubt that matching the clubs to the golfer can bring benefits and that the shaft is the most important element of the club in this respect.

At present we can often do no better than carry out this matching on the basis of personal preference stated by the golfer and observed performance - a rather long winded way of saying trial and error. The understanding of the biomechanics of the golf swing is still in its infancy. It appears that the computer technology now available to measure and record the swing is far in advance of the ability to analyse and deduce from this information what characteristics of the club best suit an individual golfer which would put the matching of the golfer and equipment on a sound technical footing.

While this remains the case the shaft manufacturers should aim to offer the widest possible range of shaft characteristics to the club makers and provide clear unambiguous information so that informed choices can be

made. In short educate rather than baffle with hype.
Here there is a fundamental problem because there are no
agreed standards for shafts which adds to confusion. It
would be quite wrong to standardize the actual
characteristics but nobody would be penalized by
standardisation of the test methods used to measure these
characteristics. The first tentative steps in this
direction have been taken by the recently reformed ASTM
Committee. Whether it is appropriate for such an
organization outside the industry to attempt this task is
perhaps arguable but in the absence of any other
initiative we should wish them success.

All the characteristics of a golf shaft ultimately
depend on the geometry and material used for its
construction. The rules of golf impose severe
limitations on the geometry but fortunately say nothing
about which materials can be used.

The adoption of different materials allows the
envelope of characteristics relating weight, strength and
stiffness to be enlarged. This is important as at the
simplest level the shaft designer aims to achieve a
defined stiffness at a particular weight with an
acceptable strength. The potential benefits of candidate
materials can be assessed by examining their specific
properties.

Fig. 6 shows a comparison of properties for some
materials which could be or have been used for golf
shafts. The specific strength (UTS/density) and specific
stiffness (elastic modulus/density) are shown and for
ease of comparison the specific properties of steel are
taken as unity.

Notice firstly that the specific properties of steel,
aluminium and titanium are very similar. Although
aluminium is a light material with a density
approximately $1/3$ that of steel, the elastic modulus and
tensile strength are similarly lower. This means that in
a golf shaft where the stiffness and strength
requirements are defined by its use, it is difficult to
make a lighter shaft using aluminium than achievable with
steel if the shaft is to have the same overall fitness
for purpose ie. playability and durability.

This does not mean that good golf shafts cannot be
made from aluminium and titanium as well as steel, but
that it is difficult to significantly extend the envelope
of characteristics using other monolithic metals
regardless of the claims made for these materials. Some
may see this as a simplistic view and admittedly
secondary advantages can be gained such as higher damping
and absence of corrosion, but when manufacturing and
material costs, especially for titanium, are added to the
equation the real advantages of these materials become
questionable.

MATERIAL	ELASTIC MODULUS (E) GPa	TENSILE STRENGTH (σ) MPa	DENSITY (ρ) Mg/m^3	SPECIFIC STIFFNESS E/ρ	SPECIFIC STRENGTH σ/ρ
HS CARBON FIBRE	235	3400	1.79	5	7.5
VHS CARBON FIBRE	245	5000	1.8	5	11
IM CARBON FIBRE	294	5500	1.8	6.5	12
HM CARBON FIBRE	390	3400	1.86	8	7
UHM CARBON FIBRE	517	1860	1.96	10.5	4
KEVLAR 49 FIBRE	127	3445	1.45	3.5	9.5
E - GLASS FIBRE	72	3170	2.54	1	5
S - GLASS FIBRE	88	4600	2.49	1.5	7
BORON FIBRE	410	3450	2.6	6.5	5
EPOXY RESIN	4	50	1.3	0.12	0.15
STEEL	193	2070	7.8	1	1
ALUMINIUM 7075	69	565	2.8	1	0.8
TITANIUM 6A-4V	103	1070	4.5	1	1
METAL COMPOSITE (7075 + 17% SiC)	93	650	2.83	1.3	0.86

NOTE :   THE SPECIFIC PROPERTIES ARE SHOWN FOR COMPARITIVE PURPOSES. STEEL HAS BEEN TAKEN AS UNITY

FIG 6   PROPERTY COMPARISON FOR SOME MATERIALS USED FOR GOLF SHAFTS

The table shows the dramatic increase in specific properties available from some high technology fibres. Unfortunately these values are rather misleading in isolation and cannot be achieved in an actual golf shaft. For example a graphite shaft is a composite of carbon fibre and epoxy resin usually containing between 35-45% by volume resin. While the properties of the fibre are very high the properties of the resin are very poor which reduces the overall properties of the structure. The properties also only apply along the fibres and fibre placement in the structure is critical.

Even so, graphite shafts can be made with lower weights than metal shafts and this must be their main advantage. A rational technical explanation for the current interest in "heavy weight" graphite shafts with properties similar to shafts made from steel is hard to provide.

The average golfer is unlikely to be aware of the
fibre used in his graphite shafts except when they
contain boron. The supposed advantages of using boron in
a golf shaft have been heavily promoted but this has led
to many incorrect perceptions and beliefs being held.
Boron has been associated with high torsional stiffness
in shafts and extra distance but the properties of this
fibre and the amount used in a shaft, commonly around 4%
by weight, cannot substantiate these claims. Boron can
be shown to have impressive compressive strength which
may help in re-inforcement of the tip end of shafts but
many shaft designs which do not use boron fibre have been
proven to have adequate tip strength.

Most graphite shafts are made from prepreg sheets of
carbon fibre wrapped around tapered mandrels using labour
intensive methods. Inevitably this produces seams or
discontinuities in the structure of the shaft where the
plies start and end. Coupled with the lack of tension in
the fibres this can lead to nominally identical shafts
having very different bending properties and even
individual shafts having different bending properties in
different planes.

Achieving with graphite the consistency expected from
metal shafts is challenging and some of the most poorly
made graphite shafts may technically not conform to the
rules of golf. Although automated manufacturing
techniques using filament winding or developments of the
pultrusion process coupled with over winding are now
being used which produce "seamless" structures, such
automated processes cannot yet fully compete with the
labour intensive prepreg wrapping method.

New metal composite materials are now becoming
available which on paper at least hold considerable
promise for use in golf shafts. First generation metal
composites are usually made from aluminium alloys
reinforced with ceramic powders or short fibres. The
reinforcement can provide improvements of up to 40% in
specific stiffness and modest gains in strength which
should make it possible to approach graphite shaft
weights. The cosmetic durability of such shafts would be
very good compared to todays painted graphite shafts.
The poor formability and especially the toughness (impact
strength) of these materials are the main barriers to
bringing them to the market place.

Golf still remains today more an art than science.
Although our technical understanding will continue to
improve it is unlikely that the element of magic will
ever be totally removed and this is probably for the good
if the game is to retain its attraction.

Of course it is valid to use technical feature to
promote product and we must hope for the health of the
industry that people continue to change their equipment

in order to improve their game. However shaft designers should always guard against believing their own hype and remember that golf is played on golf courses and not in the laboratory.

39 The dynamic performance of the golf shaft during the downswing

J.H. Butler and D.C. Winfield
True Temper Sports, Olive Branch, Mississippi, USA

Abstract
This paper analyzes the performance of golf shafts by using
the computer as well as experimentation. The finite
element method was used to analyze the effect centrifugal
loading has on the natural frequency of the club during the
swing. An experimental technique was established to
measure the shaft deflection and twisting during the swing.
Different variables relating to the overall dynamic
performance of the shaft during the downswing were analyzed
and discussed.
Keywords: Shaft Deflection, Centrifugal Loading, Natural
Frequency, Downswing.

1 Introduction

One of the more interesting aspects of the golf shaft is
how it responds dynamically during the swing. Many times
oversimplifications are made concerning how the shaft
deflects during the swing. The main goal of this paper is
to seek a better understanding of shaft dynamics and to
find key variables that characterize the dynamic
performance of the shaft during the swing.

2 Computer Modeling of the Club

The finite element method was used to analyze different
golf clubs in the computer. Different shafts were divided
into over 100 beam elements per shaft and properties
including frequency, torsional stiffness, mass, and center
of gravity were verified. A typical clubhead was attached
to the shafts using point inertia and rigid massless bar
elements. A modal analysis was then performed to extract
the frequencies and mode shapes of the club with a grip
that was clamped at the butt end. Mode 1, which occurred
at 4.26 Hertz, consisted of the shaft twisting 0.33 degrees
for every one inch of lateral deflection closely resembling
that of a cantilevered beam. This means if the shaft is

Science and Golf II: Proceedings of the World Scientific Congress of Golf. Edited by A.J.
Cochran and M.R. Farrally. Published in 1994 by E & FN Spon, London. ISBN 0 419 18790 1

deflected forward 1 inch, the clubhead is twisted 0.33 degrees causing the clubhead to close or hook. This ratio relates the bending stiffness of the shaft, the torsional stiffness of the shaft, and the amount of center of gravity offset of the club. It should be emphasized that the club when gripped by a human is not actually clamped and will exhibit natural frequencies that are slightly lower than that of a rigidly clamped shaft as indicated by Okubo and Simada (1990).

During the downswing the club is moved in a double pendulum configuration where the clubhead can be traveling as fast as 120 mph with a rotational velocity of more than 50 radians per second at impact. During this type of rotational motion, a centrifugal force which can be higher than 50 pounds stiffens the club. In this stiffened state when the club has a rotational velocity of 50 radians per second, mode 1 of the shaft is stiffened up to 10.01 Hertz. The centrifugal load also causes the club to deflect in the toe down direction relative to the clubhead as well as kick forward in the lead/lag direction.

It should be noted that the stiffness of the club is constantly changing during the downswing. In order to calculate the deflection of the shaft during the swing, the applied forces and torques supplied by the golfer must be known. These forces and torques can be derived using high speed photography as performed by Vaughan (1981). However, an experimental method can be used to actually measure the deflections of the shaft during the downswing and analyze the performance of the shaft under different types of loading conditions supplied by different golfers.

3 Experimental Analysis

3.1 Measurements of Shaft Deflection During Downswing
In order to measure the deflection of the shaft during the downswing, longitudinal strain gauges were attached to the club near the grip end in the toe up/down and lead/lag directions. These strain gauges were calibrated to measure the shaft tip deflection due to cantilever bending. As indicated in section 2, cantilever bending deflection closely resembles the lateral deflection of mode 1. Other experimental work by the authors using multiple strain gauges along the shaft in the toe up/down and lead/lag directions has indicated that mode 1 deflection predominates over the entire downswing. Shear strain gauges placed near the tip end of the shaft were calibrated to measure the shaft tip twisting angle. During the swing, strain data was taken at 50000 Hz on each gauge.

A typical set of data is shown on Fig. 1. Deflection in the toe up/down direction was plotted so that positive deflection relates to toe up defection. Lead/lag deflection was plotted so that positive deflection relates

the shaft bent forward or leading the hands. Positive
rotation in degrees related the shaft twisting where the
clubhead is closed or "hooked". The data in the graph
starts when the toe up/down defection is zero. This
instant was used to flag the initiation of the shaft
loading which usually occurs just prior to the downswing.
    As shown on Fig. 1, the shaft experiences almost all of
its deflection during the start of downswing in the toe
up/down direction. The centrifugal load causes the shaft
to deflect in the toe down direction just prior to impact.

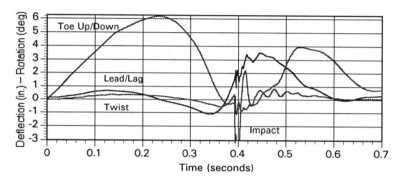

Fig. 1.   Deflection curves number 1.

    After the toe up/down deflection reaches its peak and
the golfer rolls his wrists, the shaft then kicks forward
in the lead/lag direction where it is bent forward or
leading at impact. The optimum condition is where the
shaft is straight at impact so that kinetic energy is
maximized and stored potential energy is minimized.
    The shaft during the entire downswing did not twist more
than 0.6 degrees and at impact the clubhead is closed by
about 0.5 degrees. This would indicate that the torsional
stiffness of the shaft was great enough to prevent the
shaft and clubhead from twisting too much during the swing.

3.2 Comparison of different types of swings
After hundreds of test trials, it has been found that most
swing profiles fit into one of three categories where the
first type is described in Fig. 1. Graphs from two other
types of swings are shown on Fig. 2 and Fig. 3. It should
be noted that each swing was done by a different golfer
with the same club. The shaft deflection in Fig. 2, has
two distinct peaks in the toe up/down direction. The first
peak in the toe up/down curve in Fig. 2 is caused by the
shaft simply loading up and unloading. When the golfer
feels the shaft start to unload, a strong wristbreak or
shoulder turn probably caused the shaft to load up a second
time causes the second peak. The downswing in Fig. 2 is

longer that of Fig. 1, but the shaft in Fig. 2 was also bent forward at impact. This type of swing generating this deflection pattern could be called a "double peak" swing.

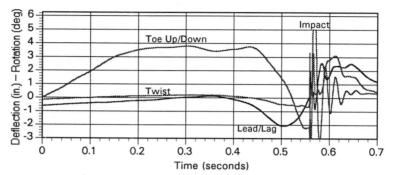

Fig. 2. Deflection curves number 2.

The swing in Fig 3 has a almost linear deflection slope up to the peak deflection in the toe up/down direction. The loading up of the shaft covers a much longer period of time than the unloading of the shaft. Again, the shaft is slightly bent forward at impact. This type of deflection pattern could be called a "ramp-like" pattern.

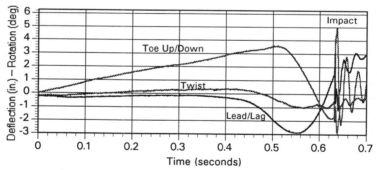

Fig. 3. Deflection curves number 3.

The swing in Fig 1 has a much faster downswing time than that of the other two swings and was loaded with the highest overall swing force as indicated by the peak defection being the greatest of the three. This type of deflection pattern could by named a "single peak" swing pattern.

The experimental measurements of shaft deflection not only show the overall shaft performance, but also show how each golfer loads the shaft. It should be noted that the clubhead velocities at impact on all three swings shown

were measured by a speed indicator to be 103 mph.
Conventional wisdom might say that each golfer needs to use
the same shaft flex. However, that assumption is a great
oversimplification of the problem. In order to select the
proper shaft for a golfer as well as analyze the
performance of the shaft, other swing variables associated
with shaft dynamics must be considered.

3.3 Analysis and discussion of variables that relate the overall shaft performance during the swing

In order to truly characterize the shaft performance during
the downswing, selected variables on the shaft deflection
curves need to be analyzed. A computer program written in
FORTRAN was used to read the swing data shown on the graphs
and pick out the following keypoints of interest on the
shaft deflection curves:

1. load up time: LT (in)
2. peak deflection: PD (in)
3. time at peak deflection: TPD (sec)
4. lead/lag deflection at impact: LDI (in)
5. toe up/down deflection at impact: TDI (in)
6. twist angle at impact: TI (deg)
7. maximum twist angle: MT (deg)
8. kick velocity at impact: KV (in/sec)
9. toe up/down velocity at impact: TV (in/sec)

The load up time or LT occurs approximately at the start of
downswing and is defined as the time from impact to the
start of loading the shaft in the toe up direction. The
peak deflection or PD is simply the maximum deflection of
the shaft in the toe up/down direction during the downswing
while the time at peak deflection points out the amount of
time for the shaft to reach its peak deflection during the
downswing. The lead/lag and toe up/down deflection as well
as the twist angle at impact relate the relative deflection
and rotation of the shaft at the impact position. The
maximum twist angle MT is the maximum relative angle in
degrees that the clubhead is twisted during the swing. The
kick velocity KV relates the speed that the shaft is
deflecting in the lead/lag direction just prior to impact
while the toe up/down velocity TV relates the speed the
shaft is deflecting just prior to impact in the toe up/down
direction. The nine variables for the swings shown are
given below in Table 1.

It is interesting to note the range of certain
variables. For instance, the values for the toe down
deflection at impact TDI ranged from -2.140 to -0.206.
Certainly the golfer used to generate Fig. 2 would need a
different lie angle than that of the golfer used to
generate Fig 1. The peak deflection in Fig. 1 was by far
the highest of the three. Obviously, the golfer in Fig. 1
loads the shaft more rapidly than the other two golfers.

It would seem logical that the golfer used in Fig. 1 would be more suited to using a stiffer shaft than the other two golfers.

Table 1. Values for the variables of the three swings

Variable	Fig. 1	Fig. 2	Fig. 3
LT (sec)	0.391	0.557	0.630
PD (in)	6.181	3.797	3.615
TPD (sec)	0.234	0.304	0.510
LDI (in)	1.531	0.111	1.490
TDI (in)	-0.206	-2.140	-1.709
TI (deg)	0.413	-0.341	-0.472
MT (deg)	0.550	0.677	1.021
KV (in/sec)	89.414	89.414	97.764
TV (in/sec)	13.086	16.641	19.537

Another important factor in analyzing the performance of the shaft would be to take multiple swings for each golfer and take the average and standard deviation of each variable. Also it would be interesting to have golfers swing different clubs with different shaft flexes.

4 Conclusions

The experimental measurements certainly help in understanding how the golf shaft responds dynamically during the swing and allows analysis of a whole new set of variables when considering how the shaft deflects during the swing. With further experimentation with many golfers, the importance of each variable will be better understood. This information could be useful in developing a method to match a particular golfer to the proper shaft stiffness without making the usual oversimplifications that are so common in the golf industry today.

5 References

Okubo, N. and Simada M. (1990) Application of CAE (computer aided engineering) to golf club dynamics, in **Science and Golf: Proceeding of the First World Scientific Congress of Golf** (ed A. J. Cochran), E. and F.N. Spon, London pp. 270-273.

Vaughan, C. L. (1981) A three-dimensional analysis of the forces and torques applied by a golfer during the downswing, in **Biomechanics VIIB** (ed Morecki, A.), University Park Press, Baltimore, pp. 325-331.

40 An investigation of three dimensional deformation of a golf club during downswing

A.M. Brylawski
Department of Mechanical Engineering and Mechanics, Lehigh University, Bethlehem, Pennsylvania, USA

Abstract
A study was undertaken to investigate the influence of shaft flexibility on the positioning of the club face during the downswing. To accomplish this task, a computerized model of deflections occurring in the shaft over the period of the down-swing was developed. Employing Lagrangian dynamics, equations of motion for bending and for twist coordinates of the shaft are produced. In addition to being dependent on stiffness, these deformations are a function of the forces generated by the acceleration of the shaft during the swing. To determine these forces, video images of a real swing are converted to digital data using a motion analysis software package. The equations of motion can then be solved numerically, yielding the position and orientation of the club face over the course of the swing.
Key Words: Stiffness, Shaft Deflections, Mathematical Model.

1 Introduction

Currently, golf shafts are available with different stiffness ratings ranging from regular to extra-stiff. The standard practice is to recommend a more flexible shaft for weaker players, while stronger golfers play with a stiffer shaft. Until recently there has been limited scientific insight into the rational for this advice. An investigation into the significance of shaft stiffness by Milne and Davis (1992) concluded that shaft flexibility does not play an important dynamic role in the golf swing, meaning that there is no advantage gained by a "whipping" effect of a flexible shaft. The only contribution of the deformations is to change the effective loft and lie angles of the club face at impact. This suggests that a golf club with a stiff shaft and the desired loft and lie angles will produce more consistent shots because the initial and the effective loft and lie will be the same. Of course, this is only true if the golfer is able to bring the club head back to the exact address position at the bottom of the downswing. This study is the primary step of an investigation into the magnitude of the deflections occurring in the shaft during the downswing and the effect they have on the position of the club head at impact.

A computerized model has been developed that calculates deformations due to forces and moments applied to the shaft. The computed parameters include the rotation of the shaft about its centerline, the deflection in a direction normal to the club face, and the deflection parallel to the plane of the club face. These three parameters define the position of the club face at any time during the swing.

Science and Golf II: Proceedings of the World Scientific Congress of Golf. Edited by A.J. Cochran and M.R. Farrally. Published in 1994 by E & FN Spon, London. ISBN 0 419 18790 1

The approach of the model development was to determine the equations of motion and boundary conditions using Lagrangian dynamics for a flexible shaft and to solve the equations numerically. The solutions required knowledge of the forces and moments applied to the golf club over the duration of the swing. A motion analysis package that converts video images from multiple cameras to digital data was used to obtain this information.

2 The Model

2.1 Equations of Motion

Three equations of motion and boundary conditions were constructed using Lagrangian dynamics (Meirovitch, 1967). Figure 1 illustrates the coordinate system fixed to the shaft, where the x direction is parallel to the club face, the y direction is the outward normal direction of the club face, and the angle of twist, θ, is measured from the x axis in a counter clockwise direction.

A golf club has a tapered shaft that results in mechanical properties that are a function of its length. The change in these properties result in variable stiffness along the shaft and

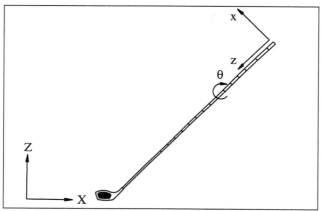

Figure 1 - Coordinate Systems

therefore influences the deflections. For this model, it was assumed that deflections were generated perpendicular to the shaft and a rotation was produced about the centerline of the shaft. The deformation along the length of the shaft was neglected because it does not adversely affect either the loft or the lie angle of the club head. Equations (1), (2), and (3) are the equations of motion in the x, y, and θ directions respectively.

$$\frac{\partial^2 x}{\partial t^2} = \frac{1}{m_z}\left[P_x(z) - \frac{\partial^2}{\partial z^2}\left(EI_z\frac{\partial^2 x}{\partial z^2}\right) + \frac{\partial}{\partial z}\left(P_z\frac{\partial x}{\partial z}\right)\right] \tag{1}$$

$$\frac{\partial^2 y}{\partial t^2} = \frac{1}{m_z}\left[p_y(z) - \frac{\partial^2}{\partial z^2}\left(EI_z\frac{\partial^2 y}{\partial z^2}\right) + \frac{\partial}{\partial z}\left(p_z\frac{\partial y}{\partial z}\right)\right] \tag{2}$$

$$\frac{\partial^2\theta}{\partial t^2} = \frac{1}{I_m}\left[\frac{\partial}{\partial z}\left(GJ_z\frac{\partial\theta}{\partial z}\right)\right] \tag{3}$$

Where,

θ	Deflection in θ direction (radian)
x	Deflection in x direction (m)
y	Deflection in y direction (m)
z	Distance along shaft (m)
t	Time (second)
I_m	Mass moment of inertia per unit length (kg$*$m)
m_z	Mass per unit length (kg/m)
GJ_z	Torsional stiffness (N$*$m^2)
EI_z	Bending stiffness (N$*$m^2)
p_z	Force per unit length in z direction (N/m)
p_x	Force per unit length in x direction (N/m)
p_y	Force per unit length in y direction (N/m)

Forces applied to the shaft are produced by gravity and the acceleration of the club during the swing. The forces that contribute to the bending and twisting of the shaft are primarily due to the club head's center of mass being located off the centerline of the shaft. Local distributed forces are also generated along the length of the shaft as a result of the accelerations of the shaft itself.

Along with the equations of motion, the equations dictating the boundary conditions of the shaft are obtained The boundary conditions incorporate the forces and moments applied to the ends of the shaft (refer to appendix A for these equations).

2.2 Experimental Data

To determine the forces generated during the swing a motion analysis package is used. The package consists of multiple video cameras (operating at a speed of 180 frames/second) which simultaneously record, from different positions, the path of reflectors attached to the shaft. The data for this paper is from a golfer swinging a number 1 metal-wood driver marked with three reflectors attached to the shaft from which an orthogonal coordinate system is defined. A motion analysis soft-ware package converts the marker images into three-dimensional position vectors relative to an inertial coordinate system. The second derivative with respect to time of the position data provides the linear acceleration of the moving coordinate system. Knowing the unit vector in the direction of the shaft and assuming the shaft is rigid, the position vectors along the length of the shaft are obtained. The second derivative of these vectors provide the local accelerations along the shaft. The rotation of the shaft about an instantaneous axis of rotation yields the angular velocity and acceleration of the moving coordinate system (Craig, 1989). Knowing the mass, position, and moments of inertia of the club head the forces applied to the end of the shaft, through the club head, are calculated. This data is then transformed into the moving coordinate system to conform with the coordinates of the equations of motion.

2.3 Solving the Equations of Motion

A procedure called the Numerical Method of Lines (Schiesser, 1991) is used to solve for the deflections. It involves replacing the partial derivatives in the equation of motion by numerical approximations, thereby reducing the partial differential equation (PDE) to a set of ordinary differential equations (ODEs) in time. This process discretizes the equations of motion along the length of the shaft consequently generating an ODE for each segment. The ODEs are solved with a state-of-the-art numerical integrator, LSODE (Livermore Solver for Ordinary Differential Equations) for each section along the shaft (Hindmarsh, 1980). The boundary condition equations for the PDEs are also reduced to ODEs. The results are deflection and torsional data at each discretized segment of the shaft as a function of time.

To demonstrate the model, a solution to the torsional equation (3) is presented. A simplified version of the problem, where the shaft was assumed to have a uniform cross section, was solved. Equation (4) is the simplified equation of motion, where c is the damping factor. The damping term is added to speed up the numerical solution of the problem. The magnitude of this term (c=15) was arrived at experimentally. Through experimenting with different values for damping it was determined that the utilized value did not have an adverse effect of the overall solution. Figure 3 demonstrates the effect of the damping term, the impact of this term is to damp out the fundamental frequency of the shaft.

$$\frac{\partial^2 \theta}{\partial t^2} = \frac{GJ}{I_m} \frac{\partial^2 \theta}{\partial z^2} - c \frac{\partial \theta}{\partial t} \tag{4}$$

Equations (5) through (8) have been selected as plausible boundary and initial conditions applied to this problem. M_z is the moment applied to the end of the shaft about the z-axis.

$$\theta |_0 = 0 \qquad\qquad \frac{\partial \theta}{\partial z}|^L = \frac{M_z|^L}{GJ} \tag{5} \quad (6)$$

$$\theta(t=0) = 0 \qquad\qquad \frac{\partial \theta}{\partial t}(t=0) = 0 \tag{7} \quad (8)$$

3 Results and Discussion

The solution to equation (4) is presented in Figure 2 along with the analytical solution of the torsional deflection of a static shaft subjected to the same boundary conditions. Observe that there is negligible differences between the static and dynamic solution. The static solution was calculated using an analytic model for torsion of a simple tube, while the dynamic solution was determined numerically. Both solutions used the experimentally determined moment applied to the end of the shaft. The peak observed at 1.4 seconds corresponds to the time of impact with the ball. The experimentally determined moment is at a maximum at this time yielding a maximum deflection of approximately 1.5 degrees at the club head. Keep in mind that this calculation was for a simplified steel tube with a uniform cross section.

In addition, an oscillation can be observed in the dynamic solution which corresponds to the fundamental frequency of torsional oscillation for the problem. The frequency of this oscillation is 1056 Hz, which lies between the fundamental frequency of a tube with cantilever boundary conditions (743 Hz) and a tube that is fixed at both ends (1485 Hz). This is due to the torsional stiffening effect of the moment applied to the end of the shaft. Figure 3 depicts the initial part of the solution, where the oscillations are more pronounced. These oscillations die out with time as a consequence of the damping term added to the equation of motion.

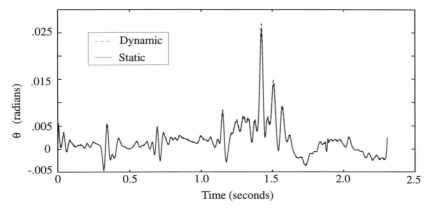

Figure 2 Static and dynamic torsional deflection of a constant diameter shaft

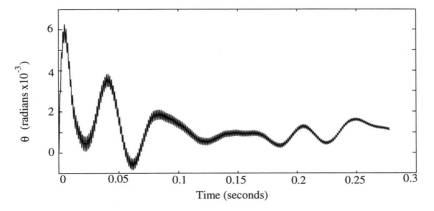

Figure 3 Initial part of torsional solution, illustrating damping of fundemental frequency

4 Conclusion

Initial results support the conclusions reached by Milne and Davis (1992), there was no observable difference between the dynamic and static solution in the presented data. However, further work needs to be completed before an absolute agreement can be made. The bending in the x and y directions need to be determined and the solution for a real shaft (ie. tapered) needs to be solved. Solving the equations of motion has proved to be difficult due to the oscillation in the initial part of the solution. The integrator required excessively small time steps to reach a solution, which resulted in exceedingly long running times.

5 References

Craig, John J. (1989) **Introduction to Robotics, Mechanics and Control**. Addison-Wesley Publishing Company, Reading, MA.

Greenwood, Donald T. (1988) **Principles of Dynamics**. Prentice-Hall, Inc., Englewood Cliffs, NJ.

Hindmarsh, A. C. (1980) **ACM SIGNUM Newsl.**, 15, No. 4, 10.

Meirovitch, Leonard (1967) **Analytical Methods in Vibrations**. Macmillan Publishing Co., Inc., New York, NY.

Milne, Robert D. and Davis, John P. (1992) The Role of the Shaft in the Golf Swing. **J. Biomechanics.**, 25, 975-983.

Schiesser, W.E. (1991) **The Numerical Method Of Lines.** Academic Press, Inc., San Diego, CA.

6 Appendix A. Boundary Conditions

The boundary conditions obtained from the derivation of the equations of motion are presented below. Equations (9) and (10) apply to the x direction equation. The y direction boundary conditions are identical, with y replacing x and M_y replacing M_x. Equations (11) is the boundary conditions for the θ direction.

$$\frac{\partial^2 x}{\partial z^2}\Big|^L = \frac{1}{EI_z|^L}\left[M_y\Big|^L - F_z\frac{\partial x}{\partial z}\Big|^L\right] \tag{9}$$

$$\frac{\partial}{\partial z}\left(EI_z\frac{\partial^2 x}{\partial z^2}\right)\Big|^L = P_z\frac{\partial x}{\partial z}\Big|^L - F_x\Big|^L \tag{10}$$

$$\frac{\partial \theta}{\partial z}\Big|^L = \frac{M_z}{GJ_z}\Big|^L \tag{11}$$

Where, M_x, M_y, M_z are the moments applied to end of the shaft about x, y, and z axis, and F_x, F_y, and F_z are the forces applied to the end of the shaft in the x, y, and z directions.

41 The attitude of the shaft during the swing of golfers of different ability

J.S.B. Mather and M.A.J. Cooper
Department of Mechanical Engineering, University of Nottingham, UK

Abstract
Modern golf shafts are made from a variety of materials. By using composites it is now theoretically possible to match a shaft or a set of shafts to the playing ability of the golfer. Important inputs to this design process are the forces and swing accelerations which different golfers apply to the club. This paper shows how those forces affect the motion of the club during the swing. Time based photographs show the development of the bending properties and calculations based on an FE programme are also given.
Keywords: Golf shaft, golf swing, finite element analysis, photogrammetry.

1 Introduction

For many years manufacturers of golf clubs have advocated the use of different shafts for different swings. The basic concept propagated is that swings achieving high head velocity at impact with high speed rotation of the club about the wrists in the last phase of the swing will require a stiff shaft, whereas those with the same tempo but at a slower speed (particularly the hand action) will require a more flexible shaft. The operative word in that statement of the concept is *tempo*, which implies the same relative timing of the swing pattern i.e. whatever the swing speed, the correct timing is achieved. This situation accounts only for a very small percentage of amateur golfers in the world. Many golfers produce swings where the phasing is totally different (see for instance reference 3), with the wrists uncocking very early in the downswing, and the club moving out of the normal plane. The club is then brought back to the ball on a plane which causes a slicing effect at impact. The clubhead velocity maximises during the *first* part of the downswing at a value very similar to that of the good golfer but then slows to a value at impact some 60% of the maximum. Much of the potential is wasted which, added to the slicing effect on the ball, results in a very poor shot with no appreciable distance and often in the rough to the right of the fairway.

It may be argued that such golfers should learn the correct timing to the swing - a timing to match their ability, but it could be that this is precluded by the unsuitability of the clubs for the amateur golfer. Thankfully, manufacturers are at last beginning to address this situation. Many golfers therefore come to accept the inevitability of the situation and either abandon the game altogether or learn to play by compensating for their deficiencies. Neither of these need happen, if equipment could be produced which

Science and Golf II: Proceedings of the World Scientific Congress of Golf. Edited by A.J. Cochran and M.R. Farrally. Published in 1994 by E & FN Spon, London. ISBN 0 419 18790 1

amateur golfers are able to use and control. That equipment can only be designed if the force/time values for different swings are known. Such swings and their differences are presented in this paper and comments are made on shaft suitability.

The shaft is known to bend notably during the swing. For a driver, the measured amplitudes of head displacement at impact for a good swing can be up to 50 mm in both the plane of the swing and perpendicular to it, which, depending on the geometry of the shaft, could increase the club loft by some 5°. For a poor swing the dynamic loft will be different because of the different phasing of the forces. One aim of this paper is to show how that difference can be accurately measured and predicted.

2 Experimental Methods

The primary aim of our experimental work is to find the accelerations of and hence the forces between the golfer and the club during the swing for a variety of golfers. Realising the difficulties that will arise with the boundary condition in the theoretical calculations, the following method was adopted. Markers were placed on the shaft of the club near to the bottom of the grip (see figure 1) at point O, defined as the origin. At this location

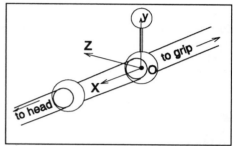

Figure 1

(confirmed by our tests) the deflection and gradient of the shaft are both zero. The markers are simply two spherical balls mated to the shaft at a distance apart of 50 mm with a third sphere placed on a thin bar some 30 mm from the line of the shaft and in the plane of the face of the club. This arrangement defines the undeformed axis of the shaft and the position of the head.

Three high speed strobes were used to illuminate different parts of the swing. Strobe rates of between 50 and 100 flashes per second were found to give satisfactory results for different swing speeds.

Two 35 mm SLR cameras with motorised drives were placed at a distance of 3 metres from the subjects and 1 metre from each other (see next section). A laser switch, which was broken at the upper part of the upswing, was used to trigger the electronic delays from which the shutters on the cameras were opened and closed. In this way different parts of the swing can be studied.

Subjects were chosen for the variety of their swings, judged initially by handicap. All were golfers of some experience. In most of the tests the golfers were asked to strike a lightweight ball. Surprisingly, at least to us, some evidence has emerged from our tests that there is a significant difference between the swings of the same golfer when the ball is present.

3 Photographic analysis of the swings

In our early studies, the cameras were placed orthogonally and a three dimensional picture of the swing was derived by digitising the two photographs and smoothing the data with splines of different order. From this the velocities and accelerations could be found. It was discovered that, even with corrections for lens distortion, the system is very inaccurate, leading to even larger inaccuracies in the forces. It was replaced with a method based on photogrammetry which is described more fully in references 1 and 2. This uses the same cameras (but now placed at any convenient location) and corrects for lens distortion, and film flatness by incorporating into the picture control points whose positions are very accurately known from measurements using surveying equipment. Such a system is described more fully in reference 3 and results in spatial accuracies of less than 2 mm. In fact, the cameras are in close proximity at one end of the laboratory and each takes in the whole of the swing pattern together with all of the control points in the swing area. The authors would strongly advise any researcher wishing to study the golf swing experimentally to embark at the outset on photogrammetry, either using metric cameras (which are very expensive) or a recognised calibration method for non-metric cameras.

4 Theoretical calculations

Any procedure to calculate the deflection of the clubhead will depend on the boundary condition assumed for the grip of the hands. This has proved to be troublesome for many researchers who have used a variety of conditions from fully encastre to free. The real case must be somewhere between. In our case no such difficulty exists. Since we have the markers on the club we can determine the accelerations of this area of the club. From a knowledge of this, the position of the markers in space and the geometry and material properties of the club, the movement of the shaft and the position on the clubhead in space can be calculated.

Commercial finite element packages are available but are cumbersome to use especially when the forces applied vary with time and space and the club to which they are being applied is moving. It was therefore decided that a finite element programme would be written specifically for the situation of a thin shaft and an eccentric mass of known geometry.

The acceleration of the club is conveniently expressed in terms of the displacements of its centre of gravity. This takes the form

$$a_G = A + \ddot{u}_G + \alpha \times (r_G + u_G) + \Omega \times \dot{u}_G + \Omega \times (\dot{u}_G + \Omega \times (r_G + u_G))$$

where A and α are the translational and rotational accelerations and Ω is the rotational velocity about the origin O on the club, and r_G and u_G respectively the position of the CG and its displacement relative to its undeformed position.

This leads to the solution of the system of equations

$$[M]\ \ddot{u} + [C]\ \dot{u} + [K]\ u\ =\ R$$

where R represents the forces in the system. These are solved by sub-dividing the shaft into many small sections and assembling the mass and stiffness matrices for the whole club. The Newmark integration scheme is used to solve for the displacements and

rotations in each subdivided section throughout the whole swing.
Again it is suggested that other researchers in the field should consider adopting similar methods to this either with specific or general FE packages.

5 Results of the analyses

Figures 2 to 6 show the linear and rotational accelerations of the club and the force along the shaft and the torques about the two axes perpendicular to the shaft in the swing of a **good player**. The reader is referred to figure 1 for an explanation of the notation of the axes.

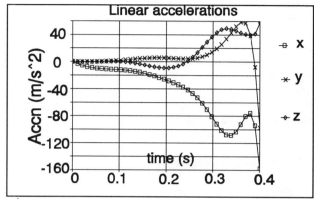

Figure 2

At the start of the downswing the club is at rest and the shaft may be deflected downwards (depending on whether the golfer introduces a pause at this stage). The acceleration is first mainly along the shaft (x-direction) with little rotation of any component. After about 0.1 seconds, the shoulder geometry moves the club forwards relative to the original plane and accelerates it slightly in a downwards direction. Uncocking of the wrists starts after about 0.2 seconds shown by the negative rotation about the z axis. The pull along

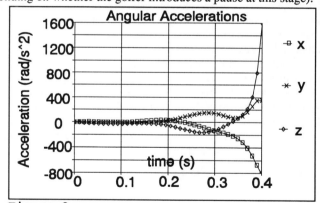

Figure 3

the shaft (x-axis) continues to increase and the arms now drag the club downwards across the original plane of the swing. From 0.3 secs to ball impact (at about 0.36 secs) the wrists rotate the club rapidly about the shaft to bring the face square, and the linear hand velocity decreases.

The effect on the shaft can be deduced by considering the forces and torques on it. Staying with a good swing, from a downwards deflection at the start there is no further acceleration (linear or rotational) to affect the deflection and the club returns through zero deflection to a positive state. The return from this condition is accompanied by the application of a moderate negative torque which promptly deflects the club with a slightly larger amplitude in the negative sense. On the return from this oscillation a large positive torque is applied which produces an even higher amplitude in the positive sense. Finally the rotation of the wrists takes the main motion of the club out of the Oxy plane. The effect is to produce a large negative y deflection. The club is bent downwards at impact.

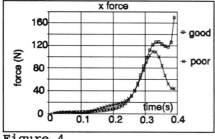

Figure 4

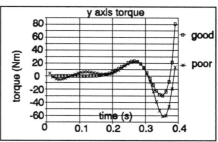

Figure 5

By similar arguments, it is found that the movement of the club first forward of and then behind the original plane of the swing coupled with the rotation of the club from the Oxy to the Oxz planes produces a similar oscillation of the clubhead in the Oxz plane. The final deflection in this plane is forwards, as expected. This descriptive analysis of the club deflection in good swing is summarised in figure 7.

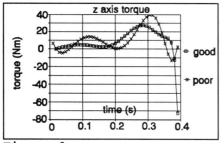

Figure 6

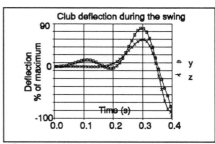

Figure 7

What is also shown in figures 4, 5 and 6 are the corresponding forces and torques for a poor golfer (> 20 handicap). Calculations based on these results show that at ball impact the clubhead velocity for the poor golfer is about half that of the good golfer. The torque about the z axis shows that the poor golfer produces a larger oscillatory pattern than the good player. The phasing is also slightly delayed. This is brought about by the early uncocking of the wrists at the start of the downswing which also throws the club into a different plane to that of the good golfer. This difference in phase and amplitude means that the deflection of the shaft at impact in both planes is quite different to that for the good golfer.

Experimental results from one of the tests (on a driver with a regular shaft) show that both the in plane head deflection and the gradient of the shaft at impact vary as shown in the table.

Golfer	Def(mm)	Grad (rads/°)
Good	19.4	0.06/3.4
Poor	43.9	0.11/6.3

An important conclusion therefore is that the head deflection does not depend only on the speed of the clubhead but also on the time history of the input accelerations. It also shows that investigations with robots using ideal swings will not test the efficiency and suitability of a club for *average* golfers.

6 Conclusions

An experimental system based on photogrammetry techniques has been developed whose spatial accuracy is much greater than could be attained by standard orthogonal camera systems. Displacements, linear and angular velocities and forces and torques throughout the swing can now be obtained. The calculations are done using a programme based on FE methods but specifically written for golf clubs.

The results invite speculation on the relationship between shafts and swing pattern. Assuming that composite shafts are available with different bending and torsional characteristics the following might apply:

Good swing			Poor swing		
Swing	Bending	Twist	Swing	Bending	Twist
Professional	Stiff	Stiff	Out-to-in pull	Stiff	Flex
Amat upright	Stiff	Medium flex	Out-to-in slice	Flex	Stiff
Amateur flat	Stiff	Flex	Smother	Flex	Stiff

At this time, we cannot put exact figures on the flex values. As an aside, we would also suggest that clubs with much lighter heads are needed to give the poor golfer better control so as to develop the correct timing to the swing.

An obvious consequence is that robotic testing with ideal swings may not produce good club designs for the high handicap golfer. We have also noticed that there are major differences between tests done with and without the target of a ball.

7 References

1. Naftel, A.J., Boot, J.C. *An iterative linear transformation algorithm for solution of the collinearity operators.* Photogrammetric Engineering and Remote Sensing. **57**, No. 7 1991
2. Abdel-Aziz, Y.I., Karara, H.M., *Direct linear transformation from comparator co-ordinates into object space co-ordinates in close range photogrammetry.* Proc. ASP/VI Symposium on Close Range Photogrammetry. Urbana, Illinois, 1971.
3. Cooper, M.A.J., Mather, J.S.B. *Categorisation of golf swings* Proc 2nd World Scientific Congress of Golf. St. Andrews. 1994.

8 Acknowledgements

The authors wish to acknowledge Wilson Sporting Goods Co of Chicago who sponsored part of the work, Dr. J.J. Webster of the Department of Mechanical Engineering at the University of Nottingham for his help and advice on the finite element programme, Dr, M.J. Smith of the Department of Civil Engineering for his help in photogrammetry and the use of survey instrumentation and to Mr. D. Vardy and Mr. A. Smith of the Department of Psychology for their help with the experimental instrumentation.

42 Golf shaft flex point – an analysis of measurement techniques

A. Chou and O.C. Roberts
Titleist and Foot-Joy Worldwide, Carlsbad, California, USA

Abstract

This paper provides a brief view of the accuracy of several popular methods of shaft flex point measurement in terms of predicting resulting ball trajectory. A review of flex point terminology is first presented along with the concept that shaft performance can be measured in absolute terms by analyzing the ball flight that is produced. Steel and composite test shafts are measured for mechanical specifications and then tested under both machine (robot) and live golfer conditions. The resulting ball flight information is recorded and analyzed. Conclusions are made regarding the general lack of accuracy of the flex point measurements that were tested and additional research is suggested.

Keywords: Flex point, Bend point, Kick point, Balance point, Frequency, Torque, Trajectory.

1 Introduction

The role of the golf shaft in the total performance of the golf club has traditionally been the subject of much discussion. The effects of shaft properties such as weight, flex, and frequency have been discussed and acknowledged. Various methods of measurement have been recognized and some have even been standardized. However, a minimal amount of scientific research has been published towards establishing a direct cause and effect relationship between shaft properties and club performance or, more notably, ball flight.

One of the more misunderstood of these properties is flex point. There is even a variety of terms used to describe "the position of maximum bending of the shaft" as it is referred to by Maltby (1982) and Wishon and Summitt (1992). The terms *flex point, bend point,* and *kick point* are all used (sometimes interchangeably) for this purpose and often different methods of measurement are even used to establish each value. Whatever terminology is used, however, it is traditionally believed that flex point has the major effect of influencing ball trajectory height. Common theory holds that a flex point that is lower, or closer to the shaft tip, creates a higher trajectory and that a higher flex point results in a lower trajectory.

The goal of this paper is to evaluate the accuracy of three popular methods of flex point measurement in determining relative ball trajectory height. We will discuss our experimental methodology, establish our experimental results, and then draw conclusions based on these results. Our aim is not to endorse any methods in particular but more to assign scientific ball flight data to what has traditionally been a laboratory measurement.

Science and Golf II: Proceedings of the World Scientific Congress of Golf. Edited by A.J. Cochran and M.R. Farrally. Published in 1994 by E & FN Spon, London. ISBN 0 419 18790 1

2   Experimental Methodology

A major shaft manufacturer was asked to submit six driver shafts (3 steel, 3 composite) for testing. These shafts were requested to represent the widest range of flex points available while keeping the other shaft characteristics as similar as possible. The shafts were trimmed to identical cut lengths (41.88") and measured for basic mechanical specifications as shown in Table 1.

Table 1. Test shaft specifications

Shaft	Weight(g)	Balance Pt(in.)	Frequency*(cpm)	Torque(deg)
Steel 1	113.4 ± 0.1	22.25 ± 0.10	259 ± 2	2.9 ± 0.1
Steel 2	112.1	22.25	259	2.9
Steel 3	114.6	22.25	259	2.7
Composite 1	79.9	22.50	281	3.6
Composite 2	79.8	24.00	279	2.4
Composite 3	80.9	22.25	267	4.4

*All frequencies measured using a standard headweight of 209 g.

All six shafts were then subjected to three different methods of determining maximum bending point. We will refer to these methods as Bend Point, Kick Point "A" and Kick Point "B" and they are described as follows:

2.1 Bend Point
A static measurement of shaft deflection under axial compressive loading. The shaft is axially compressed a specified distance and the point on the shaft that has experienced the most deflection from the original shaft centerline is determined. The distance from this point to the shaft tip (at rest) is then recorded.

2.2   Kick Point "A"
Cantilever beam measurement while clamping at the butt. The shaft is placed in a "flex board" apparatus where the butt is clamped and a specified amount of weight is hung at the tip. The point of maximum deflection is defined as the point on the shaft that is furthest from the straight line that is drawn between the butt and tip ends when the shaft is in the bent or weighted position. Again, this is measured in distance from the shaft tip (at rest).

2.3   Kick Point "B"
Cantilever beam measurement while clamping at the tip. Identical to Kick Point "A" except that the tip end is clamped and the weight is applied to the butt end.

2.4 Club Assembly and Testing
After laboratory measurements were completed, each shaft was used to construct identical 10.5 degree metal drivers. The six heads used were identical in all aspects including weight(±.5g), loft(±.25°), face attitude(±.25°), and center of gravity location(±.1"). All clubs were 43.5" in length.

The six drivers were machine tested using an indoor Iron Byron-type of hitting robot. Fifteen (15) shots per club in the same location on the clubface were measured for launch angle and backspin using proprietary instrumentation and peak trajectory heights were calculated based on the launch data. In addition, each driver was then tested by ten (10) expert golfers (handicap <5). Five solid shots per club were measured for launch angle, backspin, and peak trajectory. All live testing was conducted outdoors with peak trajectory height being calculated based on initial ball launch data. Test format was double blind, where neither the test subjects nor the test operator were made aware of any differences between clubs.

3   Test Results

Results for both the machine and live testing are shown in Table 2.

Table 2. Machine and live test results

	BendPt (in.) (±0.1)	KickPt"A" (in.) (±0.1)	KickPt"B" (in.) (±0.1)	Launch(M) (deg) (±0.2)	Spin(M) (rpm) (±130)	Height(M) (yds) (±1.1)	Launch(L) (deg) (±1.0)	Spin(L) (rpm) (±200)	Height(L) (yds) (±1.6)
Steel 1	17.0	18.9	17.0	6.9	2764	15.4	8.3	2777	17.7
Steel 2	16.8	17.9	16.5	7.8	3031	19.0	7.8	2705	16.3
Steel 3	18.0	20.0	18.5	7.7	3318	19.9	8.4	2505	16.5
Comp 1	18.0	18.5	18.5	8.3	3657	23.7	9.2	2918	20.7
Comp 2	17.3	19.0	17.8	8.4	3343	22.5	7.7	2541	15.4
Comp 3	17.5	20.3	16.9	8.6	3821	25.2	9.0	2809	20.3

(M) - machine test   (L) - live test   All flex point distances are measured from the shaft tip

4   Analysis of Results

4.1   Machine Results

Peak trajectory height is used as the measuring stick for changes in trajectory. This may be an over-simplification of sorts, but it is assumed to be more appropriate than analyzing any of the individual components of ball speed, launch angle, or backspin. Peak trajectory height is calculated assuming no wind conditions and one particular ball type.

The plots of Peak Trajectory Height versus Bend Point, Kick Point "A", and Kick Point "B" for the machine (robot) testing are shown in Figure 1. Each plot contains the corresponding flex point and trajectory heights for all six shafts. The points for each shaft material have been joined together for ease of comparison. Due to major differences between specifications of the steel and composite samples, it is not as appropriate to draw any relationships between materials.

Common flex point theory believes that trajectory height will increase with decreasing (closer to the tip) flex point. Although no specific ratio of flex point/trajectory exists at this time, the general trend should show that higher flex point shafts produce lower peak trajectory heights. This general relationship is shown in the charts as the dotted line labeled "theory". There is no significance to the particular slope of these lines as they are drawn; they merely serve to depict the trend as predicted by common theory.

Figure 1 shows that the test results do not follow the behavior as predicted by traditional golf theory. In general, no solid conclusions can be drawn from the machine test data. No firm relationships can be established between bend point, kick point "A", kick point "B" and peak trajectory height based on the machine results, especially when considering the relative standard deviations of the measured properties,.

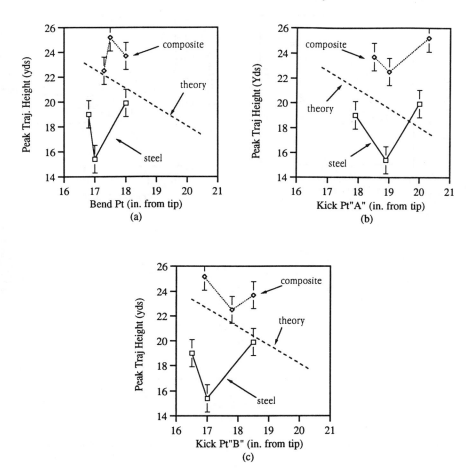

Figure 1. Machine test results for (a) Bend Pt (b) Kick Pt"A" and (c) Kick Pt"B" vs Peak Trajectory Height.

4.2   Live   Results

The plots of Peak Trajectory Height versus Bend Point, Kick Point "A", and Kick Point "B" for the live golfer results are shown in Figure 2.

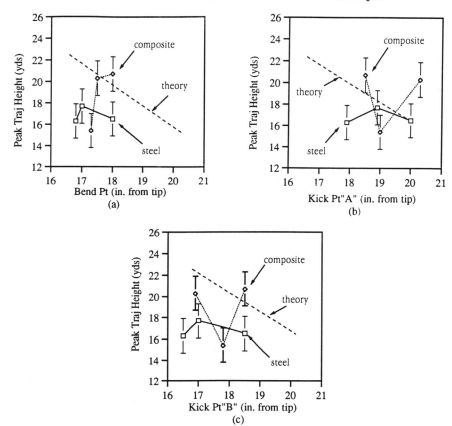

Figure 2. Live test results for (a) Bend Pt (b) Kick Pt"A" and (c) Kick Pt"B" vs Peak Trajectory Height.

The live results for both the steel and composite shafts show no consistent relationship whatsoever between Bend Point, Kick Point "A", or Kick Point "B" and Peak Trajectory Height. On the contrary, the charts show that these results were quite scattered. Note the uneven nature of all of the plots shown in Figures 2(a)-(c). Once again, no firm relationships can be established between bend point, kick point"A", kick point"B" and peak trajectory based on the live results.

4.3   Other Results
Although our results showed no major relationship between the three methods of flex point measurement and peak trajectory height, other data was discovered to be more enlightening. Figure 3 shows the plot of Balance Point versus Peak Trajectory Height for the composite shafts.

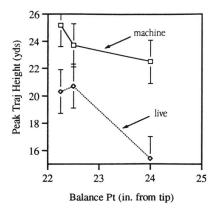

Figure 3. Balance Pt vs Peak Trajectory Height for composite shafts only.

It appears that a relationship exists that describes a decreasing trajectory height as balance point moves further from the shaft tip. A simple curve fit of average values reveals an increase of 3 yards in trajectory height for every 1 inch the balance point moves closer to the tip for the live tests. The machine test shows a more modest increase of 1.3 yards in trajectory for every 1 inch change in balance point. Factoring in the standard deviations affects the slope of the two relationships but does not change the general trend.

The balance point versus peak height relation for the steel shafts is not shown. However, because the steel samples all had identical balance points, it is difficult to draw any major conclusions regarding these clubs.

5   Conclusions

Whereas these experiments have been far from thorough and probably raise more questions than answers, a few quick conclusions can be made:

a) None of the three flex point measuring methods were very accurate or consistent in predicting relative changes in ball trajectory. This would suggest that the terms "low" , "mid", or "high" flex point are meaningless when used solely as references to describe the shaft/trajectory relationship.

b)Balance point may be more accurate in defining relative differences in resulting ball trajectory. The relation between shaft balance point, total club balance point, and ball trajectory has been studied by Wishon and Summitt (1992) and certainly warrants further research.

c) Additional research should also be aimed at the effect of shaft torque on ball trajectory. Our initial results show that torque may provide a greater contribution in determining relative trajectory heights than total shaft frequency.

6   References

Maltby, R. (1982) Golf Club Design, Fitting, Alteration and Repair (2nd Edition).   Ralph Maltby Enterprises, Inc., Newark, OH.

Wishon, T. and Summitt, J. (1992) The Modern Guide to Shaft Fitting. Dynacraft Golf Products, Inc., Newark, OH.

43 Kick back effect of club-head at impact

M. Masuda and S. Kojima
Shonan Institute of Technology, Fujisawa, Japan

Abstract
This paper reports the experimental results of kick back
effect of the club-head at impact. The kick back effect
comes with a newly discovered behavior of the shaft near
the club-head at impact. To make clear this effect, eight
strain gauges are attached along the shaft and very fast
output signals at impact are recorded and analyzed. Thus
the experiment revealed the propagation of a deformation
wave from the club head to the grip end with the sound
velocity, approximately 10Km/s. At the same time, the kick
back effect has been observed.
Keywords: Golf Shaft Vibration, Frequency Resonance, Driving Distance.

1. Introduction

For many years, it has been talked among professional and
low handicap players that the club-head chases the ball
just bouncing out from the club-head after impact. We
called it the kick back effect.

When the club-head impacts the ball, the ball is de-
formed and at the same time the shaft bends near the clubhead as shown in Fig.1(a). After a very short time
(several hundred micro-second) the shaft will bend again
but in the reverse direction and kick backs the ball. This
is a kind of local vibration of shaft caused by the impact
with the ball. The vibrational deformation will propagate
along the shaft with the sound velocity towards the grip.
If the frequency of such local shaft vibration would just
meet the characteristic frequency of the ball, then pushing
the ball by the club-head will synchronize with the ball
bouncing out from the club-head as shown in Fig.1(c). This
is the kick back effect.

Supposing the moment when the club head travels with the
ball during impact as shown in Fig.(b), a part of initial
momentum of club-head is transferred to the ball and the
velocity of club-head decreases by the following equation,

Science and Golf II: Proceedings of the World Scientific Congress of Golf. Edited by A.J.
Cochran and M.R. Farrally. Published in 1994 by E & FN Spon, London. ISBN 0 419 18790 1

$$V_c = \{M/(M+m)\}V_0$$

where M, m, V_c and V_0 are a mass of club-head, a mass of ball, a velocity of club-head during impact and an initial velocity of club-head before impact respectively.

When the club characteristic properties can meet the requirement of kick back effect described above, the velocity of the club-head once killed by an impact with ball can be recovered quickly by the return force of the bent shaft. For the most ideal case, the ball can bounce from the head with a velocity of V_0 but not V_c. This results in a great improvement in initial velocity of the ball and so thus the distance. But if such matching is missed, the ball will bounce from the head with a velocity of V_c.

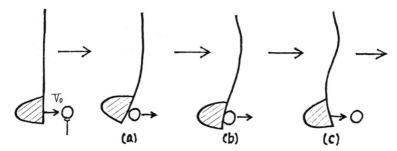

Fig.1. Kick back behavior of shaft at impact.

2. Experiment

2.1 Instrument and experimental results

The grip of the club, mainly the driver in this experiment, is fixed at the testing stand of 1 ton in weight as shown in Fig.1. Then the air-gun shoots the ball to the target at the club-head as shown in Fig.2. Two types of drivers are used for testing. The difference is the hosel configuration. One is the conventional and the other is the short hosel. The common specifications of such clubs are given in Table 1.

Table 1. Specifications of driver

Head	Length of shaft	Shaft	Total weight	Loft (degrees)	Swing weight
Persimmon	44-inch	Carbon Regular Flex	320 gr	10.5	C-9

The 8 strain gauges are attached at 4 local points on a
shaft with 10cm displacement from the hosel towards the
grip. One group picks up the signal of the strain gauge in
a bending direction and another group is one of the perpen-

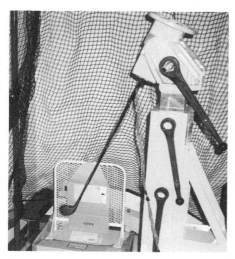

Fig.2. Photograph of stand.   Fig.3. Photograph of air-
                               gun.

dicular to this direction.
    The phenomena of the impact are very fast, shorter than
several hundred micro-seconds. Therefore the conventional
amplifier having a bandwidth of 200 KHz is not meeting with
such experimental requirements. We used a faster amplifier
for this purpose with a bandwidth of 1MHz. The total 8
channel signals are recorded. The waveforms of output
signal from 4 channel amplifiers in bending direction are
summarized in Fig.4. The other 4 channel wave forms in the
different direction have no significant meaning in the
present experiment and are not given here. The details of
the initial portion of each wave forms are shown in Fig.5.
From the figure, we can see the time delay between sequential wave forms coming from the strain gauges and so can
estimate the propagation velocity. This is estimated to be
approximately 10km/s.
    The most important wave form to discuss in the kick back
phenomenon is from the gauge attached nearest the hosel.
This is shown in Fig.6.

2.2 Experimental Analysis
We assumed first, the local deformation of shaft near the
hosel by an impact force and such deformation propagates

along the shaft with sound velocity depending on the physical constant of the shaft materials. We used a shaft made of carbon composite. These physical constants are given in Table 2.

Table 2. Physical constants of the carbon composite

Young modulus	Density	Carbon content
14 ton/mm^2	1.4 gr/cc	60%

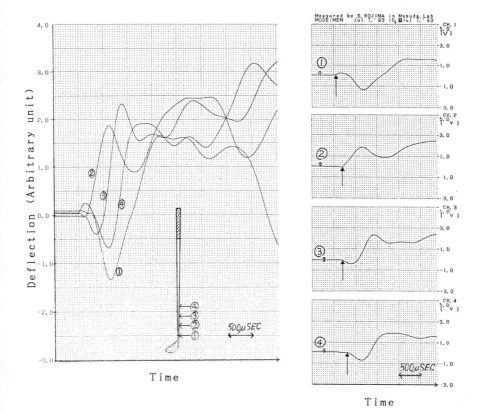

Fig.4. Output signals from 4 channel strain gauges.

Fig.5. Sequential time delay between signals. Arrows indicate the starting point of signals.

The sound velocity of given material is estimated by the following equation.

$$C = (E/\rho)^{1/2}$$

where E and ρ are Young modulus and density of carbon composite for shaft.

Substituting the constants in Table 1 to the equation, we can obtain the theoretical sound velocity. This is approximately 10Km/s and well agreed with the experimental results. Thus we can confirm that the assumption in the present work is correct. That is the local deformation is formed near the hosel and it will propagate along the shaft with sound velocity.

After confirmation of such hierarchy of shaft behavior, we could recognize the first peak shown in Fig.6 as corresponding to the kick back signal. The figure shows also two signals from gauges fixed at the same position of two different clubs of which specifications are already given in Table 1. One signal has 600 microseconds in width and another one has 250 microseconds.

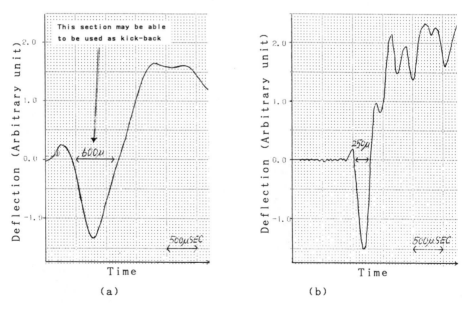

Fig.6. Kick back signals from two different clubs.
(a) kick back club   (b) conventional club

The deformation time of the ball at impact, or, the contacting time during impact is measured as something like 400 to 600 microseconds depending on the compression value

of the ball. If so, the club having a characteristic frequency of 600 microsecond in local bending mode near the
hosel   can meet the requirement of kick back condition but
the 250 microsecond club can not.

On the other hand, the distance test performed by robot
have been carried out for such two clubs. The average
distance for 10 shots for each clubs are 192.3 and 178.6
meters at 40m/s head speed for 600 and 250 microsecond club
respectively. Using the same clubs except the stiffness of
shaft near the hosel, the distance difference is surprising.

3. Conclusion

The kick back effect is a beneficial characteristic
feature of the club for improvement of distance. This is
the matching of the shaft properties very near the hosel to
the ball characteristic properties. If the matching would
be adequately performed, the club could yield an additional distance. The paper reports the effect for the distance
improvement by robot test. However, the theoretical analysis for distance issue is not totally understood yet. The
most optimistic understanding is that the ball bounces from
the club-head of a velocity of V_0 rather than V_c as described already. However, 200 gr head will bear the burden
of 46 gr ball during kick-back. It is unlikely that the
ball bounces from the club-head at a velocity of V_0. Therefore, how much head speed can be improved by the kick-back
effect is not completely understood yet.

Many investigations have to be carried out to confirm
that these concept are in fact real. One direct confirmation is to measure the ball distance by different clubs
changing only the stiffness of the shaft near the hosel.
However it seems that the more kick back effect can be
expected by the less stiffness of the shaft near the hosel.
This is understood by the fact that the short hosel gave
the better result in the distance testing by robot. The
shorter hosel can give the more flexibility to the shaft.
Therefore not only the stiffness of the shaft is a key
factor for the kick back but also the stiffness of the
hosel itself will give the same effect. It depends on the
configuration of hosel-- hard metal hosel, no hosel and
soft persimmon hosel.

In the present work, the fixed club struck by the ball
has been tested and confirmed a part of the kick back effect. However more realistic experiment by the fixed ball
and the swing club by robot or golfers should be performed
in order to fully understand the kick back effect.

44 Experimental determination of inertia ellipsoids

S.H. Johnson
Lehigh University, Bethlehem, Pennsylvania, USA

Abstract
This paper presents a method for measuring the elements of
the inertia matrix of an irregular rigid body like a golfclub head by use of a simple pendular device. The examples
demonstrate the use of the inertia ellipsoid as a means for
visualizing and interpreting inertia properties.
Keywords: Inertia Matrix, Inertia Ellipsoid, Clubhead
Inertias, Clubhead Moments

1 Introduction

Indirectly, the rules of golf require that clubheads be
rigid bodies. As such, the contribution of the club to an
impact with a ball is controlled by the face shape, the
location of the face relative to the center of mass, the
frictional properties of the face, the clubhead mass and
the inertia matrix. The inertia matrix represents the
dynamic consequences of the arrangement of the clubhead
mass. The ellipsoid of inertia is a graphical way to
portray an inertia matrix.

The following body axis system is used here:
z-axis: centerline of the hosel
xy-plane: plane of the hosel end
x-axis: a line in the xy plane parallel to the face
y-axis: completes a righthanded coordinate system

The origin of this xyz axis system is at the center of the
hosel end. With this axis system, the coordinates of the
center of mass will normally be three positive numbers.
An apparatus for determining the coordinates of the
center of mass is shown in the photograph, Figure 1. A
transverse rod is attached to the device shown and a
hanging weight is moved along the rod until static balance
is achieved. This allows calculation of the distance from
the pivot line to the center of mass. The process is
repeated for two mutually perpendicular orientations.

Science and Golf II: Proceedings of the World Scientific Congress of Golf. Edited by A.J.
Cochran and M.R. Farrally. Published in 1994 by E & FN Spon, London. ISBN 0 419 18790 1

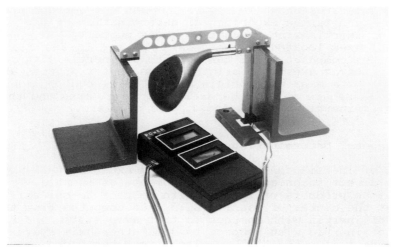

Figure 1. Experimental apparatus with a clubhead in place
and configured for moment of inertia determination. An
electronic counter/timer is shown also. The same basic
device is used to locate the clubhead center of mass.
Three additional adapters for positioning the clubhead for
rotation about various axes are not shown.

2 Moments of Inertia

If a rigid body with a fixed axis of rotation is allowed to
swing with small amplitude as a compound pendulum, the
moment of inertia about the axis of rotation is

$$I = lmg/\omega^2$$

where I is the moment of inertia in slug-ft^2,l is the
distance from the axis of rotation to the center of mass in
ft, m is the mass of the rigid body in slugs, g is the
acceleration due to gravity in ft/sec^2 and ω is the
undamped natural frequency of oscillation in rad/sec. For
larger amplitude swinging, one can derive the equivalent
large-amplitude relationship, or corrections from a table
in Beer and Johnston (1984) can be used to adapt this
equation to large-amplitude experiments. Then the
parallel-axis theorem can be used to compute the moment of
inertia about an axis through the center of mass from
knowledge of the moment of inertia about an axis of
rotation and the distance from the rotation axis to the
axis through the center of mass, the two axes being
parallel.

The apparatus shown in Figure 1, with the appropriate adapters, permits the experimental determination of the moments of inertia with respect to three mutually orthogonal axes located at the hosel end, I_{xx}, I_{yy} and I_{zz}, and then the computation of the moments of inertia with respect to three axes with origin at the center of mass and parallel to the axes with origin at the hosel end, I_{XX}, I_{YY} and I_{ZZ}. These are not, in general, principal axes and the products of inertia, I_{XY}, I_{XZ} and I_{YZ} are not zero.

3 Experimental Determination of Products of Inertia

Products of inertia cannot be determined experimentally by the same direct technique used for moments of inertia. However, the products of inertia with respect to one axis system at the center of mass, XYZ, can be computed from the moments of inertia with respect to that axis system and the moments of inertia with respect to some other axis system at the center of mass, X'Y'Z'. The direct technique above can be used to determine the moments of inertia in this other axis system.

Consider a new coordinate system, X'Y'Z', that results from a 45° rotation about the original Z axis. The product of inertia, I_{XY}, can be computed from moments of inertia in the two axis systems (see Greenwood [1988]),

$$I_{XY} = I_{X'X'} - \frac{(I_{XX}+I_{YY})}{2} \ (a), \quad I_{XY} = \frac{(I_{XX}+I_{YY})}{2} - I_{Y'Y'} \ (b). \quad (1)$$

If another coordinate system, X"Y"Z", is created by a 45° rotation about the original Y axis, the resulting two equations are

$$I_{XZ} = \frac{(I_{XX}+I_{ZZ})}{2} - I_{Z''Z''} \ (a), \quad I_{XZ} = I_{X''X''} - \frac{(I_{XX}+I_{ZZ})}{2} \ (b). \quad (2)$$

Finally, if a third coordinate system is established by a 45° rotation about the original X axis, the two alternative equations are

$$I_{YZ} = \frac{(I_{YY}+I_{ZZ})}{2} - I_{Y'''Y'''} \ (a), \quad I_{YZ} = I_{Z'''Z'''} - \frac{(I_{YY}+I_{ZZ})}{2} \ (b). \quad (3)$$

The $I_{X'X'}$, $I_{Y'Y'}$, $I_{X''X''}$, $I_{Z''Z''}$, $I_{Y'''Y'''}$ and $I_{Z'''Z'''}$ can be determined experimentally by the direct method above.

4 Golf-club Head Examples

Two distinctly different clubheads have been measured.   One
is a widely used, conventionally shaped six-iron head and
the other is an also widely used, medium-sized metal driver
head.   The inertia matrix of the six iron has been
determined independently by Professor Steve Nesbit at
Lafayette College by careful finite-element modeling, and
the inertia matrix of the metal driver has been determined
independently by Mr. Douglas Winfield of True Temper Sports
using a competing experimental procedure.   The comparable
principal moments of inertia agree within 10 percent, with
one exception, and the directions of principal axes agree
within 20°.   The inertia matrices are

$$[I]_{six\ iron} = \begin{bmatrix} 89.4 & -24.3 & -50.9 \\ -24.3 & 195.8 & 0.2 \\ -50.9 & 0.2 & 124.9 \end{bmatrix} \times 10^{-6} \quad slug\text{-}ft^2$$

$$[I]_{metal\ driver} = \begin{bmatrix} 119.3 & -0.6 & -35.7 \\ -0.6 & 143.9 & -12.9 \\ -35.7 & -12.9 & 139.4 \end{bmatrix} \times 10^{-6} \quad slug\text{-}ft^2$$

$$1.0\ slug\text{-}ft^2 = 1.356\ kg\text{-}m^2$$

The principal moments of inertia are the eigenvalues of the
inertia matrices.   For the metal driver, the principal
moments of inertia are

$$I_1 = 0.0001703 \quad I_2 = 0.0000909 \quad I_3 = 0.0001414 \quad slug\text{-}ft^2$$

and for the six iron, the principal moments of inertia are

$$I_1 = 0.0002032 \quad I_2 = 0.0001564 \quad I_3 = 0.0000505 \quad slug\text{-}ft^2$$

The relative orientations can be estimated from the two
eigenmatrices

$$\begin{bmatrix} 0.284 & -.500 & 0.818 \\ -.940 & -.312 & 0.136 \\ -.187 & 0.808 & 0.559 \end{bmatrix}_{6 iron} \quad \begin{bmatrix} 0.532 & 0.774 & -.343 \\ 0.362 & 0.158 & 0.919 \\ -.766 & 0.613 & 0.196 \end{bmatrix}_{driver}$$

with the eigenvectors ordered the same way as the
eigenvalues.   For both clubs the y axis is approximately a
principal axis; the axis of the largest principal moment of
inertia in the case of the 6 iron and the axis of the
intermediate moment of inertia for the driver.

5 Ellipsoids of Inertia

The inertia ellipsoid is a graphical means of representing
the moments of inertia about arbitrary axes with the
principal axes coinciding with the axes of the ellipsoid.
The inertia ellipsoid is given by Greenwood (1988) as

$$I_{XX}x^2 + I_{YY}y^2 + I_{ZZ}z^2 + 2I_{XY}xy + 2I_{YZ}yz + 2I_{XZ}xz = 1 \quad (4)$$

The radius vector to any point on the inertia ellipsoid is
inversely proportional to the radius of gyration about the
direction of that vector. The major axis of the ellipsoid
is the axis of smallest moment of inertia of a body. The
minor axis is the axis of largest moment of inertia. Both
are principal axes. Figure 2 shows the inertia ellipsoid
of the six iron rotated so that the axes are aligned with
the coordinate axes. Superimposed on the six-iron
ellipsoid is the ellipsoid of inertia of the metal driver,
also rotated to align the principal axes with the
coordinate axes.
A homogeneous spherical shell with uniform wall
thickness would have a spherical ellipsoid of inertia.
Inertia ellipsoids for oversized metal drivers without
hosels tend toward a spherical shape. By comparison,
wooden or synthetic drivers with prominent hosels and steel
sole plates tend to have slender, elongated ellipsoids of
inertia but the differences are not large. Even unusually
shaped, nonconforming heads intended to be inertially
different have ellipsoids of inertia that do not differ
markedly from the conventional midsized driver portrayed in
Figure 2. Clearly, the hollow driver and the back-weighted
iron have inertial properties that are quite similar.
The inertial properties of the two clubs are compared
by plotting both ellipsoids with their principal axes
aligned with the same cartesian coordinate axes. However,
two clubs with decidedly nonspherical ellipsoids that
appear to be identical when plotted as in Figure 2 could
have substantially different effects on the ball if their
ellipsoids are differently oriented at impact.
The inertia of the shaft of a driver can probably be
neglected, as pointed out by Cochran and Stobbs (1973).
Part of the shaft of an iron probably should be added to
the clubhead when computing the effective inertia matrix.
This would distort the ellipsoid somewhat.
The similarities between ellipsoids are more striking
than the differences, particularly among the drivers that
have been measured. Even radically shaped, nonconforming
heads have inertia ellipsoids that are not very different
from the driver ellipsoid shown in Figure 2. Jumbo heads
are inertially similar also. In contrast, wooden and
synthetic heads with significant added weighting can have
somewhat different, elongated ellipsoids.

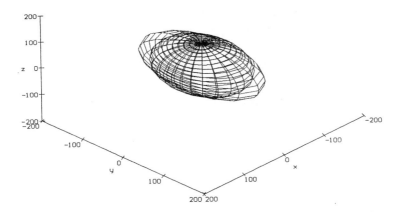

Figure 2. Superimposed inertia ellipsoids for an APEX #6 iron and a Tour Series midsized driver. The units are $(\text{slug}^{1/2}\text{ft})^{-1}$. These ellipsoids have been rotated to bring their principal axes into coincidence with the coordinate axes. The inner ellipsoid is for the driver which is closer to being spherically symmetric and weighs 0.450 lbs(1.0 lbs = 0.454 kg). The outer ellipsoid is for the less symmetric iron that weighs 0.583 lbs.

6 Patent Rights

A patent has been granted to the USGA covering the apparatus and procedure for determining the inertia matrices of irregularly shaped rigid bodies.

7 Acknowledgements

The author wishes to express his gratitude to Mr. Frank Thomas, technical director of the United States Golf Association, and to Dr. Ronald E. Philipp, manager of the USGA Test and Research Center, for their generous support, cooperation, and encouragement. The author appreciates the cooperation and help of Mr. Douglas Winfield of True Temper Sports.

8 References

Beer, F.P., and E.R. Johnston, Jr., 1984, **Vector Mechanics for Engineers – Dynamics**, 4th edition, McGraw-Hill Book Co., New York, NY.

Greenwood, D.T., 1988, **Principles of Dynamics**, Prentice-Hall, Englewood Cliffs, NJ.

Cochran, A. and J. Stobbs, 1973, **The Search for a Perfect Swing**, J.P. Lippincott Co., Philadelphia, PA.

45 Contact forces, coefficient of restitution, and spin rate of golf ball impact

P.C. Chou, D. Liang, J. Yang
Drexel University, Philadelphia, U.S.A.
and W. Gobush
Titleist and Foot-Joy Worldwide, New Bedford, USA

Abstract
Experimental and finite-element results of golf ball impact
are presented. These include the tangential and normal
forces acting on golf balls, the normal coefficient of
restitution, and the spin rate. Good agreements are obtained
between the experimental and finite-element results.
Different parameters and mechanisms affecting the impact are
discussed.
Keywords: Golf Ball Impact, Coefficient of Restitution,
Normal and Tangential Forces, Spin Rate, Viscosity, PGA No..

1   Introduction

Cochran and Stobbs (1989) gave a very thorough and clear
discussion of the impact between a golf ball and a clubhead.
They pointed out that some of the initial kinetic energy of
the clubhead is lost. They did not provide any explanation
of the mechanisms of the energy loss process. For a lofted
club face, they showed experimental results that the
smoothness of the club face does not affect the ball spin
rate. They hypothesized that the friction force which causes
the spin is resulted from sliding, and when sliding stops,
the "rolling" friction retards the spin.

   In this paper, we show that our experimental and finite-
element results agree with Cochran and Stobbs'. In addition,
we provide details on what physical properties contributed to
the loss of impact energy. In the lofted club face case, our
finite-element results show that for loft angles less than
30°, the friction force is caused mainly by the ball's
sticking to the club face, sliding occurs only partially and
does not contribute appreciably to the friction and spin.

2   Experimental measurement

In our experiment, a golf ball was launched from an air gun
into a plywood box. It struck a steel block of dimension

Science and Golf II: Proceedings of the World Scientific Congress of Golf. Edited by A.J.
Cochran and M.R. Farrally. Published in 1994 by E & FN Spon, London. ISBN 0 419 18790 1

8" x 4" x 12" which was on a turn-table adjustable to various
impact angles. For impact force measurement, a three
component force transducer was mounted on the steel block.
The top of the plywood box was covered with plexiglass to
allow a film camera to overlook and record the position and
orientation of the ball. Strobe lights were placed on the
surface of the plexiglass, and were fired at a constant time
interval. Twelve marks were made on the ball's surface. If
the camera could record the positions of at least three of
these marks, it would provide enough information to calculate
the velocity and spin of the ball. More details about the
experimental arrangement and additional result may be found
in Gobush (1976).

3.   Finite element code

The two-dimensional computer code DEFEL, Chou et al.(1991,
1992),was used in the simulation. It is a Lagrangian finite-
element hydrocode designed for the analysis of dynamic impact
problems. It includes compressibility, strength, and
viscosity effects, and has a sophisticated slide line routine
which can properly handle material interfaces. The ball's
viscosity is treated as viscous stresses which are added to
the elastic stresses in the stress-strain relation.
   There are two types of Coulomb friction, kinetic and
static. In the kinetic case, there must be "sliding" or
relative motion between the contacting bodies, and a kinetic
coefficient of friction is used. For the static case, the
friction force exists when there is a tendency to slide. The
magnitude of the friction force can vary from zero to a
maximum value equal to the normal force times a static
coefficient of friction. In general, the kinetic and static
coefficients are of different values.

4 Results

4.1 Impact forces
At the First World Scientific Congress of Golf, Gobush(1990)
presented results of measured normal and tangential forces of
a ball impacting a rigid anvil. In this section, we shall
compare our calculated results by finite-element code with
his measured data of a two-piece ball at a loft angle of 40°.
   In this paper, plane-stress simulations have been made,
where a disc, with the diameter of the golf ball and a
thickness of one inch, obliquely impacts a rigid surface.
   Figure 1 gives both measured and calculated normal and
tangential forces on the ball. Realizing that the plane-
stress calculation is an approximation, and the coefficient
of friction is an estimated one, these results do show that
the experimental and calculated results are qualitatively in
agreement.

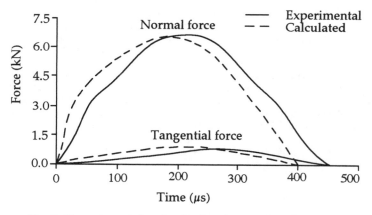

Fig. 1 Experimental and calculated normal and tangential
forces (V=28.96 m/s, α = 40°, μ_v= 2758 Poise, μ_f = 0.15)

A similar comparison between the measured and calculated
forces for the 20° loft angle case may be found in
Chou(1992).

4.2 Coefficient of restitution
The coefficient of restitution, C_r, of the normal impact
between a golf ball and a club of very large mass is given by

$$C_r = \frac{\text{rebound velocity}}{\text{impact velocity}} \qquad (1)$$

This equation is applicable to both the case of a ball
hitting a stationary club, and the case of a club hitting a
stationary ball.   In the latter case, the ball velocities are
those relative to the club.   The square of C_r gives the
percentage of the input kinetic energy that is recovered as
rebound energy.   The rest of the input energy is distributed
into: vibration energy, plastic work, and viscous work. Thus,

Input kinetic energy = rebound energy + vibration energy
+ plastic work + viscous work   (2)

The vibration energy consists of the motion of the ball
mass relative to the center of gravity and the elastic strain
energy.   Eventually, after a few milliseconds, the vibration
energy will be dissipated into heat.   The plastic work is due
to the permanent deformation of the ball.   The viscous work
is dependent on the coefficient of viscosity and the strain
rate of the ball.

Figure 2 shows the finite element grid geometry at different times during the 400μs-period when the ball is in contact with the club. The one-piece solid ball has a diameter of 4.276 cm and a mass of 45.4 gram. The initial ball velocity is 45.72 m/s. For this normal impact, our simulation is exact, using cylindrical coordinates. Baseline values used for other parameters are, Poisson's ratio = 0.49, coef. of viscosity = 5429 Poise, yield stress = 62.1 MPa, Young's modulus = 103.4 MPa.

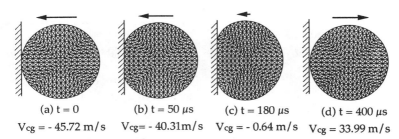

(a) t = 0 (b) t = 50 μs (c) t = 180 μs (d) t = 400 μs

V_{cg} = - 45.72 m/s V_{cg}= - 40.31m/s V_{cg} = - 0.64 m/s V_{cg} = 33.99 m/s

Fig.2 Mesh deformation of a golf ball normally impacting a rigid surface at 45.72 m/s

In order to study the mechanisms that contribute to the energy loss, we have performed a parametric calculation. For a typical impact velocity of 45.72 m/s, the maximum stress in the ball is about 34.47 MPa, much below the yield stress of 62.1 MPa of conventional ball materials. This indicates that most of energy lost is due to vibration and viscosity.

The ball vibration is directly influenced by its elasticity, or Young's modulus. In Chou (1992), it has been shown that a ball's Young's modulus can be represented by its PGA compression number. In Figure 3, the calculated value of C_r is plotted as a function of the PGA number, with coef. of viscosity, μ_v, as a parameter. It can be seen that with fixed μ_v, the C_r decreases with PGA. More energy is lost due to vibration for low PGA balls. For a fixed PGA number, the C_r increases with decreasing viscosity. Unfortunately very little information about the value of the viscosity of ball materials are known.

Gobush (1976) measured the ball velocity, launch angle, and spin rate of a few ball constructions. He also calculated the normal coefficient of restitution by taking the ratio of the normal component of rebound to that of the impact velocity. Figure 4 shows the plots of the coefficient of restitution versus the impact velocity of a one-piece ball with a PGA of 112. The measured data are taken from two series of tests, each with a fixed absolute value of impact velocity, but with different loft angles. The calculated curve is obtained from normal impact simulations, with a

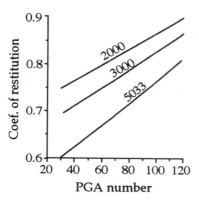

Fig. 3 Coefficient of restitution
vs. PGA number, with viscosity
μ_v (Poise) as a parameter

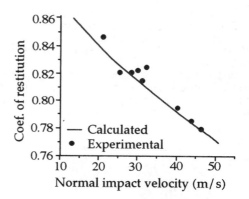

Fig. 4 Coefficient of restitution vs.
normal impact velocity
(PGA No. = 112)

selected value of μ_v = 5429 Poise to match the C_r at one
experimental point. The calculated curve agrees fairly well
with the measured data.

As expected, the value of C_r decreases as the impact
velocity increases. A smaller percentage of the initial
kinetic energy is recovered as rebound energy at higher
impact velocities.

4.3 Spin rate

The spin rate of a solid one-piece ball with a PGA number of
98, at different loft angles, is also measured and calculated
by the finite-element code as shown in Fig.5. Two types of
club surfaces are used, one smooth and the other rough. For
the calculation, a static coef. of friction μ_{fs} = 0.3 and a
kinetic coef. of friction μ_{fk} = 0.23 are used in the case of
the smooth surface, and a single coef. of μ_f=0.4 is used for
the rough surface.

At loft angles below 40°, the spins of both surfaces are
approximately the same; the coef. of friction between the
ball and the club has no effect on the spin. This is in
agreement with the observations by Cochran and Stobbs (1989).
Our code simulations show that at low and moderate loft
angles, the contact between the ball and the club is mostly
"sticking", and no gross slip occurs. The friction force is
the same with both surfaces. At higher loft angles, the ball
slides on the smooth surface club, thus reducing the
frictional force and spin rate.($\mu_{fk} < \mu_{fs}$).

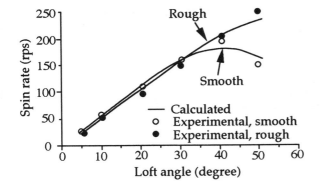

Fig. 5 Experimental and calculated spin rate vs. loft angle (V = 45.9 m/s, μ_v = 2758 Poise)

5   Discussion

The experiments reported in this paper were conducted in a well instrumented laboratory. The finite-element simulations include all possible physical parameters. The simulated results are in agreement with the experimental ones.

The loss of impact energy is primarily due to elastic vibration and viscous damping. For most impacts, the spin rate is independent of the club surface condition. The contact between ball and club is mostly sticking, where the friction force is less than the maximum static friction of the smoothest surface.

The plane-stress simulation of an oblique impact is an approximation. Values of the coefficients of viscosity and friction are all selected to match the experimental data. There is a need to measure the exact value of these coefficients.

6   References

Chou, P.C., Hashemi, J., Chou, A., and Rogers, H.C. (1991) Experimentation and finite-element simulation of adiabatic shear bands in controlled penetration impact. **Int. J. of Impact Engng**, 11(3), 305-321.

Chou, P.C. and Liang, D. (1992) Finite-element simulation of golf ball impact. Final report, Center for ballistics, Drexel University.

Cochran, A. and Stobbs, J. (1989) **The Search of The Perfect Swing.** The Booklegger, Grass Valley, Calif.

Gobush, W. (1976) Impact Properties of Golf Balls, Progress Report, Titleist Golf Division.

Gobush, W. (1990) Impact Force Measurements on Golf Balls, Science and Golf (edited by A.J. Cochran), **Proc. of the First World Scientific Congress of Golf**, London, 219.

46 Measurement of dynamic characteristics of golf balls and identification of their mechanical models

S. Ujihashi
Tokyo Institute of Technology, Faculty of Engineering,
2-12-1 Oh-okayama, Meguro-ku, Tokyo 152, Japan

Abstract
In this paper, the dynamic characteristics of golf balls during impact is measured by using a newly developed experimental apparatus, in which a golf ball fired by an air gun hits on a steel target of load cell and the contact force and the deformation of the golf ball are measured by the load cell and a high speed camera respectively. Some commercial golf balls are tested in order to clarify the restitution characteristics and mechanical models consisting of mass, spring and damper for golf balls are identified and are proposed to be used for investigating the dynamic characteristics of golf clubs as a subsequent stage of the research. The mechanical models would be a powerful idea which enables to simulate golf shots by a computer with higher accuracy and less computing time.
Key Words: Golf Ball, Dynamic Characteristics, Air Gun, High Speed Camera, Load Cell, Contact Force, Deformation, Mechanical Model,

1. Introduction

Recently the method of computer–aided design (CAD) has been introduced to manufacturing golf clubs in order to enhance the specifications and also to reduce the cost of designing.(Iwata et al, 1990) In the CAD the finite element analysis is generally employed and golf clubs are replaced by mathematical models so that a golf shot can be simulated by a computer. Here the basic understanding of a golf shot consisting of ball, club and swing by a human is required to create a precise mathematical model for a club and the computer simulation of a golf shot to be realistic.

In this paper the impact phenomenon between a ball and a club is focused among several boundary conditions surrounding a golf club such as the contact problem with a ball and the grip and swing problems of the human. Then it is attempted to obtain more understanding of what actually happens during golf impact and also it is examined how the impact velocity and the construction and the type of balls, which are available in golf shops, affect the restitution characteristics on the basis of most precise measurements ever tried using an original load cell and a high speed camera. Finally a mechanical model for golf balls is proposed and identified from the measured characteristics and can be used as one of the boundary conditions surrounding a club in computer simulations of a golf shot.

Science and Golf II: Proceedings of the World Scientific Congress of Golf. Edited by A.J. Cochran and M.R. Farrally. Published in 1994 by E & FN Spon, London. ISBN 0 419 18790 1

2. Experimental Apparatus and Golf Balls Tested

In order to investigate the dynamic characteristics of golf balls an experimental apparatus shown in Fig.1, in which a golf ball fired by an air gun hits on a steel target, is constructed instead of hitting a placed golf ball by a club.   It was observed in advance by the high speed camera that the fired ball flies without vibration and spin.   Therefore the impact by the experimental apparatus should be equivalent to the impact by hitting a placed ball.   A ball can be accelerated up to the velocity of 60m/s by the pressure of only 0.2MPa by the air gun.   The steel target of a circular bar, 30mm in diameter, has the function of a load cell, as shown in Fig.2, which measures the load variations in time happening at the impact end of the target with high and reliable accuracy on the basis of the strain measurements at the centre of the bar and the one–dimensional wave propagation theory. (Ujihashi,1990)   An acceleration transducer is attached on the opposite end of the target.   The impact and rebound velocities and the deformations of the ball are measured by the high speed camera DYNAFAX MODEL 350 (maximum speed: 35,000 frames/s, number of

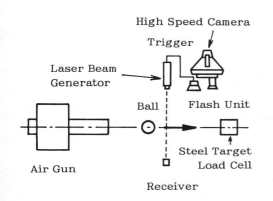

Fig.1 An Experimental Apparatus

Table 1 Golf Balls Tested

Ball ID	Construction	Type
WD-R1	Wound	Red (Promodel)
WD-R2	Wound	Red
WD-B1	Wound	Black (Promodel)
TP-P1	Two-Piece	Pink (ladies)
TP-R1	Two-Piece	Red (1)
TP-R2	Two-Piece	Red (2)
TP-R3	Two-Piece	Red (3)
TP-R4	Two-Piece	Red (4)
TP-B1	Two-Piece	Black

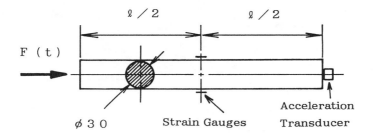

Fig.2 A Load Cell

frames: 224).   Commercial golf balls listed in Table 1, ranging from professional models to ladies models, were provided for the experiment.
First it is examined how the mass, that is, the length of the target affects contact forces and whether an acceleration transducer is capable as a load cell.   Fig.3 shows that the length (the mass) of the target does not change contact force variations in time very much within the range of from 200mm (1.17kg) up to 1,500mm (8.10kg) and the period of contact stays approximately 400 μ s and the peak height depends mostly on the impact velocity.   In Fig.4 the contact force variations in time created from the outputs of the acceleration transducer are compared with the strain gauge based measurements.   Raw signals from an acceleration transducer include unwanted signals due to the fundamental vibrations of the target and the transducer itself.   Then the processing of the low pass filtering must be undertaken in order to remove the unwanted high frequencies components and afterwards the amplitudes should be tuned to the real responses given by the strain gauge based method.   Via the above processing the measurements by an acceleration transducer can be roughly fitted to the real measurements especially in case of a lighter target and will be capable

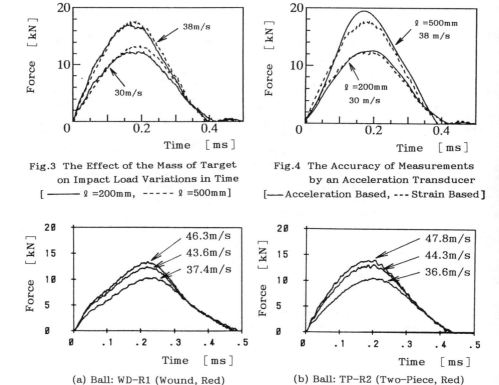

Fig.3 The Effect of the Mass of Target
on Impact Load Variations in Time
[——— ℓ =200mm, - - - - - ℓ =500mm]

Fig.4 The Accuracy of Measurements
by an Acceleration Transducer
[—— Acceleration Based, - - - Strain Based]

(a) Ball: WD–R1 (Wound, Red)

(b) Ball: TP–R2 (Two–Piece, Red)

Fig.5 The Effect of Type of Balls on Impact Load Variations in Time

to measure the contact force between a ball and a club in the subsequent stage of the research.

3. Dynamic Characteristics of Golf Balls

The golf balls in Table 1 are tested by using the longest load cell(1,500mm) and a part of the results of contact force variations in time is shown in Fig.5 which indicates the influences of the different types of balls.   The

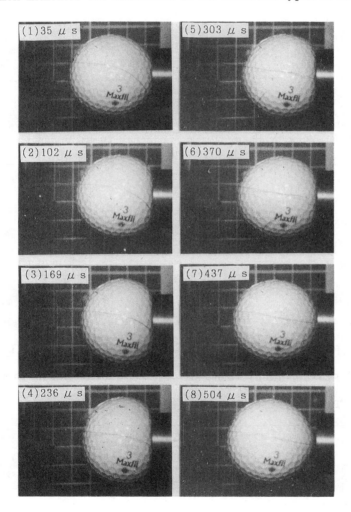

Fig.6 Photographs of a Golf Ball Taken by a High Speed Camera
[Ball: Wound WD–R2, Impact Velocity: 46.1m/s]

peak heights have almost the same values independently of the type of balls unless either the impact velocity or the ball construction is different, and change proportionally to the impact velocity only. However as far as the period of contact is concerned, a significant difference is observed between

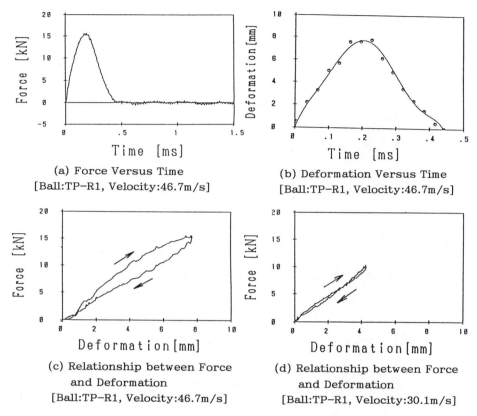

(a) Force Versus Time
[Ball:TP–R1, Velocity:46.7m/s]

(b) Deformation Versus Time
[Ball:TP–R1, Velocity:46.7m/s]

(c) Relationship between Force
and Deformation
[Ball:TP–R1, Velocity:46.7m/s]

(d) Relationship between Force
and Deformation
[Ball:TP–R1, Velocity:30.1m/s]

Fig.7 The Relationship between Force and Deformation During Impact

Table 2 The Restitution Characteristics of Golf Balls

Ball	Impact Velocity Vi [m/s]	Rebound Velocity Vr [m/s]	Impact Energy Ei [J]	Rebound Energy Er [J]	Absorbed Energy Ea [J]	Restitution Coefficient $e = Vr/Vi$
Two-	30.1	24.6	20.4	13.6	0.45	0.82
Piece	46.7	35.9	49.1	29.0	15.3	0.77
Wound	30.7	25.6	21.2	14.7	0.56	0.83
	46.1	37.2	47.8	31.1	15.6	0.81

wound–balls and two–piece balls, that is, wound–balls have longer period roughly by 15% than two–piece balls and the time to reach peaks in case of two–piece balls is much shorter because of the difference of the shape of contact force variations in time. This difference can possibly influence the golf performance. Fig.6 shows typical photographs taken by the high speed camera and the deformations of balls are obtained by measuring the longitudinal decreases of the diameter.

Fig.7 shows typical force and deformation relationship, in which (c) is a combined figure of (a) and (b) by eliminating time at the velocity of 46.1m/s and (d) is obtained by the same processing at the lower velocity of 30.7m/s. At a level of low impact velocity such as 30m/s the ball behaviour is almost perfectly elastic. However as the velocity increases the response becomes more and more visco–elastic and energy absorption by the deformation of ball is outstanding. This fact corresponds with that the restitution coefficient reduces as the impact velocity increases. The restitution characteristics by typical testings are summarized in Table 2, where energy absorption is calculated as the enclosed area by the force and deformation relationship.

4. A Mechanical Model for Golf Balls

If the dynamic characteristics of balls are expressed by mechanical models consisting of mass, spring and damper, the process of mesh generation for balls can be omitted and also the computing time can be reduced in the simulation of golf shots using the Finite Element Method. This is the reason why mechanical models for balls must be introduced. First a mechanical model of one–degree of freedom is considered as shown in Fig.8 on the basis of experimental measurements and another mechanical model of two–degree of freedom is identified as an alternative model with higher fidelity. Dynamic responses of the above two models are simulated by the models hitting on a rigid target and the comparison of the simulated contact force and deformation versus time by the models with the experimental results is made in Fig.9. The proposed mechanical models can simulate roughly the real impact by actual golf balls within the possible velocity range. It is evident that models of higher degree of freedom have better dynamic characteristics than of lower degree, however the elementary

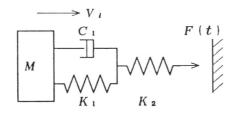

Fig.8 A Mechanical Model for Golf Balls

[M=45.1g, K_1=4.9x10^{6}N/m, K_2=4.7x10^{6}N/m, C_1=250 N/(m/s)]

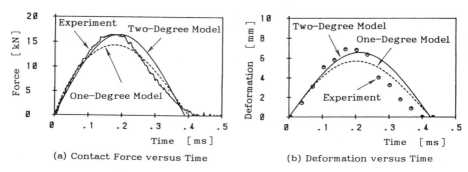

(a) Contact Force versus Time   (b) Deformation versus Time

Fig.9 The Comparison of Force and Deformation Variations
in Time by Simulation and Experiment

models shown in Fig.9 could be sufficient because the dynamic responses of
only clubs are observed when clubs are designed.   The idea of using
mechanical models would be useful in order to reduce the computing time
and also to keep the accuracy of results.

5. Conclusions

Production of golf balls are controlled by the regulations provided by R & A
and USGA, and then manufacturers cannot decide the specifications of golf
balls freely, such as the size, the mass and the restitution.   So golf balls
listed in Table 1, whose mass and diameter are approximately 45.1g and
42.7mm respectively, have almost uniform dynamic characteristics and
especially as far as concerned with the hardness of balls (red, black and so
on) any significant difference cannot be distinguished as easily as
manufacturers advertising suggests.   The dynamic measurements in this
research are with the highest accuracy ever tried especially regarding the
contact force in Fig.5 and the photographs in Fig.6.   Mechanical models for
golf balls are helpful in the computer simulation of a golf shot.   The
identification of an elaborate mechanical model is very difficult because the
behaviour of golf balls under high velocity impact of over 40m/s is strongly
non–linear and visco–elastic.
However, the impact by golf balls is just one of boundary conditions for a
golf club, and then simple linear mechanical models with lower degree of
freedom should be acceptable at the point of view of designing golf clubs.

6. References

(1) M. Iwata, N. Okubo and F. Satoh (1990), Designing of golf club heads by
    Finite Element Method analysis, Science and Golf, Proc. 1st World
    Scientific Congress of Golf; edited by A.J.Cochran, E & F N Spon,
    London, pp.274–279.
(2) S. Ujihashi (1993), An intelligent method to determine the mechanical
    properties of composites under impact loading, Composite Structures,
    23–2, pp.149–163.

47 An analytical model for ball–barrier impact

Part 1: Models for normal impact

B.B. Lieberman
Polytechnic University, Brooklyn, New York, USA
and S.H. Johnson
Lehigh University, Bethlehem, Pennsylvania, USA

Abstract
The golf ball-barrier collision has proven to be too
complicated to be characterized successfully by
conventional coefficients of restitution and spin
restitution, even if the coefficients are velocity-
dependent and angle-dependent. An alternative is to use
the parameters of an ordinary differential equation model
of the transient viscoelastic deformation of a ball during
impact. A five-parameter, nonlinear model of normal impact
of solid balls has been successful in representing ball-
barrier collisions over a wide range of approach
velocities. A new, six-parameter version successfully
represents wound balls in normal impact. With the addition
of a torsion model, oblique impact can be simulated.
Keywords: Normal Impact, Oblique Impact, Impact Modelling

1 Introduction

A first step to understanding the impact between a golf
ball and a golf club requires that one be able to model the
impact of a solid elastic sphere upon a massive plate. A
minimum result for the study would be the ability to
predict rebound angle, velocity, and spin-rate for a given
ball and plate from knowledge of the incoming velocity,
angle, and spin-rate for a set of values which could range
in velocity from 0 to 180 fps and in angle from 0 to 60
degrees. It would be desirable to characterize the
interaction in the simplest possible manner.

For the model to be successful it must reflect well-
known facts and recent results obtained during the 1987
groove study. A list of some of these features include:
(1) energy is lost during the impact; (2) the ball's
coefficient of restitution (COR) decreases very slowly with
increasing velocity; (3) the contact time during the impact
decreases with increasing velocity; (4) the compression
phase of the impact is less than one-half of the contact

Science and Golf II: Proceedings of the World Scientific Congress of Golf. Edited by A.J.
Cochran and M.R. Farrally. Published in 1994 by E & FN Spon, London. ISBN 0 419 18790 1

time; (5) the ball's diameter at the end of impact has
returned to more than 98% of its original value; (6) the
maximum deformation of the ball increases with velocity a
little faster than linearly; (7) the normal force of the
wound ball on the barrier exhibits multiple local maxima
(Gobush 1990); (8) the spin-rate increases nearly linearly
with the incoming tangential velocity for a fixed
coefficient of friction between the ball and plate
(Lieberman 1990); (9) for small incoming angles and for a
fixed incoming tangential velocity an increase in the
coefficient of friction decreases the spin-rate (Lieberman
1990); (10) a change in the cross-section of the grooves
affects the rebound response (Thomas 1987).

The use of a rigid body model with velocity and angle
dependent coefficients of restitution (Goldsmith 1960) was
not satisfactory since it was not possible to determine
functional relations for these coefficients from
experimental data. Without some simplification this would
require an enormous amount of empirical data to represent
each particular ball and plate configuration and therefore
this approach was deemed unsuitable.

2 One-degree-of-freedom models

A first step to developing the oblique model would be to
construct a successful normal impact model. Two parameter
linear visco-elastic solids such as the Voigt model (a
spring in parallel with a dashpot) or the Maxwell model (a
spring in series with a dashpot) would not be appropriate
because the former would imply that the contact time as
well as the COR are independent of initial velocity and the
latter would not permit the ball to return to its original
shape at the end of the impact. Non-linearizing the Voigt
model by introducing a Hertzian spring would give rise to a
solution for which an increase in impact velocity would
increase the COR which would be contrary to empirical
results.

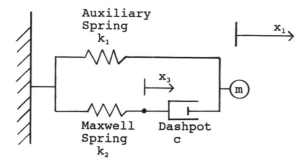

Figure 1. Ball model

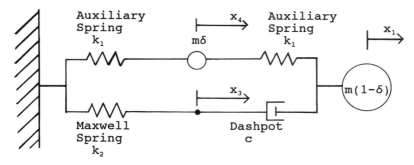

Figure 2. Two-mass ball model

Consider a three parameter model, as in Figure 1, consisting of a Maxwell model in parallel with a spring (Kolsky 1952). Elements of the model must be nonlinear, otherwise the contact time and COR would not change with initial velocity. In addition assume: (1) the elastic components behave in such a way that the stress is proportional to a power of the strain and (2) the damping component behaves in such a way that the stress is proportional to the rate of change of strain.

Thus one obtains the following initial value problem for the ball deformation, x_1, the center of mass velocity, x_2, and the position of a point between the hypothetical dashpot and spring, x_3, during normal impact:

$$\dot{x}_1 = x_2 \qquad x_1(0) = 0$$

$$\dot{x}_2 = -\frac{k_1}{m}x_1^\alpha - \frac{k_2}{m}x_3^\beta \qquad x_2(0) = V_0$$

$$\dot{x}_3 = -\frac{k_2}{c}x_3^\beta + x_2 \qquad x_3(0) = 0$$

where
m = ball mass V_0= initial velocity
V_1= exit velocity τ = contact time
α = spring 1 power k_1= spring constant 1
β = spring 2 power k_2= spring constant 2
c = dashpot constant.

The parameters, α, k_1, and τ, are obtained experimentally for each ball. Because of the singular nature of these equations one has to employ a gradient technique to estimate the constants, c, k_2, and β. The measured value of velocity and zero acceleration at the end of contact provide two equations for determining c, k_2, and β. The third equation is obtained by measuring the COR at another impact velocity. This method was applied to the modelling of two-piece, solid, and wound balls.

Table 1. Estimates of ball parameters

Bl	α	k_1	τ	V_0	$-V_1$	β	$k_2^{1/\beta}$	c
			msec	fps	fps			
1	1.25	11500	.425	122.1	93.9	2.05	235	2.75
				163.9	120.1			
2	1.34	14035	.430	119.9	89.2	2.55	123	2.18
				160.9	112.8			

In the first two types the estimates of the parameters correspond well with theory and data. The above model is not adequate to describe the wound ball. The results for the two-piece and solid balls are presented in Tables 1 and 2. Table 2 shows that the predicted COR is off by at most 1% in the velocity range tested.

Table 2. Predictions from model

Ball	Initial Velocity	Pred. Contact Time	Pred. Maximum Deform.	Pred. COR	Actual COR
	fps	msec	in		
1	100.0	.441	.17	.792	----
	122.1	.425	.20	.769	.769
	146.4	.410	.24	.747	.748
	163.9	.401	.26	.733	.733
	180.0	.394	.28	.721	----
2	100.0	.448	.18	.770	----
	119.9	.430	.20	.744	.744
	145.1	.412	.23	.715	.722
	160.9	.403	.25	.701	.701
	180.0	.393	.27	.685	----

In another approach to a similar problem, the parameters of a linear, one-mass model are adjusted by direct search to minimize the sum of the squared errors at each time denoted by an × or a + in Figure 3. The × data are for a two-piece ball fired at a barrier at 95 ft/sec and an angle of approach (AOA) of 20°. The + data are for

a two-piece ball fired at 95 ft/sec and an AOA of 40°. The
plain curves are the best fits obtainable from a linear,
constant-coefficient, three-parameter, one degree-of-
freedom model. The estimated parameters for these two
cases are given in Table 3.

Table 3. Estimated parameters from the Gobush data

at 95 ft/sec	k_1/m	c/m	k_2/c
	sec^{-2}	sec^{-1}	sec^{-1}
40° AOA	35080000	2260	7040
20° AOA	35920000	47800	420

   In the future, the direct-search coefficients will, in
turn, be used as initial values for a quasilinearization
procedure for refining these parameter estimates.

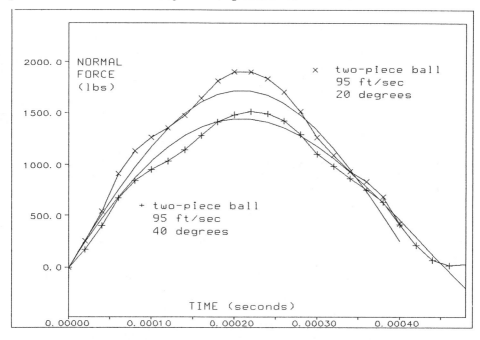

Figure 3. Comparison of linear, single-degree-of-freedom
model results with experimental force data from Gobush
(1990). The units for the vertical scale are pounds and
the horizontal scale units are seconds.

3 Two-degree-of-freedom model

The force time histories published by Gobush (1990) and Figure 3 suggest that the impact of two-piece balls against a barrier may be adequately described by a five-parameter model, but that wound balls would be less adequately represented. The Gobush results suggest that a two-degree-of-freedom, two-mass, fifth-order, six-parameter model may be sufficient to represent the major features of the force time histories for wound balls. Among several possible configurations the following, depicted in Figure 2, proved to be the most successful at mimicking the published results

$$(1-\delta)\,m\ddot{x}_1 = -k_1 x_1 - c\dot{x}_1 + c\dot{x}_3 + k_1 x_4$$

$$0 = -c\dot{x}_3 + c\dot{x}_1 - k_2 x_3$$

$$\delta m\ddot{x}_4 = -2k_1 x_4 + k_1 x_1$$

where x_1, x_2, and x_3 are as defined above and x_4 is the displacement of some fraction of the total mass, δ, assigned to an intermediate internal location. The remaining mass is lumped at the center of the ball.

4 Acknowledgements

The authors wish to express their gratitude to Mr. Frank Thomas, technical director of the United States Golf Association, and to Dr. Ronald E. Philipp, manager of the USGA Test and Research Center, for their generous support, cooperation, and encouragement.

5 References

Gobush, W., (1990) Impact force measurements on golf balls, in **Science and Golf**, (ed by A.J. Cochran), E. & F.N. Spon, Chapman and Hall, London, pp 219-224.
Goldsmith, W. (1960) **Impact**. Edward Arnold Ltd., London, pp 19, 266, 267.
Kolsky, H. (1952) **Stress waves in solids**. Dover Publications, New York, pp 106-115.
Lieberman, B.B., (1990) The effect of impact conditions on golf ball spin-rate, in **Science and Golf**, (ed by A.J. Cochran), E. & F.N. Spon, Chapman and Hall, London, pp 225-230.
Thomas, F.W., (1987) Groove study - phase II. USGA Technical Report, Far Hills, NJ.

48 An analytical model for ball–barrier impact

Part 2: A model for oblique impact

S.H. Johnson
Lehigh University, Bethlehem, Pennsylvania, USA
and B.B. Lieberman
Polytechnic University, Brooklyn, New York, USA

Abstract
The golf ball-barrier collision has proven to be too
complicated to be characterized successfully by
conventional coefficients of restitution and spin
restitution, even if the coefficients are velocity-
dependent and angle-dependent. An alternative is to use
the parameters of an ordinary differential equation model
of the transient viscoelastic deformation of a ball during
impact. A five-parameter, nonlinear model of normal impact
of solid balls has been successful in representing ball-
barrier collisions over a wide range of approach
velocities. A new, six-parameter version successfully
represents wound balls in normal impact. With the addition
of a torsion model, oblique impact can be simulated.
Keywords: Normal Impact, Oblique Impact, Ball Deformation,
Impact Modelling

1 Introduction

A model of oblique impact can be constructed by adding a
torsion model to a model of normal impact. The normal
model gives the radial deformation and the normal force.
The transverse force is either the coefficient of sliding
friction times the normal force during sliding or the
constraint force necessary to maintain rolling. The
external moment is the instantaneous radius times the
transverse force. Any of the models from Part I of this
paper is suitable for computing the normal force.

The equations of motion are referenced to an inertial
coordinate system located at the center of the undeflected
ball when it just comes in contact with the target barrier.
The state variables for the normal model are x_1: the
position of the center of mass of the ball in the y or
normal direction, which is the negative of the progress of
the center of mass toward the target from the time of first
contact and is also the negative of the deformation of the

Science and Golf II: Proceedings of the World Scientific Congress of Golf. Edited by A.J.
Cochran and M.R. Farrally. Published in 1994 by E & FN Spon, London. ISBN 0 419 18790 1

ball in the normal direction; x_2: the normal or y component of the velocity of the center of mass of the ball; and x_3: the position of the juncture between the spring, k_2, and dashpot, c, in the normal model. The first-order differential equations are

$$\dot{x}_1 = x_2 \qquad\qquad x_1(0) = 0$$

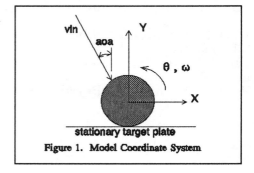

Figure 1. Model Coordinate System

$$\dot{x}_2 = \left\{ \begin{array}{c} -\left(\dfrac{k_1}{m}\right)x_1|x_1|^{\alpha-1} - \left(\dfrac{k_2}{m}\right)x_3|x_3|^{\beta-1} \\ 0 \quad if \quad \dot{x}_2 < 0 \end{array} \right\} \qquad x_2(0) = -v_{in}\cos(\theta_{aoa})$$

$$\dot{x}_3 = -\left(\frac{k_2}{c}\right)x_3|x_3|^{\beta-1} + x_2 \qquad\qquad x_3(0) = 0$$

where the condition $\dot{x}_2 \le 0$ indicates end of contact.

2 The torsional model

During periods of relative transverse movement between the surface of the ball and the target plate, the normal acceleration times the ball mass times the friction factor is the magnitude of the transverse friction force. The direction is such that the friction force opposes the x-direction motion of the portion of the surface of the ball in contact with the target plate. The transverse friction force times the instantaneous radius of the ball is the torque on the ball for the torsional model. The transverse

force is $f_t = -\mu m \dot{x}_2 \, signum(velocity)$ and the torque

exerted on the ball during sliding is $\tau = f_t(r_o + x_1)$. The torsional model state variables are x_4: the angular position of the core of the ball (thinking of the ball as consisting of a core and shell with the possibility of relative angular movement); x_5: the angular velocity of the core; x_6: the angular position of the juncture between the torsion spring, k_{2t}, and the torsional dashpot, c_t, in the torsional model; x_7: the angular position of the outer shell; and x_8: the angular velocity of the outer shell; and the first-order differential equations to be integrated are

$$\dot{x}_4 = x_5 \qquad x_4(0) = 0$$

$$\dot{x}_5 = \frac{1}{I_{core}} \{k_{1_t}(x_7 - x_4) + c_t(\dot{x}_6 - x_5)\} \qquad x_5(0) = 0$$

$$\dot{x}_6 = \frac{1}{c_t} \{c_t x_5 + k_{2_t}(x_7 - x_6)\} \qquad x_6(0) = 0$$

$$\dot{x}_7 = x_8 \qquad x_7(0) = 0$$

$$\dot{x}_8 = \left\{ \begin{array}{c} \dfrac{1}{I_{shell}}[k_{1_t}(x_4 - x_7) + k_{2_t}(x_6 - x_7) + \tau] \\ 0 \quad during\ rolling \end{array} \right\} \qquad x_8(0) = 0$$

where $I_{core} = \dfrac{2}{5} m r_o^2 (1-\gamma)^{5/3}$ and $I_{shell} = \gamma m r_o^2$.

3 The transverse model

The transverse motion state variables are x_9: the velocity of the center of mass of the ball in the x direction; and x_{10}: the position of the ball in the transverse direction. The first-order differential equations to be solved are

$$\dot{x}_9 = \left\{ \begin{array}{c} f_t/m \\ 0 \quad during\ rolling \end{array} \right\} \qquad x_9(0) = 0$$

$$\dot{x}_{10} = x_9 \qquad x_{10}(0) = 0$$

The ball is assumed to slide when it first contacts the target plate. Friction retards the outer shell motion and, if the velocity of the point of contact on the surface drops to zero, the ball subsequently rolls on the target surface, i.e., when $(r_o + x_1)x_8 + x_9 = 0$. During the initial sliding motion, the shell and core of the ball undergo separate angular accelerations while the transverse motion is retarded. The transverse velocity of the point of contact becoming zero signifies the onset of constant velocity rolling. When rolling is achieved the shell angular acceleration ceases, but the core angular acceleration does not and the relative motion of the shell and core continues. The core tries to drag the shell after it. This is prevented by friction. However, during

rebound, the friction force decreases until it can no
longer sustain rolling, and sliding resumes.
Sliding is assumed to cease and rolling begin when the
relative velocity between the surface of the ball and the
target plate drops below an arbitrary small number.
Rolling is assumed to cease and sliding to resume when the
back torque applied to the shell by the core exceeds by a
specified amount the torque due to friction. This
specification allows for the introduction of stiction. The
back torque is

$$\tau_b = k_{1_t}(x_4 - x_7) + k_{2_t}(x_6 - x_7)$$

The coding of such a model is complicated by the fact that
under some conditions three periods of sliding can occur,
separated by two periods of rolling, before disengagement.
The logic is straightforward during compression, but more
intricate during rebound.
   The discontinuities in the model make fixed-step
forward Euler integration a better choice of solution
algorithm than higher-order, variable-step alternatives.

4 Example

Guessed values for torsional parameters have been combined
with typical experimentally determined normal-model
parameters to create an example simulation. The values
used are k_1=985965 lbs/ft$^{-\alpha}$, k_2=764.48 lbs/ft$^{-\beta}$, k_{1t}=1000 ft-
lbs/rad, k_{2t}=1000 ft-lbs/rad, α=1.6, β=2.6, γ=0.1, c=21.17
lbs-sec/ft, c_t=2.6 ft-lbs-sec/rad, and μ=0.23. The
stiction factor is set at 2. The time step used for
numerical integration is 1 μs. As can be seen from Figure
2, while the ball is in contact with the target barrier, as
evidenced by nonzero normal force, the behavior is
credible. After contact is lost, the relative displacement
between the hypothetical core and shell continues to
oscillate, indicating that the torsional damping factor is
probably too small. The weighted average of the core and
shell angular velocities is constant after loss of contact,
as it should be with no external moment applied. Rolling
takes place at all angles of approach except 55°. Similar
behavior has been observed during air-gun testing of two-
piece balls. The model predicts the following spin rates:

Table 1.   Computed spin rates based on guessed parameters.

rps	aoa=15°	25°	35°	45°	55°
80 ft/s	−30.3	−45.5	−75.5	−100.6	−96.0
100	−32.5	−56.0	−98.6	−126.6	−116.0
120	−33.8	−67.6	−123.1	−151.7	−134.9

Example   319

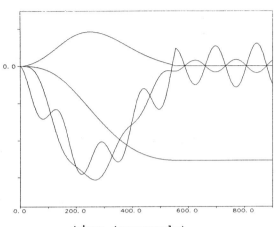

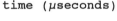

time (μseconds)

Figure 2.
Simulated ball-
barrier impact.
The vertical axis
is unscaled as
the various time
histories are
attenuated by
different amounts
to permit their
being plotted
together. This
is the 120 ft/sec
approach velocity
and 55° approach
angle case from
Table 1.   The
positive-going
time history is
normal force.
Contact ends when
the normal force
goes to zero.
The smooth
negative-going
time history that
is constant after
loss of contact
is the spin rate.
The remaining two
time histories
are the angular
accelerations of
the hypothetical
core and shell.
The shell leads
the core at early
times. Clearly,
there is too
little torsional
damping.

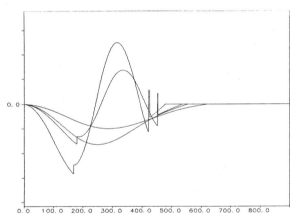

time (μseconds)

Figure 3.   Simulated transverse forces between ball and
barrier. In order of peak height, positive to negative, the
four transverse force time histories are 120 ft/sec
approach velocity and 15° angle of approach, 80 ft/sec &
15°, 80 ft/sec & 55° and 120 ft/sec & 55°.   The
discontinuities during the 15° simulations indicate that
rolling ensues and ceases before contact is lost.
Simulated stiction extends the time of rolling. At 55°
sliding continues throughout the time of contact.

The model portrays some features of ball-barrier impact correctly and misrepresents others. It is probably true that sliding is often followed by rolling and rolling may be followed by a brief period of sliding before loss of contact. Sliding-rolling-sliding-rolling-sliding probably doesn't happen, although the model does have two separate periods of rolling under some conditions. In reality, the sliding-to-rolling and rolling-to-sliding transitions are certainly less sudden than the simulation predicts.

The persistence of the angular accelerations of the hypothetical core and shell predicts persistent torsional flexure of the real golfball that is unlikely to be real. The model needs more torsional damping.

The model indicates that rolling promotes windup between the shell and core which, in turn, increases the spinrate. There is no rolling for any of the three cases in Table 1 at 55° angle of approach and the spinrates are reduced below those at 45°.

5 Future work

Part I of this paper describes the work that has gone into determining the parameters of a normal impact model. That model is successful in representing solid and two-piece ball behavior. An extension of that model seems able to portray two-piece and wound ball behavior but has an additional parameter. The additional parameter and uncertainty about strainrate effects dictate a switch to parameter estimation based on force transducer data following the precedent of Gobush (1990). An existing airgun facility is being equipped for such testing on a routine basis. The torsion model introduces four additional parameters, not including stiction or coefficient of friction, which defy identification by means other than parameter estimation from transient force data. The method of quasilinearization, (Graupe,1972) is being incorporated into the procedure.

6 Acknowledgements

The author wishes to express his gratitude to Mr. Frank Thomas, technical director of the United States Golf Association, and to Dr. Ronald E. Philipp, manager of the USGA Test and Research Center, for their generous support, cooperation, and encouragement.

7 References

Gobush, W. (1990) Impact force measurements on golf balls. Golf and Science, A.J. Cochran, editor, pp 219-224.
Graupe, D. (1972) Identification of Systems. Robert E, Krieger Publishing Co., Malabar, FL.

49 The effects of driver head size on performance

T. Olsavsky
Titleist and Foot-Joy Worldwide, Fairhaven, Massachusetts, USA

Abstract
This paper describes a scientific study to determine the performance
advantages of increased driver head size for a wide range of golfers.
The methodology includes human and mechanical performance tests. Size
comparisons were made for 3 classes of heads based on total volume and
face area. For this limited study, overall driving performance
improved as clubhead size increased.
Keywords: Metal Woods, Large Head, Moment of Inertia, Face Mapping,
Mechanical Golfer, Driver.

1 Background

1.1 Equipment advances in driving clubs

The development of driving clubs has been an enthusiastic passion of
golfers since the invention of the sport. The difficult goal of
increased distance and improved accuracy has challenged golfers and
clubmakers as much as any other aspect of the game.

One of the most successful recent developments in clubheads is that
of wood shaped metal heads, namely metal woods. While iron heads were
often cast in stainless steel, the first investment cast metal woods
were made of aluminum. These thick walled heads were used at driving
ranges because of the improved durability when compared to wooden
clubheads. As the material and casting technology evolved, thinner
stainless steel castings were developed, although they were smaller
than the wooden heads of the time. As foundries became more proficient
and club designs more sophisticated, larger heads became possible with
both oversize and midsize versions being prevalent today. Even larger
clubheads can be made with other lightweight metals as well as
composite constructions.

Science and Golf II: Proceedings of the World Scientific Congress of Golf. Edited by A.J.
Cochran and M.R. Farrally. Published in 1994 by E & FN Spon, London. ISBN 0 419 18790 1

1.2 Measurement of size

The measurement of clubhead size is typically done by two methods,
total head volume and face area. Typical driver volumes range from
140-170 cm^3 for conventional size, and 170-220 cm^3 for the midsize and
oversize categories. Even larger heads above 220 cm^3 will be classified
for this discussion as supersize. Face area is not categorized as
often but will affect performance as well as the player's perception
at address. The face area is a measure of the clubface that is
designed for striking the ball. Polar moment of inertia is measured
about the vertical axis of the clubhead through the center of gravity.
The center of gravity location is measured parallel to the ground from
the face rearwards to the center of gravity. Table 1 shows the
differences between the three clubhead types.

Table 1.   Clubhead characteristics by size category

Category	Volume (cm^3) ± 4	Face area (mm^2) ±50	Polar moment of inertia (*) (kg m^2) ±1%	CG Location from face (mm) ±1
Standard	145	2000	2.1 * 10^{-4}	21.1
Midsize	185	2450	2.4 * 10^{-4}	23.6
Supersize	250	3350	3.1 * 10^{-4}	27.9

1.3 Differences due to size

The size, shape, material and thickness distribution of the clubhead
will determine the characteristics by affecting the center of gravity
and moment of inertia. As size increases, the center of gravity of the
clubhead will move away from the face and away from the shaft
centerline. To adjust for the center of gravity location from the
face, the bulge and roll radii of the supersize club is slightly more
rounded (smaller radii) than the standard and midsize heads. The
moment of inertia will also increase with size.

   A larger clubhead also affects the player's visual perception at
address. This will vary greatly among players with a variety of skill
levels, ages, or handicaps. However, especially among higher handicap
players, a larger clubhead gives more confidence in driving the ball.

---

* - Polar moment of inertia provided by Butler J.H. et al, True
Temper Sports (1993) See Reference section 5.

1.4 Head construction

A typical metal clubhead is made by separately casting the main body of the head and the sole plate. These two pieces are then welded together to form the hollow clubhead. Minimum thicknesses are determined based on castability and metal flow through the thin walled sections. Using current technology the weight distribution can be adjusted by changing the thickness of the head in different areas.

However, while a size increase is desirable, the weight needs to remain the same or sometimes even be reduced. This is required to maintain the swingweight of the club. The physical properties of the material type will determine the size limits of the clubhead. To make the supersize driver, a lighter metal than stainless steel must be used.

2 Mechanical golfer face map tests

2.1 Test procedure for face mapping

A mechanical golfer was used to examine the various factors of club design. The standard test performed for clubhead analysis is called a face map and consists of hitting the ball at specific varied locations of the clubface to determine the head performance. Measurement is done with a ball monitoring system which provides fast and efficient data collection. This system measures the launch conditions of the ball (velocity, launch angle and spin rate), and computes the trajectory to provide distance and direction data.

2.2 Comparison of the face map sizes

There were two sets of locations used for face mapping in this comparison. These shot locations are measured from the geometric center of the face. The first grouping is smaller and represents mishits for a conventional size clubhead. Heel and toe shots are ± 19 mm from center while high and low shots are ± 9.5 mm from center. The second group of hit locations are spaced farther apart to account for the larger clubfaces of midsize, oversize and supersize designations. They consist of ± 25.4 mm for heel and toe and ± 12.7 mm for high and low positions. Therefore, each face map has five hit locations.

2.3 Results from machine test

A comparison of these three club head sizes was performed with the same type shaft and produced nearly identical initial ball velocity within 2 ft/sec. Launch conditions will vary slightly with clubhead type. As shown in Table 2 the larger headed clubs produced more launch angle and backspin than the standard size driver when hit in the geometric center of the clubface. This occurs because the more rearward center of gravity of the larger heads increases the dynamic loft at impact.

Table 2.   Mechanical golfer launch condition data

Category	Ballspeed (ft/sec) ± 2	Launch Angle (°) ±.5	Backspin (rpm) ±180	Carry (yd) ±3	Total (yd) ±3
Standard	220	8.0	3300	233	260
Midsize	220	9.3	3500	237	263
Supersize	218	9.5	3400	235	262

The most important summary comparison for the face map test is the landing areas of both carry and total distance with lateral deviation from target line. This measurement incorporates a variety of factors including ball velocity, launch angle, azimuth angle, backspin and sidespin. It also gives a consistent measure for judging the effects of clubhead loft angle, center of gravity location, bulge and roll, and weight distribution. Landing area is the ellipsoid area which would statistically enclose 95% of the landing locations in a given test. The axes of the ellipse are distance and lateral deviation from the target line. The smaller the landing area the more accurate the club or ball.

As shown in Table 3 the supersize driver performed better than the smaller clubheads based on all measures of landing area performance. This would be predicted by the larger moment of inertia value. The distance range is a measure of maximum separation from the best to worst landing location. Notice that the standard club performs very poorly at the oversize map locations. These locations would represent extreme mishits for the smaller club. This fact alone suggests that large headed drivers have better performance on off-center hits because they can have full face contact with the ball at extreme locations.

There is also less energy loss at off-center locations with the larger clubhead. This is measured by the ball velocity difference from the center hit locations versus the off center locations. At the most extreme hit locations the supersize club only loses 15 ft/sec of ball velocity the other drivers lose 22 ft/sec of ball velocity.

Table 3.   Mechanical golfer impact area data

| Category | Standard Map | | Oversize Map | |
	Landing Area (yd^2) ± 80	Distance Range (yd) ± 3	Landing Area (yd^2) ± 200	Distance Range (yd) ± 5
Standard	2200	22	3900	48
Midsize	1200	23	2370	36
Supersize	1000	14	1100	28

3 Player tests

3.1 Test procedure

16 players were tested with a variety of ages, launch conditions, and handicaps from 3-18. Players were asked to hit clubs in succession with 1 shot recorded for each club before switching to the next club. 4 shots were recorded for each player with each club for a total of 12 shots. The sequence of the three clubs was randomized to help reduce experimental error from player performance variations. Because of mishits these 12 test shots could require 20 to 25 shots depending on player ability. This is a reasonable amount of shots for most golfers for this type of test and results in the best exchange of consistency versus player fatigue.

3.2 Results of live tests

As shown in Table 4 the supersize driver provided more distance and consistency than the other drivers due to the larger size and greater moment of inertia. Subjective feedback from the players also indicated the ease of hitting increased with head size.

The ball to club speed ratio increases with head size, indicating a more consistent energy transfer even with off center hit locations. The distance produced by the supersize is slightly more than the other two classes. The landing area comparison of player tests showed that the supersize club was more consistent than the other drivers as measured by the reduced landing area. While these results do not duplicate the mechanical golfer tests exactly, they do indicate improved performance for the supersize driver. However, with all player testing the data will have larger variations than machine testing making real differences harder to detect.

Table 4.   Player launch condition data   (Averages)

Category	Ball/Club speed Ratio ± .03	Launch ang. (°) ± 2	Backspin (rpm) ± 600	Distance (yd) ± 15	Landing area (yd²) ± 300
Standard	1.42	10.2	3270	212	2830
Midsize	1.44	9.3	2900	214	2780
Supersize	1.46	10.4	3260	219	2410

4 Conclusions

4.1 Does a larger clubhead offer improved performance?
These test results have shown that the Supersize driver performs better than midsize and standard size metal woods, as measured by smaller landing area and longer distance. For off center hit locations and typical player impacts the larger clubhead performed better because of the higher moment of inertia and larger face area.

4.2 Is a bigger head easier to hit?
The larger clubhead was easier to hit for the majority of players tested based on their feedback and observations by test personnel. It inspired more confidence and produced more consistent results than the other two classes of drivers. Players also commented that because the face is longer, the supersize driver was easier to line up at address.

4.3 Future studies
While this study was limited to overall clubhead size, further efforts to examine size and driving performance might include face depth, CG location, size aspect ratio, face thickness, face radii and other head variables. We have only touched one of the head design features and have not talked about shaft or complete club variables. A superior club has been designed but an improved version can and will be developed. The search for the perfect driver continues.

5 Reference

Butler, J.H. et al, True Temper Sports (1993) Inertia Dyadic and Equivalent Mass System of a Titleist Driver. True Temper Sports, Memphis, Tennessee USA

50 Video monitoring system to measure initial launch characteristics of golf ball

W. Gobush, D. Pelletier and C. Days
Titleist and Foot-Joy Worldwide, Fairhaven, Massachusetts, USA

Abstract
A video data acquisition system is described which takes two snapshot views of selected markers on a golf ball in the immediate post-launch time period. The analysis of the combined snapshot images allows the initial ball speed, launch angle and spin rate to be measured in real time. The mathematical and photogrammetrical techniques are described that solve this motion analysis problem.
Keywords: Video, Pixels, Retroreflector, Strobe, Translational Velocity, Angular Velocity, Photogrammetry.

1 Introduction
The measurement of ball velocity, spin rate and launch angle is critically important in assessing new ball and club designs. Once the ball has left the tee, the flight motion is essentially prescribed by the velocity and spin rate created by the impact and the aerodynamic characteristics of the golf ball. In automating these kinematic measurements for outdoor use, computerized video technology has been utilized and resulted in a compact, automatic and portable measuring system.

2 Background
The study of high speed motion analysis has frequently used the medium of 16mm film or Polaroid film. The film is usually projected onto a digitizing tablet and points of interest can be selected frame by frame. However, high-speed film results in excessive film developing time and the inability to rapidly digitize frames make film a less than perfect medium for the study of golf ball motion. Recently, the advances in computerized video technology permits video to compete with film as a convenient, accurate and cost-effective research tool.

A solution to the motion blur problem caused by the fast ball speeds is the addition of the strobe lamp to the video camera. Although the typical electronic shutter is not fast enough for stilling the image of a golf ball, it results in a high level of contrast by only allowing outdoor light to photosensitize the video sensor for the duration of the scene to be measured (see Figure 1). The real motion freezing of markers on a golf

Science and Golf II: Proceedings of the World Scientific Congress of Golf. Edited by A.J. Cochran and M.R. Farrally. Published in 1994 by E & FN Spon, London. ISBN 0 419 18790 1

ball for dynamic analysis requires a strobe light of one microsecond duration and sufficient light output to overcome the shuttered background illumination.

Since the standard video signal from a video camera has a 1/60th of a second field rate, the scene of interest for analyzing ball speed and ball spin rate requires strobing the scene twice during one field period. The sound of impact captured by an acoustical sensor can be used to trigger the camera's shutter and two positions of the ball are captured within close proximity of each other (typically a one millisecond time separation).

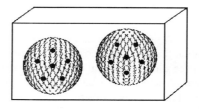

Fig. 1. Golf Ball Launch Scene

3 Photogrammetrical Analysis in Three Dimensions
Using a mathematical technique called triangulation, the simultaneous sighting from two viewpoints allows the location of markers on the ball to be measured in three dimensions. This technique requires two cameras to be located at an acute angle to each other so both cameras can image common markers on the ball from different viewpoints. This results in the camera locations shown in Figure 2 in which the optical axes of the two cameras converge on the scene of interest.

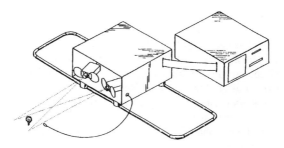

Fig. 2. Computerized Video Acquisition System

A very popular technique for three dimensional film analysis was developed in the 1970's to utilize non-metric film cameras. This technique is the Direct Linear Transformation (DLT) developed by Adbel-Aziz and Karara (1971, 1974). One reason why DLT was developed is that only linear equations need be solved. The equations which describe this approach are as follows:

$$U = \frac{C_1 x + C_2 y + C_3 z + C_4}{C_9 x + C_{10} y + C_{11} z + 1} \qquad (1)$$

$$V = \frac{C_5 x + C_6 y + C_7 z + C_8}{C_9 x + C_{10} y + C_{11} z + 1} \qquad (2)$$

where U and V are the coordinates of an imaged marker on the two dimensional video sensor and x,y,z are the actual positions of the markers in space. The $C_1..C_{11}$ calibration parameters are related to camera orientation, position and magnification factor.

To evaluate the eleven DLT parameters, a calibration of the camera is done by locating a calibration frame in the field of view common to both cameras and the initial flight zone of the golf ball. The accuracy of marker locations in the calibration frame should be less than one thousandth of an inch and contain several planes of points. The eleven constants are found by solving equation (1) and (2) by knowing the position of the premeasured x,y,z calibration markers and the computerized measurements of the imaged points U and V in the captured video image. The least squares method is used to handle the redundant equations and give a statistical analysis of the model equations fit to the measured data.

Once the two cameras are calibrated, a set of four linear equations can be solved for a point common to the field of view of both cameras. Using single prime (') for the left camera image and double prime (") for the right camera image, the following equations are obtained from equations (1) and (2) that allow the x,y,z position of any marker in the view of the two cameras to be calculated.

$$(C_9'U'-C_1')x + (C_{10}'U'-C_2')y + (C_{11}'U'-C_3')z + (U'-C_4') = 0 \qquad (3)$$

$$(C_9'V'-C_5')x + (C_{10}'V'-C_6')y + (C_{11}'V'-C_7')z + (V'-C_8') = 0 \qquad (4)$$

$$(C_9''U''-C_1'')x + (C_{10}''U''-C_2'')y + (C_{11}''U''-C_3'')z + (U''-C_4'') = 0 \qquad (5)$$

$$(C_9''V''-C_5'')x + (C_{10}''V''-C_6'')y + (C_{11}''V''-C_7'')z + (V''-C_8'') = 0 \qquad (6)$$

4 Analysis of Computerized Video Imagery

In the previous analysis, we discussed the mathematics of marker points in space and not the discrete pixel cells found in video imagery. In a typical captured video image, one field of a frame is digitized into 240 lines of data, each containing 510 pixel elements. The center of a circular marker on the calibration fixture gets digitized in the computer's memory as a cluster of rectangular cells with a gray level ranging from 0 to 255. To calculate the center of a circular marker, a centroid averaging procedure is utilized. In centroid averaging, the center position of a highly contrasted marker is found by summing over the pixel position of all pixels about the marker that have an intensity level above a threshold gray level and dividing by the number of pixel elements in the sum. The thresholding operation segments the image into distinctly contrasted regions that result in the image shown in Figure 3. To enhance the contrast of the circular marker in the image, a retroreflective marker is used that reflects strobed light approximately 900 times more than a circular white marker. This reflecting ability is highly dependent on locating the strobe lighting as close as possible to the optical axis of the camera.

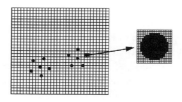

Fig. 3. Computer Enhanced Image Scene

5 Motion Analysis in Three Dimensions

The motion analysis of a golf ball is analyzed by first calculating the location of its center of mass and its orientation relative to a global coordinate system. The global coordinate system (x,y,z) is created by aligning the z axis of our calibration plate along the direction of preferred flight and the y-direction parallel to gravity.

The golf ball coordinate system called the body coordinate system is created by the location of retroreflective markers on the surface of the golf ball and measured relative to its center of mass. In practice, six reflectors are used in a pentagonal pattern shown in Figure 1. The conversion of the marker location in the body coordinate system to the reference global system of our calibrated cameras is given in matrix algebra by the equation

$$\begin{pmatrix} x \\ y \\ z \end{pmatrix}_{global} = \begin{pmatrix} T_x \\ T_y \\ T_z \end{pmatrix} + \begin{pmatrix} M_{11} M_{12} M_{13} \\ M_{21} M_{22} M_{23} \\ M_{31} M_{32} M_{33} \end{pmatrix} \begin{pmatrix} x \\ y \\ z \end{pmatrix}_{body} \tag{7}$$

The column vector, T_x, T_y, T_z, is the location of the center of mass of the ball in the global coordinate system. The matrix elements, M_{ij} (i=1,3; j=1,3), are the direction cosines defining the orientation of the body coordinate system relative to the global system. Three angles, a_1, a_2, a_3, describe the elements of matrix M_{ij} in terms of periodic functions. Substituting matrix equation (7) for the global position of each reflector into equations (3), (4), (5) and (6), a set of 24 equations result for the six unknown variables $(T_x, T_y, T_z, a_1, a_2, a_3)$. A similar set of 24 equations must be solved for the second ball strobed in the video scene shown in Figure 1. Typically, the solution of the three variables T_x, T_y, T_z and the three angles a_1, a_2, a_3 that prescribed the rotation matrix, M, is solvable in four iterations for the 24 equations that must be simultaneously satisfied.

The kinematic variables, three components of translational velocity and three components of angular velocity in the global coordinate system, are calculated from the relative translation of the center of mass and relative rotation angles that the ball makes between its two strobed positions.

The velocity components of the center of mass V_x, V_y, V_z along the three axes of the global coordinate system are given by equations to follow:

$$V_x = \frac{T_x(t+\Delta T) - T_x(t)}{\Delta T} ;\ V_y = \frac{T_y(t+\Delta T) - T_y(t)}{\Delta T} ;\ V_z = \frac{T_z(t+\Delta T) - T_z(t)}{\Delta T} \tag{8}$$

in which t is the time of the first strobed measurement of T_x, T_y, T_z and $t+\Delta T$ is the second strobed measurement of T_x, T_y, T_z.

The spin rate components in the global axis system result from obtaining the product of the inverse orientation matrix, $M^T(t)$, and $M(t+\Delta T)$. The resulting relative orientation matrix, A, measures the angular difference of the two strobed ball images.

$$A(t, t+\Delta t) = M(t+\Delta T)M^T(t) \tag{9}$$

The magnitude, Θ, of the angle of rotation about the spin axis during the time increment ΔT is given by:

$$\Theta = \sin^{-1}(R/2) \quad \text{where } R = \sqrt{l^2 + m^2 + n^2} \tag{10}$$

$$l = A_{32} - A_{23}; \quad m = A_{13} - A_{31}; \quad n = A_{21} - A_{12} \tag{11}$$

The three orthogonal components of spin rate, W_x, W_y, W_z, are given by:

$$W_x = \Theta l/(R\Delta T) ;\ W_y = \Theta m/(R\Delta T) ;\ W_z = \Theta n/(R\Delta T) \tag{12}$$

These equations can be derived from the rotation speed equations given in most kinematic books (e.g. Appendix B of <u>Rimrott</u>).

6 Typical Testing Results

A typical driving test on six balata wound golf balls and six two-piece solid balls hit under the same conditions with four replications gives results as follows:

Units	Ball Speed mph	Launch Angle degrees	Side Angle degrees	W_x Rate rpm	W_y Rate rpm	W_z Rate rpm
Average (Wound)	156.7	8.5	-0.7	-4403	3	193
Standard Deviation	0.8	0.4	0.2	184	78	115
Average (Two-Piece)	156.6	8.8	-0.7	-3202	3	-23
Standard Deviation	1.0	0.3	0.2	126	197	137

These results illustrate the effect of two different golf ball constructions on launch conditions. The launch variable primarily affected is the resulting backspin of the ball (W_x rate) on squarely hit golf shots. A secondary effect is the lower launch angle of wound construction versus two-piece solid balls with high modulus ionomer cover material.

Five error factors that contribute to the standard deviation of the measurements are:

(a) variation in the swinging speed of the test machine;
(b) variation in the compression and resilience of the golf balls;
(c) variation in the positioning of markers on the golf balls;
(d) pixel resolution of video sensor; and
(e) accuracy of premeasured markers on calibration fixture.

Computer simulations of a ±.25 pixel error model for marker centroid location on a 240 square pixel sensor result in a ±15rpm standard deviation in backspin (W_x rate) and ±70rpm for sidespin components. Therefore, most of the standard deviation in the measured data is attributed to error factors (a) and (b).

7 Conclusions

The union of computer and video technology has resulted in an automatic and portable launch monitoring device. Its use on the actual golf course allows faster data acquisition under realistic playing conditions and is a major step forward in collecting data for designing and testing new golf equipment. Measurement errors are small compared with those introduced by test machine or ball to ball variation.

8 References

Abdel-Aziz, Y.I. and Karara, H.M. (1971), Direct Linear Transformation into Object Space Coordinates in Close-Range Photogrammetry, Symposium on Close-Range Photogrammetry, University of Illinois at Urbana-Champaign, Urbana, Illinois, January 26-29, 1-18.

Abdel-Aziz, Y.I. and Karara, H.M. (1974) Photogrammetric Potential of Non-Metric Cameras, Civil Engineering Studies Photogrammetry Series No. 36, University of Illinois at Urbana-Champaign, Urbana, Illinois, March.

Rimrott (1989) F.P.J., Introductory Attitude Dynamics, Springer-Verlag, 321-328.

9 Acknowledgements

The authors thank Herbert Boehm of Acushnet Company for his support and initiation of this project. We also wish to acknowledge the assistance of Kam W. Wong for photogrammetric consulting and Clarke Hottel of Clarke Engineering for electrical development.

51 The relationship between golf ball construction and performance

M.J. Sullivan and T. Melvin
Spalding Sports Worldwide, Chicopee, Mass., USA

Abstract
The development of new materials in the golf ball industry over the past few years has fueled a virtual explosion of new product offerings that are transforming the game. No longer is there a clear choice between either a wound ball giving feel and control or a durable but hard two piece ball. Construction (i.e. simply wound versus 2-piece) no longer dictates performance. The critical design parameters are not whether the core is wound, solid, liquid filled, or balata or Surlyn covered but rather the hardness, thickness, and dynamic mechanical properties of the cover, the flexural properties of the ball, and size of the ball.
Keywords: Golf ball, Ionomer, Balata, Spin, Cover Hardness, Compression, Moment of inertia, Size

1 Introduction

One of the earliest golf balls, the feathery, was a stitched leather pouch soaked in water and stuffed with goose feathers which upon drying formed a hard sphere. This construction was the standard from about the 1400s until about 1850 when a solid gutta percha ball proved to be much less expensive, more durable and consistent than the feathery. Soon after golfers noticed that a scratched or nicked surface imparted greater distance and more uniform flight to the ball. Manufacturers soon offered textured, patterned balls, the most popular being the bumpy bramble ball. Dimples would eventually make their debut in 1909 (Martin,1968).

By the turn of the century a measure of added feel and control was added by winding continuous rubber thread under high tension around a small solid rubber core, and wrapping in a gutta percha cover. Balata, chemically similar to gutta percha and a trans isomer of polyisoprene obtained from South America, soon replaced gutta percha due to its improved adhesion to the rubber windings, better color and toughness. Over the past several years natural balata has been replaced by various blends of synthetic polymers that give greater consistency and better durability.

The pace of development of golf ball materials is tied directly to the popularity of the two piece golf ball. The drive to develop a performance two piece ball began in 1968 when the Spalding Executive ball was introduced with a core of a highly crosslinked polybutadiene composition and a polyurethane/ABS blended cover. This ball was soon eclipsed by the Spalding Top-Flite golf ball which was the first solid core ball to use DuPonts' new super tough Surlyn ionomer resins. This ball created the durable distance ball that the average golfer was looking for. While this ball has remained popular for over 20 years and fulfills the needs of the average golfer, it was considered by many better players as too hard and harsh feeling. Surlyn covered wound-core balls pioneered by the Metropolitan Golf and Ram Golf Companies and made popular by the Titleist DT ball have filled the void to some extent by offering a cut proof ball having a softer feel than the solid-core version, but these balls generally lack the distance of the two piece.

Science and Golf II: Proceedings of the World Scientific Congress of Golf. Edited by A.J. Cochran and M.R. Farrally. Published in 1994 by E & FN Spon, London. ISBN 0 419 18790 1

A balance of properties can be obtained by combining soft cover materials with solid core technology thereby creating a new category of golf balls that offer the feel and spin of a wound ball with the distance previoulsy found only in two-piece balls. Todays' golf balls generally fall into one of four performance categories: distance/durability, distance/feel/accuracy, distance/feel/spin, and high spin/feel (**Figure 1**).

Distance/[1] Durability	Distance/[2] Feel	Spin/Feel/[3] Distance	High Spin/Feel[4]
2-piece hard ionomer cov'd	oversized 2-piece hard cover	2-piece soft covered or hard ionomer cover over a wound core	2-piece or wound core with a synthetic balata cover

Figure 1. Performance Categories
1-this group includes the Top-Flite XL, Ultra, Maxfli MD, and Titleist HVC; 2-Top-Flite Magna; 3-Top-Flite Tour, Titleist DT, Titleist HP 2, Ultra Competition; 4- Top-Flite Tour Z-Balata, Maxfli HT Balata, Titleist Tour Balata

Comparison of spin rates demonstrates how the performance characteristics of two-piece balls often overlap those of wound balls (Table 1).

Table 1. Spin Rates of Popular Ball Types

Ball Type	Spin Rate (RPM)[a]
1.68", 2-pc., Synthetic Balata Cover[1]	10,011
1.68", wound core, Syn. Balata Cover[2]	9,805
1.68", wound core, Syn. Balata Cover[3]	9,426
1.68", 2-pc., Intermed. Softness Ionomer Cov.[4]	9,386
1.68", 2-pc., Intermed. Softness Ionomer Cov.[5]	9,078
1.68", wound core, Hard Ionomer Cov.[6]	8,931
1.68", 2-pc., Hard Ionomer Cov.[7]	8,593
1.68", 2-pc., Hard Ionomer Cov.[8]	8,455
1.68", 2-pc., Hard Ionomer Cov.[9]	8,125
1.72", 2-pc., Hard Ionomer Cov.[10]	6,985

a-Measured using a 9-iron and clubhead speed of 105 feet/second. 1 is a Top-Flite Tour Z-Balata 100; 2 is a Maxfli HT 100; 3 is a Titleist Tour 100; 4 is a Top-Flite Tour 100; 5 is a Titleist HP-2; 6 is a Titleist DT 100; 7 is a Top-Flite XL; 8 is a Wilson Ultra; 9 is a Titleist HVC 100; and 10 is a Top-Flite Magna

Finally, larger diameter balls have been introduced which have unique performance characteristics versus similar constructions in a smaller version.

While little published literature outside of patents exists on golf ball construction (Statz, 1990) we will present some recent findings of our work in this area concerning specific construction/performance interaction.

2 Experimental

2.1 Hardness
Shore Hardness was measured in general accordance with ASTM Test D-2240, measured on the parting line of a fixtured, finished ball..

2.2 Compression

Compression was measured using a Riehle compression device (Riehle Bros. Testing Machine Co., Philadelphia, PA.) that determines the deformation in thousandths of an inch under a fixed static load of 200 pounds (a Riehle compression of 61 corresponds to a deflection under load of 0.061 inches). PGA compression is determined by manually applying a spring loaded force to a ball using a device manufactured by the Atti Engineering, Union City, New Jersey. An approximate relationship for balls of the same diameter, between Riehle compression and PGA compression is PGA compression equals 160 minus Riehle compression. Thus, a PGA compression of 80 equals a Riehle compression of 80; 90 PGA=70 Riehle; 100 PGA=60 Riehle, etc. All reported compressions were measured as Riehle and converted to PGA compression.

2.3 Spin Rate

Spin rate was measured by striking a ball with a nine iron wherein the clubhead speed is about 105 feet per second and the ball is launched at an angle of 26 to 34 degrees with a velocity of about 110-115 feet per second. The spin rate was determined by observing the rotation of the ball in flight using stop action strobe photography.

2.4 Moment of Inertia

Moment of inertia was measured using an instrument model 5050 made by Inertia Dynamics of Wallingford, CT. It consists of a horizontal pendulum with a top-mounted cage to hold the ball. The moment of inertia is calculated using the formula:
$I = 194.0 * (t^2 - T^2)$, where 194.0 is the calibration constant for the instrument , T the period of oscillation of the instrument when empty, and t the period of oscillation of the instrument with the ball loaded.

3 Construction

In addition to proper selection of materials, other important factors governing golf ball performance are cover thickness, cover hardness, core stiffness typically measured as compression, overall ball size, dimple pattern and ratio of land area to dimpled area.

Proper choice of cover and core materials is critical to achieving distance, durability and playability . Just as important however is the way core and cover are combined and the many possible combinations give the golf ball designer considerable latitude in building in certain benefits for the desired skill level player.

Finally, the golf ball designer must adhere to the rules of golf as put forth by the USGA and R & A Golf Club. These governing bodies enforce the following rules: (1) the ball weight must not exceed 1.62 oz, (2) the ball size must be at least 1.68 inches in diameter, (3) Initial velocity must not exceed 250 ft/sec with a 2% maximum tolerance when struck at 143.8 ft/sec, (4) Overall distance must not exceed 280 yards with a 6% tolerance when hit with a USGA specified driver at 160 ft/sec (clubhead speed) at a 10 degree launch angle as tested by the USGA, and (5) the ball must pass the USGA administered symmetry test, ie. fly consistently (in distance, trajectory and time of flight) regardless of how it is placed on the tee. With this in mind we shall briefly discuss a few of the more important parameters used in designing modern golf balls.

3.1 Cover Hardness

Cover hardness is directly related to the spin rate one can impart to the ball with softer covers giving higher revolutions per minute (RPM)(**Figure 2**).

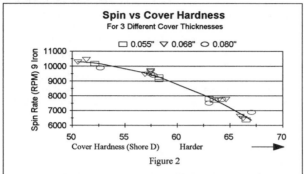

Figure 2

Spin rates are relatively independent of cover thickness except to the extent that thickness may tend to influence overall ball compression and ball compression does have some influence over spin rates.

A softer core will give a lower spin rate than a harder core having the same cover material at the same thickness. It is believed that at impact a hard core serves to compress the cover of the ball against the face of the club to a much greater degree than a soft core thereby resulting in more "grab" of the ball on the clubface and subsequent higher spin rates. In effect the cover is squeezed between the relatively incompressible core and clubhead. When a softer core is used, the cover is under much less compressive stress than in the harder core case and therefore does not contact the clubface as intimately and hence lower spin rates are obtained (**Figure 3**).

Therefore the best combination for a low spinning golf ball is a hard thick cover over a soft, low compression core. Conversely the highest spinning ball is a ball having a firm core covered by a soft, thin cover material.

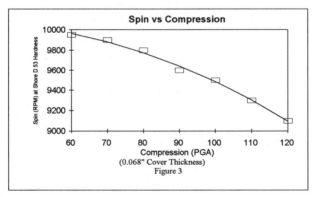

3.2 Cover Thickness

As we discussed above cover thickness can affect spin rates via the added stiffness a thick hard cover may add (or the lack of stiffness a soft thin cover contributes) to the overall ball compression. More importantly cover thickness must be carefully considered if one is to optimize distance. The distance a golf ball will travel is a function of the speed and mass of the club, and the size, density and resilience of the ball and other factors. Since the governing bodies of golf have rules that prohibit us from making a ball too small or too heavy, we concentrate on maximizing the resilience of the ball. Simply put, resilience is a measure of energy retained to energy lost when the ball is impacted with the club.

While proper selection of materials is critical to obtaining high resilience, it is also important to consider cover thickness when designing a ball. For example, a soft covered golf ball is preferred by the better golfer because he can impart high spin rates that give him better control or workability of the ball. However, soft covers such as balata or low modulus ionomers tend to have lower resilience than hard covers such as the high modulus ionomers used in the original two piece balls. These soft materials detract from resilience by absorbing some of the impact energy as it is compressed. Therefore for soft covered balls it is best to use the thinnest cover possible while relying on a high resilience core to provide the distance. With hard covered balls (of the distance/durability category) the cover increases the resilience of the ball versus that of the core and cover thickness is not critical for maximum resilience. In fact thicker covers are advantageous when greater distance off shorter irons is looked for.

3.3 Compression

Compression of itself has little bearing on overall ball performance. It will strongly influence the sound and this is what the golfer perceives as feel, particularly in chipping and putting. How much the ball compresses against the clubface and (more importantly) how soft the cover is determines the resultant spin rate. As we've already discussed a softer core will contribute to a lower spin rate than a harder core. Historically in wound ball manufacture compression was the result of an inconsistent process that required sorting of relatively hard and soft balls into two categories, 90 and 100. Even today, many wound balls are still sorted into 90's, typically having a compression of about 85 to about 100, and 100's having a compression of about 95 to 105. Solid core technology allows for much more precise control of compression since the amount of deformation is tightly controlled by the chemical formula used in making the cores.

3.4 Ball Size

Studies performed over 25 years ago comparing the 1.62 inch diameter ball to the 1.68 ball (Cochran and Stobbs, 1968) suggest significant differences in performance, namely distance between the two balls. Because of its greater area one would expect a larger ball to experience greater drag and lift and therefore have less carry distance and greater sideways deviation. In these early studies , the response of both balls to the same impact was very similar in launch angle, spin rate, and velocity leaving the clubface, however the smaller ball did carry about 2 to 4 % further and the larger ball experienced much greater deviation in a headwind.   While there was a general acceptance that the larger ball would putt truer, and be easier to hit since its larger diameter provides an improved lie, it was clear that significant changes in design must be made to make an oversized ball that provides net benefits over a smaller ball.

Advances in aerodynamic design and materials for golf ball construction over the past 25 years have made possible the design of a 1.72 inch diameter ball (adhering to all USGA and R&A rules) that does not sacrifice carry distance or sideways deviation when compared to a typical 1.68 inch diameter ball. The ball has a thick (0.090 inches), hard cover of ionomer over a very soft , solid core and has a greater moment of inertia (Table 2) then smaller balls.   This combination gives reduced spin rates (Table 1) and therefore reduced slicing and hooking. Further the increased size along with the soft core/hard cover combination results in higher launch angles off the clubface which is belived to contribute to increased distance under at least some circumstances.

A larger ball also allows the use of wider dimples than are possible (without overlap) on a 1.68 inch diameter ball. While studies have been limited in this area, wider dimples generally contribute reduced drag for greater carry distance. The combination of a rigid cover, a low compression core and high percent coverage (greater than about 70 %) dimple designs unique to a larger surface area give interesting benefits that we continue to investigate. Balls having diameters even larger than 1.72 inches at a weight not exceeding 1.62 ounces present greater challenges with respect to maintaining acceptable carry distance and sideways deviations but may find some utility in the form of a ball for very low clubhead speeds and for low skill level play such as for beginning golfers.

Table 2. Moment of Inertia of Popular Ball Types

Ball Type	Moment of Inertia(g/cm^2)[a]
1.68", wound core, hard ionomer cov.[1]	0.398
1.68", wound core, synthetic balata cov.[2]	0.400
1.68", wound core, synthetic balata cov.[3]	0.415
1.68", 2-pc., intermed. softness ionomer cov.[4]	0.437
1.68", 2-pc., intermed. softness ionomer cov.[5]	0.441
1.68", 2-pc., intermed. softness ionomer cov.[6]	0.443
1.68", 2-pc., intermed. softness ionomer cov.[7]	0.444
1.68", 2-pc., synthetic balata cov.[8]	0.445
1.72", 2-pc., hard ionomer cov.[9]	0.458

a-See Experimental Section for Test Description
1 is a Titleist DT 100; 2 is a Titleist Tour 100; 3 is a Maxfli HT 100; 4 is a Wilson Ultra Competition; 5 is a Top-Flite Tour 90; 6 is a Top-Flite Tour 100; 7 is a Titleist HP-2 100; 8 is a Top-Flite Tour Z-Balata 100; 9 is a Top-Flite Magna

4 Conclusions

The golf ball has been the object of extensive industrial and academic research for well over 100 years with more than 5000 patents issued on golf ball technology since 1900. This considerable effort has provided the user with a number of significant improvements. The ball that once lasted only a few holes before it became unplayable if struck less than perfectly square is now available in a version that is virtually indestructible, has excellent distance and gives a soft responsive feel. Products with these seemingly contradictory characteristics are the result of a fiercely competitive business place that rewards innovation with market share.

The main technical conclusions drawn from the work presented herein are:
1. Past distinctions between two piece and three piece balls or wound versus solid core balls are no longer pertinent due to a better understanding of the effect of core and cover on performance, and;
2. Increased ball size does not necessarily give reduced performance.

References
Cochran, A. and Stobbs, J. (1968) The Search for the Perfect Swing. The Booklegger (USA).

Martin, J. (1968) The Curious History of the Golf Ball. Horizon Press.

Statz, R. (1990) Surlyn Ionomers for Golf Ball Covers. First World Scientific Congress of Golf, St. Andrews.

52 A new aerodynamic model of a golf ball in flight

A.J. Smits
Princeton University, Princeton, NJ, USA
and D.R. Smith
IMST, Marseille, France

Abstract
A new aerodynamic model of a golf ball is proposed based on recent wind tunnel
measurements. The primary features of the model are the inclusion of a spin rate decay
law, and a non-linear dependence of the drag on Reynolds number. This term is necessary
to represent accurately the decrease in drag coefficient observed at Reynolds numbers
greater than about 200,000.
Keywords: Golf ball, Aerodynamics.

1 Introduction

Accurate measurements of the lift and drag characteristics of golf balls are necessary to
predict the golf ball trajectory and its point of impact. The first comprehensive
measurements of the lift and drag of a spinning golf ball were made by Davies (1949) who
measured the aerodynamic forces acting on the ball by dropping it through the horizontal air
stream of a wind tunnel. By measuring the point of impact of the ball on the tunnel floor,
and by repeating this measurement for balls with clockwise and counterclockwise spin, the
lift and drag could be determined. The spin rate was varied up to 8000 rpm (corresponding
to a spin rate parameter $W = \omega r/V$ of 0.089), but only one tunnel speed was used (105
ft/s, corresponding to a Reynolds number $R = 2Vr/v$ of about 94,000). Davies also
presented some trajectory calculations using the measured lift and drag information, but, as
he stated: "Neither the manner in which L and D vary with translational speed nor the time
rate of change of rotational speed are known."

   The next major contribution was made by Bearman and Harvey (1976), who
suspended a large model of a golf ball in a wind tunnel using fine wire supports. The ball
could be spun in either direction using a motor mounted inside the ball. The interference
due to the support wires was determined by reference to previous results for spinning
smooth spheres, and it was found that when the ratio of the support wire diameter to the
ball diameter was less than about 0.005 the interference effects were negligible. Results
were obtained for Reynolds numbers between 0.4×10^5 and 2.5×10^5 (equivalent golf ball
velocities of 46 and 289 ft/s respectively) , and spin rate parameters of 0.02 to 0.3. No
information was obtained on the time rate of change of rotational speed.

   More recently, Aoyama (1990) adapted Davies method for finding lift and drag from
drop tests by recording the trajectory of the ball as it fell using short exposure video
techniques. This approach can give more accurate results for lift and drag since there is no
need for simplifying assumptions regarding the trajectory shape, the equations of motion or
the relative velocity differences between the ball and the airstream. Lift and drag
coefficients were presented for ball velocities of 100 to 250 ft/s, and spin rates from 1000

Science and Golf II: Proceedings of the World Scientific Congress of Golf. Edited by A.J.
Cochran and M.R. Farrally. Published in 1994 by E & FN Spon, London. ISBN 0 419 18790 1

to 3500 rpm. They showed that the lift and drag coefficients for the balls using the 384 icosahedron dimple pattern were consistently lower than the 336 Atti patterned balls.

Here we present further lift and drag measurements on a golf ball, with the aim of improving the prediction of golf ball performance. To do so, we have also measured the spin rate decay. Based on these results, we tentatively propose a new aerodynamic model for a golf ball for the flight regime experienced during a typical driver shot.

2   Description of the Experiments

The wind tunnel was of the suction type, designed and manufactured by Aerolab, with an entrance section modified to help improve the uniformity of the flow. The test section was 18"x12" in cross-section, with a maximum air speed of about 325 ft/s. The turbulence level was between 0.4% and 0.8% over the entire speed range.

The tunnel was equipped with a two component strain-gauge balance. The golf balls were mounted in the balance using thin metal spindles which were drilled and glued into the casing of the ball and allowed the ball to rotate freely. A high speed motor was used to spin up the ball, and when the desired rotation rate was reached (as determined using an encoder on the spindle mount), the motor was withdrawn from the tunnel. As the spin on the ball decreased, lift and drag measurements were taken simultaneously at each spin rate. Spin rate decay measurements were taken separately.

The spindles had a diameter of 1/16", so that the ratio of the spindle diameter to the ball diameter was .037, considerably larger than the recommendation given by Bearman and Harvey (1976) for negligible interference effects on drag measurements. To determine the level of interference, a number of test were performed using smooth spheres. The drag coefficient of a smooth sphere at subcritical Reynolds numbers is almost constant and equal to 0.5 ± 0.02 (see Bearman and Harvey 1976). Smooth spheres of 1" and 1.68" diameter were mounted in the balance using the 1/16" spindles. The drag coefficient of the smaller ball was nearly constant at a value of 0.67 for Reynolds numbers between 0.42×10^5 and 1.33×10^5, whereas the value for the larger ball was about 0.65 for Reynolds numbers 0.74×10^5 to 1.82×10^5. The drag coefficient of a 1/16" rod mounted in the balance was found to be nearly constant at a value of 0.17 over the same range of conditions (using the ball area as a basis). Therefore a tare correction of -0.17 applied to the drag coefficient to account for interference effects. When this correction was applied to the drag coefficients obtained for *spinning* smooth spheres, the agreement with the data from Maccoll (1928) and Davies (1949) was within ± 0.03. Data were also obtained for non-spinning golf balls, and the corrected results agreed well with the work of Davies (1949). Better agreement with Bearman and Harvey (1976) for non-spinning balls was obtained with a correction of -0.18, and this particular value was then chosen to correct all the golf ball drag data presented here.

Similar studies were made to investigate the interference effects on the lift coefficient, and they were found to be negligible. A correction is also required for the spin rate decay measurements to take account of the friction in the bearings. This correction was determined by measuring the spin rate decay at zero tunnel speed.

The range of Reynolds numbers and spin rates tested in our experiments covered the flight conditions experienced by the ball when using the full range of clubs. The typical Reynolds numbers and spin rate parameters for shots made by a driver, a #3 iron, a #5 iron and a #7 iron are shown below.

The results presented here are for one brand of golf ball, the Slazenger two-piece ball with a Surlyn cover. This brand was chosen because previous tests had indicated that the balls are highly symmetrical, thereby avoiding many of the mechanical resonance problems experienced when using the balance with some other brands. In all major respects, however, the data for the Slazenger balls were typical of other balls tested, which included the Doyle 384, Kasco, Ping Zing 4, Flying Lady and Worthington two-piece balls.

Club	Min. R#	Max. R#	Min. W	Max. W
Driver	72,000	208,000	0.08	0.20
#3 iron	60,000	152,000	0.18	0.55
#5 iron	52,000	162,000	0.29	0.85
#7 iron	39,000	112,000	0.50	1.3

Table 1. Typical values of Reynolds number and spin rate parameter

3   Results

All the data are presented in non-dimensional form. Here we define the lift and drag coefficients C_L and C_D, and the spin rate decay parameter SRD according to:

$$C_L = \frac{L}{\frac{1}{2}\rho V^2 \pi r^2} \qquad C_D = \frac{D}{\frac{1}{2}\rho V^2 \pi r^2} \qquad SRD = \left(\frac{d\omega}{dt}\right)\frac{r^2}{V^2}$$

where L is the lift force, D the drag force, ρ the density of air, μ its viscosity, V is the tunnel velocity, r the ball radius, and ω is the rotation rate (rads/s). By dimensional analysis, we would expect all three parameters to be a function of the Reynolds number R and spin rate parameter W. Note that W is defined as the ratio of the peripheral velocity to the velocity through the air $(W = \omega r/V)$.

3.1   Lift coefficient
Typical results for the lift coefficient as a function of spin rate are given in Fig. 1. In all respects, the data are very similar to the data obtained by Bearman and Harvey (1976). First, the lift coefficients monotonically increase with spin rate, as expected, although the current values are higher than the values obtained by Bearman and Harvey for their hexagonally dimpled ball by a constant increment in lift coefficient of about 0.04. Second, the Reynolds number dependence is very weak, at least for Reynolds numbers greater than 90,000. At Reynolds numbers less than 90,000 the lift coefficient decreases with Reynolds number, and it can actually become negative (not shown in Fig. 1). These trends were also observed by Bearman and Harvey, who suggested that at low Reynolds numbers and high spin rates transition to turbulent flow can take place asymmetrically, that is, transition may occur only in the boundary layer on the surface advancing against the main flow (normally the underside of the ball), whereas the boundary layer on the opposite side of the ball will remain laminar. This could lead to negative lift coefficients. Third, the lift coefficients at spin rates less than about 0.04 decrease rapidly with spin rate but they do not extrapolate to zero lift at zero spin rate. A similar behavior was observed by Bearman and Harvey, who noted that it could not be explained by any simple attached flow circulation theory.

3.2   Drag coefficient
Typical results for the drag coefficient as a function of spin rate are shown in Figs. 2 and 3. Again the data are in broad agreement with the observations made by Bearman and Harvey, although our results indicate a stronger dependence on spin rate parameter over the entire spin rate regime. For Reynolds numbers greater than about 50,000 the drag

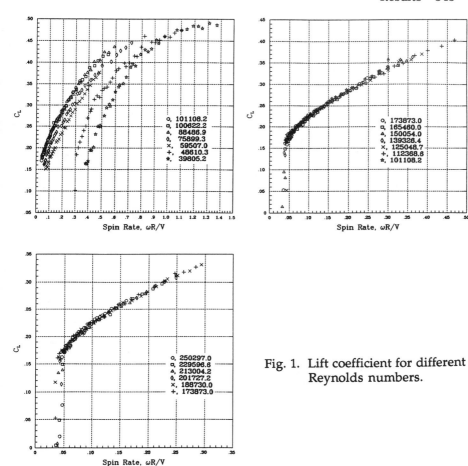

Fig. 1. Lift coefficient for different Reynolds numbers.

coefficient monotonically increases with spin rate parameter (see Fig. 2), but for Reynolds numbers less than this value the drag coefficient at low spin rates increases as the spin rate decreases. A similar trend was seen by Bearman and Harvey, although they did not offer an explanation. However, the minimum observed in the variation of drag coefficient with spin rate parameter corresponds closely with the point where the lift coefficient tends to negative values at the same Reynolds numbers (see Fig. 1), and it appears that the asymmetric transition behavior in this flow regime has a strong effect on the strength of the wake, and therefore the drag, as well as producing relatively low and sometimes negative lift, as discussed earlier.

For Reynolds numbers greater than about 50,000, the drag coefficient increases with Reynolds number until a Reynolds number of approximately 200,000. Interestingly, at higher Reynolds numbers there appears to be a subsequent *decrease* in drag coefficient. These trends are more evident in Fig. 3 where the data of Fig. 2 are replotted as a function

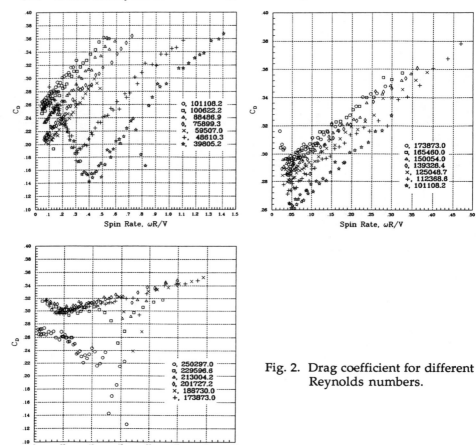

Fig. 2. Drag coefficient for different Reynolds numbers.

of Reynolds number. A decrease in drag coefficient at high Reynolds numbers has not been reported previously in the literature, and at first we suspected the results to be anomalous. In particular, the data shown in Fig. 2 indicated that a mechanical resonance occurred in the ball suspension system at high Reynolds numbers, at a rotational speed of about 85 rps. However, the decrease in drag coefficient occurred over the entire range of spin rates studied. Furthermore, wind tunnel data on other brands, including the Doyle 384, Kasco, Ping Zing 4, Flying Lady and Worthington two-piece balls indicated a similar decrease in drag coefficient at Reynolds numbers greater than about 200,000, to a greater or lesser degree. The fact that there is no corresponding change in the lift coefficient in this Reynolds number regime is also interesting: the drag decrease must happen through some symmetrical mechanism affecting the flow on the upper and lower sides of the ball equally, since an asymmetrical mechanism would also affect the lift.

This observation of a second critical Reynolds number is provocative in that it is not in agreement with previous investigations, although it should be noted that the data presented

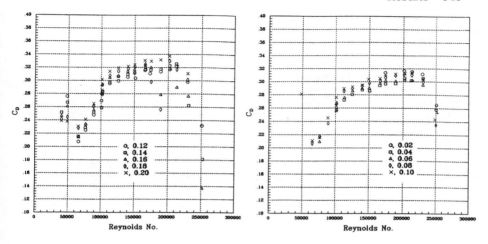

Fig. 3. Drag coefficient for different spin rates.

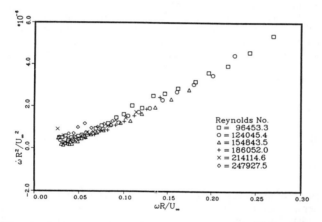

Fig. 4. Spin rate decay for different Reynolds numbers.

here are far more detailed than those obtained in any previous study. Furthermore, there is no obvious physical explanation for this phenomenon. An explanation based on transition behavior does not seem possible since the Reynolds numbers are well above the critical value, even taking into account the effects of the peripheral velocity. However, compressibility may provide a possible cause. At the maximum Reynolds number, the freestream Mach number is only about 0.25, but as the flow speeds up over the ball the local Mach number can exceed 0.5. The change in the density is only about 5%, but the flowfield may be altered more substantially. Although we would generally expect to see an increase in the drag coefficient due to compressibility, it is not clear that this expectation would continue to hold in the present case. Compressibility effects would help to explain the differences between the present data and those of Bearman and Harvey, since in their work a model 2.5 times larger than a golf ball was used at a correspondingly lower velocity to obtain the desired Reynolds numbers. Therefore their Mach number was lower by the same factor.

There remains the possibility that our data are flawed in some way. For example, the interference effects caused by the spindles may not be as well behaved as we have assumed in our use of a constant tare correction. To confirm this behavior at high Reynolds numbers and provide a check on the wind tunnel data, further work is currently in progress using the Indoor Testing Range described by Zagarola et al. (1994). These results will be available at the Congress for additional discussion.

3.3   Spin rate decay

Typical spin rate decay measurements are given in Fig. 4. By using the non-dimensional representation shown, the results for all Reynolds numbers collapse onto a single curve, which is close to a straight line. This suggests that at a constant velocity the spin rate decreases exponentially with time, or exponentially with distance if the velocity varies.

4   Aerodynamic Model

The data indicate that a "universal" aerodynamic model which predicts the flight performance of the ball over the wide range of spin rates and Reynolds number experienced in the game of golf may have to be extremely complex to capture all the subtleties associated with the variations in lift and drag coefficients that occur. Based on the data presented here, we propose a restricted aerodynamic model which is applicable only to driver shots, where the Reynolds number is usually between 70,000 and 210,000, and the spin rate is between 0.08 and 0.20. That is:

$$C_D = C_{d_1} + C_{d_2} W + C_{d_3} \sin\{\pi(\mathrm{Re} - A_1)/A_2\}$$

$$C_L = C_{l_1} W^{0.4}$$

$$SRD = R_1 W$$

The principal features of the model are: (1) The drag coefficient depends linearly on the spin rate parameter and non-linearly on the Reynolds number (the sine function is just a convenient curve-fit). This differs from other models in the literature such as that used by Lieberman (1990) where the effects of Reynolds number and spin rate parameter are neglected entirely. (2) The lift coefficient is independent of Reynolds number, and it is proportional to the spin rate parameter raised to the 0.4 power. In contrast, Lieberman used a linear function of R plus a square root function of W. (3) The spin rate decay is proportional to the spin rate. This relationship was also used by Lieberman, although he did not have the direct experimental evidence in hand.

The functions given above represent curve fits to the experimental data obtained for the Slazenger ball. Additional tests on other brands suggests that the general form may be widely applicable. From the wind tunnel data on the Slazenger ball, the following approximate values for the constants were suggested: $C_{d_1} = 0.24$, $C_{d_2} = 0.18$, $C_{d_3} = 0.06$, $C_{l_1} = 0.54$, $R_1 = 0.00002$, $A_1 = 90,000$, $A_2 = 200,000$. These values are representative of the other balls tested in the wind tunnel.

Values for these constants were also derived by comparing the predictions made using the trajectory program developed by Lieberman (1990) with trajectory data for driver shots obtained by the USGA for a variety of brands. The constants in the model were varied in a systematic way to optimize the agreement between the predictions and the experimental data on carry and time of flight. For the 7 driver trajectories tested, using a variety of brands, C_{l_1} was given by 0.51 ± 0.02, and C_{d_1} was given by 0.21 ± 0.01, in reasonable agreement with the results obtained for the Slazenger ball in the wind tunnel.

5 Conclusions

A revised aerodynamic model of a spinning golf ball has been proposed. The model includes a nonlinear dependence on Reynolds number and an allowance for the spin rate decay. The model appears to perform well in matching the available wind tunnel data for a variety of brands, and the available trajectory data for carry and flight time for a number of driver shots, all with fairly small changes in the model constants. Further verification of this aerodynamic model is currently underway using the Indoor Testing Range described by Zagarola *et al.* (1994).

This work was performed at the USGA Research and Test Center under their sponsorship.

6 References

Aoyama, S. (1990) A modern method for the measurement of aerodynamic lift and drag on golf balls. **Science and Golf**, (ed. A.J. Cochran), E. & F.N. Spon, London, pp. 199-204.

Bearman, P.W. and Harvey, J.K. (1976) Golf ball aerodynamics. **Aeronautical Quarterly**, 27, pp. 112-122.

Lieberman, B.B. (1990) Estimating lift and drag coefficients from golf ball trajectories. **Science and Golf**, (ed. A.J. Cochran), E. & F.N. Spon, London, pp.187-192.

Davies, J.M. (1949) The aerodynamics of golf balls. **J. Applied Physics**, 20, pp. 821-828.

Maccoll, J. (1928) Aerodynamics of a spinning sphere. **J. Royal Aeronautical Soc.**, 32, p. 777.

Zagarola, M.V., Lieberman, B. and Smits, A.J. (1994) An indoor testing range to measure the aerodynamic performance of golf balls. Proc. Second World Scientific Congress of Golf, E. & F.N. Spon, London.

53 An indoor testing range to measure the aerodynamic performance of golf balls

M.V. Zagarola
Princeton University, Princeton, NJ, USA
B. Lieberman, Polytechnic University, Brooklyn, NY, USA
and A.J. Smits
Princeton University, Princeton, NJ, USA

Abstract
The design of an Indoor Testing Range is described. The test range uses a calibrated launching machine to provide a precisely known initial velocity and spin rate. The velocity and arrival time of the ball is then measured at three down range stations, along with the vertical and horizontal position. The data can be used to derive the coefficients in the aerodynamic model of the ball. The model may then be used in a trajectory program to predict the total carry.
Keywords: Golf Ball, Aerodynamics.

1 Introduction

In flight, a golf ball experiences lift and drag forces, where its lift is derived from its spin by the Magnus effect and its drag is caused in large part by the formation of a wake with a significant momentum deficit. As the ball moves along its trajectory, its spin rate decreases with time, which affects the lift and the drag. The aerodynamic characteristics of the ball must be known precisely in order to predict the trajectory accurately. Specifically, we need to know how the lift and drag coefficients, and the spin rate decay, depend on the spin rate and the Reynolds number.

Outdoor range tests employing hitting machines, routinely used for conformance testing, have a limited utility in this regard. With some care the initial conditions (launch angle, initial spin rate and ball velocity) can be measured accurately, but in-flight trajectory measurements are difficult, and usually limited to features such as the maximum height of the trajectory, distance to impact, etc. The precise trajectory, as in position versus time, is difficult to obtain, although some limited measurements are now available (see, for example, Chikaraishi *et al.* 1990). The limitations of range tests mean that it is difficult to obtain information regarding the basic aerodynamic characteristics of the golf ball, that is, lift and drag coefficients, and the rate of spin decay.

Science and Golf II: Proceedings of the World Scientific Congress of Golf. Edited by A.J. Cochran and M.R. Farrally. Published in 1994 by E & FN Spon, London. ISBN 0 419 18790 1

Wind tunnel tests are more useful in this regard, but they are also limited. Two principal means exist for obtaining the aerodynamic coefficients. First, over a range of wind tunnel speeds, the ball is mounted on spindles, spun up to speed, and the spin rate, lift and drag are monitored as the ball spins down. Second, the ball is spun up to speed outside the tunnel and then dropped into the test section, where the subsequent trajectory is recorded, over a range of wind tunnel speeds and initial spin rates. In the first technique, the spindles introduce an extraneous drag which can constitute a significant fraction of the total drag (see, for example, Smits and Smith 1994). A tare correction must be applied to the results, but the accuracy of this procedure can always be questioned since the spindles interfere with the flow field over the ball in a way that is not precisely known. In the second technique, the trajectory needs to be recorded in considerable detail to infer the aerodynamic coefficients, and it is doubtful that results of high accuracy can be obtained. Neither technique is simple to implement, and both methods are restricted to basic studies of golf ball performance, where only limited data are required. They do not present a serious challenge to the outdoor tests for routine testing of golf ball performance.

To avoid some of these difficulties, an Indoor Testing Range (ITR) has been designed and constructed which combines the advantages of indoor testing with the free flight characteristics of outdoor testing using, for example, a mechanical golfer. This new testing range may be used to fulfill basic test requirements (designed to obtain fundamental aerodynamic data) and outdoor test functions (designed to do conformance tests).

2 Design of the Indoor Testing Range

The ITR was designed to determine the aerodynamic characteristics of golf balls by making measurements during the initial part of the ball trajectory. Before this indoor testing range could be designed and constructed, however, some basic questions needed to be answered. In particular, we needed to know what kind of measurements could be made, and with what degree of accuracy? The answers to these questions dictated the type of instrumentation and data analysis which were required, and the length of the testing range (since a longer range will reduce the level of accuracy required on the data).

2.1 Accuracy Requirements for ITR Measurements
The first question in the design is really "In terms of the Overall Distance Standard (as set forth in the Rules *of Golf*), how accurately do we need to know the input to the trajectory program?" That is, how accurately do we need to know initial launch angle, initial velocity, initial spin rate, lift coefficient, drag coefficient, and spin rate decay? Some estimates are already available, either from experience or from existing trajectory predictions. These estimates were defined more precisely using the trajectory model

developed by Lieberman, together with the aerodynamic model described by Smits and Smith (1994).

From these calculations, the following minimum specifications were derived, using the criterion that if the uncertainties were independent (as they almost certainly will be) the total uncertainty in estimating the carry distance would be less than 1 yard. Hence:

1. For launch angles in the range of 8° to 12°, we require that the uncertainty in launch angle be less than ± 0.20°;

2. For initial velocities in the range of 220 to 250 fps (67 m/s to 76 m/s), we require that the uncertainty in the initial velocity be less than ± 0.48 fps (± 0.15 m/s);

3. For initial spin rates in the range of 40 to 50 rps, we require that the uncertainty in the initial spin rate be less than ± 1.0 rps;

4. We require that the arrival time at each location be known to better than ± 2.5 µsec; and,

5. We require that the vertical position at the second station (most restrictive) be known to better than ± 1.2 mm.

2.2   Instrumentation

The keys to the success of the ITR are the launching machine, which produces an initial spin rate and launch velocity to within the accuracy requirements given above, and the use of ballistic screens which allow the ball velocity, vertical and horizontal position, initial launch angle, and arrival time to be measured to within the requirements on accuracy given above. Schematics of the facility and the ballistic screen arrangement are shown in Figures 1a and 1b.

The launching machine used in the ITR consists of four 25" wheels, approximately arranged in a square, with the upper pair and the lower pair connected by a timing belt and driven separately in opposite directions by individually controlled motors. The gap between the two belts is slightly smaller than the diameter of a golf ball, so that when a ball is introduced into the gap by a pressure-driven air gun, it is firmly gripped by the belts. The differential velocity of the belts dictates the spin given to the ball, and the ball velocity is equal to the average velocity of the belts.

An extensive survey of timing screens and velocity measuring devices was made before selecting the ballistic screens manufactured by MV Ordnance. These devices produce a pulse when the ball breaks a light screen, and they have a very short rise time (less than 20 nanoseconds) with a high degree of accuracy among different shots (i.e. different angles, heights, and velocities). They can be used to give velocity and position using time-of-flight measurements, where the velocity is determined using two parallel screens separated by a known distance, and the vertical and horizontal position is determined using an additional screen set at a known angle (typically 45°). Each array of three screens constitutes a station.

The initial velocity produced by the launching machine was calibrated against the ballistic screens. The launch angle was found using Stations 1a

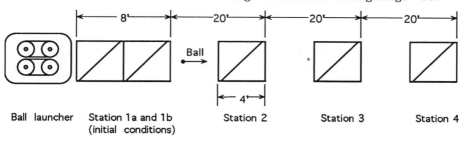

Fig. 1a: Schematic of ITR (not to scale).

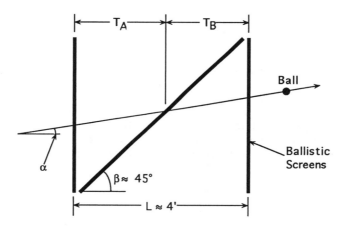

Fig. 1b: Arrangement of ballistic screens within each station.

and 1b to precisely determine the vertical and horizontal position of the ball at two locations. The spin rate produced by the launching machine was calibrated by photographing marked balls at two locations. The velocity, vertical and horizontal position, and arrival time of the ball were also measured using Stations 2, 3, and 4, located approximately 20', 40', and 60' down range of Station 1b.

The aerodynamic model used in the trajectory program is described in detail by Smits and Smith (1994). There are seven constants in the model. By fixing the value of the least critical constant, the six down range measurements (velocity and position at three stations) provide sufficient information to determine the six remaining constants.

2.3 Calibration Procedure
For the measurement of the vertical and horizontal position, each station had

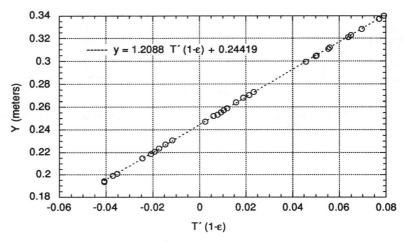

Fig. 2: Calibration data for the vertical position at Station 1a.

to be calibrated to attain the accuracy required by the model. To understand the calibration procedure the governing equations will be briefly described.

From the arrangement shown in Figure 1b the position (x, y) of the ball relative to some origin a distance of (x_0, y_0) away can be found from

$$x = L(1-\varepsilon)T' + x_0 \qquad\qquad y = \frac{L}{\tan\beta}(1-\varepsilon)T' + y_0$$

where T´ is a non-dimensional time defined as $T' = \dfrac{T_A - T_B}{2(T_A + T_B)}$,

and ε is a very small number (of order 0.001) that is dependent on the decrease in velocity between the two vertical screens.

Also, from the arrangement shown in Figure 1b the velocity (V) can be found from

$$V = \frac{L}{(T_A + T_B)\cos\alpha} + (\Delta V)T'$$

where ΔV is the change in velocity between the two vertical screens and α is the local trajectory angle which can be estimated from the position data at two stations. Note that for a typical driver shot of 240 fps (73 m/s) the second term is less than ± 0.05 fps (± 0.015 m/s), and α is less than 1° (i.e. cos α = 1).

The calibration for each station consisted of launching thirty balls through the station and measuring the position by photographing the ball as it crosses the 45° screen. For each ball launched an accurate calibration grid was first placed in the plane of the ball trajectory and photographed, and then slid aside. A strobe triggered by the ball crossing the 45° plane triggered the camera a second time, producing a clear double-exposed picture of the ball

Fig. 3: Photographs from the spin rate calibration (410° CW revolution).

superimposed on the grid. The positions were then plotted versus the non-dimensional time (corrected with ε) and a straight line was fitted to the data. A typical plot is shown in Figure 2. The overall uncertainty in position (including referencing the grid) was estimated as ± 1.5 mm for the horizontal position and ± 0.5 mm for the vertical position which is within the requirements set forth in the design specifications.

The ball launcher was calibrated for both launch velocity and spin rate. For the launch velocity stations 1a and 1b were used to find the decrease in velocity which was then used to extrapolate the velocity to the launcher exit. This velocity was compared to the average periphery velocity of the wheels to determine the calibration factor.

The spin rate was calibrated by photographing a marked ball at the first and third vertical ballistic screens. Figure 3 shows two of these photographs. By measuring the time between photographs and the angular rotation relative to a horizontal string, the rotation rate can be calculated. To calibrate the launcher this rotation rate was compared to that calculated with the differential velocity of the wheels. Ninety balls were launched at speeds of 240 fps (73 m/s) and rotation rates of 30 rps through 50 rps. The overall uncertainty of this technique is ± 0.5 % of the rotation rate. The repeatability of the launcher was found to be ± 0.7 rps which is within the limits set forth in the design specifications.

3 Results and Discussion

At this stage, the ITR instrumentation has been calibrated and checked for repeatability and accuracy. It has been shown to provide initial conditions and trajectory data to within the limits indicated by the preliminary sensitivity estimates determined using the trajectory program. We are now commencing indoor tests for a wide range of ball brands and initial conditions. By launching different brands of balls over the entire range of Reynolds numbers and spin rate parameters encountered in the game of golf, we will be able to check the aerodynamic model establish from the wind tunnel tests, as given by Smits and Smith (1994).

Full trajectory data will also be obtained for the same balls using the launching machine to make outdoor tests. By checking the predictions made using the coefficients in the aerodynamic model obtained from the ITR against the results from the full trajectory data obtained in outdoor testing, we hope to establish the reliability and accuracy of the aerodynamic model and the ITR concept.

This work was performed at the USGA Research and Test Center, under their sponsorship.

4 References

Chikaraishi, T., Alaki, Y., Maehara, K., Shimosaka, H. and Fukazawa, F. (1990) A new method on measurement of trajectories of a golf ball. **Science and Golf**, (ed. A. J. Cochran), E. & F. N. Spon, London, pp. 193-198.

Smits, A. J. and Smith, D. R. (1994) A new aerodynamic model of a golf ball in flight. Submitted to Second World Scientific Congress of Golf. To appear E. & F. N. Spon, London.

54 Changes in golf ball performance over the last 25 years

S. Aoyama
Titleist and Foot-Joy Worldwide, Fairhaven, Massachusetts, USA

Abstract
A golf ball popular on the professional tours around 1970 is replicated using similar and actual materials, methods and tooling. Objective techniques such as wind tunnel testing, computer simulated trajectory analysis, and mechanical golfer flight tests are used to compare its distance and slicing characteristics to those of a contemporary tour ball. Commonly held perceptions about the differences are evaluated in light of the findings.
Keywords: Wind Tunnel Testing, Trajectory Analysis, Flight Testing, Flight Performance, Distance, History.

1 Introduction

Twenty-five years ago, the golf balls used by touring pros were very similar to one another. They shared the same kinds of materials, the same wound/balata construction type, and the same 336 octahedron dimple pattern. But in golf, as in other equipment related sports, technology has since taken a front-and-center position in the minds of many participants. New materials, new construction types, and new dimple patterns are now the rule rather than the exception. It is common to hear television commentators, ex-tour players, and senior tour players remark about how this technology has made today's golf ball 20, 40, or even 60 yd longer than the ones from earlier times. It is often said to be straighter as well, forgiving accidental hooks and slices. Adding to these perceptions is the continual presence of advertising claims encouraging such beliefs.

The Rules of Golf have for some time included four golf ball restrictions which, when combined, act to severely restrict the distance a golf ball will fly. By limiting the size to a minimum diameter, the effect is to establish a minimum amount of aerodynamic drag that the ball must generate. The maximum weight and maximum initial velocity rules combine to limit the amount of kinetic energy which is available to overcome that drag. Finally, the Overall Distance Standard places an explicit distance limit on all approved balls when launched under a prescribed set of conditions.

Science and Golf II: Proceedings of the World Scientific Congress of Golf. Edited by A.J. Cochran and M.R. Farrally. Published in 1994 by E & FN Spon, London. ISBN 0 419 18790 1

This casts some doubt on any notion of dramatically longer golf balls. If today's players really are driving the ball substantially farther, then it seems likely that some of the improvement is due to other factors. This study was designed to determine how much of the last 25 years' distance gain can be attributed to the ball, and how much must have come from other sources. The question of straightness will also be examined.

2   Experimental procedure

2.1 Test balls
A fundamental problem encountered in measuring the performance of historical golf balls is that actual balls cannot be used. Even if sufficient quantities of good condition balls could be found, the material properties would certainly have changed during storage over the years. For this study, it was decided to manufacture new "old" balls using the original materials, specifications, processes, and tooling to the extent possible.

The ball chosen for reproduction was the most popular ball on the US tour in 1970, commonly referred to as the Titleist "K2". It was a balata covered, wound construction, liquid center ball having the then-standard 336 octahedron dimple pattern. Since the rubber envelope containing the center liquid of this ball contained lead, environmental concerns made replication of this component impractical. Therefore, original K2 balls were dissected to recover the centers, which were found to be in excellent condition. These centers were wound with rubber thread made to the original dimensions and using the original winding specifications. A balata coverstock was formulated to match the original as closely as possible, given the current unavailability of natural balata.

The balls were formed in original production mold cavities, and finishing was performed using 1970 procedures. The paint and clearcoat formulations were very similar to the originals, and they were applied to original coat weights and thicknesses.

The Titleist Tour Balata was chosen to represent contemporary tour balls, since it is currently the most popular ball among touring professionals. Standard production balls were selected to match the compression of the reproduction K2 balls.

2.2 Wind tunnel testing
The aerodynamic characteristics of the test balls were evaluated in the Titleist wind tunnel, a facility specifically designed and built for that purpose (Aoyama, 1990). Lift and drag coefficients were measured over a spin rate range of 1500 to 4500 rev/min and a Reynolds number range of 60,000 to 200,000 (equivalent to a ball velocity range of 70 to 233 ft/sec or 21 to 71 m/s under typical atmospheric conditions). These ranges blanket the typical conditions experienced by wound balata balls when struck with a driver.

2.3 Trajectory simulations

Due to differences in golf swings and clubs, golfers generate a wide range of launch conditions (initial velocity, launch angle, and initial spin rate). When comparing the distance performance of two balls, it is therefore necessary to consider a range of launch conditions which take into account the possibility of differing reactions in different situations. The typical test method of hitting balls to a fairway using a driving machine is impractical for such an experiment, due to the time required for multiple setups and tests. Atmospheric and fairway conditions will change over the course of the experiment, resulting in data which is not comparable from beginning to end.

A solution is to conduct the experiment using computer simulations of flight trajectories. Knowing the lift and drag characteristics from wind tunnel testing, it is possible to calculate a trajectory given any set of conditions. Beginning with the initial velocity, launch angle, and spin rate, the trajectory is built up step by step over small time increments until the altitude reaches zero, indicating ground impact. The amount of roll is then calculated as a function of those impact conditions using an empirically based model.

A computer program incorporating this technique was used to calculate trajectories over a matrix of nominal launch conditions covering launch angles from 4 to 12° and spin rates from 2000 to 4500 rev/min, all at an initial velocity of 230 ft/sec. These ranges were chosen to encompass virtually all tour caliber players. The Tour Balata balls were found to spin 5% less than the K2 balls, so this difference was preserved in the trajectory simulations. Similarly, K2 trajectories were run at 2 ft/sec lower initial velocity to take into account the lower ball speeds typical of its era.

2.4 Flight testing

To verify the computer simulation, True Temper driving machine tests were conducted at two launch conditions: a high launch/high spin condition of 10°/3600 rev/min, and a low launch/low spin condition of 7°/2600 rev/min. Initial velocity for both tests was 230 ft/sec.

3   Results and analysis

3.1 Wind tunnel tests

Figure 1 is a contour plot showing the difference in drag coefficient (C_D) between the Tour Balata and K2 balls. Positive numbers (dashed contour lines) indicate that Tour Balata is greater than K2 (a convention followed throughout this study). Clearly, over the majority of the field the current ball has equal or lower C_D than the old ball. In general, the difference is in the 0 to 9% range.

Similar information is shown for lift coefficient (C_L) in Figure 2. The Tour Balata is again equal to or lower than the K2 over most of the range, this time by 0 to 20%. At very low Reynolds numbers, however, there are large differences of the opposite sign.

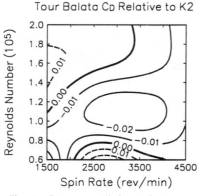

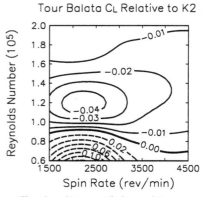

Fig. 1. Drag coefficient difference   Fig. 2. Lift coefficient difference

Lift and drag differences of these magnitudes would be expected to produce significant differences in trajectory shape and distance.

3.2 Trajectory analysis

Figure 3 shows the total distance results from the computer trajectory simulation. The distance difference between the new and old balls is presented as a contour plot versus launch condition (note the dual spin axis, showing the 5% spin difference). Overall, the graph shows a distance advantage for the new ball for a majority of the tested launch conditions. Golfers launching the ball higher and with more spin get more distance with the Tour Balata; those launching lower and with less spin do better with the K2. This is not surprising, given the generally lower C_L and C_D levels previously noted for the Tour Balata. At the high launch/high spin corner of the

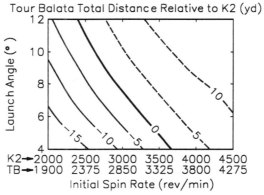

Fig. 3. Total distance difference

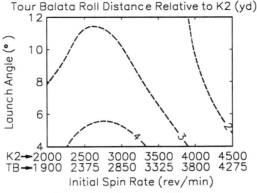

Fig. 4. Roll distance difference

graph, the advantage for the current ball approaches 15 yd, but this is not a launch condition typically found among professional level players. The large differences found at the low launch/low spin corner are essentially academic for the same reason. Based on tour player launch condition measurements reported by Drumm (1993), very few would see more than a 5 yd advantage for the old ball or a 10 yd advantage for the contemporary one. These measurements were performed over the last two years on 281 professional tour players from the US PGA and Volvo tours.

The difference in roll distance between the two balls is shown in a similar manner in Figure 4. The Tour Balata ball rolls farther than the older ball over the entire range of tested launch conditions. Once again, the generally lower C_L and C_D characteristics of the new ball, resulting in a lower and "hotter" trajectory, form the obvious explanation for this. However, there is an additional factor at work here. Referring back to Figure 2, notice that in the low Reynolds number/low spin rate region of the graph, the Tour Balata ball has dramatically larger C_L values than the K2. Thus, near the end of the trajectory, where the Reynolds number and spin rate are low, the Tour Balata generates substantially more lift. This results in a shallower ground impact angle (a more glancing impact), which gives more rolling distance.

Returning to Figures 3 and 4, it is apparent that in the region where the contemporary ball exhibits a total distance advantage, its roll advantage is about 2 to 3 yd. For the high launch/high spin players who enjoy a 10 yd gain with the Tour Balata, about 8 yd is due to increased carry, and only 2 yd comes from increased roll.

Computer simulations can also be used to study lateral performance such as hooking and slicing behavior. To simulate a right-hand player's slice, the previous launch condition matrix was rerun with the ball's spin axis inclined 10° clockwise (from the player's viewpoint). This produces a sidespin component of sin(10°) or about 17%, resulting in slices in the range of 10 to 25 yd, depending upon ball and launch condition. This could be characterized as a substantial slice for a tour level player.

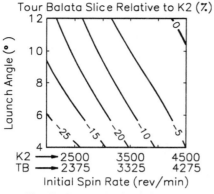

Fig. 5. Percent slice difference

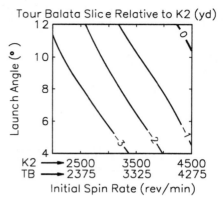

Fig. 6. Slice difference

The results of this simulation are presented in Figure 5, which is a contour plot of the percentage slice difference between the Tour Balata and the K2, using the latter as the base. For nearly all launch conditions, the new ball is found to slice less than the old one. This might have been predicted, considering the K2's higher lift coefficient and spin. As before, however, the amount of difference is a strong function of launch condition. Extreme low launch/low spin golfers get the greatest reduction of around 25%, while their counterparts at the opposite corner see no difference at all. Real world tour players fall in the range of 2 to 20% reduction.

For a better assessment of effect on the game, Figure 6 presents the same data as yards of slice difference rather than percentage. The magnitude of the largest slice reduction is found to be only about 3 yd.

3.3 Flight tests
The results of the conventional driving tests are summarized in Table 1. Carry distance differences between the new and old balls are compared with computer simulation results. The flight test and computer simulation numbers agree very well, considering that the flight test data has a standard deviation on the order of 3 yd.

Table 1. Distance difference comparison

Launch condition	Flight test carry distance diff (yd)	Simulation carry distance diff (yd)
High launch/high spin	+4.7	+5.9
Low launch/low spin	-9.0	-10.8

4   Conclusions

The contemporary Titleist Tour Balata ball exhibits generally lower aerodynamic lift and drag characteristics than the Titleist K2 ball of around 1970. Combined with a lower spin rate, this creates a trajectory which is lower and flatter, with more ground roll. Depending on the golfer's swing, this may result in substantially more or less distance than the older ball. Over the range of launch conditions typically generated by today's professional tour players, no player is likely to gain much more than 10 yd, and no player is likely to lose more than 5 yd by playing the Tour Balata versus the K2. This finding is supported by historical PGA Tour driving distance statistics reported by the USGA Research and Test Center (1993), which indicate that among the longer hitters, driving distance has only increased by about 10 yd since 1970.

If, in spite of this, some of today's players really are driving the ball 20, 40, or 60 yd farther than they would have in 1970, then there are other factors at work. Likely candidates would be better player conditioning, better swing mechanics, improved clubs, and more closely mown fairways.

On the question of straightness, there is some basis for the belief that today's ball hooks and slices less than that of 1970. This is a consequence of the contemporary preference for lower, flatter trajectories. The same factors which reduce trajectory height also reduce hooking and slicing. The reduction, however, is only on the order of 0 to 3 yd for a fairly severe slice.

5   Acknowledgements

The author wishes to acknowledge, with gratitude, the tireless efforts of Ms. Judy Concepcion, who researched and directed the manufacturing of the new "old" golf balls which were so vital to this study, and Ms. Karen Richard, who performed the endless legwork to get them made.

6   References

Aoyama, S. (1990) A Modern Method for the Measurement of Aerodynamic Lift and Drag on Golf Balls. **Science and Golf - Proceedings of the First World Scientific Congress of Golf** (ed A. J. Cochran), E. & F. N. Spon/Chapman and Hall, London, UK.

Concepcion, J.L. (1991) Back to the Future II. Internal memorandum JLC91-7, Titleist and Foot-Joy Worldwide, Fairhaven, MA, USA.

Drumm, J.D. (1993) Tour Player Launch Conditions. Internal memorandum dated 12/2/93, Titleist and Foot-Joy Worldwide, Fairhaven, MA, USA.

USGA Research and Test Center (1993) P.G.A. Tour Statistics - Graphical Representations, United States Golf Association, Far Hills, NJ, USA.

55 Does it matter what ball you play?

T. Hale, P. Bunyan and I. Sewell
Centre for Sports Science, Chichester, UK

Abstract
Manufacturers of golf balls set out to persuade the club golfer of the special qualities
of their own particular brands. This paper examines the relative performance in terms
of accuracy and distance of balls regularly advertised in the popular golf magazines to
test the assertions made by manufacturers. Eighteen golfers were divided into three
equal groups of low (LH), middle (MH) and high handicaps (HH). Each subject
played eight shots with two clubs - a three wood and a five iron with six different
balls. The distance of each shot and its deviation from a target line were recorded. The
balls from 3 different manufacturers were tested. Balls A and C were 2-piece surlyn
covered and B a 3-piece balata from the same company. Balls D and E were 2-piece
surlyns from two different companies and F a 3-piece surlyn covered ball recovered
from a water hazard. The results showed that LH group were significantly longer and
more accurate with each ball than both other groups ($P<0.05$), but there were no
significant differences between the MH and LH groups. The claims for greater
distance for balls C and D are confirmed for LH but at the expense of a slight loss in
accuracy. The MH group received no significant advantage in distance or accuracy
from any of the balls on trial. The cheaper Lake balls were significantly shorter for the
high handicappers.
Keywords: Golf balls, Distance, Accuracy.

1 Introduction

The history of the development of the golf ball is one of steady progress in terms of
distance and controllability and has now reached a point where, at the very highest
levels, some believe the very nature of the game may be threatened. At the other end
of the spectrum, the handicap golfer is always looking for some feature, usually new
equipment, that will enhance their game. One of the features that occurs regularly in
golf magazines is the number of advertisements describing the particular
characteristics of high performance balls.

At present there are two basic forms of construction - 2-piece or 3-piece. These are
combined with surlyn, surlyn-lithium or balata coverings offering a mixture of

Science and Golf II: Proceedings of the World Scientific Congress of Golf. Edited by A.J.
Cochran and M.R. Farrally. Published in 1994 by E & FN Spon, London. ISBN 0 419 18790 1

durability, distance and feel, different compression, and several arrangements of dimple patterns designed to affect ball aerodynamics and optimise ball flight.

Most manufacturers support the claims made for their particular ball by calling on data collected from controlled tests using a machine known as the "Iron Byron" which can deliver repeatable swings. These tests have led to contradictory claims by the manufacturers regarding distance and accuracy of particular brands of ball.

The Acushnet Company, for example, states "Hitting machine tests prove that the Titleist HVC is two to seven yards longer off the driver than other competitive two-piece distance balls. In the same tests, the HVC averages 30% tighter dispersion off the tee. That's a lot more fairways hit in the heart." At the same time the Wilson Sports company claimed that their Ultra AR432 was "Better known as the world's longest hitting ball. It not only out-distanced every other professional but it even stretched the old Ultra claim to fame by a good 17 feet." The force of this latter argument was reinforced when ".....under the supervision of independent auditors we invited 700 golfers to add flesh to our findings in the Ultra Challenge."

The use of a machine as a test device has distinct advantages in terms of repeatability and experimental control but has limited ecological validity. Hence the procedure adopted by the Wilson Company of involving 700 players more nearly mirrors the true interaction between golfer and golf ball, but the methods used may not have been well-enough controlled and the results thus open to some question.

This study examined the claims about the accuracy and distance characteristics made by various manufacturers by comparing the relative performances of widely available balls amongst golfers of differing abilities.

2 Methods

Eighteen college golfers, seventeen men and one woman, aged between 19 and 28 years and ranging in ability from scratch to a 28 handicap were selected and assigned to one of three ability groups, - low- (LH 0-10), mid-(MH 11-18) and high-handicap (HH 19-28). The purpose of the test was explained but the subjects were ignorant of the type of ball they were striking. Attendance at the trials was dependent on availability and was therefore essentially random.

The tests began with a 15 min controlled warm-up of stretching exercises followed by 5 shots with practice balls with the odd numbered clubs starting with the wedge. Alternate shots were then taken with a three wood and a 5 iron; club order was randomised within the groups. Two targets were provided at 200 and 150 m. Measuring flags were placed at 2 m intervals along a straight line to the targets. A second tape measure was laid at right angles to this line.   The total distance the ball travelled - i.e. the flight and roll combined - and the dispersion from the target line, were measured by triangulation. All shots, including mis-hits, were recorded.

Balls from 3 different manufacturers were tested. Balls A and C were 2-piece surlyn covered and B a 3-piece balata from the same company. Balls D and E were 2-piece surlyns from two different companies and F a 3-piece surlyn covered ball recovered from a water hazard in the United States. The balls were heated to about 75^0 F and stored in an insulated box during each trial. 8 balls of each brand were selected at random from the container and placed in turn on a practice mat with the manufacturers name turned away from the subject. Each subject was then instructed to aim at the appropriate target and urged to make their best swing for each trial. They were also required to take their time between shots to minimise any fatiguing effects.

Each subject acted as their own controls. The means of the eight shots with each ball with both clubs - i.e. 96 shots in all- were calculated. A 2-way ANOVA with two repeated measures was performed on the data with the critical level for alpha set at the 5% level.

3 Results

The data are reported for the three groups separately. Each table gives the means ($\pm$ S.D.) of 288 shots with each club arising from eight strokes by six subjects with the six balls.

3.1 The low handicap group

The age of the LH group was 22.67 ± 2.88 years with a handicap of 4.7 ± 3.67. Table 1 below gives the distances achieved with each brand for the two clubs

Table 1. Distances (metres) achieved by the low handicap group

Club	A	B	C	D	E	Lake
3 wood	187	183.4	183.7	192.6	192.4	184.7
	± 6.85	6.14	12.36	2.98	5.54	2.88
5 iron	143.5	142.4	142.2	148.1	145.3	142.2
	± 7.12	7.95	6.83	9.04	8.15	8.03

The two 2-piece balls with surlyn covers from different manufacturers (D and E) were the two longest balls off both clubs, but the difference was significant for the 3 wood only. However, when the distances for the two clubs were combined ball D travelled significantly further than the balls B, C and the Lake balls, and ball E travelled further than B and C.

Table 2. Dispersion distances (metres) of the low handicap group for each club

Club	A	B	C	D	E	Lake
3 wood	13.0	13.5	16.2	17.3	15.3	15.0
	± 4.69	4.24	3.41	3.29	3.49	5.69
5 iron	8.8	9.1	9.9	10.2	10.9	10.1
	± 2.74	2.28	4.19	3.31	4.36	2.27

The accuracy of the two clubs is given in Table 2. The higher the figure the greater the distance from the tee- to-target line. However, it is important to recognise that the method of calculating dispersion gives a limited a picture of the overall spread of the shots. Consecutive shots may be an identical distance from the target line - say 5 yards- but one may have been sliced the other hooked. Thus the deviation from the target line would be 5yds for each shot, but the actual spread of the two shots is 10 yards. Furthermore, according to central limit theory, the pooling of a relatively large

number of shots for each group will tend to mask the often considerable individual
variability. There was a significant difference between the clubs (P<0.01) but although
the dispersions of balls A and B were the smallest, the differences in ball performance
were not statistically significant.

3.2 The middle handicap group
The mean age of this group was 20.67 ± 0.52 years with a handicap of 16. The general
pattern of results mirrored the LH group in that the combined distances showed that
the balls D and E were the longest and ball B, the balata, the shortest. None of the
differences were significant. However, there was a significant reduction in the overall
performance of the MH compared to the LH group . The data are given in tables 3 and
4 below.

Table 3. Distance (metres) for the middle handicap group for each club

Club	A	B	C	D	E	Lake
3 wood	166.6	154.5	165.1	171.3	173.1	162.5
	±11.53	19.26	17.28	14.35	14.11	11.18
5 iron	137.8	136.7	132.0	133.5	135.8	131.7
	±10.29	9.61	13.28	10.29	9.9	6.2

The accuracy scores were generally poorer than for the LH group; the balata ball (B)
revealed the smallest dispersion but not significantly so.

Table 4. Dispersion distances (metres) of the middle handicap group for each club

Club	A	B	C	D	E	Lake
3 wood	16.6	15.7	20.8	16.9	16.7	18.5
	±3.51	4.65	4.08	5.48	4.6	3.76
5 iron	11.8	10.8	13.2	11.9	13.6	15
	±4.44	2.27	2.75	2.54	2.91	3.9

3.3 The high handicap group
The mean age for the HH group was 20.2 ± 0.98 years with an handicap of 27.5.

Table 5. Distances (metres) for the high handicap group for each club

Club	A	B	C	D	E	Lake
3 wood	170.6	164.4	163.2	162.5	169.5	155
	±12.51	12.54	3.16	9.31	6.76	10.83
5 iron	130.9	124.3	134.1	127.6	116.7	125.2
	±12.11	17.2	14	16.7	14	9.18

The pattern changed for this group in that balls D and E no longer occupied the first two rankings. Ball A was just the longest but the only significant differences lay between the Lake balls and the balls A and C.

Table 6. Dispersion distances (metres) for the high handicap group for each club

Club	A	B	C	D	E	Lake
3 wood	28	20.4	23.2	22.9	22.4	18.9
	±8.44	7.86	4.47	8.81	9.38	4.14
5 iron	20.1	20.9	15.1	18	15.9	17.4
	±6.3	8.46	5.14	5.91	5.26	6.04

No clear pattern emerged from the dispersion data and there were no significant differences between the balls for either club.

4 Discussion

The subjects fell into three distinct groups. The LH group contained one golfer each at scratch, 2, 3, 6, 7 and 10. The MH group contained one each at 14 and 18, with the remainder at 16. The HH group contained one each at 26 and 27 with the rest on 28. This clear distinction between the groups enabled differences in ball performance to emerge. The LH group were the best group; they hit the ball consistently further than the other two groups and, except for ball D with the 3 wood, were consistently more accurate. The MH group were more accurate than the HH group but there were few differences in distances achieved. A more useful picture of distance performance occurs when the performance of all the balls with both clubs is combined and ranked. These data are shown in Tables 7 and 8 below.

Table 7. Combined 3 wood and 5 iron distances (metres) for the three groups and the six balls

Group	A	B	C	D	E	Lake
LH	330.5	325.8	325.9	340.7	337.7	326.9
MH	304.4	291.2	297.1	304.8	308.9	294.2
HH	301.5	288.7	297.3	290.1	286.2	280.2

Table 8. Ball rankings for the three groups based on combined distances

Group	A	B	C	D	E	Lake
LH	3	6	5	1	2	4
MH	3	6	4	2	1	5
HH	1	4	2	3	5	6

The balata ball (B) was the shortest of the balls on trial. It was a 90 compression three-piece wound ball with a liquid centre with a balata covering. According to Graham (1993), it is the kind of ball chosen by professional and low handicap golfers because, "it comes with a lot of natural backspin". Spin rates for such balls are greater than for both 2- and 3-piece surlyn balls, thus offering more control for good strikers. However, the greater the backspin the higher the trajectory with an accompanying reduction in roll distance. Furthermore, no restrictions were placed on the make of club used by the subjects nor the material used in the manufacture of the club head. It is suggested (Graham 1993) that heads constructed of mild metal tend to impart more backspin on balata balls. Some subjects may have used such clubs and both of these factors would go some way towards explaining the shorter distances recorded for the balata ball in these experiments.

However, many high and middle handicap golfers are faced with a dilemma between lowering their handicap and economic considerations. The popular choice is two-piece balls designed to give greatest distance, are more durable and thus cheaper than balata balls. However, this strategy may mitigate against improved performance leading to lower handicaps. Casual observation of mid- and high handicap students practising at this Institute reveals very little time spent on the short game. There is some suggestion that a major weakness of many handicap golfers is their limited effectiveness on and around the greens and an inability to consistently save par with a good short game. For example, Anderson (1989) remarks " Even though putting well is one of the most difficult parts of the game, too little thought is spent on it and far too little time is spent on practising. Indeed, it is very rare for a player to ask his pro for a putting lesson.....". The same may be said about the short game in its entirety. Indeed, Watson (1983) goes as far as saying " Go to any professional golf tournament and you will see as much practice on and around practice greens as on the driving range. I venture to say you will not see most amateur golfers spend the same amount of time practising the short game." It is conceivable that greater attention to practising their short game combined with the use of balata balls may lead to greater ball control around and on the greens and lowered handicaps. This hypothesis may be worth testing.

The Lake balls also performed poorly. Marketed in the USA these are 3-piece balls of wound construction with a lithium-surlyn covering. They are second-hand balls which are collected from water hazards, but it is unclear how long they have been immersed and whether they have been treated in any way to enhance their appearance. The main attraction is the low price. Those interested in lowering their handicap may find these kinds of ball unhelpful.

If distance is the prime consideration there seems to be little difference between balls D and E for both the LH and MH groups. The significantly greater distances achieved by these balls for the LH group means that about one club less will be needed to reach the green. The HH group, however, seemed to have some difficulty with these balls and were more successful with balls A and C and there seems no logical explanation for this difference.

Accuracy is important and hitting the green in regulation is therefore advantageous. But the dispersion figures give no clear difference between the balls. If the data from the 5 iron only is ranked by group there is some evidence to suggest that the balls A and B are best for the LH and MH groups and ball C performs best for the HH.

Table 9. Ball rankings for dispersion (metres) of the three groups.

Group	A	B	C	D	E	Lake
LH	1	2	3	5	6	4
MH	2	1	4	3	5	6
HH	5	6	1	4	2	3

Part of the explanation for may be that accuracy increases as distance falls. This is logical since any shot off line will diverge further from the target line the longer it is in flight. In this respect the LH group demonstrates its superiority with the iron club. The average distance off-line is 9.8 metres compared to 12.7 and 17.9 for the other two groups.

Although the ANOVA revealed significant differences between the six golfers in each of the groups, few of the differences in distance and none of the differences in dispersion arising from this study reached statistical significance. The claims of the manufacturers based on the use of the Iron Byron are not entirely refuted here, but neither are they strongly confirmed; the general impression gained is that the modern golf ball is very similar in performance no matter where it originated. Thus taste and price are likely to affect golf ball purchases and regular lessons with the professional rather than the search for a "magical" ball may be a better way of lowering a handicap.

5 References

Anderson, M.A. (1989) **Better Golf.** W. H. Allen & Co. London.
Graham, D. (1993) **The Guinness Guide to Golf Equipment.** Guinness Publishing, Enfield, Middlesex.
Watson, T. S. (1983) **Getting Up and Down** Hodder & Stoughton, London.

56 The golf equipment market 1984–1994

S.K. Proctor
Sports Marketing Surveys Ltd, Byfleet Business Centre, Chertsey
Road, Byfleet, Surrey, UK

Abstract
Since 1984 Sports Marketing Surveys Ltd has conducted
about 10,000 interviews each year with regular golfers in
the UK. During this period we have also carried out an
equipment census of competitors at the Open Championship
and major events on the PGA European Tour.
　This paper demonstrates the major trends in the
equipment market over this period and shows that the
amateur equipment market does not always reflect the
equipment in vogue on the tour. Some forecasts for future
trends in the equipment market are made.
Keywords: Driver Head Type, Driver Shaft Type, Iron Head
Type, Iron Shaft Type, Golf Ball Construction, Future
Trends.

1 Introduction

Every year since 1984 Sports Marketing Surveys Ltd has
carried out golf equipment research amongst both amateur
and professional golfers. We interview 10,000 amateur
golfers each year at golf courses throughout England,
Scotland and Wales. The questions asked have been kept
broadly comparable over the years. This paper shows some
of the main trends and suggests a few future forecasts.
　To cover professional usage, we carry out an equipment
census each year at 12 events on the PGA European Tour
and the Open Championship. In order to reflect the most
international of these fields, we have chosen the results
from the Open Championships to use in this paper.
　It is interesting to compare the amateur and professional games. The professionals are used widely in
product advertising but there is no clear pattern between
professional usage and amateur product acceptance. We
have used recent purchases in the amateur game rather

Science and Golf II: Proceedings of the World Scientific Congress of Golf. Edited by A.J.
Cochran and M.R. Farrally. Published in 1994 by E & FN Spon, London. ISBN 0 419 18790 1

than usage because the trends are more apparent and
technology available at the time of purchase is better
illustrated.

2 Driver head type

The change in the driver market has been substantial
since 1984. There has been a major switch to the metal
headed driver. In 1986, the first year we have comparable
figures, 23% of amateur driver purchases were metal
headed woods whilst only 11% of tour pros were using a
metal driver.

From 1987 onwards the switch to metal drivers in the
amateur game and the professional game went almost hand
in hand. Now three quarters of new purchases and three
quarters of professional usage are metal headed. This is
shown in Figure 1.

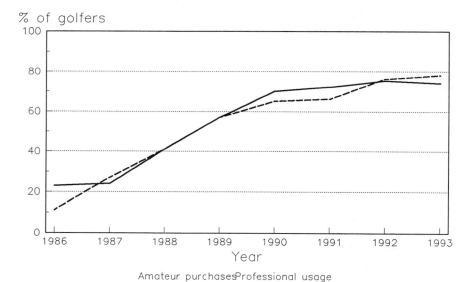

Fig. 1   Metal Drivers 1986–1993 – Amateurs vs professionals

Drivers with an oversize head now account for 10% of the
market and the trend away from purchasing matched sets of
woods continues. Individual wood purchases now account
for 60% of wood purchase occasions.

3 Driver shaft type

Whereas the switch to metal headed drivers went almost
hand in hand between the amateur and the professional
games the switch to graphite shafted drivers has been
much more rapid in the professional game. This is probably to be expected due to the premium prices of graphite
shafts compared to steel shafts.

In fact three quarters of drivers used by professionals currently have a graphite shaft compared to
only 39% of recent driver purchases by amateurs. Figure 2
shows the progress of graphite shafts for the two
markets.

As prices come down graphite shafted drivers will continue to spread into the amateur game who, after all,
probably stand to benefit the most from new technology.

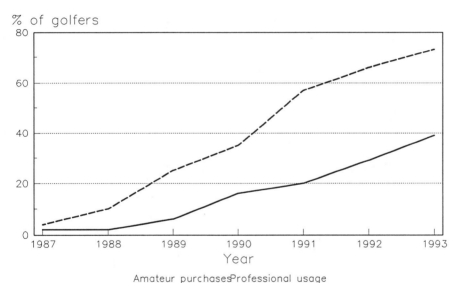

Fig. 2   Graphite shafted drivers 1987-1993 - Amateurs vs
professionals

4 Iron head type

Traditionally the "cavity back" iron was considered a game improver club, so it is to be expected that it is more prevalent in the amateur game than on the professional tour.

The cavity back iron has accounted for about 20% of professional usage on the Tour for most of the last 10 years with the Ping brand predominant. However, in 1992 and 1993 we have seen cavity back irons increase to 39% of professionals on tour. This is still considerably short of the amateur game where 78% of new purchases are cavity backed. Figure 3 shows this trend.

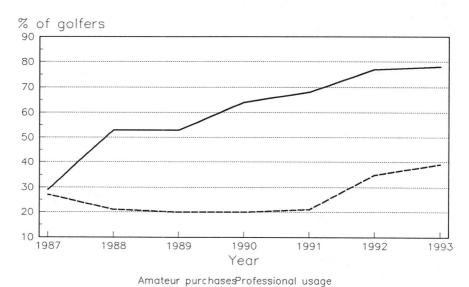

Fig. 3 Cavity backed irons 1987-1993 – Amateurs vs professionals

In the same way as woods, there is a move towards more purchases of individual irons with 20% of purchases now of individual irons such as 1 irons or extra wedges.

Over half of the professionals on tour now use an extra wedge. The trend is likely to move to the amateur game but only perhaps to the better golfers.

5 Iron shaft type

As you might expect the switch to graphite in the full
set of irons has been much slower than the switch to
graphite shafts in drivers. However, whereas the switch
to graphite in drivers is more rapid in the professional
game, the switch to graphite shafts in irons has been
more noticeable in the amateur game.

Only 10% of tour pros currently use graphite shafted
irons. This compares to 24% of recent purchases in the
amateur game. Figure 4 shows this clearly. It may be that
professionals are content with the distance they achieve
with steel shafts and amateurs are always looking for
extra distance particularly those with slower swing
speeds such as older and lady golfers. There is also some
evidence from Sports Marketing Surveys' regular golfer
interviews that younger golfers readily accept graphite
in golf as they are used to the technology from tennis
and squash.

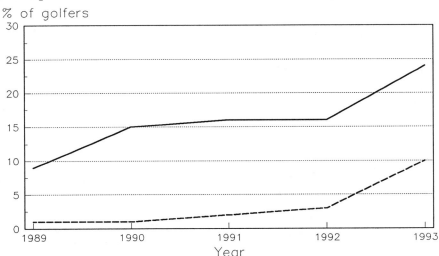

Fig. 4 Graphite shafted irons 1989-1993 - Amateurs vs
professionals

As prices of graphite shafts come down the switch to
graphite in irons is likely to continue. Amateurs, however, are unlikely to use the very low torque shafts that
some of the professionals are using but generally both
the amateur and professional game will see increased
usage of high technology shafts.

6 Golf ball construction

Almost all of the professional players still use a three
piece balata ball. This has changed little over the last
10 years.

Through the 1980s the amateur game saw a gradual
increase in the two piece surlyn ball as a result of the
success of "distance" balls such as Ultra, Pinnacle and
Top Flite. At their peak in 1989 these two piece balls
accounted for 75% of the market. Since then the three
piece wound ball made a recovery to 35% of the market in
1992 as "feel" and "control" became more important than
"distance".

The latest trend in 1993 is the "performance" two
piece which now accounts for 10% of the market. This is
similar to the two piece surlyn but has a higher spin
rate and therefore better "stopping" characteristics than
the traditional distance ball.

Figure 5 charts the movements in the ball construction
market. Please note the two piece surlyn category
includes "x-outs".

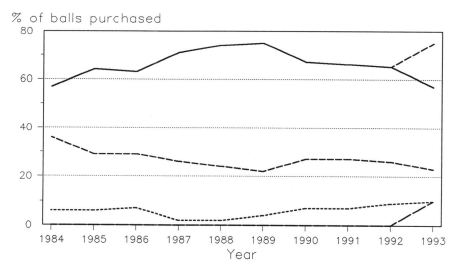

Fig. 5 Golf ball construction 1984-1993 - Amateur
golfers

7 Conclusion and Future forecasts

The overall conclusion is that the links between equipment usage in the professional and amateur games are not always clear. Generally new technology will filter through to both professional and amateur games but only where technology is appropriate for the standard of play. For example, amateurs are unlikely to use balata balls or very low torque graphite shafts in any great number.

Although the switch to metal drivers was almost simultaneous for the amateur and professional game, the link is not so clear in other areas. The professionals are well ahead in the switch to graphite shafts in drivers. Conversely the amateurs are ahead in the switch to graphite shafts in irons. Amateurs, traditionally, have been bigger users of the cavity back iron although professionals have increased their usage in the last two years.

Trends we expect to see over the next few years are:
  a) Better amateur golfers to purchase extra wedges in line with professional usage on the Tour.
  b) Amateurs to continue to purchase cavity back irons especially mid-sized. More professionals to use cavity back irons.
  c) Amateurs to increasingly purchase two piece performance balls at the expense of both traditional distance two piece and three piece surlyn. A few professionals are also starting to use performance two piece balls.
  d) The switch to graphite shafts in irons to continue in both the amateur and professional games.
  e) Gradual switch to high technology materials such as inserts in irons but only for clubs that are not outrageously styled.

57 Chemistry and properties of a high performance golf ball coating

T.J. Kennedy III
Manager Coatings and Analytical Chemistry, Spalding Sports World Wide
and W. Risen, Jr
Professor of Chemistry, Brown University

Abstract
Golf balls typically utilize two part polyurethane coatings due to the abrasion resistance, adhesion and weatherability. The isocyanate portion of these materials was historically a toluene diisocyanate (TDI) prepolymer. However, with the advent of high whiteness golf balls, it is important that the coating for the golf balls maintains its water white appearance, along with maintaining all of the other properties (adhesion, abrasion resistance, gloss retention, etc.). It is also important to decrease the amount of volatile organic carbon (VOC) that evaporates from the coating during the spraying and curing of the golf ball coating.
Keywords: Golf balls, Polyurethane, Biuret, Trimer, Ultraviolet.

1 Introduction

The golf ball has under gone a great deal of metamorphosis over the past 100 years. One aspect that has changed dramatically are golf ball coatings, the thin layers of material that are the outer surface of the golf ball.

In the past, the golf ball was finished with up to five layers of coating. These consisted of an epoxy primer, two layers of a titanium dioxide (TiO_2) containing white paint, and two layers of a clear top coat. This process required a great deal of handling and resulted in a large amount of organic solvent emission from the finishing process.

The golf ball that is manufacture today has a much simplified coating process. A water borne primer is applied to the golf ball as a tie layer between the ionomer cover and the clear top coat. The golf ball logo is then applied on to the primer. The final step is the application of a solvent borne polyurethane clear coat. This final clear coat contains small amounts of additives to enhance the coatings performance. One such additive that may be utilized is a narrow range u.v. absorber. This paper will describe in depth the chemical nature of the solvent borne polyurethane top coat and one of the enhancing additives, a narrow range u.v. absorber.

2 Biurets And Isocyanurate Trimers As Polyurethane Crosslinkers

Science and Golf II: Proceedings of the World Scientific Congress of Golf. Edited by A.J. Cochran and M.R. Farrally. Published in 1994 by E & FN Spon, London. ISBN 0 419 18790 1

2.1 Polyurethane Polyols

The material that comprises the outer surface of a golf ball provides the abrasion resistance that is necessary to protect the golf ball during play. This coating also imparts a high gloss to the golf ball that is aesthetically pleasing. This outer coating has undergone a great deal of transformation, due mainly to two reasons; increasing performance and environmental awareness.

The outer coating on the golf ball is a solvent borne two part polyurethane. The first part of the system is a hydroxyl functional polyol. These materials are characterized mainly by the functional group (-O-H) to molecular weight ratio. This value is known as the equivalent weight of the polyol. The polyols that are employed for golf ball coatings typically have a hydroxyl equivalent weight in the range of 50 to 1500. The polyol is ethylenically saturated and is typically one of the following: 1. a polyether polyol that is derived from propylene oxide or ethylene oxide, 2. a polyester polyol, such as a poly(oxydiethylene adipate) or 3. an acrylic polyol comprised of methyl methacrylate, co-polymerized with hydroxy-ethyl methacrylate.

2.2 Isocyanate Crosslinkers

The second part of the polyurethane system is composed of the biuret or isocyanurate trimer of hexamethylene diisocyanate (HDI). These derivatives of HDI have been found to have the desirable characteristics of abrasion resistance, u.v. stability, and adhesion to a primed ionomer cover. Derivatives of toluene diisocyanate (TDI) were formerly employed as crosslinkers for polyurethane coatings. These materials were not as abrasion resistant, they had very poor u.v. stability, and the adhesion was not as good as the HDI derivatives. Other diisocyanate derivatives of methylene diisocyanate (MDI) and isophorone diisocyanate (IPDI) were also inferior to the HDI derivatives.

Another attribute of the biuret and trimer derivatives is low viscosity and high functionality. These two properties allow the total coating system to have a higher solid content and still have a viscosity that facilitates spray painting / air atomization of the coating system on the outer surface of the golf ball. A viscosity between 50 centiPoise and 5000 centiPoise is the range for the biuret and trimer derivatives. CentiPoise and milliPascal*seconds are equivalent viscosity measurements.

The functional group of isocyanates is -N=C=O. The biuret and isocyanurate trimer derivatives of HDI typically have equivalent weights between 100 and 300. The biuret molecule is shown in Figure 1 and the trimer molecule is depicted in Figure 2.

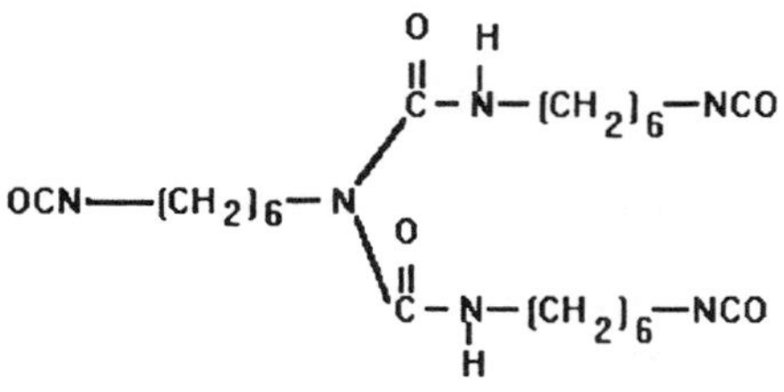

Fig. 1 Biuret of HDI

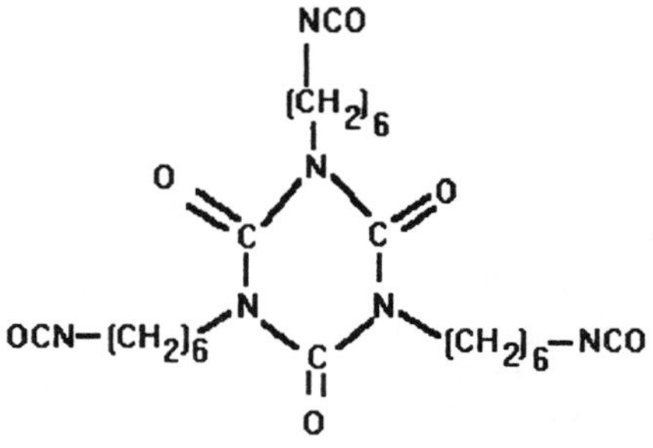

Fig. 2 Isocyanurate Trimer of HDI

2.3 Polyurethane Coating System

The polyurethane coatings are compounded with a stoichiometricly excess amount of isocyanate. The reason for this excess is to compensate for any water that may be in the coating system. The stoichiometric equation for a polyol / isocyanate system is shown in Equation 1.

$$1.0 \ R\text{-}N\text{=}C\text{=}O + 1.0 \ R'\text{-}O\text{-}H \Rightarrow 1.0 \ R\text{-}N\overset{\displaystyle H}{\underset{\displaystyle O}{\overset{|}{\underset{\parallel}{C}}}}\text{-}O\text{-}R'$$

Equation 1

When excess isocyanate is introduced into Equation 1, along with water molecules from either the air or the polyol, the isocyanate reacts as seen in Equation 2.

$$1.05R\text{-}N\text{=}C\text{=}O + 1.0R'\text{-}O\text{-}H + 0.025H\text{-}O\text{-}H \Rightarrow 1.0R\text{-}N\overset{H}{\underset{O}{\overset{|}{\underset{\parallel}{C}}}}\text{-}O\text{-}R' + 0.025CO_2 + 0.025R\text{-}N\overset{H \ \ H}{\underset{O}{\overset{| \ \ |}{\underset{\parallel}{C}}}}\text{-}N\text{-}R$$

Equation 2

The excess isocyanate reacts with the water in the coating system and the water vapor in the air. The products are polyurea and carbon dioxide.

The stoichiometric balance of the isocyanate to the polyol (R-N=C=O / R'-O-H) is typically greater than 1.00 to compensate for moisture in the air and water in the polyols, due to their hydroscopic nature. The excess R-N=C=O reacts with the H_2O to form polyurea and carbon dioxide. If the stoichiometric balance, R-N=C=O / R'-O-H, is less than 1.00, there is excess polyol. The excess R'-OH groups of the polyol will not react and tend to plasticize the coating film. This plasticizing effect is desirable in some applications, giving the coating film better adhesion to the substrate. However, the plasticized coating film does not have as good mechanical properties, such as stain resistance and abrasion resistance, as the same coating system with a stoichiometric excess of isocyanate.

3 Ultra Violet Light Absorbers And Optical Brighteners

3.1 Optical Brighteners
Optical brighteners work by taking up some of the ultraviolet (UV) radiation in sunlight and emitting some of that energy as light in the visible range through fluorescence. They typically are selected to emit blue light, because it is blue light that is missing most importantly when white light is reflected from an object that is yellowish. The blue light emitted by optical brighteners adds to the visible light reflected from the yellowish object to make it appear white. If a white object contains the optical brightener, it appears even whiter than white because the object gives off more visible light than it would if it were only reflecting white light.

3.2 UV Stabilizers
Typically, polymeric objects become yellowish because they contain compounds that absorb light in the short wavelength (blue or UV) regions more strongly than they do in the longer wavelength visible regions. These compounds can be there for a number of reasons. One is the set of reactions known as aging. It is a complex set of reactions which includes thermally induced processes, oxidation, and many chemical processes that result from the absorption of UV radiation. To prevent, or at least slow down, the aging processes that result ultimately from the absorption of UV light, it is common practice to add ultraviolet absorbers. These compounds are selected to absorb as much UV light as possible without absorbing it in the blue region of the visible spectrum (otherwise, they would contribute to yellowing).

Thus, to prevent the degradation of an object caused by absorbed UV light one incorporates another compound (UV absorber) to absorb the UV light. However, to make an object optically bright, one adds an optical brightener to take up some incident UV light and fluoresce it into the blue end of the spectrum.

3.3 UV Stabilizers With Narrow Range Absorption
This presents the dilemma of wanting the UV light to be absorbed but also have enough of it transmitted to permit the optical brightener to function. The typical solution is to compromise on both. The compromise usually involves incorporating less of the UV absorber and more of the optical brightener than is optimal, but it can also mean putting the optical brightener only in the thin topcoat layer on an object.

It has been found in this work that a different approach leads to a superior result. The idea is to use a UV absorber whose UV absorbance spectrum leads to high absorption of the types (wavelengths) of UV light that cause the greatest damage while transmitting to a significant extent the types (wavelengths) of UV light that do not cause much damage but which do excite the optical brighteners. That type of UV absorber is a narrow band, short wavelength UV absorber.

The use of this type of narrow band UV absorber permits both high absorbance of the most harmful radiation and highly efficient use of an optical brightener. Both functions can be performed well and economically.

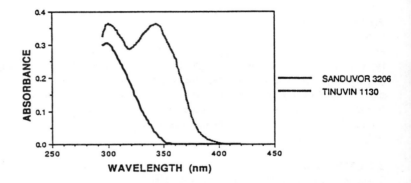

Fig. 3 ABSORBANCE SPECTRA

In Figure 3, the absorption spectra of Sanduvor 3206 and Tinuvin 1130 are shown after the solvent (THF) and background effects and concentration effects have been removed so they are both on an equivalent concentration basis of $1.13 * 10E-5$ g/mL. Clearly, the Sanduvor 3206 absorbs UV light of wavelengths below 320 nm quite well, as does Tinuvin 1130 on a mass equivalent basis. Thus, both absorb well the most energetic photons (Y <= 320 nm). However, the narrow band absorption characteristics of the Sanduvor 3206 allow the lower energy photons, which make up UV light in the 340-380 nm range, to be transmitted much better than the Tinuvin 1130 does. If an optical brightener is in the system as well, it can be excited by this 340-380 nm light and fluoresce blue. Even though it is possible to get some optical brightener function using a broad band UV absorber, use of the narrow band one increases the efficiency of the combination so much that it is possible to use less optical brightener and the optimal amount of UV absorber.

The experimental data in Figure 4 show the value of this approach quite clearly. To obtain the data in Figure 4, some golf ball covers were prepared with Tinuvin 1130 incorporated and others were made with the same amount of Sanduvor 306 in place of the Tinuvin 1130. Both contained the same concentration of Uvitex OB optical brightener. Their fluorescence spectra was measured. When excited by UV light at 320 nm, the fluorescence in the blue region was somewhat greater for the Sanduvor 3206 containing sample, as shown in Figure 4. This is expected because Sanduvor 3206 absorbs somewhat less of the source light at 320 nm.

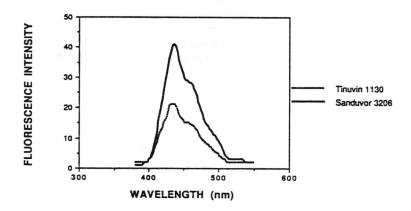

Fig. 4 OPTICAL BRIGHTENING; 320 nm EXCITATION

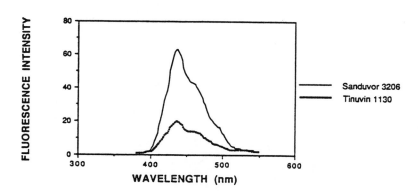

Fig. 5 OPTICAL BRIGHTENING; 350 nm EXCITATION

This effect is even more dramatic in the regions where the differences in UV absorption are greater. As shown in Figure 5, when the samples are excited with 350 nm UV light, the optical brightener's fluorescence intensity is much greater for the cover containing the narrow band absorber.

4 Conclusions

The use of biuret and isocyanurate trimers of hexamethylene diisocyanate as crosslinkers for polyurethanes produce a superior coating for golf balls. The golf balls have improved abrasion resistance, excellent weatherability, excellent adhesion to primed golf balls, and lower levels of VOC emission during processing.

The incorporation of a narrow range ultraviolet radiation absorber allows for protection of the coating from harmful UV radiation while allowing the excitation of an optical brightener in the golf ball cover. The optical brightener thus provides a greater whiteness for the golf ball.

References

Woods, G. (1982) Flexible Polyurethane Foams, Applied Science Publishers Ltd., pp 1-27.

Miles Corporation (1988) The Chemistry of Polyurethane Coatings, pp 1-15.

58 Novel high acid ionomers for golf ball cover applications

M.J. Sullivan and R.A. Weiss
Spalding Sports Worldwide, Chicopee, USA and the University of
Connecticut, Storrs, USA

Abstract
The use of Surlyn ionomers in golf ball covers is well documented and deal
exclusively with neutralized copolymers of ethylene and methacrylic acid
typically containing 15 wt-% or less methacrylic acid. In 1971, R.P. Molitor
at Spalding discovered that blends of zinc and sodium ionomers gave enhanced
distance and improved low temperature durability over previous covers. It has
now been demonstrated using materials developed in our laboratories that
ionomers containing about 20 wt-% acid neutralized with a variety of different
cations, give golf balls having dramatically lower spin rates and greatly
improved distance.
Keywords: Golf balls, Ionomers, Cations, Acid Copolymer, Ionomer Blends.

1 Introduction

Ethylene ionomers are copolymers of ethylene and a partially neutralized
unsaturated carboxylic acid such as methacrylic acid or acrylic acid (Rees,
1968 and Bush, 1972). They are commonly available commercially as metal salts
under the trademarks of Iotek (Exxon Chemical Co.) and Surlyn (E.I.DuPont de
Nemours & Co.). Free-acid derivatives are also commercially available as
Nucrel (E.I.DuPont de Nemours & Co.) and Primacor (Dow Chemical Co.). Because
of their excellent resilience, toughness and durability, the metal salt
ionomers have replaced trans-polyisoprene as the most commonly used cover
material for golf balls.

Molitor (Molitor, 1972) discovered that blends of zinc and sodium ionomers
not only provided dramatically improved low temperature cracking resistance
but also gave a synergistic improvement in initial velocity over that of
either ionomer alone. Today, blends of zinc, sodium and lithium ionomers are
commonly employed in golf ball cover compositions. The specific salts used,
the level of neutralization of the ionomer and the blend composition influence
not only the distance and durability of the ball but also such playing
characteristics as spin rate, sound, and feel. Recently, terpolymers prepared
from ethylene, a partially metal-neutralized unsaturated carboxylic acid and
an acrylate monomer such as butyl or methyl acrylate (Statz,1989), have been
used in golf ball covers to soften the composition (Sullivan, 1989).
Historically, commercially available ionomer resins used in golf ball cover
applications contained at most 15 to 16 wt-% carboxylic acid. Higher acid
ionomers are now commercially available and golf balls with covers molded from
blends of high acid zinc, sodium and magnesium ionomers exhibit enhanced
coefficient of restitution (C.O.R.) values and higher hardness compared to
blends of low acid ionomers.

This paper reports our initial studies of the effect of cation and salt
concentration on the performance of golf balls molded from high-acid ionomers
and their blends.

Science and Golf II: Proceedings of the World Scientific Congress of Golf. Edited by A.J.
Cochran and M.R. Farrally. Published in 1994 by E & FN Spon, London. ISBN 0 419 18790 1

2 Experimental

2.1 Hardness

Shore Hardness was measured in general accordance with ASTM Test D-2240, measured on the parting line of a fixtured, finished ball.

2.2 Coefficient of Restitution

Coefficient of restitution (COR) was measured by firing a golf ball from an air cannon at a velocity of 125 feet per second against a rigidly mounted 2 inch thick steel plate which is positioned 12 feet from the muzzle of the cannon. The ingoing and rebound velocity are measured electronically and th COR is the ratio of outgoing to ingoing velocities. All numbers reported herein represent the average of 24 balls tested.

2.3 Spin Rate

Spin rate was measured by striking a ball with a nine iron wherein the clubhead speed is about 105 feet per second and the ball is launched at an angle of 26 to 34 degrees with a velocity of about 110-115 feet per second. The spin rate was determined by observing the rotation of the ball in fligh using stop action strobe photography.

2.4 Materials

The high acid ionomers were prepared from a single ethylene-acrylic acid copolymer, Primacor® 5981 (Dow Chemical Co.), which contained 8.9 mol% acryl acid (20 wt.%) and had a density of 0.960 g/cm^3 and a melt index (2150 g lc at 190°C) of 300 g/10 min. Partially neutralized metal salts were preparec by adding the specific neutralizing agent and the ethylene acrylic acid copolymer to a 1000 cc Banbury mixer at room temperature. The neutralizing agents used were sodium hydroxide (NaOH), lithium hydroxide (LiOH), potassi hydroxide (KOH), manganese acetate tetrahydrate ($(C_3H_5O_2)_2Mn--4H_2O$), zinc acetate dihydrate ($(C_3H_5O_2)_2Zn--2H_2O$), magnesium actetate tetrahydrate ($(C_3H_5O_2)_2Mg--4H_2O$), calcium acetate ($(C_3H_5O_2)_2Ca$), nickel acetate ($(C_3H_5O_2)_2Ni$) and magnesium oxide (MgO). All neutralizing agents were added as crystalline solids except the calcium acetate, which due to problems encountered in soli form was added as a 30 wt% aqueous solution. It was assumed that the neutralization reaction was quantitative. 50/50 blends were prepared in the same fashion, either by adding the two or more cations simultaneously or by post melt mixing the individually reacted ionomers. The neutralization agen dissolved in the acid copolymer above the melting point of the copolymer anc vigorous reaction took place with considerable foaming occurring as the base reacted with the carboxylic acid groups of the acid copolymer and the volat: by-products of water (in the case of the oxides or hydroxides) or acetic ac: (when acetates are used) were evaporated. The reaction was continued for about 30-45 minutes at ca. 120-149°C until foaming ceased, at which point th batch was removed from the mixer. Mixing was continued on a hot (80-120°C) two-roll mill to ensure complete reaction. The extent of reaction was monitored by measuring melt flow index according to ASTM D-1238-E.

Golf balls were prepared by injection molding over a pre-positioned core a closed mold at a melt temperature of about 205-216°C. All balls were 1.68 inches in diameter molded over a 1.545 inch diameter solid core. Balls were tested in both the molded and finished state. Molded balls were simply equator-trimmed prior to testing whereas finished balls were also lightly abraded with nylon bristles, washed thoroughly in water and two coats of cle polyurethane were applied at a total dry thickness of about 1.5 mils (38 μm. The finishing operation also subjected the balls to about 4 to 5 hours at 6 71°C.

3 Results and Discussion

3.1 Effect of cation and salt concentration on COR

COR of golf balls with molded covers consisting of a single ionomer was determined as a function of the type of metal cation used and the salt concentration. The samples and properties are summarized in Table 1. The COR values were measured on unfinished balls, i.e., without the top-coat and the thermal history that accompanied the finishing operation. Partially neutralized ionomers may be considered as terpolymers consisting of ethylene, acrylic acid and metal acrylate units.

The data for the different salts can be divided into three categories that depend on the class of cation used: 1) alkali metal salts (Li^+, Na^+, K^+), 2) alkaline earth metal salts (Ca^{2+}, Mg^{2+}) and 3) transition metal salts (Zn^{2+}, Ni^{2+}, Mn^{2+}). For the alkali metal salts, increasing neutralization or increasing cation size (i.e., the ionic radius of Li is 0.68 Angs., Na is 0.97 Angs. and K is 1.33 Angs.) corresponds to decreasing COR. In contrast, for the transition metal salts, the COR increases with increasing neutralization. The trend for the alkaline metal salts is not as apparent, and from the limited data, COR appears to be relatively insensitive to level of neutralization. These data indicate that in a single cation golf ball, COR is optimized by minimizing the neutralization for alkali metal salts and maximizing the neutralization for transition metal salts.

Table 2 also lists the synergistic effect of blending on the COR of golf balls prepared from high-acid blends. The predicted COR, $(COR)_{calc}$, was calculated from a weighted average of the coefficients for the as-molded, unfinished balls prepared from the component ionomers. $(COR)_{exp}$ was the coefficient for the as-molded, unfinished balls with ionomer blend covers and the synergism was defined as $\Delta \equiv (COR)_{exp} - (COR)_{calc}$.

The most significant positive synergism was observed for the balls that were prepared from the combination of an alkali metal salt and a transition metal salt, specifically zinc (samples B4, B13 and B16 though one sample (BThe high acid ionomers as a group are significantly harder and higher in COR than the lower acid versions most commonly found in golf ball cover applications, which typically have a maximum hardness of 66D. The effect of this increased hardness on spin rates will be discussed in section 3.4.

3.2 Effect of blending different ionomers on COR

In order to balance low temperature properties, room temperature properties and cut resistance of a cover for a golf ball, a blend of ionomers is usually used in the construction of a cover for a two-piece golf ball. Most common is a blend of a zinc and sodium ionomer, though recently other salts such as lithium and magnesium have been used.

Covers were prepared from 50/50 binary blends of different ionomers as summarized in Table 2; the ionomers used to prepare the blends were chosen from the list in Table 1. In general, the golf balls with covers molded from blends of the high-acid ionomers showed a much greater COR pickup upon finishing, ca. 0.005-0.009, than similar balls using straight ionomer or blends of lower-acid ionomers such as the control in Table 2. This COR gain following finishing (and the associated thermal treatment) is thought to be a result of an annealing of the ionic crystallites and/or polyethylene crystallites resulting in a slightly harder, more resilient composition (Hirasawa, et.al., 1991).

A surprising, though poorly understood result of blending ionomers is that often the COR for a golf ball based on a blend is higher than that of golf balls constructed from either ionomer alone.

25) that contained nickel also showed a high positive synergism. This synergism is also prevalent in covers constructed from conventional lower-acid

Table 1: Golf Ball Compositions

Sample	Cation	c_{COOM}[a]	c_{COOH}[a]	WT-% Neutral- ization	MI (g/10 min)	COR[b]	Shore D Hardnes
1	Na	0.029	0.060	68	0.9	.804	71
2	Na	0.041	0.048	54	2.4	.808	73
3	Na	0.056	0.033	36	12.2	.812	69
4	Mn	0.025	0.064	72	7.5	.809	73
5	Mn	0.010	0.079	88	3.5	.814	77
6	Mn	0.042	0.047	53	7.5	.810	72
7	Li	0.026	0.063	71	0.6	.810	74
8	Li	0.042	0.047	53	4.2	.818	72
9	Li	0.057	0.032	36	18.6	.815	72
10	K	0.057	0.032	36	19.3	na	70
11	K	0.038	0.051	58	7.2	.804	70
12	K	0.021	0.068	77	4.3	.801	70
13	Zn	0.026	0.063	72	0.2	.806	71
14	Zn	0.042	0.047	53	0.9	.797	69
15	Zn	0.057	0.032	36	3.4	.793	67
16	Na	0.065	0.024	27	17.5	.812	na
17	Mn	0.000	0.094[c]	106	0.7	.813	na
18	Mg[d]	0.026	0.063	71	2.8	.814	74
19	Mg[d]	0.011	0.078	87	1.5	.815	76
20	Mg[d]	0.041	0.048	54	4.1	.814	74
21	Mg[e]	0.041	0.048	54	2.5	.813	na
22	Mg[e]	0.025	0.064	72	2.8	.808	na
23	Mg[e]	0.009	0.080	89	1.1	.809	na
24	Ca	0.027	0.062	69	1.1	.813	na
25	Ca	0.058	0.031	35	10.1	.808	na
26	Ni	0.035	0.054	61	0.2	.802	71
27	Ni	0.046	0.043	49	0.5	.799	72
28	Ni	0.056	0.033	37	1.8	.796	69
29	Ni	0.067	0.022	24	7.5	.786	64
Primacor	H	0.089	0.000	0	300	.774	na

a- mole fraction
b- unfinished two-piece balls
c- overneutralized
d- neutralized with magnesium acetate tetrahydrate
e- neutralized with magnesium oxide

TABLE 2.   COR of golf balls prepared with ionomer blend covers

Sample	Cation 1[a]	Cation 2[a]	$(COR)_{exp}$ (unfin.)	$(COR)_{exp,f}$ (fin.)	$(COR)_{calc}$ (unfin.)	100Δ
B1	Na	Mn	0.813	0.818	0.813	0.0
B2	Na	Li	0.813	0.818	0.815	−2.0
B3	Na	K	0.809	0.816	0.808	1.0
B4	Na	Zn	0.811	0.818	0.8045	6.5
B5	Na	Mg	0.813	0.819	0.813	0.0
B6	Na	Ca	0.811	0.819	0.8125	−1.5
B7	Mn	Li	0.811	0.817	0.816	−5.0
B8	Mn	K	0.811	0.818	0.809	2.0
B9	Mn	Zn	0.807	0.814	0.8055	1.5
B10	Mn	Mg	0.809	0.816	0.814	−5.0
B11	Mn	Ca	0.809	0.816	0.8135	−4.5
B12	Li	K	0.810	0.817	0.811	−1.0
B13	Li	Zn	0.813	0.819	0.8075	5.5
B14	Li	Mg	0.812	0.820	0.816	−4.0
B15	Li	Ca	0.811	0.819	0.8155	−4.5
B16	K	Zn	0.810	0.815	0.8005	9.5
B17	K	Mg	0.811	0.820	0.809	2.0
B18	K	Ca	0.810	0.817	0.806	4.0
B19	Zn	Mg	0.807	0.814	0.8055	1.5
B20	Zn	Ca	0.808	0.814	0.805	3.0
B21	Mg	Ca	0.810	0.818	0.8135	−3.5
B22	Na	Ni	0.809	0.815	0.8055	3.5
B23	Mn	Ni	0.807	0.814	0.8065	0.5
B24	Li	Ni	0.809	0.816	0.8085	0.5
B25	K	Ni	0.809	0.816	0.8015	7.5
B26	Zn	Ni	0.799	0.804	0.798	1.0
B27	Mg	Ni	0.805	0.813	0.8065	−1.5
B28	Ca	Ni	0.807	0.815	0.806	−1.0
Control[b]	Zn[b]	Na[b]	0.808	0.810	0.803	5.0

a-ionomers correspond to samples listed in Table 1 with Na referring to sample 3, Mn to sample 5, Li to sample 8, K to sample 11, Zn to sample 14, Mg to sample 18, Ca to sample 24, and Ni to sample 27; all blend compositions were 50/50 by weight
b-control sample was a 50/50 blend of Iotek® 8000 and 7030
$\Delta \equiv (COR)_{exp} - (COR)calc$

zinc/sodium blends (Table 2, control sample).

The synergism increased as the size of the alkali metal ion increased (Li < Na < K); this can be seen by comparing the three blends involving the zinc salt. Although none of the other blends exhibited as large a positive synergism, the same trend was followed when alkali metal salts were involved as one of the components in the blend. For example, blends of K/Ni (B25) gave greater synergy than Na/Ni (B22) which in turn gave higher synergy than Li/Ni blends, and this trend was also observed for blends of the alkali metals with Mn, Ca, and Mg ionomers.

3.3 Effect of Cover Composition on Spin Rate

The degree of spin one is able to impart to a golf ball is directly related to the balls' cover hardness, therefore the high hardness ionomers described in this paper are useful in producing golf balls having significantly lower spin rates than those currently available. It is believed that lower spinning golf balls are beneficial to the less skilled player who tends to impart unwanted sidespin to the ball. Table 3 gives the spin rates of some selected examples from Table 2 as well as some commercially available balls for comparison purposes.

Table 3. Spin Rates of High Acid Ionomer Covered Golf Balls

Sample	Cation Blend	Spin Rate (RPM) 9-Iron	Shore D Hardness
Control	Na/Zn	8,547	65
B4	Na/Zn	5,729	69
B13	Li/Zn	5,233	71
B16	K/Zn	5,530	70
B25	K/Ni	5,386	71
1.68", 2-pc. Hard ionomer cov'd[a]	Na/Zn	8,455	65
1.68", 3-pc. Hard Ionomer Cov'd[b]	Na/Zn/Li	8,931	65
1.72", 2-pc. Hard Ionomer Cov'd[c]	Na/Zn	6,985	65

a-ball type tested is a Wilson Ultra; b-ball tested is a Titleist DT-100; c-Ball tested is a Top-Flite Magna

4 Conclusions

Ionomers prepared from a high acid copolymer of ethylene and acrylic acid exhibit interesting properties for golf ball cover applications. These new ionomers are higher in hardness and modulus compared to existing lower acid conventional ionomers still in use on most golf balls. By blending certain cation neutralized ionomers one obtains a synergistic pick-up in COR above and beyond those found in conventional zinc/sodium blends as discovered by Molitor (Molitor, 1968). Golf balls having very low spin rates and considerably higher resilience are obtained using these ionomers and will likely find an application in commercial products in the near future.

5 References

Bush, J.L., Milligan, C.W. (1972), U. S. Pat. 3,649,578.
Hirasawa, E., Yamamoto, Y., Tadano, K., Yano, S., (1991), J. Appld. Poly. Sci., Vol. 42, 351-362.
Molitor, R.P., (1972), U.S.Patent 3,819,768.
Rees, R.W. (1968), U. S. Pat. 3,404,134.
Statz, R.J. (1989), U. S. Pat. 4,801,649.
Sullivan, M.J. (1989) U.S. Pat. 4,884,814 and 5,120,791.

59 A design system for iron golf clubs

S. Mitchell, S.T. Newman, C.J. Hinde and R. Jones
Manufacturing Engineering Department, Loughborough University, UK

Abstract
This paper describes a prototype computer based design system for iron golf clubs. The design method uses proprietary surface modelling software and is based on an extended form feature method (EFFM). This method enables clubs to be designed or built by the assembly of pre-defined features. Modifications to designs can be effected by either feature substitution or manipulation. A golf club anatomy is described which specifies the relationships between features and thus enables club sets to be automatically generated. The system interface has been developed for use by non-experts.
Key Words: Golf Clubs, Design, Features.

1 Introduction

Golf clubs have been made for hundreds of years by craftsmen who in early days were frequently professional golfers. The club head has acquired a traditional shape and the rules of golf (R&A 1982) have generally restricted shape innovation. Statements such as "the club head shall be generally plain in shape" ... "features such as holes ..., or appendages to the mainbody etc ... are not permitted" have meant that relatively little change has taken place, and so the general club shapes have varied little from 70 years ago. Golf clubs represent a good example of a sculptured product where the set is developed from parametric rules. Some of the design rules have been specified such as loft, weight and offset, but there are many others which are the result of the designers aesthetic perception or quasi scientific performance related reasoning.

A golf club is easily recognisable and most design activity is based on variations of the basic product. The major problem the majority of manufacturing companies have at present is concerned with the speed with which they can introduce new products to the market. At present the majority of the world's club heads are sourced from the Far East, and for Western companies this places severe demands on communications, particularly if design iterations are required. It is apparent that faster design and prototyping systems are required in order to develop innovations quickly. Smith and Reinertson (1991) indicate that the principal benefits from early product introduction are extended product sales life, increased market share and higher profit margins.

While it is important to develop club designs and view the concepts in three dimensions, the nature of club design requires artefacts for appreciation and modification. The more concepts and prototypes that can be made the better the

Science and Golf II: Proceedings of the World Scientific Congress of Golf. Edited by A.J. Cochran and M.R. Farrally. Published in 1994 by E & FN Spon, London. ISBN 0 419 18790 1

chances of a successful design. Since the second world war computer aided design and manufacturing systems have been developed to enable the rapid development of the aerospace industries. Recently many manufacturers have appreciated that these methods can also be used for golf equipment. Unfortunately they require considerable engineering expertise for operation.

2 System Requirements

Irrespective of whether the club designer is an artisan or an expert professional the rapid capture of design concepts is a considerable development aid. The basic requirements for a club design system would be:

(a) Ease of operation by non-computer experts.
(b) Ability to generate and modify designs quickly.
(c) Automated generation of club sets by specifying parameter variation.
(d) Integration with automated prototype production.
(e) Design analysis.

3 Surface Generation

The description of full 3-D sculptured surfaces is probably best achieved using surface modelling methods (Jones 1990). If the product is described as a single surface then shape changes require considerable manipulation, and the generation of edges is particularly difficult. This situation is easily overcome by generating the object from a series of biparametric surfaces. Most designers of sculptured products will define their products in terms of features which are meaningful to them, but it is often difficult to determine the exact position of their start and finish e.g. where the toe ends and the sole starts on a club. It is apparent that there are certain features (primary) which strongly affect the design, these primary features are often blended together with secondary features to give aesthetic acceptability. To enable features to be manipulated or substituted independently from mating features the extended form feature method (EFFM) was developed (Jones et al 1993). With this method the primary product feature surface is extended far beyond its likely boundaries and is intersected with similarly extended features or limited by blend tangency curves. The excess surface is trimmed away. Figure 1 illustrates the EFFM concept by showing the interaction of top sole and toe features. It is possible to successfully model an iron club typically using 13 primary form features and 13 secondary blend features (depending on the back cavity's existence and complexity, and the feature blending algorithm and strategy).

4 Design System

Each club in a set is related to others by a set of rules. Simple club set rules such as lie, loft, offset and weight are well established, but unfortunately rules governing surface and shape progression have yet to be formalised.

The relationships between product features can be established and expressed using an entity relationship model which can be used to develop data structures. These, together with geometry modelling software are capable of describing a product.

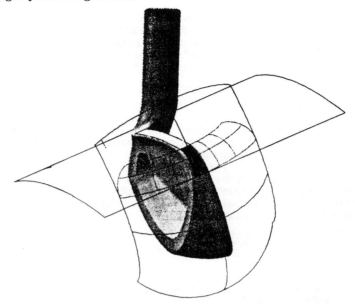

Fig.1. Extended Form Features

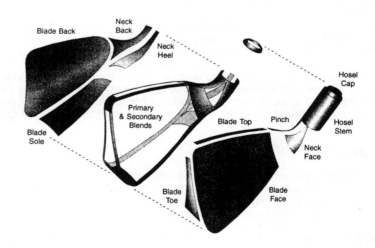

Fig.2. Typical Golf Club Features

The club needs to be described as a series of primary and secondary features and Figure 2 shows typical features for a golf club. These features need to be related by an anatomy which contains the full set of features or possibilities needed to build the product. The anatomy may be considered the shopping list or skeleton for assembling specific features to define the club. A library of shapes may exist for any particular feature type to enable the design of particular product types. Figure 3 shows a typical iron golf club feature anatomy hierarchy. It can be seen in this example that structural and ornamental features are categorised. Further subdivisions can be specified to include materials, finishes, manufacture etc.

In order to develop designs it is necessary to establish a co-ordinate reference system with which to position features. This is a matter of considerable importance, and one that has caused many problems since the methods presently used by the golf industry are subjective. In this instance the club datum has been defined at the intersection of the centre line of the hosel and the horizontal sole tangecy plane when the club is at address.

With the exception of the face and hosel the shape of a feature is generally free form since it has been generated by a craftsman's eye and skill. It is possible that a class of feature shape could be used by more than one feature, for example, the sole and toe feature shapes could well be interchangeable. However, they would be identified by different terminology and their spatial position would be different. Because many of the features are reverse engineered the patches can contain irregularities, undulations or ripples, which cannot be detected by the designer's eye. Futhermore, when the patch is extended to enable it to be mated with other features, undesirable folds can occur on the surface. Consequently it is often desirable to approximate the digitised surfaces with parametrically generated equivalents. This not only supports better automatic set generation, but also corrects feature shape irregularities. Clearly this modifies the shape, but work on existing club models has shown that it is possible to define existing club shapes through parametric features with sufficient accuracy for them to be indistinguishable from the original.

5 Design Interface and System Use

The majority of club design is performed by golf experts, such as professional players, golf enthusiasts and sales and marketing personnel. These designers are generally not engineers or scientists and if design innovation is to be pursued on a computer based system it must be easy to use and use terminology and methods with which they are familiar. Unfortunately, the engineering modelling tools which are currently available require considerable expertise and learning. In order to increase usage a "point and click" menu driven interface has been developed with an interactive window requesting information, such as, club name, dimensions etc. when required. Clubs can either be built from scratch or by using templates of existing models and affecting modifications.

The system is still in an early stage of development and has a limited set of design rules to enable club set generation. The current system enables parameterisation of the major parameters, such as, loft and lie angles, and blade offset. Further rules need to be established for different club families, but the data structure has been designed such that easy incorporation is possible. For automated set generation the design normally proceeds along the traditional approach of designing a 5 or 6 iron. Parametric variation through the set is established by altering values in a table provided in the interactive window.

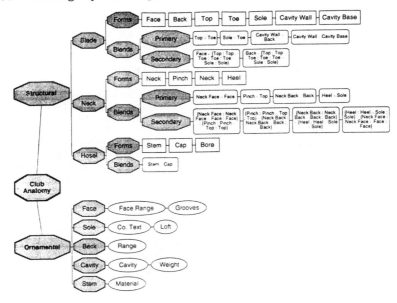

Fig.3. Iron Golf Club Feature Anatomy Hierarchy

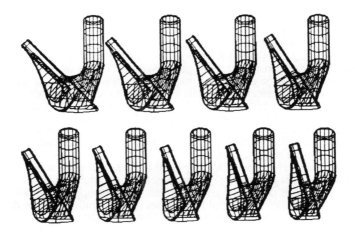

Fig.4. Automatically Generated Club Set Using Parametric Rules

Automated set generation can then proceed and the complete design of the base club and set can be completed in a matter of hours. An example of a set of clubs generated by the system is shown in Figure 4.

6 Conclusions and Future Work

An iron club design system has been developed, which uses a feature based approach to design. The system is simple to use and results in significant savings in time for club designs. A generic data structure has been developed which depends on the identification of a club feature anatomy that can be modified to user requirements. The system has been extensively tested by developing blade and cavity back clubs already on the market. Parametric design of a set of irons is possible enabling automated set generation from a single club design.

Further work is in progress on the application of the methods to woods and putters. The integration of design analysis tools to enable iterative development of the design to include mechanical properties is proposed, together with the automated generation of manufacturing data for the rapid production of prototypes.

7 Acknowledgements

The authors would like to thank:
The SERC/ACME Directorate for providing grant funding. Dunlop-Slazenger International Limited and Delcam International for their support and funding.
The Department of Manufacturing Engineering and its engineering support staff at Loughborough University of Technology.

8 References

The Royal and Ancient Golf Club of St Andrews, **"The Rules of Golf"**, 1982.
Smith P G and Reinertson D G, **Developing Products in Half the Time,** Van Nostrand Reinhold, 1991.
Jones R, Computer Based Methods for the Design of Golf Clubs, **Science and Golf Proc. 1st World Scientific Congress of Golf**, E&FN Spon., pp 280-285, 1990.
Jones R, Mitchell S and Newman S T, Feature Based Systems for the Design and Manufacture of Sculptured Products, **Int.J.Prod.Res.**, Vol.31, No.6, pp 1441-1452, 1993.

Part Three
The Golf Course
and the Game

60 Environmental protection and beneficial contributions of golf course turfs

J.B. Beard
International Sports Turf Institute, College Station, Texas, USA

Abstract
During the past decade allegations concerning the adverse effects of
golf courses on the quality of our environment have received headlines
in nearly every country where golf is played. Unfortunately, these
allegations tend to be based on pseudo-scientific arguments that are
not germane, but rather are focused to draw on the popular press to
promote such allegations by preying on the ignorance of the general
populace. Research is ongoing to identify those allegations that are
invalid as well as those environmental concerns that can be supported
by sound scientific data in order that appropriate adjustments can be
made to eliminate or minimize any potential problems. Equally important is the need to recognize and quantify the beneficial contributions of turfgrasses when properly maintained as part of a positive
golf course environment. This paper presents our current state of
knowledge concerning the benefits of golf course turfs as documented
by sound scientific data.
Keywords: environmental-quality, grasses, heat/noise-abatement,
mental/physical-health, quality-of-life, soil-stabilization, water-
quality, wild-life habitat

1 Introduction

An 18-hole golf course facility in the United States typically is
comprised of (a) 0.8-1.2 ha of putting green area, (b) 0.6-1.2 ha of
teeing area, and (c) 10-20 ha of fairway area (Table 1). In other
words, only 20 to 30% of the area on a golf course is used and maintained to specific criteria as part of the playing requirements of the
game (Beard, 1982). Except for the varying types of physical
structures that may be constructed on site, a majority of the golf
course property is devoted to a low maintenance, natural landscape. A
properly planned and maintained golf course facility offers a
diversity of functional benefits to the overall community, in addition
to the physical and mental health benefits provided from the game
itself. These benefits are significant when compared to alternate
uses such as industry, business, and residential housing, especially
in the case of urban areas where a majority of the golf courses are
located. In addition, greater benefits are derived from golf course
facilities when compared to agricultural production operations in
rural areas.

Science and Golf II: Proceedings of the World Scientific Congress of Golf. Edited by A.J.
Cochran and M.R. Farrally. Published in 1994 by E & FN Spon, London. ISBN 0 419 18790 1

Table 1.   Comparative turf use by area for a representative 18-hole
golf course in the United States.

Turf use	Area (ha)	Percent of area
Rough-water-woodland	52.65	72.2
Fairways	16.2	22.2
Buildings-parking lots	2.11	2.9
Putting greens	1.01	1.4
Tees	0.93	1.3
Total	72.9	100.0

2 Turfgrass benefits

Turfgrasses have been used by humans to enhance their environment
for over 10 centuries.   The complexity and comprehensiveness of the
environmental benefits that improve our quality-of-life are just now
being quantitatively documented through research.   Turfgrass benefits
may be divided into (a) functional, (b) recreational, and (c) aesthetic components (Beard, 1973).   The major benefits of a golf course
derived from the extensive use of turfgrasses, plus the associated
trees, shrubs, and flowering plants, are summarized as follows.

2.1 Soil erosion control and dust stabilization - vital soil resource
protection
Turfgrasses serve as inexpensive, durable ground covers that protect
our valuable, non-renewable soil resources.   Turfgrasses offer one of
the most cost efficient methods to control wind and water erosion of
soil, and thus are very important in eliminating dust and mud problems.

Generally, a few large storms each year are responsible for most
soil erosion losses (Menzel, 1991).   Gross et al. (1991) reported
sediment losses of 10 to 60 kg ha^{-1} from turfgrass during a 30 min.
storm that produced 76 mm h^{-1} of rainfall; while soil loss for bare
soil plots averaged 223 kg ha^{-1}.   They concluded that well-maintained
turfgrass stands should not be a significant source of sediment
entering bodies of water.   Other studies and reviews (Gross et al.,
1990; Morton et al., 1988; Petrovic, 1990; Watschke and Mumma, 1989)
have concluded that quality turfgrass stands modify surface water flow
so that runoff is insignificant in all but the most intense rainfall
events.

The erosion control effectiveness of turfgrasses is the combined
result of a high shoot density and root mass for soil surface stabilization, plus a high biomass matrix that provides resistance to lateral
surface water flow, thus slowing otherwise potentially erosive water
velocities.   Mowed turfgrasses have a dense ground cover matrix, with
a high shoot density ranging from 75 million to 20 billion shoots ha^{-1};
while putting greens possess in the order of 66 billion shoots ha^{-1}
(Beard, 1973; Lush, 1990).   Regular mowing, as practiced in turf
culture, increases the shoot density substantially because of enhanced
tillering when compared to ungrazed grassland (Beard, 1973).

2.2 Enhanced ground water recharge and protection of surface water quality

A key mechanism by which turfgrasses protects water is a superior capability to essentially trap and hold water runoff. This results in more water infiltrating and filtering downward through the soil-turfgrass ecosystem.

A mowed turfgrass possesses a leaf-stem biomass ranging from 1,000 to 30,000 kg ha^{-1}, depending on the grass species, season, and cultural regime (Lush, 1990). This biomass is composed of a matrix of relatively fine-textured stems and narrow leaves with numerous, random open spaces. The matrix is porous in terms of the water infiltration capability. Also, turfgrass ecosystems often support abundant populations of earthworms (*Lumbricidae*) in the range of 200 to 300 m^{-2} (Potter *et al.*, 1985, 1990a). Earthworm activity increases the amount of macropore space within the soil, which results in a higher soil water infiltration rate and water-retention capacity (Lee, 1985).

Studies conducted on the same research site have shown that surface-water runoff losses from conventionally cultivated tobacco (*Nicotiana tabacum* L.) averaged 6.7 mm ha^{-1} month^{-1} during the May to September growing season, whereas the surface-water runoff loss from turfgrass averaged 0.6 mm ha^{-1} month^{-1} (Angle, 1985; Gross *et al.*, 1990). Surface runoff losses of total nitrogen and total phosphorus for tobacco were 2.34 and 0.48 kg ha^{-1} month^{-1}, respectively, during the growing season. Losses for the same parameters from turf averaged 0.012 and 0.002 kg ha^{-1} month^{-1}, respectively. Other studies have shown a similar ability of a grass cover to reduce runoff, and therefore enhance soil water infiltration and ground water recharge (Bennett, 1939; Gross *et al.*, 1991; Jean and Juang, 1979; Morton *et al.*, 1988; Watschke and Mumma, 1989). Finally, the reduced runoff volume, due to a turfgrass cover, may decrease costly storm-water management structural requirements for urban tract development (Schuyler, 1987).

2.3 Improved biodegradation of organic chemicals and ground water protection

A diverse, large population of soil micro-flora and -fauna are supported by the decomposition of turfgrass roots and rhizomes. These same organisms offer one of the most active biological systems for the degradation of organic chemicals and pesticides trapped by the turf. Thus, this turf-ecosystem is important in the protection of ground water quality.

The runoff water and sediment that occurs from impervious surfaces in urban areas carries many pollutants (Schuyler, 1987), including metals such as lead, cadmium, copper, and zinc; hydrocarbon compounds from oil, grease, and fuels; and household-industrial hazardous wastes such as waste oils, paint thinners, organic preservatives, and solvents. Turfgrass areas can function in the catchment and filtration of these polluted runoff waters (Schuyler, 1987).

It is significant that large populations of diverse soil microflora and microfauna are supported by this same soil-turfgrass ecosystem. Microflora constitute the largest proportion of the decomposer biomass of most soils. The bacterial biomass component ranges from 30 to 300 g m^{-2} and the fungi from 50 to 500 g m^{-2}, with actinomycetes probably in a similar range (Alexander, 1977). Soil invertebrate decomposer biomass ranges from 1 to 200 g m^{-2}, with the higher values occurring in soils dominated by earthworms (Curry, 1986).

The bacterial population in the moist litter, grass clippings, and thatch of a turf commonly is in the order of 10^9 organisms cm^{-2} of litter surface (Clark and Paul, 1970). The average microbial biomass pool is 700, 850, and 1,090 kg C ha^{-1} for arable, forest, and grassland systems, respectively (Smith and Paul, 1990). A microbial biomass of 1,200 kg C ha^{-1} has been reported for grasslands in the United States (Smith and Paul, 1988). Microbial biomass values of mowed turfgrasses are not yet available, but are probably even higher because of the high carbon biomass contained in the senescent leaves and grass clippings that accumulate near the soil surface and the more favorable soil moisture regime due to irrigation (Smith and Paul, 1990).

The turfgrass ecosystem also supports a diverse community of non-pest invertebrates. For example, a *Poa pratensis* - *Festuca rubra* polystand supported 83 different taxa of invertebrates including insects, mites (*Acarina*), nematodes (*Nematoda*), annelids (*Annelida*), gastropods (*Gastropoda*), and other groups (Streu, 1973). Similarly, dozens of species of *Staphylinidae* (rove beetles), *Carabidae* (ground beetles), *Formicidae* (ants), *Araneae* (spiders), and other groups of invertebrates have been recovered from turfgrass sites (Arnold and Potter, 1987; Cockfield and Potter; 1983; 1984; 1985). Earthworms (*Lumbricidae*), oribatid mites (*Cryptostigmata*), Collembola, and other invertebrates also are abundant in turfgrass soils (Arnold and Potter, 1987; Potter et al., 1985; Potter et al., 1990a,b; Vavrek and Niemczyk, 1990).

Finally, there is the gaseous dimension of atmospheric pollution control. Carbon monoxide (CO) concentrations greater than 50 μl often occur in urban environments, especially near roadsides (Jaffe, 1968). Gladon, et.al. (1993) reported that certain turfgrasses, such as *Festuca arundinacea*, may be useful as an absorber of CO.

2.4 Soil Improvement and restoration

An extremely important function of turfgrasses is soil improvement through organic matter additions derived from the turnover of roots and other plant tissues that are synthesized in part from atmospheric carbon dioxide via photosynthesis. A high proportion of the world's most fertile soils has been developed under a vegetative cover of grass (Gould, 1968).

The root depth potential of turfgrasses ranges from 0.5 to 3 m, depending on the species, extent of defoliation, and soil/environ-mental conditions. Generally, C$_4$ warm-season turfgrasses produce a deeper, more extensive root system than the C$_3$ cool-season species (Beard, 1989b). The root system biomass of a *P. pratensis* turf is in the range of 11,000 to 16,100 kg ha^{-1} (Boeker, 1974; Falk, 1976). In the upper 150 mm of soil there are approximately 122,000 roots and 6.1 x 10^7 root hairs per liter of soil, with a combined length of over 74 km and a surface area of about 2.6 m^2 (Dittmer, 1938).

Falk (1976) estimated the annual root system turnover rate at 42% for a turf. Using Falk's estimate, 6,761 kg ha^{-1} of root biomass would be turned over into the soil each year. This estimate is low because it did not account for root secretions, death and decay of fine roots and root hairs, and consumption of roots by soil animals. The amount of root biomass annually produced and turned over into the soil, or root net productivity, for a defoliated grassland is higher than the amount reported for ungrazed prairie ecosystems (Dahlman and Kucera, 1965; Sims and Singh, 1971 and 1978). Similarly, the net effect of regular mowing on prostrate growing turfgrasses would be to concentrate energies into increased vegetative growth, as opposed to reproductive development, and to form a canopy of numerous dense, short, rapid growing plants with a fibrous root system. Also, many prairie lands show decreased productivity under regular defoliation, as by mowing, since most native grass species found in these ecosystems form meristematic crowns that are elevated higher above the soil where their removal is more likely when compared to turfgrass species.

Accelerated soil restoration of environmentally damaged areas by planting perennial grasses is employed effectively on highly eroded rural landscapes, burned-over lands, garbage dumps, mining operations, and steep timber harvest areas. These areas may then be developed as golf courses and recreational areas.

2.5 Enhanced heat dissipation - temperature moderation

Through the cooling process of transpiration, turfgrasses dissipate high levels of radiant heat in urban areas. The overall temperature of urban areas may be as much as 5 to 7°C warmer than that of nearby rural areas. Maximum daily canopy temperature of a green *Cynodon* turf was found to be 21°C cooler than a brown dormant turf and 39°C cooler than a synthetic surface (Table 2). The transpirational cooling effect of green turfs and landscapes can save energy by reductions in the energy input required for interior mechanically cooling of adjacent homes and buildings (Johns and Beard, 1985).

Table 2. Maximum diurnal temperatures of four surfaces assessed on an August day in College Station, Texas (Johns and Beard, 1985).

Type of surface	Maximum temperature in °C	Percent temperature increase over green turf
Green, growing *Cynodon* turf	31.1	--
Dry, bare soil	38.9	16
Brown, dormant *Cynodon* turf	52.2	43
Synthetic turf	70.0	80

2.6 Noise abatement, glare reduction, and visual pollution control

The surface characteristics of turfgrasses function in noise abatement, as well as in multi-directional light reflection that reduces glare. Studies have shown that turfgrass surfaces absorb harsh sounds significantly better than hard surfaces such as pavement, gravel, or bare ground (Cook and Van Haverbeke, 1971; Robinette, 1972). These benefits are maximized by an integrated landscape of turfgrasses, trees, and shrubs. Unfortunately, the proper use of these diverse species in concert to maximize noise abatement has received little attention within the scientific community.

2.7 Decreased noxious pests, allergy-related pollens, and human disease exposure

Closely mowed turfs reduce the population of nuisance pests such as snakes (*Ophidia (Serpentes)*), rodents (*Rodentia*), mosquitoes (*Culicidae*), ticks (*Ixodoidea*), and chiggers (*Trombiculidae*).

Allergy-related pollens can cause human discomfort and potentially serious health concerns to susceptible individuals. Dense turfs typically are void of the many weedy species that often produce allergy-related pollens. In addition, most turfgrasses that are mowed regularly tend to remain vegetative with minimal floral development, and thus have reduced pollen production.

Exposure to a number of serious human diseases is facilitated by key insect vectors such as mosquitos and ticks. Of current concern is Lyme disease, which is spread by a tick commonly found in unmowed tall grass and woodland-shrub habitats. Chigger mite (*Trombicula irritens*) population densities were highest at the ecotone or transition area of neighboring 600 mm tall grass beyond a mowed turf. This is due to the distinct decrease in temperature and solar radiation at the ecotone. Closely mowed turfs offer a less favorable habitat for unwanted nuisance insects and disease vectors (Clopton and Gold, 1993).

2.8 Favorable wildlife habitat

The 70+% of a golf course that is allocated to rough and non-play area encompasses (a) turfgrasses, trees, and water in the primary rough and (b) turfgrasses, flowers, shrubs, trees, and water in the secondary rough and perimeter areas. A diverse wildlife population can be achieved on such golf courses by an integrated landscape composed of turfgrass, tree, shrub, and water features (Green and Marshall, 1987; Maffei, 1978).

A study of golf courses and parks has shown conclusively that passerine birds benefit from golf courses, even to the extent that golf courses may be described as bird sanctuaries (Andrew, 1987). Ponds, lakes, and wetlands are very desirable features as used in golf courses because they create aquatic habitats, as well as diversity in visual landscape aesthetics. Properly designed urban green areas, such as golf courses, can maintain and even promote plant and animal diversity, natural habitats, and wet-lands when compared to intensive agriculture and urban residential-business usages. Thus, golf courses are important naturalized open spaces, especially in areas of urban development and intensive agriculture.

2.9 Enhanced physical health of golf participants

The enjoyment and benefits of improved physical/mental health derived from golfing activities on turfgrasses are important to a contemporary industrialized society, especially in densely populated urban areas. There are 15,000+ golf courses in the United States offering 24 million golfers more than 2.4 billion hours of healthy, outdoor recreation.

2.10 Improved mental health via a positive therapeutic impact
Most city dwellers attach considerable importance to urban green areas
with views of grass, trees, and open space (Ulrich, 1986). Cities can
be very dismal without green turfgrasses, with the result being a loss
of productivity, more susceptibility to anxieties, and mental disease.
    Kaplan and Kaplan (1989) addressed the role of nature, including
parks, woodland areas, and large landscape sites in contributing to a
person's quality-of-life within urban areas. The role encompassed the
opportunity to use nature facilities in recreational activities as
well as aesthetics, i.e. the appreciation of natural beauty. They
reported an increased sense of residential neighborhood satisfaction
and of general well-being when there was a nearby nature landscape.
Similarly, Ulrich (1984) reported that an outdoor view contributed to
more rapid recovery for hospital patients.

2.11 Enhanced beauty and aesthetics.
Turfgrasses provide beauty and attractiveness that enhance the quality-of-life for human activities. The clean, cool, natural green of
turfgrasses provides a pleasant environment in which to live, work,
and play. Such aesthetic values are of increasing importance to the
human spirit and the mental health of citizens because of rapid-paced
lifestyles and increasing urbanization.

2.12 Substantial contribution to the national economy
From a monetary standpoint, the golf industry contributes in excess of
US $18 billion annually to the United States economy. This represents
substantial employment opportunities.

3 References

Alexander, M. (1977) **Introduction to Soil Microbiology**, 2nd ed. John
    Wiley and Sons, Inc., New York, N.Y.
Andrew, N.J. (1987) Wildlife and related values of park golf course
    ecosystems. **Res. Project Rep.** Hamilton County Park District,
    Cincinnati, OH.
Angle, J.S. (1985) Effect of cropping practices on sediment and nutri-
    ent losses from tobacco. **Tob. Sci.**, 29,107-110.
Arnold, T.B and Potter, D.A. (1987) Impact of a high-maintenance lawn-
    care program on non-target invertebrates in Kentucky bluegrass turf.
    Environ. Entomol., 16,100-105.
Beard, J.B. (1973) **Turfgrass: Science and Culture.** Prentice-Hall,
    Inc., Englewood Cliffs, N.J.
Beard, J.B. (1982) **Turfgrass Management for Golf Courses.** Macmillan
    Publishing Co., New York, N.Y.
Beard, J.B. (1989) The role of Gramineae in enhancing man's quality of
    life. **Symp. Proc. Nat. Comm. Agric. Sci.**, Japanese Sci. Council,
    Tokyo, Japan. pp. 1-9.
Bennett, H.H. (1939) **Soil Conservation.** McGraw-Hill Book Co., Inc.
    New York, N.Y.
Boeker, P. (1974) Root development of selected turfgrass species and
    cultivars, p. 55-61. in **Proc. Int. Turfgrass Res. Conf.**, (ed. E.C.
    Roberts), Blacksburg, VA., 2,55-61.

Clark, F.E. and Paul, E.A. (1970) The microflora of grassland. **Adv. in Agron.**, 22,375-435.

Clopton, R.E. and Gold, R.E. (1993) Distribution, seasonal and diurnal activity patterns of *Eutrombicula alfreddugesi* (Acari: Trombiculidae) in a forest edge ecosystem. J. **Med**. Entomol., 30,47-53.

Cockfield, S.D. and Potter, D.A. (1983) Short-term effects of insecticidal applications on predaceous arthropods and oribatid mites in Kentucky bluegrass turf. **Environ**. **Entomol**., 12,1260-1264.

Cockfield, S.D. and Potter, D.A. (1984) Predation on sod webworm (*Lepidoptera: Pyralidae*) eggs as affected by chlorpyrifos application to Kentucky bluegrass turf. J. **Econ**. **Entomol**., 77,1542-1544.

Cockfield, S.D. and Potter, D.A. (1985) Predatory arthropods in high- and low-maintenance turfgrass. **Can**. Entomol., 117,423-429.

Cook, D.I. and Van Haverbeke, D.F. (1971) Trees and shrubs for noise abatement. **Nebraska Agric**. **Exp**. **Stn**. **Res**. **Bull**. 246, Lincoln, NE.

Curry, J.P. (1986) Effects of management on soil decomposers and decomposition processes in grassland, in **Microfloral and faunal interactions in natural and agro-ecosystems**. (eds M.J. Mitchell and J.P. Nakus), Dordrecht, Boston, MA., pp. 349-399.

Dahlman, R.C. and Kucera, C.L. (1965) Root productivity and turnover in native prairie. **Ecology**. 46,84-89.

Dittmer, H.J. (1938) A quantitative study of the subterranean members of three field grasses. **Amer**. J. **Bot**., 25,654-657.

Falk, J.H. (1976) Energetics of a suburban lawn ecosystem. **Ecology**. 57,141-150.

Gladon, R.J., Brahm, D.J., and Christians, N.E. (1993) Carbon monoxide absorption and release by C_3 and C_4 turfgrasses in light and dark. **Intl**. **Turfgrass Soc**. **Res**. J., 7,649-656.

Gould, F.W. (1968) **Grass Systematics**. McGraw-Hill, Inc., New York, N.Y.

Green, B.H. and Marshall, I.C. (1987) An assessment of the role of golf courses in Kent, England, in protecting wildlife and landscapes. **Landscape and Urban Planning**. 14,143-154.

Gross, C.M., Angle, J.S., Hill, R.L. and Welterlen, M.S. (1991) Runoff and sediment losses from tall fescue under simulated rainfall. J. **Environ**. **Qual**., 20,604-607.

Gross, C.M., Angle, J.S., and Welterlen, M.S. (1990) Nutrient and sediment losses from turfgrass. J. **Environ**. **Qual**., 19,663-668.

Jaffe, L.S. (1968) Ambient carbon monoxide and its fate in the atmosphere. J. **Air Pollut**. **Control Assoc**., 18,534-540.

Jean, S. and Juang, T. (1979) Effect of bahiagrass mulching and covering on soil physical properties and losses of water and soil of slopeland (First report). J. **Agric**. **Assoc**. **China**., 105,57-66.

Johns, D., and Beard, J.B. (1985) A quantitative assessment of the benefits from irrigated turf on environmental cooling and energy savings in urban areas, in **Texas Turfgrass Research--1985**. Texas Agric. Exp. Stn. PR-4330, pp. 134-142.

Kaplan, R. and Kaplan, S. (1989) **The Experience of Nature**. Cambridge Univ. Press, New York, N.Y.

Lee, K.E. (1985) **Earthworms**. **Their ecology and relationships with soil and land use**. Academic Press, New South Wales, Australia.

Lush, W.M. (1990) Turf growth and performance evaluation based on turf biomass and tiller density. **Agron. J.**, 82,505-511.

Maffei, E.J. (1978) Golf courses as wildlife habitat. **Trans. North-east. Sect. Wildl. Soc.**, 35,120-129.

Menzel, R.G. (1991) Long term research on water and environmental quality. **Agron. J.**, 83,44-49.

Morton, T.G., Gold, A.J. and Sullivan, W.M. (1988) Influence of over-watering and fertilization on nitrogen losses from home lawns. J. **Environ. Qual.**, 17,124-130.

Petrovic, A.M. (1990) The fate of nitrogenous fertilizers applied to turfgrass. **J. Environ. Qual.**, 19,1-14.

Potter, D.A., Bridges, B.L. and Gordon. F.C. (1985) Effect of N fer-tilization on earthworm and microarthropod populations in Kentucky bluegrass turf. **Agron. J.**, 77,367-372.

Potter, D.A., Powell, A.J. and Smith, M.S. (1990a) Degradation of turfgrass thatch by earthworms (Oligochaeta: Lumbricidae) and other soil invertebrates. **J. Econ. Entomol.**, 83,205-211.

Potter, D.A., Buxton, M.C., Redmond, C.T., Patterson, C.J. and Powell, A.J. (1990b) Toxicity of pesticides to earthworms (Oligochaeta: Lumbricidae) and effect on thatch degradation in Kentucky bluegrass turf. **J. Econ. Entomol.**, 83,2362-2369.

Robinette, G.O. (1972) **Plants, people, and environmental quality.** U.S. Dept. Interior, National Park Service. Washington, D.C. and Am. Soc. Land. Arch. Foundation.

Schuyler, T. (1987) **Controlling urban runoff: A practical manual for planning and designing urban BMPs.** Metropolitan Washington Council of Governments, Washington, D.C.

Sims, P.L. and Singh, J.S. (1971) Herbage dynamics and net primary production in certain ungrazed and grazed grasslands in North America, in **Preliminary Analysis of Structure and Function in Grasslands.** (ed N.R. French) Range Sci. Dept. Sci. Series. No. 10. Colorado State Univ., Fort Collins, CO., pp. 59-123.

Sims, P.L. and Singh, J.S. (1978) The structure and function of ten western North American grasslands. III. Net primary production, turnover and efficiencies of energy capture and water use. J. **Ecology.**, 66,573-597.

Smith, J.L., and Paul, E.A. (1988) The role of soil type and vegeta-tion on microbial biomass and activity, in **Perspectives in Microbial Ecology.** (ed. F. Megusar and M. Gantar) Slovene Soc. for Microbiol-ogy, Ljubljana, Yugoslavia, pp. 460-466.

Smith, J.L., and Paul, E.A. (1990) The significance of soil microbial biomass estimations, in **Soil Biochemistry.** Vol. 6. (ed J.M. Bollag and G. Stotzky) Marcel Dekker Inc., New York, N.Y., pp. 357-396.

Streu, H.T. (1973) The turfgrass ecosystem: impact of pesticides. **Bull. Entomol. Soc. Am.**, 19, 89-90.

Ulrich, R.S. (1984) View through a window may influence recovery from surgery. **Science.** 224,420-421.

Ulrich, R.S. (1986) Human responses to vegetation and landscapes. **Landscape and Urban Planning.** 13, 29-44.

Vavrek, R.C. and Niemczyk, H.D. (1990) The impact of isofenphos on non-target invertebrates in turfgrass. **Environ. Entomol.**, 19,1572-1577.

Watschke, T.L. and Mumma, R.O. (1989) The effect of nutrients and pesticides applied to turf on the quality of runoff and percolating water.   Penn State Univ. Environmental Resources Res. Inst.   ER 8904, University Park, PA.

Note: The paper is based on a publication in the May-June 1994, issue of the Journal of Environmental Quality, which was partially funded by a grant from the United States Golf Association.

61 The playing quality of golf greens

S.W. Baker
Sports Turf Research Institute, Bingley, UK

Abstract
The playing quality of golf greens is influenced by the way in which the ball interacts with
the surface following an approach shot and by the ball roll characteristics during putting.
There has been increasing interest in the characterisation of components of playing quality
for golf greens, as this produces objectives for both green management and for future
research work on golf greens. Techniques to measure green speed have existed for well over
forty years, but most of the published work on hardness and ball impacts has been
restricted to the last eight years. Both construction materials and grass type have important
effects on playing quality and these properties are subsequently modified by management,
in particular fertiliser application, irrigation and cutting height. Management operations
can bring about not only immediate changes in playing quality, but there are also indirect
and longer-term changes caused by modification of the species composition of the sward
and this must be considered in any management programme.
Keywords: Golf Greens, Playing Quality, Green Speed, Ball Impact, Hardness,
Construction, Maintenance.

1 Introduction

A high proportion of the shots played in a round of golf take place onto or on the putting
green. For example, Lodge and Baker (1991), using data for professional players given by
Jones (1990), concluded that approximately two-thirds of the shots would involve
interaction between the ball and golf green turf, either in the form of approach shots
played onto the green or as putts. The quality of golf greens will therefore have a profound
influence on a player's enjoyment of his or her game, as well as their final score for a round.

Playing quality for any sport can normally be subdivided into a number of components
of which interaction between the player and the surface and interaction between the ball
and the surface are usually considered to be the most important characteristics (Baker and
Canaway 1993). Player/surface interaction is relatively unimportant in golf as the nature
of the game means that players do not usually fall or land heavily on the playing surface
and usually have sufficient grip, except perhaps on steep slopes in wet weather or surfaces
affected by algal slimes. Ball/surface interaction is, however, critical in golf and the player
must continually adjust his or her game to anticipate how the ball will respond to the
prevailing conditions of the turf surface.

Ball/surface interaction on golf greens can in turn be subdivided into two components,
firstly, ball roll and secondly, ball impact on the green. Ball roll properties determine what

Science and Golf II: Proceedings of the World Scientific Congress of Golf. Edited by A.J.
Cochran and M.R. Farrally. Published in 1994 by E & FN Spon, London. ISBN 0 419 18790 1

is generally described as the "speed of the green" and are relatively easily measured by releasing a ball down an appropriate ramp and recording the distance travelled. In consequence, green speed has been widely studied and indeed, performance guidelines have been developed (Radko 1977, 1980).

The processes of ball impact on a surface are more complex and are governed primarily by ball rebound resilience (i.e. the energy returned to the ball after impact), the hardness or stiffness of the surface (i.e. the amount of deflection for a given force) and the amount of spin which is retained after impact, which in turn is influenced by ball/surface friction. As impact conditions vary considerably in terms of approach angle, velocity and backspin (depending on the shot played and the club which is used), an enormous range of impact conditions need to be considered and until the 1980's, little work had been undertaken on this aspect of the game of golf.

Players are concerned with overall turf performance as it governs playing quality, but also with uniformity. One of the five justifications given by Radko (1980) for making green speed measurements using the USGA's Stimpmeter, was to establish whether all greens are uniform on a given course. Similarly, consistency within a green is important to the player who is making an approach shot and nothing can be more frustrating than seeing a well struck shot fly off a dry, compacted area when an identically struck shot landing less than a metre away would have retained its backspin and held on the green.

The playing quality of golf greens is influenced by a number of highly inter-related factors, i.e. sward composition, soil type, management (e.g. mowing height, fertiliser input and irrigation), the amount of play and external factors, most noticeably weather conditions, but also the incidence of pests and diseases (Canaway 1990). The purpose of this paper is therefore to review work which has been undertaken on the playing quality of golf greens, with regard to ball roll and ball impact and to identify future research requirements. There are, however, many other facets determining the quality of a green, for example its drainage performance, its visual appearance and its surface levels, particularly as they influence the "bumpiness" of the putting surface. These, however, fall outside the scope of this work, but their importance in terms of the quality of golf greens must be fully recognised.

2   Methodology

Most of the work on ball roll on putting greens has used a Stimpmeter (Stimpson 1974, Thomas 1978, Radko 1980). Current versions consist of an aluminium bar 0.914 m in length with a 145° v-shaped groove extending along its entire length. It has a ball-release notch 0.762 m from the tapered end which rests on the ground. In use, the ball is placed in this notch and the angle of the bar is gradually increased until the ball starts to roll. The ball-release notch is designed so that the ball will always be released when the Stimpmeter is raised to an angle of approximately 20° to the horizontal.

Ramps with fixed angles have been used by Dudeck and Peacock (1981) and Lodge (1992a). Lodge (1992a) lists a number of problems with the Stimpmeter which his ramp is intended to overcome, these include: the ball being released with top spin, possible variation in the initial release angle as a result of operator error and roll lengths exceeding those of experimental plots. Comparative data from experimental plots with various construction, irrigation and nutrition treatments suggested that roll lengths were more reproducible when a fixed ramp was used (Lodge, unpublished data).

Brede (1991) reported that a 2.1% slope, which he suggests is virtually undetectable under golf course conditions, can introduce a 6.2% error in green speed measurements if the mean of ball roll values in opposite directions is used and has introduced an appropriate method for calculating green speed to compensate for the effects of slope.

A number of other aspects of ball roll have also been measured. Dudeck and Peacock (1981) examined the deflection of roll from a straight line and Barr (1993) used a subjective method to examine bounce or deviation of the ball in the last 12 m of a putt. In addition, Haake (1989) examined ball/ surface friction by measuring both the horizontal force required to initiate movement of three golf balls mounted on a triangular plate and the rotational force required to initiate movement of three balls mounted on a weighted disc.

The firmness of the putting surface has been examined in three main ways. Buchanan (1984) measured the penetration depth of a lead golf ball which was dropped onto the putting surface. Cooper and Skogley (1981) and Haake (1989) have used a penetrometer to measure surface strength. Lawson (1987), Canaway et al. (1987), Colclough (1989), Baker and Richards (1991), Lodge and Baker (1991) amongst others have characterised the hardness of greens by measuring the deceleration of a falling mass on impact with the turf using a Clegg Soil Impact Tester (Clegg 1976). Haake (1989) has extended this work by using a falling mass with a golf ball attached to the end.

For work on ball/surface impacts two main assessment techniques have been used: firstly, vertical rebound behaviour and secondly, the impact response of a ball fired into the turf with various velocities, rates of backspin and angles of incidence so that different shots can be simulated. Vertical rebound has been recorded by video by Colclough and Canaway (1988) and Colclough (1989) after the ball was released from a height of 5 m. Measurements of angled ball behaviour are probably more realistic and Haake (1987, 1991a) developed a machine based on two independently rotating pneumatic wheels, whereby a golf ball can be projected to simulate the impact conditions of different golf shots. Two different ways have been used to measure impacts. Haake (1987, 1991a) developed a photographic method using a stroboscope to "freeze" motion of golf balls before and after contact with the turf. Changes in velocity, spin and the angles of arrival and departure could be examined in detail (Haake 1991b). The photographic method gives valuable detail about ball behaviour, but is too slow for routine use. The alternative method has been to measure the stopping distance of the ball after impact, i.e. the distance between the position of impact (the pitch mark) and the final resting point of the ball. The measurement is of direct relevance to the golfer as he is concerned with how quickly a ball will stop when chipped onto a green. A number of impact conditions have been simulated, e.g. angle = $45°$, velocity = 15 m s^{-1}, backspin = 484 rad s^{-1} (Colclough and Canaway 1988), angle = $55°$, velocity = 19 m s^{-1}, backspin = 570 rad s^{-1} (Colclough 1989, Baker and Richards 1991), angle = $53°$, velocity = 22 m s^{-1}, backspin = 770 rad s^{-1} (Lodge and Baker 1991). Lodge (1992b) extended this approach to examine the length and height of the first bounce as well as the total distance travelled, thus giving greater insight into ball movement following impact.

Haake (1991c, 1991d) developed a mathematical model for evaluating ball response after impact on putting green surfaces, based on a two layered system. The upper layer had an elastic as well as a damping component, whilst the lower layer had only a damping component. For oblique impacts the coefficient of friction was included to account for the effects of spin. The model was used to predict the outcomes of 5-iron and 9-iron shots, with a variety of backspin and good agreement was found against experimental data.

Where discrepancies arose they were thought to be caused by the dependence of the coefficient of friction on the velocity of the ball.

3   Effect of construction type and rootzone composition

There is very little published information on the effects of different types of putting green construction on playing quality. In addition, it is often difficult to isolate the direct effects of rootzone composition from associated variation in ground cover, species composition, thatch depth etc. For example, Baker (1991) and Lodge *et al.* (1991) both recorded more *Festuca* spp. and less *Agrostis* ssp. as the sand content of their construction plots increased. These changes in sward composition would interact with any direct effects of construction type on playing performance and should be borne in mind when interpreting the results from any construction trials.

Baker and Richards (1991) examined the effects of 16 different rootzone materials formed by the combination of four different sand types and four mixing ratios of sand to soil. Rootzone composition had very little effect on green speed and significant differences were only recorded on one out of six sampling dates. On this occasion (January 1990) distance rolled increased for those rootzone materials with a greater sand content, mainly because of drier surface conditions. Sand-dominated rootzones gave more consistent conditions with regard to hardness than those containing more than 8% silt plus clay, which tended to be softer in wet winter conditions, but harder in the summer months. Similarly, there was less seasonal variation in stopping distances for angled ball impacts for sand- dominated rootzones than those containing more soil. There was also an effect of sand type in that balls tended to stop more quickly on rootzones containing finer grades of sand, whilst the highest values were associated with a medium-coarse sand and a sand with a wide range of particles. This effect can be attributed to greater moisture content on the finer sands and particle interpacking on the sand with a wider spread of particle size.

Lodge and Baker (1991) and Lodge (1992b) examined the effects of three different golf green constructions on playing quality. The three constructions were a sandy loam soil with pipe drains, a sand/soil/peat rootzone conforming to USGA standards (USGA 1989) and a pure sand rootzone. A gravel drainage layer was present in the latter two constructions. The pure sand constructions were consistently found to produce the fastest putting surfaces and the least variation in hardness throughout the year. The soil constructions produced the slowest surfaces and showed considerable variation in hardness, whilst the performance of the USGA construction was intermediate (Lodge and Baker 1991). Lodge (1992b) measured the stopping distance of balls fired to simulate a 5-iron shot on the same three constructions. Values were more consistent over time on the pure sand rootzone, intermediate on the USGA rootzone and ranged from approximately 0.4 m to 3.5 m on the soil construction.

4   Effect of grass type and method of establishment

There are a number of papers examining the effects of grass species or cultivars on ball roll characteristics but very little appears to have been published on the effects of grass type on other aspects of playing quality. Batten *et al.* (1981) compared ball roll distances for various cool-season turfgrasses oversown onto dormant Bermudagrass (*Cynodon* spp.). Ball roll distances ranged from 1.65 m to 2.17 m and were greatest where *Lolium perenne* L. was used, compared with *Agrostis palustris* Huds. and *Festuca* spp. There were significant differences amongst *L. perenne* cultivars with the coarse-textured varieties having shorter ball roll distances than fine-textured varieties.

Dudeck and Peacock (1981) examined the effects of *L. perenne* and *L. multiflorum* Lam. seeded into *Cynodon* putting greens. The use of *L. multiflorum* gave the fastest surface (2.14 m), whilst where *L. perenne* was used for overseeding, ball roll distances ranged from 1.90 m to 2.13 m, with significant differences between cultivar types. The angle of deflection from a straight line was not influenced by cultivar selection.

In Britain, Canaway and Baker (1992) examined ball roll on five turfgrass species commonly found on golf greens. Averaged over five dates, ball roll distances ranged from 1.57 m for *Poa annua* L. to 1.96 m for *F. rubra* ssp. *litoralis* G.F.W. Meyer. *F. rubra* ssp. *commutata* Gaud. also gave high ball roll distances, whilst *A. capillaris* L. and *A. castellana* Boiss. & Reuter were intermediate between the *Festuca* spp. and *P. annua*. Lodge and Baker (1991) examining the effects of construction, irrigation and nutrition on a *Festuca/Agrostis* sward found positive correlations between *Festuca* content and ball roll distances, whilst distance rolled decreased as *Agrostis* became more dominant.

Haake (1991b) found that ball/surface friction increased as *P. annua* content increased, whilst the putting surfaces were less firm when more *P. annua* was present in the sward.

Canaway (1993) examined different methods of grass establishment using two seed rates and four types of sod to establish a primarily *Festuca/Agrostis* sward on a sand rootzone. Before simulated wear started, the seeded plots were considerably harder than those established using sod. The effect diminished with wear, but after nine months of wear there were still significant differences, ranging from a hardness value of 66 gravities when seed was used at a rate of 100 g m^{-2} to 83 gravities where sod, grown originally on a heavy textured soil, was used. Similarly, after nine months of wear, ball roll ranged from 1.53 m for the sod development on heavy soil (referred to above) to 1.78 m for a juvenile sod grown on a netted, organic, soil-less mulch.

5   The effect of fertiliser input

There is probably more published work on the effects of fertiliser input on playing quality than on the effects of any other aspect of turf management. Increasing nitrogen content generally decreases green speed (Throssel and Duich 1981, Colclough 1989, Lodge and Baker 1991) and the hardness of putting surfaces (Lawson 1987, Canaway *et al.* 1987, Colclough 1989, Lodge and Baker 1991). There is a slight exception at very high nitrogen rates and Lodge (1992b) found that on a *Festuca/Agrostis* sward with more than 400 kg ha^{-1} year^{-1} of nitrogen ball roll distances started to increase again on sand-dominated constructions, especially those receiving lower levels of irrigation, because of reduced grass cover.

As an example of the effect of nitrogen applications, data from Lodge and Baker (1991) for July 1990 showed that ball roll on a topsoil rootzone decreased from 1.62 m to 1.27 m as nitrogen application was increased from 35 to 635 kg ha^{-1} year^{-1}. On a pure sand rootzone the roll length decreased from 1.82 m to 1.33 m as the nitrogen input changed from 35 to 410 kg ha^{-1}year^{-1}, but with a slight increase in distance rolled at higher nitrogen rates. Similarly, over the 35-635 kg ha^{-1}year nitrogen range, hardness decreased from 100 to 91 gravities on the soil construction and from 94 to 74 gravities on the sand rootzone.

Colclough and Canaway (1988) and Colclough (1989), working on a pure sand rootzone with nitrogen levels ranging from 100-400 kg ha[-1] year[-1], found that ball rebound resilience increased at higher nitrogen rates and attributed this to the elastic effect of more dense, springy turf. Responses of the stopping distance of angled ball impacts are more complex. Colclough (1989) found that stopping distance decreased as nitrogen content increased. Lodge and Baker (1991) found that the total distance travelled after impact was greatest at their 235 kg ha[-1] year[-1] nitrogen rate and declined either side of this value and Lodge (1992b) found that the response of bounce length and bounce height to nitrogen content was very dependent on construction type. For sand-dominated rootzones, bounce length and height were greatest at intermediate nitrogen contents (around 110-235 kg ha[-1] per year) but on a sandy loam soil construction, bounce length was shortest when nitrogen inputs were in this range.

Colclough and Canaway (1988) and Colclough (1989) found that ball rebound resilience increased as the amount of potassium increased from 0-300 kg ha[-1] year[-1] K_2O, but at these rates potassium had little effect on green speed or hardness. Colclough (1989) also found that rebound resilience decreased as phosphate content increased from 0-50 kg ha[-1] year[-1] P_2O_5 and for green speed there was also an interaction between phosphate and lime content with green speed decreasing with phosphate content on the limed plots.

Lodge and Baker (1991) found an interaction between phosphate and nitrogen inputs on pure sand constructions, but not on topsoil or USGA rootzones. At higher rates of nitrogen (>200 kg ha[-1] year[-1]) green speed and hardness decreased when phosphorus input was increased from 0 to 50 kg ha[-1] year[-1].

Colclough and Canaway (1988) and Colclough (1989) found green speed, hardness and stopping distance decreased with the addition of lime on a pure sand rootzone. In contrast, ball rebound resilience was greater on plots having a higher pH.

As with the effects of construction, it is impossible to isolate entirely the effects of nutrition in terms of increased ground cover, vigour and structure of the leaf tissue from changes in species composition which can arise, particularly when more than one grass species is included in the original seeds mixture.

6 Effect of irrigation

There is little published information on the effects of irrigation on playing quality. Lodge and Baker (1991) examined playing performance for three irrigation treatments of 25% less than the theoretical evapotranspiration, direct replacement of evapotranspiration and 25% more than the theoretical evapotranspiration requirement. There was a significant effect on the hardness of the putting surface for the topsoil and USGA constructions, but not on a sand rootzone. There was no significant effect on ball roll or stopping distance following angled impacts. Lodge (1992b) increased the under-watering and over-watering treatments to - 40% and + 40% of the theoretical evapotranspiration demand and found that on the topsoil and USGA constructions hardness increased as less irrigation was applied, but the pure sand construction became firmer at the highest irrigation rate. With the greater range of irrigation treatments there was also a major effect of irrigation on angled ball behaviour. For example, using data for October 1991 for the topsoil and USGA constructions, the ball travelled forward after the first bounce for the 40% under-watering treatment, but checked and spun back for the 40% over-watering treatment.

Canaway and Baker (1992) examined the effect of applying 1.2 mm of water shortly before ball roll measurements were carried out and found an average reduction in distance rolled of 6%, compared with earlier readings carried out in dry conditions.

7   Effects of other maintenance practices

Cutting height has a strong influence on green speed. Engel *et al.* (1980), combining results from an assortment of courses, primarily in north-eastern United States (all *Agrostis* with varying amounts of *P. annua*), found variation of between approximately 13-57% between cutting heights of ¹/₄ inch (c. 6.4 mm) and ³/₁₆ inch (c. 4.8 mm). The contrast in speed between uphill and downhill was considerably greater (i.e. 57%) at the lower cutting height. Their data also revealed a significant effect of cutting direction, with ball roll distances in the direction of cut being between 7-15% greater than those against the direction of cut. Throssell and Duich (1981) showed that mowing at ³/₃₂ inch (c. 2.4 mm) increased distance rolled by about one-third compared with mowing at ⁶/₃₂ inch (c. 4.8 mm). They also found that mowing seven times per week, as opposed to thrice weekly, increased green speed from approximately 1.95 m to 2.23 m.

Baker and Richards (1991) and Canaway and Baker (1992) showed general increases in distance rolled when the cutting height was reduced from 6 mm to 5 mm, but the effect cannot be entirely isolated from changes in moisture content which may have occurred between the different sampling dates. Radko (1978) found that on more liberally fertilised greens, speed decreased during the course of the day after they had been cut in the morning. He also found that frequency of cut affected green speed, with double-cutting on successive days giving a faster surface. Radko's work also indicated that heavy top dressing of greens with a soil mixture slowed the green until the material was worked well into the turf. Heavy, infrequent top dressings caused speeds to oscillate whereas light, frequent top dressings improved speed and consistency.

Cooper and Skogley (1981) found that significant differences in green speed eventually developed when four different top dressing programmes were used on experimental plots containing *A. palustris* and *A. canina* L. Turf receiving a dressing of 9000 l ha⁻¹ of a sand-soil mix based on a loamy coarse sand every four weeks had significantly lower green speeds than turf receiving semi-annual top dressing treatments.

8   Discussion

On the basis of this review, there is a considerable amount of published work, demonstrating the importance of mowing practices, species composition and fertiliser input on green speed. Construction methods and rootzone materials generally have a smaller direct effect on green speed, except in wet conditions when surface drainage becomes important. There can, however, be many indirect effects of construction materials, particularly on species composition and thatch development and this will affect playing performance. Irrigation, top dressing practices and cultivar selection have been shown to have some effects on green speed, but the amount of published data is relatively small. There is very little quantitative data available on the effects of wear, thatch development, verticutting/grooming and aeration practices on green speed, especially for the *Festuca/Agrostis* swards used in the United Kingdom. This is surely an area where more research is needed.

Ball impact and surface hardness have been shown to be strongly influenced by rootzone composition and changes in soil moisture content caused by both natural rainfall and supplementary irrigation. Fertiliser input also influences impact properties and hardness, but there has been very little analysis of the effect of species composition and cultivar selection on impact values and this could be important in terms of ball/surface friction and hence the retention of backspin on impact. Similarly, there is very little quantitative information on the effects of mowing practices, thatch development, verticutting/ grooming and top dressing operations on ball impact and surface hardness.

It should be recognised that responses in playing quality need to be considered over a wide range of turf conditions, as there are major interactions between construction and management (Canaway 1990, Lodge and Baker 1991, Lodge 1992b). Thus, for example, the response of turf quality to nutrient input is significantly affected by the underlying rootzone composition, the irrigation regime and indeed the age of the green.

The other outstanding requirement for future research is to determine the range of values for each component of playing quality which are preferred or accepted by the players. With the exception of work on green speed (discussed below), there are no available data to relate measured values of, for example, hardness or stopping distance after impact to players' opinions of turf quality. Preferred and acceptable ranges of values need to be established so that the test methods which have been developed can be used to set objectives in future research and indeed, more generally for turf managers. The range of values which is set must be compatible with good turf management practices and one of the most frequent complaints against the USGA's Stimpmeter is that it encourages pressure from players to speed up greens by closer mowing and excessive verticutting, practices which can leave the turf weak and subject to weed and moss invasion (Oatis 1990). In addition, any requirements, although eliminating unacceptable turf conditions, must inevitably cover a broad range : one of the joys of golf is tackling a variety of course conditions and excessive uniformity between courses would detract from the pleasure of the game, as well as having very expensive management implications. For example, many existing golf greens are developed on heavy soils and cannot be expected to have the playing performance of sand-dominated rootzones during wet weather.

With regard to the needs for performance requirements for golf greens, a major study started at the Sports Turf Research Institute during 1993. The aim will be to survey around 150 golf greens over a two year period for playing quality, soil and sward characteristics, whilst maintenance inputs are also being determined. Questionnaire surveys of players on the same day that our physical measurements are being made will assist in the interpretation of the data, allowing performance requirements to be established. Similar work has successfully been completed for soccer, Rugby, hockey and bowls (see Baker and Canaway 1993) – there is no reason why such requirements cannot also be determined for golf.

9 Acknowledgements

The financial support of the Royal and Ancient Golf Club of St Andrews for our work on the playing quality of golf greens is greatly acknowledged.

10 References

Baker, S.W. (1991) Rootzone composition and the performance of golf greens. I. Sward characteristics before and after the first year of simulated wear. **J. Sports Turf Res. Inst.**, 67, 14-23.

Baker, S.W. and Canaway, P.M. (1993) Concepts of playing quality : criteria and measurement. **Int. Turfgrass Soc. Res. J.**, 7, 172-181.

Baker, S.W. and Richards, C.W. (1991) Rootzone composition and the performance of golf greens. II. Playing quality under conditions of simulated wear. **J. Sports Turf Res. Inst.**, 67, 24-31.

Barr, D.A. (1993) An assessment and diagnostic system for golf greens. **Int. Turfgrass Soc. Res. J.**, 7, 937-940.

Batten, S.M., Beard, J.B., Johns, D., Almodares, A. and Eckhardt, J. (1981) Characterizations of cool season turfgrasses for winter overseeding of dormant Bermudagrass. **Proc. 4th Int. Turfgrass Res. Conf.** (ed. R.W. Sheard), Ontario Agric. College/International Turfgrass Society, pp. 83-94.

Brede, A.D. (1991) Correction for slope in green speed measurement of golf course putting greens. **Agron. J.**, 83, 425-426.

Buchanan, W.G. (1984) Why don't the greens hold? **USGA Green Section Record**, 22, 4, 1-5.

Canaway, P.M. (1990) Golf green agronomy and playing quality - past and current trends. **Science and Golf**, Proc. 1st World Scientific Congress of Golf (ed. A.J. Cochran). E. & F.N. Spon, pp. 336-345.

Canaway, P.M. (1993) Effects of using seed, sod and juvenile sod for the establishment of an all-sand golf green turf and on its initial performance under wear. **Int. Turfgrass Soc. Res. J.**, 7, 469-475.

Canaway, P.M. and Baker, S.W. (1992) Ball roll characteristics of five turfgrasses used for golf and bowling greens. **J. Sports Turf Res. Inst.**, 68, 88-94.

Canaway, P.M., Colclough, T. and Isaac, S.P. (1987) Fertiliser nutrition of sand golf greens I. Establishment and pre-wear results. **J. Sports Turf Res. Inst.**, 63, 37-48.

Clegg, B. (1976) An impact testing device for *in situ* base course evaluation. **Australian Road Res. Bureau Proc.**, 8, 1-6.

Colclough, T. (1989) Fertiliser nutrition of sand greens IV. Playing quality. **J. Sports Turf Res. Inst.**, 65, 64-72.

Colclough, T. and Canaway, P.M. (1988) Fertiliser nutrition of sand golf greens II. 1987 results. In: **Proc. 6th Discussion Meeting of Amenity Grass Res.** (eds. R.J. Gibbs and W.A. Adams), University College of Wales, Aberystwyth, pp. 177-192.

Cooper, R.J. and Skogley, C.R. (1981) An evaluation of several topdressing programs for *Agrostis palustris* Huds. and *Agrostis canina* L. putting green turf. **Proc. 4th Int. Turfgrass Res. Conf.** (Ed. R.W. Sheard). Ontario Agric. College/International Turfgrass Society, pp. 129-136.

Dudeck, A.E. and Peacock, C.H. (1981) Effects of several overseeded ryegrasses on turf quality, traffic tolerance, and ball roll. **Proc. 4th Int. Turfgrass Res. Conf.** (ed. R.W. Sheard). Ontario Agric. College/International Turfgrass Society, pp. 75-81.

Engel, R.E., Radko, A.M. and Trout, J.R. (1980) Influence of mowing procedures on roll speed of putting greens. **USGA Green Section Record**, 18, 1, 7-9.

Haake, S.J. (1987) An apparatus for measuring the physical properties of golf turf. **J. Sports Turf Res. Inst.**, 63, 149-152.

Haake, S.J. (1989) **Apparatus and Test Methods for Measuring the Impacts of Golf Balls on Turf and Their Application in the Field.** PhD Thesis, University of Aston, Birmingham.

Haake, S.J. (1991a) The impact of golf balls on natural turf. I. Apparatus and test methods. **J. Sports Turf Res. Inst.**, 67, 120-127.

Haake, S.J. (1991b) The impact of golf balls on natural turf. II. Results and conclusions. **J. Sports Turf Res. Inst.**, 67, 128-134.

Haake, S.J. (1991c) The impact of golf balls on natural turf. III. Physical model of impact. **J. Sports Turf Res. Inst.**, 67, 135-144.

Haake, S.J. (1991d) The impact of golf balls on natural turf. I. A physical model of impact. **Applied Solid Mechanics - 4** (eds. A.R.S. Ponter and A.C.F. Cocks). Elsevier Applied Science, pp.72-89.

Jones, R.E. (1990) A correlation analysis of the Professional Golf Association (USA) statistical rankings for 1988. In: **Science and Golf. Proc. First World Scientific Congress on Golf** (ed. A.J. Cochran). E. & F.N. Spon, pp. 165-167.

Lawson, D.M. (1987) The fertiliser requirement of *Agrostis castellana-Festuca rubra* turf growing on pure sand. **J. Sports Turf Res. Inst.**, 63, 28-36.

Lodge, T.A. (1992a) An apparatus for measuring green "speed". **J. Sports Turf Res. Inst.**, 68, 128-130.

Lodge, T.A. (1992b) A study of the effects of golf green construction and differential irrigation and fertiliser nutrition rates on golf ball behaviour. **J. Sports Turf Res. Inst.**, 66, 95-103.

Lodge, T.A. and Baker, S.W. (1991) The construction, irrigation and fertiliser nutrition of golf greens. II. Playing quality assessments after establishment and during the first year of differential irrigation and nutrition treatments. **J. Sports Turf Res. Inst.**, 67, 44-52.

Lodge, T.A., Baker, S.W., Canaway, P.M. and Lawson, D.M. (1991) The construction, irrigation and fertiliser nutrition of golf greens. I. Botanical and reflectance assessments after establishment and during the first year of differential irrigation and nutrition treatments. **J. Sports Turf Res. Inst.**, 67, 32-43.

Oatis, D.A. (1990) It's time we put the *green* back in green speed. **USGA Green Section Record**, 28, 6, 1-6.

Radko, A.M. (1977) How fast are your greens? **USGA Green Section Record**, 15, 5, 10-11.

Radko, A.M. (1978) How fast are your greens? An update. **USGA Green Section Record**, 16, 2, 20-21.

Radko, A.M. (1980) The USGA stimpmeter for measuring the speed of putting greens. In: **Proc. 3rd Int. Turfgrass Res. Conf.** (ed. J.B. Beard). Am. Soc. of Agronomy, pp. 473-476.

Stimpson, E.S. (1974) Putting greens - how fast? **USGA Golf J.**, 27, 2, 28-29.

Thomas, F. (1978) The stimpmeter and the Open. **USGA Green Section Record**, 16, 6, 7-9.

Throssel, C.S. and Duich, J.M. (1981) Management factors affect golf course green speeds. **Science in Agriculture**, 28, 4, 9.

USGA Green Section Staff (1989) **Specifications for a Method of Putting Green Construction** (ed. W.H. Bengeyfield). United States Golf Association, Far Hills, New Jersey, 24 pp.

62 A method for classifying the quality of golf green turf

T.A. Lodge
STRI, Bingley, West Yorkshire, UK
and D.J. Pilbeam
Department of Pure and Applied Biology, University of Leeds, Leeds, West Yorkshire, UK

Abstract
A method of classifying the quality of golf greens on the basis of a small number of objective measurements was tested. Test data were obtained from a field trial in which the effects of differing rates of irrigation, nitrogen and phosphate fertiliser on three different types of golf green construction were examined. The objective tests used for the classification were measurements of the botanical composition and ground cover, shoot density, turfgrass colour and soil pH, phosphate, potassium and calcium content. Classification of the surfaces was achieved using the multivariate analysis techniques of principal components analysis and complete linkage cluster analysis. Ten classes of greens were identified and a key was prepared which enabled similar surfaces to be placed in a class. The classes of greens were described in terms of their average visual merit, green "speed", golf ball behaviour after impact and the construction, irrigation and fertiliser treatments which they had received.
Keywords: Golf greens, Quality, Classification, Multivariate analysis.

1 Introduction

The quality of a golf green is determined by its appearance, its quality of play and its capacity to provide a suitable surface throughout the year. Quality is therefore a multi-faceted feature. Measurement of, for example, botanical composition, drainage rate or green speed may therefore be viewed as assessments of individual facets of the overall quality. The number of such objective measurements which could be carried out is open ended, and many correlations will exist between such measurements.

A classification of data from a survey of a large set of golf green surfaces which took into account these correlations would enable workers to identify particular types, or classes, of greens. General characteristics pertaining to the quality of each class may then be described. Subsequently, a small number of observations of any green may be used to place that green into the most appropriate class. Statements about the quality of the surface, and hence how it compares with others, may then be made on the basis of the characteristics associated with the class. Techniques for achieving such a classification are to be found in the field of multivariate analysis.

In this paper, a data set from a large field trial investigating the construction, irrigation and fertiliser nutrition of UK golf greens is re-examined with a view to testing the workability of a method of classification of golf greens. Most of the data, and the trial itself, have been analysed by conventional analysis of variance and are described elsewhere (Lodge *et al.* 1991, Lodge & Baker 1991, Lodge 1992a,b, Lodge & Lawson 1993, Lodge 1994 - in preparation).

Science and Golf II: Proceedings of the World Scientific Congress of Golf. Edited by A.J. Cochran and M.R. Farrally. Published in 1994 by E & FN Spon, London. ISBN 0 419 18790 1

2 Materials and methods

2.1 Trial design and maintenance
The construction, experimental treatments and maintenance of the trial is described in Lodge *et al.* (1991). To summarise, experimental treatments consisted of three types of golf green construction, three rates of irrigation, five rates of nitrogen and two rates of phosphate fertiliser. On 25 August 1988, the trial was sown with an 80:10:10 mix of *Festuca rubra* ssp. *commutata* (Gaud.), *Agrostis castellana* (Boiss. & Reut.), *A. capillaris* (L.), and was maintained as golf green turf. Simulated wear treatments were applied.

The three types of green construction were a sandy loam topsoil with pipe drainage and two suspended water table constructions, one with a rootzone of pure sand, the other with a rootzone conforming to the United States Golf Association specifications (USGA 1989). The irrigation treatments represented replacement of 60%, 100% and 140% of evapotranspiration (ET) losses in 1991 and 1992. The nitrogen fertiliser treatment rates were 35, 110, 235, 410 and 635 kg N ha^{-1} yr^{-1} and the phosphate fertiliser rates were 0 and 50 kg P$_2$O$_5$ ha^{-1} yr^{-1}. The trial was in two blocks, with 180 plots in total.

2.2 Classification data
The data from 12 objective measures were used for classifying the surfaces. These included the total live cover, total cover of the sown species, cover of *P. annua* (percent) and the shoot density (shoots m^{-2}) in October 1992. The means of three colour assessments during the growing season of 1992, were also included, as were the rootzone pH, phosphate, potassium and calcium content (mg l^{-1} air dried rootzone - ADR), in October 1991, and the organic matter content (percent) in March 1992.

Cover and botanical composition were assessed using an optical point quadrat frame (Laycock & Canaway 1980). Shoot density counts were made of *Agrostis* spp., *P. annua* and *F. rubra* in each of nine 10 mm diameter cores taken from each plot. The colour of the grass clippings was measured using a D25L - PC2 Delta Tristimulus Colorimeter System (Kirstol Ltd, Stalybridge) with a 95 cm viewing port. This measured brightness, greenness and yellowness. The more negative the "a" figure, the greener the grass, and the more positive the "b" value, the more yellow the grass.

Flame photometry was used to determine K$_2$O content of ADR samples, and P$_2$O$_5$ was measured by the method of Murphy & Riley (1962). This estimated the total amount of labile phosphate extracted from the sample. Calcium content of a 1 M ammonium nitrate extract was measured with an atomic absorption spectrophotometer. The pH was determined using a combined glass-reference electrode inserted into a sample/water mixture. Organic matter content was measured by the loss in weight after ignition in a muffle furnace at 400°C for 8 hours.

2.3 Classification method
Principal components analysis (PCA) was performed on the 12 objective measures of the 180 sub-sub-plots. The first five principal components accounted for 85 % of the variation in the data. The scores for each plot on these axes were then used to derive a similarity matrix. The similarity measure (s_{ij}) used was called "City Block", and was derived from the equation:

$$s_{ij} = 1 - \frac{\lfloor x_i - x_j \rfloor}{\text{range}} \tag{1}$$

in which x_i and x_j are the component scores of the ith and jth sub-sub-plots respectively.

The matrix was then analysed by complete linkage cluster analysis (Chatfield & Collins 1980). This is an agglomerative procedure which built up a hierarchical tree by grouping individuals into sets of increasingly dissimilar clusters. The "distance" between two clusters was defined by this method as the dissimilarity between their most remote pair of individuals. Groups of plots were selected by eye within the resulting hierarchical tree or dendrogram. The criteria used for their definition, or for "chopping the tree" at appropriate branches, were that approximately ten classes, with an average membership of 18 sub-sub-plots, should be identified.

The mean values for each of the objective measures were calculated for each class. From this information, and from the loadings of each measured variable on the first five principal components, a dichotomous key was prepared. This facilitated the placing of any turf type into the appropriate class by means of a series of questions and answers.

2.4 Additional performance evaluation of the classes

Visual merit evaluations of all sub-sub-plots were performed throughout 1991 and 1992. Evaluators were asked "Please score the turf on the basis of how nice, in your view, it appears to be." A 1 to 9 scale for visual assessments of turf quality, in which 9 represented the most desirable, was used. The scores were converted to z-scores prior to analysis. ie

$$\text{z-score} = \frac{\text{plot score - mean score for the evaluator}}{\text{standard deviation}} \quad (2)$$

"Green speed" was assessed using the technique described by Lodge & Baker (1991) using a semi-tubular steel ramp (Lodge 1992b). The method of golf ball impact simulation and recording was described by Lodge & Baker (1991) and Lodge (1992a). This involved measuring the distance of bounce and roll, or check, of golf balls hitting the turf with backspin and velocity comparable to 5-iron shots. The spin and trajectory characteristics were imparted by a machine developed by Haake (1991). The "average" construction type, irrigation and fertiliser regime associated with each class were also deduced.

3 Results

3.1 Classification

The complete link cluster analysis dendrogram divided the 180 sub-sub-plots into 9 classes (A to I) with 3 outlying plots, the classification of which was rejected. The dendrogram is shown in Fig. 1. As examples, the positions of classes B and D, and C, H and I, are indicated in the scattergrams of the plot component scores on the first and second and second and fourth PCA axes respectively in Fig. 2.

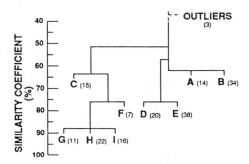

Fig. 1. Dendrogram produced by complete link cluster analysis of the first 5 PCA axes. Numbers in brackets indicate the numbers of plots assigned to each group.

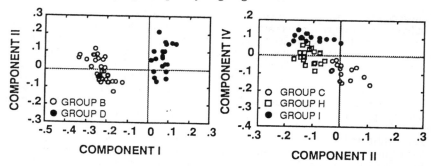

Fig.2. Scattergrams of Component I/Component II and Component II/Component IV showing the distribution of the plots in classes B and D and C, H and I respectively.

3.2 Artificial key to classes and class descriptions

From the information given in Fig.1, and the means for each class of each of the 12 objective measurements, an "Artificial Key to Classes" was derived. This comprises a series of statements enabling a particular green to be allocated to one of the classes and is shown in Table 1.

Table 1. Artificial Key to Classes in a set of 177 Field Trial "Golf Greens"

1 *P. annua* cover > 10 %, rootzone pH > 6.0, rootzone calcium content > 15 mg l⁻¹
ADR, organic matter content > 3 %....Go to Question 3.
Not this collection of attributes....Go to Question 2.
2 Total live cover < 60 %, sown species contribution < 60 %....Question 4.
Not this collection of attributes....Go to Question 5.
3 *P. annua* cover > 50 %, Colorimeter "a" values > 9, total live cover > 90 %, rootzone
potassium content > 35 mg l⁻¹ ADR....CLASS A.
P. annua cover < 50 %, Colorimeter "a" values < 9, rootzone potassium content < 35
mg l⁻¹ ADR....CLASS B.
4 Rootzone phosphate content > 10 mg l⁻¹ ADR....CLASS D.
Rootzone phosphate content < 10 mg l⁻¹ ADR....CLASS E.
5 Total live cover < 80 %, P. annua cover > 10 %, organic matter content > 2 %,
rootzone pH > 5.5, rootzone calcium content > 5 mg l⁻¹ ADR....CLASS C.
Total live cover > 80 %, *P. annua* cover < 10 %, organic matter content < 2 %,
rootzone pH < 5.5, rootzone calcium content < 5 mg l⁻¹ ADR....Go to Question 6.
6 Cover adjusted shoot density > 100 000 shoots m⁻², rootzone phosphate content > 10
mg l⁻¹ ADR material, rootzone calcium content > 2 mg l⁻¹ ADR....CLASS F.
Cover adjusted shoot density < 100 000 shoots m⁻², rootzone phosphate content < 10
mg l⁻¹ ADR material, rootzone calcium content < 2 mg l⁻¹ ADR....Go to Question 7.
7 Colorimeter "a" values < 8, rootzone phosphate levels > 7 mg l⁻¹ ADR....CLASS G.
"a" values > 8, rootzone phoshate levels < 7 mg l⁻¹ ADR....Go to Question 8.
8 "a" values < 9, "b" values < 19, rootzone phosphate levels < 6 mg l⁻¹ ADR...CLASS H.
"a" values > 9, "b" values > 19, rootzone phosphate levels > 6 mg l⁻¹ ADR...CLASS I.

The classes were described individually in terms of their overall visual and playing quality and the management procedures which the respective surfaces had received. These descriptions are provided in Table 2. By converting the ball roll data to Stimpmeter green speeds (Lodge 1992b), the classification of green speeds by Radko (1977) allowed these values to be expressed in Radko's terminology of slow, medium/slow, medium,

medium/fast and fast for regular and tournament play. Class descriptions comprise visual quality, as assigned by the evaluators, green speed, the spin retention and rebound velocities of impacting golf balls, the construction type, the mean rate of nitrogen and whether or not phosphate fertiliser was applied. A statement concerning the irrigation rate of Class "I" was also appropriate.

Table 2. Class Descriptions

CLASS A: Visually good. Regular play - medium, tournaments - very slow. Iron shots show good spin retention but rebound at high speed. All soil constructions. Mean nitrogen rate - 540 kg N ha^{-1} yr^{-1}.

CLASS B: Visually fair to good. Regular play - medium, tournaments - slow. Iron shots show medium spin retention and rebound at high speed. All soil constructions. Mean nitrogen rate - 153 kg N ha^{-1} yr^{-1}.

CLASS C: Very variable. Visually poor. Regular play - medium, tournaments - slow. Post-impact ball behaviour too variable for general statements. 60% soil construction, 33% USGA. Mean nitrogen rate - 247 kg N ha^{-1} yr^{-1}. 80% received no phosphate.

CLASS D: Visually poor. Regular play - medium/fast, tournament - medium/slow. Iron shots show poor spin retention and low rebound velocities. 60% - pure sand, 40% - USGA. Mean nitrogen rate - 50 kg N ha^{-1} yr^{-1}. 80% received phosphate.

CLASS E: Visually very poor. Regular play - medium, tournament play - slow. Iron shots show poor spin retention and rebound at low velocities. 71% - sand, 29% - USGA. Mean nitrogen rate - 393 kg N ha^{-1} yr^{-1}. 13 % received phosphate.

CLASS F: Visually fair. Regular play - medium, tournament play - slow. Iron shots very variable but rebound velocities fairly low. 71% - USGA, 29% both sand and soil. Mean nitrogen rate - 238 kg N ha^{-1} yr^{-1}. Phosphate applied to all.

CLASS G: Visually fair. Regular play - medium, tournament play - slow. Iron shots show medium spin retention and rebound velocity. 73% - USGA, 27% - sand. Mean nitrogen rate - 180 kg N ha^{-1} yr^{-1}.

CLASS H: Visually good. Regular play - medium, tournament play - slow. Iron shots show medium spin retention and rebound velocity. 68% - USGA, 32% - sand. Mean nitrogen rate - 180 kg N ha^{-1} yr^{-1}. 50 % received phosphate.

CLASS I: Visually excellent. The slowest putting speeds of the trial. Regular play - medium, tournament - very slow. Iron shots show good spin retention and medium rebound velocities. 50% - sand, 50% - USGA . Mean nitrogen rate - 382 kg N ha^{-1} yr^{-1}. 94 % received phosphate. 80 % received irrigation above ET demand.

4 Discussion

The method used was successful in producing a classification of the surfaces. The set of classes appeared to be logical and therefore could possibly have been identified subjectively, rather than by the chosen algorithm, were this practicable. The key to the classes could be used to classify any one of the 177 plots, or any similar surfaces, if the user were provided with the appropriate objective data.

One obvious limitation is that greens not included in the original classification may not "fit" into a class because their particular range of objectively measured characteristics were not encompassed within that of the original similarity matrix. For example, it is quite possible for a pure sand golf green to have a pH of more than 6.0, but an organic matter content considerably less than 3 %. Such a surface could not get past question 1.

If more greens were sampled the range of characteristics would be increased, and also a more realistic assessment of overall quality could be obtained by using additional objective measures. These should be chosen to summarise differences in, for example, soil texture, structure, depth and infiltration rate in order to accurately locate greens within a similarity matrix and a subsequent classification. Also, seasonal variation in the measured parameters would need to be taken into account by taking more than one assessment per year for each site. A practicable classification scheme for golf greens would therefore require an initial survey of greens in which many objective tests were carried out as well as assessments of playing quality and perceived merit. The data set must also encompass as large and wide-ranging a set of golf greens as possible. The initial labour requirements for such a classification would be great, but the methodology has been shown to work and the benefits for the sport would be considerable.

5 Acknowledgements

The authors would like to thank the Royal and Ancient Golf Club of St Andrews for financial support, Mrs C.W. Richards, Ms. J. Wicket, Messrs. Baines, Husband, Laybourn, Pronczuk and West for technical assistance, and the ground staff of STRI for trial maintenance.

6 References

Chatfield, C. & Collins, A.J. (1980). *An introduction to multivariate analysis.* Chapman & Hall. London, England. 246 pp.

Haake, S.J. (1991). The impact of golf balls onto natural turf I. Apparatus and test methods. *J. Sports Turf Res. Inst.* **67**, 120 - 127.

Laycock, R.W. & Canaway, P.M. (1980). A new optical point quadrat frame for the estimation of cover in close mown turf. *J. Sports Turf Res. Inst.* **56**, 91-92.

Lodge, T.A., Baker, S.W., Canaway, P.M. & Lawson, D.M. (1991). The construction, irrigation and fertiliser nutrition of UK golf greens. I. Botanical and reflectance assessments after establishment and during the first year of differential irrigation and nutrition treatments. *J. Sports Turf Res. Inst.* **67**, 32-43.

Lodge, T.A. & Baker, S.W. (1991). The construction, irrigation and fertiliser nutrition of UK golf greens. II. Playing quality during the first year of differential irrigation and nutrition treatments. *J. Sports Turf Res. Inst.* **67**, 44-52.

Lodge, T.A. (1992a). A study of golf green construction and differential irrigation and fertiliser rates on golf ball behaviour. *J. Sports Turf Res. Inst.* **68**, 95-103.

Lodge, T.A. (1992b). Technical note : An apparatus for measuring green "speed". *J. Sports Turf Res. Inst.* **68**, 128-130.

Lodge, T.A. & Lawson, D.M. (1993). The construction, irrigation and fertiliser nutrition of UK golf greens. Botanical and soil chemical measurements over 3 years of differential treatment. *J. Sports Turf Res. Inst.* **69**, 59-73.

Lodge, T.A. (1994). *The construction, irrigation and fertiliser nutrition of UK golf greens.* PhD thesis. University of Leeds, Leeds.

Murphy, J. & Riley, J.P. (1962). A modified single solution method for the determination of phosphate in natural waters. *Analytica Chimica Acta* **27**, 31-36.

Radko, A.M. (1977). The USGA Stimpmeter for measuring the speed of putting greens. In *Proc. 3rd. Int. Turf Res. Conf.* (Ed. J.B. Beard), Munich, Germany. pp 473 - 476.

USGA. (1989). *Specifications for a method of putting green construction.* (Ed.W.H.Bengeyfield). The USGA Green Section Staff, USGA, Far Hills, New Jersey, USA. 24 pp.

63 The effects of light-weight rolling on putting greens

G.W. Hamilton, Jr, D.W. Livingston and A.E. Gover
Penn State University, University Park, USA

Abstract
The rolling of golf course putting greens to increase ball roll distance is becoming more popular with golf course superintendents. Light-weight rolling may increase compaction, which can be detrimental to the turfgrass stand. An experiment was conducted to evaluate the effects of light-weight rolling on ball roll distance, bulk density, and water infiltration. Plots were rolled 0, 1, and 2 times per week for 14 weeks. Light-weight rolling increased ball roll distance an average of 38 cm. The increase in distance lasted less than 48 hours. Bulk density in the surface 2.5 cm of soil and saturated infiltration were not affected by rolling.
Keywords: Rolling, Green Speed, Compaction, Infiltration, Golf Green, Putting Green.

1 Introduction

The distance a golf ball travels on a putting green is typically a concern for the golfer and golf course superintendent. The distance a ball rolls can be measured with a Stimpmeter (USGA, 1979). The distance the ball rolls may be a function of how fast the ball is traveling, however, to term this measurement "green speed" or "speed" may be misleading since the variable being measured is distance. A more appropriate term to use concerning Stimpmeter readings might be Ball Roll Distance (BRD).

Practices to increase BRD (e.g. low mowing heights, reduced fertilization, reduced watering) are not agronomically correct for proper turfgrass management. Some supplementary cultural practices, such as topdressing and verticle mowing, have also been tried to increase BRD (Throssell, 1981 and Langlois, 1985).

Langlois (1985) also evaluated rolling as a means to increase BRD. A Jacobsen hand mower modified with additional weight was used to roll bentgrass plots. Rolling did increase BRD, but the effect only lasted for a day or two.

Rolling has been used extensively on lawn bowling greens and cricket pitches. Many types of commercial rollers have been developed for this purpose. The use of commercial rollers on golf course putting greens has increased in recent years and continues to gain acceptance, however, detrimental effects of rolling are unknown and need to be thoroughly researched and documented.

2 Objective

To evaluate the effects of light-weight rolling on ball roll distance, bulk density, and water infiltration on putting greens.

Science and Golf II: Proceedings of the World Scientific Congress of Golf. Edited by A.J. Cochran and M.R. Farrally. Published in 1994 by E & FN Spon, London. ISBN 0 419 18790 1

3 Materials and Methods

This experiment was conducted on a research putting green located at the Joseph Valentine Memorial Turfgrass Research Center on the Penn State campus in University Park, PA. The site was relatively level, non-undulating and consisted of 16 year-old "Penncross" creeping bentgrass (Agrostis palustris Huds.) infested with Poa annua L.. The root zone contained more than 70% sand and the thatch layer averaged 17 mm deep across the area.

Mowing was done once per day on Monday through Saturday with a Jacobsen Greensking triplex with a bench set height of 4 mm. The area was core cultivated in early May with 13 mm tines and topdressed with an 80% sand, 20% peat topdressing mix.

Plots were 0.9 by 9.1 m and arranged in a randomized complete block design with three replications. The rolling was done with a Smooth Roll roller. The roller was rolled from one end of the plot to the other and then returned back across the plot in the opposite direction. In essence, the plot was rolled twice, but it was considered one rolling for this experiment. Plots were rolled approximately 4 hours after mowing and it was done at about 1400 hours. The treatments were as follows: rolled once per week; rolled twice per week, two days apart; and a control. Rolling was usually done on Mondays and Wednesdays. Rolling began on June 28 and ended on October 6.

Ball rolling distance was measured with a Stimpmeter and metal measuring tape. Three balls were rolled in one direction from the same position of each plot and the distances recorded. The balls were then rolled in the opposite direction and the distances recorded. The average ball roll distance for that plot was calculated from the six distances. Only the balls that rolled within 15 cm of the edge of the plot were rolled again. Measurements were made on all plots on all days in which rolling occurred.

Infiltration rate and bulk density were measured prior to the start of rolling and after the last rolling. Five areas were sampled in each plot. Infiltration rate was measured using a double-ring infiltrometer (Bouwer, 1986). The outer ring was 35.6 cm and the inner ring was 20.3 cm, both rings were 10.2 cm high. The rings were driven into the ground 6.4 cm. The rings were saturated for 30 minutes prior to the initial reading, to ensure that saturated flow was being measured. Bulk density soil samples were collected with a Uhler soil sampler. The thatch was removed at the thatch-soil interface. The soil cores were 5.0 cm in diameter and 2.5 cm in length and oven-dried at $105^{\circ}C$ for 24 hours.

The data was subjected to analysis of variance and means were compared using Fisher's Protected LSD test with $p = 0.05$.

4 Results and Discussion

4.1 Ball Roll Distance

Ball roll distance significantly increased on every day the plots were rolled (Figure 1). The average increase in distance was 36 cm and 41 cm for the once per week and twice per week treatments, respectively (Table 1). For the once per week treatment the maximum gain was 53 cm and the minimum gain was 31 cm. For the twice per week treatment the maximum gain was 66 cm and the minimum gain was 41 cm. An interesting note is the control had a maximum gain of 28 cm. This was probably due to the inaccuracies of the Stimpmeter.

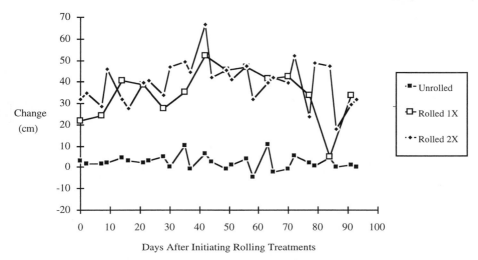

Figure 1. Gain in ball roll distance (cm) for all treatments measured on days when rolling occurred.

Table 1. Range and average gain in ball roll distance.

	Once/Week	Twice/Week	Control
Max.	53	66	28
Min.	30	18	-12
Avg.	36	41	5

The gain in distance due to rolling did not last long. The once per week treatment (measured on the non-rolled day) was significantly different than the control only once (Figure 2). Hence, the effect of rolling lasted less than 48 hours. This was also reported by Langlois (1985).

A single day experiment was conducted on an area directly adjacent to this experiment. Plots were rolled once and distance was measured every two hours. The initial gain in distance measured directly after rolling was 23 cm (Table 2). The increase in distance varied between 13 and 22 cm through 6 hours after rolling. The gain in distance was only 5 cm at 8 hours after rolling, which was the last time distance was measured.

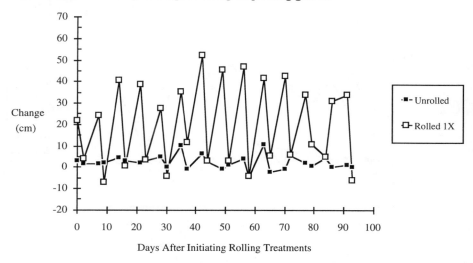

Figure 2. Gain in ball roll distance (cm) measured on days when rolling did and did not occur.

Table 2. Effect of time after rolling on ball roll distance.

Hours after rolling	Cm increased
0	23
2	15
4	23
6	13
8	5

4.2 Bulk Density

Pressure that is applied to soil (i.e., rolling) may compact soil particles, which can result in decreased air and water movement, as well as an increased resistance to root penetration.

The average bulk densities for all treatments before the rolling began was 1.10 g/cm^3 and ranged from 1.13 to 1.15 g/cm^3 after all rollings were completed (Table 3). There was no significant difference between treatments.

The amount of thatch present (17 mm) may have had an effect on the potential for compaction due to rolling. Thatch is a highly compressible material and the pressure caused by the roller may have been primarily absorbed by the thatch.

Since bulk density was measured in the top 2.5 cm of soil, the bulk density measurements may not have been an effective method to detect a thin layer of soil compaction.

Table 3. Bulk densities prior to and after rolling.

Treatment	Before (g/cc)	After (g/cc)
Rolled once per week	1.10 ns*	1.15 ns*
Rolled twice per week	1.10 ns	1.13 ns
Check	1.10 ns	1.14 ns

*according to Fisher's Protected LSD, p=0.05.

4.3 Infiltration Rates

Infiltration rates may be able to detect minimum soil compaction. Carrow and Petrovic (1992) states that a "thin layer of compacted soil at the surface can greatly reduce water infiltration."

There was no significant difference between infiltration rates prior to rolling or after all rollings were completed (Table 4). This is another indication that there was no serious compaction due to rolling.

Table 4. Infiltration rates prior to and after rolling.

Treatment	Before (cm/hr)	After (cm/hr)
Rolled once per week	12.2 ns*	6.7 ns*
Rolled twice per week	11.0 ns	5.9 ns
Check	11.7 ns	7.4 ns

*according to Fisher's Protected LSD, p=0.05.

5 Conclusions

Light-weight rolling of putting greens can significantly increase ball roll distance. The effect is short lived (less than 24 hours). The amount of thatch present may have an effect on how much increase in ball roll distance is gained, how long the effect last, and how much compaction is caused by the rolling. Bulk density and infiltration were not affected by rolling.

6 References

Bouwer, H. (1986) Intake rate: Cylinder infiltrometer, in **Methods of Soil Analysis**. (ed A. Klute), Agronomy Monograph 9. ASA and SSSA, Madison, WI, pp. 825-844.

Carrow, R.N. and Petrovic, A.M. (1992) Effects of traffic on turf, in **Turfgrass** (eds. D.V. Waddington, R.N. Carrow, and R.C. Shearman), Agronomy Monograph 32. ASA, CSSA, and SSSA, Madison, WI. pp. 286-325.

Langlois, S.R. (1985) Practices affecting putting green speed. M.S. Thesis. The Pennsylvania State University.

Throssell, C. S. (1981) Management factors affecting putting green speed. M.S. Thesis. The Pennsylvania State University.

United States Golf Association (1979) Stimpmeter instruction booklet. Golf House, Far Hills, NJ.

64 Golf ball impacts, greens and the golfer

S.J. Haake
University of Sheffield, UK

Abstract
This paper gives a brief overview of the results of a 3 year project to study the relationship
between the characteristics of golf greens and the impact of golf shots on them. To this
end, an apparatus was developed to project spinning golf balls directly onto golf greens
with the resulting impacts recorded on film. The apparatus was used on eighteen golf
courses resulting in 721 useful photographs of impacts. Two types of green emerged
from analysis of the photographs;. on the first, the ball tended to rebound with topspin,
while on the second, the ball retained backspin if the initial backspin was large enough.

Eleven tests were used to determine the characteristics of greens and the relationships
between the characteristics were linked to the impact study. It was found that it was easier
to retain backspin on the rebounding ball on a green that was freely drained and had a low
amount of *Poa annua* in its sward.

A mathematical model was developed to simulate the impact of the ball with the turf. The
model gave sensible results for oblique impacts with backspin.
Keywords: Golf, Impact, Turf, Playing Quality.

1 Introduction

This project was carried out at the Sports Turf Research Institute in conjunction with the
University of Aston in Birmingham. Manufacturers of golf balls have carried out many
tests to study the behaviour of the ball on impacting with the golf club face. There has also
been much work done on the aerodynamics of the golf ball (Bearman and Harvey 1976).
There is little information, however, on what is a fundamental part of the game of golf - the
impact of the ball with the green. With a better understanding of the process of impact it
may be possible to define a given turf using a few easily measurable quantities and hence
to predict how a golf green will play. These tests could then be used to aid the
maintenance and construction of golf greens.

2 Apparatus

2.1 Recording golf ball impacts

The apparatus has been described in detail by Haake (1991a). Briefly it comprises a
modified baseball practice machine to project the golf balls directly at the green and a light
tight tent covering the impact zone to enable stroboscopic photographs of the impact to be
recorded. The complete set of apparatus is shown in Figure 1. The projection apparatus
has two identical wheels with pneumatic tyres with their axes parallel. The wheels rotate in
opposite directions and when a ball rolls down the chute it enters the gap between the
wheels. It is then gripped and fired out of the other side. The speeds of the two motors

Science and Golf II: Proceedings of the World Scientific Congress of Golf. Edited by A.J.
Cochran and M.R. Farrally. Published in 1994 by E & FN Spon, London. ISBN 0 419 18790 1

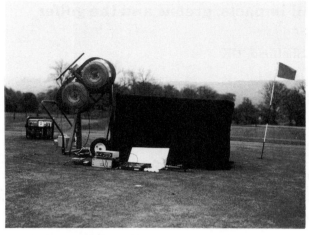

Fig. 1. Apparatus used to photograph impacts of golf balls on golf greens.

can be altered independently in order to impart spin to the balls; if the bottom wheel rotates faster than the top wheel then the ball is projected with backspin.

The system described in this paper used a stroboscope to illuminate the ball along its trajectory before, during and after impact. The images of the ball are recorded using a still camera whose shutter is activated along with the stroboscope by an infra-red beam across the chute of the ball projection device. To enable analysis of the motion of the ball a grid was placed in the vertical plane containing the impact point and the direction of flight of the ball and was exposed onto the same frame of the film as the impact. A typical photograph of a golf ball impact is shown in Figure 2.

2.2 Measurement of playing characteristics
Eleven quantities of the green were determined to try to discover the characteristics that were important in the golf ball impacts (Haake 1991b). The measures included the inherent characteristics of the turf such as moisture content, soil type and grass type as well as measures of the "hardness" of the turf. Not all of the characteristics were found to be significant in relation to the golf ball impacts, however, and only the most important are described here:

Clegg impact soil tester (Clegg 1976; Lush 1985). The Clegg impact soil tester uses an accelerometer to measure the peak deceleration of a hammer as it is dropped on a surface. The results are given in multiples of g, where g is the acceleration due to gravity.
Traction. The traction of the green was measured using an apparatus described by Bell *et al.* (1985). Three golf balls were adhered to the bottom of a test disc and the torque required to twist the disc was measured.
Soil moisture content. Ten three quarter inch diameter cores were taken from each green and were weighed, dried at 105°C for 24 hours and then reweighed for determination of their moisture content.
Soil type. A particle size analysis of the soil from each green was carried out.
Ground cover and species composition. This was studied with an optical frame point quadrat as described by Laycock and Canaway (1980).

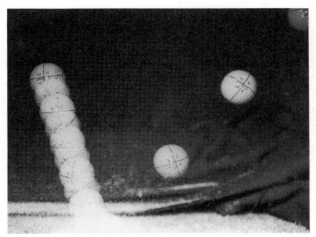

Fig. 2. Stroboscopic photograph of a typical golf ball impact. The ball entered from the right at a velocity of 23.4 m s^{-1} and with a backspin of 127 rad s^{-1}. The rebounding ball had a velocity of 3.9 m s^{-1} and topspin of 160 rad s^{-1}.

3 Results

3.1 Impacts
Eighteen golf greens were studied using the apparatus described resulting in 721 useful photographs of impacts. One of the most important results is shown in Figure 3. This shows the relationship between the spin after impact versus the velocity after impact for all the impacts studied. If no slip occurred then $v=\omega r$ where v is the velocity of the ball across the surface, ω is the rotational velocity of the ball and r is the ball radius. This relationship is represented by the line on Figure 3. It can be seen that the majority of the points lie close to this line and points below the line represent impacts which slipped off the surface and rebounded with backspin.

The characteristics of the greens were related to the golf ball impacts and it was found that the greens could be roughly categorised in two types. On the first type backspin was retained after impact if the initial spin was large enough. On these greens the ball slipped throughout impact and rebounded at relatively low angles. The depth of the pitchmark was found to be relatively shallow. On the second type of green the backspin of the ball was nearly always converted to topspin. The ball rebounded at high angles and the depth of the pitchmark was quite deep.

3.2 Playing characteristics
Statistical analysis was carried out on the green characteristics and the interdependency of the characteristics of the turf was shown; high moisture contents implied high levels of clay in the soil and high amounts of organic matter. It was also shown that soils high in moisture, organic matter and clay content had predominantly *Poa annua* (annual meadow grass) growing on them. Those greens with higher proportions of *Poa annua* tended to have lower measures of hardness and higher measures of traction.

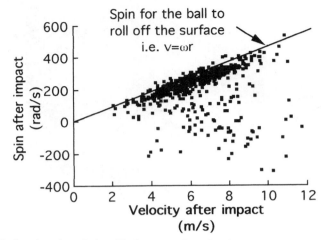

Fig 3. Graph showing the relationship between the spin after impact and the velocity after impact for all 721 impacts studied. The impacts nearest the line are more likely have rolled off the surface.

The significance of these results and their relationship to golf ball impacts can be seen in Figure 4. The crosses represent the greens on which most of the impacts rolled off the surface while the filled circles represent the greens on which the ball slipped throughout impact if the initial backspin was high enough. Figure 4 (a) shows that the "slipping" greens tend to have less than 30% fines (clay) in their soil composition and moisture contents of less than 30%. Figure 4(b) and (c) show that these greens have less than about 60% of *Poa annua* in their ground cover while having high hardness (peak deceleration) values and low traction values.

The analysis of the green characteristics thus showed that the greens on which balls slipped throughout impact were relatively resistant to the vertical component of the impact (hardness) while being less resistant to the horizontal motion of the ball (traction). This was supported by the difference in the depth and shape of the pitchmark created during impact. On the "slipping" greens the pitchmark was relatively shallow and long in the direction of motion of the ball. On the "rolling" greens the pitchmark was both deeper and shorter. The difference between the two different types of green was indicated by the amount of *Poa annua* present on the green.

4 A mathematical model of impact

Space does not allow a full description of the mathematical model to predict the rebound of golf balls developed during the project. Essentially the model of the turf was composed of two layers. The upper layer represented the grass, thatch and root layer while the second layer represented the soil layer underneath. The model predicted well simple vertical impacts and was further modified to include obliquely spinning impacts. The complete model was described by Haake (1991c). Figure 5 shows some predictions of the model for a 5-iron and a 9-iron shot. Both types of green discussed previously have been modelled and the incoming ball given low, medium and high amounts of backspin.

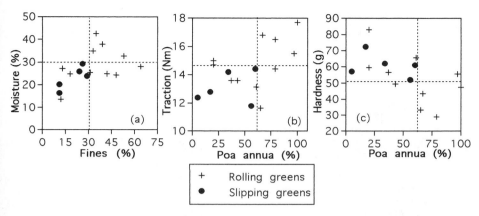

Fig. 4. Graphs showing the relationships between measurable quantities of the green and an indication of the characteristics of greens on which balls were seen to slip during impact.

Consider first the 5-iron shot. On the slipping green shots with high and medium amounts of backspin stop within a metre of the second bounce. The shot with low amounts of backspin is penalised however and rolls over 2 m further. On the softer rolling green there is less difference between the shots and the balls end up roughly 1.5 to 2.5 m from the initial landing point.

For the 9-iron shots the effect of spin is much more marked. On the slipping green the highly spinning ball screws back a long way, the medium spin ball less so and the ball with low spin screws back a small distance to end up just in front of the initial landing point. On the rolling green the spin again has much less effect with the ball with low amounts of backspin stopping just in front of the landing point and the highly spinning ball coming to rest about 1 m behind the landing point.

The results of the model show, in an exaggerated way, that the golfer has much less control of his or her shot on the rolling green as opposed to the slipping green. Conversely, shots with low spin are penalised more on the slipping greens since they roll further after the first bounce.

5 Conclusions

It was found that the greens studied could be classified into two categories; in the first type the ball was able to slip throughout impact if the initial backspin was high enough and, thus retaining backspin after impact. These type of greens were generally hard but had low surface tractions and had low amounts of moisture, clay in their soil composition and low amounts of *Poa annua* on their sward. A mathematical model of impact was created which was able to predict simple vertical impacts well and which gave sensible results for oblique golf shots with backspin.

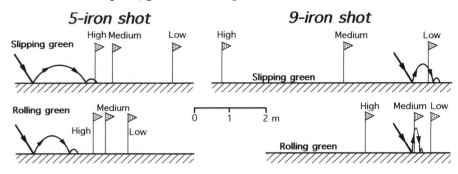

Fig. 5. Diagrams to show the simulated behaviour of 5-iron and 9-iron shots with different amounts of backspin on a green on which the ball rolls throughout impact and on a green which allows the ball to slip. The ball arrives in the direction of the arrow, bounces twice and then rolls along the ground. The flags indicate the end positions of impacts with high, medium and low amounts of backspin.

6 References

Bearman, P.W. & Harvey, J.K. (1976). Golf ball aerodynamics. **Aeronautical Quarterly, 27**, 112-122.

Bell, M.J., Baker, S.W. & Canaway, P.M. (1985). Playing quality of sports surfaces: a review. *J. Sports Turf Res. Inst.*, **61**, 9-35.

Clegg, B. (1976). An impact testing device for *in situ* base course evaluation. *Australian Road Res. Bureau Proc.*, **8**, 1-6.

Haake, S.J., (1991a). The impact of golf balls on natural turf. I. Apparatus and test methods. *J. Sports Turf Res. Inst.*, **67**, 128-134 .

Haake, S.J., (1991b). The impact of golf balls on natural turf. II. Results and conclusions. *J. Sports Turf Res. Inst.*, **67**, 128-134.

Haake, S.J., (1991c). The impact of golf balls on natural turf: A physical model of impact. *Applied Solid Mechanics, 4*, Ed. by A.R.S. Ponter and A.C.F. Cocks, Published by Elsevier Applied Science, 72-79.

Laycock, R.W. & Canaway, P.M. (1980). A new optical point quadrat frame for the estimation of cover in close mown turf. *J. Sports Turf Res. Inst.*, **56**, 91-92.

Lush, W.M. (1985). Objective assessment of turf cricket pitches using an impact hammer. *J. Sports Turf Res. Inst.*, **61**, 17-79.

Acknowledgements
The author would like to thank Dr Alastair Cochran and Mr Mike Canaway for their guidance during this project. Grateful thanks also go to the Royal and Ancient Golf Club of St Andrews, Acushnet Co. and SERC for their generous support.

65 Improving the performance of golf turf soils by cultivation

K.W. McAuliffe, R.J. Gibbs and A. Glasgow
NZ Turf Culture Institute, Palmerston North, New Zealand

Abstract

Soil conditioning and/or artificial drainage offers a cost-effective solution to many poorly drained golf greens, tees and fairways.
A scientific analysis of the site and soil profile is a pre-requisite with any drainage improvement programme.
Measuring the permeability of soil profile horizons allows the depth to and thickness of any barrier layer to be identified.
A national study into the permeability of soil profiles carried by agronomists of the NZ Turf Culture Institute provided an insight to the drainage characteristics of golf greens. Permeability measurements illustrated that drainage performance is site specific, depending on properties such as construction type, nature of the sand used and age of green.
The cultivation equipment selected to rectify a drainage problem must also be site specific. A cultivation trial carried out on a fine sandy loam practice golf green showed significant, relatively long term improvement in root zone permeability using the HydroJect and Verti-drain.

1 Introduction

A fundamental requirement for successful turf management is a deep, healthy plant root system. In turn a good root system will result only if the soil environment is adequately maintained.

In many parts of the world golf courses with poorly drained greens, tees and fairways are the norm rather than the exception. Many courses have been built using local soil materials and to a budget, so it is not surprising that when coupled with high water loading and player pressure, they perform badly from the drainage viewpoint.

Reconstruction is undoubtedly one way to resurrect a poorly performing green, tee or fairway. But reconstruction need not be the most cost effective

Science and Golf II: Proceedings of the World Scientific Congress of Golf. Edited by A.J. Cochran and M.R. Farrally. Published in 1994 by E & FN Spon, London. ISBN 0 419 18790 1

approach. An option that should always be considered at the outset is modification of the existing soil medium by cultivation and/or artificial drainage.

For a cultivation programme to be successful it is important to select the right equipment and use it under the right conditions.

2   Reconstruction or modification - which option?

Any club faced with the decision to upgrade their greens, tees or fairway drainage should at the very outset carry out an in-depth, scientific study into the problem. In particular, reference should be made to the soil profile characteristics (Carrow, 1993). A soil profile study should determine the rate of water movement (the permeability) through the profile and to identify the depth to and thickness of any impeding or barrier layer.

3   Measuring soil permeability

The agronomists of the NZ Turf Culture Institute use a simple "*in situ*" technique to measure permeability. The technique, termed the NZTCI permeameter method, (Howard & McAuliffe 1993) allows accurate identification of the incremental permeability down the soil profile in order to identify any low permeability zones. In turn this indicates the depth of cultivation required to bring about improvement.

A national survey, produced by combining more than 60 different drainage feasibility studies carried out by the NZTCI agronomists, paints an interesting picture. Although each turf system and soil profile portrayed unique characteristics, it was apparent that some generalisations can be derived. Key points noted include:

> The drainage performance of sand constructed greens depended on the type of sand used, particularly the particle size distribution, and the age of the green. Permeability decreased as sand greens aged (Fig 1a). This effect was largely attributable to organic matter accumulation; a study into the effect of organic matter accumulation on physical properties of golf greens is currently underway in New Zealand through AgResearch Grasslands.
> Some young sand greens (2-5 years) accumulated organic matter in the surface 50mm to the point where permeability was restricted. This illustrated a need for physical treatment even in relatively young sand constructions.

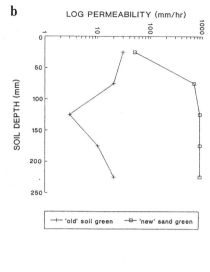

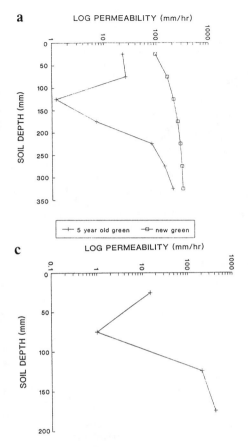

Fig. 1a.   Soil profile permeability of an old (5 years) and a new fine 'dune' sand golf green.

Fig. 1b.   Soil profile permeability of soil-based greens (mean of 15 greens) compared with a new sand green at the Tauranga Golf Club, N.Z.

Fig. 1c.   Soil profile permeability for a soil green topdressed with 50mm approx. of a medium grade sand.

In older greens (5 years plus) the most limiting
permeability zone was invariably below the depth
of coring (Fig 1b). This observation was
consistent in both sand and soil greens. Where
older greens had been built using good quality
topsoil permeability at depth was generally
satisfactory (e.g. Fig 1b).

Native soil greens topdressed with sand (a common
procedure in New Zealand) invariably had
impermeable conditions at or just below the
sand/soil interface (Fig 1c). In some cases
where the topdressing sand layer was shallow it
was possible to reach more permeable subsoil
layers with conventional cultivation equipment.
In other cases the depth of sand topdressing had
built up so that the sand/soil interface was
beyond the reach of conventional cultivation
equipment.

4   Interpreting permeability information

The NZTCI permeameter method serves to quantify the
drainage performance of the soil profile. In doing so
it enables the identification of any physical problems
that may exist.
    The next step involves matching the information
obtained with the attributes of available cultivation
treatments, in particular the depth of penetration and
anticipated extent and longevity of permeability
improvement (McAuliffe, 1992). For example, in cases
where the most restricting zone is at or near the soil
surface (e.g. a young green or tee) it is likely that
treatments such as coring and spiking alone would
improve drainage. In contrast an area with deep set
compaction (e.g. a sand topdressed green or older
green which has developed a "coring pan") would
require deep penetrating cultivation treatment. Yet
further, if no free draining zone is encountered in
the surface 350-400mm it is likely that some form of
artificial (pipe) drainage or even reconstruction is
warranted.

5   Selection of a cultivation treatment

Having identified the depth to and thickness of any
soil profile layer(s) which restrict permeability, an
appropriate cultivation treatment can then be
selected. The treatment must be capable of
penetrating through to a satisfactorily drained zone
and provide long lasting improvement without undue
surface disruption.

Sports turf cultivation methods produce only modest soil improvement relative to agricultural cultivation methods. This is naturally understandable given the pre-requisite in turf of maintaining acceptable surface levelness at all times. Yet results using soil physical treatment in turf, especially if repeated on a regular basis, can be spectacular.

A trial conducted in Palmerston North, New Zealand in 1991 illustrates the permeability improvement brought about by turf cultivation techniques (McAuliffe *et al.*, 1993). The trial compared the effects of a single pass with three commonly used cultivation methods; a multi-bladed oscillating mini-mole plough,Verti-drain unit and HydroJect. The trial site was a fine sandy loam practice putting green.

Results showed that the HydroJect and Verti-drain treatments gave significant soil improvement in the zone of limiting permeability (50-150mm depth). In contrast the multi-bladed oscillating mini-mole plough did not confer a significant response (Fig 2).

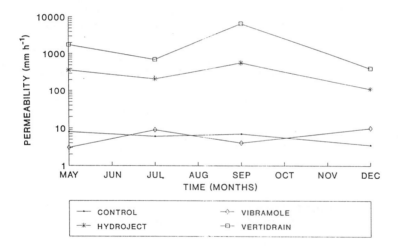

Fig.2. The effect of three cultivation treatments on soil permeability in the 100-150mm depth compared with an untreated control.

The results also highlight the importance of timing, particularly in relation to soil moisture content, when carrying out cultivation.

The improvement in permeability with both the HydroJect and Verti-drain was due to the formation of continuous holes through the restricting zone. There was no evidence to suggest any improvement in soil

condition outside the direct point of impact by the
machine. This could reflect to some degree at least
the relatively high soil moisture content at the time
of treatment.

The information gained from this trial illustrates
a number of points in relation to the selection and
use of a cultivation technique. In particular it
highlights:

> The need to select a treatment which gives
> significant improvement in the zone restricting
> the permeability.
> The need for repeat treatments if the effect is
> to be totally effective and continuous.

Summary

Sub-standard drainage is a problem faced by golf clubs
throughout the world. In many instances
reconditioning of the soil profile offers a cost
effective option for drainage improvement. Clubs must
however acknowledge that drainage problems are site
specific and there is no single recipe for solving all
problems.

An intensive study of a site is needed to gauge the
nature and extent of the drainage problem. Soil
permeability measurement or assessment should be part
of this study.

Having identified the depth to and thickness of any
impeding layer it will then be possible to select an
appropriate cultivation treatment. The ideal treatment
would be capable of giving long lasting permeability
improvement in the limiting zone, without undue
surface disruption.

References

Carrow, R.N. (1993) Developing a cultivation
programme for a golf course. **Greenmaster** Sept/Oct.
1993, 18-20.
Howard, D.R. & McAuliffe. K.W. (1993) The NZTCI
permeameter method for identifying soil drainage
problems. **Int. Turfgrass Society Research Journal** 7,
422-425.
McAuliffe, K.W. (1992) Drainage improvement -
Remedy without reconstruction in New Zealand. **USGA
Green Section Record 30** (2), 6 - 10.
McAuliffe, K.W., Rieke, P.E. and D.J. Horne (1993) A
study of three physical conditioning treatments on a
fine sandy loam golf green. **Int. Turfgrass Society
Research Journal** 7, 444 - 450.

66 Soil macropore effects on the fate of phosphorus in a turfgrass biosystem

S.K. Starrett, N.E. Christians and T.A. Austin
Civil and Const. Engineering Dept., Hort. Dept., Civil and Const.
Engineering Dept., respectively, Iowa State University, Ames, Iowa,
USA

Abstract
Phosphorus (P) is commonly applied to turfgrass areas as a
fertilizer. It has been associated with detrimental
effects on the environment by causing eutrophication of
surface waters. The objective of this study was to
investigate the effect of irrigation regimes on the
movement of P when applied to undisturbed soil columns
with intact soil macropores. The soil columns were
collected by encasing undisturbed soil columns 20 cm in
diameter by 50 cm deep, in concrete. Two irrigation
treatments that included one 2.54-cm application compared
to four 0.64-cm applications over a 7-day test period were
applied to the column surface, after a 33 kg P ha^{-1}
application. Fifty-four percent more P was transported
below 20 cm and P leaching was increased from 0.0 mg to
1.0 mg with the one 2.54-cm irrigation treatment than the
four 0.64-cm irrigation applications. Whereas heavy
irrigation or rainfall events can potentially move P
through the macropores in the soil profile, carefully
controlled irrigation practices can prevent P movement.
Keywords: Nutrient Fate, Preferential Flow, Turfgrass.

1 Introduction

Phosphorus (P) is an essential element for plant growth
and can become a limiting factor during establishment and
growth of mature grasses (Turgeon, 1985). Low P
concentrations can result in delayed maturity, reduced
yields, and stunted leaf growth (Munson, 1982).

With the current elevation of public concern, all
industries are being questioned about their effect on the
environment. The turfgrass industry is often criticized
for applying fertilizers and pesticides as part of their
management system to grasses. An understanding of the
fate of these chemicals is needed to manage turfgrass
maintenance better, and to determine the chemicals that
pose an environmental threat. Little research has been
done concerning their environmental effects of chemicals
applied to turfgrasses (Walker et al., 1990). Phosphorus
is of concern because it is commonly applied to turfgrass
areas and can have detrimental effects. Eutrophication,
excessive algae growth that decreases dissolved oxygen of
surface waters, can occur if P and nitrogen (N) are

Science and Golf II: Proceedings of the World Scientific Congress of Golf. Edited by A.J.
Cochran and M.R. Farrally. Published in 1994 by E & FN Spon, London. ISBN 0 419 18790 1

abundant.   Availability of P is considered the limiting
factor in eutrophication.

Phosphorus and all surface applied chemicals are more
likely to leach when soils have a macropore system created
by worms, insects, cracks, and other factors.   Everts
(1989), who conducted a thorough review of macropore flow
research,   states that macropores increase water and
solute flux through soils and that the influence of
macropores is negated when experiments are done in a
laboratory using dried, sieved, and repacked soil columns.

The objective of this study was to investigate the
effects of 2 irrigation regimes on the movement of P
applied to undisturbed soil columns with intact
macropores.

2   Materials and Methods

Fourteen undisturbed columns of mostly Nicollet (fine-
loamy, mixed, mesic Aquic Hapludoll) soil that had been
graded in 1968 were taken from a 400 m^2 area at the Iowa
State University Horticulture Research Station.   The area
had been established with Premium Sod Blend®, a blend of
'Parade', 'Adelphi', 'Rugby', and 'Glade' Kentucky
bluegrass (*Poa   pratensis* L.), in 1979 and maintained at
fairway mowing height (2.54 cm) since 1989.   The columns
measured 20 cm in diameter and were excavated to a 50-cm
depth using the method described by Priebe and Blackmer
(1989).   According to this method, a free standing column
of soil was excavated by removing the surrounding
material.   Water was misted on the free-standing column to
prevent drying of the soil.   A 30-cm heating-duct pipe was
placed around the column, leaving 5 cm between the soil
column and the pipe.   Masonry concrete was poured between
the pipe and soil column (Fig. 1).   The concrete was
allowed to set for ten days in the field, and the columns
were then moved to the greenhouse on 15 October 1990.

The soil columns were watered with approximately 1.3 cm
of distilled water twice a week.   Natural light was
supplemented with high pressure sodium lights with an
average intensity of 870 μmol m^{-2} s^{-1} measured at 90 cm.   A
14-hr photoperiod was used for supplemental light in the
winter months.   The greenhouse was maintained between a
nighttime temperature of 19 ± 2 °C and a daytime
temperature of 27 ± 2 °C.

The columns were slowly lowered into distilled water
over a 6-hr period (8.3 cm hr^{-1}) and left submerged for 24
hr to obtain saturation and reach water-holding capacity.
The columns were slowly raised out of the water and
allowed to drain for 24 hr (Priebe and Blackmer, 1989).

Monobasic calcium phosphate [Ca(H$_2$PO$_4$)$_2$] was dissolved
in distilled water and applied to the surface of the

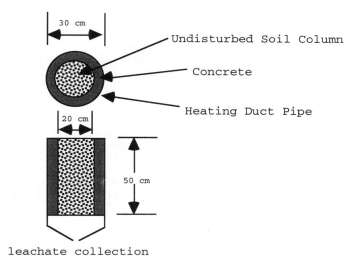

Fig. 1   Description of undisturbed soil columns.

Kentucky bluegrass turf at 33 kg P ha^{-1} using a spray-mist
atomizer attached to an air pressure pump.   Experimental
treatments included two irrigation regimes.   One treatment
(# 1) consisted of watering the column with 2.54 cm of
distilled water immediately after the P was applied.   The
second treatment (# 2) included a 0.64-cm application
immediately after applying P, with three additional 0.64-
cm applications at 42-hr intervals.   This gave a total of
2.54 cm of irrigation spread evenly over the 7-day test
period.   The two treatments were replicated seven times.
The initial water applications were applied over a time of
4 min with a Teejet® Conejet TXVS 4 nozzle.
Volatilization chambers were placed on the columns
following the initial water applications to collect
volatilized ammonia (Starrett, 1992).   For the three later
applications of the light irrigation regime, the stopper
on top of the chamber was removed, and the spray nozzle
inserted into the hole.
   A plastic bag was placed around the bottom of the column
and fastened to the sides to act as a leachate collection
device and to prevent the bottom of the soil column from
drying.   Leachate was collected daily and was immediately
placed into a plastic bottle and frozen.
   The soil was excavated in 10-cm layers at the end of the
7-day test period.   It was spread into a thin layer and
air dried for 3 day according to the method of Priebe and

Blackmer (1989). It was then placed in plastic bags, thoroughly mixed, and sampled for analysis. The soil layers and the leachate were tested for available P by the Bray P-1 method (Bray and Kurtz, 1945; Murphy and Riley, 1962).

3   Results and discussion

Soil properties, including water-holding capacity, bulk density, porosity, specific surface, and specific yield, were consistent between the two treatment groups (Starrett, 1992). When the soil columns were excavated, numerous earth worms were observed. Many of the worm holes extended below a depth of 50 cm. The upper soil layers of columns with treatment 1 irrigation level were dryer at the end of the test period. Water that was lost to evapotranspiration was not being replaced as it was with the smaller, but more frequent, irrigation levels in treatment 2.

Concentrations of elemental P were highest in the thatch mat layer (Table 1). The thatch mat layer under treatment 2 contained 1.5 times the amount found under treatment 1 (P = 0.073). The 20 to 30-cm layer under treatment 1 contained 1.6 times the amount found under treatment 2 (P = 0.031). Leachate collected under treatment 1 contained 1.0 mg of P compared with 0.0 mg collected under treatment 2.

Table 1. Available phosphorus concentrations (mg kg^{-1}) in the soil and total P in the leachate (mg)†.

	Treatment 1‡		Treatment 2§		
Category	Mean	Std.Dev.	Mean	Std.Dev.	Probability¶
Thatch Mat	18.5	2.9	27.5	8.3	0.073
0-10 cm	6.7	1.5	6.4	1.6	0.735
10-20 cm	2.7	1.0	2.4	0.5	0.502
20-30 cm	2.3	0.8	1.4	0.5	0.031
30-40 cm	2.4	1.3	1.6	1.1	0.208
40-50 cm	3.0	1.6	2.0	1.7	0.288
Leachate††	1.0	1.0	<0.1	<0.1	0.024

†   Values are from 7 replications.
‡   Treatment 1, one 2.54-cm irrigation application.
§   Treatment 2, four 0.64-cm irrigation applications over a 7-day period.
¶   t - test.
††   Total P found in leachate (mg).

Phosphorus is considered highly immobile, but under treatment 1, P was found in some of the leachate samples. No P was detected in the leachate for 8 of the 14 soil columns (two from treatment 1, six from treatment 2). The P that leached through the soil column did so in the first five hr of the test period and showed evidence of preferential flow through macropores.

One way to calculate the depth that P could be transported without preferential flow is by dividing applied irrigation (volume) by the area of the column and water-holding capacity (whc), moisture content, mass basis, (depth = [volume of irrigation] / [area * (whc)]) (Priebe, 1989). Average depth of P calculated in this manner is 8.3 cm.

The results of this study demonstrate that macropores may play a role in chemical movement even for relatively immobile materials such as P. Heavy irrigation or rainfall immediately after application may also have a major effect of the movement of other chemicals through the soil profile. By properly managing the time of application and irrigation levels after application, the risk of detrimental effects of P on the environment can be decreased. More work is being conducted to investigate the effect that different irrigation regimes have on the fate of pesticides.

4   Acknowledgments

The authors would like to thank the United States Golf Association (USGA) Green Section for funding, and the Horticulture, Civil and Construction Engineering, and Agronomy Departments at Iowa State University for additional support.

5   References

Bray, R.H. and L.T. Kurtz. 1945. Determination of total, organic, and available forms of phosphorus in soils. **Soil Sci.** 59:39-45.

Everts, C.J. 1989. Role of preferential flow on water and chemical transport in a glacial till soil. Ph. D. Dissertation. Iowa State University. Ames, Iowa. (disser. abst. no. dew8920130).

Munson, R.D. 1982. Soil fertility, fertilizers, and plant nutrition. *In* V.J. Kilmer (ed.). **Handbook of soils and climate in agriculture.** CRC Press, Inc. Boca Raton, Florida. p. 269-293.

Murphy, J. and J.P. Riley. 1962. A modified single solution method for determination of phosphate in natural waters. **Anal. Chem. Acta.** 27:31-36.

Priebe, D.L. and A.M. Blackmer. 1989. Preferential movement of oxygen-18-labeled water and nitrogen-15-labeled urea through macropores in a Nicollet soil. **J. Environ. Qual.** 18:66-72.

Starrett, S.K. 1992. Fertilizer fate under golf course conditions in the midwestern region. Master's thesis. Iowa State University. Ames, Iowa. 50011.

Turgeon, A.J. 1985. **Turfgrass management**. Reston Pub. Co., Inc. Reston, Virginia. p. 170.

Balogh, J.C., and W.J. Walker 1992. **Golf course management & construction environmental issues.** Lewis Pub. Chelsea, Michigan.

67 Experimental studies on black layer

W.A. Adams and J.N.G. Smith
Institute of Biological Sciences, University of Wales, Aberystwyth,
UK

Abstract
Samples of rootzone materials were incubated anaerobically in the
laboratory to investigate factors influencing the production of metal
sulphide which is the cause of black layer. Treatments examined
included the addition of different sources of oxidised S, the addition
of an organic adjuvant, seaweed extract and a comparison between
soils with different reserves of reducible Fe. Where the oxidised
S source decreased soil pH ($FeSO_4$) sulphide production did not occur.
Seaweed extract concentrations greater than recommended caused
sulphide production. Larger amounts of reducible iron compounds
decreased sulphide production.
Keywords: Sulphide, Redox Potential, Seaweed Extract, Anoxic
Conditions, Iron Sulphate, pH.

1 Introduction

A continuous or discontinuous black layer is a morphological feature
present in sections of greens on many golf courses. Typically, black
layers, composed in the main of FeS, occur within the top 60mm of
rootzones (Adams and Smith, 1993) and root development stops at these
layers (Lubin, 1987). The occurrence of a black layer is reflected
in poor turf quality, probably through the toxicity of H_2S to
turfgrass roots (Fitter and Hay, 1981).
    The redox potential (E_h) of aerated soils is typically in the
range +400 to +600mV. Saturation by water virtually prevents oxygen
diffusion into soils and following the utilisation of the residual
oxygen by aerobic organisms the E_h falls as a sequence of electron
acceptors is utilised by anaerobes (Adams and Gibbs, 1994). The
rate and extent of the fall in E_h in anoxic soils is determined by
the nature and amount of organic substrates, the presence of redox
buffers including nitrate (Connell and Patrick, 1969) and other
factors including pH. Sulphate reduction, which is carried out by
a range of bacterial species does not occur until E_h's lower than
+100mV are reached (Vainshtein and Gogotova, 1987).
    Despite the more extensive use in golf green construction of
rootzone specifications designed to provide good aeration (eg USGA
Green Section Staff, 1993), black layer seems to be an increasingly
evident phenomenon. There are probably several contributing factors
including the use of biocides affecting components of the soil

Science and Golf II: Proceedings of the World Scientific Congress of Golf. Edited by A.J.
Cochran and M.R. Farrally. Published in 1994 by E & FN Spon, London. ISBN 0 419 18790 1

microflora (Beard, 1988), vertical heterogeneity in particle size distribution (Burpee and Anderson, 1987) and the wider occurrence of neutral or alkaline rootzones (Adams and Smith, 1993).

The aim of the work was to provide more evidence on potentially causal factors in sulphide production in golf greens by incubating rootzone materials anaerobically under controlled temperature conditions in the laboratory. The aspects investigated were 1) the effect of source of oxidised S addition, 2) the effect of seaweed extract on the progress of reduction processes and 3) the significance of redox buffering by oxidised iron compounds.

2 Materials and Methods

2.1 General
All incubations were carried out on saturated samples of rootzones or soil mixes at 20°C ± 0.5°. Samples of 30g were incubated in sealed screw-top vials 78mm x 22mm diam of 30ml capacity. After each period of incubation, E_h and pH were determined on replicate vials. E_h was measured at a depth of 30mm using a Pt electrode with calomel reference electrode. The pH was determined using a combination electrode after mixing the top 40mm of sample. Vial contents were then harvested destructively for the measurement of metal sulphides and extractable Fe. The rootzone material was washed into a 500ml conical flask using 25ml of distilled water. To this was added 50ml of 5M HCl and the evolved H_2S force bubbled through 2 x 25ml of 40mM $CuSO_4$ using a small aquarium pump. After 15 min the $CuSO_4$ solutions were combined and filtered to remove CuS. The decrease in Cu concentration was determined spectrophotometrically and used to calculate the metal sulphide-S in the rootzone. The rootzone plus acid was shaken for a further 15 min and then filtered. Extracted Fe^{2+} and total Fe were determined spectrophotometrically using ααdipyridyl as chromophore.

2.2 Experiments
2.2.1. A commercial golf green rootzone was used which had 1.8% organic matter, a pH of 6.2, 79% in the particle size range 125-500μm and a D_{20} of 164μm. It was incubated anaerobically with either added $FeSO_4$ or K_2SO_4. The sulphate sources were added and mixed in at the rate of 1g SO_4-S kg^{-1}. 30g samples of rootzone were added incrementally to vials to ensure complete saturation with a solution of 1% sodium lactate in de-oxygenated distilled water. A 2mm depth of lactate solution was maintained over the rootzone. Sufficient vials were prepared to enable triplicate samples to be taken at zero time and at 4, 8, 12, 16 and 20 days. At each occasion the following were determined: E_h, pH, metal sulphide-S, extractable Fe^{2+} and total Fe.

2.2.2. The same rootzone material was incubated as in experiment 1. In this case the rootzone samples were saturated with a range of dilutions of seaweed extract (Maxicrop Garden Products, Corby, Northants). The rates of dilution were 0.3ml, 3ml, 30ml and 300ml of extract per litre of distilled water. A water control was also included. E_h was determined on quadruplicate samples at intervals up to 20 days. At 20 days, pH was measured and samples were analysed for metal sulphide-S, extractable Fe^{2+} and total Fe.

Table 1. Particle size distribution and total extractable iron in three soil mixes

Soil	2-0.5mm	500-125μm	125-20μm	20-2μm	<2μm	Extr Fe (g kg^{-1})
			% by weight			
A	10	16	13	29	32	8.52
B	6	49	9	17	19	4.90
C	0	88	5	2	5	1.22

2.2.3. Three 'soils' were prepared by mixing different proportions of a clay loam agricultural topsoil with dune sand. Particle size distributions of the mixes is summarised in Table 1. Samples (30g) of each of the mixes was saturated as described using a 5% solution of sodium lactate containing 2g L^{-1} of K_2SO_4 and incubated over a period of 24 days. At 1, 4, 7, 12, 17 and 24 days triplicate samples were used for the determination of E_h, pH, metal sulphide-S and extractable Fe^{2+} and total Fe.

3. Results and Discussion

Adams and Smith, (1993) suggested that the acidifying effect of $FeSO_4$ may be quite important by producing conditions unfavourable for sulphate reducing bacteria even though it does provide a source of reducible S. This prediction is supported by the results in

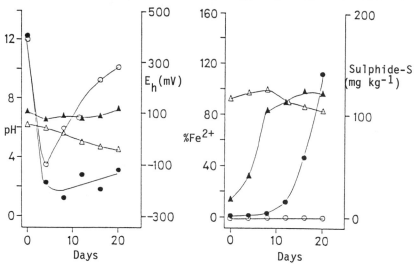

Fig. 1. Changes in pH, E_h, proportion of Fe^{2+} in total extractable Fe and sulphide production during anaerobic incubation of a rootzone with different sulphate sources; pH and %Fe^{2+} are triangles, E_h and sulphide are circles; $FeSO_4$ is open symbols, K_2SO_4 is closed symbols.

experiment 1 (Fig 1). There was a progressive decrease in pH in the $FeSO_4$ treatment down to around pH4.5 whereas with K_2SO_4 the pH remained reasonably constant at around pH7. In both treatments E_h fell to values of -100mV or lower although these values were not maintained in the $FeSO_4$ treatment. The proportion of Fe^{2+} remained greater than 80% in the $FeSO_4$ treatment for the entire experiment. In the K_2SO_4 treatment the %Fe^{2+} reached 80% after 8 days of anaerobic incubation. Sulphide began to occur soon afterwards and increased progressively. No sulphide was produced in the $FeSO_4$ treatment. The results suggest that rootzone pH is important and support the contention that rootzones which are of near neutral pH are predisposed to black layer production when other conditions are favourable for its formation.

Table 2. Change in E_h with time of anaerobic incubation in rootzone samples saturated with different concentrations of seaweed extract

Concentration of seaweed extract	Days of incubation					
	0	1	4	7	14	20
				E_h (mV)		
0	+400	+374	+358	+370	+363	+400
0.3ml L^{-1}	+400	+383	+345	+363	+379	+386
3.0ml L^{-1}	+405	+388	+331	+380	+363	+384
30ml L^{-1}	+395	+237	+148	+159	+130	+131
300ml L^{-1}	+395	+ 70	-418	-377	+ 70	+ 24

LSD (P = 0.05) = 60

The recommended dilution for the seaweed extract used in experiment 2 is 6ml L^{-1} and the closest dilution to this, 3ml L^{-1}, did not cause a significant depression of E_h below the control (Table 2). Despite the long period of waterlogging, the control showed no lowering of E_h and no measurable reduction of Fe suggesting that there was very little utilisable organic matter in the rootzone

Table 3. Percent of total extractable Fe as Fe^{2+}, pH and presence of metal sulphide after 20 day anaerobic incubation of rootzone samples saturated with different concentrations of seaweed extract.

Concentration of seaweed extract	pH	% Fe^{2+} in total	Sulphide-S (mg kg^{-1})
0	6.7	6.5	0
0.3ml L^{-1}	6.8	6.7	0
3.0ml L^{-1}	6.8	6.7	0
30ml L^{-1}	6.8	51	16
300ml L^{-1}	7.2	93	50

material. At the 30ml and 300ml L^{-1} dilutions, E_h fell rapidly over the first four days. At the highest concentration of seaweed extract virtually all the acid extractable Fe was in the reduced form at the end of the experiment and a substantial amount of metal sulphide was produced (Table 3). Thus organic adjuvants or ameliorants which are biodegradable have the potential to increase the risk of sulphide production in anoxic conditions.

The Fe^{3+}/Fe^{2+} redox couple has a higher standard electrode potential than the $SO_4{}^{2-}/H_2S$ couple so that Fe reduction would be expected to occur prior to SO_4 reduction and also the presence of reducible Fe^{3+}-iron compounds might act as a redox buffer delaying sulphide production. In experiment 3 the amount of extractable Fe in Fe^{3+} form was eight times greater in soil A than soil C (Table 1). There was a rapid fall to negative E_h values over 4 days in all three soils (Table 4) and the E_h remained negative throughout the experiment. Iron reduction was most rapid in all three soils between days 4 and 7 with the greatest proportion of Fe being reduced in the sandiest soil (Table 5).

Table 4.   Change in E_h with time of anaerobic incubation in three soil mixes

Soil	Days of incubation						
	0	1	4	7	12	17	24
				E_h (mV)			
A	+390	+341	- 99	-399	-395	-390	-380
B	+410	+343	-169	-390	-395	-399	-378
C	+390	+196	- 44	-245	-300	-379	-410

LSD (P = 0.05) = 65

Table 5.   Percent Fe^{2+} in the total extractable Fe and occurrence of metal sulphide in anaerobic incubations of three soil mixes.

Soil	Days of incubation							24
	0	1	4	7	*12	17	24	Sulphide-S $(mg\ kg^{-1})$
				% Fe^{2+}				
A	3.0	2.0	5.6	34	52	51	56	50
B	3.0	3.5	10	40	55	52	60	71
C	13	15	24	54	63	60	67	176

* Black metal sulphide first visible in vials on day 12.

Black metal sulphide was first evident visually in the vials at day 12 and it was most apparent in soil C. It was only in this soil that all replicates developed clear black staining. At the end of the incubation period substantially more sulphide was present in soil C. In this experiment the large differences in reducible

Fe had a rather small apparent effect on reduction processes. It seems likely that the redox buffering effect was masked to some extent by the large input of lactic acid. In field conditions less readily utilisable organic matter would have been present and therefore the fall in E_h less dramatic. A semi-quantitative estimate of sulphide was made on days 12 and 17 by the PbAc paper blackening method described by (Adams and Smith, 1993). The results suggested that a given amount of metal sulphide was more visible the sandier the soil so that the smaller specific surface area of sandy soils may increase the 'visibility' of any sulphide present.

4. Conclusions
Black layer formation is less likely in acidic soils than in neutral or near neutral ones.

A biodegradable adjuvant or ameliorant applied to golf greens will contribute to other naturally produced sources of energy for soil microorganisms and increase the risk of black layer formation in anoxic conditions.

Reducible Fe^{3+} compounds in soils, can act as a redox buffer delaying the onset of sulphide production. These are present in smaller amounts in golf green rootzones.

References

Adams, W.A. and Gibbs, R.J. (1994) **Natural Turf for Sport and Amenity: Science and Practice.** CAB International, Wallingford, UK.

Adams, W.A. and Smith, J.N.G. (1993) Chemical properties of rootzones containing a black layer and some factors affecting sulphide production, in **International Turfgrass Society Research Journal,** 7 (eds. R. N. Carrow, N.E. Christians and R.C. Sherman. Intertec Publishing Corp. Overland Park, Kansas, pp136-141.

Beard, J.B. (1988) Why has black layer increased? **Grounds Maintenance,** 22, 10.

Burpee, L.L. and Anderson, A. (1987) The cause of black layer in golf greens: an alternative hypothesis. **Greens Master,** 23, 24.

Connell, W. and Patrick, W. (1969) Reduction of sulphate to sulphide in waterlogged soil. **Soil Sci. Soc. Amer. Proc.** 33, 711-715.

Fitter, A.H. and Hay, R.K.M. (1981) **Environmental Physiology of Plants,** Academic Press.

Lubin, T. (1987) Black layer: a western view. **Divot News,** 25, 26-42.

USGA Green Section Staff (1993) USGA recommendations for a method for putting green construction. **USGA Green Section Record,** Mar/Apr 1993 pp1-3.

Vainshtein, M. and Gogotova, G. (1987) Effect of redox potential of the medium on sulphide production by sulphate-reducing bacteria. **Mikrobiologiya** (English translation) 56, 31-35.

68 The role of fungi on the development of water-repellent soils on UK golf greens

C.A. York
STRI, Bingley, UK
and N.W. Lepp
School of Biological and Earth Sciences, Liverpool John Moores
University, Byrom Street, Liverpool, L3 3AF, UK

Abstract
This paper outlines results obtained from assessments of *Marasmius oreades* fairy rings, which indicate that this fungus is capable of conferring a state of water-repellence to the soil through which it has passed. Soil sampled from the inner zone of *M. oreades* rings demonstrated a higher degree of water-repellence compared with soil sampled from the outer zone through which the fungal mycelium has not passed. Scanning electron microscopy has confirmed the presence of active fungal mycelium only within the so-called dead zone of the ring. This supports the conclusion that it is not the presence of the fungal mycelium itself which is causing the development of the water-repellence, but deposition of some metabolic or decay product originating from the fungus.
Keywords: *Marasmius oreades*, Water-repellent Soil, Fine Sports Turf

1 Introduction

Dry patch (localised dry spot) is a term used to describe a condition found on areas of amenity turf, characterised by the presence of water-repellent soil. The factors contributing to the development of the soil's water-repellence have been the subject of much research world-wide (Danneberger and Hudson, 1994; Howard, 1983; Karnok and Tucker, 1989; Oades, 1987), but the causal factors for this phenomenon have not been specifically identified. Much speculation exists regarding the possibility that certain soil fungi may be contributing/causing water-repellence to develop (Danneberger, 1987; Hubbell et al, 1983). Superficial fairy rings (SFR), caused by a number of basidiomycete fungi, have frequently been implicated in the development of dry patch, but soils taken from affected areas show no presence of active fungal growth (Wilkinson and Miller, 1978). Due to the fact that identification of specific fungi responsible for SFR and their isolation from the soil is extremely difficult, this study was completed on another basidiomycete, *Marasmius oreades*, which is readily identifiable on amenity turf. *M. oreades* rings have been used because of the characteristic nature of their development. The rings increase annually in diameter as the fungus moves radially outwards, producing a clearly defined 'dead' zone of bare soil which contains a high concentration of active mycelium. Inside the ring the soil contains no active mycelium, but in previous years the fungus will have passed through it. Outside the dead zone the soil does not contain the fungus, but the mycelium from the dead zone will pass into this area in subsequent years as the ring increases in size (Smith et

Science and Golf II: Proceedings of the World Scientific Congress of Golf. Edited by A.J. Cochran and M.R. Farrally. Published in 1994 by E & FN Spon, London. ISBN 0 419 18790 1

al, 1989). Thus, the *M. oreades* ring provides a clear model in which to observe changes in soil characteristics, both whilst colonised and following colonisation of the fungus compared with the same, but unaffected soil.

2   Materials and methods

Two sites were selected for this study: Ganton golf course (SE 982778) and Shipley golf course (SE 109380), which are areas of sandy loam and loam soil respectively. The *M. oreades* rings selected for sampling were located on the practice area of both golf courses.

2.1 Identification of sampling intervals
The centre of each ring included in the study was determined by measuring the radius through 360°. A marker pin was placed at the centre of the ring and a tape measure taken from the centre across the radius of the ring. Sampling locations were then identified across the radius by the placement of marker pins – one through each of the inner, dead and outer zones. The inner and outer zone markers were located 45 cm inside and outside of the dead zone marker respectively.

2.2 Sampling techniques
[1] Soil cores (25 mm diameter and 120 mm in length) were removed at each sampling interval using a zero contamination tube (Aquatrols Corporation, USA). The samples were retained inside UPVC liners and sealed at both ends to retain moisture levels. Such samples were used for the assessments of moisture content, organic matter content and severity of water-repellence, as detailed below. [2] Soil samples (10 mm x 80 mm x 120 mm) were removed using a 'plate' sampler. These samples were used for the assessment of the presence of active mycelium. Three intact and distinct rings were identified at each site and used for collection of soil samples for the following analyses:

2.3 Moisture content
Soil samples were sectioned at intervals with depth and their mass recorded. The samples were then air-dried at 20°C for 1 week before being reweighed and the percentage loss of moisture (% MC) determined.

2.4 Organic matter content
The air-dried soil samples used to determine the % MC were placed in a muffle furnace at 400°C for 6 hours to burn off the organic matter. After ignition the mass of the samples was recorded and the percentage change in mass (% OM) determined.

2.5 Severity of water-repellence (MED)
To quantify the severity of the soil's water-repellence within each zone and with depth, soil cores were sectioned at intervals with depth, air-dried, milled and sieved to ≤1.3 mm particle size, to remove both stones and the bulk of the organic matter (root material and thatch), which is in itself water-repellent and which would affect results. The sieved soil was then levelled in Petri dishes (85 mm diameter) and drops (36 µl) of increasing concentrations of aqueous ethanol solutions placed on the surface. The MED value ascribed to each sample identifies the molarity of the ethanol (drop) required to penetrate the soil in <60 seconds. This method is based on that of King (1981). MED values ≥2 are considered to represent water-repellent soil.

2.6 Presence of active mycelium

The location of active fungal mycelium within each zone and at depth, was determined by placing soil samples in humid chambers at 20°C for 5 days. After incubation the presence or absence of mycelium was recorded at each depth interval. Soil samples taken from the inner, dead and outer zones of one ring at Ganton were observed using a scanning electron microscopy (SEM).

3   Results

The mean values obtained for moisture content (%), organic matter content (%) and MED value from three *M. oreades* rings at each of the two sites are shown in Figures 1-6. Linear or curvilinear models were fitted to the observed values of measurements collected in relation to depth. Statistical analysis was not completed on the raw data collected, due to the magnitude of the differences identified between soils in the two zones and the complication which would have been included due to defining the sampling depth intervals. Results of assessments completed on soil samples taken from the dead zone of the fairy rings sampled are not shown because it is the comparison between results obtained from the inner and outer zones which has most relevance to this work. Assessments of the presence of active fungal mycelium with depth in each of the three zones of the *M. oreades* rings at both of the sites selected for study, indicated that active mycelium was present at all depth intervals observed within the dead zone only. No active mycelium was seen in soil from either the inner or the outer zone at either site. SEM observations on soil samples taken from the inner, dead and outer zones of the *M. oreades* rings at Ganton golf course, confirm the absence of fungal mycelium from within both the inner and outer zones. The active fungal mycelium was confirmed as being present only within the dead zone, as shown by the growth of the mycelium within a humid chamber. Figures 1-3 inclusive show results obtained from fairy rings sampled at Ganton golf course. Mean moisture content values are shown to be 8% higher at 20-40 mm depth in soil taken from the outer zone when compared with those recorded for soil from the inner zone of the rings (Figure 1). A similar result is seen with the data obtained for mean organic matter content of soil taken from the same areas where values are 3% higher at 20-40 mm depth in the outer zone compared with the inner zone (Figure 2). Figure 3 shows that the MED values obtained were greater for soil taken from the inner zone, compared with soil from the outer zone at all depths assessed. The same trend can also be seen in Figures 4-6 inclusive, which show results obtained from the same assessments completed on soil taken from fairy rings sampled at Shipley golf course.

4   Discussion

The results from this study show that irrespective of the course sampled (soil type), the outer zone through which the fungal mycelium has not passed, shows higher levels of organic matter and correspondingly higher levels of moisture content, compared with the same soil within the inner zone. This reduction in organic matter content of soils from the inner zone will result from the action of the mycelium which has previously passed through it, breaking down the organic matter to release nutrients in a form which will become available to the fungus for its development and progress through the soil. With a lower

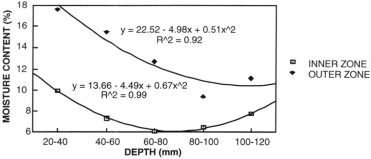

Figure 1. Moisture content of soil with depth across *M. oreades* rings at Ganton golf course

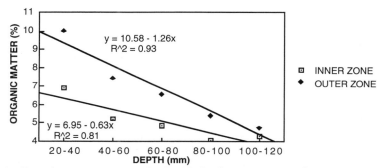

Figure 2. Organic matter content of soil with depth across *M. oreades* rings at Ganton golf course

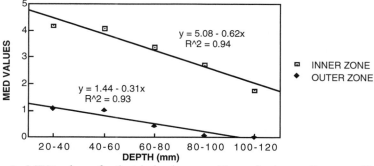

Figure 3. MED values of soil with depth across *M. oreades* rings at Ganton golf course

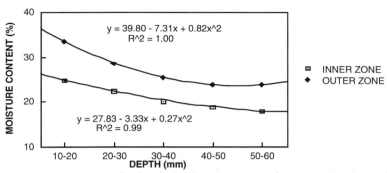

Figure 4. Moisture content of soil with depth across *M. oreades* rings at Shipley golf course

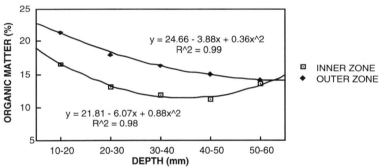

Figure 5. Organic matter content of soil with depth across *M. oreades* rings at Shipley golf course

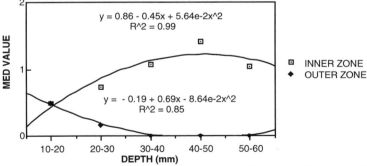

Figure 6. MED values of soil with depth across *M. oreades* rings at Shipley golf course

organic matter content the soil will be capable of holding less available moisture, as observed in these results.

The results obtained relating to the level of water-repellence within the soil could in part be explained by the presence of organic matter within the soil fractions. However, the observation that higher levels of water-repellence are present within soil fractions taken from the inner zone, where the corresponding levels of soil organic matter content are low, suggests that some other factor is present which is contributing to this repellence as observed. It has been suggested (Howard, 1983) that water-repellence may be the result of the deposition of a compound within the soil profile and if this theory is to be believed, the higher the sand content of the soil and hence the lower the surface area : volume ratio, the greater the severity of water-repellence present.

The mean MED values obtained from the soil of the inner zone of the rings at Ganton golf course are higher than those observed from the corresponding zone of the rings sampled at Shipley golf course. This can be accounted for by the nature of the soil present at each of the sites. At Ganton golf course the soil has a higher sand content than that at Shipley golf course. If the fungus is effecting a deposition and subsequent build up of a water-repellent material within the soil through which it passes, either directly via its metabolism or as a result of its decomposition, the severity of the symptoms resulting from this build up of repellent material should be greater in a soil offering a smaller surface area to allow the deposition to occur.

The results included in this account are part of an extensive study of *M. oreades* rings and their possible involvement in the development of water-repellence in soils. The results show that the severity of water-repellence is increased in soils through which the fungus has passed, when compared with soil which has not been colonised. This suggests that in some way the fungus has a role to play in the development of this condition. Further research is necessary to fully identify the precise nature of the water-repellent material which is present in these soils and to show conclusively the actual means by which this water-repellence develops.

5   References

Danneberger, K. (1987) Those summertime blues : localised dry spot. **Grounds Maintenance**, 22, 5, 30-32.

Danneberger, T.K. and Hudson, R.A. (1994) Characterisation of localised dry spots on creeping bentgrass turf in the United States. In this volume.

Howard, D. (1983) Dry patch. **New Zealand Turf Culture Inst.**, 143, 4-5.

Hubbell, G.D., Isabell, R.F. and Northcliffe, K.H. (1983) Water-repellence. In: **Soils, an Australian Viewpoint**. Div. Soils, CSIRO, Town, County/Country.

Karnok, K.J. and Tucker, K.A. (1989) The cause and control of localised dry spot on bentgrass greens. **Golf Course Management**, 57, 8, 28-34.

King, P.M. (1981) Comparison of methods for measuring severity of water repellence of sandy soils and assessment of some factors that affect its measurement. **Aust. J. Soil Res.**, 19, 275-285.

Oades, J.M. (1987) Non-wetting sands. **Uni. Adelaide, Waite Agric. Res. Inst. Report**, pp. 8-15.

Smith, J.D., Jackson, N. and Woolhouse, A.R. (1989) Fairy rings. In: **Fungal Diseases of Amenity Turfgrasses**. E. and F.N. Spon, London.

69 Subterranean insects and fungi: hidden costs and benefits to the greenkeeper

A.C. Gange
Department of Biology, Royal Holloway, University of London

Abstract
It is suggested that long-term application of fungicide to golf
courses has reduced the abundance of mycorrhizal fungi in the
soil. These fungi are abundant in nature and are beneficial to
plants, as they increase growth and competitive ability by enhancing nutrient uptake. They also render plants more resistant
to insect attack. It is shown that in one golf course the fungi
were sporadic and that their occurrence may be related to insect
distribution and the prevalence of desirable grasses. By re-in-
troducing these fungi into turf, we could perhaps establish a
natural pest protection system, and favour the growth of desirable grasses relative to weeds.
Keywords: Mycorrhiza, Poa annua, Agrostis stolonifera, Agrostis
capillaris, Insects, Pests.

1 Introduction

The production of fine quality turf is the prime concern of the
greenkeeper. However, root-feeding insects or foliar pathogenic
fungi can disrupt the process of turf culture, resulting in
poorer quality playing surfaces. The two most common pest insects in turfgrass are subterranean larvae of chafer beetles
(Coleoptera: Scarabaeidae) and crane flies (Leatherjackets; Diptera: Tipulidae) (Gratwick, 1992). The presence of larvae in
golf turf may pass unnoticed until damage levels are extensive.
In addition, as the larvae may be deep in the soil, insecticide
application is often ineffective. Although various pesticides
are approved for the larval control, sometimes these may have to
be applied frequently and in large quantities, to achieve some
level of adequate control. Clearly, this is not a satisfactory
situation, as large volumes could result in runoff and the entry
of pesticides into groundwater (e.g. Sudo and Kunimatsu, 1992).
   Arbuscular-mycorrhizal fungi are found in the soil of all ter-
restrial ecosystems, where they form mutualistic associations
with the roots of over 70% of plant species (Allen, 1991). The
association is considered to be beneficial to both partners, as
the fungus has a much greater ability than the plant to take up
nutrients (nitrate and phosphate), which it donates to the plant.
In return there is a transfer of carbon from plant to fungus, as
the fungus cannot obtain this on its own. However, it has been

Science and Golf II: Proceedings of the World Scientific Congress of Golf. Edited by A.J.
Cochran and M.R. Farrally. Published in 1994 by E & FN Spon, London. ISBN 0 419 18790 1

stated that mycorrhizal fungi could be detrimental in turfgrass, as the donation of carbon to the fungus could mean that the fungus becomes parasitic on the plant, thus reducing its growth (Smith, et al., 1989). This idea is contrary to current ideas of mycorrhizal functioning and there is therefore an urgent need to establish whether these fungi are beneficial or detrimental to grass plants in a golf course.

A recent paper (Gange et al., 1994) has shown that mycorrhizal fungi may provide a hitherto unrecognised benefit to plants, in that they can render plant roots less susceptible to insect attack. Clearly, if this can be exploited, then we may have a naturally occurring method of plant protection against these pests.

Currently, we have no information on the abundance of mycorrhizal fungi in golf turf. The aim of this paper is to provide an example of chafer presence in turf and present some of the first evidence of mycorrhizal occurrence in golf greens.

2 Materials and methods

2.1 Insect sampling

In October 1990, a golf tee measuring 144m^2, known to have an infestation of *Phyllopertha horticola* (Garden Chafer) was selected for sampling. Details of the tee preparation and history are provided in Gange et al. (1991). One hundred quadrats, each 25cm x 25cm, were randomly positioned and the abundance of all plant species in each quadrat estimated by counting the number of 5cm x 5cm 'cells' in which they occurred. The quadrat was then excavated to a depth of 10cm, and all chafer larvae counted. The main data set was reported in Gange et al. (1991) and a subset is presented here.

2.2 Fungal sampling

In October 1993, five soil cores (each 1.5cm diameter) were taken from random positions in all 18 greens on a golf course. Each core was examined under a binocular microscope and the number of tillers of each grass species present were counted. The roots of each grass species in each green were pooled and a random sample were stained for mycorrhizal fungi, using the method of Koske and Gemma (1989). Linear regression analysis was used to examine the relations between mycorrhizal infection and grass abundance, using each green as a replicate. Mycorrhizal spores were extracted from soil by centrifugation and identified to species using Schenck and Perez (1990).

2.3 Interactions between insects and fungi

Larvae of *P. horticola* were reared on the roots of *Agrostis capillaris* in a constant environment room, maintained at 20°C. Plants were grown in 13cm diameter flower pots, in sterilized compost. There were two treatments: 1) mycorrhizal, in which plants were infected with an inoculum of the fungus, *Glomus mosseae* and non-mycorrhizal, in which plants received sterilized inoculum. Two first instar larvae were introduced into each pot; this density is equivalent to 150m^{-2}. Larvae were weighed before

and after the experiment (90 days) and growth rates calculated.
There were ten replicates of each treatment.

3 Results

3.1 Insect abundance
The mean number (± standard error) of chafer larvae per quadrat
was 20.55 ± 1.1; this equates to a mean of 328.8 m^{-2} , with a
range of 16-784 m^{-2}. This was clearly a bad infestation, being
greatly in excess of the recognised economic damage levels for
this insect in pasture (Gratwick, 1992). The larvae were found
to be highly aggregated, with the overall distribution closely
fitting a negative binomial (Gange et al., 1991).
   There was a significant, positive, non linear relation between
the abundance of chafer larvae and that of A. capillaris in each
quadrat (F$_{2,97}$ = 26.4, P < 0.001; r^2 = 0.352) (Fig. 1). Larvae
were therefore aggregating towards this species and accentuating
damage to the grass.

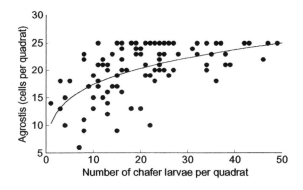

Fig.1. Relation between A. capillaris and P. horticola

3.2 Fungal abundance
The dominant grass in all greens was Poa annua (Annual Meadow
Grass). A. stolonifera and Festuca rubra were also present.
   There was a significant positive relation between the abundance (number of tillers per core) of A. stolonifera and mycorrhizal fungi (F$_{1,15}$ = 5.5, P < 0.05; r^2 = 0.269) (Fig. 2).
Therefore, greens which contained the greatest levels of fungal
inoculum in the soil also had the greatest density of tillers of
this grass. It must be acknowledged that the r^2 value in this
case is relatively low and clearly a number of other factors,
such as mowing height and frequency and trampling by golfers, are
likely to determine A. stolonifera abundance.

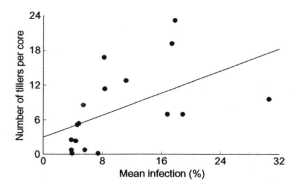

Fig. 2. Relation between abundance of *A. stolonifera* and mycorrhizal fungi.

In contrast to *A. stolonifera*, there was a significant negative relation between abundance of *Poa annua* and mycorrhizal infection ($F_{1,16}$ = 5.2, P < 0.05; r^2 = 0.244) (Fig. 3)

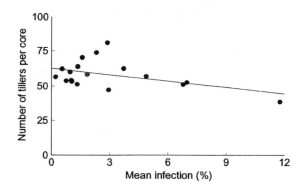

Fig. 3. Relation between abundance of *P. annua* and mycorrhizal
fungi.

The important features of Figs. 2 and 3 are the differences in
the axes. *P. annua* was considerably more abundant than *A. stolonifera*, but was also much less mycorrhizal. Even in cores
where the *A. stolonifera* was heavily infected with fungus, the *P.
annua* consistently had very low levels of infection. The dominant fungus in the greens was *Glomus mosseae*, comprising 63% of
all spores identified. *G. fasciculatum* was the next abundant at
26%. In total, 7% of spores could not be identified with cer-
tainty.

3.3 Interactions between insects and fungi

Mycorrhizal presence significantly reduced the survival of insect larvae. In fungus pots, survival was 43.2% , while in fungus-free pots it was 65.8% (t = 3.44, P < 0.001). The mean growth rate of the larvae was also significantly reduced by the mycorrhiza. With the fungus present, this was $0.023 mgmg^{-1}day^{-1}$, while without fungus it was 0.035 $mgmg^{-1}day^{-1}$ (t = 3.97, P < 0.001). Therefore, the presence of a mycorrhizal association in the roots of *A. capillaris* renders these roots considerably more resistant to larval attack.

4 Discussion

Insect pests, such as chafer larvae can cause serious damage to golf turf. The damage is often sporadic and does not appear to be easily predictable in time or space (Gange *et al.*, 1991). One reason for this is the highly aggregated nature of the larvae, meaning that large areas of turf will always be unaffected in any one year. Part of this aggregation stems from the clumped oviposition habit of the female (Milne 1963), but these results show that the larvae also aggregate towards grass roots. This may seem surprising as the mycorrhizal fungus renders roots less susceptible to insect attack, but infects grasses in the turf.

However, a striking feature of these results is the low level of mycorrhiza which appears to be present in golf turf. In natural grasslands of similar age, one would expect the infection level of *A. stolonifera* (or *A. capillaris*) roots to be about 80%. However, in this study, only one green had a mean infection of 30%, while the majority were below 10%. A number of fungicides are regularly applied to golf turf and one (iprodione) has been shown to be very effective in reducing mycorrhizas in developing grassland (Gange *et al.*, 1990). In that study, reducing mycorrhizal infection led to significant decreases in the growth of a number of plants. Therefore, fungicides may have reduced mycorrhizas in golf turf, so that the grass plants receive little growth benefit. Any potential resistance against subterranean insects demonstrated here and with other root feeders (Gange *et al.*, 1994) could also be lost. Chafer larvae can therefore aggregate towards grasses because the grass has lost much of its natural protection. It remains to be seen if these conclusions hold true for leatherjackets, the most prevalent pest of golf turf.

Another feature of the greens was the abundance of *P. annua* and its negative relation to mycorrhizal infection. As *P. annua* is an annual grass, one would not expect it to form strong mycorrhizal associations, unlike the perennial *A. stolonifera* (Allen, 1991). I suggest that reducing mycorrhizal inoculum means that the growth of *A. stolonifera* is impaired, as its nutrient uptake is reduced. As a result, this grass species is less vigourous and less able to compete with the fast growing *P. annua*. In addition, as *P. annua* can continually regenerate from seed in a golf green (Lush, 1988), it will always dominate the sward if the *A. stolonifera* is weak. Fungicide thus alters the balance of competition in favour of the non-mycorrhizal grass. Fertilizer application is unlikely to alleviate the situation as the *A. stolonifera* root system, without the fungus, cannot take advantage of the increased nutrients to the extent which it could with the fungus.

It is generally agreed that the combined action of mowing and trampling tips the competitive balance in favour of *P. annua*. As the results here are from regularly-used greens, it is suggested that despite these other factors, mycorrhizas may also affect the competitive balance. However, another interpretation of these results could be that patches of *A. stolonifera* result in high fungal inoculum availability. This is unlikely, as the same fungus infects both grasses, but *P. annua* was not more colonised when *A. stolonifera* was most infected. In addition, fungal presence was measured as root infection, not inoculum availability.

Clearly, we now need to perform laboratory experiments with the grasses under different management regimes, with and without mycorrhizas. In addition, we need to establish the generality of these results with other insects and in different soil types. However, these results suggest that mycorrhizal fungi are beneficial and not detrimental to golf turf production. If inoculum could be re-introduced into turf, then we may have a natural pest protection system, as well as favouring the growth of desirable grasses against weed species.

5 References

Allen, M.F. (1991) **The Ecology of Mycorrhizae.** Cambridge University Press, Cambridge.

Gange, A.C. Brown, V.K. and Farmer, L.M.(1990) A test of mycorrhizal benefit in an early successional plant community. **New Phytol.**, 115, 85-91.

Gange, A.C. Brown, V.K.Barlow, G.S. Whitehouse, D.M. and Moreton, R.J. (1991) Spatial distribution of garden chafer larvae in a golf tee. **J. Sports Turf Res. Inst.**, 67, 8-13.

Gange, A.C. Brown, V.K. and Sinclair, G.S. (1994) Reduction of black vine weevil larval growth by vesicular-arbuscular mycorrhizal infection. **Ent. Exp. Appl.**, in press.

Gratwick, M. (1992) **Crop Pests in the U.K.** Chapman and Hall, London.

Koske, R. E. and Gemma, J. N. (1989) A modified procedure for staining roots to detect VA mycorrhizas. **Mycol. Res.**, 92, 486-488.

Lush, W.M. (1988) Biology of *Poa annua* in a temperate zone golf putting green (*Agrostis stolonifera/Poa annua*). II. The seed bank. **J. Appl. Ecol.**, 25, 989-997.

Milne, A. (1963) Biology and ecology of the garden chafer, *Phyllopertha horticola* (L.) IX. Spatial distribution. **Bull. Ent. Res.**, 54, 761-795.

Smith, J.D. Jackson, N.J. and Woolhouse, A.R. (1989) **Fungal Diseases of Amenity Turf Grasses.** E. and F.N. Spon, London.

Schenck, N.C. and Perez, Y. (1990) **Manual for the Identification of VA Mycorrhizal fungi.** Synergistic Publications, Gainesville, Florida.

Sudo, M. and Kunimatsu, T. (1992) Characteristics of pesticide runoff from golf links. **Water Sci. Technol.**, 25, 85-92.

70 A golf club on a volcano

J.R. Gomez
Department of Golf Studies, Royal Golf Club of Las Palmas, Grand
Canary, Canary Islands

Abstract
This paper describes a golf club on a volcano and evaluates
possiblites it offers. The optimal location was made taking into
consideration several geographic peculiarities. These included
sea level, benign wind and volcanic drainage.
Keywords: Volcanic Material, Bioclimatic Pocket, Drainage,
Natural contours.

Introduction

The Royal Golf Club of Las Palmas , (founded 1891), located
inside the Bandama Natural Park on the Atlantic island of Grand
Canary, haves an unusual character. This is brought about by the
peculiarities of the geography (plate 1) and soils amongst
other factors and particularly the climatic circumstance of the
zone.

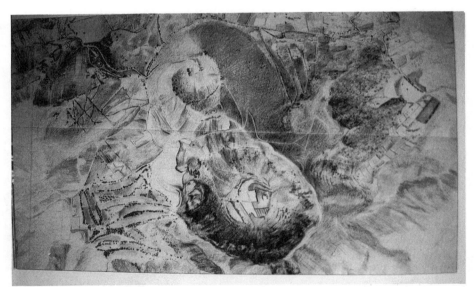

Plate 1 - An aerial view : the crater of La Caldera and the new
course at Royal Golf Club of Las Palmas, in Bandama, Grand
Canary.

We place special emphasis on the fact that 18 holes of this
club, one of the oldest in Europe, are constructed in a situation

Science and Golf II: Proceedings of the World Scientific Congress of Golf. Edited by A.J.
Cochran and M.R. Farrally. Published in 1994 by E & FN Spon, London. ISBN 0 419 18790 1

not normally associated with the practice of the sport of golf. That is, land evolved over thousands of years by successive volcanic eruptions into now dormant mountains and craters and juxtaposed with the club buildings, constructed some decades ago.

From the above circumstances and because of the intrinsic value of familiarising you with this club, we make reference to the three hundred and ninety one thousand square metres which constitute the club, located on a plateau three hundred metres above sea level on the extreme north east of the island of Grand Canary. To get a better grasp, we must picture the course, laid out among accumulated volcanic material and tempered by an erosion process from over nine millions years ago during a period known as Pleistoceno-Holoceno in which the most recent deposits are from eruptions dating fron 6 thousand and 3 thousand year B.C. This explains how this place developed from magma and lava extrusions in an age between the middle Miocene and recent history. A geomorphological accident which has thrown up a unique location.

2   Location, climate and layout

Let us contemplate this promontory at six hundred metres above sea level, and evaluate what possiblities it offered as a location for a golf course (plate 2) and the climatic micro system it created. The location enjoys a gentle sub-tropical breeze during the greater part of the year. The architect and designer of the course was Philip Mackenzie Ross (1890- 1974), his was the felicitous idea to wed the two elements of landscape and breeze which are so characteristic of this course.

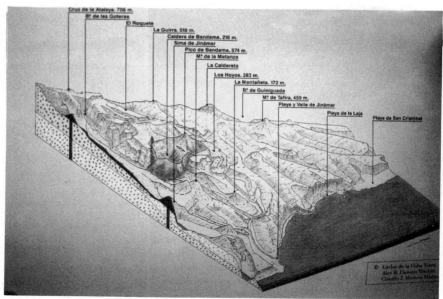

Plate 2   - Profile of the landforms in the canarian relief of Bandama (a work by De la Coba / Hansen / Moreno)

Furthermore, Mackenzie, this notable son of Edimburgh, took

advantage of the circumstances and adapted the course to them, planning various holes in different directions, most notably the first nine, which are adapted to take into consideration the prevailing breeze. This benign wind around 15 or 20 kilometres an hour contributes new and tantalizing difficulties to the terrain in play, this constitutes one of the course's great attractions.

Mackenzie's work on the island of Grand Canary throws up other facets. For example, it is worth mentioning the way he employed the channels created by the volcanic extrusions, all this in the most scrupulous fashion, resulting in a golf course so personal and distinctive it carried his fingerprint. Contrary to some theories of course design prevalent at the time, he opted, with the exception of the second hole, to adapt his project to the natural contours of the Bandama-Atalaya Plain as the maps of the period designate the zone. Similarly he took into account the existing bioclimatic pockets in his location of the greens.

It is obvious that the Royal Golf Club of Las Palmas, the second to be built on the island (an early course had been built in what is now the city of Las Palmas), can, in every respect, be considered an outstanding example of the unusual in the context of this particular sporting discipline. We might add to those points already mentioned, the extraordinary capacity of the terrain to absorb, in the shortest time, substantial rainfall. In fact, in this zone which receives annually 300 to 400 litres per square metre and as much as 179 litres in the winter period, the volcanic drainage is so efficient that the course can be played at whatever time. Apart from allowing the game to be played this same phenomenon helps preserve the course in the state in which it was initially conceived.

Table 1   Average temperature and rains (1992)

MOUNTH	DEGREES	RAINS(days)
January	18C	7
February	18C	8
March	19C	5
April	20C	5
May	23C	2
June	25C	1
July	26C	0
August	27C	0
September	25C	1
October	22C	2
November	20C	3
December	20C	6

3 Conclusions

Whichever way we look at it, this golf course on the Canary Islands is here (plate 3) to be enjoyed with all its peculiarities and idiosyncracies; as mentioned some natural, some fortuitous and some by the art of the course designer. All this enveloped by the uniquely benign Canarian weather. The mean average temperature in winter is 17 degrees Celsius, and there is a wealth of flora (such species as <u>Phoenix canariensis</u>, <u>Pistacia lentiscus</u>, <u>Laurus azórica</u>, <u>Olea europecea</u>, <u>Pinus canariensis</u>, <u>Draco draconea</u>,etc.).

All in all a portfolio of peculiarities and distinctly unique personality, a combination of exotic nature and inspired human intervention have contrived together to produce a most peculiar phenomenon, almost as peculiar, were it possible, as the game of golf itself!

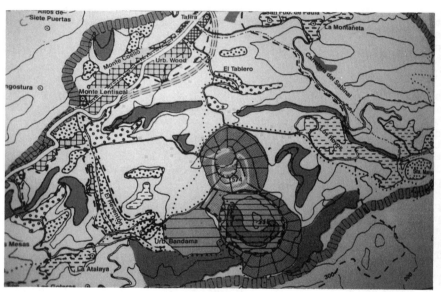

Plate. 3.   A pictorial view : La Caldera and Royal Golf Club of Las Palmas, in Bandama, Grand Canary (a work by Carlos Arocha Isidro).

References

Hansen Machin, (1993), "Bandama , paisaje y evolución". Cabildo Insular de Gran Canaria, área de Política Territorial, Arquitectura y Medio Ambiente y Vivienda. Las Palmas of Grand Canary. Canary Islands.

Antonio Santana Santana/Agustín Naranjo Cigala (1992), "El relive de Gran Canaria", Libreria Nogal Ediciones, Las Palmas of Grand Canary, Canary Islands.

Montelongo / Acosta ,(1994), Consejería de Urbanismo, Arquitectura y Medio Ambiente ,Cabildo Insular de Gran Canaria,

Cornish S./ Whitten E., (1981)"The Architects of the golf " (1981) HarperCollins Publishers, New York. United States of America.

71 Response of creeping bentgrass (*Agrostis palustris*) to natural organic fertilizers

C.H. Peacock and J.M. Dipaola
North Carolina State University, Raleigh, North Carolina

Abstract

Response of creeping bentgrass (*Agrostis palustris*) maintained under putting green conditions to nitrogen (N) fertilizers can be characterized based on turf quality, growth response and N uptake. With the natural organic materials, source of the N carrier can influence longevity of turf response and N availability. This study evaluated natural organic and synthetic N carriers and combinations. Creeping bentgrass was fertilized at either 5 or 7.5 g N m^{-2} rates with ten N sources over a two year period. Turf performance was evaluated during the fall and spring based on turf quality, growth rates, and N uptake rates. A rate response was found for all parameters. Based on nitrogen uptake rates, products containing natural organic carriers combining bone meal, feather meal, wheat germ and soybean meal were most efficient at providing N for plant growth. By comparison, these materials had a N uptake rate seasonal average 100% higher than a sewage sludge based material which had the same water insoluble nitrogen (WIN) content.
Keywords: Bentgrass, Nitrogen, Turfgrass growth.

1 Introduction

Probably no category of turf fertilizer has seen expansion like that which has occurred among the "organics" over the last few years. Materials which have been used as nitrogen (N) carriers in natural organic fertilizers include blood meal, bone meal, animal tankage, soybean meal, feather meal, sewage sludge and compost. These materials vary greatly in the percent nitrogen from a low of 1% up to 14% which is close to the maximum of pure protein at 16% N. The sustained release of N from these materials can vary from 6 to 16 weeks depending on mineralization rate which is dependent on environmental conditions which favor degradation, adequate soil moisture and temperature, and the source of the carrier and how it is processed resulting in the percent Water Insoluble Nitrogen in the actual product

Science and Golf II: Proceedings of the World Scientific Congress of Golf. Edited by A.J. Cochran and M.R. Farrally. Published in 1994 by E & FN Spon, London. ISBN 0 419 18790 1

(Power and Papendick, 1985). Comparisons among different natural organic carriers with similar water insoluble nitrogen (WIN) content and in contrast to synthetic carriers are not well documented.

　　　　This study was conducted to compare the performance of creeping bentgrass (*Agrostis palustris*) to commercial fertilizer products based on natural organic, synthetic, and a combination of natural organic and synthetic carriers. Performance was evaluated by comparing turf quality, growth rates and nitrogen uptake rates over a period of regrowth.

2 Methods and Materials

An existing area of 'Penncross' creeping bentgrass grown on a USGA soil profile was used for the study. Plot size was 1 x 2 m with 4 replications. Fertilizer materials and application dates were as shown in Table 1. Plots were mowed at

Table 1. Fertilizer materials evaluated in study. Applications were made in 1991 on 10/25 and 12/9; in 1992 on 2/10, 5/1, 10/2, 11/13; and in 1993 on 2/11, 3/25 and 5/7. All poultry manures were composted materials.

Product	Analysis	Percent WIN	Nitrogen Carriers
Harmony	9-0.9-3.3	60	Poultry manure, urea ureaformaldehyde
Harmony	14-1.3-5	60	Poultry manure, urea ureaformaldehyde
Harmony	6-0.9-9.9	60	Poultry manure, urea ureaformaldehyde
Ringer[†]	6-0.4-2.5	90	Bone meal, feather meal wheatgerm, soybean meal
Ringer[†]	10-0.9-5	90	Bone meal, feather meal wheatgerm, soybean meal
Milorganite[‡]	6-0.9-0	90	Sewage sludge
IBDU[‡]	31-0-0	90	Isobutylidenediurea
Nutralene[‡]	41-0-0	36	Methylene urea polymer
Urea[‡]	45-0-0	0	Urea
Ammonium nitrate[‡]	33-0-0	0	Ammonium nitrate

[†] An inoculum was added to the material consisting of a proprietary blend of soil microorganisms containing, but not limited to, *Bacillus* sp., *Trichoderma* sp., enzymes, and actinomycetes with approximately 1.25×10^6 CFU g^{-1}.
[‡] Phosphorus and potassium were added to match the Harmony 14-1.3-5 ratio. All P and K ratios are expressed as elemental content, not oxides.

4.8 mm three times weekly and irrigated to prevent moisture stress. Turf quality was periodically evaluated on a 1 to 9 scale, 9=best. Growth rates were determined by mowing, allowing a period of regrowth, harvesting all leaf tissue above the cutting height and drying at 80 C for 48 hrs. A growth rate was calculated averaged over the regrowth period. An aliquot of the harvested tissue was analyzed for nitrogen content. All data were subjected to analysis of variance and mean separation was by the Waller-Duncan K ratio t-test, K ratio=100.

3 Results and Discussion

For the 1991-92 growing season, there was an overall rate response for turf quality with all materials (Table 2). At the 5 g N m^{-2} rate the best performance was from

Table 2. Seasonal averages of creeping bentgrass turf quality (TQ), growth rates (GR) and nitrogen uptake rates (NUP) in response to fertilizer sources, 1991-92.

Material	5 g N m^{-2} rate			7.5 g N m^{-2} rate		
	TQ[†]	GR[†]	NUP[†]	TQ	GR	NUP
Harmony 9-0.9-3.3	5.5lm[‡]	0.71h-k	27i-k	6.2h-k	1.07de	44def
Harmony 14-1.3-5	6.1ijk	0.66i-l	25i-m	6.8def	0.96efg	39fgh
Ringer 6-0.4-2.5	5.7klm	0.85fgh	34ghi	6.9cde	1.74a	80a
Ringer 10-0.9-5	5.3lm	0.80ghi	32hij	7.0b-e	1.25c	58c
Milorganite	4.5o	0.51lm	17m	5.7klm	0.73hij	29ijk
IBDU	6.1ij	0.65i-l	26i-m	6.8def	1.06de	48de
Nutralene	6.3g-j	0.70h-k	28i-l	7.4abc	1.13cd	50cde
Urea	6.8efg	1.15cd	51cd	7.4abc	1.58ab	78a
Ammonium Nitrate	6.7e-h	0.99def	42efg	7.5ab	1.50b	67b

† TQ on a 1 to 9 scale, 9=best; GR in g m^{-2} d^{-1}; NUP in mg m^{-2} d^{-1}.

‡ Means in columns for the same parameter followed by the same letter are not significantly different.

urea and ammonium nitrate although performance with Nutralene was equivalent to urea. The Harmony 14-1.3-5 and IBDU were intermediate in performance. At the 7.5 g N m^{-2} rate, urea, ammonium nitrate and Nutralene performed best with IBDU and all of the organics intermediate. In the 1992-93 growing season, there was an overall rate response from urea, Nutralene, IBDU, Harmony 14-1.3-5, Ringer 6-0.4-2.5 and Ringer 10-0.9-5 (Table 3). At both the 5 and 7.5 g N m^{-2} rates, urea, ammonium nitrate, Nutralene and IBDU performed best. The organic materials were not equivalent, but performance was good.

There was an overall rate response with growth rates for all materials in 1991-92 (Table 2). With the 5 g N m^{-2} the greatest rates were with urea and ammonium nitrate with Nutralene, IBDU, the Ringer and Harmony materials intermediate. At the 7.5 g N m^{-2} rate the Ringer 6-0.4-2.5 and urea were greater. Among the organic materials the Ringer product was best. In 1992-93, there was an overall rate response for growth rates for the Harmony 14-1.3-5, Ringer 6-0.4-2.5, Ringer 10-0.9-5, IBDU and Nutralene (Table 3). At 5 g N m^{-2} all materials were

Table 3. Seasonal averages of creeping bentgrass turf quality (TQ), growth rates (GR) and nitrogen uptake rates (NUP) in response to fertilizer sources, 1992-93.

Material	5 g N m^{-2} rate			7.5 g N m^{-2} rate		
	TQ[†]	GR[†]	NUP[†]	TQ	GR	NUP
Harmony 6-0.9-9.9	6.0hij[‡]	1.2b-f	49g-k	6.2fgh	1.5bcd	67d-h
Harmony 14-1.3-5	5.9h-k	1.3c-g	59f-j	6.5ef	1.7b	81cde
Ringer 6-0.4-2.5	5.5lm	1.4b-e	68d-g	6.3efg	2.4a	115a
Ringer 10-0.9-5	6.1ghi	1.4b-e	64e-i	6.5de	2.0a	101ab
Milorganite	5.3m	0.9ghi	40jkl	5.6klm	1.1d-h	52g-k
IBDU	7.1c	1.1e-i	49h-k	7.6a	1.6bc	88bc
Nutralene	6.9cd	1.0f-i	47i-l	7.6a	1.4b-e	73c-f
Urea	7.0c	1.2c-g	60f-i	7.5ab	1.6bc	85bcd
Ammonium Nitrate	7.2bc	1.3b-e	64e-i	7.5ab	1.5bcd	74c-f

† TQ on a 1 to 9 scale, 9=best; GR in g m^{-2} d^{-1}; NUP in mg m^{-2} d^{-1}.

‡ Means in columns for the same parameter followed by the same letter are not significantly different.

equivalent. At 7.5 g N m^{-2} the best growth performance was with the Ringer 6-0.4-2.5 and 10-0.9-5, although there was good growth from all others except Milorganite.

For the nitrogen uptake rates in 1991-92 there was an overall rate response for all materials. At 5 g N m^{-2} urea had the highest rate followed by ammonium nitrate with the organic materials, IBDU and Nutralene intermediate and Milorganite lowest. At 7.5 g N m^{-2} urea and Ringer 6-1-3 were highest followed by ammonium nitrate. Ringer 10-2-6, Harmony, IBDU and Nutralene were intermediate and Milorganite lowest. In the 1992-93 growing season there was a rate response for all materials except Milorganite. At 5 g N m^{-2} the Ringer 6-1-3 was highest although not different from all but Milorganite. At 7.5 g N m^{-2} the

Ringer materials had the highest rates with all others intermediate except for Milorganite which was lowest.

Nitrogen uptake efficiency based on seasonal averages and individual observation dates found that with the natural organic materials the source of the carrier did play a pivotal role in performance. In 1991-92, the Ringer 6-0.4-2.5 product performed equally to urea and better than ammonium nitrate; in 1992-93 the Ringer 6-0.4-2.5 material was the best performer with the Ringer 10-0.9-5 equivalent. While few differences in N uptake rates are noted as temperatures are declining in the fall and through early winter (Figs. 1 & 2), as temperatures warmed, the Ringer products had quicker N availability based on uptake rates. This would indicate the bone meal, feather meal, wheat germ, soybean meal combination is more readily decomposed than the manure or sewage sludge materials. The addition of inoculum to this material has not been shown to be a factor in N release based on previous work (Peacock and Daniel, 1992).

Figure 1. Creeping bentgrass nitrogen uptake rates, 1991-92.

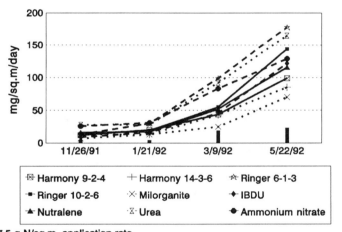

7.5 g N/sq.m. application rate
Bar indicates MSD at p=0.05.
Treatments applied 10/25, 12/9, 2/10, 5/1.

4 Conclusions

The less temperature dependent more water soluble materials gave better performance based on turf quality, although the performance from the slowly available synthetic and natural organic materials was good with the exception of

Milorganite. The greatest growth rates occurred with the less temperature dependent and more water soluble materials, but good growth occurred with most products except Milorganite. The nitrogen uptake rates were similar to growth rate data. This is consistent with previous work which had found that N release was

Figure 2. Creeping bentgrass nitrogen uptake rates, 1992-93.

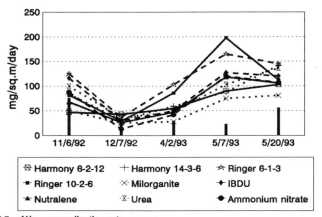

7.5 g N/sq.m. application rate
Bar indicates MSD at p=0.05.
Treatments applied 10/25, 12/9, 2/10, 5/1.

more favorable at temperatures > 16 C (Engle, 1969). Adequate nitrogen release occurred from the slowly available products to have good growth and turf quality, but not better than urea or ammonium nitrate, probably because of the time of year and the temperature dependency for nitrogen release. Among the N carriers, the Ringer products provided more readily available N for plant growth during the spring period than the other natural organic based materials.

5 References

Engle, R.E. 1969. Slow release nitrogen fertilizers on turf. Proc. 1st Int. Turgrass Res. Conf., pp. 180-184.

Peacock, C.H. and P.F. Daniel. 1992. A comparison of turfgrass response to biologically amended fertilizers. HortScience 27(8):883-884.

Power, J.F. and R..J. Papendick. 1985. Organic sources of nutrients. In Englestad, O.P. (ed) Fertilizer Technology and Use. pp. 503-520. Soil Science Soc. of Amer., Madison, WI.

72 Characterization of localised dry spots on creeping bentgrass turf in the United States

T.K. Danneberger and R.A. Hudson
Department of Agronomy, The Ohio State University, Columbus, Ohio and Ecogen, Inc., Langhorne, Pennsylvania, USA

Abstract
Localised dry spots (LDS) are a serious problem on creeping bentgrass turfs in the United States. The cause of LDS is not fully understood. Studies were conducted to provide a more complete characterization of LDS and the effect of nitrogen on the severity of LDS. Results obtained showed increased levels of extracted organic matter associated with non-wettable soils than wettable soils. The only structural difference in the extracted organic matter was observed following a methanol extraction of 3-yr-old green. It appears there is either a unique organic structure, or interaction between several structures occurring in LDS areas. Nitrogen applications tended to reduce the severity of LDS.
Keywords: Localised Dry Spots, Turfgrass, *Agrostis palustris*, Nitrogen

1 Introduction

Localised dry spots (LDS) are irregular shaped turf areas appearing to suffer from drought stress, due to the presence of a water-repellent agent in the soil (York and Baldwin, 1992). Symptoms of LDS appear initially as irregular shaped patches of wilting turf. The turf patches progress to a brownish to tan colored turf. Frog-eye type patches, characteristic of some turfgrass patch diseases, have been observed but do not predominate. Soils underling LDS are lighter in color and lower in moisture content compared to adjacent soil profiles under healthy turf which are darker in color and higher in moisture content. In turf, LDS is primarily associated with high sand content golf greens (Tucker et al., 1990; Hudson and Danneberger, 1992). However, LDS have been observed on soils with

Science and Golf II: Proceedings of the World Scientific Congress of Golf. Edited by A.J. Cochran and M.R. Farrally. Published in 1994 by E & FN Spon, London. ISBN 0 419 18790 1

relatively high clay content (McGhie and Posner, 1980).
Generally, creeping bentgrass (*Agrostis palustris*
Huds.) is the predominant turfgrass species associated
with LDS (York and Baldwin, 1993; Danneberger,
unpublished data).

A soil is hydrophobic if the water penetration
time (WDPT) is greater than 20 seconds (Miller and
Wilkinson, 1977; Tucker et al. 1990). The
hydrophobicity has been attributed to quantitative or
qualitative difference in soil organic matter
associated with hydrophobic soils. The classes of soil
organic fractions most frequently reported as being
responsible for the non-wetting are lipids (Ma'Shum et
al. 1988), proteinaceous compounds (Bond 1964), and
alkaline extractable compounds (Miller and Wilkinson,
1977). Alkaline extractable compounds include humic
and fulvic acids; lignin, lignocellulose, and suberin
in various stages of decomposition and transformation
(Stevenson, 1984). Analysis of the organic coating on
sand particles associated with LDS yielded substances
with an infrared spectra characteristic of fulvic acids
(Miller and Wilkinson, 1977). Fulvic acids are a
diverse group of macro-molecules, common in most soils,
that are extractable in solutions with a high pH and do
not precipitate when the pH is lowered to 1 or below.

Management practices for the control of LDS are
inconsistent at best, yet the following practices have
aided in reducing symptom severity. Topdressing with
sand that contains a minimal amount of "fine"
particles. Small particles may tend to aggravate the
problem over time (Hudson and Danneberger, 1992).
Repeated core cultivation has helped reduce the
severity of LDS (Danneberger and White, 1988). Wetting
agents, which reduce the surface tension of water, have
given some degree of control for LDS, but are best used
in a preventative program (York and Baldwin, 1993).
Syringing of the greens may be used as a stop-gap
measure, but primarily serve to lower the canopy
temperature and rarely will alleviate symptoms
(Danneberger and White, 1988; Tucker et al., 1990).
Frequently, various combinations of the above
strategies are necessary, and a trial and error type
approach is needed, to achieve adequate control of LDS.

The cause of LDS is not fully understood. The two
most likely causes of LDS are soil microflora or
turfgrass plant decay (York and Baldwin, 1992). Fungi
have been implicated as a possible cause of LDS
(Wilkinson and Miller, 1978; Danneberger, 1987). Fungi
associated with the development of superficial fairy
rings on bentgrass putting greens have been shown to
have hydrophobic mycelium, although their role in the

development of soil hydrophobicity has not been
determined (Smith et al., 1989). If fungi are
potential causes of LDS, it is interesting to speculate
on what effect nitrogen might have as a cultural
control for LDS. In turf, a number of diseases caused
by fungi are known to be enhanced or reduced through
nitrogen applications (Smith et al., 1989). Nitrogen
may be a means of reducing the severity of LDS.

Studies were conducted to provide a more complete
characterization of LDS. In the first study, organic
matter found in both wettable and non-wettable sand
greens were characterized and compared. The second
study determined the role of nitrogen as a potential
management practice for controlling LDS.

2 Organic Matter Characterization

Several common classes of soil organic matter were
extracted from two different sites. Samples from both
wettable and non-wettable areas were taken from two
United States Golf Association (USGA) constructed
putting greens located at The Ohio State University
Turfgrass Research Center, Colombus with a history of
LDS (Miller and Wilkinson, 1977; Wilkinson and Miller,
1978). The greens consisted of creeping bentgrass cv.
Penncross mowed at 4.7 mm and irrigated when needed.
Samples were collected from a second site at Bent Tree
Golf Club in Sunbury, Ohio. The greens were 3-yr-old
and constructed to USGA specifications and seeded with
creeping bentgrass cv. Penneagle. Soil organic matter
extractions were done using several extraction
sequences (Hudson et al., 1993). Structural analysis
of lipids were accomplished by gas chromatography/mass
spectroscopy and the large molecules that were
extracted in alkaline solution were analyzed by
infrared spectra and nuclear magnetic resonance
spectroscopy (NMR) (Hudson et al., 1993).

All extracted organic matter fractions were
quantitatively greater in association with non-wettable
soils (Table 1). Additionally, qualitative
differences were observed following a methanol
extraction of the 3-yr-old green for the fulvic acid
NMR, as well as the presence of a C-16 lipid in the
subsequent hexane extract of the non-wettable soil that
was not observed in the wettable sample. It appears
that there is either a unique structure, or
interaction between several structures occurring in the
LDS sample. One possible scenario is that a unique
structure or structures act to "prime" the LDS areas,
and then the LDS is intensified by subsequent drying

Table 1. Comparison of relative levels of various
organic compounds between wettable and non-wettable
USGA constructed sand mixes.

Organic Fraction	Non-wettable (LDS)	Wettable
Humic acids	> quantities	< quantities
Fulvic acids	> quantities different with methanol extraction	< quantities spectra same
Lipids	> quantities C16 fatty acid present	< quantities No C16 fatty acid present

cycles, which after several years may mask the unique
component that initiated the LDS. The origin of the
organic compounds could not be determined in these
studies, but it is probably derived from bentgrass
roots, soil microflora, or both.

     Quantitative and structural differences of the
organic matter may impact the environmental fate of
various compounds applied to LDS. In a recent study,
the sorptive characteristics of carbazole and fenarimol
which have different polarities varied between the
wettable and non-wettable soils (Hudson, unpublished
data). The least polar compound (carbazole) displayed
increased sorption on non-wettable soils and the
resulting isotherm was positively correlated with
organic carbon, while no correlation occurred between
the isotherm slope and organic carbon for the more
polar compound (fenarimol). These sorption differences
may indicate different environmental fates and efficacy
of compounds applied to greens exhibiting LDS.

3 Effect of Nitrogen Rate and Carrier

A study was initiated to evaluate the effect of various
nitrogen carriers on LDS suppression. Ten nitrogen
fertiliser products were applied to a USGA constructed
"Penncross" creeping bentgrass putting green at The
Ohio State University Turfgrass Research Center with a
history of LDS. The fertilisers were applied 31 March
1993 at a nitrogen rate of 0.8 kg ha[-1]. Subsequent
applications were made every 28 d. The treated plots
measured 1.5 x 1.8 m and all treatments were replicated
four times. Visual assessment of the severity of LDS

was made 21 July and 29 July.

Nitrogen applications tended to reduce the severity of LDS but did not eliminate them (Table 2). Given the variability, CV of 54% and 46% for 21 July and 29 July rating dates respectively, no clear delination of carrier can be made. LDS appears to be more of a problem on creeping bentgrass turfs receiving minimal nitrogen applications. Increasing the nitrogen fertility program may reduce the severity of LDS. Since nitrogen alone will not control LDS, a combination of cultural practices including adequate nitrogen applications may decrease the severity of LDS.

In summary, a unique extracted organic matter structure was associated with LDS. The source of the unique structure could not be determined. However, the positive affect that nitrogen fertilization had on reducing the severity of LDS might imply that the cause is microbial in nature.

Table 2.   Effect of Nitrogen carrier on LDS applied at a rate of 0.8 kg ha^{-1} actual nitrogen on a four week schedule.

Nitrogen Source	Analysis	---- LDS Severity ---- 7/21/1993	7/29/1993
Methlylene urea (Scott's Winterizer)	19-3-12	1.3[+] a	1.8 a
Calcium nitrate	20-0-0	2.8 ab	3.3 ab
Urea	46-0-0	3.0 ab	2.3 ab
Potassium nitrate	13-0-38	3.0 ab	5.0 abc
Sulfur-coated Urea	28-3-10	3.0 ab	3.8 ab
Ammonium nitrate	34-0-0	4.5 ab	4.5 abc
Isobutyldiene diurea (Par Ex IBDU)	24-4-12	4.8 ab	3.0 ab
Resin-coated urea (Grace-Sierra's Once)	34-0-7	4.8 ab	2.0 a
Ammonium chloride	26-0-0	4.8 ab	3.0 ab
Ammonium sulfate	21-0-0	6.0 b	5.5 bc
Control	--	6.5 b	7.5 c
Coefficient of Variation (CV)		54%	46%

[+] Visual rating was on a scale of 1 to 9 with 1 being no localised dry spots; and 9 being severe localised dry spot damage. Values followed by the same letters are not significantly different (P=0.05) as analyzed by Duncan's Multiple Range Test.

4   References

Bond, R.D. 1964. The influence of microflora on the physical properties of soils. II. Field studies on water repellant soils. **Aust. J. Soil Res.**, 2, 123-131.

Danneberger, T.K. 1987. Those summertime blues: localised dry spots. **Grounds Maintenance**, 22(5), 30-32.

Danneberger, T.K. and S. White. 1988. Treating localised dry spots. **Golf Course Management**, 56(2), 6-10.

Hudson, R.A., S.J. Traina, and W.W. Shane. 1993. Organic matter comparison of wettable and non-wettable soils on bentgrass sand greens. **Soil Sci. Soc. Amer. J.**, (in press).

Hudson, R.A. and T.K. Danneberger. 1992. The biology and control of localised dry spots on sand greens. **TurfCraft Australia**, 29, 28-29.

Ma'Shum, M., M.E. Tate, G.P. Jones, and J.M. Oates. 1988. Extraction and characterization of water-repellant materials from Australian soils. **J. Soil Sci.**, 39, 99-110.

McGhie, D.A. and A.M. Posner. 1980. Water repellence of heavy textured Western Australian surface soils. **Aust. J. Soil Res.**, 18, 309-323.

Miller, R.H. and J.F. Wilkinson. 1977. Nature of the organic coating on sand grains of nonwettable golf greens. **Soil Sci. Soc. Am. J.**, 41, 1203-1204.

Smith, J.D., N. Jackson, and A.R. Woolhouse. 1989. **Fungal Diseases of Amenity Turf Grasses.** E. & F.N. Son. London.

Stevenson, F.J. 1984. **Humus chemistry: Genesis, composition, reactions.** Wiley-Interscience. New York.

Tucker, K.A., K.J. Karnok, D.E. Radcliffe, G. Landry, Jr., R.W. Roncadori, and K.H. Tan. 1990. Localized dry spots as caused by hydrophobic sands on bentgrass greens. **Agron. J.**, 82, 549-555.

Wilkinson, J.F. and R.H. Miller. 1978. Investigation and treatment of localized dry spots on sand greens. **Agron. J.**, 70, 299-304.

York, C.A. and N.A. Baldwin. 1992. Dry patch on golf greens: A review. **J. Sports Turf Res. Inst.**, 68, 7-19.

York, C.A. and N.A. Baldwin. 1993. Localised dry spot of UK golf greens, field characteristics, and evaluation of wetting agents for alleviation of localised dry spots symptoms. **Int. Turfgrass Soc. Res. J.**, 7, 476-484.

73 Australian bunker sands – quantifying playability

R.B. Dewar, G.W. Beehag
Australian Turfgrass Research Institute, Sydney, NSW, Australia
and K.Y. Chan
Biological and Chemical Research Institute, NSW Agriculture,
Rydalmere, Australia

Abstract
The playing quality of a bunker sand is described in terms of ball lie, the extent of compaction of the sand, the degree of crusting, ball plugging and the firmness of footing.

A survey sent to golfers and golf course superintendents across Australia identified these criteria as the most important properties in a bunker sand. These criteria are quantified by laboratory analysis of 17 bunker sands collected from around Australia.

Evaluation of playing characteristics of a bunker sand is made, with emphasis on the physical characteristics of particle size distribution (PSD), particle shape and packing density. These characteristics exert the dominant influence over bunker sand in terms of playability and are significant indicators of sand performance. Packing density and PSD predominantly affect ball plugging and crusting. Large values of Pmax (maximum packing density) and a widely graded PSD are associated with a higher crusting incidence and a lower plugging incidence respectively. Particle shape predominantly affects angle of repose and the crusting incidence, with low values of roundness and sphericity associated with higher angles of repose and crusting.

Keywords: Bunker, Sand, Particle Size Distribution, Packing Density, Grain Shape.

1 Introduction

Specifications for golf bunker sands exist in the United States and in Britain. The United States require sands in the range of .25mm to 1mm, preferably with 75% of the particles between 0.25mm to 0.5mm (USGA Green Section Staff, 1974). Sand should be light in colour, silica in composition, with angular grains preferred as they shift less under foot and provide the best stance and less buried balls (Beard, 1982). Britain's specification is similar for inland courses, with recommendations for links courses being in the range 0.125mm to 0.5mm (Baker, 1990).

Currently there are no guidelines for the selection of bunker sand in Australia. Although bunkers are meant to be a hazard, it is important that Australia has some means of reducing the disparity between and within golf courses to allow golf course superintendents, tournament organizers and golfers to make the most informed choices.

Science and Golf II: Proceedings of the World Scientific Congress of Golf. Edited by A.J. Cochran and M.R. Farrally. Published in 1994 by E & FN Spon, London. ISBN 0 419 18790 1

The objective of this study is to provide a clearer understanding of the physical relationships and processes influencing bunker sand quality by exploring the characteristics of the sand which are related to sand performance. Ultimately, this study aims at providing a set of standards based on reproducible laboratory techniques for the selection of golf bunker sand in Australia.

2 Experimental methods

2.1 Sand materials and methods

17 sands were collected from golf clubs around Australia. The following laboratory methods shown in Table 1, were performed after a national survey identified these criteria as important;

Table 1. Methods used to quantify criteria

CRITERIA	METHODS *unless otherwise stated 3 replicates were taken. Sands were air dried before use and initial moisture content determined by drying at 105°C.
Particle Size Analysis	Dry sieve analysis used an automatic shaker. Wet silt/clay analysis method of Gee & Bauder (1986). The D60/D40 stability index was obtained by dividing the D60 value (a diameter where 60% of the grains are smaller) by the D40 value (a diameter where only 10% of the grains are smaller). These were inferred from the grading curve.
Particle Shape	Photographs of the dominant sieve fraction were taken. Sand grains were then chosen randomly to determine sphericity and roundness of the grains. Sphericity method after Wu (1976). Rapid visual roundness estimate after Krumbien (1941).
Packing Density	A computer model (Gupta & Larson, 1979) was used to calculate the maximum bulk density, known as Pmaximum (Pmax).
Crusting Strength	Sand was wetted by sprinkling until saturated and then dried in an oven. A pocket penetrometer was used to determine the degree of crusting. Modified method of Brown & Thomas (1986) with 6 estimates in 1 replicate.
Angle of Repose	500 cm^3 of sand was dropped from a height of 15 cm onto a flat surface, the angle the sand forms with the flat surface under these condition was measured using a clinometer. Method of Baker et al (1990).
Ball Plugging	A pocket penetrometer with a flat tip determined the force used to push a ball into 1000cm^3 of sand from a half way mark indicated on the ball. Method of Brown & Thomas (1986). 6 replicates.
Infiltration	Measured by a drainage and compaction study using samples equilibrated to field capacity on a tension table. Hydraulic conductivity was derived from constant head infiltration under ponded conditions. Modified method from Elrick et al (1981).

3 Results and discussion

3.1 Summary of criteria under test

Table 2 summarises the results of the sands under test. The values suggest some initial findings for Australian sand characteristics as a whole. These include being light in colour and not plugging or crusting to a great extent. The majority of samples here have a high bulk density, therefore 'fluffiness' of the sand is less common than firmer, more packed sand, with firmness more common in widely graded sands. However, one sample had a bulk density of 1.08 g/cm^3 which may cause problems associated with 'fluffy' sand, such as ball plugging and unstable footing.

The 17 sands tested did not have a great susceptibility to ball plugging as measured by penetrometer resistance, nor did sands crust as the maximum clay reading was only 2.4% and statistical analysis indicated relationships between clay and crusting were not significant at a 95% confidence interval. Sands having a high penetrometer measurement i.e. > 98kPa tended form a crust as deep as the water penetrates (Brown & Thomas, 1986), rather than form a crust on the sand surface.

Table 2. Characteristics of sands under test and their range of values

	Characteristic	Unit	Mean	Min.	Max.
	Wetness w	g/g	0.065	0.026	0.15
Physical	Sphericity	-	1.73	0.47	3.31
Characteristics	Angularity	-	0.42	0.30	0.53
of the sand	Gradation Index (D60/D40)	-	1.29	1.13	1.63
	Bulk Density after compaction	g/cm^3	1.52	1.08	1.79
	P maximum (Pmax)	g/cm^3	1.83	1.51	2.30
	Silt+Clay	%	1.1	0.1	2.4
	Angle of repose	degrees	32.83	31.08	35.00
	Plugging force	kPa	341.0	245.0	433.2
Performance	Crusting Strength	kPa	78.0	49.0	135.2
Criteria	Infiltration	mm/h	1129.1	105.8	2400.6
	Munsell Colour	-	-	5YR 8/1 White	10YR 5/2 Greyish/Brown

3.2 Particle size distribution

Size analysis showed three dominant sieve fractions at 1) 250-106 μm, 2) 300-250 μm and 3) 500-455 μm and gives rise to four distinct groups. Sands were allocated to a particular group based on their PSD. Figures a to d below and over page show the four dominant groups based on PSD. Group 1 is a very uniform unimodal sand with a dominant peak in the 250-106μm range. Group 2 is a moderately uniform unimodal sand with a dominant peak at 300-250μm. Group 3 represents a very well graded unimodal sand with a major peak at 250-106μm. Group 4 is a very well graded unimodal sand leading to a peak at 500-455μm.

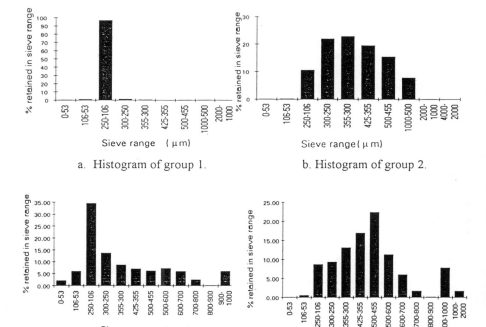

a. Histogram of group 1.

b. Histogram of group 2.

c. Histogram of group 3.

d. Histogram of group 4.

Fig. 1. Histograms of the 4 groups of sands.

3.3 One way analysis of variance

In order to test whether sands similar in particle size distribution have similar playing characteristics, sands falling into particular groups based on their PSD, were subjected to one way analysis of variance of PSD groups against all criteria measured in the laboratory. The results in Table 3 show which criteria were significant at a 95% confidence interval (C.I). These indicate that based on PSD alone, sands falling into a particular group are likely to have similar stability, maximum bulk densities, angle of repose and crusting measurements, than sands that do not have a similar PSD. This suggests there may be a predictive power of the PSD to determine playing characteristics, the extent of this however is yet to be explored.

Table 3. Criteria established as significantly different between groups at a 95% C.I.

Characteristics	F ratio	Significance Level
Angle of repose	10.21	0.002
Crusting	4.45	0.022
Pmax	6.80	0.006
D60/D40	7.90	0.03

3.4 Effects of physical attributes on performance criteria

The regression equations in Table 4 indicate some interesting relationships between the playing characteristics and the physical characteristics of the sand. Of particular interest is the overall significant impact the maximum bulk density and the D60/D40 stability measurement have over plugging incidence and crusting, both of which are important criteria affecting play. 1) Plugging incidence was most significantly related to the D60/D40 stability index although the correlation was relatively weak (R^2 =22.3). This relationship was expected as the D60/D40 measurements are an overall summary of the PSD and it is the PSD which affects the packing density and hence the degree of resistance a ball may face when it is forced into the sand. The positive relationship suggests that lower plugging incidence are expected in more widely graded sands.

2) Crusting incidence was not related to the clay content in this instance, as no evidence of a significant relationship between the two exist and clay levels were consistently low.

Table 4. Prediction of performance criteria from physical attributes.

Regression Equation	R^2
Plugging = 1.48 + 1.56 D60/D40	22.3
Crusting = -0.235 + 0.579 Pmax	21.3
Angle repose = 35.8 - 7.25 roundness	21.4
Angle repose = 33.9 - 0.643 sphericity	28.8
Angle repose = 32.1 + 0.595 clay	23.5
Angle repose = 30.7 + 2.64 crusting	56.8
Crusting = 1.81 - 2.45 roundness	30

However, a form of crusting known as 'set up', is evident. Set up is the formation of a hard layer or crust as deep as the water penetrates (Brown & Thomas, 1986). Thus penetrometer resistance increases not as a result of clay content, but the maximum bulk density. A positive correlation between Pmax and crusting indicates that the incidence of crusting or 'set-up' will increase as the bulk density increases. This means that as sand is wet and dried particle sorting and settling occurs and the sample density increases. Packing is primarily a result of the PSD and the shape of the sand, with roundness having a significant, negative relationship with crusting. Therefore indicating as roundness decreases, crusting present as 'set-up' increases.

3) Angle of repose is significantly related to the four parameters of crusting, roundness, sphericity and clay content. Angle of repose is related to sphericity and roundness as the shape of the sand grain exerts the dominant influence over this parameter (Baker *et al*, 1990). A point of interest is the significance of clay and crusting on the angle of repose. As clay levels are generally low and are not related to crusting levels in this study, it is uncertain why there is such a significant relationship between angle of repose and clay. Crusting, however is more related to the grain shape ($R^2 = 30$), hence the strong link between angle of repose and crusting.

However, multiple regression of the angle of repose against crusting and sphericity accounts for 58.1% of variation as opposed to a model containing all four parameters of crusting, roundness, sphericity and clay content, which has an R^2 of 62.6% i.e. the extra two parameters of clay and roundness only account for 4.5% more variation.

4 Conclusion

Research on this project is continuing. However, the data analysed so far indicate that;

1) The sands analysed can be divided into four groups based on similarities in particle size distribution. Sands falling into a group based on a particular PSD were more likely to have similar stability, maximum bulk densities, angle of repose and crusting measurements, than sands that do not have a similar PSD.

2) On the whole, the sands tested suggested some preliminary findings that Australian sands are generally light in colour and do not plug the ball or crust to a great extent.

3) The variance accounted for by the regression analysis is not high. However, relationships do exist and seem to indicate that Pmax, the D60/D40 index and grain shape (measured as roundness and sphericity), are significant indicators of sand performance. Pmax predominantly affects crusting or 'set-up' incidence, while the D60/D40 index exerts the main influence over plugging incidence. Pmax and D60/D40 are directly related to the PSD, this indicates that the PSD is one of the most important criteria influencing the physical and playing characteristics of bunker sands. Grain shape is also an important physical characteristic affecting angle of repose and crusting strength.

5 References

Baker, S.W. (1990). *Sands for sports turf construction and maintenance*. Sports Turf Research Institute, Bingley.

Baker, S.W., Cole, A.R. & Thornton, S.L. (1990). The effect of sand type on ball impacts, angle of repose and stability of footing in golf bunkers. p. 352-357. *In*: A.J. Cochran (ed.) Science and Golf. Proceedings of the First World Scientific Congress of Golf, University of St. Andrews, July 1990. E. & F.N. Spoon.

Beard, J.B. (1982). *Turf management for golf courses*. Burgess Publications Co., Minneapolis, Minnesota.

Brown, K.W. & Thomas, J.C. (1986). Bunker sand selection. Golf Course Management; 54(7): 64-70.

Elrick, D.E., Sheard, R.W. & Baumgartner, N. (1981). A simple procedure for determining the hydraulic conductivity and water retention of putting green soil mixtures. p. 189-200. *In*: R.W. Sheard (ed.) Proceedings of the fourth international turfgrass research conference. University of Guelf, Canada, July 19-23, 1981. Ontario Agricultural College, Univ. of Guelph & The International Turfgrass Society.

Gee, G.W. & Bauder, J.W. (1986). Particle size analysis. *In*: A. Klute (ed.) Methods of Soil Analysis. Part 1. 2nd ed. Agronomy 9: 383-411.

Gupta, S.C. & Larson, W.E. (1979). A model for predicting packing density of soils using particle size distribution. *Soil Science Society of America Journal* 43, 758-764.

Krumbien, W.C. (1941). Measurement and geological significance of shape and roundness of sedimentary particles. *Journal of Sedimentary Petrology*, 11(2), 64-72.

United States Golf Association Green Section Staff (1974). Sand for golf courses. USGA Green Section Record 12 (5), 12-13.

Wu, T.H. (1976). *Soil Mechanics*. 2nd ed. Allyn and Bacon, Inc. Boston, London & Sydney.

74 Nutrient transport in runoff from two turfgrass species

D.T. Linde, T.L. Watschke and J.A. Borger
Penn State University, University Park, PA, USA

Abstract
Increased environmental awareness has generated a need to better understand nutrient transport from turfgrass systems, especially golf courses. This study assessed the effects turfgrasses, maintained as a golf turf fairway, had on runoff water quality. Sloped (9 to 14%) plots, each 123 m^2, of creeping bentgrass, *Agrostis palustris* Huds., and perennial ryegrass, *Lolium perenne* L., were maintained as a golf course fairway. Plots were treated on five dates with a 32-1.3-8.3 (N, P, K) fertilizer at 15.3 g/m^2, and on one date with urea (46-0-0) at 10.6 g/m^2. Within 24 h following fertilization, and on other selected dates from Aug 1991 to Oct 1992, plots were irrigated at 152 mm/h for the generation of runoff and leachate samples.
Water samples were analyzed for nitrate-N, phosphate, and total Kjeldahl-N. Nutrient concentrations and loading rates found in runoff and leachate samples were consistently low and generally reflected those found in the irrigation water. Concentrations of NO_3-N, phosphate, and total Kjeldahl-N rarely exceeded 7, 5, and 2 mg/L, respectively. Although bentgrass reduced runoff more than ryegrass (Linde, 1993), both turfs, when maintained as a golf fairway, did not allow significant transport of NO_3-N, phosphate, or total Kjeldahl-N.
Keywords: Bentgrass, Ryegrass, Nitrogen, Phosphorus, Fertilizer, Surface Runoff, Overland Flow

1 Introduction

The assessment of nutrient transport for turfgrass systems is essential for developing environmental models that determine potential nonpoint impacts of nutrient management on water quality. However, limited information regarding nutrient transport from turfgrass systems has been published. Balogh and Watson (1992) stated "government agencies regulating the allocation of water resources and environmental impacts of turfgrass systems currently are using simulation software that is not specifically modified for turfgrass conditions."

Golf courses have a potential for nutrient transport because of large areas, mainly fairways, of intensely maintained turfgrass. To better determine this potential, nutrient transport needs to be assessed for turfs maintained as a golf fairway.

Two turfgrasses commonly used for golf fairways in the northeastern and pacific northwestern U.S. are creeping bentgrass and perennial ryegrass. Creeping bentgrass is a fine-textured, stoloniferous (produces above-ground stems called stolons) species, which, when closely mowed, forms a turf with superior shoot density (>200 shoots/dm^2) and turfgrass quality (Turgeon, 1985). Also, creeping bentgrass has a

Science and Golf II: Proceedings of the World Scientific Congress of Golf. Edited by A.J. Cochran and M.R. Farrally. Published in 1994 by E & FN Spon, London. ISBN 0 419 18790 1

medium slow establishment rate, requires a high cultural intensity, and forms a definite thatch layer.

Perennial ryegrass is a medium-textured, bunch-type (noncreeping tufts) species, which, when closely mowed, forms a turf with good shoot density (100 to 200 shoots/dm^2) and turfgrass quality (Turgeon, 1985). Also, perennial ryegrass is quick to establish, requires a medium cultural intensity, and forms no definite thatch layer.

In the limited publications concerning runoff from turfgrass, runoff, sediment, and nutrient transport were significantly reduced by turfgrass systems (Bennett, 1979; Gross et al., 1990, 1991; Harrison et al., 1993; Morton et al., 1988; Watson, 1985).

Petrovic (1990), in a review of the fate of nitrogenous fertilizers applied to turf stated that runoff losses of fertilizer N were minimal, since natural precipitation rarely produced runoff. He also stated that leaching losses of fertilizer N were generally far less than 10% of the applied N and suggested certain management strategies that can be used to minimize or eliminate NO_3^- leaching.

Harrison et al. (1993) had to use high rates of irrigation to force runoff from turf maintained as a home lawn and observed that concentrations of soluble NO_3-N, P, and K in runoff and leachate rarely exceeded 5, 2, and 6 mg/L, respectively. Also, no specific pattern developed between nutrient concentrations in runoff and fertilizer application dates.

The studies conducted by Gross et al. (1990, 1991), Harrison et al. (1993), and Morton et al. (1988) utilized mature turfs. No published studies were found that included information concerning nutrient loss in runoff from immature turfs and/or turfs maintained as a golf fairway. This study was conducted to help fill these voids in research by assessing runoff and nutrient transport on two commonly used fairway turfs, creeping bentgrass and perennial ryegrass, from seedling stage through maturity. The objective was to assess the transport of NO_3-N, total Kjeldahl-N, and phosphate applied to sloped plots of creeping bentgrass and perennial ryegrass maintained under fairway conditions.

2 Methods and Materials

This research was conducted concurrently with a study designed to characterize surface runoff from bentgrass and ryegrass stands (Linde, 1993). Briefly, the site had a variable slope (9 to 14%) and the surface soil was a severely eroded Hagerstown series classified as a clay (23% sand, 36% silt, 41% clay).

In July 1991, three runoff plots, each 6.5 by 19 m, were seeded with 'Penneagle' creeping bentgrass and three plots were seeded with a perennial ryegrass blend ('Citation II', 'Commander', 'Omega II'). Only triple-superphosphate was applied prior to seeding.

Plots were mowed with a reel mower at a height of 1.9 cm with clippings remaining. Cultivation practices such as core cultivation, verticutting, and spiking were not used during the study. Irrigation, other than that scheduled to provide adequate runoff and leachate samples, was conducted only when the turf was under moisture stress and for durations which would not produce runoff or leachate samples.

Fertilizers used in the study were urea (46-0-0) and a 32-1.3-8.3 (N-P-K) fertilizer (O. M. Scott & Sons, Marysville, OH), with 0.5% NH_4-N, 24.8% urea and methylene urea-N, and 6.7% water insoluble methylene urea-N, and with P derived from monoammonium phosphate and K from K_2SO_4. The turfs were fertilized on six dates during the study (Table 1).

Table 1. Fertilizer application dates and rates

Date	Fertilizer applied (N-P-K)	Rate (g/m^2)
__1991__		
3 Oct	32-1.3-8.3	15.3
__1992__		
5 May	32-1.3-8.3	15.3
11 June#	32-1.3-8.3	15.3
5 July#	46-0-0	10.6
8 Sept	32-1.3-8.3	15.3
13 Oct	32-1.3-8.3	15.3

Runoff event was not conducted 24 h after application.

2.1 Water Sampling Procedures

Water samples were collected from runoff events forced with irrigation (152 mm/h) and, on occasion, from natural rainstorms. Irrigation was applied approximately 24 h following an application of fertilizer to provide runoff and leachate samples for nutrient concentration analyses. Irrigation duration varied from 7 to 35 minutes depending on species and date.

Runoff was sampled at the rate of 16 ml/min throughout an event's duration to form a composite sample (Harrison et al., 1993). Leachate samples were taken from four subsurface samplers per plot (Harrison et al., 1993), which were located 150 mm below the soil surface. A composite leachate sample for each plot was made by taking equal parts from the four samplers.

2.2 Nutrient Analysis Procedures

Nutrient concentration analyses were based on samples collected from a total of 14 irrigated and rainfall runoff events that occurred between August 1991 and October 1992. Within 24 h following collection, each sample was analyzed colormetrically using a Hach DR/3000 Spectrophotometer (Hach Co., Loveland, CO) for NO_3-N, and soluble P (phosphate). Nitrate-N was determined using a cadmium reduction procedure, and soluble P as orthophosphate via amino acid reduction of molybdophosphoric acid (Hach Co., 1986).

Prior to NO_3-N and phosphate analyses, samples were filtered through Millipore prefilters and Millipore 0.45 um membrane filters (Millipore Corp., Bedford, MA). Total Kjeldahl-N concentrations were determined by the Penn State University Nutrient Analysis Lab using the methods developed by the Methods Development and Quality Assurance Research Lab, Cincinnati, OH (U.S. EPA, 1974). This method for determining total Kjeldahl-N excluded NO_3-N. Following analyses, the remaining sample water was frozen and archived.

2.3 Statistical Designs and Procedures

The two treatments were arranged in a randomized complete block design with three replications. Blocking was based on surface slope of the experimental units. Statistical analyses were conducted for each nutrient and sample source to determine species effects for a given event. Means were separated using Fisher's protected LSD (Steel and Torrie, 1980).

Due to major differences in environmental and hydrologic conditions for each runoff event, analyses were limited to individual dates. Also, runoff events from natural rainfall often did not provide full data sets because runoff did not occur on all plots. In these cases, averages were based on the number of plots that provided data and were not included in statistical analysis.

3 Results and Discussion

Mean nutrient concentrations, by runoff event and sample source, are presented in Table 2. Nutrient concentration and runoff volume per unit area, as determined in a concurrent runoff study (Linde, 1993), were used to calculate loading rates in runoff and leachate for each turf (Tables 3, 4, and 5).

Table 2. Mean nutrient concentrations in runoff and leachate water samples.

Date	Nitrate-N (mg/L)		Phosphate (mg/L)		Kjeldahl-N (mg/L)	
	Runoff	Leachate	Runoff	Leachate	Runoff	Leachate
1991						
Aug	6.5	7.5	1.65	0.89	-	-
4 Oct	3.8	4.4	1.61	1.64	0.1	0.2
1992						
6 May	7.2	5.8	4.17	2.16	3.5	1.1
9 May§	2.8#	1.5	6.06#	1.90	1.4#	0.6
10 Jun	6.7	5.6	2.13	2.34	0	0
19 Jun§	5.4#	1.2#	5.31#	0.97#	-	-
24 Jun	6.7	6.1	2.03	1.61	0	0.2
26 Jun§	1.8	1.3	3.54	1.65	-	-
14 Jul§	1.8#	1.1	3.61#	1.13	-	-
15 Jul	7.2	6.0	2.93	1.95	0.7	0.4
19 Aug	6.7	5.6	2.14	1.81	0	0
28 Aug§	3.1#	1.0	3.05#	1.42	-	0.6
9 Sep	4.3	4.8	4.98	3.53	2.0	0.1
14 Oct	6.6	5.4	2.77	1.91	0.3	0

§ Rainfall caused runoff.
# All replications did not produce a sample.

3.1 Nitrate-N

Nitrate-N concentrations were consistently lower than the 10 mg/L drinking water standard set by the USEPA. This information concurs with recent turf runoff studies done by Harrison et al. (1993), Gross et al. (1990), and Morton et al. (1988). No significant species effect was detected for any runoff event, therefore, the species were averaged for each sample source (Table 2). The highest mean NO_3-N concentration was 7.2 mg/L which was found in the runoff samples on two dates, 6 May and 15 July 1992.

Runoff and leachate loading rates of NO_3-N for each turf were consistently lower than irrigation inputs of NO_3-N (Tables 3 and 4). Also, runoff loading rates, which ranged from 0 to 0.09 g/m^2, were lower than leachate loading rates, which ranged from 0.04 to 0.32 g/m^2.

Table 3. Chronology of inputs and runoff loading rates of total N
(Kjeldahl-N + nitrate-N) and nitrate-N for bentgrass and ryegrass.

Date	Fert. inputs of N	Irrigation inputs (g/m^2) Bent		Rye		Found in runoff (g/m^2) Bent		Rye	
		N	NO_3^-N	N	NO_3^-N	N	NO_3^-N	N	NO_3^-N
1991									
Aug						-	0.05	-	0.04
3 Oct	4.9								
4 Oct		0.82	0.82	0.82	0.82	0.05	0.05	0.07	0.07
1992									
5 May	4.9								
6 May		0.29	0.29	0.23	0.23	0.03	0.02	0.05	0.03
9 May§									
10 Jun		0.62	0.62	0.67	0.67	0.05	0.05	0.09	0.09
11 Jun	4.9								
19 Jun§								-	0.01
24 Jun		0.69	0.69	0.38	0.38	0.05	0.05	0.06	0.06
26 Jun§						-	0	-	0.01
5 Jul	4.9								
14 Jul§								-	0
15 Jul		0.40	0.35	0.25	0.22	0.01	0.01	0.03	0.03
19 Aug		0.72	0.72	0.39	0.39	0.01	0.01	0.03	0.03
28 Aug§						-	0	-	0
8 Sep	4.9								
9 Sep		0.41	0.41	0.30	0.30	0.03	0.02	0.04	0.02
13 Oct	4.9								
14 Oct		0.81	0.81	0.24	0.24	0.04	0.04	0.03	0.03

§ Rainfall caused runoff.

3.2 Phosphate

A significant species effect for phosphate ($P=0.05$; Fisher's protected LSD) was
detected only 3 times for 23 tests (24 Jun 1992 in leachate, bent=1.49 mg/L, rye=1.74
mg/L; 26 Jun 1992 in runoff, bent=3.15 mg/L, rye=3.94 mg/L; and 14 Oct 1992 in
runoff, bent=2.24 mg/L, rye=3.30 mg/L). These differences were of little practical
significance because values remained low, thus the species were averaged for each
sample source (Table 2). The highest mean phosphate concentration was 6.06 mg/L
which was found in the runoff samples taken 9 May 1992.

Runoff and leachate loading rates of phosphate-P were consistently lower than
fertilizer and irrigation inputs of phosphate-P (Table 5). Also, runoff loading rates,
which ranged from 0 to 0.011 g/m^2, were lower than leachate loading rates, which
ranged from 0.009 to 0.045 g/m^2.

Table 4. Chronology of inputs and leachate loading rates of total N (Kjeldahl-N + nitrate-N) and nitrate-N for bentgrass and ryegrass.

Date	Fert. inputs of N	Irrigation inputs (g/m^2) Bent		Rye		Found in leachate (g/m^2) Bent		Rye	
		N	NO$_3$-N	N	NO$_3$-N	N	NO$_3$-N	N	NO$_3$-N
1991									
Aug						-	0.25	-	0.32
3 Oct	4.9								
4 Oct		0.82	0.82	0.82	0.82	0.18	0.17	0.17	0.17
1992									
5 May	4.9								
6 May		0.29	0.29	0.23	0.23	0.26	0.21	0.26	0.23
9 May§						-	0.06	-	0.05
10 Jun		0.62	0.62	0.67	0.67	0.22	0.22	0.22	0.21
11 Jun	4.9								
19 Jun§						-	0.05	-	0.04
24 Jun		0.69	0.69	0.38	0.38	0.23	0.23	0.24	0.24
26 Jun§						-	0.05	-	0.05
5 Jul	4.9								
14 Jul§						-	0.05	-	0.04
15 Jul		0.40	0.35	0.25	0.22	0.23	0.22	0.25	0.24
19 Aug		0.72	0.72	0.39	0.39	0.21	0.21	0.22	0.22
28 Aug§						-	0.04	-	0.04
8 Sep	4.9								
9 Sep		0.41	0.41	0.30	0.30	0.17	0.17	0.20	0.19
13 Oct	4.9								
14 Oct		0.81	0.81	0.24	0.24	0.25	0.25	0.16	0.16

§ Rainfall caused runoff.

The Aug 1991 event was conducted before fertilization to provide information on background nutrient levels. Background levels were similar to levels found throughout the study.

Nitrate-N and phosphate concentrations were slightly higher than those found by Harrison et al. (1993). However, in this study, NO$_3$-N and phosphate concentrations rarely exceeded 7 and 5 mg/L, respectively. The higher values may be attributed to the higher concentrations detected in the irrigation water.

As Harrison et al. (1993) had found, there was little indication in the runoff and leachate samples that fertilizer was ever applied. Also, concentrations and loading rates in runoff and leachate generally reflected those detected in the irrigation water. Gross et al. (1990), investigating nutrient losses from tall fescue/Kentucky bluegrass turf, also found limited losses of NO$_3$-N and phosphate in runoff and leachate.

3.3 Total Kjeldahl-N

No significant species effect was found for any event, therefore, the species were averaged for each sample source (Table 2). Mean total Kjeldahl-N concentrations in runoff and leachate ranged from 0 to 3.5 mg/L. The higher concentrations were detected in runoff samples on 6 May and 9 Sept 1992, dates that fertilizer was

Table 5. Chronology of inputs and runoff and leachate loading rates of phosphate-P for bentgrass and ryegrass.

Date	Fert. inputs of P	Irrigation inputs of P (g/m^2)		P found in runoff (g/m^2)		P found in leachate sampler (g/m^2)	
		Bent	Rye	Bent	Rye	Bent	Rye
1991							
Aug				0.003	0.004	0.013	0.009
3 Oct	0.2						
4 Oct		0.092	0.092	0.006	0.008	0.022	0.019
1992							
5 May	0.2						
6 May		0.029	0.023	0.003	0.007	0.027	0.027
9 May§						0.024	0.023
10 Jun		0.064	0.069	0.005	0.011	0.021	0.038
11 Jun	0.2						
19 Jun§				0	0.003	0.010	0.014
24 Jun		0.052	0.029	0.004	0.006	0.019	0.022
26 Jun§				0	0.004	0.020	0.021
14 Jul§				0	0.004	0.014	0.014
15 Jul		0.028	0.017	0	0.003	0.023	0.025
19 Aug		0.069	0.037	0	0.004	0.021	0.024
28 Aug§				0	0	0.016	0.019
8 Sep	0.2						
9 Sep		0.051	0.037	0.009	0.009	0.044	0.045
13 Oct	0.2						
14 Oct		0.061	0.018	0.004	0.006	0.025	0.022

§ Rainfall caused runoff.

applied 24 h before runoff. Also, rainfall events seldom produced large enough samples to conduct Kjeldahl-N analysis, therefore limiting such data.

Mean total Kjeldahl-N results and mean NO_3-N results were added together for estimates of total N in the samples. Total N loading rates were seldom greater than NO_3-N loading rates, even for events that N fertilizer was applied 24 h before runoff (Tables 3 and 4). The greatest mean total N loading rate, 0.26 g/m^2, was detected in leachate samples for 6 May 1992. A nitrogen fertilizer input of 4.9 g N/m^2 was made approximately 24 h prior to the event.

Total Kjeldahl-N analyses were conducted to determine if there were any amounts of the N fertilizer in the samples that had not yet been converted to the NO_3-N form. Because total Kjeldahl-N concentrations were very low, it was assumed that most of the N fertilizer applied was in the soil above the subsurface sampler and/or did not become soluble and remained on the soil surface. To a lessor extent, the fertilizer could have possibly been converted to NO_3-N, absorbed by foliage and roots, utilized by the plants, and/or lost due to denitrification.

4 Conclusions

Although bentgrass reduced runoff more than ryegrass (Linde, 1993), appreciable transport of NO_3-N, phosphate, and total Kjeldahl-N did not occur from either turf. Concentrations of NO_3-N, phosphate, and total Kjeldahl-N rarely exceeded 7, 5, and 2 mg/L, respectively. In fact, nutrient concentrations and loading rates generally reflected those found in the irrigation water. Clearly the nutrients in the fertilizer used in this study did not move in runoff or into leachate collectors in amounts greater than found in irrigation water.

5 References

Balogh, J.C. and Watson, Jr, J.R. (1992) Role and conservation of water resources, in **Golf Course Management and Construction: Environmental Issues** (eds J.C. Balogh and W.J. Walker), Lewis Publ., Chelsea, MI, pp. 39-104.

Bennett, O.L. (1979) Conservation, in **Tall Fescue** (eds R.C. Buckner and L.P. Bush), ASA, CSSA, SSSA, Madison, WI, **Agron. Monogr.** 20, 319-340.

Gross, C.M. Angle, J.S. Hill, R.L. and Welterlen, M.S. (1991) Runoff and sediment losses from tall fescue under simulated rainfall. **J. Environ. Qual.**, 20, 604-607.

Gross, C.M. Angle, J.S. and Welterlen, M.S. (1990) Nutrient and sediment losses from turfgrass. **J. Environ. Qual.**, 19, 663-668.

Hach Company (1986) **D/R 3000 spectrophotometer instrument manual.** 3rd ed. Hach Company, Loveland, CO.

Harrison, S.A. Watschke, T.L. Mumma, R.O. Jarrett, A.R. and Hamilton, G.W. (1993) Nutrient and pesticide concentrations in water from chemically treated turfgrass, in **Pesticides in Urban Environments: Fate and Significance** (eds K.D. Racke and A.R. Leslie), ACS Symposium Series No. 522, pp. 191-207.

Linde, D.T. (1993) **Surface Runoff and Nutrient Transport Assessment on Creeping Bentgrass and Perennial Ryegrass Turf.** M.S. Thesis, The Pennsylvania State Univ., University Park, PA.

Morton, T.G. Gold, A.J. and Sullivan, W.M. (1988) Influence of overwatering and fertilization on nitrogen losses from home lawns. **J. Environ. Qual.**, 17, 124-130.

Petrovic, A.M. (1990) The fate of nitrogenous fertilizers applied to turfgrass. **J. Environ. Qual.**, 19, 1-14.

Steel, R.G.D. and Torrie, J. H. (1980) **Principles and Procedures of Statistics: A Biometrical Approach.** 2nd Ed. McGraw-Hill, New York.

Turgeon, A.J. (1985) **Turfgrass Management**. Prentice-Hall, Englewood Cliffs, NJ.

U.S. Environmental Protection Agency (1974) **Methods for Chemical Analysis of Water and Wastes**. Developed by Methods Development and Quality Assurance Lab, Cincinnati, OH. Office of Technology Transfer, Washington, DC.

Watson, Jr., J.R. (1985) Water resources in the United States, in **Turfgrass Water Conservation** (eds V.A. Gibeault and S.T. Cockerham), Univ of Calif., Riverside, Division of Agric. and Natural Resources, pp. 19-36.

75 Impact of golf courses on ground water quality

A.M. Petrovic
Cornell University, Ithaca, New York, USA

Abstract
This paper summaries the results from both research studies
and actual golf course monitoring of ground water for
pesticide and nitrate contamination. In both cases there
have been few studies conducted. For the most part, the
real life golf course results compare well with the controlled research studies. Where differences exist, a more
careful examination of the nature of the studies revealed a
good explanation of the differences. A newly established
site with limited turf cover appears to have the greatest
potential for excessive pesticide leaching.
Keywords: Pesticide, Fertilizer, Leaching, Environment,
Ground Water.

1. Introduction

Turfgrass sites such as golf courses have been under considerable pressure to defend the unregulated use of pesticides and fertilizers in relationship to ground water
quality. The concern over the impact of pesticides and
fertilizers on groundwater quality has been fueled by
impacts noted from other systems, mostly tradition agriculture.
   There is only a recent history associated with pesticides and/or fertilizers and groundwater quality. In the
1970s, nitrates were found in community wells in several
states in excess of drinking water standards. Flipse et
al.(1984) suggested that lawn fertilization could be a
significant source of nitrate contamination of groundwater
in sewered suburban watersheds. Pesticides (atrazine,
aldicarb and 1,2-dibromochloropropane) used in traditional
agriculture were first detected in groundwater of seven
states in the USA in 1979/80.
   The first extensive sampling of community and private
wells for pesticides and nitrate in the United States was
conducted during 1988-1990 by the US Environmental Protection Agency (EPA), as reported by Cohen (1991). Samples

Science and Golf II: Proceedings of the World Scientific Congress of Golf. Edited by A.J.
Cochran and M.R. Farrally. Published in 1994 by E & FN Spon, London. ISBN 0 419 18790 1

were collected from 1292 wells and analyzed for 101 pesticides, 25 pesticide transformation products and nitrate.
Based on the results from actual well samples, it was
estimated that 10.4% and 4.2% of community wells and rural
domestic wells, respectively, had at least one detectable
pesticide. None of the community water system wells had any
pesticide residue in concentrations greater than maximum
contaminant level (MCL), while 0.6% of the rural domestic
wells had pesticide concentration in excess of the MCL.
Nitrates on the other hand were frequently detected in
either community water system wells (52%) and rural domestic wells (57%). In this case 1.2% of the community water
system wells and 2.4% of the rural domestic wells had
nitrate concentration in excess of the MCL. Though most of
these site were not associated with golf courses, it does
suggested that pesticides and fertilizers can be detected
in ground water and be present at levels that exceed MCL
from land application (agriculture).

One of the most pointed charges that pesticides applied
to golf courses may impact ground water quality was made by
the Attorney General of the New York State (Jaffe et al.,
1991) in a report entitled "Toxic fairways; risking groundwater contamination from pesticides applied to Long Island
golf courses". In this report the rate of pesticide use on
Long Island, NY golf courses was determined by survey to be
5 times higher than the national average use for all of
agriculture. Though no golf course had any of it's groundwater tested, there were implications that pesticides
applied to Long Island golf courses could contaminate
groundwater based on the detection of some of the pesticides used on golf courses in wells; some of the pesticides
applied to these golf courses were known to have a high
probability for leaching; and the soils/hydrology of Long
Island is conducive for pesticide leaching.

2 Pesticide and fertilizer impacts on ground water quality

The impacts of pesticides and fertilizers applied to golf
courses on ground water quality can be viewed from studies
done on actual ground water sampling from existing golf
courses or from research studies conducted under pseudo-
golf course conditions. Each type of study has strengths
and weaknesses. The following is a review of some of the
available golf course ground water monitoring studies and
results from several research projects.

2.1 Golf course monitoring studies
The big advantage of monitoring the ground water from
actual golf courses is the 'real' nature of such studies
which integrate the actual conditions of an operating golf
course. Conditions that are hard to mimic in research

studies include the stresses caused by the golfer (traffic, divots, fast green speed, etc.) and the management variables of a golf course that can be influenced by the golfer (off hours irrigation, early morning mowing, restrictions on the timing of application of pesticides/fertilizers and desire for high quality turf).

The big disadvantages to golf course monitoring studies are: the sampling is often done infrequently (quarterly to monthly) in which a pulse of either fertilizer nitrate or pesticide may be missed, the hydrology of the golf course may not be well understood, inputs of rainfall/irrigation, fertilizers and pesticides may not be well quantified, and the inability of extrapolating such data to other golf courses. The poor understanding of the hydrology of the golf course can often led to improper placement of monitoring wells and uncertainty associated with the detection in ground water of either a pesticide or nitrate as to the origin of such chemicals which may be from the adjacent or upstream property not applied to the golf course. In any event, the monitoring of the ground water under golf courses is often required in the approval process on many new golf course projects in the United States.

The published literature on ground water quality from golf courses in the United States is limited. The most widely cited example is from four golf courses on Cape Cod, Massachusetts (Cohen et al., 1990). This study involved a federal agency (USEPA), local government (Barnstable County) and golf course superintendents. Cape Cod was chosen based on the hydrological vulnerability of the aquifer system (principal drinking water source). Four golf courses were selected as worst-case assessments out of a possible 30 based on the following criteria: sites with high risk of leaching (glacial outwash plains with sandy soils and shallow water tables), heavy usage of fertilizers/ pesticides, and courses older than 30 years (higher risk since more time available for migration to ground water). Samples for pesticides were collected quarterly for one and a half years and monthly to semi-monthly for two years for nitrates.

From the 16 wells on the 4 golf courses (background, under green, tee and fairways), 7 out of 17 pesticides and related compounds were never detected (mecoprop, siduron, anilazine, iprodione, diazinon, dacthal). Pesticides were most often detected in samples from greens and tees and seldom were detected from wells under fairways or background wells. A summary of the results is shown in Table 1. The toxicological significance of these results are that none of the 12 currently registered pesticides studied in this project (chlordane is no longer registered or used) were detected in concentrations greater than one fifth of the health guidance levels in the United States.

The results on leaching of nitrates into ground water

from fertilizers applied to the four golf courses is also found in Table 1. Several interesting points can be made from results of this study. First, the average concentration of nitrate in the wells under the golf course sections was reduced significantly in the second/third year (1987-88). This was attributed to lower rates of application (nitrogen application rates dropped 10 to 25%). Even though twice as much fertilizer nitrogen was applied to greens, the fairways had the highest nitrate concentration in ground water wells.

Table 1. Range in pesticide concentration (ug/L) and average nitrate concentration (mg/L) found in Cape Cod golf course ground water wells

Material	Detection limit	Well location Greens	Tees	Fairways
Pesticides				
Chlordane				
technical	0.125	BDL*-7.2	BDL-1.7	BDL-1.39
metabolite	0.03	BDL-0.08	BDL-0.16	BDL-0.08
Chlorothalo-nil	0.015	BDL-0.38	BDL-0.22	BDL
Chlorpyrifos				
technical	0.05	BDL-0.1	BDL	BDL
metabolite	0.10	BDL	BDL-0.76	BDL
2,4-D	0.05	BDL-0.24	BDL	BDL
Dacthal				
metabolite	0.20	BDL-1.07	BDL-0.35	BDL
Dicamba	0.05	BDL	BDL	BDL-0.06
Isofenphos	0.75	BDL-1.17	BDL	BDL
Nitrate				
1986	0.1(2.2)+	5.7(4.6)#	1.8(2.8)	6.4(2.4)
1987/88	0.1(1.8)+	3.4(3.4)	1.0(2.5)	4.3(1.7)

* BDL=below detection limit. + Concentration of nitrate in background wells. # Values in () were the average amount of nitrogen applied, lbs./1000 sq.ft.

One of the major concerns raised in the Cape Cod Study was the fact that only older golf courses were evaluated. Does a new or very recently built golf course pose a greater threat to ground water quality than older courses with more developed soil organic matter/thatch and a microbial population that can enhance the pesticide decomposition?

Monitoring the ground water quality on a new golf course
would help address this concern. This was done at the Queenstown Harbor Golf Links, Queenstown, Maryland (Roy, 1993),
with the results on nitrate concentrations shown in Table
2. There are several important features about this site.
First it was originally agricultural fields (corn and
wheat) with some area still under production. Second, the
site is located within 1000 feet of the tidal waters of the
Chesapeake Bay, an area with intense environmental pressure
to improve the water quality of the Chesapeake Bay. It is
interesting to note that conversion of this site from
tradition agriculture to a golf course resulted in a substantial improvement in the groundwater quality to the
point that the nitrate concentration in water from wells on
the tees and fairway are below MCL for nitrate of 10 mg/L.
It should be noted that this golf course follows good
management practices for nitrogen fertilization which has
resulted in a drastic improvement in ground water quality.

Table 2. Concentration of nitrate (mg/L) from ground water
wells at the Queenstown Harbor Golf Links, Maryland

| Well location | Sampling date | | | Average | Range |
	11/90	10/92	6/93		
Back-ground	<0.1	0.4	0.1	0.1	<0.1-0.4
Tee (1)	0.1	1.7	2.0	1.7	<0.1-2.9
Agri-culture	19.0	21.0	12.7	17.6	12.7-23
Fairway	2.6	7.1	3.5	6.2	2.6-10.2
Tee (2)	n/a	<0.1	1.8	0.3	0.01-1.8

2.2 Research results

Research conducted at universities on the leaching of
pesticides applied to turfgrass (including golf course type
turf) involves measuring the concentration of pesticides in
drainage water or below the root zone, not ground water.
Since the drainage water or leachate below the root zone
must still travel some distance to reach groundwater, it is
assumed that these values will be lower once ground water
is reached, since further reactions and dilution can occur
at greater depths in the soil.

Table 3 summarizes the findings from several studies on
the leaching of pesticides similar to the ones studied on

the Cape Cod golf courses. For the pesticides chlorothalonil, 2,4-D and dicamba, the research results were very
similar to actual ground water concentrations from the Cape
Cod golf courses for sandy loam soil. However, the maximum
concentration of pesticides found in water from the research studies on sand (with the exception of chlorothalonil) and clay were substantially higher than from the Cape
Cod golf course wells.

The results of nitrate leaching studies have been summarized in a previous review article (Petrovic, 1990). With
few exceptions the nitrate concentrations observed on
actual golf courses agreed well with the research findings.

Table 3. Summary of pesticide leaching research studies
from turfgrass applications

Pesticide	Site conditions location	soil	Range in conc.(ug/L)	Reference
chloro-thalonil	lawn	sand	0	Borromeo, 1992
		sandy loam	0	
		silt loam	0-0.1	
2,4-D	lawn	sandy loam	0.6-0.9	Gold et al., 1988
		sand	0-105	Borromeo, 1992
		sandy loam	<1	
		silt loam	0-25	
		clay	0-312	Watschke and Mumma, 1989
	green	sand/peat	<10	Smith, 1993
dicamba	lawn	sandy loam	0.3-0.6	Gold et al., 1988
		sand	0-56	Borromeo, 1992
		sandy loam	<1	
		silt loam	0-14	
		clay	0-251	Watschke and Mumma, 1989
mecoprop	fairway	sand	0-1250	Petrovic, 1993
		sandy loam	0-50	
		silt loam	0-60	

3 Discussion

It is not surprising that controlled research studies had

different results than actual ground water values from real golf courses. One reason is that none of the studies were conducted with the identical soils and climatic variables which can significantly alter the leaching potential of a given chemical (pesticide or nitrate). A closer inspection of the research studies can shed some light on some of the difference noted. For pesticides, the greatest difference observed between research results and actual golf course data occurred on sand (Borromeo, 1992 and Petrovic, 1993) and clay (Watschke and Mumma, 1989) soils. These studies were designed to produce leachate water for study purposes. As was the cases with the clay soil, irrigation was applied at a rate of 15 cm/hr, an intensity seldom observed. The studies done on sand also were irrigated to produce leachate water for analysis. On the real golf courses, the rainfall or irrigation may not have occurred for a considerable time after application, thus not encouraging leaching. On the other hand, the actual golf courses only sampled groundwater four times per year and it is possible that higher concentrations could occurred but were not sampled. Conversely, all the water that leached was analyzed from the research studies.

One other example needs further explanation. Mecoprop was not detected in any of the well water samples from the Cape Cod golf courses, whereas the research results (Petrovic, 1993) showed high concentrations of mecoprop in samples. The research studies was conducted on a 4 month old seeding compared to the 30 + old golf courses. The newly established site was sparely covered with turf (especially the sand site) compared to the very dense actual golf course turf. It is apparent the thinly covered turf sites (especially on sandy soils) are more prone to pesticide leaching than well established sites and some caution should be exercised when applying pesticides under those conditions.

Another reason for differences in extent of leaching observed between research and actual golf course ground water monitoring studies is that the research studies are done in shallow lysimeters (< 2 m deep). The concentration of pesticide/nitrate would be expected to decrease in field ground water monitoring studies due to dilution with soil water/ground water and further chemical transformations that may take place deeper in the soil.

Nitrate leaching from either actual golf courses or controlled research studies were in agreement when similar timing, rates of application and material were compared. Thus, it appears that proper fertilizer management practices can easily results in minimal to no impact on ground water quality.

In the next several years there will be a tremendous amount of both research and actual golf course studies published on pesticide and fertilizer effects on both surface and ground water. Some care must be exercised in making direct comparisons of such studies and extrapolating the information to any turfgrass or golf course site. Solute (pesticide and nitrate) fate models have the greatest potential for accomplishing this task assuming they can be validated for golf course sites.

4   References

Borromeo, N.R. (1992) Leaching of pesticide applied to turf. **M.S. Thesis**, Cornell Univ., Ithaca, NY.

Cohen, S.Z., Nickerson, S., Maxey, R., Dupuy, A., and Senita, J.A. (winter, 1990) A ground water monitoring study for pesticides and nitrate associated with golf courses on Cape Cod. **Ground Water Monitoring Rev.** 160-173.

Cohen, S.Z. (winter, 1991) Agricultural chemical news (results of national pesticide-ground water survey). **Ground Water Monitoring Rev.** 85-87.

Flipse, W.J.,Jr., Katz, B.G., Lindner, J.B., and Markel, R. (1984) Sources of nitrate in ground water in a sewered housing development, central Long Island, NY. **Ground Water**, 32, 418-426.

Gold, A.J., Morton, T.G., Sullivan, W.M., and McClory, J. (1988) Leaching of 2,4-D and dicamba from home lawns. **J. Soil, Air and Water Poll.**, 37, 121-129.

Jaffe, S., Surgan, M.H., Goldweber, A., Volberg, D.I., and Sevinski, J.A. (1991) Toxic fairways: Risking groundwater contamination from pesticides on Long Island golf courses. New York State Department of Law, Albany, NY.

Petrovic, A.M. (1990) The fate of nitrogenous fertilizers applied to turfgrass. **J. Environ. Qual.**, 19, 1-14.

Petrovic, A. M. (1993) Leaching:research update. **J. Intern. Turfgrass Res. Soc. 1,**

Roy, S.P. (1993) Water quality report #8, Queenstown Harbor Links. Apogee Research, Inc. Bethesda, MD.

Smith, A. (1993) Pesticide leaching from greens. **J. Intern. Turfgrass Res. Soc. 1,**

Watschke, T.L., and Mumma, R.O. (1989). The effect of nutrients and pesticides applied to turf on the quality of the runoff and percolating water. Environ. Re sources Res. Inst. Report ER 8902, Penn. State Univ., University Park, PA.

76 Dislodgeable and volatile residues from insecticide-treated turfgrass

K.C. Murphy, R.J. Cooper and J.M. Clark
University of Massachusetts, Amherst, MA, USA

Abstract
Two insecticides were applied separately to a 10 m radius
plot of 'Penncross' creeping bentgrass (*Agrostis palustris*
Huds.) in order to determine levels of dislodgeable and
volatile residues. Source flux was estimated using the
Theoretical Profile Shape (TPS) Method. The effect of
post-application irrigation on residue dissipation was
assessed. Maximum residue levels were compared to
published dermal and inhalation "no-effect" values. As
judged by this preliminary comparison, golfer exposure to
airborne and dermal residues are deemed within safe
levels, except in selected situations.
Keywords: Theoretical Profile Shape Method, Inhalation
"No-Effect" Values, Dermal "No-Effect" Values,
Evapotranspiration , Pesticide Fate, Turfgrass

1 Introduction

In order to maintain golf courses in acceptable conditions
for play, pesticide application is sometimes necessary.
Because of the potential for environmental contamination
and human and non-target exposure however, there is
increasing opposition to pesticide use. In order to
assess the environmental fate and magnitude of pesticide
exposure, foliar dislodgeable and airborne residues were
measured from pesticide-treated turfgrass.

2 Experimental design

All experiments were conducted at the University of
Massachusetts Turfgrass Research Facility in South
Deerfield, MA. Isazofos(O-5-chloro-1-isopropyl-1H-1,2,4-
triazol-3-yl O,O-diethyl phosphorothioate)and trichlorfon
(dimethyl 2,2,2-trichloro-1-hydroxyethylphosphonate)were
applied separately at the manufacturers' highest
recommended rate to an established plot of 'Penncross'
creeping bentgrass. For each application, a 10 m radius

Science and Golf II: Proceedings of the World Scientific Congress of Golf. Edited by A.J.
Cochran and M.R. Farrally. Published in 1994 by E & FN Spon, London. ISBN 0 419 18790 1

plot was sprayed. Isazofos application was followed immediately by 1.3 cm of irrigation. Two applications of trichlorfon were made; one with 1.3 cm of irrigation immediately after application and one without post-application irrigation. Dislodgeable and volatile residues of dichlorvos (DDVP), the toxic metabolite of trichlorfon, were measured as well. Wind speed, wind direction, surface and air temperature, solar radiation, and rainfall were monitored throughout each two week sampling period using a Campbell CR10 measurement and control system (Campbell Scientific, Logan, Utah).

Dislodgeable residue samples were obtained by wiping pesticide-treated turf with a piece of dampened cheese-cloth (Thompson *et al.*, 1984). The Theoretical Profile Shape (TPS) method (Wilson *et al.*, 1983) was used to estimate source flux of volatile pesticides. Airborne residues were collected on 120 ml of XAD-4 resin with a Staplex high volume air pump located at 70 cm above the center of the treated surface.

3 Methodology

3.1 Sample collection, preparation and analysis
Dislodgeable residue samples were obtained 15 min, three and eight h after application on Day 1, and at 1200 h on subsequent days. Volatile residues were collected immediately after application(i.e., during application and continuing for an additional 30 min)and during consecutive four-hour-sampling periods until 1900 on Day 1. Sampling continued from 0700 to 1900 h on Days 2 and 3, and 0900 to 1700 h on Days 5,7,10 and 15. Approximately 40 min after application, isazofos (Fig. 1) and trichlorfon-treated plots (Fig. 3) received 1.3 cm irrigation.

Pesticide residues were extracted from the cheesecloth and XAD-4 resin using acetone or methanol. Field samples were extracted immediately after collection and stored in a freezer until analysis. Aliquots from the extract were diluted or concentrated so the pesticide concentration fell within the linear working range (i.e., between 0.1 and 5.0 ug/ml). Recoveries for all compounds ranged between 80 and 100% (Murphy, 1994). Pesticide fortified cheesecloth and XAD-4 resin showed no observable loss of pesticide over the maximum storage time of four months (Murphy, 1994).

All samples were analyzed by gas chromatography utilizing capillary columns and a flame photometric detector. Isazofos was analyzed as described in the method of Perez (1985) and trichlorfon and DDVP were analyzed according to the method of Cox (1989).

3.2 Quantification of pesticide residues
Final extract concentration was determined using standard

curves (r>0.98).   Pesticide residues on cheesecloth and
XAD-4 resin were determined by using the appropriate
dilution or concentration factors and correcting with
established laboratory recoveries.

Airborne concentration ($\mu g/m^3$) was determined by
dividing the amount of pesticide on the XAD-4 resin (μg)
by the volume of air drawn through the pump during that
sampling period (m^3).   Volatile source flux ($\mu g/m^2/h$) was
estimated by incorporating the airborne concentration and
the wind speed at 70 cm above the treated surface into
Wilson's TPS model (1983).

4 Results and discussion

Irrigation reduced dislodgeable residues of isazofos from
3920 $\mu g/m^2$ measured at 15 min to 6 $\mu g/m^2$ measured 8 h after
application (Fig. 1).   Dislodgeable isazofos residues were
nondetectable after Day 3.   The source flux of isazofos
volatile residues was reduced from 4164 $\mu g/m^2/h$ immediately
after application to 1399 $\mu g/m^2/h$ measured from 1100 to
1500 h on Day 1.   Overall source flux decreased with time,
resulting in 10 $\mu g/m^2/h$ being rendered as volatile residues
on Day 13 (0.02% of applied isazofos).

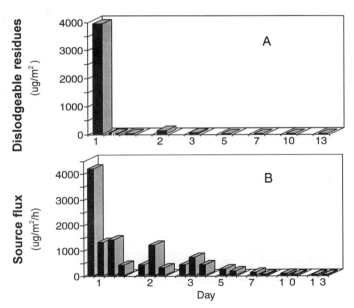

Figure 1.   Isazofos applied at 2142 g/ha followed by 1.3
cm of irrigation: (A) dislodgeable residues; (B) volatile
residues.   Each bar represents one sampling period.

In the absence of irrigation, dislodgeable residues of
trichlorfon measured 47570 $\mu g/m^2$ immediately after
application (Fig. 2) and declined to 10 $\mu g/m^2$ by Day 15
(0.001% of applied trichlorfon). Source flux of
trichlorfon was greatest immediately after application
(4570 $\mu g/m^2/h$) and dissipated to 3 $\mu g/m^2/h$ (0.002% of
applied trichlorfon) by Day 15.

Dislodgeable residues of trichlorfon were reduced from
105660 $\mu g/m^2$ measured immediately after application to 182
$\mu g/m^2$ measured three h after application on Day 1 as a
result of post-application irrigation (Fig. 3). By Day
15, dislodgeable residues measured 28 $\mu g/m^2$ (0.003% of
applied trichlorfon). Irrigation reduced source flux of
trichlorfon from 1154 $\mu g/m^2/h$ immediately after application
to 646 $\mu g/m^2/h$ during the 1100 to 1500 h sampling period on
Day 1. However, mid-day source flux on Days 2 (2046
$\mu g/m^2/h$) and 3 (2029 $\mu g/m^2/h$) was greater than on Day 1
after the irrigation process (645 $\mu g/m^2/h$). This may be
due to soil drying via evapotranspiration resulting in
subsurface water moving upward translocating more water-
soluble and non-bound pesticides to the surface.
Pesticide residues which were moved into the soil by
irrigation immediately after application appeared to be
available as dislodgeable and volatile surface residues on
Days 2 and 3. By Day 15, trichlorfon flux declined to 26

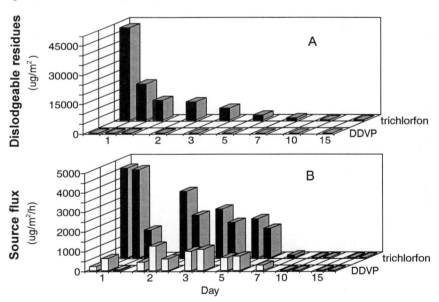

Figure 2. Trichlorfon applied at 9155 g/ha: (A) dislodgeable
residues; (B) volatile residues. Each bar represents one
sampling period.

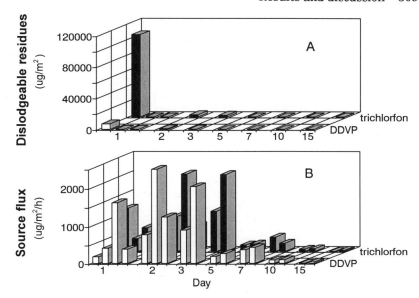

Figure 3. Trichlorfon applied at 9155 g/ha followed by 1.3 cm of irrigation: (A) dislodgeable residues; (B) volatile residues. Each bar represents one sampling period.

$\mu g/m^2/h$ (0.03% of applied trichlorfon).

Without irrigation, maximum dislodgeable residues of DDVP (30 $\mu g/m^2$) were found immediately after application on Day 1 and were nondetectable by Day 15 (Fig. 2). Maximum source flux occurred on Day 2 (1240 $\mu g/m^2/h$) and declined to 2 $\mu g/m^2/h$ by Day 15.

When irrigation followed application, DDVP dislodgeable residues were maximal on Day 2 (785 $\mu g/m^2$) and were nondetectable by Day 5 (Fig. 3). Consistent with trichlorfon source flux after irrigation, maximum DDVP source flux occurred on Days 2 and 3 (2046 and 2028 $\mu g/m^2/h$, respectively). Post-application irrigation of trichlorfon enhanced conversion to DDVP, the more toxic metabolite. DDVP volatile flux following irrigation was equal to or greater than trichlorfon flux (Fig. 3), however, without irrigation, DDVP source flux was approximately 30% of trichlorfon source flux (Fig. 2).

Following determination of dislodgeable and volatile residues, an attempt was made to relate those measurements to potential human exposure. Dislodgeable residue measurements were used to estimate dermal exposure using the method of Zweig et al. (1985) and were compared to published dermal "no-effect" values. Air concentrations estimated from volatile residues for each compound were compared to published inhalation "no-effect" values. Published "no-effect" values are determined from laboratory animal studies. Estimated human dermal and inhalation exposures less than 100-fold below published "no-effect" values may be of toxicological significance because of the many assumptions made in equating animal "no-effect" and human "no-effect" values.

Using these estimated exposures, isazofos was the only compound that resulted in dermal exposure levels less than 1000-fold below dermal "no-effect" values. On Days 2 and 3, the estimated dermal exposures for isazofos were 30 and 80-fold, respectively, below dermal "no-effect" values. Thus, dislodgeable residues of isazofos were considered to be of possible toxicological significance through Day 3.

DDVP was the only compound that produced air concentrations less than 1000-fold below inhalation "no-effect" values. Without irrigation, DDVP air concentration levels were 100 and 60-fold below the inhalation "no-effect" values on Days 2 and 3, respectively. With irrigation, DDVP air concentration levels were only 30 and 60-fold below inhalation "no-effect" values.   In conclusion, a golfer could be exposed to concentrations of DDVP causing non-lethal toxic effects for up to 3 days following after application.

5 Acknowledgement

The authors would like to thank the United States Golf Association and the Massachusetts Turf and Lawngrass Association for their generous financial support of this research.

6 References

Cox, C.L.; Timmons, L.L.; Ridlen, R.L. (1989) Capillary gas chromatographic analysis of trichlorfon in dosed feed formulations. **J. Anal. Toxicol.**, 13, 84-88.
Murphy, K.C. (1994) Ph.D. thesis, University of Massachusetts at Amherst, unpublished results.
Perez, R. (1985) Method No. 479, Ciba Geigy Corp., Greensboro, NC.
Thompson, D.G.; Stephenson, G.R.; Sears, M.K. (1984) Persistence, distribution and dislodgeable residues of 2,4-D following its application to turfgrass. **Pest. Sci.**, 15, 353-360.
Wilson, J; Catchpoole, V.; Denmead, O.; Thurtell, G. (1983) for estimating the rate of gaseous mass transfer from the ground to the atmosphere. **Agric. Met.**, 29, 183-189.
Zwieg, G.; Leffingwell, J.T.; Popendorf, W. (1985) The relationship between dermal pesticide exposure by fruit harvesters and dislodgeable foliar residues. **Environ. Sci. Health,** B 20 (1), 27-59.

77 Fate and mobility of pre-emergent herbicides in turfgrass

H.D. Niemczyk and A.A. Krause
OARDC/The Ohio State University, Wooster, Ohio, USA

Abstract
Much of the groundwater quality concern, related to the use of herbicides on golfcourses, is based on extrapolation from agricultural situations rather than data developed from studies conducted in field turfgrass situations. To address this data gap, a two-year field project evaluating the behavior and mobility of the commonly used preemergent herbicides, benfluralin, trifluralin, bensulide, oxadiazon, pendimethalin, and DCPA with its two metabolites was conducted at OARDC/The Ohio State University, Wooster, Ohio, in 1988-89. Plots were located on a site with thatch (WT) and one with no thatch (NT) to further clarify the impact of thatch on herbicide behavior. Treatments were applied in April and samples of thatch and four zones of soil (0-2.5, 2.5-5, 7.5-10 and 22.5-25 cm) were collected throughout the year and analyzed for residue dissipation. Residues of pendimethalin, benfluralin, and trifluralin in the 22.5-25 cm zone were below the limit of determination. No detectable oxadiazon residues were found in this zone at the WT site in 1988 but on two occasions, residues of 0.01 and 0.02 kg/ha were found in 1989. At the NT site, residues in this zone on one occasion were 0.02 kg/ha in 1988 and none in 1989. Residues of bensulide in the same zone ranged not detectable (ND)-0.02 kg/ha in both locations. The DCPA residues in the 22.5-25 cm zone ranged ND-0.10 kg/ha (WT), ND-0.27 kg/ha (NT) in 1988, and ND-0.02 kg/ha (WT), ND-0.04 kg/ha (NT) in 1989. The residues of SDS 1449, the less stable of two dacthal metabolites, were very low but higher in 1988 than in 1989 in both locations. The SDS 954 residues in 22.5-25 cm zone ranged ND-0.1 kg/ha (WT), and ND-0.16 kg/ha (NT) in 1988, and ND-0.26 kg/ha (WT), and ND-0.27 kg/ha (NT) in 1989.

Some amount of all herbicides applied carried over into the spring of the year following application but oxadiazon and bensulide were the most persistent.
Keywords: thatch, benfluralin, trifluralin, pendimethalin, bensulide, oxadiazon, DCPA, leaching

1 Introduction

The vertical mobility of pesticides is influenced by many factors including the properties of the pesticide, the medium to which they are applied and the frequency - intensity of precipitation or irrigation. Computer simulation has enabled many researchers to study the impact of these and other factors on mobility in soil (Enfield et al. 1982, Carsel et al. 1984, Knisel and Leonard 1986, Wagenet and Hutson 1989). Theoretical screening techniques have also been developed (Dean et al. 1984, Rao et al. 1985, Wilkerson and Kim 1986, Jury et al. 1987, Gustafson 1989) to identify compounds with high leaching potential. Field data are needed to calibrate such models and verify their applicability to the turfgrass situation. Turfgrass field studies on vertical mobility and persistence of some insecticides (Kuhr and Tashiro, 1978, Niemczyk et al., 1977, Sears and Chapman, 1979, Niemczyk and Krueger, 1987, Petrovic et al., 1993) have been reported. While Gold et al. (1988) and Petrovic et al. (1993a) reported on the leaching of the postemergence herbicides 2,4-D and mecoprop, except for studies of Stahnke et al. (1991) on pendimethalin, relatively little field data developed in established (≥5 years) turfgrass situations, have been published on the preemergent herbicides most commonly used on turfgrasses. The purpose of this study was to evaluate fate and mobility of these herbicides in turfgrass.

Science and Golf II: Proceedings of the World Scientific Congress of Golf. Edited by A.J. Cochran and M.R. Farrally. Published in 1994 by E & FN Spon, London. ISBN 0 419 18790 1

2 Materials and methods

2.1 Experiment site

Experiments were conducted on two sites, each consisting of Kentucky bluegrass (Poa pratensis L. var. unknown) turf mowed at 7.5 cm, and located at The Ohio Agricultural Research and Development Center (OARDC), The Ohio State University, Wooster, Ohio. One site (WT) established in 1965 and reseeded in 1985, had 0.6 - 1.3 cm of thatch and the second (NT) established in 1959, had no thatch. Prior to establishment of the experiment in 1988, both sites received annual applications of isobutylidene diurea (IBDU) fertilizer, preemergent (Dacthal®75W - NT site, Betasan®7G - WT site) and postemergent (combination of 2,4-D, MCPP and dicamba) herbicides in 1987. In 1988 both sites were fertilized with one application of IBDU and received two applications of postemergent herbicide (2,4-D alone or combination of 2,4-D, MCPP and dicamba). No postemergent herbicides were applied to either site in 1989 but each was fertilized once with IBDU.

The physical properties of thatch and soil were assayed by CLC Labs, Westerville Ohio. Organic matter (OM) content (determined by loss on ignition) was 34.04, 7.44, 4.20, 4.59 and 2.56% for thatch, 0-2.5, 2.5-5, 7.5-10 and 22.5-25 cm sample zone, respectively (WT) and 9.77, 6.25, 5.00 and 2.60% for 0-2.5, 2.5-5, 7.5-10 and 22.5-25 cm sample zone, respectively (NT). The soil at both sites was Wooster silt loam (level fine - loamy, mixed, mesic, Typic Fragiudalf).

In 1988 the experiment was conducted under moisture deficient conditions. During that year of the experiment the majority of the rainfall occurred between 90 and 140 DAT. In 1988, rainfall was 32.0 and 13.2 mm during May and June, respectively which was 69.1 and 87.9 mm below the 101 year average for these months. In 1989, rainfall for these two months was 114.3 and 182.9 mm, 13.7 and 80.5 mm above the 102 year average.

2.2 Treatments

The following herbicides were applied at labelled rates to single plots 3.1 x 7.6 m at both WT and NT sites on April 19 1988, and 1989: benfluralin [N-butyl-N-ethyl-α,α,α-trifluoro-2,6-dinitro-p-toluidine] as Balan®2.5G at 2.2 kg a.i./ha and as a component of Team®2G[a] at 1.5 kg a.i./ha, bensulide [S-2-benzenesulphonamidoethyl O,O-di-isopropyl phosphorodithioate] as Betasan®12G at 13.4 kg a.i./ha, oxadiazon [5-tert-butyl-3-(2,4-dichloro-5-isopropoxyphenyl)-1,3,4-oxadiazol-2(3H)-=one] as Ronstar®2G at 2.7 kg a.i./ha, pendimethalin [N-(1-ethylpropyl)-2,6-dinitro-3,4-xylidine] as Pre-M®60WDG[b] at 1.7 kg a.i./ha, trifluralin [α,α,α-trifluoro-2,6-dinitro-N,N-dipropyl-p-toluidine] as Team®2G at 0.8 kg a.i./ha, and DCPA [dimethyl tetrachloroterephthalate] as Dacthal®75WP at 11.2 kg a.i./ha. Granular formulations were applied with a 0.6 m wide drop spreader, and liquids with a pressurized CO_2 sprayer, Tee-Jet® 8015 nozzles that delivered 0.16 L/m^2. Plots were irrigated by hand immediately after treatment with 1.3 cm (12.7 L/m^2) of water.

Prior to initial application of the herbicides, samples of thatch and soil (-1 DAT) from each plot at both sites were analyzed to determine possible background and carryover from previous herbicide applications. The analyses showed a total carryover of 5.59 and 0.02 kg a.i./ha for bensulide and benfluralin, respectively, in the WT site and 0.01 kg a.i./ha bensulide in the NT site.

2.3 Sample collection

Samples for residue analyses were obtained using a standard soil probe, 3.2 cm inside diameter at 0, 2, 7, 13, 20, 27, 56, 84, 111, 149, 173 days after treatment (DAT) in 1988, and 0, 2, 7, 14, 29, 64, 89, 114, 146, 180, 208 DAT in 1989. Cores (10-12) from both sites were taken across the

---

[a] Team®2G is a herbicide formulation containing 1.33% of benfluralin and 0.67% of trifluralin.

[b] Pendimethalin applied in 1988 only.

width of the plot in a line perpendicular to the direction of application, and sectioned into zones of thatch (if present), 0-2.5, 2.5-5.0, 7.5-10.0, and 22.5-25 cm of underlying soil. Cores from each zone were pooled into separate plastic bags and stored at -18°C until analyzed.

2.4 Residue analyses

Samples of turfgrass thatch and soil were analyzed without prior drying. The content of each plastic bag of pooled samples was weighed and the number of cores counted. Grass blades were removed from all cores and discarded. Thatch cores were cut manually with scissors into small pieces and mixed thoroughly to produce a homogenous sample. Soil cores were manually disintegrated and thoroughly mixed. Each sample of thatch and/or soil was prepared in a separate, disposable laboratory aluminum pan. New rubber gloves were used for mixing each sample and the scissors used for thatch cutting rinsed with acetone to prevent sample cross-contamination. Oxadiazon, DCPA/degradates, and trifluralin/benfluralin residues were solvent extracted, reextracted/purified using a solid-phase extraction (SPE) system, and measured by gas-liquid chromatography (GLC) according to methods of Krause and Niemczyk (1990, 1990a, 1992), respectively. Pendimethalin residues were assayed according to a modified (no concentration of the final SPE extract) method of Smith (1984). Average pendimethalin recoveries were 98.9 ± 0.7 and $96.4 \pm 1.5\%$, for soil and thatch respectively. The residues of bensulide were extracted with acetone, an aliquot of clear extract was diluted with water, and reextracted/purified on a preconditioned C_8 SPE tube. The residues were measured by GLC with nitrogen/phosphorus detection. Average bensulide recoveries were 102 ± 1.9 and $96.0 \pm 3.2\%$, for soil and thatch respectively. The limits of determination for thatch/soil were 0.08/0.04, 0.01/0.02, 0.01/0.01, 0.02/0.01, 0.05/0.02, 0.05/0.02, 0.13/0.05 and 0.20/0.05 ppm for oxadiazon, DCPA, SDS1449, SDS954, trifluralin, benfluralin, pendimethalin and bensulide, respectively. Analyses of all samples collected during the study were completed by May 1990.

2.5 Data expression

In taking samples, the thatch zone was always broken off from the core at the natural visible division between thatch and underlying soil. As samples were taken, we observed that the depth of thatch varied considerably across the plots. Though the number of cores remained the same, the mass of pool material collected varied through the sample period. When for example, the dissipation curve of DCPA residues (ppm) in the thatch zone for 1988 was plotted we observed that the curve minimum point (27 DAT) corresponded to the highest thatch sample dry weight, and the maximum point (56 DAT) to the lowest. This variation was corrected when ppm residues were recalculated based on the formula of Johnson et al.[a] (1990) and expressed in kg/ha.

3 Results

3.1 Dinitroanilines (DNA)

No detectable residues of benfluralin, trifluralin, pendimethalin (1988 only) were found in the 22.5-25 cm sampling zone during 1988 and 1989.

---

[a] Residue (lb/A)=Residue (ppm) x WT x CF

where WT = total weight (kg) of the sample collected including any sand added prior to mixing
        CF (conversion factor)= $4.395/(r^2 \times N)$

where

        r = inside radius (inches) of the tip of the sampler probe
        N = number of cores collected and composited into a single sample

3.1.1 Benfluralin (Balan®)
Residues in the thatch zone at the WT site ranged 66.7-98.5 and 81.8-99.5% of the total residues recovered and 85.7-100 and 81.8-100% in the first 2.5 cm zone at the NT site in 1988 and 1989, respectively.

3.1.2 Benfluralin (Team®)
Residues in the thatch zone at the WT plot ranged 88-100 and 75-100% of the total residues recovered, and 75-100 and 50-98.9% in the first 2.5 cm zone at the NT plot in 1988 and 1989, respectively.

3.1.3 Trifluralin
Residues in the thatch zone at the WT plot ranged 87.5-100 and 75-100% of the total residues recovered, and 75-100 and 66.7-98% in the first 2.5 cm zone at the NT plot in 1988 and 1989, respectively.

3.1.4 Pendimethalin
Residues in the thatch zone at the WT plot ranged 47.4-93.3% of the total residues recovered, and 27.3-100% in the first 2.5 cm zone at the NT plot.

3.2 Oxadiazon
No detectable residues occurred in the 22.5-25 cm sampling zone at the WT site in 1988, however on two sampling occasions in 1989,-1 DAT, 0.01 kg/ha (0.5% of the total residues recovered) and 64 DAT 0.02 kg/ha (0.4% of the total residues recovered) were found. In 1988 residues of 0.02 kg/ha (1.7% of total residues recovered) were found in the same zone at the NT site on one sampling occasion 8 DAT but none were found in this zone in 1989.

Residues in the thatch zone at the WT site ranged 98.5-100 and 96-100% of the total residues recovered, and 76.5-98.8 and 73.6-95.2 in the first 2.5 cm zone at the NT site in 1988 and 1989, respectively.

3.3 Bensulide
Residues of bensulide in the 22.5-25 cm sampling zone, at both sites and in both years, ranged from ND to 0.02 kg/ha which was ≤0.8% of the total residues recovered from all sampling zones. Residues in the thatch zone at the WT site ranged 77.1-96.8 and 69.3-97.2% of the total residues recovered and 91.5-98.6 and 88.1-94.6% in the first 2.5 cm zone at the NT site in 1988 and 1989, respectively.

In 1988, fifty percent or more of the bensulide residues found in each of the five sample zones from the WT plot at 0 DAT were carryover from applications of bensulide to the site prior to initiation of the study.

3.4 DCPA and metabolites

3.4.1 DCPA
DCPA residue in the 22.5-25 cm zone ranged ND-0.10 kg/ha (WT), ND-0.27 kg/ha (NT) in 1988, and ND-0.02 kg/ha (WT), ND-0.04 kg/ha (NT) in 1989. Residues in the thatch zone at the WT site ranged 68.3-100 and 60-100% of the total residues recovered, and 71.3-95.6 and 50-91 in the first 2.5 cm zone at the NT in 1988 and 1989, respectively.

3.4.2 SDS 954
The SDS 954 residue in the uppermost zone in both sites reached its highest level 29 DAT in 1989, and in 1988 at 112 and 84 DAT in the NT, and WT sites, respectively. The SDS 954 residues in the 22.5-25 cm zone ranged ND-0.1 kg/ha (WT), and ND-0.16 kg/ha (NT) in 1988, and ND-0.26 kg/ha (WT), and ND-0.27 kg/ha (NT) in 1989. SDS 954 residues in the 22.5-25 cm

zone were greater in 1989 than in 1988 in both locations.

3.5 Maximum residue levels

A summary of the maximum seasonal residue levels, including background and carryover, found in all zones at both sites is presented in Table 1.

Table 1. Maximum Seasonal Residues Found in All Zones Sampled, 1988-1989.

Sample Zone (cm)	Benfl. Balan®	Bensul.	Oxadiaz.	Pendimeth.	Triflu. Team®	Benfl. Team®	DCPA	SDS1449	SDS954
			Maximum Seasonal Concentration Observed (kg/ha)[1]						
With Thatch									
Thatch 1988	0.67	14.43	2.36	0.78	0.25	0.47	5.70	0.21	1.32
1989	2.21	14.27	5.40		0.20	0.34	7.21	0.09	1.36
0-2.5 1988	0.04	1.53	0.03	0.09	0.02	0.03	0.60	0.02	0.60
1989	0.09	1.00	0.08		0.03	0.07	0.52	0.01	0.57
2.5-5 1988	0.01	0.22	0.01	0.06	ND	ND	0.53	0.04	0.72
1989	0.01	0.20	0.06		0.01	0.02	0.07	0.01	0.52
7.5-10 1988	0.01	0.13	ND	0.07	ND	ND	0.36	0.02	0.27
1989	0.01	0.04	0.06		ND	ND	0.15	0.01	0.43
22.5-25 1988	ND	0.02	ND	ND	ND	ND	0.03	0.01	0.10
1989	ND	0.02	0.02		ND	ND	0.02	ND	0.26
With No Thatch									
0-2.5 1988	1.57	11.61	1.77	0.74	0.46	0.90	4.16	0.11	2.09
1989	1.16	10.43	2.68		0.48	0.90	7.41	0.07	0.81
2.5-5 1988	0.02	0.46	0.08	0.07	0.02	0.04	0.59	0.01	1.37
1989	0.07	0.60	0.35		0.02	0.03	0.92	0.01	0.39
7.5-10 1988	0.01	0.08	0.09	0.03	ND	0.01	0.25	0.01	0.78
1989	0.01	0.53	0.09		ND	0.01	0.26	ND	0.24
22.5-25 1988	ND	0.01	0.02	ND	ND	ND	0.27	0.01	0.16
1989	ND	0.02	ND		ND	ND	0.04	ND	0.27

[1] Includes background and carryover, ND - below the limit of determination

4 Discussion

The properties of pesticides having the greatest effect on their potential for vertical mobility are soil sorption coefficient (K_{OC}), and field half-life ($t_{1/2}$) (Cohen et al. 1984, Jury et al. 1987, Gustafson, 1989), and rarely water solubility (Nicholls, 1988, Truman and Leonard, 1991). The K_{OC} and $t_{1/2}$ for the herbicides applied in this study are 9000 and 40, 8000 and 60, 5000 and 90, 5000 and 100, 3200 and 60 and 1000 and 120 for benfluralin, trifluralin, pendimethalin, DCPA, oxadiazon and bensulide, respectively (Wauchope et al., 1991). Soil sorption coefficients do not fully reflect the mobility of the pesticides seen in this study. With soil K_{OC} of 5000 and $t_{1/2}$ of 100 one would not expect to find DCPA residues in the 22.5-25 cm zone of either site but residues were found in this zone. Residues of pendimethalin, with similar K_{OC} and $t_{1/2}$ of 5000 and 90, respectively, were not found.

Thatch, a medium for which sorption coefficients have not been established, is an important factor in many aspects of turfgrass management (Ledeboer and Skogley 1967; Beard 1973; Niemczyk et al. 1977; Turgeon et al. 1977; Turgeon 1979, 1988; Carrow 1979; Hurto and Turgeon 1979; Shearman 1979; Hurto et al. 1980; Shearman et al. 1983; Potter et al. 1990). The sorptive capacity of the thatch in the WT site (34.04% OM) and the 0-2.5 cm zone of the NT site (9.77% OM) in this study was the major factor responsible for finding high residues of DNAs, oxadiazon, bensulide and DCPA in these zones. The major reason for this was that the OM content of this zone was sufficiently high to cause adsorption of a major fraction of the herbicides applied. While the OM level of thatch is naturally high, the OM content of the 0-2.5 cm zone in established turf ($\geq$5 years) with no thatch is normally higher than that of most agricultural soils (range for Wooster silt loam, Wooster, Ohio is 1-5% OM) because in the absence of tillage (34 years at the NT site), continual senescence and death of plant parts lead to an accumulation of organic matter. The field data on the mobility of benfluralin, bensulide, and DCPA in WT versus NT sites we present in this paper do not support the findings of laboratory studies by Hurto and Turgeon (1979) who showed mobility of these herbicides to be greater in undisturbed thatch than in undisturbed soil from sites with no thatch.

While the OM level and sorptive potential of the zone to which pesticides are applied are key factors in their availability to degradation and transport processes, this study showed that rainfall was a more important factor in the residue levels found at both the surface and subsurface. In this study, the mobility of herbicides into the lower sampling zones was correlated to major rainfall events that occurred prior to sampling. Generally, the data show little movement of DNAs, and oxadiazon to the soil of 0-2.5cm sampling zone under the thatch (WT sites), and 2.5-5 cm zone (NT sites). Among DNAs, pendimethalin showed most of the movement into the second sampling zone of both sites. This may be attributed to the fact that pendimethalin has the lowest K_{OC} and longest $t_{1/2}$ of the DNAs applied.

Finding residues of bensulide in the 7.5-10 and 22.5-25 cm sampling zones (both sites) may be explained by the fact that the $t_{1/2}$ for bensulide (120 days), is significantly longer than for the DNAs and oxadiazon, and its affinity for organic matter (K_{OC}=1000) is much lower than that of DNAs and oxadiazon. Apparently the herbicide persists in the soil long enough to be translocated into deeper soil layers.

The mobility of DCPA and its two degradates SDS 1449 and SDS 954 into the lower sampling zones were monitored during this study. Rapid degradation of DCPA occurred between 84 and 111(112) DAT and 29 and 64(65) DAT in 1988 and 1989, respectively, after major rainfall events. Residue pattern of SDS 1449, the less stable of two DCPA metabolites, also corresponded to major rainfall events.

Generally, weak organic acids do not readily move through acidic media high in OM. Based on the small amount of SDS 1449 found in the lower sample zones, where pH was $\leq$5.6, we theorize that the acidic pH of these zones suppressed its mobility because it is a weak acid. Residues of SDS 954 were common in the lower zones indicating increased mobility. Evidence of its reduced affinity for organic matter was confirmed during the development of an analytical method (Krause and Niemczyk, 1990a) which showed that SDS 954 had no affinity for the C_{18} sorbent at pH =1. The K_{OC} of tetrachloroterephthalic acid (SDS 954), the second metabolite of DCPA is 90 in sandy, 4 in silty clay soils, and its $t_{1/2}$ is unknown (Smith, 1990). The K_{oc} and $t_{1/2}$ for monomethyltetrachloroterephthalate (SDS 1449), the first acidic metabolite of DCPA were not available.

The residue data obtained in this study show that each year some amount of all the herbicides applied carried over into the spring of the next year, however, oxadiazon and bensulide were most persistent. In 1989, 74%(1.9 kg a.i./ha) of the 2.57 kg a.i./ha oxadiazon residues in the thatch and 0-2.5 cm zones 0 DAT were carryover from 1988. Of the maximum residues (5.14 kg a.i./ha) found in these zones 27 DAT, 55% (2.82 kg a.i./ha) were carried over into 1990. In the same year, 39% (3.33 kg a.i./ha) of the 8.54 kg a.i./ha bensulide residues in these zones 0 DAT were carryover from 1988. Of the maximum residues (14.39 kg a.i./ha) found in these zones 27 DAT, 13% (1.87 kg a.i./ha) carried over into 1990. These data indicate a need to consider the carryover of these two herbicides in relation to the need for and rate of application necessary for continued preemergent weed control in turfgrass.

5 References

Beard, J. B. (1973) Turfgrass Science and Culture. Prentice-Hall, Inc., Engelwood Cliffs, N. J.

Carrow, R. N. (1979) Integration of Control Methods Necessary to Prevent Thatch Buildup. **Weeds Trees and Turf**, 18(4), 58-59.

Carsel, R., Smith, C., Mulkey, L., Dean, J., Jowise, P. (1984) Users Manual for the Pesticide Root Zone Model (PRZM), Release 1., EPA-600/3-84-109, EPA, Athens, GA.

Cohen, S., Creeger, S., Carsel, R., Enfield, C. (1984) Potential for Pesticide Contamination of Ground Water Resulting From Agricultural Uses. in: Krueger, R. F. and Seiber, J. N. Eds., **Treatment and Disposal of Wastes** Am. Chem. Soc. Symposium Series 325, pp 297-325.

Dean, J. D., Jowise, P. P., Donigian, A. S. Jr. (1984) Leaching Evaluation of Agricultural Chemicals (LEACH), EPA-600/3-84-068, EPA, Athens, GA.

Enfield, C., Carsel, R., Cohen, S., Phan, T., Walters, D. (1982) Approximating Pollutant Transport to Ground Water with PESTAN. **Ground Water**, 20, 711-722.

Gold, A. J., Morton, T. G., Sullivan, W. M., McClory, J. (1988) Leaching of 2,4-D and Dicamba from Home Lawns. **Water, Air, and Soil Pollution**, 37, 121-129.

Gustafson, D. I. (1989) Groundwater Ubiquity Score: A Simple Method for Assessing Pesticide Leachibility. **Environ. Toxicol. Chem.** 8, 339-357.

Hurto, K. A., Turgeon, A. J. (1979) Influence of Thatch on Preemergence Herbicide Activity in Kentucky Bluegrass (*Poa pratensis*) Turf. **Weed Sci.**, 27(2), 141-145.

Hurto, K. A., Turgeon, A. J., Spomer, L. A. (1980) Physical Characteristics of Thatch as a Growing Medium. **Agronomy J.** 72, 165-167.

Johnson, W. H., Sieck, F., Griggs, R. D. (1980) **Personal communication**. Agricultural Analytical Chemistry Department, Eli Lilly and Co., Greenfield, Indiana.

Jury, W., Focht, D., Farmer, W. (1987) Evaluation of Groundwater Pollution Potential From Standard Indices of Soil-Chemical Adsorption and biodegradation. **J. Environ. Qual.**, 16, 422-428.

Knisel, W., Leonard, R. (1986) Impact of Irrigation on Ground-Water Quality in the Humid Region. **Proc. Am. Soc. Civil Eng. Water Forum 86: World Water Issues in Evolution**, Long Beach, CA, pp 1508-1515.

Krause, A. A., Niemczyk, H. D. (1990) Gas-Liquid Chromatographic Analysis of Oxadiazon Residues in Turfgrass Thatch and Soil Using a Solid-Phase Extraction Technique. **J. Environ. Sci. Health, Part B**, B25, 347-355.

Krause, A. A., Niemczyk, H. D. (1990a) Gas-Liquid Chromatographic Analysis of Chlorthal-Dimethyl Herbicide ad Its Degradates in Turfgrass Thatch and Soil Using a Solid-Phase Extraction Technique. **J. Environ. Sci. Health,** Part B, B25, 587-606.

Krause, A. A., Niemczyk, H. D. (1992) Simultaneous Gas-Liquid Chromatographic Analysis of Trifluralin and Benfluralin Residues in Turfgrass Thatch and Soil by Solid-Phase Extraction Technique. **J. Environ. Sci. Health, Part B**, B27(1), 39-51.

Kuhr, R. J., Tashiro, H. (1978) Distribution and Persistence of Chlorpyriphos and Diazinon Applied to Turf. **Bull. Environ. Contam. Toxicol.**, 20, 652-656.

Ledeboer, F. B., Skogley, C. R. (1967) Investigations Into the Nature of Thatch and Methods of its Decomposition. **Agronomy J.**, 59, 320-323.

Nicholls, P. H. (1988) Factors Influencing the Entry of Pesticides into Soil Water. **Pest. Sci.**, 22, 123-137.

Niemczyk, H. D., Krueger, H. R., Lawrence, K. O. (1977) Thatch Influences Movement of Soil Insecticides. **Ohio Report**, 62(2), 26-28.

Niemczyk, H. D., Krueger, H. R. (1987) Persistence and Mobility of Isazofos in Turfgrass Thatch and Soil. J. Econ. Entomol. 80, 950-952.

Petrovic, M. A., Young, R. G., Sanchirico, C. A., Lisk, D. J. (1993) Downward Migration of Trichlorofon Insecticide in Turfgrass Soils. Chemosphere, 27(7), 1273-1277.

Petrovic, M. A., Gutenman, W. H., Ebel, J. G. Jr., Lisk, D. J. (1993a) Leaching of Mecoprop Herbicide Through Turfgrass Soils. Chemosphere, 26(8), 1541-1547.

Potter, D. A., Powell, A. J., Smith, M. S., (1990) Degradation of Turfgrass Thatch by Earthworms (Oligochaeta: Lumbricidae) and Other Soil Invertebrates. J.Econ. Entomol., 83(1), 205-211.

Rao, P. S. C., Hornsby, A. G., Jessup, R. E. (1985) Indices for Ranking the Potential for Pesticide Contamination of Groundwater. Proc. Soil Crop Sci. Soc., 44, 1-8.

Sears, M. K., Chapman, R. A. (1979) Persistence and Movement of Four Insecticides Applied to Turfgrass. J. Econ. Entomol. 72, 272-274.

Shearman, R. C. (1979) Latest Thatch Information is Helpful but Controversial. Weeds Trees and Turf 18(4), 46.

Shearman, R. C., Bruneau, A. H., Kinbacher, E. J., Riodan, T. P. (1983) Thatch Accumulation in Kentucky Bluegrass Cultivars and Blends. HortScience, 18(1), 97-99.

Smith, J. (1984) Analytical Method M-1453, American Cyanamid Company, Princeton, New Jersey.

Smith, L. (1990) Personal communication, Fermenta ASC, Mentor, Ohio.

Stahnke, G. K., Shea, P. J., Tupy, D. R., Stougaard, R. N. (1991) Pendimethalin Dissipation in Kentucky Bluegrass Turf. Weed Sci., 39, 97-103.

Taylor, A. W., Caro, J. H., Freeman, H. P., Turner, B. C. (1985) Sampling and Variance in Measurements of Trifluralin Disappearance from a Field Soil. ACS Symp. Ser. 284, pp. 25-35.

Truman, C. C., Leonard, R. A. (1991) Effects of Pesticide, Soil, and Rainfall Characteristics on Potential Pesticide Loss by Percolation - a GLEAMS Simulation. Trans. of the ASAE, 34(6), 2461-2468.

Turgeon, A. J. (1979) Influence of Thatch on Soil is Both Positive and Negative. Weeds Trees and Turf 18(4), 48-50.

Turgeon, A. J., Hurto, K. A., Spomer, L. A. (1977) Thatch as a Turfgrass Growing Medium. Illinois Res. 19(3), 3-4.

Turgeon, A. J. (1988) Landscape Management, March, 58-61.

Wagenet, R. J., Hutson, J. L. (1989) LEACHM Leaching Estimation and Chemistry Model. Continuum: Vol. 2, Version 2. NYS Water Resources Institute, Center for Environmental Research, Ithaca, NY.

Wauchope, R. D., Buttler, T. M., Hornsby, A. G., Augustijn-Beckers, P. W. M., Burt, J. P. (1991) The SCS/ARS/CES Pesticide Database for Environmental Decision-Making. in: Rev. Environ. Contam. Toxicol., 123, 1-164.

Wilkerson, M. R., Kim, K. D. (1986) The Pesticide Contamination Prevention Act: Setting Specific Numerical Values. California Dep. of Food and Agric., Sacramento, CA.

78 Reducing the environmental impact of golf course insect management

R.L. Brandenburg
Professor, Department of Entomology, North Carolina State
University, Raleigh, NC, USA

Abstract
Concern over the environmental impact of golf course
management has triggered many new approaches to pest
management. Pesticide selection in concert with the site
of application can reduce problems associated with drift,
runoff, and other contaminations. New application
technology can help reduce drift, surface residues,
runoff risk, exposure to wildlife, and odor. Many new
biological control agents are available for managing
turfgrass insect pests. These vary from entomogenous
nematodes to the use of *Bacillus thuringiensis* sprays.
Improved ability to monitor and predict insects helps
manage the pests.
Keywords: Integrated Pest Management, Pesticides, Insect
Management, Turf Pest Management, Pesticide Application.

1 Introduction

While the golf course industry in the United States
continues to grow at a record pace, the concerns
associated with such growth also increase at an equal or
greater pace. Some concerns such as those expressed
through the recent banning by the Environmental
Protection Agency of diazinon on golf courses due to bird
kills have been legitimate. Other concerns, perhaps less
well documented, are perceived as equal or greater risks
by various environmental groups. This increased concern
over the potential environmental consequences of
pesticide use and increasing regulation of pesticides on
turfgrass comes in light of more demand for high quality
turfgrass on golf courses by the public.
   The concepts of Integrated Pest Management(IPM) are
well established and have been recently reviewed for
turfgrass (Tashiro 1987, Potter and Braman 1991). While
IPM has been quite successful in agricultural crops, its
effective use in turfgrass is more difficult. Reasons
for this include: a) the perennial nature of turfgrass,

Science and Golf II: Proceedings of the World Scientific Congress of Golf. Edited by A.J.
Cochran and M.R. Farrally. Published in 1994 by E & FN Spon, London. ISBN 0 419 18790 1

b) shortage of reliable, cost-effective alternatives to pesticides, c) limited sampling and decision-making guidelines, and d) limited tolerance for damage by golfers. This paper summarizes several new approaches to reducing environmental risk while effectively managing insect pests on golf courses.

2 Product and Site Selection

Pesticides vary in their toxicity to fish, wildlife and humans. Pesticide selection for reduced environmental impact must also consider the formulation, the use rate, persistence, water solubility, and other factors. One of the greatest concerns is runoff and this isn't always a direct reflection of water solubility. In general, turfgrass has been demonstrated to be an effective filter and virtually eliminates pesticide runoff (Cohen et al. 1990, Rhodes and Long 1974, and Niemczyk and Krueger 1987). Leaching through the soil is also of great concern although it appears to be minimal in turfgrass (Branham and Wehner 1985, Snyder and Cisar 1993, Cohen et al. 1990, and Miles et al. 1992). However, individual pesticides and sites have shown some reason for concern (Petrovic 1993, and Loffredo et al. 1991). This confirms the suggestion that each site and each pest problem must be evaluated separately.
  Course construction can play a role in reducing environmental concerns with pest management. This has been recently reviewed although much of the information is from the study of agricultural crops (Balogh and Walker 1992). Recent trends in the United States have been to use relatively low maintenance plantings in environmentally-sensitive areas to reduce the area that requires pest management.

3 Subsurface Pesticide Application

Recent advances in the ability to apply pesticides below the soil surface for soil pests such as white grubs or mole crickets have offered new options for pest management. The many advantages include: a) reduced surface residue, b) reduced odor, c) improved efficacy, d) reduced pesticide rates, e) reduced drift, f) reduced need for post-treatment irrigations. While such equipment would be effective only against soil-borne pests, these are often the most difficult to control and require the highest rates of pesticides.

3.1 Liquid Application
Two main types of subsurface application equipment are currently available. One is designed to use very high

pressure (13,000 kilopascals (kPa)) to deliver the spray
solution in a steady stream through small nozzle orifices
spaced 5.0 to 7.5 cm apart placed on the turf surface and
directed into the soil. This approach does no mechanical
damage and is capable of placing the pesticide 2.0 to 4.0
cm deep in sandy soil with approximately 800 liter of
water/ha. Commercial units used in our trials have been
built by Cross Equipment Company, Albany, Georgia, U.S.A.
Several other companies have also been involved in the
production of similar prototype or commercial units.
These units are generally useful for emulsifiable
concentrates and flowable concentrations, but not for
wettable or soluble powders.

In our trials, the subsurface application of
chlorpyrifos was found to be efficacious against mole
crickets (*Scapteriscus vicinus*) at one half the labeled
rate for surface feeders (Table 1). Chlorpyrifos has a
very low water solubility and is a good choice for sandy
soils because of its limited mobility. Our study
determined that subsurface placement made the use of this
pesticide with long residual activity not only
efficacious, but the reduced rate enhanced the cost-
effectiveness. Studies in the state of Massachusetts
found improved efficacy results with the pesticide
isazophos against grubs of the Japanese beetle (*Popilla
japonica*) (Vittum 1993).

Table 1. Subsurface application of Dursban® 4E
          (chlorpyrifos) for mole cricket control on
          bermudagrass fairway, damage = degree of insect
          tunneling on surface, North Carolina, U.S.A.
          1991

Treatment	Kg(AI) per ha	Damage rating (0-9, 0=no damage, 9=total damage)		
		7 days post-treat	14 days post-treat	21 days post-treat
Dursban® 4E (chlorpyrifos)	1.1	3.25a	2.08a	4.00a
Dursban® 4E	2.2	2.58a	2.67a	3.92a
Untreated	---	5.58a	7.75b	8.58b

Means followed by the same letter are not significantly
different (DMRT, P = 0.05).

3.2 Granule Application
Other application equipment is designed to apply granular
formulations of pesticides below the soil surface. These

units usually involve a coulter wheel or other slicing device to create a slit in the turf. Tubes deliver the granules into the slice that has been opened. Different pieces of equipment open varying widths of slits and most have adjustments for depth of placement. In general, these are all gravity-feed devices with varying levels of calibration accuracy. Some are simply modifications of slit seeder/dethatcher devices where the dethatcher cuts the slit and others are basic slit seeders.

Comparative studies found that the subsurface application was superior to the surface broadcast application of two different pesticides, chlorpyrifos and bendiocarb (Tables 2 and 3).

Table 2. Comparison of subsurface and surface application of Dursban® 2.32G (chorpyrifos) for mole cricket control on bermudagrass fairways, North Carolina, U.S.A. 1992

Treatment	Kg (AI) per ha	Damage rating (0-9) 47 days
	Location 1	
Dursban® 2.32G (chlorpyrifos) subsurface	2.2	0.44a
Untreated	--	6.56b
	Location 2	
Dursban® 2.32G surface	2.2	4.80a
Untreated	---	6.30a

These studies indicate definite advantages to the use of such equipment in golf course soil insect management in reducing total pesticide use. Such equipment is not without disadvantages. The speed of application is somewhat slower than conventional approaches, especially with the liquid injection. In addition, the cost of some equipment is relatively high.

4 Biological Control

There is increasing interest in the development of microbials and other biorational insecticides. In general, biological control is slower acting, more expensive, more difficult to implement, and less readily available. These limitations are slowly being overcome for many products. Advantages include target specificity and limited environmental consequence.

Table 3. Comparison of subsurface and surface
         applications of Turcam® 2.5G (bendiocarb) for
         mole cricket control on bermudagrass fairway,
         North Carolina, U.S.A. 1992

Treatment	Kg (AI) per ha	No. crickets/ sq. meter 27 days post-treat	Damage rating (0-9) 47 days post-treat
Turcam® 2.5G (bendiocarb) subsurface	2.3	1.17a	2.00a
Turcam 2.5G surface	4.6	0.50a	1.33a
Untreated	---	12.00b	6.56b

Means followed by the same letter are not significantly
different (DMRT, P = 0.05).

    Probably the best-known biorational control is for
control of the Japanese beetle. This bacterium, *Bacillus
popilliae* Dutky, has been used extensively for many
years, but its efficacy is under question (Klein 1992).
Bacillus thuringiensis is receiving considerable
attention in the turfgrass area. Past studies have found
them to be rather slow acting and erratic, but recent
advances in biotechnology are providing a much improved
array of *B.t.* based insecticides (Feitelsen et al. 1992).
    Recent work has greatly improved the efficacy of
various entomogenous nematodes. Formulations to improve
shelf life and mixing are now available. Exhibit®, sold
by Ciba-Geigy, is an example of a U. S. product
distributed by a large agrichemical company (Table 4).
This product is a formulation of *Steinernema carpocapsae*
with efficacy against a limited number of surface turf
feeders. Other products are being sold by other
companies with reported efficacy against a number of
pests. Research trials have shown activity against white
grubs, cutworms, billbugs, sod webworms, mole crickets
and other soil-inhabiting pests (Klein 1990).
    Studies in North Carolina have evaluated a strain of
Steinernema scapterisci (biosys, Palo Alto, CA) against
the adult stage of the mole cricket (Table 5). This
product offers an alternative to the continual use of
pesticides on a year round basis against this pest.
Concerns of pesticide resistance, microbial degradation,
and the presence of this pest near water makes
alternative strategies quite attractive.

Table 4. Black cutworm control on bentgrass green. North Carolina, U.S.A. 1992

Treatment	Kg (AI) per ha	Live worms/sq. meter 24 hrs. post-treat	72 hrs. post-treat
Sevin® 90DF (carbaryl)	2	2.67a	3.33b
Dursban® 4E (chlorpyrifos)	1	0.67a	0.00a
Exhibit® (S. carpocapsae)	480g/93.6m^2	25.00b	9.00b
Untreated		23.67b	24.33c

Means followed by the same letter are not significantly different (DMRT, P - 0.05).

Table 5. Use of the entomogenous nematode, *Steinernema scapterisci*, for adult mole cricket control on bermudagrass fairways, North Carolina, U.S.A. 1993

Treatment	Kg (AI) per ha	Damage rating (0-9) ave. of 20 damage ratings
Steinernema scapterisci	2.54 billion	1.1a
Untreated	--	2.1b

Means followed by the same letter are not significantly different (DMRT, P = 0.05).

5 Predicting Pests

Entomologists have been working with predictive "models" of insects for many years. Current research focuses more on empirical models that provide guidance in pest management decisions. Increasing regulations that force a prescription pesticide application approach on the golf industry in the United States will benefit greatly from an "expert system" that provides guidance to the superintendent. An informed superintendent with the knowledge of insect development is more likely to look

for the pest at the appropriate time and implement
control strategies at the most effective time.

Only limited work has been done on specific turf pests
in the United States. Some of these studies, such as the
model for the Japanese beetle (Regniere et al. 1979) was
done on agricultural crops. Other studies, such as that
on sod webworm (Tolley and Robinson 1986) have shown the
successful use of degree days to predict moth flights.
Additional degree day models are available on masked
chafers (Potter 1981), chinch bugs (Liu and McEwen 1979),
and frit fly (Tolley and Niemczyk 1988). Pheromone and
sex attractants have been identified for a number of
turfgrass pests and make excellent monitoring devices
from which to develop predictive models. There has been
little success, however, in relating trap catches of
adult stages to the subsequent abundance of damaging
larval stages (Potter and Braman 1991).

Work in North Carolina is relating soil and air
temperature degree day accumulations (Base 10°C) from
January 1 of each year and adult trap catches with the
subsequent timing of damaging larval populations. This
is then coupled with computerized weather monitoring
equipment and appropriate software to provide an
automatic visual reminder of insect activity to the
superintendent.

6 References

Balogh, J.C. and Walker, W.J. (1992) Golf course
    management and construction: environmental issues.
    Lewis Publishers, Chelsea, MI.
Branham, B.E. and Wehner, D.J. (1985) The fate of
    diazinon applied to thatched turf. **Agronomy J.**,
    77:101–104.
Cohen, S.Z., Nickerson, S., Maxey, R., Dupuy, A., Jr.,
    and Senita, J.A. (1990) Groundwater monitoring study
    for pesticides and nitrates associated with golf
    courses on Cape Cod. **Ground Water Monit. Rev.**,
    10(1):160–173.
Feitelsen, J.S., Payne, J. and Kim, L. (1992) *Bacillus
    thuringiensis*: Insects and beyond. **Bio/Technology**,
    10:271–276.
Liu, H.J. and McEwen, F.L. (1979) The use of temperature
    accumulations and sequential sampling in predicting
    damaging populations of *Blissus leucopterus hirtus*.
    Environ. Entomol., 8:512–15.
Loffredo, E., Senesi, N., Mellilo, V.A. and Laberti, F.
    (1991) Leaching of fenamiphos, fenamiphos sulfoxide,
    and fenamiphos sulfone in soil columns. **J. Environ.
    Sci. Health**, B26(1) 99–113.

Miles, C.J., Leong, G. and Dollar, S. (1992) Pesticides in marine sediments associated with golf course runoff. **Bull. Env. Contam. Toxicol.**, 49:179-185.

Niemczyk, H.D. and Krueger, H.R. (1987) Persistence and mobility of isazofos in turfgrass thatch and soil. **J. Econ. Entomol.**, 80(f):950-952.

Petrovic, A.M. (1993) Leaching: Current status of research, inIntl. **Turfgrass Soc. Res. J. 7** (eds R. N. Carrow, N. E. Christians, R. C. Sh arman). Intertec Publishing Corp., Overland Park, KS.

Potter, D.A. (1993) Integrated insect management in turfgrasses: prospects and problems, in Intl. **Turfgrass Soc. Res. J. 7** (eds R. N. Carrow, N. E. Christians, R. C. Shearman). Intertec Publishing Corp., Overland Park, KS, pp. 69-79.

Potter, D.A. (1981) Seasonal emergence and flight of northern and southern masked chafers in relation to air and soil temperature and rainfall patterns. **Environ. Entomol.**, 10:793-97.

Regniere, J., Rabb, R. L. and Stinner, R.E. (1979) *Popilla japonica* (Coleoptera: Scarabeidae): A mathematical model of oviposition in heterogenous agroecosystems. **Can. Ent.**, 111:1271-1280.

Rhodes, R.C. and Long, J.D. (1974) Run-off and mobility studies on benomyl in soils and turf. **Bull. Env. Contam. Toxic.**, 12(4):385-393.

Snyder, G.H. and Cisar, J.L. (1993) Mobility and persistence of pesticides in a USGA-type green II. Fenamiphos and fonofos. **Intl. Turfgrass Soc. Res. J. 7** (eds R. N. Carrow, N. E. Christians, R. C. Shearman). Intertec Publishing Corp., Overland Park, KS, pp. 978-983.

Tolley, M.P. and Niemczyk, H.D. (1988) Seasonal abundance, oviposition activity, and degree-day prediction of adult frit fly (Diptera: Chloropidae) occurrence on turfgrass in Ohio. **Environ. Entomol.**, 17:855-62.

Tolley, M.P. and Robinson, W.H. (1986) Seasonal abundance and degree-day prediction of sodwebworm (Lepidoptera: Pyralidae) adult emergence in Virginia. **J. Econ. Entomol.**, 79:400-404.

Vittum, P.J. (1993) Enhanced efficacy of isazophos against Japanese beetle larvae using sub-surface placement technology, in **Intl. Turfgrass Res. J. 7** (eds R. N. Carrow, N. E. Christians, R. C. Shearman). Intertec Publishing Corp., Overland Park, KS, pp. 364-369.

79 Health risk assessment from pesticide use in golf courses in Korea – Part two

Y.H. Moon, D.C. Shin and K.J. Lee
Department of Preventive Medicine and Public Health, College of
Medicine, Yonsei University, Seoul, Korea

Abstract
This study aims to investigate the amount and kinds of
pesticide applied on 59 golf courses in Korea. In the
previous studies with similar themes as this one, we have
referred to only 4 golf courses in general concerning the
pesticides and their orders frequently used on golf
courses in Korea. The total amount of pesticides used on
all the golf courses in Korea in 1991 was 78,555 kg, and
thereby the average amount of pesticides per golf course
was 1,331 kg. Most frequently used pesticides were
thiophanate-methyl, bensulide, polyoxin D-thiram,
fenitrothion, triadimefon, carbofuran, napropamide,
tolclos-methyl, iprodione, etc.. The applied amount of
pesticides on golf courses located in the vicinity of big
cities was twice as much as used in other areas.
Key words: Pesticide, Golf course, Korea

1. Introduction

Recently, with the economic growth in Korea, the number of
people visiting golf courses for health promotion and
recreation is increasing. Along with this increase in the
golfing population, the health risks caused by pesticide
application in golf courses have begun to attract social
attention. Around 80 kinds of pesticide were used on golf
courses in Korea. Presently, there are over 1.5 millions
golfers in Korea.

Pesticides have been a serious health problem for Korean
people. Korea had been predominantly an agricultural
nation where rice farming was an important part until it
has been changed into a industrial country since 1970.
Therefore, pesticides are still widely used on rice fields.
Since no special license or qualification are required for
handling pesticides in Korea, pesticides can be easily
purchased and sprayed anywhere. Such use of pesticides by
nonprofessional persons results in many problems
specially in the aspects of selection of pesticides,
methods of the spraying of pesticides, body protection

Science and Golf II: Proceedings of the World Scientific Congress of Golf. Edited by A.J.
Cochran and M.R. Farrally. Published in 1994 by E & FN Spon, London. ISBN 0 419 18790 1

methods from pesticides, recognition of the toxicity of pesticides, etc.. Health risk is always imminent not only to the sprayer of pesticides but also to golfers and caddies.

Also due to such non-controlled management of pesticides, they are also being widely used for the purpose of suicide in Korea.

About 3 years ago, we reported on the use of pesticides in a survey of 4 golf courses. This study includes 59 golf courses in nationwide and intends to clarify the difference between the past and the present pattern of use of pesticides. It is believed that this study will provide information to develop a policy for the management of health concerning the sprayers of pesticides, golfers, and caddies.

2. The amount of pesticides and most frequantly used pesticides

The total amount of pesticides used on 59 golf courses in Korea in 1991 was 78,555 kg(table 1). This is 3 % of the total amount of pesticides(23,280,000 kg) used in Korea in 1991.

Table 1. The amount of pesticides used on golf courses in 1991

No. of golf course	Average applied amount	Total amount
59	1,331 kg	78,555 kg

Table 2 shows 20 kinds of pesticides most frequently used. Pesticides in the family of carbamate have been most frequently used; they are thiophanate-methyl, thiram, carbofuran, iprodione, etc.. Such pesticides inhibit acetylcholine esterase which is reversible. No death by carbamate has been reported in America. Pesticides in the group of organophosphate such as fenitrothion, trichlorofon, ethroprohos, diazinon, etc. are often used on golf courses, thereby result in a serious problem of intoxication.

Besides, pesticides antibiotics such as polyoxin D and B, and so on, napropamide, etc. in the family of amide, and lamda-cyhalothrin, etc. in the family of pyresroid are also being used.

In the study of 4 golf courses in 1988, it was reported that pesticides in the family of organochlorine such as chlorothalonil, captan, dicofol, captafol, etc., and in the family of organophosphate such as demeton, methidathion, trichlorofon, diazinon, thiophanate- methyl, etc. were frequently used. However, in 1991, it was observed that

pesticides in various families were also used on golf
courses, thereby indicating some pattern of using
pesticides(table 2 and table 3).
     It is interesting to note that the kind of pesticide,
chlorothalonil, which was frequently used on 4 golf
courses in 1988 has not been used on any other golf courses
since then. Moreover, 3 kinds of pesticide in a family of
organochlorine such as captan, dicofol, and captafol which
had been widely used in the past were excluded in the 20
major pesticides inspected in 1991. This clearly indicates
that such a problem concerning the pesticides used on golf
courses risen since 1989 has resulted in a disappearance
of pesticides in the family of organochlorine whose
toxicity is more serious and a decomposition in natural
environment is slower(table 3).
     The total amount of 20 kinds of pesticide most
frequently used in 1991 was 71,179 kg , which represents
90.6% of the amount of all the kinds of pesticide used.

Table 2. Mainly applied pesticides on the golf courses
         in 1991

Rank	Pesticides	Family	Amount(kg)	Toxicity*
1	Thiophanate-methyl	CA	11,617	6,640-7,500
2	Bensulide		7,851	770
3	Polyoxin D	Anti	7,666	800(mice)
4	Polyoxin D + thiram	Anti+CA	7,591	640-800
5	Fenitrothion	OP	5,912	570-740
6	Triadimefon		5,710	363-568
7	Carbofuran	CA	5,544	8.2-14.1
8	Napropamide	Amide	3,422	> 5,000
9	Tolclofos-methyl		2,897	> 5,000
10	Iprodione	CA	2,249	3,500
11	Mecoprop	Phenoxy	1,867	700-1,500
12	Polyoxin B	Anti	1,464	800(mice)
13	Trichlorfon	OP	1,391	450-630
14	Metalaxyl	Acyl	1,165	669
15	Ethoprophos	OP	1,051	62
16	Oxine-copper+iprodine	OCu+HI+CA	1,048	
17	lamda-cyhalothrine	Pyresroid	953	
18	Lime-sulfur	Sulfur	897	
19	Diazinon	OP	884	300-850
20	Others		7,376	
Total			78,555	

* : oral LD50 in rat(mg/kg)
OP : Organophosphate   CA : Carbamate
Anti : Antibiotics   OCu: Organocopper
Acyl : Acylalanine   HI : Hydantoin

Table 3. Pesticides most frequently used, 1988 and
         1991, Korea

1988	1991
Chlorothalonil	Thiophanate
Captan	Bensulide
Dicofol	Polyoxin D
Demeton	Polyoxin D + thiram
Methidathion	Fenitrothion
Trichlorofon	Triadimefon
Diazinon	Carbofuran
Thiophanate-methyl	Napropamide
Captafol	Tolclofos-methyl
Napropamide	Iprodione

3. The pesticides application according to region

As seen in table 4, this study compares the difference in
the application of pesticides among the 6 regions in Korea
(i.e., Seoul, Kangwon, Choongchung, Cholla, Kyungsang, and
Cheju island. We divided 6 regions because there used to be
differences in the information sources, type of fungi and
bacteria on grass. In the light of these differences we
thought that the administrative boundaries would be more
reasonable.

Table 4. The amount of pesticides applied according to the
         region in Korea

Region	No. of golf course	Amounts of applied(kg)(%)		Average amount/ golf course(kg)
Seoul	33	49,597	(63.1)	1,503 ·
Kangwon	4	2,775	(3.5)	694
Choongchung	4	2,680	(3.4)	670
Cholla	2	740	(0.9)	370
Kyungsang	13	19,403	(24.7)	1,493
Cheju Island	3	3,360	(4.3)	1,120
Total	59	78,555	(100.0)	1,331

It is noteworthy that Seoul region, Kyungsang region
including Pusan city, second largest city in Korea, and
Cheju island, a resort area, had used average amount of
pesticides per golf courses 2 times more than 3 other
regions. This may be partially attributed to the
communication differences for the information of

pesticides. That is big cities such as Seoul and Pusan had an easy access to the most recent information about pesticides. If such phenomenon continues, it can be foreseen that the amount of pesticides nationwide will be rapidly increased. It is argued that the nationwide application of pesticides is dangerous without extensive studies on how much of pesticides should be sprayed.

4. The use of pesticides according to the purpose

In the study of the use of pesticides according to the purposes, the proportion of fungicide was 56.6%, insecticide was 24.1%, and herbicide was 18.2% in 1991(table 5). In comparison with the proportion using pesticides on farming fields according to the purposes in 1988, fungicide was 34.5%, insecticide was 34.1%, and herbicide was 21.0%. The proportionate rate of the amount of fungicides out of all the pesticides used on the golf courses was much higher than that of the amount of fungicides used on the farm fields.

Table 5. The amount of pesticides according to the purpose of use

Purpose	Freq. of application	Total amount(kg)	Percent
Fungicides	309	44,470	56.6
Insecticides	219	18,952	24.1
Herbicides	128	14,303	18.2
Others	23	830	1.1
Total	679	78,555	100.0

Table 6. The amount of pesticides according to the type of formulations

Type of formulation	Freq. of application	Amount(kg)	Percent
Soluble powder	369	43,279	55.1
Emulsifiable concentrates	152	16,473	21.0
Granular(dust)	19	6,800	8.7
Others	139	12,003	15.3
Total	679	78,555	100.0

Table 6 shows the type of formulation of pesticide used. Pesticides in forms of soluble powder or emulsifiable concentrates are used with proper amount of water. Soluble powder(55.1%) and emulsifiable concentrates(21.0%) were most widely used, and granular(dust) pesticides in a form of particles were used for only 8.7%. And most of the pesticides were used in a liquid form.

5. Conclusion

In the result of both surveys on use of pesticides on 4 golf courses in 1988 and 59 golf courses in 1991, it is apparent that the use of organochlorine pesticides has been on the ebb, on the other hand the use of other kinds of pesticides such as carbamates or in other family has been remarkable. It was observed that the applied amount of pesticides on golf courses located in the vicinity of big cities was twice as much as used in other areas.

Since there have been few studies concerning the health of golfers, caddies, and sprayers in Korea, and there is no valuable information about various kinds of pesticide now in use and pesticides are being sprayed by nonprofessional persons at present, it is urgent that there should be some studies concerning their health from the perspective of public health. Therefore, there should be strict control and management over the use of pesticides at a governmental level, Actually, since August of 1993, the Korean Environmental Control Office has been controlling the use of pesticides by setting permissible limits of residual amount for 14 different kinds of pesticides including thiophanate, bensulide, triadimefon, iprodione, etc. In order to reduce health risk caused by the use of pesticides, further toxicological studies by health experts on various kinds of pesticides and stricter governmental control on the use of pesticides are necessary.

6. References

American Conference of Governmental Industrial Hygienists. (1990) Documentation of the threshold limit values and biological exposure indices. 6th ed., Cincinnati, Ohio.

Doull,J., Klassen,C.D., and Amdur,M.O. (1986) Casarett and Doull's Toxicology. 2nd ed., Macmillan Publishing Co., New York., pp. 357-408

The Royal Society of Chemistry. (1984) The agrochemicals handbook, Unwin Brothers Limited, London.

Hayes,A.W., Principles and Methods of Toxicology. 2nd ed., Raven Press, New York, pp. 137-67

Spencer,E.Y. (1968) Guide to the chemicals used in crop protection. Canada Department of Agriculture.

Windholz M. (1983) The Merck Index. 10th ed., Merck & Co., Rahway, N.J.

Zenz, C. (1988) **Occupational Medicine.** 2nd ed., Year Book
   Medical Publishers Inc., Chicago., pp. 933-957

80 Course design with precision and control

R.A. Ryder
Ryder Golf Services, Hampshire, UK

Abstract
This paper describes how computer aided design (CAD) can be and has been of benefit to golf course architects.

With "natural" golfing sites becoming very rare the golf course architect has increasingly to compromise because of difficult terrain, conflicting local interests and budgetary constraints. Traditional design skills need to be supported by modern techniques which enhance precision and control.

CAD enables the existing site and the proposed golfing landforms to be accurately modelled and analysed. Computer generated course, golf hole or feature prototypes may be evaluated for environmental impact, golfing quality and cost and if necessary modified before commitment to major development and construction costs.

The paper identifies the scope for CAD in course design, describes the basic techniques involved and gives recent case studies. In conclusion the cost effectiveness of using CAD in golf course design is reviewed.

Keywords: CAD, Course Design, Computer Aided Design, Digital Ground Modelling, Digital Terrain Modelling, DGM, DTM.

1 Introduction

Designing courses to challenge and stimulate all types of golfer requires imagination. Indeed, for natural golfing terrain of the links and heathland variety imagination may be said to be the overiding requirement, as visible human intervention should be kept to a minimum. However, sites on ideal terrain are increasingly rare and of more significance than a natural suitability for golf will almost certainly be proximity to centres of population, major transportation routes, or holiday resorts.

Although imaginative design can transform a less than sympathetic site, if the proposals involve major site alterations development costs can escalate. Extensive earthmoving may be envisaged to make steep or rocky hillsides playable, a featureless locality challenging, or to provide storage lakes for irrigation. Compliance with environmental and land use planning conditions and integration with the local infrastructure may present complex problems. In such cases the golf course architect can benefit from the precision and control available via computer aided design (CAD), whereby alternative solutions may be evaluated quickly in terms of form, function and cost prior to final commitment to major development and construction expenditures.

Science and Golf II: Proceedings of the World Scientific Congress of Golf. Edited by A.J. Cochran and M.R. Farrally. Published in 1994 by E & FN Spon, London. ISBN 0 419 18790 1

2 The scope for CAD in course design

2.1 The nature and capability of CAD

Computer aided design in the context of this paper is the process whereby three-dimensional geometry and associated attributes defining an existing or proposed physical object are held within a computer database. The object may be an area of terrain or a single golf hole, green complex, teeing ground or bunker. The 3D database constitutes a digital model of the site or feature from which analyses, graphic images and drawings can be generated automatically.

CAD is unique in enabling the designer to create prototype landforms which can be viewed, analysed, quantified and refined at will until they exactly meet the design requirement. No longer need the built landform also be the prototype, and thus costly surprises and changes at the construction stage can be avoided. The precision of the model can be as coarse or fine as is appropriate to the stage of the project, with the complete process through to construction controlled as follows:-

(a)   Analyse site
(b)   Design course routing
(c)   Create prototype landforms (digital models)
(d)   Test, refine, optimise digital models
(e)   Produce and issue contract documents
(f)   Review construction bids
(g)   Adjust design if budget exceeded
(h)   Confirm construction budget
(i)   Construct to budget.

2.2 Specification and analysis of landforms

(a) Existing site features or proposed landforms may be specified by means of points, lines, arcs, contours or random three-dimensional strings.

(b) Contours at any required interval may be generated from digital models of existing and proposed surfaces. Surface elevation may be identified at any location within a model.

(c) Profiles through a number of surfaces may be generated along any path of straight line segments. Sections through a number of surfaces may be generated at any orientation or spacing. Drawing and anotation can be automatic.

(d) Development potential may be analysed by displaying the site surface in terms of user defined categories of gradient - e.g. 0 to 5%; 5% to 10%; etc. For existing or proposed landforms directions of steepest slope may be displayed for the analysis of surface water run-off and the definition of watersheds.

(e) Aspect analyses - site surfaces may be displayed and colour coded by user defined categories of orientation - e.g. Southeast to Southwest facing; North to Northeast facing; etc.

(f) Shade analysis - the shadow cast by a site feature or any object may be generated for a given point in time or as a footprint throughout a period.

(g) Visibility analyses - zones of visibility of a specific point or from a specific point for any height of observation may be generated as a surface footprint. Surface profiles taken along specific lines of sight may also be used to check visibility.

2.3 Earthworks design

The elevation of a proposed surface to meet a specified balance between cut and fill may be calculated automatically. User defined batter slopes may be inserted automatically between surfaces. Isopachytes - contours of cut and fill - may be generated between any two surfaces. The effects of settlement in areas of fill may be simulated.

2.4 Quantity take-off
Item counts, lengths, plan areas and surface areas may be extracted directly from individual models. Earthworks cut and fill calculations are performed by comparing volume differences between two digital ground models.

2.5 3D visualisation
Both isometric and perspective views may be generated from a 3D model and be used for design verification and promotional purposes.

   In isometric projections measurements along the edges are true to scale and both the nearest and the furthest parts of the view are equally represented, there being no foreshortening of the distant detail due to perspective. In combination with carefully spaced and coloured surface meshes, sometimes with vertical exaggeration also, isometric views can provide highly informative design checks, course shaping references and eye-catching images for presentation. Fig.1 is a reproduction of part of a full colour isometric view.

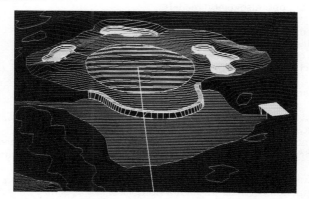

Fig.1. Isometric view of 17th. green and surrounds, Ingon Manor Golf Club.

   True perspectives may be generated to verify the future view from a particular location for design or planning purposes, or to confirm the effectiveness of screening. For such design purposes unshaded wire frame or line drawings may be adequate. For promotional illustrations realistically portrayed natural features and surfaces are desired but surface shading by computer can be either too crude or time consuming and expensive. Photomontage and/or enhancement by a graphic artist may produce more cost effective results.

3 Digital modelling

3.1 Survey data input
Site survey details may be supplied on traditional paper plans or in digital form on disc from aerial surveys, scanned contour drawings, electronic theodolites or CAD drawing files. Where systems are compatible site information can be loaded and

displayed on screen on receipt and modelling can commence immediately. If traditional survey drawings are the source, digitising will be necessary - the electronic transfer of the relevant survey detail by tracing on a digitiser tablet or table.

3.2 Digital ground/terrain modelling
A 3D computer simulation of a ground surface is termed a Digital Ground (or Terrain) Model (DGM or DTM). A DGM is a digital representation of the surface from which specialist software can generate reports, calculations, drawings and 3D views. Natural surfaces are random in form and the most efficient means of accurate representation is that of triangulation - the generation of planar triangles whose vertices are individual survey points or the nodal points along contour or feature strings recorded by the surveyor. The ground model surface is thus generated from the survey data as a set of triangular facets, each face of which can be identified by location, altitude, slope and orientation.

3.3 Design modelling
DGMs defining proposed course elements and landforms are created from points, lines, arcs, contours and 3D feature strings defined or implied by the architect. Where the design has been drafted traditionally onto a base plan the details may be digitised to create three-dimensional model entities. Alternatively, design details can be input freehand using the digitiser mouse or puck as an electronic pencil, superimposing the design in 3D directly onto the survey drawing displayed on screen. In either case the data input phase will be completed by merging the corresponding new and existing site contours where they are to coincide. The proposed surface DGMs can then be built and design optimisation commence.

4 Case Studies

4.1 Site Analysis
Chateau Montcalm near Quebec, Canada, is in an area of lakes and rocky outcrops with a backdrop of steep hillsides. The site varies in altitude by 80 metres and the average surface gradient is approximately 17%. The requirement was to analyse and quantify the physical nature and potential of the site for golf.

Data input was by digitising a 1:2000 scale base map, all 25 feet interval plus significant 5 feet interval contours, building outlines, road limits and soil type boundaries being recorded. From this data a DGM composed of 24,450 triangles was built to model the 170 hectare site. For convenience of use on site two A1 size 1:2500 scale site plans with contour intervals of 1 metre and 5 metres were generated from the DGM.

The course designer required slope gradients to be identified within the ranges 0-5%, 5-10%, 10-15%, 15-20% and greater than 20%. Accordingly the model triangles were sorted into the five categories and colour coded for on screen display. Individual triangles within each category were then aggregated to improve legibility when plotted and a Site Gradient Analysis drawing produced. For slope aspect analysis the categories chosen were northwest to northeast facing (shaded slopes), NE to SE facing (morning sun), SE to SW facing (midday sun) and SW to NW facing (afternoon sun). As for gradients, all 24,450 triangles were sorted into each category and aggregated to produce the Slope Aspect Analysis drawing. The production of further drawings showing directions of surface water run-off and the location of soil and rock formations completed the analysis of the site for golfing suitability.

4.2 Balancing cut and fill

Mount Panther Park is in an area of rolling hills overlooking the Mountains of Mourne in County Down, Northern Ireland and is the site of 27 holes, a practice ground and 4-star hotel currently under construction.

The initial task was to achieve an earthworks balance across an area of the site having an altitude difference of 40 metres and required to accommodate a full length 18 hole course, practice ground and training hole. Preliminary design contours defining outline course shaping and lake configurations were merged with 1 metre interval existing contours digitised from the site plan. From DGMs of the site and the proposed surfaces the initial cut and fill balance was calculated, the first pass showing an excess of 135,000 cubic metres of fill. Separate calculations were performed to determine the earthworks consequences of terracing the practice ground.

Revisions to the proposed course and lake contours reduced the imbalance to 55,000 cubic metres cut, and the third pass (including the practice ground) proved acceptable at 224,000 cubic metres cut and 212.000 cubic metres fill. The downward sloping practice ground was the subject of a study to compare the merits of terracing against a straight grade throughout. Surface profiles were taken along the alternatives to determine how adequate visibility could best be achieved using a minimum volume of fill.

With an overall earthworks balance achieved, further fully detailed surface models were built for green, tee and bunker complexes on all 27 holes and the training area, from which were produced final quantities and 37 contract drawings.

4.3 Earthworks control and pre-contract budgetary adjustment

Allen Park is a municipal course currently under construction in Antrim, Northern Ireland. Built to a firm budget on a flat site, CAD was employed to ensure that the excavations required to create three multi-purpose water features would provide precisely the fill required to create landforms for golfing interest. Lake perimeters were to be randomly curved on plan and the profile of each lake bed was to be terraced. Storage capacity was required for the irrigation of the golf course and several sports pitches, and the largest lake had to accommodate fishing from an island reached by causeway. Survey details were on disc in DXF format.

DGMs were built of the site and each lake configuration, from which were calculated areas of topsoil strip, volumes from ground level to water levels and from water levels to each bed terrace level, and perimeters at each water level. Adequate water storage capacities to meet irrigation demand under drought conditions were established.

DGMs of each proposed golf course landform were then built and adjusted until the gross volume of fill required balanced the subsoil to be excavated from the lake areas. Contract drawings, quantities and earthworks mass haul calculations were then produced. Receipt of the completed tenders revealed that savings would have to be made to be within the available budget. Lakes and landforms were therefore rapidly remodelled to reduce earthmoving costs, drawings were amended, a revised contract price was accepted and construction begun without delay to the planned programme.

4.4 3D Visualisation

For Ingon Manor Golf Club, Stratford-on-Avon, the CAD brief was to create 3D views to evaluate proposed enhancements around two greens from design notes added to existing plans. With the existing course survey details (provided as a DXF file on floppy disc) displayed on screen the new greenside features were modelled directly by specifying new contours, 3D strings and spot heights. Individual DGMs were built for tees, greens, bunkers, roughs, fairways and water features and over each was "draped" an appropriately spaced and coloured surface mesh. Isometric views from various viewpoints, photographed from the screen using standard 35mm. colour print film and a tripod, confirmed that the greenside improvements would achieve the desired result. Fig.1 is a reproduction of a colour print taken in this manner.

The same technique is to be used to assist in the marketing of a new and an extended course throughout their construction periods. Colour isometric views will be used to show prospective members how the courses will appear when mature and open for play.

4.5 Environmental protection

Established on the fringe of a Hampshire village in 1891, Hartley Wintney Golf Club is now being extended from 9 to 18 holes. Most of the site is in a conservation area and seven of the new holes are within the flood plain of the River Hart. The design of the new holes is required to conform to golf course development guidelines issued by both the local authority and the National Rivers Authority.

Harmony with the existing landscape and protection of existing hydrological patterns were prerequisites for planning approval. To ensure that there is no loss of flood storage or impact on flood flow, where ground levels are to be raised within the flood plain the NRA require compensatory excavation on the flood plain edge. The provision of balancing ponds to delay increased surface water discharge due to irrigation and improved drainage was also requested.

Earthmoving is required for moderate course featuring, the excavation of a storage lake for irrigation, the raising of tees, fairway landing areas and greens above the flood level, the provision of wetland areas for surface water storage and habitat enhancement, and compensatory excavation. A means of accurately evaluating various design options and their re-landscaping and cut and fill implications was essential. Digital ground modelling was the key to identifying speedily and precisely a solution which satisfied environmental, hydrological, budgetary and golfing objectives.

5 The cost effectiveness of CAD for golf course design is proportional to :-

(a)   the need to change the existing surface of the site
(b)   the scope for achieving an optimum solution from a number of options
(c)   the need to produce design amendments quickly
(d)   the importance of presentation
(e)   the skill and perception of the CAD operator.

Experience in providing CAD services for golf course and landscape design shows that 3D modelling for the purposes of site analysis, design appraisal and optimisation, quantity calculation and 3D visualisation are the areas of greatest benefit. Traditional 2D detailing and draughting alone may gain little or no benefit from CAD unless there is much repetitive detail and a large number of drawings. Where 3D modelling is justified for analysis and design purposes however, the resulting capability to generate plans and sections automatically is a highly productive bonus.

CAD cannot be successfully implemented on a casual or intermittent basis and intensive and continual use of the system is required to gain and maintain an acceptable level of expertise. The CAD system itself must also be backed by specialist training and responsive hardware and software support services from the supplier.

CAD enables design solutions to be precisely tuned and budgets to be closely controlled. Used with imagination, it is a uniquely powerful and creative weapon in the golf course architect's armoury.

81 The role of management planning and ecological evaluation within the golf course environment

A.-M. Brennan
The Durrell Institute of Conservation and Ecology, The University,
Canterbury, Kent CT2 7NX, UK

Abstract

This paper reviews the basic principles of management planning and their role in golf course management. It also considers the nature of management for areas with multiple uses. In addition to this, the paper includes an overview of ecological survey and evaluation techniques such as habitat mapping protocols, sieve mapping, presence/absence recording, abundance scoring and community analysis along with evaluation methods such as the Nature Conservation Review (NCR) criteria. The role of evaluation procedure as part of Environmental Impact Assessment (EIA) is also discussed.

Keywords: Environmental Evaluation, Environmental Impact Assessment (EIA), Golf and Environment, Management Planning.

1 Introduction

The nature and extent of the nature conservation resource provided by golf courses has been well documented (Brennan 1992, Dair and Schofield 1990). In Great Britain over 100 courses lie partially or wholly within Sites of Special Scientific Interest. An awareness of golf courses as part of the 'wider countryside' and their wildlife value has lead to initiatives which bring golf and nature conservation together (Nature Conservancy Council 1989). Golf courses are ideally suited to pro-active conservation as, unlike many other areas, management rather than cultivation is the primary objective. As a result, much of the course is available for wildlife.

2 Management planning

As with any human endeavour, conservation management requires foresight and planning. Not only to ensure that human and material resources are not

Science and Golf II: Proceedings of the World Scientific Congress of Golf. Edited by A.J. Cochran and M.R. Farrally. Published in 1994 by E & FN Spon, London. ISBN 0 419 18790 1

wasted but also to provide a means of setting clearly defined objectives and a framework within which these can be met (Nature Conservancy Council 1988). In order to achieve this an environmental management plan should view the course as a single entity integrating areas both in and out of play. In recognition of need for management planning, the former Nature Conservancy Council produced a document introducing the basic principles of environmental management planning to golf courses (Nature Conservancy Council 1990). The publication outlines a mini-environmental plan which precedes the production of a full plan. As no two golf courses are identical, each management plan will be different. There is, however, a basic structure common to all management plans and this is shown below in Table 1.

Table 1.   A generalised course management plan format

Course Management Plan Outline

Summary
Introduction
    aims & objectives of the course management plan
Description
    introduction
    site history
    landscape
    wildlife (by habitat referring to key species)
Evaluation
    introduction to evaluation methods and criteria used
    evaluation by habitat
Management objectives: opportunities and constraints
    ideal management objectives
    ecological constraints
    legal constraints
Management recommendations
    by habitat/site
    special policy measures
        tree planting policy
        agrochemicals policy
        potential pest species policies
    phasing and implementation of management works (including monitoring and review)
Bibliography
Acknowledgements
Appendices
    species lists
    environmental guidelines for golf course development and management

As can be seen in the above table, it is necessary to describe the site and be aware of its possibilities and limitations before a management and monitoring programme for a course can formulated. Survey and evaluation techniques therefore form a key part of the management planning process.

2.1 Survey and mapping techniques

Environmental management planning seeks to adopt an integrated approach and surveys the species, communities (groups of species which live together as a biological unit) and habitats.

The simplest form of ecological survey consists of a species list providing information about a species' presence or absence which can in turn be compared with previously recorded data for the locality. This type of survey identifies uncommon or sensitive species and the presence of rarities and other protected species (as listed in Red Data Book and legislation for the respective countries) and is important in formulating management prescriptions for the course as their needs will have to be taken into account.

Presence or absence data has limitations and so when undertaking a survey an indication of numbers of a particular species by abundance scoring makes the resulting data of even greater use. The two most commonly used systems are the DAFOR (an acronym for Dominant Abundant, Frequent, Occasional, Rare) and percentage-cover based Domin scales (a 10 point score where $10 = 100\%$ and $1 = \; <5\%$ cover).

There are a range of habitat classification and mapping protocols available. In the United Kingdom, Phase 1 is the most widely used and recognised habitat mapping scheme (Nature Conservancy Council 1990).   Originally designed as a basic, user-friendly means of mapping which can be rapidly learnt, undertaken and assimilated, each habitat is allocated an alphanumeric code under the major categories A-woodland, B-grassland C-tall herb and fern, D-heathland, E-bog, F-swamp G-open water, H- coastland, I-rock, J-miscellaneous (*e.g.* A.1.3.2. mixed plantation woodland) and has a colour-coded mapping equivalent which can be drawn onto a base map (usually at a scale of 1:10,000) to produce a visual representation of the major habitats present.

Interesting features are located and earmarked for further investigation in a Phase 2 survey. This more detailed survey shifts the emphasis away from habitats and looks at the plant communities and the species within them using the recently published National Vegetation Classification scheme (NVC) (Rodwell 1991). The NVC uses a list of plant species and their relative abundance (in form of the Domin scale) as a botanical fingerprint, matching them with known communities and sub-communities. Once again, the classification takes the form of written description and codes which can also be mapped to show the location and extent of the different communities. The scheme is even more powerful as it indicates how one community can shift into another over time as a result of a change in or lack of management. In this way it can be used in pro-active management and habitat restoration. For example, the management of a former heathland course could included a habitat creation scheme to bring back the heather the site supported at the turn of the century.

2.2 The role of evaluation
A key element of management planning is the use of information produced by survey and review in assessing the ecological value of a given site.

The Nature Conservation Review criteria (NCR) represent the standard commonly used criteria for nature conservation in the United Kingdom and has similar counterparts in other countries (Ratcliffe 1978).   The criteria listed below in Table 2 are the ten most important and commonly used: they include the familiar concepts of environmental value such as rarity, area (attributes which can be quantified in numerical terms) along with criteria which depend on the relative values of features within the site.
The NCR criteria link in with other aspects of environmental evaluation, in particular landscape and heritage considerations. Heritage and landscape tend to be important aspects of on-course conservation as many long established golf courses have within them sites of historic importance (in the form of Scheduled Ancient Monuments) or are themselves wholly or partially designated historic or protected landscapes (*e.g.* historic parks and gardens, Areas of Outstanding Natural Beauty *etc.*). In most cases, the needs of golf, nature, landscape and heritage conservation can be met in the course of the management planning process.

Once the survey and evaluation processes have been completed, management prescriptions- the recommendations for objectives which have to be met and the methods by which they will be achieved- are formulated.

Important and vulnerable aspects of the site, once identified, can be used to build a composite map featuring all the sensitive areas. This process, known as sieve mapping, presents an overall picture of the site in terms of increasing levels of environmental information. Before the advent of Geographical Information Systems (GIS), maps were physically overlain to produce a composite master map: now computer graphics enable digitised maps to be manipulated permitting even greater detail to be achieved. Such maps can be used to indicate the relative environmental sensitivity of different parts of course by means of a constraints map, an envelope in which course development, management can be undertaken without appreciable environmental impact. It can also be used as a guide to areas of the course which though presently having limited conservation interest, possess potential value which can be enhanced by habitat creation/restoration measures.

Table 2.   Nature Conservation Review criteria

Nature Conservation Review Criteria

The process of evaluation may appear complex but, by applying the criteria systematically, a proper appreciation of a site can be made as a prerequisite to defining the objectives of management. On some sites it may be necessary to apply the criteria to each feature of major conservation value. The criteria are:-

Size   In general, larger sites are more highly valued than smaller ones, all else being equal. Amongst aspects of size to be considered are the relative size of the site compared with sites of similar type, the extent of individual components of the site, and whether the site is of sufficient size that the small changes within will not lead to the loss of a site's interest.

Diversity   One of the most important site attributes is variety in numbers of both communities and species, which are usually closely related, and in turn depend largely on a diversity of habitat. Diversity is sometimes related to habitat instability which will affect management prescriptions.

Naturalness   Ecosystems least modified by man tend to be rated more highly. However, the vast majority of sites of conservation interest have been influenced by man's activities to some extent. The degree and nature of this influence should be noted.

Rarity   Rarity is concerned with communities and habitats as well as species. Presence of one or more rare components on a site gives it higher value than a comparable site with no rarities.

Fragility   This reflects the degree of sensitivity of habitats, communities and species to environmental change. Fragile sites often represent ecosystems which are highly fragmented, dwindling or difficult to re-create.

Typicalness   The typical and commonplace in a field of ecological variation are also of value.

Recorded History   The existence of a scientific record of long-standing adds considerably to the value of the site. Note should also be made of the recorded land-use practices.

Position in an ecological unit   In the event of two sites representing a certain formation being of equal intrinsic value, the close proximity of one site to a highly rated example of another type increases the value of that site.

Potential value   Certain sites could, through appropriate management or even natural change, eventually develop a nature conservation interest substantially greater than that existing at present. Note may also be made of those factors which would limit such potential being achieved.

Intrinsic appeal   While science may well view all creatures as equal, pragmatism dictates that in nature conservation it is realistic to give more weight to the more popular appeal of some species and groups than others.

2.3 Environmental Impact Assessment

Unlike some other countries, there is no mandatory requirement in the United Kingdom for environmental impact assessment (EIA) to be undertaken for golf course development (HMSO 1989). However, the European Community Directive on which the law is based makes provision for the discretionary inclusion of such projects and as a result many planning authorities incorporate elements of EIA into their decision-making process. EIA enables full consideration of the environmental impact of a development, whilst also allowing management planning, regular monitoring and review, for a course.

3 Conclusions

Great similarities exist between the management of golf courses and nature reserves. In the historic past management was minimal... indeed it could be said that the very first greenkeepers had four legs! However, the twentieth century has brought changes in land use and management with golf itself moving from a game of coastal links and heaths into a worldwide leisure industry. New technology can alter ecosystems dramatically and irrevocably either directly (as in the use of heavy plant/machinery and agrochemicals) or indirectly (*e.g.* the consequences of habitat loss, pollution, climate change *etc.*). Environmental management planning is therefore essential if the nature conservation resource is to be protected, enhanced and created on both new and existing courses.

4 References

Brennan, A-M. (1992) The management of golf courses as potential nature reserves. **Aspects of Applied Biology**, 29, 241-248.

Dair, I. and Schofield, J.M. (1990) Nature conservation and the management of golf courses in Great Britain. in: **Science and Golf.** (ed A.J. Cochran), Spon, London, pp. 330-335.

HMSO (1989) **Environmental assessment: a guide to the procedures.** HMSO, London.

Nature Conservancy Council (1988) **Site management plans for nature conservation- a working guide.** English Nature, Peterborough.

Nature Conservancy Council (1989) **On Course Conservation: Managing Golf's Natural Heritage.** English Nature, Peterborough.

Nature Conservancy Council (1990) **Your Course... Preparing a conservation management plan.** English Nature, Peterborough.

Nature Conservancy Council (1990) **Handbook for Phase 1 habitat survey- a technique for environmental audit.** English Nature, Peterborough.

Ratcliffe, D.A. (1977) **A nature conservation review.** Vols. 1 & 2, Cambridge University Press, Cambridge.

Rodwell, J. (1991 *et seq.*) **British plant communities.** Cambridge University Press, Cambridge.

82 The development and growth of the U.S. golf market

J.F. Beditz
National Golf Foundation, Jupiter, Florida, USA

Abstract
This paper analyzes the growth of golf in the United States and the
applicability of the U.S. experience to other markets. Three distinct growth periods are identified: the 1920's, the 1960's and the
third, and current, growth period that began in the mid-eighties.
Barriers to further growth of the game are then examined. Finally,
the paper discusses the development of an industry-wide strategic
plan to overcome the growth barriers.

Keywords: U.S. Golf History, Participation, Growth of Golf, Market
Development, Consumer Research, Strategic Plan.

1 Introduction

In 1995 the United States Golf Association will celebrate its, and
arguably the game of golf's, one hundredth anniversary in America.
In that centennial year, approximately twenty five million Americans
will play over five hundred million rounds of golf on more than
15,000 golf courses.

Because of the relatively rapid growth of the game in the U.S. and
owing to the fact that the U.S. market represents about half of the
world market for golf, many observers look to the States as a model
for growth in other parts of the world. Is this emulation appropriate, or are there uniquenesses in the U.S. Market that can not be
replicated? To answer this question one needs to take a closer look
at the development of golf in the U.S. and develop an understanding
of the factors that have contributed to that growth.

2 Golf in the U.S. - The Early Years

While the exact date of golf's introduction in the U.S. is a point of
argument, it seems the start of golf's acceptance as a sport in the
United States occurred in the 1920's. During this period there was
an aggressive development of golf facilities so that by 1931, there
were over 5,600 golf facilities in the United States.

Golf in the U.S. during this early development period was primarily a private club sport, with golf participation estimated at 2% of

Science and Golf II: Proceedings of the World Scientific Congress of Golf. Edited by A.J.
Cochran and M.R. Farrally. Published in 1994 by E & FN Spon, London. ISBN 0 419 18790 1

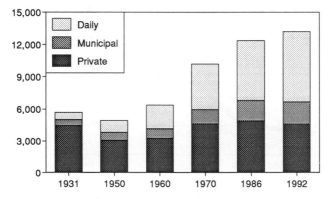

Fig. 1. Facilities By Type

the overall U.S. population. It is also estimated that approximately
90% of all U.S. golfers were men at that time.

After this first significant growth period ended in approximately
1931, the game of golf remained relatively unchanged for the next 30
years. Between 1931 and 1960, the number of facilities grew by only
0.4% per year, totalling approximately 6,400 by 1960. However, a
subtle, but important change took place during this time.

In 1931, approximately 78% of all golf facilities were private
clubs and accessible only to members. By 1960, approximately 50% of
all facilities in the U.S. were private clubs. The significance of
this shift from primarily private clubs to an equal mix of public and
private facilities can not be overstated. For it was this shift that
essentially postured the game for rapid expansion during the final
third of its first one hundred years.

3 The Democratization of Golf in the U.S.

It was during the 1960's that golf experienced a second boom period,
measured by growth in both golf facilities and golfers. The number
of facilities grew from 6,385 in 1960 to 10,188 in 1970. This expansion equated to an annual growth rate of nearly 5%, or 380 new facilities per year.

Accessibility to the public also increased in the 1960's. The
number of facilities available to the public increased by 77%, while
private facilities grew by only 43% in the same period.

In terms of participation, golf experienced similar growth. The
number of golfers increased from 4.4 million in 1960 to 11.2 million
in 1970, with the participation rate more than doubling from 3.3% in
1960 to 7.1% of the total U.S. population in 1970.

The growth in the 1960's was supported by two major factors.
First, the U.S. government provided financing for the development of
public golf facilities. From 1931-1960, the number of municipal golf
facilities increased 1.7% per year from 543 in 1931 to 895 in 1960.
In the next ten years, municipal facilities grew by 4% annually to

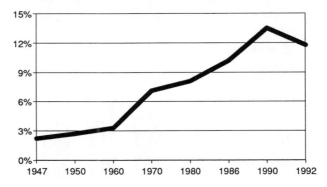

Fig. 2. Participation Rate

1,321 in 1970. Overall, publicly accessible golf facilities grew from 48% of all facilities in 1960 to 55% of all facilities in 1970.

The second factor supporting the growth of golf in the 1960's was the media exposure of the professional tour. Television introduced the World and the United States to such golfing personalities as Arnold Palmer, Gary Player and Jack Nicklaus.

It is interesting to note that in spite of the rapid expansion of public facilities in the 1960's, golf's accessibility differed widely from one region of the U.S. to another. The majority of facilities were in the North-Central region. This region accounted for nearly 37% of all public facilities in the U.S. Conversely, the South-Central region contained less than 13% of all public facilities. This disparity existed in spite of a more conducive golfing climate in the southern regions.

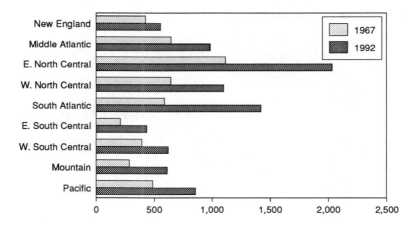

Fig. 3. Number of Public Facilities

4 The Latest Growth Era

The boom of the 1960's slowed considerably in the 1970's. The recession, high interest rates, and inflation combined to slow golf facility development. In 1980 there were 12,005 facilities in the country, which equates to an annual growth rate of 1.7% since 1970.
Private facilities grew the slowest, at less than 1% per year, while
municipal facilities led the growth at 3.1% annually.

Coinciding with the slowed facility development, was a slowed
growth in participation rates. After growing by nearly 4% in the
previous decade, the participation rate in the 1970's increased by
only 1%, to 8.1 in 1980.

The slowed growth experienced in the 1970's continued into the
early 1980's. Between 1980 and 1986, 379 golf facilities were developed, an average of only 63 per year. Development of private facilities was virtually stagnant at 0.2% annually, while the annual growth
of public facilities was just under 1%.

In spite of the sluggish growth of facilities through the early to
mid-1980's, golf participation began to increase. This increase
would be the harbinger of the third major growth era of golf in the
U.S. From 1980 to 1986, the participation rate rose by 2.1% to 10.2.
The participation increase in these six years more than doubled the
growth from the entire previous decade.

By the middle of the 1980's, golf-course development was beginning
to recover from the slowdown that started in the 1970's. The rate of
new-facility development between 1986 and 1992 more than doubled the
rate of development in the first half of the 1980's. The golf participation rate also grew during this period peaking at 13.5% in
1990, before declining to 11.9% in 1992.

Over this period, the mix of public and private facilities continued to change. From 1986 to 1992, the number of publicly accessible
facilities grew by nearly 15% from approximately 7,500 to over 8,600.
In fact, approximately 1,000 of this 1,100 facility growth occurred
in the daily-fee market. These facilities are typically developed by
private real-estate and golf-facility developers. The number of
truly private facilities actually declined by nearly 7% during that
same period.

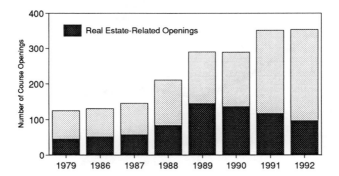

Fig. 4. Golf Course Openings / Real Estate-Related

Two related factors significantly enhanced the recent growth in U.S. golf facilities. First, golf courses became a major part of the real-estate resort-development profile. In 1986, 51 of the 131 total course openings were real estate and resort related. By 1989, real-estate resort related course openings peaked at 144, and accounted for approximately 50% of that years total course openings. Since 1989, the U.S. real estate market has slowed and in 1992, real estate related course openings dropped to 96 of the approximate 350 course openings that year.

The second factor contributing to the growth of golf in the United States since 1986, was the increase in available funding. Deregulation of the banking industry in the United States gave rise to Savings & Loan institutions aggressively funding new-development activities of all kinds. Golf course and golf-related real-estate development were two of the highest profile users of the Savings & Loan capital.

The North-Central region of the United States continues to account for the largest number of public facilities. In 1992, this region had 3,137 public facilities, which equated to 36% of all U.S. public facilities. The South-Central region of the United States remains primarily a private-club region and continues to be the smallest in terms of public facilities. In 1992, this region contained 1,066 public facilities, accounting for only 12% of the total U.S. public facilities.

Another indicator of the strength of the public-golf market in the U.S. is seen by using per capita ratios of population to public-golf facilities. In 1950 there were over 62,000 people for every public facility. This number has dropped dramatically in the last four decades to just over 29,000 people per public facility in 1992. This per capita analysis also magnifies the regional disparity. The North-Central Region averages less than 18,000 people per public facility. Conversely, the South-Central Region has over 35,000 people per public facility.

Not surprisingly, golf participation correlates with public-golf accessibility. In the North-Central region of the U.S. where public-golf flourishes, between 15% and 17% of the population plays golf.

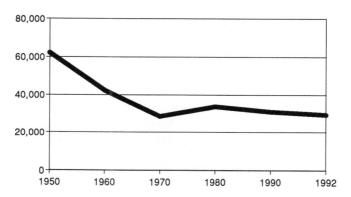

Fig. 5. Population Per Public Facility

In the South-Central region participation rates of between 8% and 9% go hand-in-hand with low public accessibility to golf.

5 Golf Consumer Research

Information provided thus far proves valuable primarily in identifying and analyzing historical trends. However, it became apparent to the National Golf Foundation that the industry needed a more consumer-oriented research database to plan for and manage the growth of golf in the United States.

The golf consumer research that was conducted on both golfers and non-golfers focused on two major areas: behaviors and attitudes. Behavioral research investigated subjects such as play frequency, spending, instruction-taking, and vacation golf travel. Another important element of this study was the behavioral differences based on family involvement, junior golf involvement, and gender of the subjects.

The attitudinal research investigated golfers' and non-golfers' feelings toward accessibility to the game of golf, speed of playing a round of golf, barriers to participating in golf, and general attitudes of non-golfers toward the game of golf. The focus of this research was to identify factors inhibiting the growth of the game in the United States.

Findings from the consumer research indicate that the frequency of participation among golfers is mainly affected by the amount of time available to play. All golfers, regardless of how often they play, identified the amount of time necessary for work and family responsibilities as a primary limitation on how often they play golf. While it is true that the cost of golf was another significant detriment, it was not identified as being nearly as important as time constraints.

While the barriers to golf participation among non-golfers also

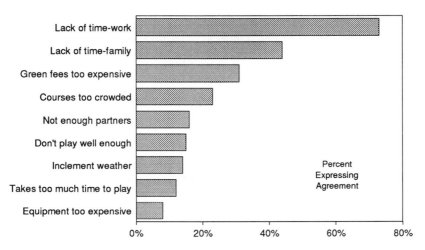

Fig. 6. Why Golfers Don't Play More Often

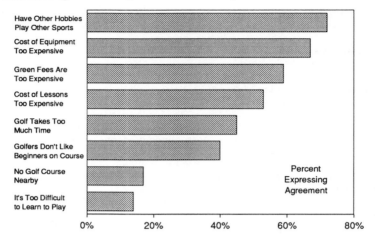

Fig. 7. Barriers to Golf Participation Among Non-Golfers

revolved around time, money was another important consideration. The
primary time barriers were family and job limitations, with participation in other hobbies and sports being another important consideration. New golfers were particularly concerned with the cost of
equipment, lessons, and green fees. One other very important finding
was the general perception by non-golfers that golfers do not like
beginners on the course. That perception does, in fact, keep them
from participating in golf.

It was not surprising to find that one of the primary reasons
people begin playing golf, and ultimately continue to play golf, is
that friends and relatives are involved in the game. Other factors
that entice people to play golf are that it is a recreational sport,
it provides a chance for exercise, and it allows the player to be
outdoors.

In addition to enhancing the industry's understanding of its con-
sumers' behaviors and attitudes, this psychographic research identified areas that required additional investigation. Extended research
was conducted on issues such as the reasons golfers quit playing golf
and what factors would lead infrequent golfers to play additional
rounds of golf.

6 Strategic Planning

The net effect of this research was that the industry was able to
recognize the key issues affecting its growth and vitality. As a
result, a strategic plan for the growth of golf in the United States
was developed in 1986 and is being implemented.

The strategic plan developed by the NGF and the U.S. golf industry
identifies the major barriers to the growth of golf in the United
States. As part of the plan, action programs have been developed to
combat or mitigate the circumstances limiting the growth of the game.

An example of one important issue is to make the beginning golfer's entrance into the game of golf easier. From the Golf Summit meetings sponsored by the National Golf Foundation, two courses of action have been recommended to overcome this limiting factor. First, the industry is sponsoring the development of numerous publications and programs to bring beginning-golfers into the game and to make the game more friendly and accessible. Second, the industry has recognized the need to develop alternative golf facilities, short courses, practice ranges, and other resources for the beginning golfer to hone their skill before graduating to the regulation facilities.

There are a significant number of additional issues that will affect the growth of the game of golf in the United States. Identified in the U.S. golf industry's strategic plan are issues such as golf and the environment, player attrition, golf course development and financing, accessibility, and the cost of golf. These issues have also prompted the development of specific action plans. In the U.S., organizations and companies are taking the lead on issues that impact their respective businesses.

7 Summary and Conclusions

Golf began in the U.S. as an aristocratic pastime but has evolved into a game of the masses. However, significant growth did not occur until sufficient public access golf facilities were available to cater to the interests of those who would become golfers.

Three distinct growth periods are evident in the first one hundred years of golf in the U.S. The first occurred in the 1920's and was primarily private-club golf. The second growth period occurred in the 1960's and was fueled by the emergence of golf celebrities and the development of a large number of public golf courses. The third, and current, growth period began in the mid-eighties and has occurred as a result of united industry efforts to develop and implement a strategic plan for golf's growth.

Specific consumer research on U.S. golfers has aided the development of programs aimed at reducing barriers to entry into the game as well as barriers to more frequent participation by existing golfers.

In examining the growth of golf in the U.S. and the factors that underlie that growth, it would appear that there is nothing unique that cannot be replicated elsewhere.

In fact, an understanding of the U.S. experience leads one to conclude that most if not all of the ingredients for growth are present in many markets around the world. If this is true, then it is only a matter of time before these ingredients are mixed together in a way that results in significant growth in the game of golf.

83 Development of golf courses: market research and appraisal

W.G. Deddis
The Department of Surveying, University of Ulster, Northern Ireland
and J.S. Hanna
The Department of Civil Engineering and Transport, University of Ulster, Northern Ireland

Abstract
The paper investigates market research and development appraisal as applied to golf course development in Ireland. Market research in a strategic context, relating to demand and supply, and the market for golf course development, is considered initially. Then, at the geographic location level, issues concerning market location and methods of site selection are investigated. The question of land availability (land suitable for golf course use) and the extent to which developers use market research and site selection techniques is evaluated. Finally, development appraisal in theory and practice is examined in relation to current development activity.
Keywords: Market Research, Demand and Supply, Site Selection, Development Appraisal, Golf Course Development.

1. Introduction

Golf course development is a test of appraisal expertise and management competence. Developments can and do fail, and some golf courses will always do better than others. Failures have arisen largely because developments have been design led as opposed to appraisal led, (Deddis 1992, Price 1993).

Historically, golf courses have not been significant revenue producers. Clubs operated largely on a break even basis and profit was not a consideration. However,. the increasing popularisation of golf has increased pressure on existing courses. This pressure is manifest as follows: increased club membership quotas, long waiting lists for membership, pre-booking and early morning queues to play at weekends. Demand apparently is insatiable. In the past decade (worldwide) golf has become a high profile big business with increased earning potential and investment.

The "Golf Boom" of the late 1980's produced many successful developments. Deepening economic recession in the UK led to some spectacular failures making headlines in the early 1990's. This did not mean golf course development was no longer viable. On the contrary, many experts believe that further developments may be profitable. The belief is qualified with the caveat that facilities provided must be of the right type, in the right place, well conceived, profitable and well managed. Golf course development must be the product of appropriate **market research** and rigorous **development appraisal.**

The methodology used by the authors incorporated a number of approaches. A literature review was undertaken. Person to person interviews with developers and officials of the Golf Union of Ireland were conducted. Primary research included questionnaire surveys of utilised respectively, were comprised as follows: 20

Science and Golf II: Proceedings of the World Scientific Congress of Golf. Edited by A.J. Cochran and M.R. Farrally. Published in 1994 by E & FN Spon, London. ISBN 0 419 18790 1

developers, 30 clubs, and 100 golfers. Survey work and data analysis is ongoing. Percentage figures quoted relate to that proportion of data analysed at the time of writing.

2. Market Research

In the property market it is necessary to tailor research to suit the nature and characteristics of the product. The primary objective of research into golf course development must be to establish if a product market exists. To ascertain if this is the case an analysis of wider economic variables is required. If a market exists, site identification and selection become the focus of research. Finally, at project level having selected a site, the (valuation/financial) appraisal can be undertaken to determine viability/profitability. If the scheme is profitable and capable of securing the investment, the development can proceed. Obtaining adequate funding is unlikely to present a problem in such circumstances. Lenders should not entertain a funding arrangement without proof of the financial viability.

3. Research Method

There are three distinct research stages involved:

At a strategic level	-	market analysis
At a location level	-	site selection
At the project level	-	a valuation appraisal

Research at each stage analyses different sets of variable factors. At the strategic level the key factors are demographic and economic. The factors at the location level are geographic and topographic. finally, at project level the factors to be analysed are primarily financial, (cost and value) with course design an associated factor affecting cost/revenue balances. The research progresses from the general to the particular, that is, from the wider economic context to appraisal of a specific scheme.

3.1 The strategic level
This stage establishes the potential for leisure land use. The primary activity is data specification, collection, and compilation. First the specific data requirements are established. Second the availability of the prerequisite data is ascertained. It may be necessary to obtain further data from external sources, and utilise secondary sources in the investigation. Furthermore primary research (survey/questionnaire analysis) may be required to obtain data. Having assembled the required data, an informed, objective and qualitative judgement can be undertaken. The data essential to the analysis includes:

(a) population size, growth rates and age profiles
(b) composition (males/females) of the target population
(c) community structure
(d) per capita incomes
(e) willingness to pay and travel to play
(f) recreational preferences

Surveys showed that 80% of developers sought to establish if the population was growing or static. Over 90% failed to take other factors into account.

3.2 Market Analysis

3..2.1 Demand
What population base will support a golf course? Estimates have changed significantly. In the 1950-60's a base of 20-30,000 was necessary to support an eighteen-hole course. Today opinion considers a population base of 10-15,000 to be sufficient. This is due to the following factors: more leisure time, higher disposable incomes, and increased popularity. In catchment areas (climatically suited) and with a population skewed towards the retired age group, a base of 2,500-5,000 is satisfactory (Heuer 1980). Such figures are unlikely to apply in the British Isles.

3.2.3 Factors affecting demand
Community composition affects demand. Factors such as: age structure (no age limitation), population level (declining, static, or growing) have a significant effect. Economic factors such as income levels, willingness to pay, and price are crucial. Data collected provides the material required for analysis.

Golf is no longer considered an exclusive pastime for the rich. In a survey of golfers in Northern Ireland 85% did not consider the game elitist. furthermore the surveys showed that the price elasticity of demand was highly inelastic. Eighty-five percent of respondents would not give up golf even if annual subscriptions increased significantly. One cannot conclude that costs had no effect, or that the willingness to pay (club or green fees) was unimportant. Significantly, of the golfers surveyed 41% thought golf was an expensive sport. In relation to willingness to pay, 75% of developers made no effort to assess demand.

The clubs surveyed indicated that membership fee increases exceeded the rate of retail price inflation over the past three years. This did not lead to reductions in membership, applications for membership, or waiting list numbers (only 45% of clubs have active lists).

3.2.3 Supply
What is the current level of golf course provision? All existing courses plus projects on stream and any future proposals must be included. In an Irish context only 15% of developers carried out more than a cursory assessment of the market supply. In 85% of the cases this was based on local knowledge, which could be misleading. Numerically there may be enough courses to equate with current ratios of population per course criteria, but this is only one indicator. Expanding tourism may lead to increased demand. Supply and demand will not necessarily therefore remain in equilibrium. Some courses may attract more trade than others. Some may be too difficult and others too exclusive. do enough pay-and-play type courses exist to meet the needs of beginners and golfers to whom private clubs are inaccessible? On the supply side, from the survey of golfers, 45% of the respondents perceived their course to be overcrowded at peak demand periods.

3.2.4 Factors affecting Supply
Regional environmental characteristics can affect supply, factors such as: geology, geomorphology, topography, soils, vegetation and climate. In terms of the current level of supply, the existing facilities available, there is a direct relationship with those demographic factors which determine demand. These factors include the size of the target city or town comprising the market population, population growth profiles (past, present and future), and the ration of provision per head of population currently accepted. Furthermore, in both national and regional terms, the predelictions of the sporting population can have an impact on the supply of specific sport facilities.

Eighty percent of developers ignored existing local supply and 95% did not take the regional or national level of supply into account. Additional factors were overlooked by 100% (such as regional climatic conditions and weather patters which affect the length of playing season). A thorough profile report on all information likely to affect supply will assist the decision-making process, and facilitate an accurate development appraisal.

3.3 Implications

An accurate analysis of demand potential against current supply provision will indicate if a market for golf courses exists. Furthermore it will facilitate an informed evaluation and the information will demonstrate if market gaps exist. This should clarify the types of development required to ensure financial success. The results may conclude that future developments should be Pay and Play courses. The information can only be obtained by analysis of; -

(a) demand and willingness to pay
(b) the current supply profile.

4. The location level

Land for development purposes in any location is always limited. Competition between land uses means that the choice between alternative locations must be analysed carefully. The analysis is data dependent, and the required data may not be easily accessible. In some countries high quality data for market research is provided by Geographic Information Systems (GIS). GIS facilitates integrated spatial analysis, increasing the scope for research and model building. There GIS is not available one or more site-selection methods may be utilised.

4.1 Check - List Method

A systematic evaluation of key characteristics of one or more targeted sites. The method places each option in context by using a simple preferred ranking. If a site is predetermined, the analysis becomes site specific. As an aid to decision making it is simple, quick, inexpensive, flexible, and reasonably objective. However, these advantages alone will not guarantee profitability. Considerable skill, insight and development experience are required to ensure success. No quantitative estimates of market share, investment return, or net profitability are provided.

4.2 Analogue Method

This method is used to compare potential with existing sites in profile terms. Profiles should contain site characteristics related to the development of golf courses. These will include:

Location, acreage, format and structure (9/18 holes)
Memberships/subscriptions/green fees/incomes
Population of catchment area
Other details: topography, services, accessibility.

This is a hit and miss approach for golf course development. As with the check list method significant inputs of expertise are required to facilitate evaluation.

4.3 Analysis of Residuals Method

A quantitative technique similar to the Check List method permitting examination of several location options. This method is not particularly suitable for golf course development being geared to investigations on A regional scale. However, when targeting a wider market (eg attracting overseas memberships, hosting international events) a modified form could be used.

4.4 Site Identification Method

A composite of previous techniques, utilising the same data, it is commonly used by developers. Selection is site specific. Quick, reliable and useful results can be readily obtained. This favours the approach.

The are of land required for any proposed development must be considered as acreage varies significantly with the type of course envisaged. Additional land is required if associated housing development and other facilities are included. Of those developers faced with a choice between alternative sites, 74% did not undertake (to varying degrees) an appropriate site analysis to test potential.

When all factors have been taken into account a site can be chosen, and a development appraisal undertaken. The relevant factors affecting site potential are as follows:

4.4.1 Location, accessibility and quality: A site must be close to a population centre large enough to support the facility. It must also be accessible and visible from main roads. Accessibility and the quality of a golf course are related. A poor quality course may be highly accessible, it may be over-played, and this has contributed to the poor quality. Conversely a course may be relatively inaccessible to players but of a high quality.

4.4.2 Shape, topography, soil, drainage, and vegetation. Safety is an important factor. Fairways must be adequately segregated and protected to avoid accidents. A site must not be too hilly or to flat. The composition, depth and condition of the soil are important. Sandy loam gives the best drainage and forms an adequate seed bed.

4.4.3 Water and other utilities/services: Mains services must be on hand. Water, sewers and electricity (overhead power cables should be avoided), are important site services, necessary for the use and maintenance of a golf course.

5. General observations

Significantly the survey of developers indicated that, in 95% of cases, the approach to market research and analysis in a broad context was lacking in rigour. Awareness of alternative methods for providing the data essential to informed decision making was non existent.

6. The project level

Economic principles underpin development appraisal. At project level if a site is given, the choice is simplified. The developer must decide what quantities of the variable factors of production (labour, materials, and capital) should be combined with the fixed amount of land. Marginal revenue productivity states that marginal increments of the variable factors will be added up to the point where marginal cost equals marginal revenue. As a result the cost of development (land, design, and construction costs, developer's profit, fees and interest charges) is crucial. Ultimately the value in use/market value of the product, a golf course, must secure the capital investment.   Adverse results can arise if the valuation appraisal (relative to the design component) is relegated to a subservient role. A common outcome being excessive costs and short term revenue returns which do not cover loan debt.

The survey of developers produced a number of important findings in relation to the appraisal element. Firstly, all developers undertook some form of financial appraisal. Secondly, only 35% carried out a rigorous development appraisal of the proposed project. Most developers required access to external funding, yet only 62% had to submit a development appraisal. Furthermore, in 20% of these cases the appraisal was rudimentary. In this light, the scepticism of lenders is not based on solid financial grounds, rather on preconceived notions that, by their nature, golf courses are inherently unprofitable.

Quality control is necessary for cost effectiveness. This was formerly irrelevant to the formation of a golf club. The cost/revenue elements are critical within the development appraisal. From the developer's perspective the only good golfing experience is a profitable one. Consequently, a rigorous appraisal of financial viability or value of the development is a priority.

6.1 The Appraisal/Valuation Method
Market value and value in use can differ. A golf course (in an urban environment) could maximise revenue return if sold for housing. Three methods are used to value property:-

(1) Market Basis, Capital/Rental comparative approach
(2) Income Basis, Profits/Investment approach
(3) Cost Basis, Contractors/Residual/Depreciated Replacement Cost approach

The Cost Basis is currently applicable to development appraisal of golf courses, and may be used in a variety of situations. The basic contractors approach, obtaining the total cost of the physical works to create a golf course, is most utilised (52% of developers). To determine the price to pay for land suitable for golf course use the more detailed residual cost option would be used (37% of developers). A depreciated replacement cost format is best utilised to value an existing facility for sale as a going concern/golf course. Not being dependent upon market evidence, the method is suitable for valuing most golf course facilities. When lenders required evidence of a detailed financial appraisal, the method was used by 11% of developers.

6.2 Valuation problems
Golf course valuation is complicated by a number of factors:-

(a) lack of market evidence/data due to insufficient market transactions and confidentiality
(b) the comparative data available to facilitate appraisal of true net profits can be unreliable
(c) historical factors: long leases, low fixed rents, low rental values relative to alternative uses, private clubs only had to break even financially, majority of pay
and play courses were municipal ventures with profit not a major concern
(d) rental growth failed to keep pace with a capital growth
(e) golf courses are purpose built for a specific use
(f) diversity, courses are not uniform products
(g) the need for specialist knowledge

6.3 A hypothetical case study

Assume a basic golf course is being valued for sale. The land value is assessed at opportunity cost (next best use value usually agricultural, but there may be a use producing a higher revenue).

The valuation includes;-

(1) The land value.
(2) The replacement costs of course improvements, and the cost of replacing the clubhouse etc.
(3) An estimate of accrued depreciation is then deducted.
     Depreciation arises from deterioration (physical wear and tear), functional obsolescence (lack of utility, style or design compared to modern facilities), and economic obsolescence (loss of value from environmental causes).
(4) Next the value of ancillary non-golf improvements (minor structures, car parking, etc.) is added. Producing the current value in use for the existing golf course.

6.4 The Valuation

		£
The land: 160 acres @ £2000 per acre . . . . , . .		320,000

Golf Course improvements: -	£	
Building - 18 tees @ £2000 per tee	36,000	
- 18 ladies tees @ £1500/tee	27,000	
- 18 greens @ £6500 each	117,000	
Fairway improvements	15,000	
Sand Traps/Bunkers - 38 @ £1000 each . . .	38,000	
Watering systems/greens	55,000	
Tree Planting	5,000	
Five Shelters	4,750	
Course Draining	50,000	
Developers profit . . . . .say	25,000	
Incidentals Construction Management		
Fees @ 2% of Construction cost	11,535	
	384,285	384,300

Replacement Cost less depreciation: -		
Clubhouses, Restaurant/Bar, Locker rooms,	£	
showers/Pro-shop etc. Replacement cost	750,000	
Less accrued depreciation	150,000	
=	600,000	
Add: - Non-golf course improvements	20,000	
	620,000	620,000
	TOTAL	1,324,300

VALUE IN USE . . . . say   **£1,325,000**

7. CONCLUSIONS

This sector of the leisure industry in Great Britain is now more aware of the problems. Publicised failures in Scotland and England have made developers more aware of the need for market research and rigorous development appraisals. Such publicity may be necessary in Ireland to impress this need upon Irish developers. A recent article (unspecified author) in the Property Valuer (Ireland), reported one development struggling to attract a viable membership, and two with funding problems. There is a clear message; to ensure economic viability and profitable investment, research and appraisal are crucial. Then schemes will be undertaken which are design-efficient, provide an agreeable golfing experience, and ensure optimum results, financially, socially, and indeed environmentally.

8. REFERENCES

Deddis, W.G. (1992) Golf Courses: Development Appraisal and Valuation,
   Journal of Property Valuation & Investment Vol 10 Number 3 (Spring)
Heuer, K.L. (1980) Golf Courses: A guide to analysis and Valuation.
   American Institute of Real Estate Appraisers.
Price, R. (1993) Can Scottish Golf get out of the Bunker? **The Scottish Banker,
   the Magazine of the Chartered Institute of Bankers in Scotland (May)**
Smith, S.L.J. (1989) **Tourism Analysis. Longman Scientific & Technical.**
Veal, A.J. (1992) Research Methods for Leisure and Tourism, **A Practical Guide.
   Longman Leisure Management Studies**

84 Golf course development in Japan: its abnormal supply and demand

H. Zaitsu
Kato International Design Inc., Minatoku, Tokyo, Japan
S. Takeshita
Physical Education Lab., Kokusaigakuin Junior College of Saitama,
Japan
T. Meshizuka
Graduate School, Chukyo Women's University, Japan
and K. Kawashima
Biomechanics Lab., College of Agriculture and Veterinary Medicine,
Nihon University, Japan

Abstract
As in Scotland and the U.S.A., the golf boom in Japan led to the
establishment of clubs and associations and the promotion of tournaments, which played a major role in golf's development.   However,
in Japan one of the biggest factors influencing the growth of golf
is the fact that golf club membership rights are the object of both
individual and corporate investment.   Behind the history of supply
and demand in the golf market after 1945 lies the history of golf as
a business, which is the subject of this paper.
Keywords: Supply and Demand, Yotaku Deposit, Membership Market.

1. Introduction

Golf development in Japan experienced rapid growth in the short
period of the almost 50 years since the end of the Second World War.
Although there were only about 30 golf courses (consisting of
ordinary 18-hole and more inclusive of some 9-hole courses) in Japan
in 1955, this number had increased to 2,109 by 1990, and was more
than 2,424 as of December, 1993, if courses now under construction
are included (Golf Tokushin, 1993). The total annual number of visits
to golf courses in Japan (n.b., this is not the same as number of
rounds played) is about 90.71 million (Ministry of International
Trading & Industry, 1992). The total annual sales at Japanese golf
courses amounts to US$ 13,987 million.   The history of Japanese golf
course development during the last 50 years has produced very
different characteristics and problems from those of Great Britain
and America, where golf has a long history.

Science and Golf II: Proceedings of the World Scientific Congress of Golf. Edited by A.J.
Cochran and M.R. Farrally. Published in 1994 by E & FN Spon, London. ISBN 0 419 18790 1

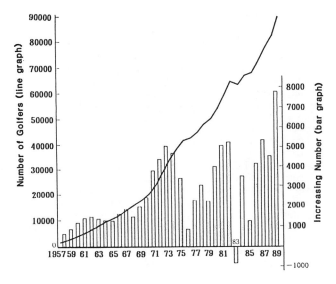

Fig.1. Total numbers of golfers (line graph, 1000)

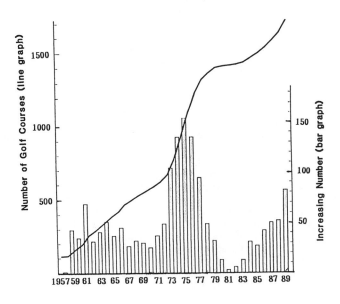

Fig.2. Total numbers of courses

2. Supply and Demand in Golf

2.1 Golf Demand

The first golf course was built at Kobe in 1901, and the first golf club, Kobe Golf Club, was established there two years later. Golf gradually spread and several other courses were built. The pre-1940 Japanese golfing population has been estimated at 110,000, whereas in 1957, 1.82 million visits to golf courses were recorded (Japan Golf Yearbook, 1991). The postwar growth in the number of golfers in Japan can be divided into three periods (Tanaka, 1993). Golf development was given a great boost by the 1964 Tokyo Olympics (which increased the popularity of sport in general) and the growth in professional tournaments and their being broadcast on television. During the first period of postwar growth (1958-1962), the standard of living improved, due to Prime Minister Ikeda's income-doubling programme, and people gradually became interested in golf (see Figure 1). During the second period (1971-1974), Japan's Gross National Product was second in the world. After that, economic factors such as the "oil shock" and the "dollar shock" had a negative effect on golf. After surviving this depression, however, golf began to boom again and in the third period of growth (1986 to the present), Japanese people began to think about ways to enjoy their increasing leisure time. If the number of visits to golf courses in 1957 (1.82 million) is compared with that in 1992 (90.71 million), it can be seen that the latter figure is almost 50 times the former.

2.2 Golf Supply

Before the Second World War, there were about 30 golf courses, whereas in 1957 this number had increased to 116 (see Figure 2). According to data of 1989 provided by the Economic Planning Agency (1992), there were about 1,700 golf courses in Japan, compared to about 12,800 in the U.S. and about 2,000 in Great Britain. This means that there is an average of 150 visits to a golf course in Japan each day. Looking at the number of golf courses in relation to the size of the country, Japan probably has one of the highest levels golf facility provision in the world.

Nowadays it is very difficult to find suitable land on which to build a golf course. Japan covers an area of 1,990,586 km² and is long from north to south. It is very mountainous and there is little flat land. Golf courses account for a total of 0.53% of the entire land area of Japan (378,126 km²). The amount of wooded land per capita is 0.002 km² in Japan, compared to the world average of 0.007 km² (Taniyama, 1991). The amount of woodland which has already been cut down to build golf courses amounts to more than 2,000 km², the equivalent of Metropolitan Tokyo.

Construction of golf courses had increased until 1975 (Figure 2), and 143 golf courses were opened in the year of 1975. However, because of the "oil shock", the number of courses under construction had decreased. The cost of construction became higher than before. After 1981, golf course constructions again increased. Since the Law of General Resort Development (sougo hoyo-chiiki seibi ho) was settled in 1987, it has been possible to construct golf courses within national parks. Figure 3 indicates how the areas for golf development have

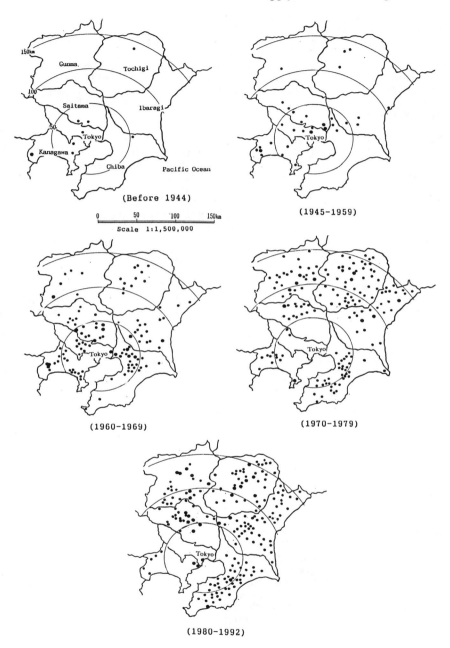

Fig.3. Location of courses in Tokyo Metropolitan Area (1945-1992)

spread further out from Tokyo into the surrounding mountains.

An average cost of construction of a golf course which is located 100 kilometers from Tokyo is US$ 2.7 million per one hole. Therefore, 18 holes will cost US$ 49 million. Cost of land and other expenses will be about US$ 45.5 and US$ 45.5 millions respectively. The total cost of a construction will therefore be about US$ 136.4 million (Kikuchi, 1993). However, the construction of a high-grade course will cost US$ 227.3 million. Construction in other localities will cost US$ 72.7 millions.

2.3 Management Style and Playing Fee

There are three management types of golf courses in Japan. The first type is a private membership course. These types of golf courses are popular in Japan. They consist of almost 90% of all courses. The second type is a public golf course. The last one is a municipal golf course which is managed by a city government. Compared with Great Britain and America, the public and municipal courses are very few in number. One character of Japanese private membership courses is to accept visitors' play. 70 % of players who play on the private courses are visitors. Even on private courses, their management style is very similar to the public course. Many private golf courses count on visitors' playing fees more than their membership fees as current income. Table 1 shows the comparison of playing fees of golf courses located in city areas of several countries. The average of the playing fee in Tokyo Metropolitan Area is higher than those of other cities.

Table 1   International comparison of playing fee

City	Public	Municipal	Private
Tokyo	$194.0	$ 87.0	$233.4
New York	$ 65.6	$ 40.8	$ 60.4
Düseeldorf		$ 14.1	$ 51.6
London	$ 52.5	$ 18.4	$ 64.9
Paris		$ 51.3	$ 97.0

(Exchange rate US$1=¥110, Economic Planning Agency, 1992)

There are several reasons why the Japanese playing fee is high. One of the reasons is that golf course development costs are very expensive. Another reason is that many players use courses as an occasion for business. For example, a course offers a set price for playing including caddy fee, expensive lunch menu, and so forth. Players usually come back to the clubhouse and eat lunch after they finish the first nine holes. Then, they start the last nine holes. According to the latest census of the Economic Planning Agency (1992), 35 % of golfers play with their superiors or colleagues; and 27 % of golfers play with their clients. Over 60 % of golfers play with persons related to their business. Golf courses produce high grade facilities and services for the occasion. As a result, the playing fee needs to be high.

3   Japanese Membership with Yotaku Deposit

3.1 Yotaku Deposit

A major characteristic of the history of Japanese golf has been that golf course owners introduced a system requiring a payment additional to the membership fee. It is a kind of deposit which is called "Yotaku". A golfer pays an entrance fee, membership fee and the Yotaku deposit when he joins a golf club. According to data of the Japan Golf Courses Management Association, 78 % of all Japanese private courses have introduce the Yotaku deposit system (Kikuchi, 1993). After the owner receives the deposit, he does not have to pay any interest to the club member. The owner can use the money for another investment. The owner is under no obligation to return the Yotaku deposit to the member after a certain number of years (usually 10 years).

3.2 Reasons for the Introduction of the Yotaku Deposit

One reason why many Japanese golf courses use this Yotaku deposit system is that a huge budget to develop a new golf course is needed. Moreover, the owner of the course has the intention to keep long term funding from the deposit. Before 1960, there were very few courses that introduced the Yotaku deposit system. Because of increasing numbers of golfers and rising construction costs, the owners intro-duced the system. The Yotaku deposit is originally a loan of money from a new member so that the borrower (the owner) does not have to pay federal tax for it under Japanese law. The golf course owner puts the Yotaku deposit in a bank. According to the Economic Planning Agency (1992), the average deposit of 500 courses located in eastern Japan was US$ 324,600 (¥ 35,700,000) per one membership. Therefore, the owner will receive US$ 233,600 (¥25,700,000) per one member after 10 years, based on 7 % of the compound interest of a half year (han-toshi fukuri). This form of Japanese business management is very convenient for the golf course owners.

Table 2   Foreign investments by Japanese Golf Business

USA	128	Brazil	3	Philippines	2
Australia	22	Spain	3	Portugal	1
France	21	Thailand	3	Bulgaria	1
G. Britain	12	Indonesia	2	Luxemburg	1
China	7	Germany	2	South Korea	1
Malaysia	5	Fiji	2	New Zealand	1
Canada	5	Vanuatu	2	Italy	1

Furthermore, money from Yotaku deposits has been invested in foreign golf development: Table 2 list 225 projects (constructions and purchases) in which Japanese firms have been invested up until October 1993 (Golf Tokushin, 1993). Many companies develop Yotaku membership golf courses in Japan and they invest abroad.

3.3 Golf Membership Market

Another characteristic of the Japanese golf business is the creation
of a membership market similar to a stock market. Whereas many British
and American golf club memberships, are either for life or until the
member resigns, Japanese golf club memberships can be traded, i.e.
bought or sold.   There are special trades who deal in golf course
memberships like stock brokers.   A membership broker receives about
3 % of the membership fee including the Yotaku deposit when it is
sold.   The market prices of the memberships are reported every week in
golf magazines and golf newspapers. Table 3 shows changes of membership market prices of 150 golf courses in the Tokyo Metropolitan Area
during the last 20 years.   The 1990's average price of Tokyo Metropolitan City memberships is 40 times higher than the 1970's.   Not only
individuals, but also corporations understand the membership as a
floating property. As a result, it can be stated that the Japanese have
tended to focus on the commercial benefits of golf club membership.

Table 3   Average membership fee market including the Yotaku
deposit of 150 golf courses in Tokyo Metropolitan Area

	1970	1980	1990
Tokyo Met. City	$193.6	$1,429.0	$8,920.0
Tokyo Met. Area	$126.0	$ 594.1	$3,967.5

(Tokyo Met. Area includes 7 prefectures)

4 Future Orientation of Japanese Golf

The numbers of golfers and courses are still increasing gradually in
Japan. Recently, people and local governments started to notice that
golf course development destroys the natural environment, therefore
the number of golf course constructions will decrease according to
regulations in order to protect nature.   The membership market is
recently inactive due to the world wide depression.   Thus, Japanese
golfers are gradually recognizing the true value of golf as a sport,
and not as an object of business. These facts, little by little force
the change of the future direction of management of Japanese golf
courses, especially the Yotaku deposit membership courses. Therefore,
more golfers will pay attention to the municipal type of golf course
in future for pure enjoyment, and not motives of business.

References

Economic Planning Agency (1992) Cost of Leisure, Tokyo: Author.
Ikki Publishing Inc. (1993) Golf Tokushin, Tokyo: Author.
Kikuchi, K.,(1993) Golf Course Management Seminar, Golf Course
    Management Research Association, Tokyo.
Kyodo Press Inc. (1991) Japan Golf Yearbook, Tokyo: Author.
Ministry of International Trading & Industry (1992) Service Industry
    Report, Tokyo, Tsusan Tokei Kyokai.
Tanaka, Y. (1993) Golf and Japanese, Iwanami Inc., Tokyo.
Taniyama, T. (1991) Japan Golf Islands, Kodansha Inc., Tokyo.

85 Market appraisals for new golf projects

M.G. Williamson
Consulting Director, TMS, Edinburgh, UK

Abstract
A market is best thought of as a productive matching of supply and demand - not just a head count of potential customers, even if that were possible. Drawing on the author's experience of carrying out research nationally for Sports Councils and locally for enterprise companies and developers, the paper describes a methodology for appraising potential demand for new golf facilities. The methodology takes account of the limited national and local data available, but also recognises the need for demand appraisals to be project-specific. In particular, the demand for any project will both influence and be influenced by the facilities to be provided, and how these are managed and marketed. Even the most rigorous demand assessments can at best provide targets, not guarantees. But, seen in this light, a good demand assessment becomes an integral part of the whole process of successful site selection, design, implementation, management and marketing of new golf facilities. The 'golf boom' is dead; long live good new golf development, where science and art combine to create facilities which meet real demand, and which can be both financially viable and environmentally friendly in so doing.
Keywords: Market Appraisal, Supply and Demand, Targets, Management and Marketing.

1 Introduction

The 1988-90 'golf boom' in the UK has much to answer for. The plethora of unresearched and over-designed projects has left developers bankrupt and the countryside, particularly in England, bearing the scars of abandoned projects. More importantly for the future, the failures that hit the headlines have left a legacy of suspicion among planners and financiers which often amounts to a clear presumption against supporting new golf projects of any kind.

At the same time, it is no bad thing that developers now have to try harder to gain support for their projects. However, there is some danger, as always, of the pendulum swinging too far in the opposite direction. The potential demand for new projects **must** be assessed, but

a) the data available for analysis are limited;
b) demand cannot be quantified - this is a social science of few certainties, and the world would be a grey place if it were otherwise;
c) demand and supply are inextricably linked - the location, design, product mix, and pricing of the proposed facilities will influence as well as be influenced by potential demand.

Science and Golf II: Proceedings of the World Scientific Congress of Golf. Edited by A.J. Cochran and M.R. Farrally. Published in 1994 by E & FN Spon, London. ISBN 0 419 18790 1

Projects therefore need to have a clear demand assessment component, in a way that many 'golf boom' projects did not, but that assessment must be seen simply as part of a comprehensive and integrated process of investigation. Just as design and construction are part-science and part-art, so judgement and experience as well as information gathering and calculation have to be brought to bear on the demand assessment process.

Projects, in other words, have to be assessed in the round - the market that has to be created to achieve success is a productive matching of supply and demand. Whether that matching can be accomplished in any particular set of circumstances is the question which market appraisals have to address.

The notes and figures that follow relate particularly to the Scottish situation, with which the author is most familiar, but the principles apply more widely.

2   National Context

The information base available on golf participation and demand at a national level is limited, but it is important to take account of the context it provides for individual project studies as well as to understand its limitations.

Statistics on the 'number of people who play golf' in any country are meaningless and potentially misleading, particularly in international comparisons, without clear and consistent definition. The most consistent, since it applies no matter the time of year at which the surveys were carried out, is the proportion of a population who have played golf at least once in the preceding 12 months. On that basis, recent studies for the Sports Council and the Scottish Sports Council show that 10% of the adult population of England and 15% of the adult population of Scotland 'play golf'. The same studies yield much more information on the key characteristics of golfers - the 5:1 ratio of male to female players, the age and social class profile of golfers, frequency of play, etc.

The limited comparisons possible with previous studies also highlight the growth in golf participation - from about 9% to 12% of adults in Great Britain between 1987 and 1990, and from about 12% to 15% of adults in Scotland between 1973 and 1990.

Other findings from the Sports Council studies challenge the conventional wisdom and are therefore particularly relevant to assessing the demand for new projects. They include:

a) Golfers travel short distances to play golf - a mean distance of only 8-10 miles, and with most golfers travelling less than 5 miles. The old saying about the three most important success factors for a hotel being 'location, location and location' is one for golf developers to take to heart too.

b) For most golfers, the sport is **not** expensive to play. A typical club member paying a subscription of £250 a year and playing once a week is paying only £5 a round for his golf, and play on many municipal courses is little more expensive. That is the context in which new projects, with their capital costs to finance - and the time lag between construction and opening - have to prove themselves viable.

c) Against the common assertion of a strong latent demand by women to play golf, situations where like for like comparisons are possible show that women often pay lower subscriptions than men, that club waiting lists for women are much shorter than for men, and that, among non-participants, levels of interest in taking up the game are much lower among women than men.

d) Similarly, only 2% of the adult population in England (1% in Scotland) who do not play golf are 'very interested' in taking up the game. The factors preventing these people playing golf are **not** lack of access to facilities, but lack of time, the cost of equipment, and not knowing how to get started.

Taken overall, these national results give some clear pointers to the factors likely to be critical determinants of the success of new projects.

Most projects, of course, have to cater for a mix of markets. National data on golf participation by tourists is very limited. In Scotland, the national tourist boards' United Kingdom Tourism Survey (UKTS) consistently shows that about 5% of visitors to Scotland play golf and that, for about half of these, golf is a main purpose of the visit. However, UKTS sample sizes are too small to yield reliable trend information, and there is no information on key aspects such as the reasons for choosing Scotland, the types of golf demanded, price-sensitivity, or market segmentation.

Corporate golf - catering for group outings of various kinds - is also an important source of business for many new projects, but one on which no good data exist at aggregate level.

Caution must also be exercised in using the results of surveys of existing providers. About 75% of courses in the UK are run by private members' clubs, many of which collect no reliable statistics on aspects such as total numbers of rounds played or types of visitor, and have no obligation to supply figures (e.g. on waiting lists) to researchers in any case. The operators of commercially-run courses have an obvious vested interest in keeping key management information to themselves, and local authorities running municipal courses similarly have the implications of compulsory competitive tendering to consider when deciding whether to respond to requests for information.

Beware, therefore, the neat tables of figures in published reports, read the small print on sample sizes and response rates carefully, and be sceptical about results which go beyond the simply factual and non-contentious.

Beware, too, the tyranny of averages and ratios. Scotland has 18 holes of golf per 12,000 population, almost the highest level of provision in the world, three times the level of provision in England where so many new projects have failed, and yet there is still clear scope in Scotland for good new projects. Regionally within Scotland, provision varies from 18 holes per 6,500 people in Highland Region to 18 holes per 16,500 people in Strathclyde.

Even within one region - Strathclyde - the variations are enormous, from 18 holes per 77,000 people in the City of Glasgow to an astonishing 18 holes per 750 people on the Isle of Arran. Within Ayrshire, the delightful 9-hole municipal course in Maybole (where people simply turn up and play for £6 a round and where the recent provision of a new shoe cleaning brush was a significant event) is less than 10 miles from the Japanese-owned golf resort of Turnberry, host to Open Championships and where the money spent on the recent replacement clubhouse would have paid for ten new Maybole courses; it is not easy to characterise Ayrshire golf, never mind Scottish or UK golf, in these circumstances.

In summary, the national context is important but inherently limited. Golf development is essentially a very localised business - every project (existing and potential) is unique, and golfers will not travel long distances to play golf on a regular basis. Market appraisals for new projects have to take this local focus as their starting point.

3   Project Appraisals

Before spending (and possibly wasting) time on an appraisal of potential demand, any project has to yield positive answers to several key questions:

a) Is it in a good **location**?
b) If so, broadly what types of demand is it in a good location for?
c) Is the **site** likely to be capable of transformation at reasonable cost into a golf facility of an appropriate type?

A project should be aborted if the location is too remote or the site physically unsuitable. If it is not discounted on either of these criteria, the next step is to broadly identify the project's market positioning. Is it a site on the urban fringe that can be inexpensively developed to provide a high volume/low cost pay as you play course? Is it a beautiful site in an exclusive resort area or stockbroker belt that can be developed into a low volume/high cost visitors' complex or members' club? Or is it, as most are, geographically and financially somewhere between these two extremes, where the aim is to create an attractive but carefully-funded golf course which will target a mix of markets and be managed to the highest standards of the leisure industry to maximise revenue from - and harmony between - its different customers?

This focus on golf projects as part of the leisure industry also gives them a clear customer-orientation, where good business practice leaves no room for the restrictive practices that characterise many traditional members' clubs. There is a happy coincidence between commercial viability and providing the informal, open-access, reasonable cost golf facilities which the Sports Council and R+A studies have identified as the main priority.

Catering for demand from different market segments maximises throughput and revenue, while reducing the risk of over-dependence on any single group. Location and site will largely determine the potential sources of demand in each case; for many new projects in a country like Scotland, key segments are likely to be:

a) **Regular players** - who may be members, season ticket holders, or 'cardholders' offered various combinations of benefits and costs.
b) **Occasional players** - who will use the facilities on a 'pay as you play' basis, again with scales of charges to maximise revenue at peak times and throughput at off-peak times.
c) **Groups** - players on corporate and society outings who can bring good volume 'package' business if the facilities and management are geared to their needs.
d) **Golfing holidaymakers** - players on specific golfing holidays, who will use the facilities if they are attractive enough (principally seaside courses in the case of Scotland), fairly priced, available at peak times when many club courses are not, and well marketed along with accommodation.
e) **Holiday golfers** - who will play some golf while on a general holiday, and who need attractive, informal, and inexpensive facilities where there is equipment for hire and which are close to their holiday base.

The market mix will naturally vary project by project, but the aim must always be to identify a mix which is **achievable**, **compatible**, and **profitable**. The starting point is to define the physical carrying capacity of the course (and other facilities - short course, driving range, etc. - if these are to be included), i.e. the number of rounds the course can carry and still be maintained in excellent condition over the long term and at reasonable cost. This capacity will vary with location, site, design, standards required for the target markets, etc., and should be determined by the course architect and course manager in consultation with the developer and operator. In Scottish conditions, it might range from 30,000 rounds for an exclusive resort or members' course to 60,000 rounds for a simple pay as you play course, and with 40,000 rounds as a reasonable figure for a middle range mixed-market course.

The next step is to set target numbers of rounds from each of the market segments which will achieve this total - taking particular account of the limited daily carrying capacity of an 18 hole course (200-250 rounds at most on a peak summer day), and the peaked nature of demand. By targeting different market segments, and implementing careful pricing policies, the aim must be to maximise revenue at peak times and maximise throughput at off-peak times.

Thus, weekend times must be fairly shared between the competing demands of regular players (particularly for club competitions), occasional players who will be paying the 'top rate' green fee, and golfing holidaymakers who cannot get access to club courses at weekends and whose word of mouth marketing will be important in generating new business.

Off-peak midweek morning and afternoon times should be positively promoted to corporate and society outings, and to local non-working players for whom these times are attractive. Family and youngsters' tickets for such times should be promoted during school holidays when corporate demand tails off, 9-hole 'twilight' tickets should be sold to maximise throughput on summer evenings, and attractive rates should be offered to local regular and occasional players in the winter.

Unlike traditional members' clubs where capital costs have long been written off and the aim is simply to balance the books annually and maintain adequate reserves, new projects need to maximise revenue - and the market appraisal needs to demonstrate that sufficient demand is likely to be generated from the various market segments for revenue to exceed operating costs by a margin that will allow capital costs to be financed and a profit to remain.

A detailed local analysis is then carried out, covering aspects such as:

a) current provision of golf holes per head of local population, signs of excess demand at municipal courses, waiting lists at members' courses, etc.

b) if the developer can be persuaded, primary market research to test the scale and nature of potential local demand, and interest in various packages of benefits and prices.

c) an analysis, by direct contact with companies and societies in the catchment area and by inference from the facilities they already use, of potential demand from the group sector.

d) a realistic assessment of the attractiveness of the area and the project to golfing holidaymakers, and of the numbers who might be attracted by direct marketing and working with hotels, golf tour operators, etc. The different segments within the golf holiday market need to be recognised, along with the difficulties (in the case of Scotland) of having to compete with long-established traditional links courses and other destinations, like Ireland, which are aggressively promoting a broadly similar product.

e) numbers and profile of general holidaymakers visiting the area in which the project is located, and a reasonable penetration rate of this market.

Throughout the appraisal, account has to be taken of the competition not just from existing golf facilities in the area, but from potential new developments. Assessing which of these is likely to proceed can be difficult - particularly in England where the 'golf boom' gave rise to almost 2,000 proposals for new projects.

The market appraisal is then drawn together into a matrix, indicating achievable numbers of rounds from different market segments, and the revenue these should generate. In simple form, for a new project in a popular golf holiday area reasonably close to an urban population in Scotland, this might take the following form:

Table 1. Outline market appraisal

Market segment	Number of rounds	Achieved rate per round (£)	Annual revenue (£)
Regular players	15,000	4.70	70,000
Occasional players	3,000	11.00	33,000
Groups	4,000	9.00	36,000
Golfing holidaymakers	10,000	10.00	100,000
Holiday golfers	3,000	11.00	33,000
Total	35,000		272,000

In each case, the full appraisal would include the detailed workings. For instance, in this example there would be 300 regular players paying £200 for a season ticket which entitled them to 40 rounds of golf and a 50% reduction on green fees for additional rounds. Regular players playing once a week on average would therefore play 50 rounds a year and pay a total of £275 each (based on a standard green fee of £15). Deducting value added tax gives an achieved rate per round of about £4.70 and annual revenue of about £70,000 from this segment. Similar calculations are made for the other segments, with occasional players and holiday golfers paying close to the standard rate on average, but with group rates and commissions reducing the achieved rates for groups and golfing holidaymakers respectively. In each case, account would be taken of the likely breakdown of demand by day of the week, time of day, and season, and by adults and children, all of which would have a bearing on the achieved rate per round. The target number of rounds from each segment would also be distributed, ideally on a daily basis, throughout the year to ensure that each target was reasonable in relation to the limited course capacity at peak times.

The estimate of annual revenue should then be compared to capital and operating costs (both of which should be able to be estimated in advance with reasonable accuracy), and sensitivity analysis carried out on the demand and revenue estimates to test the effect on potential viability of changing assumptions on key variables. Account must also be taken of a build-up in demand, to allow marketing to take effect and the course itself to settle in. In the above example, the build-up might be from 15,000 rounds in the first year to 25,000 rounds in year two, and with the 35,000 rounds being achieved from year three onwards.

In this respect, the balance between regular players (a stable market paying a lump sum at the start of each year when cash flow is at its weakest, but generating low average revenue per round played) and other segments (less secure, requiring higher marketing expenditure, but yielding higher revenue per round), is an important aspect of the appraisal.

4   Conclusion

The process of market appraisal is a thorough one, but it is not scientific in the sense of arriving at answers which are demonstrably correct. The methodology provides as robust a framework as possible, but a lot of judgement based on wide experience and detailed local knowledge is required. The methodology reduces but does not eliminate the element of risk; it should certainly prevent no-hope projects going ahead, and it can help refine potentially good projects. The use of sensitivity analysis in particular can help identify the magnitude of various risks, while regarding the estimates of demand from specific market segments as **targets** links the market appraisal directly into the next stages of preparing detailed marketing and business plans. Demand estimates are hypothetical; spelling out **how** potential demand is to be converted into customers, and how these customers will then be served, helps both to test the reasonableness of the demand estimates themselves and to shape the operating plan which must aim to create satisfied customers out of every first-time user.

Stand-alone golf projects are not licences to print money. But with careful site selection and market appraisal, effective marketing, and customer-orientated management, they can succeed without the need for cross-funding from the built development which got so many projects into planning and financial trouble during the 'golf boom'.

Instead, we could be witnessing the early stages of a significant new wave of golf development which is much more in tune with the concerns of the late twentieth century - golf development which can be:

a) **socially and economically valuable,** by providing new opportunities to play the Royal and Ancient game to those whose needs and demands are not currently being met;
b) **financially viable,** by careful control of costs, cash flows, and funding packages, and maximising revenue, so that those who take the risks and provide the new opportunities have a fair chance of reward;
c) **environmentally friendly,** by avoiding ancillary built development, designing with rather than against nature (which also keeps down capital costs) and, wherever possible, enhancing the landscape and nature conservation value of sites which were previously derelict or under agriculture.

Good market appraisals which will help get more people swinging golf clubs are at least as important as the technical studies that analyse what happens when they do.

References

Royal and Ancient Golf Club of St Andrews (Undated) **The Demand for Golf.**
Sports Council (1992) **Study of Golf in England.**
The Scottish Sports Council (1991) **Study of Golf in Scotland.**

86 The database of golf in America: a guide to understanding U.S. golf markets

A Product of Golf Digest, The Golf Company

J.F. Rooney, Jr
Regents Professor of Geography,
Oklahoma State University
and H.J. White
V-P Research and Marketing Services, NYT Sports/Leisure Division
of the New York Times Company Magazine Group

Abstract
We introduced the U.S. Golf Facility Database at the 1990
World Scientific Congress of Golf. Since its inception, the
U.S. Golf Facility Database, now called the Database of Golf
in America, has been enhanced to include much more information
on both the supply and demand for golf facilities, equipment
and services. It is a Geographic Information System
containing golf data combined with a host of geodemographic
information. The purpose of our presentation to the 1994
Congress is to discuss the key elements of the Database of
Golf in America. We will comment on its utility to the golf
industry and present examples of its applications, and finally
we will deal with the theoretical potential of the Database
for identifying and solving the myriad of golf related
problems.
Keywords: Golf Market Database, GIS, Golf Facility Supply,
Golf Demand, Golf Market Applications, Optimal Golf Locations.

1 Introduction

The original version of the U.S. Golf Facility Database was
designed primarily to identify the best possible locations for
new golf courses and golf enterprises. It was based on supply
data from the National Golf Foundation and various state and
regional golf associations. Facility use was obtained from
approximately twenty percent of all U.S. golf courses via a
survey conducted by Golf Shop Operations; A trade publication
distributed to over 17,000 U.S. Golf professionals and
retailers. The survey was designed to collect data on rounds
played, average travel distance, percent male and female
participation, course maintenance costs, and greens fees.
Golfer demand pressure was calculated from a series of
variables including readership of golf periodicals, purchase
of golf equipment, TV viewership of golf tournaments and
support for various levels of competitive golf.

Our 1990 paper focussed on the use of the Database for the
analysis of new facility development in Prince Georges County,

Science and Golf II: Proceedings of the World Scientific Congress of Golf. Edited by A.J.
Cochran and M.R. Farrally. Published in 1994 by E & FN Spon, London. ISBN 0 419 18790 1

Maryland. We compared golf supply in the county to golf demand. We introduced the terms Golf Supply Index (GSI), Golf Demand Index (GDI), and the Golf Intensity Index (GII). We concluded that in the case of Prince Georges County that golf demand substantially exceeded current golf facility supply. Using the formula developed for the calculation of the Golf Intensity Index, we concluded that Prince Georges County could support at least six additional 18-hole equivalents. We further concluded that most of the new courses should be open to the public, since the most severe shortage was in the public golf arena.

2 The Structure of the Database

Much has happened during the past four years to improve the Database of Golf in America. We have much better data, thanks to the vision and financial support of the NYT Sports/Leisure Division of The New York Times Company Magazine Group, the parent company of Golf Digest, Golf World and Golf Shop Operations. That group sponsors a Fellowship Program at the Oklahoma State University Graduate School of Geography. Through a cooperative effort between the Research Resource Center of Golf Digest, The Golf Company, and the Oklahoma State University Department of Geography, we have improved the baseline data as well as the theory that underpins our Database.

3 Golf Facility Supply

Our supply data are more accurate than they were in 1990. We now believe that we have information on at least 99% of all U.S. golf facilities. We have combined a variety of lists on golf facilities, including the National Golf Foundation, Golf Shop Operations, State and Regional Associations, and the numerous golf course guides published over the last several years. By mixing and matching, merging and purging, we have assembled an extremely reliable supply Database.

We have gone beyond mere quantity by bringing in the qualitative information produced by the Golf Digest editorial staff over the last decade. We have included the information from "Places to Play" which is updated annually by Golf Digest. We have also utilized the Golf Digest course rating system by state, covering public, private and resort courses. In addition we are now coding data from a national survey of Golf Digest readers, dealing with courses not included in the "Places to Play" group.

The Database of Golf in America has commissioned Dr. Steve Stadler, climatologist from Oklahoma State University, to incorporate atmospheric data within the Database. Climatological guidance is of value in that long-term atmospheric conditions determine numbers of playable days and, hence, influence numbers of rounds played. The original data are from magnetic tape records of the National Climate Data Center and consist of long-term daily means of weather

variables reported from over 200 National Weather Service
hourly reporting sites. Each golf facility location has been
associated with the nearest weather reporting site.
Climatological averages -- seasonal means of temperature,
number of rainy days, etc. -- are in the Database. The
Database also includes the output of a leisure comfort model
adapted from the work of Yapp and McDonald (1978). Seasonal
weather parameters (temperature, humidity, cloudiness, wind,
and solar radiation) are used in an energy-balance metabolic
model to simulate the degree of comfort experienced by walking
and riding golfers. For each golf facility, the number of
comfortable and uncomfortable days are estimated by season and
year.

4 Golf Demand
We can now measure demand for golf facilities at several
geographic levels; the five digit zip code, county,
metropolitan, and the Area of Dominant Influence.
    We have continued to collect information through the Golf
Shop Operations annual survey of subscribers and readers. The
current questionnaire is illustrated in Table 1.

Table 1.

1. TYPE OF FACILITY

Private Country Club		A__ Military	H__
Privately Owned Daily Fee	B__	Off Course/Spec. Shop	I __
Semi Private Country Club	C__	Club Repair Shop	J __
University/College	D__	Industrial Course	K __
Munic./St./County Owned	E__	Golf Range	L __
Public Country Club	F__	Other (please specify)	
M__			
Resort	G__		

2. TITLE

Golf Professional	A__	Equipment Buyer	
I__			
Owner/Partner/Pres.	B__	Apparel Buyer	J__
Club Manager	C__	General Buyer	K__
Shop Manager	D__	Other (please specify)	
G__			

3. DO YOU MAKE GOLF SHOP BUYING DECISIONS FOR YOUR FACILITY?
   Yes _____   No _____

4. WHO ELSE MAKES BUYING DECISIONS FOR YOUR FACILITY?
   _____

5. FACILITY INFORMATION (please answer all)

a) What is the zip code and country name of each golf course's location?

_____

b) If the facility is a multi-course development, please record answers separately.

Course name 1 _____ # of holes _____

2 _____ # of holes _____

3 _____ # of holes _____

c) Is there a full service (club sales, apparel, shoes, etc.) pro shop? _____

d) Is there a driving range available? # of stalls

_____

e) If course is a resort development, please list best, (most golfers) market areas accessed (i.e. cities, states, countries)

_____

f) Is the course a residential development? _____

If yes, how many lots sold? _____

How many available? _____

The <u>Golf Shop Operations</u> questionnaire is designed to analyze the utilization of U.S. Golf Facilities. It provides data on rounds played, distance traveled to play and the type of user associated with each course. Through this survey we obtain a good measurement of demand pressure on courses throughout the nation. Over the last two years we have obtained data from over one half of all U.S. Golf Facilities and nearly 60% of all facilities containing 18 holes or more. We have supplemented the <u>Golf Shop Operations</u> mail survey with a phone interview barrage. As a result of the telephone interviews we have procurred useable data for nearly 1500 additional courses. The GSO and phone interview programs will continue until we have complete coverage of the U.S. facility market.

5 Golf Intensity

Using the supply and demand data we have developed a series of golfer to 18 hole equivalent ratios for a variety of county size and urban-rural categories. For example, large central cities such as New York, Chicago, and Los Angeles have an

overwhelming number of golfers per 18-hole facility. Three to
four thousand frequent players per facility are not uncommon
in and around the largest U.S. cities. In contrast there are
many 9-hole golf courses located in communities with
populations between 1,000 and 2,500. These populations yield
frequent golfer numbers in the 100-200 range. Research has
led us to believe that though facility to golf ratios are
population dependent, there are considerable regional
variations in these ratios. As a result we have grouped U.S.
counties into six population categories and seven golf supply
regions.

We discriminate not only between county population size but
also the counties relationship to a major city. For example
there are many suburban counties with large numbers of golf
courses per population unit. Though they appear to be well
served they are primarily geared to providing golf for
underserved central city markets. The "Edge City" phenomena
identified by Joel Garreau, represents the new urban form and
function associated with so many American cities. "Edge City"
is that area where people both live and work on the edge of
the old central cities. They are most apparent around New
York, Chicago, Dallas, Washington, and Los Angeles. It is
within these "edge cities" that golf supply is lowest relative
to demand. As a result the "edge city" zones are categorized
separately within the Database of Golf in America.

6 Applications of the Database of Golf in America
Sales Analysis

Aside from facility location, there are numerous other
applications of the Database of Golf in America. We recently
completed a study for the U.S. Senate pertaining to the
potential opening of the nearly 300 military golf courses to
public play. Working with New Mexico Senator Dennis
Deconcini, we used the Database to measure the feasibility of
adding military courses to the public sector. We concluded
that by opening military courses, particularly those located
in major metropolitan areas such as San Francisco, Washington,
D.C., and Los Angeles, critical supply shortages would be
eased substantially.

The Database of Golf in America is strongly committed to an
increase in minority golf participation. We have worked with
the USGA and a number of black golfer associations to identify
the factors that contribute to minority participation. Golf
Digest is now supporting a major research project that will
produce policy recommendations geared to increase minority
golf participation.

We have used the database to assist manufacturers in
determining the demand potential for any sales territory
within the United States. For example, a firm with 50 sales
people would be best served by allocating each sales person a
territory representing 2% of national golf product demand.

The database allocates a percentage of national product demand to each county in the United States. Hence, combinations of counties can be assembled to represent a desired percentage of national demand. The map of the U.S. portraying GDI values by county is the first step in developing a demand surface for sales analysis (Figure 1).

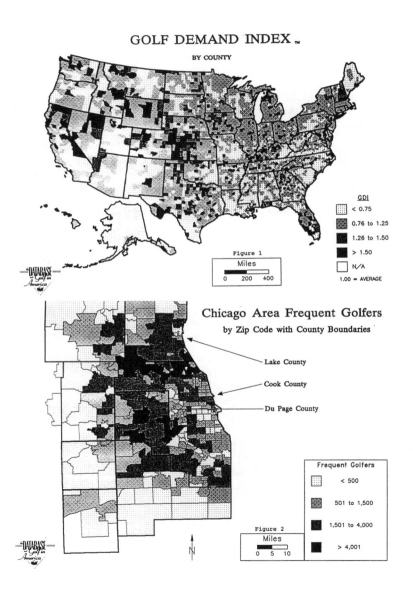

GOLF DEMAND INDEX ™

BY COUNTY

GDI
⬚ < 0.75
▨ 0.76 to 1.25
▤ 1.26 to 1.50
■ > 1.50
☐ N/A

1.00 = AVERAGE

Figure 1
Miles
0   200   400

Chicago Area Frequent Golfers
by Zip Code with County Boundaries

Lake County

Cook County

Du Page County

Frequent Golfers
⬚   < 500
▨   501 to 1,500
▤   1,501 to 4,000
■   > 4,001

Figure 2
Miles
0   5   10

N

The Database also operates at the five digit zip code level. The Chicago market illustrates the type of micro-geographical variation in frequent golfer locations (Figure 2). Knowledge of these patterns is critical to the rational bounding of sales territories as well as the positioning of off course golf retail outlets.

7 Golf Travel

Another application of the Database of Golf in America involves travel golf destinations. By combining residential golfer counts with information on occupancy rates at hotels and motels, as well as second home data, we can evaluate the current supply of golf facilities at any travel destination. The Database can assist hotel chains, golf resort developers, travel packagers and convention planners in evaluating existing and potential travel golf destinations.

Golf Digest magazine runs a regular feature on travel resort information. Readers are asked to identify various resort destinations which they are interested in visiting. By combining the home town locations of the respondents with their prefered travel destinations we are able to analyze the travel patterns of American golfers. This knowledge enables any resort manager to better understand both his existing and potential market region.

8 Tournament Site Selection

Still another application of the Database of Golf in America centers on the identification of potential tournament sites as well as the evaluation of existing sites. We know the number of frequent and total golfers within various radii of each tournament site. We also have data on tournament attendance and a sampling of the types of individuals who comprise the spectator groups. As a result we can compare all existing tournament sites against each other and against any new site under consideration.

The various U.S. golf tours are missing out on many of the most lucrative golf markets (Figure 3). This is in part a function of the winter segment of the tours, when all tournaments are held in the Sun Belt regions of the U.S.   But it is obvious from Table 2, that many large markets are untapped.

9 Analyzing New Construction Trends

Over 1300 new U.S. golf facilities and additions have been opened since 1987. This growth spurt followed the construction doldrums that plagued the industry since the federally funded boom days of the 1960s. That was the period, fueled by Palmer, Player, Nicklaus and television, that brought daily fee and municipal golf to many communities throughout the nation.

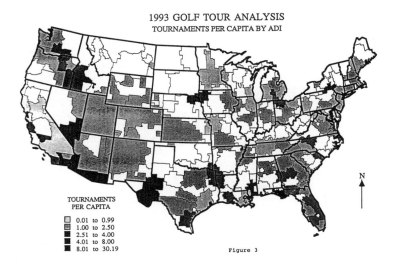

1993 GOLF TOUR ANALYSIS
TOURNAMENTS PER CAPITA BY ADI

TOURNAMENTS
PER CAPITA

☐ 0.01 to 0.99
▨ 1.00 to 2.50
■ 2.51 to 4.00
■ 4.01 to 8.00
■ 8.01 to 30.19

Figure 3

N

Table 2

TOP 25 ADI'S WITHOUT A TOUR EVENT *
Ranked by Total Population

Arbitron ADI Market Name	1993 Population	Frequent Golfers	Tourneys Per Capita	# of Holes	GDLQ	TV Golf
St. Louis	3,023,481	95,602	0.00	1,836	1.01	1.01
Baltimore	2,557,312	84,826	0.00	1,035	0.95	1
Raleigh-Durham	1,926,387	48,969	0.00	2,151	1.21	1.04
Buffalo	1,646,752	55,133	0.00	1,566	0.92	0.94
Oklahoma City	1,574,333	46,852	0.00	1,071	1.02	1.04
Louisville	1,494,874	43,097	0.00	1,179	0.92	0.99
Providence-New Bedford	1,477,029	47,619	0.00	1,197	1.04	0.93
Little Rock	1,317,208	30,625	0.00	1,071	0.8	1.01
Fresno-Visalia	1,304,340	36,391	0.00	549	0.71	1.02
Albany-Schenectady-Troy	1,301,673	46,405	0.00	1,620	1.1	1.02
Charleston-Huntington	1,300,896	33,875	0.00	675	0.69	1.01
Dayton	1,276,146	41,934	0.00	1,044	1.14	0.99
Wilkes Barre-Scranton	1,250,218	38,369	0.00	1,044	0.79	0.98
Tulsa	1,195,226	34,088	0.00	774	1.03	1.02
Mobile-Pensacola	1,185,276	31,967	0.00	936	0.8	1.01
Green Bay-Appleton	1,037,150	33,438	0.00	1,386	0.99	0.98
Roanoke-Lynchburg	1,005,671	24,317	0.00	990	0.9	1.03
Lexington	958,595	23,179	0.00	783	0.78	1.02
Des Moines	955,367	31,393	0.00	1,332	1.3	1.04
Omaha	946,088	29,915	0.00	945	1.2	1.01
Syracuse	938,943	33,473	0.00	1,296	1.21	1.03
Spokane	898,594	26,742	0.00	873	1	1.04
Jackson, MS	873,389	18,140	0.00	531	0.64	0.98
Columbia, SC	856,457	20,178	0.00	801	0.97	1.01
Huntsville-Decatur-Florence	834,664	20,958	0.00	612	0.85	1.03

* Includes PGA, Sr. PGA, LPGA, & NIKE tours

As a result of the 60s boom some places had too much golf, an over supply relative to the small numbers who were using the facilities. But in others, particularly in the Northeast, California, and the burgeoning cities of the New South, the demand for golf courses was never met. Many former and potential golfers were turned off by long waits, even longer rounds, and poor reservation systems.

And so, for many areas, the reved-up pace of construction is both heartening and well-timed. But perhaps the most important trend is the focus on public access to the game. Over 80% of the facilities opened during the last three years are public.

Developers and communities have responded to a need that has been hammered home at every national and regional golf gathering since the 1986 Westchester Summit.   Most would agree that there was a pressing need for additional facilities. The mini-boom in golf course construction, however, raises a number of pertinent questions. Were the new courses built in the right locations? Are they catering to the right market niches? How many additional courses can the U.S. support, now and in the future?

What is the minimum carrying capacity for a golf facility (for profitability)? What is the maximum carrying capacity, after which point the golf experience begins to deteriorate? Have some markets reached saturation? How many and what percent of U.S. golf courses are providing an unsatisfactory experience due to poor maintenance, poor service, over crowding, or obsolescence? The answers to these questions are important to the accessment of the resurgence in golf facility construction.

Total Course Openings 1987-1993
by State

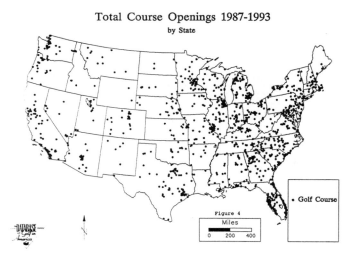

Figure 4

• Golf Course

Miles

0   200   400

The accompanying map displays the geographical variation in new golf facility development since 1987 (Figure 4). Returning to our earlier query, were these golf courses built in the right places? We know that variations in U.S. golf participation rates are largely a function of access to municipal and daily fee golf. That is why participation is so high across the northern U.S., where almost every small town has a golf course. There we have high rates of participation (15 to 20 percent) in states well supplied with public courses and low rates (5 to 10 percent) in states poorly supplied with public courses.

It is vital therefore, that the courses are built in areas with the greatest pent up demand. We measure unfulfilled demand with our Golf Intensity Index. The GII compares and relates demand (The Golf Demand Index) to supply (The Golf Supply Index). In places where the GDI exceeds the GSI, there is a shortage of golf facilities. So by using our golf demand and supply indices we can, with considerable confidence, evaluate the surge in new course development.

Our indices confirm that many metropolitan areas were in short supply of public golf. Construction since 1987 has alleviated some of those critical shortages. For example Atlanta, Dallas, Houston, Louisville-Lexington, all in the "Southern Void," have added substantially to their public sector inventory. Northern hotbeds of golf have become hotter. Chicago, Detroit, St. Louis, Columbus and Minneapolis-St. Paul have been the big winners in the construction boom.

Resort areas have also flourished. This is particularly true for Florida's east Coast, Cape Cod, northern Michigan, the Carolinas, Colorado and the desert Southwest. Our data demonstrate that most of these resort destinations are geared to northeastern and midwestern golf travelers. As such they can be viewed as an enhancement to supply in those regions.

Let us return to our initial question. Were these facilities built in the right places? In most cases the answer is yes. The construction surge has brought supply in balance with demand in some metropolitan areas; Columbus, St. Louis, Detroit, Omaha, Portland and Indianapolis. Access has improved dramatically around Atlanta, Baltimore, Washington D.C. and Boston.

But severe shortages still remain. Construction in California has barely touched the supply deficit. For example Los Angeles has less than forty percent of the courses that it could theoretically support. San Francisco and San Jose, where demand is extremely high, could support substantial additions to their course base.

Major problems continue to plague a number of eastern and southern markets, particularly in the public and daily fee arena. New York City, Philadelphia and many of the fast growing suburban or "edge cities" in New Jersey, Connecticut,

Maryland and Virginia are in desperate need of more golf
courses.

Southeastern Sun Belt cities have finally begun to identity
with the game.   Demand across the south though, is still very
low compared to the Northern Heartland.   It is still too early
to predict whether the new urban affinity for golf there will
spread to the small towns and rural communities, as it has
done throughout the North.

In summary the recent uptick in golf course construction
has helped to balance supply and demand.   It has solved the
public access problem in a number of cities.   But in other
places it has simply been a case of the rich getting richer;
more and better courses in the strongest markets.   Major
shortages still exist and it will require creative genius and
substantial capital to generate construction in California and
the Northeast.

10   Theoretical   Concerns
Both golf facility supply and golf participation rates are a
microcosm of the broader sports culture.   Golf is interrelated
to other sports, and perhaps more importantly, to overarching
cultural values.

Regional sports cultures have been delineated for the U.S.
(Rooney and Pillsbury, 1992).   The identification and mapping
of regional cultures ranging from the "Pigskin Cult" to
"Pacific Cornucopia" was based on data pertaining to the
geography of over seventy American sports (Figure 5).

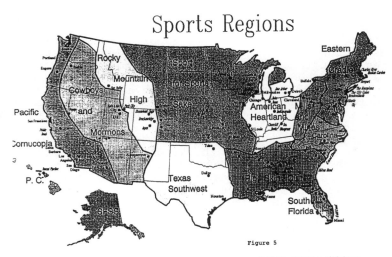

Figure 5

Source: Rooney & Pillsbury,
Atlas of American Sport
Macmillian 1992

Golf is most available and most important in the "Sports for Sports Sake Region." This region is centered in the Northern U.S. in the states of Wisconsin, Iowa, Minnesota, Kansas, Nebraska, and the Dakotas. It is an area where participation and sports fundamentals are stressed over sports specialization and the boosting of community pride through winning high school sports programs. Per capita participation in youth and high school sports exceeds national norms by two or three times. As a result there is a strong carryover to adult sports; tennis, softball, bowling and especially golf. Golf participation rates and public access to the game are 200-300 percent higher than they are in the "Pigskin Cult." Differences in women's participation are even greater. Thirty to 35% of "Sports for Sports Sake golfers" are women as opposed to 5-10% in the "Pigskin Cult."

The State of Kansas provides an excellent illustration of "Sports for Sports Sake" golf demand and golf supply indices. The population of Kansas is heavily concentrated in the eastern half of the state. The sparsely populated wheat country of the west, however, is very high on the sport of golf (Figures 6&7). There are more courses per capita in the west and a higher percentage of golf demand per capita. It is there, in nine hole golf country, where supply and demand reach their zenith.

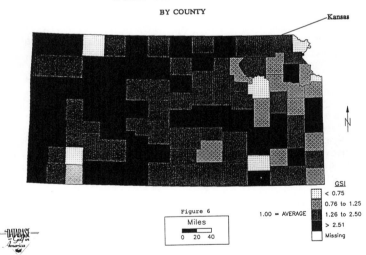

GOLF SUPPLY INDEX™

BY COUNTY

Kansas

N

Figure 6

Miles

0   20   40

1.00 = AVERAGE

GSI
: < 0.75
0.76 to 1.25
1.26 to 2.50
> 2.51
Missing

GOLF DEMAND INDEX ™

BY COUNTY

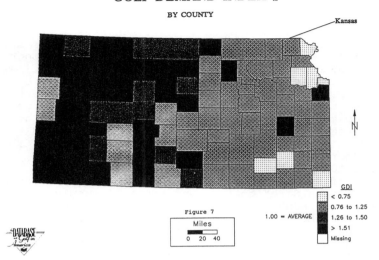

Figure 7

Miles

0   20   40

1.00 = AVERAGE

GDI

< 0.75
0.76 to 1.25
1.26 to 1.50
> 1.51
Missing

    The Database has identified many pertinent questions. Can
participation based cultures be transferred to macho-dominated
mono sports regions? Is so, what is the time frame? The
challenge is obvious. If golf is to grow to its full
potential, strategies must be developed to penetrate
unaccepting sports cultures.

    In addition we must gain a clear understanding of the
theoretically optimum carrying capacity for all types of golf
facilities. We must know more about maximum participation
rates for varying types of socio-demographic profiles. And we
must better understand the ability of golf to compete with
other sports in a limited leisure time market across a wide
range of demographic and regional settings.

11 References

John F. Rooney, Jr. and Richard Pillsbury. **Atlas of
    American Sport,** New York, Macmillian, 1992.
John F. Rooney, Jr. and Richard Pillsbury. "American Sports
    Regions," **American Demographics,** November 1992, pp 30-39.
John F. Rooney, Jr. and Hugh White. "The Utilization of the
    U.S. Golf Database for the Optimal Location of New Golf
    Facilities, **Science and Golf,** Spon, London, 1990.
John F. Rooney, Jr. and Robert A. Adams. "American Golf
    Courses: A Regional Analysis of Supply," **Sport Place
    International,** Vol. 3, No. 1, 1989, pp. 3-17.
John F. Rooney, Jr. "An Analysis of Regional Golf Supply in
    the U.S." **Golf Projections 2000,** National Golf
    Foundation, Jupiter, Florida, 1989, pp. 23-40.
G.A. Yapp and N.S. McDonald, "A Recreation Climate Model"
    Journal of Environmental Management, (1978), 7, pp 253-
    60)

87 Targeting for success – the European golf market

K.R. Storey
Sports Marketing Surveys Ltd, Byfleet Business Centre, Chertsey
Road, Byfleet, Surrey, UK

Abstract
This paper analyses the major European golf markets in
terms of number of courses and golfers. It compares
recent growth trends throughout Europe and compares the
typical profile of golfers in the major markets. A
theoretical "mature market" in terms of the number of
courses is suggested to identify which countries have the
biggest need for new courses. The paper also calls for
detailed catchment research before building new courses
and shows how geodemographic analysis can be used to
compare catchments.
Keywords: European golf market, Catchment, Geodemographics, Feasibility studies.

1 Introduction

The R&A "Demand for Golf" has been widely quoted since
its publication in 1989. The report pointed to the basic
shortfall of golf courses in the UK and the subsequent
growth in courses has been dramatic. This paper looks at
the recent growth in courses and golfers throughout
Europe and looks at future potential. It also calls for
thorough research into new developments and looks at
geodemographics as a method for analysing catchments.

This paper is in four main sections:
The growth of golf in the main European markets
The profile of golfers in the main European markets
The need for new courses in Europe
Geodemographics and their use in golf facility target-
ing.

Science and Golf II: Proceedings of the World Scientific Congress of Golf. Edited by A.J.
Cochran and M.R. Farrally. Published in 1994 by E & FN Spon, London. ISBN 0 419 18790 1

2 The growth of golf in Europe

2.1 The UK experience
Since the start of 1988 an additional 280 courses have been built in the UK. This represents nearly half of the R&A target of a further 691 courses by the year 2000.

To reach the R&A target the UK will need to build 53 courses a year. It appears however that 1993 may have been a peak year in terms of new builds. If the build rate declines through the 1990s it looks as if the total number of additional courses by the year 2000 will be in the region of 570. Figure 1 shows the two different forecasts.

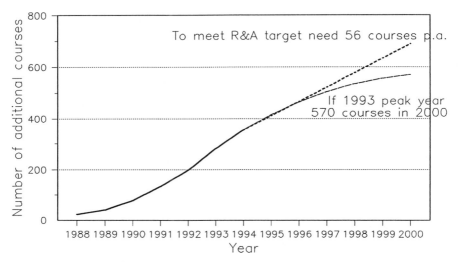

Fig. 1 Growth in UK golf courses 1987 to 2000 – Two forecasts

Obviously, these additional courses can't just be built anywhere in the UK, full feasibility studies should be carried out to establish the likely demand and the type of facility needed.

2.2 Growth in golf in continental Europe
England, Scotland and Wales (GB) has traditionally represented more than half the total number of golfers in Europe. However, recent rapid growth in Continental Europe has left GB with only 45% of the number of registered golfers. Table 1 shows this change in balance from 1988 to 1992.

Table 1. Number of registered golfers GB vs Rest of Europe

	1988		1992	
GB	807,347	52%	986,863	45%
Rest of Europe	756,222	48%	1,205,199	55%

   Please note that Table 1 shows the numbers of registered golfers so it does not represent the whole picture but it is a fair basis for comparison.
   The growth rates to achieve this change of balance in Europe have been exceptional. Norway, Netherlands, Finland and Austria have all more than doubled during the period 1988 to 1992 both in terms of numbers of courses and numbers of golfers. It should, of course, be noted that the starting bases for these countries were very low.
   Figure 2 shows the growth rates between 1988 and 1992 and the total number of courses in 1992. The number of courses clearly shows France, Germany, Sweden and Ireland as the next most important countries after GB.

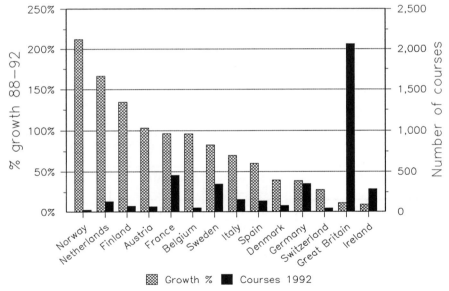

Fig. 2   European golf course growth 1988 to 1992

3 The profile of European golfers

As you might expect golf in continental Europe is still restricted to relatively affluent sections of the community. Golf in GB, where penetration rates are highest, reaches the broadest cross section of the population. The game is still very "up market" in France and Germany. Golf in Sweden reaches a broader cross-section but is still not as widespread as in GB.

For comparison purposes, the Table 2 shows the percent of golfers who fall into the top two social grades (AB) in each of the four main golfing markets. The data comes from Sports Marketing Surveys' regular interviews with golfers in the main European markets. From this work, we have built up a good profile of European golfers.

Table 2. Percent of golfers in AB social grade

Country	% in social grades AB
GB	23%
Sweden	37%
Germany	46%
France	55%

There are also differences in the age/sex profile of golfers. French golfers are the oldest on average and German golfers the youngest. Although golf has a long history in GB, it is still very male dominated with 88% of golfers being male. The German golf market is the most "liberated" but is still 64% male. Table 3 shows the male:female ratio and the average ages of golfers.

Table 3. Male:female ratio and average age of golfers

Country	Male:Female Ratio	Average age
GB	88:12	41.7
Sweden	78:22	39.4
Germany	64:36	38.0
France	73:27	43.8

4 The need for new courses

In order to assess the number of courses needed in the main countries in Europe, I have assumed a mature penetration rate for <u>regular</u> golfers of 5% of the population in GB, Sweden and Ireland where penetration is already above 1% and a mature rate of 2% of the population for countries whose penetration is currently below 1%.

I have then assumed the need for one facility for every 1200 golfers. This corresponds to 1 course for every 25,000 population for GB, Sweden and Ireland and 1 course for every 60,000 population in the rest of Europe.

On this basis a further 808 courses are needed in Italy, 698 in Germany, 513 in Spain, 485 in France and 330 in GB. It is very unlikely that these build figures could be achieved in the next 10 years on the continent although the GB level might be achievable by the end of the decade.

It should be pointed out that this analysis is for domestic demand only. There is undoubtedly scope for new courses in tourist areas around the Mediterranean without domestic demand. Away from the sun, Ireland demonstrates that even in situations of over supply a healthy tourist market can be based around golf facilities.

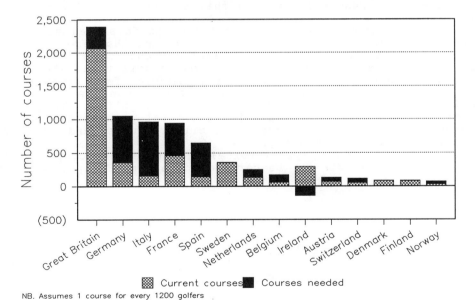

NB. Assumes 1 course for every 1200 golfers

Fig. 3   Mature golf market - Number of courses

Figure 3 shows the number of courses needed for this "mature market". If all these courses were built, there would be 7400 courses in Europe which is one course for every 46,000 population which is still considerably less than provision in the USA of one course per 20,000 population.

5 Geodemographics and their use in golf facility targeting

Using total population to demonstrate demand is clearly simplistic but has frequently been used in the past in feasibility studies. Careful analysis is needed at the catchment level to ensure the right facility is built in the right place. MOSAIC can be used to more accurately assess not just the number of people in catchments but also the types of people.

MOSAIC is a geodemographic system which classifies each postcode in the country according to the types of housing and kinds of people who live there. For example, we know that 25% of golfers come from MOSAIC Group 9 – Better off families. We can then say more about this group, for example what type of housing they live in, how many cars they are likely to own, what newspapers they are likely to read and how many children they are likely to have.

Figure 4 shows the MOSAIC profile of golfers against the profile of the GB population. The groups that are overrepresented are "Better off families" and "Older couples in leafy suburbs". "Go-getting council tenants" are also important especially at pay and play facilities.

For catchments around potential sites we can use MOSAIC to calculate the number of potential golfers. This method is more precise than using the total population method and therefore improves feasibility studies and location planning immensely.

There is a MOSAIC system for all countries in Europe so accurate analysis can be carried out across Europe.

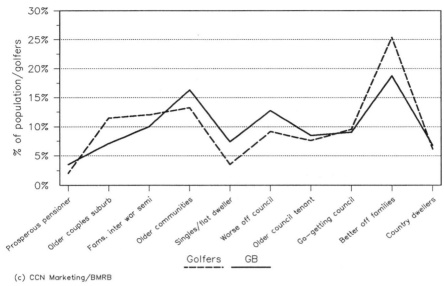

(c) CCN Marketing/BMRB

Fig. 4   MOSAIC profile of golfers and GB residents

6 Conclusion
The golf market in continental Europe has grown considerably in the last 5 years. GB is no longer over half the
total European market in terms of the number of golfers.
    Despite recent growth, golf in continental Europe is
still primarily restricted to the better off sections of
the community.
    To reach a notional "mature market" of 7400 courses in
Europe an additional 3100 courses are needed. This is
unlikely to be achieved within the next 10 years.
    Although the future for golf in Europe looks bright at
a macro-level, careful analysis is always needed at the
catchment level to ensure that the right facility is
built in the right place. Traditional population analysis
is increasingly being replaced by more sophisticated
methods such as geodemographics. This enables us to
determine who likely golfers are and where they are
likely to live which in turn gives us a better understanding of catchment suitability.

88 Spectators' views of PGA golf events

H. Hansen and R. Gauthier
University of Ottawa, Ottawa, Canada

Abstract
3019 spectators attending six PGA golf tournaments rated
the relative importance of 27 reasons to attend on a five
point Likert scale; spectators provided three phrases
describing their thoughts of the event and they completed
demographic data categories. The internal consistency of
the scale was 0.902 as measured by Cronbach Alpha. ANOVA
followed by the Tukey test was used to seek differences
between groups based on gender, age, and golf playing
frequency with an alpha level set at .05. Several
differences per grouping were found resulting in the
following observations: (1) non-golfers/infrequent golfers
attended because of reasons such as scenery, fitness
benefits, event image, and golfer personality; (2) being
close to the field of competition highlights the learning
aspect of spectating; (3) an entertainment focus appeals to
females whereas a learning focus attracts males; (4) market
segmentation can be implemented based on study results; (5)
the "scenery aspect" differentiated the PGA spectators from
other tours spectators.
Keywords: Golf, Spectator Research, Sport Marketing.

1 Introduction

Studies of the factors affecting attendance at professional
sport events involves demand studies which focus on reasons
why spectators attend games of primarily team sports
(Schofield, 1983). In a recent study of six professional
leagues eleven attendance factors were isolated as well as
differences found between baseball, football and indoor
soccer (Hansen & Gauthier, 1989). However the literature
contains but a few studies of spectator reasons to attend
golf events or factors affecting attendance at golf events
(Gauthier & Hansen, 1993; Hansen & Gauthier, 1993; Cuneen &
Hannan, 1993). Trade journals and popular press account for
much of the information pertaining to the golf industry and
specifically to the professional tours, however little or
no attention is given to spectators'views of the sport

Science and Golf II: Proceedings of the World Scientific Congress of Golf. Edited by A.J.
Cochran and M.R. Farrally. Published in 1994 by E & FN Spon, London. ISBN 0 419 18790 1

product. "A product is a complex of value satisfactions... Customers attach value to products...to help solve their problems. Hence a product has meaning ... because value can reside only in the benefits he wants or perceives" (Levitt, 1983, p. 77). Sport has many benefits and/or attributes such that spectators will seek the satisfaction of various wants and/or needs from a sport product. Identifying the viewpoints of spectators about the sport product provides a basis for understanding event markets and developing market plans to increase attendance.

Spectators, who provide a key source of revenue, enjoy and are attracted to many different kinds of sport events for a variety of reasons. For essentially all sport events, spectators are confined to a seat in potentially unattractive, crowded surroundings (Hansen & Gauthier, 1993). Although golf is unique due to such attributes as charity donations, volunteers, green spaces, and a proximity of athletes and spectators; "... the golf tour is one of the poorer spectator tickets in sport... due to four miles of arena, 150+ players...spectators do not see all the action... then what can it be that draws so many people to a golf course to watch only a portion of the contest?" (Barkow, 1989, p. 7). The purpose of this study was to seek answers to that question and to others.

2   Methodology

2.1 The instrument
A questionnaire was developed for the purpose of assessing on a Likert scale of 1-5, 27 reasons why spectators attend golf events and to isolate their views of the event. Reasons were: personality of golfers, scenery of the course, finesse of shot making, feel the excitement/drama, seeing golfers overcome adversity, seeing golfers make a 'charge', picking up tips, seeing 'live' action, seeing the best, making own decisions, being close to golfers, enjoying the excitement of weekend play, because of 'big names' in the event, promotion, charity, excitement of final round, event noted for great golf, T.V. coverage, convenience of getting to the event, ticket value, image of the event, size of the purse, entertainment value, advertising of the event, excitement of the first two rounds, media coverage, and fitness benefits of walking the course. General questions elicited demographic information including gender, age, golf playing frequency (Ericsson & Simon, 1980; Hansen & Gauthier, 1989, 1992, 1993).

2.2 Sample and procedures
Our total study involved some 4500 spectators who completed the questionnaire representing 2 LPGA, 2 Senior PGA and 6 PGA tour events. This study will focus on the 3019 spectators who attended the 6 PGA golf tournaments. (Event

A, n = 608; Event B, n = 449; Event C, n = 517; Event D, n = 624; Event E, n = 467; Event F, n = 354). Data collection consisted of a spectator intercept technique (Hansen & Gauthier, 1993) wherein the spectators were randomly selected to complete the survey and concerns of sampling were allayed. Study assumptions included: people have no reason to lie, people can recognize their own beliefs and feelings, and people who are asked to think aloud can be considered reliable (O'Shaughnessy, 1987).

3   Results

The internal consistency of the questionnaire as measured by Cronbach Alpha was found to be 0.902 (Cronbach, 1951). Males made up 72.2% (N = 2138) of the sample while females comprised 27.8% (N = 822). From a marketing perspective it is interesting to know that most (46%) decided to attend more than a month before the event and another 16% decided 2-3 weeks ahead of time. Although 42% are visitors and hence tourism implications become evident, the majority of spectators live locally in the so called 'trade area'. Thus, ticket packages and advertising can be designed to accommodate the majority of spectators well in advance of the actual event.

Descriptive statistics of the highest rated reasons for attending an event indicated an entertainment focus involving such reasons as: to see the best perform, to see the finesse of shotmaking, to feel excitement and to see live action. Further, it is noted that 'making one's own decision as to who and where to watch' and the enjoyment of course scenery are top rated reasons to attend which we think are unique attributes of golf tournaments compared to other professional sport events.

The free response question allowed for three possible words per spectator providing a maximum of 9057 (3019 X 3) responses. The response rate for all events was 49%. These free responses by spectators yielded (Krippendorff, 1980) five major attribute/image clusters containing descriptive meanings of spectator views: the Atmosphere (relaxing, social outing, fun), the Event (prestigious, well run, charity), the Golf (great players, shotmaking, competition), the Course Setting (healthy exercise, scenic, challenging), the Entertainment (close to action, talented field, great golf). These attributes are representative of spectator views of the golf product and provide the event planner with rich meanings that fans have of the event. "Marketers need to understand the meanings associated with their products and services "(Peter & Olson, 1987, p. 80).

Significant differences were found between spectators who indicated they played at private clubs compared to those who played at public courses for twelve of the reasons for attending golf events. Spectators from public

courses attended for reasons of drama and the fitness
benefits of walking in fresh air. The private club
spectators focused on reasons related to the game and the
golf playing of the professionals (finesse of shot making,
picking up tips, personality of golfers).

One purpose of the study was to analyze differences in
reasons for attendance based on gender, age and frequency
of playing golf.

3.1 Gender differences
Males placed more importance on reasons relating to shot
making and the playing of golf (5 of the 27 reasons).
Females differed from males on 8 reasons which focused on
excitement/drama, personality of golfers, fitness benefits,
event image, and charity(ies) supported; clearly some non-
performance oriented reasons compared to the males.

3.2 Age differences
Selected differences were evident for each of the four
groups for a variety of reasons except for two reasons
involving the under 35 year group and the 66+ year group.
The under 35 year group placed significantly less
importance on 'to make my own decisions about who and where
to watch' compared to all the other age groups (35-50, 51-
65, 66+). Similarly the 66+ group found 'enjoying the
scenery of the course' to be less important than all the
other age groups. This 66+ age group accounted for eleven
differences between the under 35 year and the 51-65 year
group on reasons having a marketing focus (advertising,
promotions) and an entertainment focus (personality of
golfers, seeing the best). The 35-50 year group had a focus
for entertainment and media related reasons as compared to
the 51-65 year group; overall this 51-65 year group placed
importance on live action, scenery of the course and shot
making finesse. Clearly, age group differences provide a
basis for market segmentation.

3.3 Golf playing differences
Non-golfers place importance on the fitness benefits of
walking the course when compared to the other active
playing spectators. All groups differed from the non-
golfers on a variety of other reasons to attend. Active
golfing spectators (groups playing 11 or more rounds per
year) placed more importance on several reasons related to
shotmaking, adversity, excitement and seeing the best
perform in live action situations. The frequent (26 rounds
+) golfing spectators differed from all groups on two

reasons which focus on the uniqueness of golf events as
compared to other sport events, firstly, being close to the
field of action and secondly being able to make one's own
decisions about who and where to watch.   Overall, these
frequent golfing spectators accounted for 17 differences
with spectators who play no golf or occasional golf (1 - 10
rounds per year). Again, a differentiated approach to the
marketing of the golf event would capture these preferences
based on golfing vs non-golfing groups.

3.4 Tour differences

Comparisons were made between the data obtained from
spectators attending PGA, Senior PGA, and LPGA tour events.
Significant differences were found for one reason (enjoy
scenery) where the PGA spectators differed from the other
tours spectators. The four reasons yielding significant
differences of the LPGA with the PGA and the Senior PGA
tour spectators focus on excitement and drama, shotmaking
finesse and the fitness benefits of walking the course. The
senior PGA spectators focused on 'big names' and the
personality of golfers compared to the PGA and LPGA
spectators. These differences of the respective tours
highlight perceived attributes which differentiate the
tours as sport products.

4 Implications of the study

Answers to the question posed by Barkow (1989) are many,
varied and needed if one is to understand the views of
spectators about golf events.   The six events involving
3019 interviews, although limited, provide us with
potential golf market segments and golf product attributes
such that effective market plans could be developed to
increase attendance at golf events. The summary
observations of the study are as follows: (1) non-
golfers/infrequent golfers attended golf events because of
course scenery, fitness benefits, event image, and
personality of golfers; (2) being close to the field of
competition highlights the learning aspect of spectating;
(3) an entertainment focus appeals to females whereas a
learning focus attracts males;(4) market segmentation using
various reasons attributed to age groups would enhance
market plans.   Further, there appears to be differences
between those who play at public versus private golf
courses.   This too can provide a basis for targeting
spectators; (5) course scenery differentiated the PGA
spectators from the other tours spectators; (6) five

clusters of attributes/images of the golf event product
were derived: Atmosphere, Event, Golf, Course Setting, and
Entertainment, all of which provide rich meanings upon
which to create market plans.

   This study focused on the views of spectators about
the sport product of golf. Unique spectator reasons such
as: making one's own decision as to who and where to watch,
enjoying the fitness benefits of walking a few hundred
acres of attractive landscape in the fresh air can
differentiate a golf event from virtually all other
spectator sport events.

5 References

Barkow, A. (1989). **The history of the P.G.A. Tour**. N.Y.
   Doubleday.

Cronbach, L.J. (1951). Coefficient Alpha and the internal
   structure of tests. **Psychometrika**, 16(3), 297-334.

Cuneen, J. and Hannan, M.(1993). Intermediate measures
   and recognition testing of sponsorship advertising at an
   LPGA tournament. **Sport Marketing Quarterly**, 2(1), 47-56.

Ericsson, K.A. and Simon, H.A. (1980). Verbal reports as
   data. **Psychological Review**, 87(3), 215-251.

Gauthier, R. and H. Hansen (1993). Female spectators:
   Marketing   implications for professional golf events.
   Sport Marketing Quarterly, 2(4), 21-28.

Hansen, H. and Gauthier, R. (1989). Factors affecting
   attendance at professional sport events. **Journal of
   Sport Management**, 3(1), 15-32 .

Hansen, H. and Gauthier, R. (1992). Marketing objectives of
   professional and university sport organizations. **Journal
   of Sport Management**, 6(1), 27-37.

Hansen, H. and Gauthier, R. (1993). Spectator views of LPGA
   golf events. **Sport Marketing Quarterly**, 2(1), 17-25.

Krippendorff, K. (1980). **Content analysis. An introduction
   to its methodology**. Beverly Hills, Ca. Sage
   Publications. p. 115.

Levitt, T. (1983). **The Marketing Imagination**. New York,
N.Y., The Free Press.

O'Shaughnessy, J. (1987). **Why people buy**. New York, N.Y.,
   Oxford University Press.

Peter, J. Paul and Olson, J.C. (1987). **Consumer behavior,
   marketing strategy perspectives**. Homewood, Illinois,
   USA. Richard D. Irwin, Inc.

Schofield, J.A. (1983). Performance and attendance at
   professional team sports. **Journal of Sport Behavior**,
   6(4), 196-206.

89 Golf for all? The problems of municipal provision

J.R. Lowerson
Reader in History, Centre for Continuing Education, University of Sussex, UK

Abstract
This paper rehearses and re-evaluates the history of municipal provision in England and Scotland. It examines the three main thrusts in this, which overlap chronologically but are quite distinctive. Social attitudes and trends towards exclusiveness are discussed and the regional and financial implications are assessed in the light of changes in consumption patterns and leisure expectations.
Keywords: Golf, Towns, Municipal Authorities, Class, Consumption, Land, Finance, Regions, England, Scotland, Policy.

1 Introduction

The role played by local authorities in providing golf facilities has been little examined, with the exception of a brief but important mention in Cousins' general social history (Cousins 1975, chapter 18). I have treated it **en passant** in a number of studies (Lowerson 1989, 1993, 1994), largely as a counterpoint to other factors, not least the domination of the modern game in Britain by the aspiring and established middle classes. Golf's spread since the late Victorian period, albeit in uneven spurts, has only occasionally been questioned in terms of the social limits of its clientele, their often deliberate exclusiveness and the debate over the annexation of land by what is the most territorially hungry and probably privately-minded of all sports.

Here I look at the ways in which public bodies, most noticeably urban government, have responded to this; at the tensions in social values and local pride involved; at the financial framework and the role of sporting magnets in urban development. There are also underlying issues of national differentiation within Britain itself and of myths about 'democracy'.

Science and Golf II: Proceedings of the World Scientific Congress of Golf. Edited by A.J. Cochran and M.R. Farrally. Published in 1994 by E & FN Spon, London. ISBN 0 419 18790 1

2   Accessibility and Exclusiveness

It is appropriate that this paper is being delivered in what is proudly, and largely rightly, regarded as the most 'democratic' of all golfing sites. Although it has to be said that the idea of golf as the quintessential 'people's game' owes more to Scottish romanticism than to actuality (Lowerson 1994) St. Andrews does have a long history of combining low-cost local accessibility with providing for an international and frequently affluent pilgrim group. This is less true of many of the country's other major golfing venues.

Before the late Victorian expansion in Scotland golf had enjoyed a pan-class following, albeit at a restricted level. The use of seaside 'links' as common land had allowed an apparent social mix of players which has done much to foster a myth of aboriginal 'democracy'. But growing bourgeois culture in the Enlightenment and Industrial Revolution had prompted club formation which annexed some of the playing space, increased costs and eventually prompted a considerable move towards private facilities. Scotland maintained, nevertheless, a higher level of accessibility for artisan and white-collar groups than did its southern neighbour; the lower working class's access was largely as low-wage and exploited labour, in the form of caddies.

In England the boom after the 1870's led to a wholesale alienation of common land from working-class leisure use, except where popular protest or court actions prevented it or forced a compromise. Golf became a mark of social aspiration and the recognition of personal ascent; formal clubs rather than individual play for the sake of it dominated the scene. On the whole this meant private enterprise, either as a speculative venture or, more usually, the harnessing of collective middle-class capital formation to ensure privacy and access limited as much by social acceptability as by skill, wealth or enthusiasm. By these means some 100,000 acres (40k hectares) were removed from other uses in England before the outbreak of the First World War.

Golf became a major magnet for middle-class suburban settlement and recreational patterns and this was mirrored during holidays. The popularity of 'select' seaside resorts (Walton 1983) was enhanced by local golf facilities. This became a crucial issue for each holiday town's placing in the national league table of competition for visitors upon which local economies depended. For golf this meant, as in Skegness, Great Yarmouth, and similar towns, that local councils were often prepared to enter into 'partnerships' with private individuals or groups by leasing public land at peppercorn rents for clubs to be developed (Lowerson 1993, 134). In so doing they often removed common land from working-class access or restricted it considerably.

The process moved a stage further in the 1890's when Bournemouth began the direct provision of golf facilities, extending them in subsequent decades. This 'municipal socialism' was prompted, not by the needs of local enthusiasts from the lower classes, but by an urge to move ahead of such major rivals as Brighton and Eastbourne. Brighton followed suit in 1908. In both cases one consideration was that demand from visitors was threatening to swamp the facilities offered by established private clubs. Even so, resorts which did this also tended to encourage the formation of clubs to play over municipal courses, partly because of the need to provide facilities for handicapping and amateur tournaments which served as further magnets, partly because local year-round use was necessary to sustain relatively expensive facilities. In such cases, the level of public expenditure was usually heavier than on meeting local housing needs. This was investment designed to foster financial returns for the wider community.

Where local lower-class demand existed it was sometimes met by the paternalistic provision of artisan clubs attached to private bodies, offering limited playing rights over their courses. The potential players who tended to suffer most from cost and exclusiveness were not manual workers as such but the lowest group of middle-class aspirants, white-collar workers. For them, there was a limited regional response, largely away from the resorts.

The key body in this was the London County Council although, as with so much other 'progressive' provision, its role has probably been exaggerated by its own capacity for self-advertisement. Its first purpose – built course was Hainault Forest, eventually expanded to meet the considerable demands it encountered (Cousins, 95). But play even at a shilling a round (actually doubled in the Edwardian years to meet maintenance costs) was far too expensive for most manual workers for whom the likely total costs of play at £12 a year would have represented anything up to 20 per cent of annual income.

Until 1914, outside Scotland where a limited amount of cheap play remained possible, there was little else to match London's pioneering. In the midlands and north of England two industrial cities took a tentative step; Nottingham opened a municipal course to be followed in 1911 by Sheffield whose playing charges were a quarter of London's. Sheffield attracted 10,000 players in its first three weeks (Lowerson 1993, 144) but few, if any, tried to calculate how much of the iceberg lay beneath this.

3   Paternalism and Modernity

The major constraint on any development of this type was the reluctance to spend public money on what was often regarded

as 'luxurious' rather than 'improving' leisure; ratepayers'
organisations kept a sharp eye on many local authorities.
In England this was relaxed slowly between the Wars but any
considerable degree of expansion was also hindered by the
impact of economic recession upon public expenditure,
particularly where conservative economic policies were
applied after 1932.

There were, however, some notable exceptions which
revealed, in turn, some other tensions in wider social
attitudes. In Birmingham, already strong in its claims to
be England's 'Second City', moves to provide facilities were
well-supported but opened up local debates about the whole
direction of social change which organised leisure
represented. Its first venture, in 1921, passed relatively
easily but a decision to open a second course in 1926
produced major arguments in the city. The issue was not
golf itself, nor the role of the municipality in providing
it - it was the moral implications of allowing Sunday play.

The corporation acquired an existing private course at
Harborne and redeveloped it for public play. In doing this
it proposed to follow the increasingly widespread practice
of Sunday play amongst private clubs, which had a long
history of controversy (Lowerson 1984). Birmingham was
widely regarded as the centre of the 'Nonconformist
Conscience' and this was still sufficiently strong in the
1920s to cause a local outcry. The city's Free Church
Council mounted a fierce campaign which produced 207
petitions with 27,000 signatures in a couple of weeks.
Controversy was heightened when the Lord Mayor described
them as 'interfering busybodies'. After angry debates the
Corporation voted 47 - 40 in favour of Sunday play. The
issue was not only about possible threats to worship but
also about whether the paternalism implicit in such
provision should go to the extent of denying to the local
working classes that which richer townsmen could purchase
through private memberships (**Birmingham Gazette,** 21 -31
March 1926). It would be interesting to see how far this
was matched elsewhere. In Scotland the limited evidence
suggests that new course building conformed with a stronger
sense of sabbatarianism and was not yet regarded as offering
the same threats (Lowerson 1984, 218).

Some other English towns followed Birmingham's example,
such as Birkenhead in 1931 (Merseyside, 8). There golf was
landscaped into the wider setting of a public park so that
tension over accessibility to public space was lessened.
One noticeable feature of the 1930s in particular was the
acquisition by some councils of existing private courses
less with the idea of providing for greater public demand,
since the courses were often leased back to private clubs,
than to restrain speculative housing developments over which
they had very limited planning powers. This was often
prompted as much by an urban-lung aesthetic as by any demand

for healthy and active recreation (**Parks, Golf Courses and Sports Grounds,** 1935 – 7, passim).

In Scotland there was also some limited growth, not without irony. The construction of courses seemed to some authorities to offer a convenient means of utilising the local unemployed, a minor and rather unco-ordinated version of Roosevelt's New Deal. In Aberdeen the Hazlehead course was laid out in 1927 as 'the people's golf course'. This was reported nationally, as was the use of men whose dole money was boosted very modestly before the days of the Means Test by being paid for their labour. The damp and demanding toil left a bitter memory that attracted little attention at the time. What did draw comment was the reality of access to play – it was relatively expensive and identified with minor snobbery (Lowerson 1994).

It would take a great deal more oral history work to establish how common this was but there is evidence to suggest that the class gap on the course widened as much in interwar Scotland as it did in England. What was different, however, was that the wider incidence of Scottish municipally-managed golf allowed some working-class play through their own organisations, the Thistle clubs, rather than as the grateful hangers-on of middle-class patronage.

One issue that dogged all municipal courses at this point was the relative isolation of the players. The organisation of handicapping and tournaments through the private club network tended to assume that players on public courses had little interest in competition or had failed to develop playing skills of a high enough standard. There were some exceptions. In Leeds, for instance, the municipality fostered local business patronage to provide trophies; both Schweppes and the **Yorkshire Post** were involved in club competitions and club membership for those who could afford it allowed participation in the Yorkshire Union of Golf Clubs' tournament structure (Leeds 1928, 19).

The sporadic nature of such provision led to the foundation of the National Association of Public Golf Courses in 1927. Prompted by the architect FG Hawtree and the tournament champion JH Taylor it sought to build bridges between the municipal world and what was widely seen as the mainstream private game. Although it attracted some sponsorship from **The News of the World,** always sharp to realise its readers' changing interests, its success was limited at first. Its annual championship was 'unofficial', a clear recognition of the wide gap that existed within the sport and its very organisation presupposed a degree of financial commitment beyond the reach of most municipal aspirants. It represented, however, a reluctance to accept the bounds of social snobbery within golf (Benson and Hedges 1986, 266).

4   Pay as you Play - Hopes for a Mass Game

Golf was not much of a priority in the rebuilding of Britain immediately after the Second World War. Housing, health and industry were rather more pressing. But there were forces present that eventually had a major impact upon the sport. Determination to avoid the policy mistakes and the social deprivation which followed 1918 were accompanied by assumptions about a much wider diffusion of living and leisure standards, by new ideas about the relationship between built and open spaces and by a major role for government or semi-official bodies. The Sports Council, formed in 1972, was to have a major role, particularly through its regional branches. Immediately, however, there was little impetus for the growth of public provision.

That rode on the back of the growth in consumer spending which began in the mid-1950s and accelerated rapidly in the next decade. The 1960s are usually associated with bizarre social habits and expenditure; for many they represented the opportunity to join in activities, such as golf, which financial constraints had denied them previously. But what was equally important was the shift in (not the removal of) attitudes to social class which had survived well after the War ended.

A key factor was a new stage in urbanisation. Rebuilding of war damage was accompanied by the creation of major new towns by semi-government commissions. In these leisure space was to be integrated with work and living areas. Because they were treated as industrial as well as residential magnets there was a clear need to attract managers. Despite proclaimed ideals of social integration the new towns of the 1950s and 1960s almost inevitably recreated many of the social divides of the older urban world. As in Harlow, most courses were provided by private money, albeit welcomed by public bodies (Schaffer 1970, 149).

This was even more pronounced in the second generation of new cities, Milton Keynes, Peterborough, Northampton and so on, whose growth reached its peak in the 1980s. They were much more socially zoned than the initial new towns and golf was seen as a crucial part of attracting industry which often had an international management. During the process the scale of 'public' provision rose because of the much higher course standards now expected, although both Northampton and Washington made accessibility and cheapness, as against local private clubs, a major feature of their advertising.

The key factor to influence public provision was the spread of disposable income amongst white collar and skilled manual workers during the 1960s. Coupled with the mass importing of cheap implements from the Far East (by the later 1970s half sets of clubs were available in many high street stores) this made for a potential market of players

whose aspirations could not be met by either existing
private or municipal provision. It was claimed that
participation in the game doubled during these years and
potential was much higher (Davidson and Leonard 1975, 1).

Laying out new courses moved rapidly from being an **ad hoc**
response on a local basis to becoming a part of public
policy and planning. Cousins has identified the key date in
this as 1965, when the Golf Development Council was formed
(Cousins 1975, 97). He has also argued that the planning
powers acquired by local authorities actually made it easier
for them than for private developers. That might have been
so but expansion had been limited – there were only 80
public courses in England and Wales by 1972 (Davidson and
Leonard 1975, 1). 29 of those had been started within the
previous 3 years and another 26 were in construction.

The spurt came with the development of regional
investigative groups following the founding of the Sports
Council and the spread of independent consultancy firms. A
collective pressure for the provision of golf facilities
emerged, underpinned by a considerable apparatus of research
and policy papers (Davidson and Leonard 1975, Eastern 1991,
Essex 1992, Jenkins 1991, Kent 1991, Lothian 1978, South
Western 1973, Sports Council 1990). All these, from the
Royal and Ancient downwards, assumed a huge pool of
unsatisfied demand – at one point the R and A expected that
more courses (500) would need to be constructed during the
1990s than had been between 1910 and 1970. What all the
reports realised was that golf's playing facilities were
still dominated by pre-First World War provision and, often,
social attitudes. The scale of the demand is not being
questioned here; what is significant are the tensions
revealed about the problems of social differentiation
focusing on public provision.

One author noted a significant post-war shift in emphasis
away from concern with working-class housing towards ideas
of a balanced environment (Jenkins 1991, 59). Others
claimed that golf had lost much of its earlier class-
exclusive connotations (Eastern Council, 1991, 15). The
issues were not, however, only those of course building.
Complicating these were actual levels of use – the average
public course has twice as many rounds as its private
equivalent – and assumptions about standards of play. It is
normally assumed that, largely lacking the stimulus of
organised competition (despite the considerable increase in
the work of NAPGC which now reaches 3,500 of the estimated
50,000 public golfers) and the possibility of handicapping,
public courses attract sloppier players and are more suited
to beginners. Implicit, and occasionally made explicit, is
the assumption that private membership clubs use public
courses in some instances as weeding-out grounds where
would-be members can learn the playing rudiments before
being made part of the 'respectable' playing world, if they
meet other criteria.

The social attitudes remain as significant in the
equation of providing play as ever. In fact they are
probably more complex, more subtle, than the somewhat crude
divisions which characterized private and public before
1945. But there are other significant issues to add
complications. In a sense the 1970s marked the peak of
municipal provision as such. Since the Conservative victory
in 1979 public golf has joined many other leisure activities
under suspicion for being subsidized by local taxpayers.
The air of social improvement has given way to a neo-
Victorian sense of private responsibility for leisure as
well as basic living. This is reflected in the shift of
language now used by both planners and golfing idealists.
'Pay as you play' may be an accurate description of what has
always been the case on municipal courses but it now has
moral as well as implementation provisions.

Local authorities are now unable to provide courses
directly – they can only attract or restrict private
developers. The policy became trapped in the vicissitudes
of the property and land markets, most noticeably in the
impact of 'setaside' agricultural regulation, and this has
caused major problems for local planners (East Sussex 1992,
Essex 1992, Kent 1991). Paradoxically, more land is
probably now available for golf development than at any
point since the late Victorian agricultural depression
fostered London's multilayered ring of courses. But the
situation is different. Developers so far have been
attracted by high-prestige speculations, many of which have
failed to reach their potential. Golf is still seen as
having a social cachet which tends to militate against the
high-use, low-cost, low-margins courses which are needed to
fulfil the R and A's expectations. The irony now lies in
the large number of loss-leader advertisements common in
many southern local newspapers for courses that have failed
to reach their expected potential of income generation
during the recession (**Sussex Express**, 21 January 1994).

It would be ridiculous to deny the huge advances made in
public provision since 1945. But it needs a sharpened
perspective. In England 186 municipal courses or their
equivalent represent only some 14 per cent of the total, in
'democratic' Scotland the proportion is little more that;
what is significant is the high percentage not open to
public use. The situation towards the end of this century
is perhaps more frustrating than at its beginning.
Expectations, despite the recession, are now much higher;
competition is as much to reach the first tee as to beat the
opponent. If anything, this is likely to grow and it will
require a much wider change in attitudes to public provision
to meet so many hopes.

5 References

Benson and Hedges Golfer's Handbook. (1986) London.
Birmingham Gazette. March 1926.
Cousins, G. (1975) Golf in Britain, A social history from the beginning to the present day. London.
A.W. Davidson and J.E. Leonard (eds) (1975) Land for Leisure - Golf courses. London.
Eastern Council for Sport and Recreation. (1991) Sport in the East, A strategy for the nineties - The future for golf. Bedford.
East Sussex County Council. (1992) Planning Guidance for Golf Course Developments in East Sussex. Lewes.
Essex Planning Officers' Association. (1992) The Essex Golf Report.
Jenkins, R.O. (1991) Golf Course Developments in the U.K. Sunningdale.
Kent Planning Officers' Group (1991) Planning for Golf in Kent. Maidstone.
Leeds and District Golf. (1928) Leeds.
Lothian Region Department of Recreation and Leisure. (1978) Golf: An interim strategy for provision in the Lothian region. Edinburgh.
Lowerson, J.R. (1984) 'Sport and the Victorian Sunday: the beginnings of middle-class apostasy' in The British Journal of Sports History. London.
(1989) 'Golf' in Sport in Britain: A social history. Mason, T. (ed.) Cambridge.
(1993) Sport and the English Middle Classes, 1870 - 1914. Manchester.
(1994) 'Golf and the Making of Myths' in Scottish Sport in the Making of the Nation; Ninety Minute Patriots? Jarvie, G. and Walker, G. (eds.) Leicester.
Golf in Merseyside and District. (n.d.) Liverpool.
Parks, Golf Courses and Sports Grounds. (1935 - 1937).
Schaffer, F. (1970) The New Town Story. London.
Sports Council. (1990) Planning for Sport: Golf course seminar report. Nottingham.
Sussex Express, 21 January 1994.
Walton, J.K. (1983) The English Seaside Resort: a social history, 1750 - 1914. Leicester.

90 Golf, development and the human sciences: the swing is not the only thing

B. Stoddart
University of Canberra, Canberra, Australia

Abstract
This paper attempts a reminder that golf is a major *social* phenomenon and, as such, is open to meaningful interpretation by researchers in the social sciences and the humanities. Examples are developed from issues surrounding the creation of new golf courses, especially in the developing world; from cultural shifting which results in altered social patterning, and from literary accounts. A central point is that the human passion for golf is not only an interesting case for academic observation, but also *the* principal ingredient in the worldwide boom that is so central to the economic growth of the golf industry.
Keywords: Social factors, Land, Anti-golf, Growth, Culture, Change, Literature

1 Introduction

Let us start with a simple proposition: if ever human beings became disinclined to devote time and money in search of better ways to propel a small white ball into a distant hole (and diverted that energy, say, towards solving world conflict, famine and disease), then conferences like this would never happen. A logical extension to the argument is that most, if not all the deeper problems confronting the game in its current boom are social rather than technical. At a more subtle level, solutions to the mysteries of addiction to golf are to be found more in literary and social science forms than in swing manuals which treat the symptoms rather than diagnose the disease.

In his chapter in the Badminton volume, for example, Lord Wellwood (1890) ascribed a rather simple set of social characteristics as the reason for golf's popularity: pleasurable exercise, different skill levels, available to all ages, open to women, playable at any time and not dependent on numbers, and financially accessible. On closer investigation, though, few if any of those characteristics explain the sheer human passion which has driven golf across virtually every culture and into every country on earth during

Science and Golf II: Proceedings of the World Scientific Congress of Golf. Edited by A.J. Cochran and M.R. Farrally. Published in 1994 by E & FN Spon, London. ISBN 0 419 18790 1

the last century. The ultimate explanation of that human obsession lies more with writers like Bamberger (1993) than with player-authors like Norman (1987), great though the latter are at telling us how to improve. Therein lies one key, of course - the desire to improve, progress, the drive towards excellence.

It is in that search for excellence, in all its aspects, where lie many if not all of golf's modern dilemmas and the analysis lies with the social rather than the physical sciences.

2   Purpose

The intent here, then, is to sketch out some of golf's contemporary dimensions which lie outside the realms of rational science, some of which pose problems for the future of the game, and some which help account for the deep loyalty inspired by the spirit of golf to the point of keeping substantial numbers of people employed in an industry which has now attained vast proportions.

As an aside here, it is tempting to speculate what Karl Marx might have thought of golf had it reached its current proportions in his time, because golf is a wonderful example of his capitalist theory in which enterprises feed off themselves and not necessarily in service of the common good. Perhaps, though, Antonio Gramsci might have been a better analyst in that he understood better than Marx how human passions stood frequently in the way of rational revolution.

The Marxist thread gives a connection to the ultimate dilemma of modern sport and one faced more by golf than by any other game. With rare exceptions, modern sports forms were formulated and codified during the later nineteenth century, but have been overtaken by what writers like David Harvey (1989) rightly label the "postmodern". Cricket, for example, is extremely wasteful in time, one of postmodernity's most precious commodities, hence the expansion of one-day matches. Rugby union was constructed solidly within the amateur tradition but now, in face of increasing numbers of games and rising player commitments, is moving inevitably towards a form of professionalism which is anathema to many devotees (Jones, 1993). Sumo wrestling was constructed solidly within Japanese cultural tradition but its modern rewards have attracted cross-cultural attention, leading to vigorous debate about whether or not non-Japanese might be elevated to the very elite ranking. Much of American college sport has moved from being purely about physical development to being a central line item in institutional budgets, hence the irony of many football and basketball coaches being higher paid than their college presidents.

3   Golf and land

Golf's major problem in this shift towards postmodernity is obvious - it is a vast consumer of land, a resource central to thinking in both capitalist and Marxist modes. Take some very simple and crude statistics from two countries thought to be "golf mad":

Table 1. Land and golf in Japan and Australia

	Japan	Australia
land area	145,000 sq. miles	2,900,000 sq. miles
arable area	16,000 sq. miles	435,000 sq. miles
golf courses	3,600	1,500
golf courses/total area	1.2%	.002%
golf courses/arable	10.9%	.17%

These are extreme examples, of course, but the social implications are obvious even before the environmental debate is taken into account. The pressure of golf courses upon productive land is clearly considerable in Japan and far less so in Australia. That is well-known as one of the major factors for club membership being so high in Japan, the sheer cost for purchase and development of the playing area is so considerable. Important though that factor is to golfers, it is not the essential social question concerning golf at the general community level. There the question is whether or not productive land can be spared for golf courses on which relatively few people soak up natural resources at a disproportionate rate for no apparently productive output. Given these two examples it is clear, again, that the issue is much more immediate and contentious in Japan than in Australia where the obstacles to development lie in environmental and cultural issues.

4   Anti-golf

Lest this all be considered a relatively minor problem for golfers, it is well worth considering the activities of the Global Anti-Golf Movement which recently held its second international conference in Japan. GAG'M as it is acronymed, is a coalition of three quite significant agencies: the Global Network for Anti-Golf Course Action (based in Chiba, Japan, where further course development has now been banned as a result of local action), the Asia-Pacific Peoples' Environment Network (based in Malaysia), and the Institute of Tourism and Development Studies at the

Bedford Institute of Higher Education in England. This coalition demonstrates how golf is rapidly moving from being a significant sporting subculture to a mainstream social issue which is arousing popular passions to rival those of golfers ever striving to improve their scores.

The strength of the anti-golf movement may be judged by this extract from GAG'M's first update publication of December 1993 referring to:

the increasing outcry of many local communities worldwide regarding the uncontrolled proliferation of golf courses in many parts of the world, which are causing severe social and environmental problems. Loss of forest and agricultural land, destruction of wetlands, depletion of water resources, soil contamination from run off of silt and highly toxic chemicals and air pollution from spraying pesticides in the courses have been continuously reported from many countries. Social problems such as disruption of communities, loss of natural resources which are essential for community livelihoods, increasing gap between the rich and the poor, questionable land acquisition practices by shady businesses, crime and corruption can be observed in many cases where golf course development takes place.

In the subsequent regional reporting, the strength of local movements becomes apparent.

The Movement Against Golf Course Development in Indonesia has staged demonstrations outside the national parliament. In Hawaii, the Hawaii Golf Course Action Alliance has been prominent in opposing further development and exposing the sources of foreign capital employed in such development. In several other countries, local action committees have turned their attention to golf.

There are two particular points worth making about this. First, the antagonism towards golf (and by association, in some quarters, towards its devotees) is widening far beyond the environmental debate. (While that issue is still not widely recognised by golfers in general, it is amongst industry leaders and the debate has been joined by authorities like the USGA which is funding research into environmentally friendly golf.) Rather, the focus is now more upon social impact and that has the potential to be even more damaging to the game. Dispossessing people from traditional villages and thereby destroying local economies is a sure way to breed opposition to golf.

The second point is a related one. It has been widely reported now that the real golf boom is in the Pacific Basin and on the Pacific Rim. While there is steady rather than spectacular growth in traditional golfing countries like the United States, Australia and New Zealand, there is an explosion in the so-called "New Tiger" economies like Taiwan, , Malaysia and Singapore. While the previously flamboyant Japanese economy sparked the growth, much of it is now taken over by local capital in countries like South Korea and Indonesia.

It is precisely in these new areas that the opposition is growing most rapidly and most strongly. Given that population densities there are amongst the heaviest in the world, that the disparity between rich and poor is greater there than in most other sites, and that development issues are struggles between tradition and modernity in most instances, the volatile nature of the golf debate becomes increasingly obvious.

5   Traditional views

This is all a far cry from the traditions of golf, even in relation to land use where there has been a rather idealised, even romantic attitude prevalent (Dickinson, 1990). In good part, that derives from the prevailing view about the evolution of the playing area. As Cornish and Whitten (1987) put it so clearly, "the earliest Scottish links were designed entirely by nature". The idea, that is, was of golfers being dominated by the environment rather than vice-versa. There has been a great change in that attitude. That is not to say that the playing environment is unimportant. Photographers like Brian Morgan (1988) and artists like Graeme Baxter, for example, celebrate the beauty of golf in all its exotic location. Rather, the point to make is that there is some substance to the view of golf architects now struggling to dominate the landscape rather than being directed by it.

That is a highly contentious assertion, of course, and can be debated endlessly. What is not so contentious, however, is the observation that golf course development now is driven by far more direct pressures than a piece of linksland eventually providing a site for play to a collection of local residents in search of amusement. The typical development now is with an eye to economic profit rather than to providing communities in general with the opportunity to play a wonderful sport (Strawn, 1992). In short, a love of the game is an ingredient frequently missing in the planning of a new development.

6   Change in social location of golf

This is all leading to the reaffirmation of that simple but powerful earlier point: golf is no longer a subculture. As a part of a complex social order, it is no longer satisfactory to analyse it as a subculture. When those trained and steeped in golf confront some of the modern issues, they often face confusion or, at least, major rethinking. In Australia, for example, there is an interesting debate about whether or not the playing levels are too severe for entry to club professional ranks. Critics argue that teaching and merchandising skills are far more important; supporters of the tough restrictions argue that club professionals need to be able to "play" even though the vast proportion of their clients are mid to high handicappers.

The answer to that debate might best be found in literature about teaching rather than in writings about golf.

An associated piece of cultural shifting has come with the opening of a new private club in Sydney. Funded by Japanese companies, it has set up as an avowedly and openly elitist (especially in the monetary sense) institution, and just as openly declaring that some types of people would be considered "undesirable" (Gibson, 1994). The attitudes are not new in Australia and certainly not the discriminatory practice. What is new and culturally alien is the public broadcasting of the attitude and practice. The Australian tradition (for which read "mythology") is of an open, democratic social structure (Stoddart, 1986). This is certainly not that, and is indicative of the many culturally based alterations going on across the golfing world.

7   Consequences of change

The issues about development, then, are of immense proportions for the golf industry and will not be dealt with adequately by any approach which does not employ the social sciences/cultural studies approach, because modern golf development involves intercultural contact. Historians, sociologists, economists, anthropologists and geographers hold the answers because, of all sports, golf holds the most complex social position in modern life. If those answers are not found, the swing doctors will deal with a declining constituency because without growth in courses there will be minimal growth in numbers.

The most immediate and obvious observation at this point is that modern golf has undergone a massive cultural conversion. Golf has always been migratory, of course, with the game founded in most parts of the world by expatriate Scots either as amateurs gone out to make their fortunes or as golf professionals gone out to spread the word. The results were wonderfully varied. In the United States, the rise of golf and the country club went hand in hand, but the public links movement also grew apace with the United States title beginning as early as 1922. Much the same happened in Australia where prestigious clubs headed by Royal Sydney (Tatz and Stoddart, 1993) and Royal Melbourne (Johnson, 1991) grew their traditions at one extreme while public courses like Moore Park in Sydney developed quite different social practices (interestingly enough, both those Royal institutions physically adjoin public courses).

Within those two cultures, however, golf retained much of its British heritage in playing practice, social patterning, club formation and profile. Much the same could be said of most locations where the direct British influence was evident, although there were clear local variations. In South Africa, for example, institutionalised racial segregation marked golf's evolution as it did every other social venue so that establishments like the Pretoria Country Club (Odell, 1977) represented a tiny section of the overall population.

Status, of course, was one component that ran through all these golfing cultures - while the sporting activity itself was important, who was allowed into and who was excluded from the clubs was a matter of considerably importance. Racial groups were not the only ones to feel this; so, too, did religious communities (members of the Jewish faith, for example) and women (Lord Wellwood noted that they *could* play, but that there were other matters to be considered). Whatever the pattern, structured membership of private or semi-private organisations was the locus.

That began to change dramatically in the years following World War Two, and more particularly from the 1960s onwards, as golf and social status were considered interchangeably as newer golf cultures began to take their inspiration from post-British golf models, most notably that of the United States.

8   The example of Japan

Japan provides the outstanding example, although it is now being rivalled by some of the "New Tigers". There were very few courses there pre-war, and just 196 by 1960. As the economy boomed so did golf and by 1980 there were over 1400 courses and that figure doubled in the next ten years. The status here was that golf participation became a badge for social arrival and a "new money" benchmark. Moreover, it also became part of the new economy as memberships were bought and sold on the stock market. Not only was golf a "sign" of money, it also became a means to money as developers traded in on the social frenzy for the game. While that frenzy has calmed a little in the wake of the Japanese economy overheating, it is all relative: one club membership still costs over $900,000 but is back from a 1991 high of $2.2 million (*Asia Week*, 1993). Exclusivity here was marked by money rather more than by caste as it was and is in other golf cultures.

9   Contributions to growth

In relation to overall golfing patterns, the significance of all this is that the worldwide golf industry feeds off all this enthusiasm, and alongside the proliferation of equipment to keep pace with demand has been a concomitant rise in the thirst for knowledge about playing.

That is, the social pressures propelling the growth of golf have been directly responsible for a growing desire to learn/be taught the game. One Malaysian diplomat told me during 1993, for example, that members of his foreign service must attain proficiency at either golf or tennis because they are seen as desirable social traits. To make it brutally clear, then: not all those who arrive at the teaching tee are there because they are obsessed with conquering the game, some are there for quite different reasons altogether.

10 Literary analysis

Of course, that is the fundamental reason why so many prominent literary figures have written about golf: J.M. Barrie, P.G. Wodehouse, A.A. Milne and John Updike among them (Jarvie, 1993). Many great intellects, too, have written on golf with that great polymath, Andrew Lang being one of them. Indeed, Lang (folklorist, golfer, anthropologist, fisherman, mystic, cricketer and more) is perhaps the quintessential analyst of golf in all its human dimensions. All these writers, and others like them, recognise the human passion which draws golfers to the links and they, better than any, understand why a perfectly hopeless player will return unquestioningly even though the most rigorous explanation of the perfect swing will have little or no improving impact.

11 Conclusion

None of this is to deny in any way the importance or significance of growing technical knowledge or expertise in the making of equipment, improving the swing or creating environmentally-friendly golf courses. Rather, it is to provide something of a corrective to an unconscious orthodoxy that *all* of golf is about *just* those things. Golf is about people and how they interact with the game, its playing conditions and their playing colleagues (not to mention non-playing colleagues. The evolution of the rules, for example, flows from the human ingenuity for interpretation while the revolution in equipment manufacture comes from the developed world's fetish for improvement. There is much yet to learn about the inner compulsions of the game when the Holeproof Sports Sock Company can receive a letter from a golfer thanking it for such an excellent product - half an hour after he put the socks on for the first time he hit a hole-in-one. This is the world of human understanding, of the anthropologist and sociologist, not of the rational scientist.

References

Asia Week (1993). "A Losing Round". 22-29 December.
Bamberger, Michael (1993). *To The Linksland: a Golfing Odyssey.*
   Mainstream Publishing Company, Edinburgh.

Cornish, Geoffrey S. and Whitten, Ronald E. *The Golf Course* (1987 edn). Rutledge Press, New York.

Dickinson, Patric (1951). *A Round of Golf Courses: a Selection of the Best Eighteen*. Evans Brothers, London.

Gibson, Adam (1994). "$95m Golf Club Tees Off". *Sunday Telegraph*, 13 February.

GAG'M [Global Anti-Golf Movement] (1993). *Update No.1*. December.

Harvey, David (1989). *The Condition of Postmodernity: an Enquiry into the Origins of Cultural Change*. Basil Blackwell, Oxford.

Jarvie, Gordon ed. (1993). *Great Golf Stories*. Michael O'Mara Books, London.

Johnson, Joseph (1991). *The Royal Melbourne Golf Club: a Centenary History*. The Royal Melbourne Golf Club, Melbourne.

Jones, Stephen (1993). *Endless Winter: the Inside Story of the Rugby Revolution*. Mainstream Publishing, Edinburgh.

Morgan, Brian (1988). *A World Portrait of Golf*. Gallery Books, New York.

Norman, Greg [with George Peper] (1987). *Shark Attack*. Macmillan Publishing, Sydney.

Odell, C.F. (1977) *History of the Pretoria Country Club, 1909-1975*. Pretoria Country Club.

Stoddart, Brian (1986). *Saturday Afternoon Fever: Sport in the Australian Culture*. Angus & Robertson Publishers, Sydney.

Strawn, John (1991). *Driving The Green: the Making of a Golf Course*. Harper Perennial, New York.

Wellwood, Lord (1892). "Some General Remarks" in *Golf*, ed. Horace G. Hutchinson. Longman Publishing, London.

91 Discipline and flourish: golf as a civilising process?

D. Collinson and K. Hoskin
University of Warwick, Coventry, UK

Abstract
This paper draws on the work of two writers currently influential in the social science field, Elias and Foucault, to develop a framework for the critical analysis of the dynamics of modern golf. We examine the "civilising" (Elias) and "disciplinary" (Foucault) processes that have shaped the game's emergence. While a civilised image is a distinctive feature of routine golfing practice, golf has also become a "disciplinary" field, where (i) technical and social discipline of body, mind and behaviour are seen as essential to success, and (ii) deep golfing knowledge is achievable only via the intervention of experts from technological and scientific disciplines. Yet, looking at its history, the emergence of golf as a civilising and disciplinary project was in no sense inevitable before the late nineteenth century. We therefore propose that a properly critical science of golf must confront the way that the game since then has become a field for civilising disciplinary and scientific interventions. Disciplinarity, in its various aspects, structures the way in which the game is organised, played and analysed. Even the meta-scientific framework of golf science is, we suggest, one of disciplinarity.
Keywords: Civilising Process, Disciplinarity, Meta-Scientific Analysis, Social Organisation of Golf

1. Introduction

Socio-historical studies of sport have rarely paid attention to the historical and contemporary organisation of golfing practices, focussing instead on sports such as football and cricket (e.g. Holt, 1989). While the papers by Stoddart (1990), Guest (1990) and Lowerson (1989, 1993) are partial exceptions to this rule, they tend to leave implicit the analytical framework that informs their examination of golf organization and practice. We seek to be more explicit in outlining a framework that can analyse why golf has developed both "civilising" and "disciplinary" dynamics in the way that it has over the past century. In so doing we both draw upon and modify insights developed by Elias and Foucault in other contexts and for other purposes. This is a search not for origins, for the "first golfer" or the "first country" where golf was played. It is instead a concern with how and why golf came to inherit its modern kingdom, transformed from an obscure and casual game played by an elite few---mainly in Scotland---to a worldwide global obsession.

2. Golf as a Civilising Process? The Links of History

Social scientific analyses of sport have recently begun to take up ideas from Freud, Weber, Marx, feminism and ethnic concerns among others; one particularly influential approach is the "figurational" or "process" sociology associated with the work of Norbert Elias (e.g. Elias, 1978; Elias and Dunning, 1986), an approach which has examined the historical emergence of sport as part of a "civilising process". Elias contends that sport is a central feature of broadranging cultural shifts spanning several centuries, which are reflected in changes in the personality structures of individuals. Over time definitions change as to what is "acceptable" and "decent" behaviour regarding, for example, table manners (today eating tidily with knives and forks) and such behaviours as not picking one's nose, spitting, breaking wind or urinating in public.

Elias refers to "sportisation" as the nineteenth-century introduction into competitive sports of codified and strictly observed rules and norms, thus regularising the behaviour

Science and Golf II: Proceedings of the World Scientific Congress of Golf. Edited by A.J. Cochran and M.R. Farrally. Published in 1994 by E & FN Spon, London. ISBN 0 419 18790 1

of participants, limiting levels of acceptable violence, and ensuring meritocratic processes. He notes how in pastimes from fox hunting to cricket and football, civilising processes make overt violence more socially unacceptable and encourage in individuals an increasing self-control and restraint. The move away from no-holds-barred confrontations---bear-baiting, cock-fighting, prize-fighting, and such practices as firing catapults at dogs and horses, common among English public school boys down to the 1820s (Mangan, 1981)---would seem to bear out Elias' thesis in a general way. The social world has become civilised as "sportisation" has taken hold.[1]

Sports studies have begun to connect this kind of "civilising" with the increasing normalisation of social behaviour, and a long-term rise in the social threshold of shame and embarrassment (e.g. Dunning and Rojek, 1992; Holt, 1989). Yet intriguingly, the case of golf has not been seriously raised in this respect. We find this strange, since the decline of violent and agonistic (i.e. head-to-head) contests in sport would seem to parallel the rise of golf in its apparently "civilised" phase of organisation. Like other sports, early golf was, even at the highest level, essentially agonistic. One-on-one challenges were issued and crowds gathered to watch and wager. In this guise, the sport remained a minority pastime, restricted geographically more or less to Scotland, and in its social impact even within Scotland---the existence of skilled artisan-players shows that the early game reached across class divisions, but was not universal [i.e. in Lowerson's words (1993: 135) it was "trans-class" not "pan-class"]. Yet following the playing of the first Open in 1860, within 50 years golf had been transformed into an incipient global obsession, and perhaps the exemplary non-violent sport, and thus particularly appropriate for an Elias-informed analysis.

The Elias view of "sportisation" as a historically specific kind of civilising may lead us towards a new more sociologically-aware analysis of modern golf's development. He sees the emergence of sportisation as closely associated with the appearance of a new upper-middle-class elite, consisting of commercial, industrial, professional and managerial men. Both Holt (1990: 71) and Lowerson (1989, 1993) have highlighted the predominant role played by such men in the development of organised golf clubs both in Scotland and England, in a way that would be compatible with Elias' view that the "civilising process" was largely class and gender-specific, undertaken primarily by an administrative, mercantile and professional male elite. Well before World War I private golf clubs were becoming a focal point for the enactment of "civilised" lifestyles for the middle classes in which business contacts could flourish alongside leisure activities (Holt, 1989, 71-72, 130-34). This change can be marked, even in Scotland, by tracing the founding dates of courses; of some 400 Scottish clubs traced (Lowerson, 1993: 135), only around 40 date to before 1870, with the big spurt coming in the last decade of the nineteenth century and the first decade of this (with 111 and 79 respectively).

Golf in the modern age has developed an aura as the quintessentially civilised and middle class sport: the "country club" phenomenon. It is characterised worldwide by an amateur and "gentlemanly" ethic of self-disciplined behaviour, enshrined in the code of manners known as etiquette and in the extensive and meticulous regulatory framework of rules. It is played in the relaxed pastoral setting of the countryside; players play their own ball and mark each other's scorecards without direct recourse to an umpire or referee (even, most of the time in the professional game too). There are precise notions of in-group civilised solidarity in the game's rituals and ceremonies, such as the driving-in of new club captains, and the R and A's special inauguration rite, where the new captain is required to kiss the silver balls donated by all his predecessors. Thus one finds, at the heart of contemporary golf, apparently timeless civilised and civilising traditions, embodied in formal and informal rules and practices which govern the deportment of the body, and the regulation of space and time. Yet on closer analysis

---

1.   Yet Elias also suggests that the rationalisation of paid work, education and family life makes sport today one of the few spaces for less conformist, more aggressive and passionate behaviour. The sporting "quest for excitement" is characterised by manufactured tensions and imaginary dangers (Dunning and Rojek, 1992, xii). Sport, as a competitive bodily exertion, acts as a symbolic, more "civilised", non-military form of competition between states.

these prove to be historically recent: quasi-eternal ceremonies, they lend a patina of changelessness to what has been a revolution in mores, no more than a century old.

The Elias approach, then, would seem to be one important and neglected path towards understanding both the power and fascination exerted by golf in the modern age. However, our view is that it is not in itself sufficient. On the one hand, it tends to present a rather one-sided overly-optimistic view, where civilising equates to unilinear progress reinforced by ever-increasing social learning and self-knowledge. On the other, too much is left unexplained. For instance, it is clear that the idea of golf as a civilising process goes only so far, as the game is also characterised by certain de-civilising tendencies. The politics of appearance money is at odds with the civilising principle; the kind of gamesmanship exhibited by spectators in recent Ryder Cups, and increasingly at the Masters and other major championships, is barely in line with the amateur ideals of the "royal and ancient game". And within the amateur game, the knowing maintenance of an inappropriately high handicap, the improving of lies, the miscalculation of shots taken, are features all too well-known. More generally, the continued separation of male and female time and space within many golf clubs sits increasingly at odds with changing ideas about gender relations and "civilised practice". It may now appear increasingly de-civilising to continue the private appropriation and control of countryside for golfing purposes, particularly when informed by a quasi-aristocratic sense of land and country house ownership that excludes others from its use (Stoddart 1990). Finally the Elias approach may misunderstand the dynamics of modern golf's emergence. For while the main promoters and beneficiaries of golf's modernisation appear to have been members of a class elite, was <u>class</u> membership the only reason for their focus on sport in general, and golf in particular, as a means to civilising? It is here, we suggest, that a "disciplinary" approach offers a wider understanding---one which, without denying golf's civilising dimension, frames it in a more comprehensive way, not least by recognising the gender and class implications of golf's "gentlemanly" image and its potentially de-civilising tendencies.

3.   Golf as a Disciplinary Process: Links to the Present

This approach is in large part derived from the work of Michel Foucault into the phenomenon of how power and knowledge interrelate in what he characterised as the modern "disciplinary" world: but it is Foucault with a difference. Foucault, as a theorist of power/knowledge relations, investigated the history of the small micro-technologies through which we construct our social world and our selves: technologies of writing, recording, drilling and practising, of surveillance and judgement (e.g. Foucault, 1975). Disciplinary practices can therefore be seen as ways of exerting power over bodies, as some sports researchers recognise (e.g. Andrews, 1993; Heikkala, 1994). But there is equally another side to the power-knowledge equation, the way in which forms of <u>knowledge</u> are equally the product of such practices. The process through which humans "learn to learn", it now appears, intimately affects the forms of knowledge that they internalise and produce. Foucault himself first articulated this possibility in his book <u>Discipline and Punish</u> (1975), which discusses how a new technology of examination, written graded testing, began around 1800 to turn pupils into a new "field of knowledge".

This kind of analysis can be extended to understanding the genesis of modern disciplinary knowledge in general (Hoskin, 1993), from the arts disciplines to experimental science, all of which are developed once students "learn to learn" under this new form of examination.[2] As Foucault recognised, through being constantly

---

2.   Around 1770, students began to be made to write and were graded on their writing in three new pedagogic spaces: the seminar in Germany, the laboratory in France and the classroom in Britain. From the seminars come the first PhD's, from the laboratories the first experimental scientists and the experts in all the fields, as Foucault saw, with "psycho-" as their prefix; in Britain the

examined and graded, such students also become a new kind of self, the "calculable self". We see golf as a quintessential vehicle for this double "disciplinarity", for it is both a sport which embodies the triumph of mental, physical and behavioural self-discipline, and one where the quest for perfection---in the swing, in equipment, in course lay-out, in agronomy and even in the golfing self (as defined according to handicap)--is pursued via the agency of the disciplinary expert. Golf in the modern kingdom may be an Arthurian quest, as the grail of perfection proves constantly just out of reach, but it is a search prosecuted by a whole apparatus of expert organising, teaching, drilling, experimenting, practising and reflecting---in the broadest sense of the term, "disciplining".

So Elias' "civilising" may be better interpreted as a "disciplining" of golf. The transformation of the game and how it was played can be seen as a set of disciplinary innovations, where new norms and rules were introduced, and golfers became "calculable selves". For instance, the construction of golf courses became normalised as either an 18 or 9 hole project, ending the earlier practice of cutting your course to the cloth of the acreage and topography available. Equipment began to be standardised, with the first large-scale production of clubs by named club-makers and the move towards higher-performance balls---from the guttie and the rubber-cored ball onwards. The principle of bogey and par, based primarily on length of hole, was established, and regular stroke-play and match-play events increasingly replaced the old agonistic challenge matches. Golfers began to know themselves by their handicap, particularly with the shift towards medal-play format and its emphasis upon the total quantification of performance. Finally, it became generally accepted that there should be a recognised governing body and a set of rules to regulate the game. As with all codifications, some rules were to prove universal, others binding only within different jurisdictions (as with differences between the R & A and the USGA, or with more localised rules, down to club level). Meanwhile there also emerged the archipelago of supplementary "informal rules", etiquette.

But the definitive triumph of disciplining emerged as golf became a fertile field for the exercise of disciplinary and quasi-disciplinary knowledge. Before 1900 we find the first emergence of a literature around golf: the part-instructional, part-reminiscence works by the early professionals, and golf magazines such as Golf Illustrated. Science and technology began to be applied to equipment manufacture and the swing in a process that has continued and expanded down to the present. Our concern is not to object to this process, but to point out how it has always, in the modern era, had a disciplinary underpinning. Science, after all, never exists in a vacuum; it invariably has a meta-scientific framework.[3] Since 1800, with the emergence of experimentalism, that framework has been a disciplinary one: for, as the work of Bruno Latour (e.g. Latour, 1990) has in particular observed, modern science is always a process of writing, examining and calculating in disciplined and methodical ways.

But there is a further twist to this. For as we see that both the playing and the understanding of golf are, in complementary ways, disciplinary practices, we may find emerging a new way of understanding not just golf but modern sport more generally. There was clearly some form of discontinuity in the form all sports took from around 1860. A new educated British elite, mainly from public schools and Oxbridge, invented the rule-bound versions of all forms of football, tennis, athletics, rowing, boxing, and so on (cf. Mangan, 1981). We may now see that this general "sportisation" was one more aspect of the new disciplinarity, following the change when Oxbridge students began to "learn to learn" under written, graded examinations. The invention of modern

classroom method, allied to the awarding of classified degrees, preceded the emergence of "class" as the key social metaphor in the nineteenth century.

3.   Within the philosophy of science and social science, it is now a commonplace that there is no pure scientific attitude achievable outside time and space: the practices through which scientists engage in science in any given era are not contingent but systematic features of the way in which science produces knowledge and truth. Science in any era entails some meta-scientific framework within which its understandings are constructed.

sport represents "the translation of the new examining, grading and writing practices from student work to student play" (Hoskin, 1993, p. 300). Among the results were the introduction of regular formats of play (standardised pitches, distances and number of players), uniform end-limits (the game of two halves, the five-set match, the 72-hole tournament) and winning on a numerically graded basis (points, goals, stop-watch times, strokes, etc). As with exams, sport has become a field of "calculable selves", marked by the obsession with being "number one".

In investigating the emergence of modern golf, therefore, we suggest that the role of the educated English male elite, along with their Scottish counterparts, should be a particular focus of investigation. Together they would appear to have set the "civilised", "gentlemanly" tone which is still so much a part of golf today, a tone equally cultivated when the game was exported to the US, where, we suspect, it was the Ivy League elite of the Eastern seaboard who set the parameters for the culture of the country club.

4.   Golf in the Modern Kingdom: A Civilised Discipline?

We close with some suggestions on how a more inclusive scientific understanding of contemporary golfing organisation and practices may be developed, by issuing a call, not to abandon scientific research, but to reappraise its purposes and its boundaries. We perceive certain areas in which tensions are emergent, and which particularly challenge any one-dimensional view of golf as a purely civilised and/or technocratic form of organisation or practice.[4] For instance, there is now a clear tension between the "civilising" tendencies in golf and the disciplinary pressures associated with competition in both its individual and team-based forms. Golf, as civilised discipline, has its versions of more general sporting desires: "to look young, healthy and beautiful, and to be exciting" (Andrews, 1993: 161): but also to break par, to shoot one's age, to compete not only with others but also, so much more profoundly, with one's self. The conflict between the desire to be "number one" and to remain part of a civilised golfing community constantly simmers, without definitive resolution. In the professional game the constant visibility of star players (as well as the level of rewards available) has generated pressures never experienced in golf before. In the amateur game, the preoccupation with winning and social status can inform a concern with retaining an artificially high handicap (in the US "sandbagging", in the UK "nursing your handicap"), or conversely keeping one's handicap as low as possible.

There is in all this a positive power produced through disciplinarity, as the self becomes attached to golfing drills and customs, but the civilising principle can be seriously compromised, as for instance when the Kiawah Island Ryder Cup became, for spectators and even players, the "War on the Shore". Another increasingly problematic area concerns the social and gender divisions and exclusions hitherto harboured behind the civilised disciplinary image of the sport (Guest, 1990). Notoriety accrues to *causes celebres* like the token admission of blacks to country clubs, but of more general concern is the invisible way in which forms of disciplinary masculinity continue to dominate golfing practice. From the preoccupation with the macho long drive and on-course betting through to the systematic exclusion of people from courses and clubhouses on gender, class, ethnic or age grounds there is a long list of such practices. In certain new clubs, and in different cultures, alternative and less masculinist principles sometimes emerge. But there is clearly scope for research into the continuing consequences within golf of "hegemonic masculinities" (cf. Collinson and Hearn, 1994), for example in terms of women's resistance and the institutional disciplining of young males.

---

4   In a pathbreaking social science paper, Stoddart (1990) identified three key areas requiring a more critical research approach: environmental considerations, internationalisation and social access. We anticipate that research in such areas will expand and become more theoretically sophisticated, not least as it is complemented by research into other emergent areas too.

We see other areas for future analysis based on this kind of approach: the way in which financial and business disciplines have shaped so much of emergent golf infrastructure, the customised construction of courses, the setting of profit-maximising subscriptions, green fees and equipment prices, the increasing use of examinations as entry-hurdles (from the PGA qualifying schools to the interview and playing test required by "exclusive" clubs). Whither, one may wonder, the "gentlemanly" elite in the next few decades? Yet, to conclude, it is not necessarily a counsel of despair to recognise that both the modern form of golf and our modern modes of understanding it have a joint disciplinary genesis. That is why, in the terms set out in our title, we envisage golf's modern evolution as a process of "discipline" and "flourish". For it is surely the case that golf fundamentally has flourished through discipline, albeit accompanied by certain de-civilising tendencies. At the same time, its development has been strongest where disciplinary power-knowledge has given rise to a golf that is played and appreciated with a flourish.

References

Andrews, D.L. (1993) Desperately Seeking Michel: Foucault's Genealogy, the Body, and Critical Sport Sociology. Sociology of Sport Journal, 10, 148-167.

Collinson, D. L. and Hearn, J. (1994) Naming Men as Men: Implications For work, Organization and Management. Gender, Work and Organization, 1, 1, 2-22.

Dunning, E. and Rojek, C., eds, (1992) Sport and the Civilising Process. Macmillan, London.

Elias, N. (1978) The Civilising Process, vol. 1: The History of Manners. Blackwell, Oxford.

Elias, N. and Dunning, E., eds, (1986) Quest for Excitement. Blackwell, Oxford.

Foucault, M. (1975) Discipline and Punish. Allen Lane, London.

Guest, R.H. (1990) Golf Organisation: Challenges of Growth and Change--a Preliminary Social Science Perspective, in Science of Golf (ed A.J. Cochran), Chapman and Hall, London, 295-302.

Heikkala, J (1994) Discipline and Excel - Techniques of the Self and Body and the Logic of Competing. Sociology of Sport Journal (forthcoming).

Holt, R. (1989) Sport and the British, Oxford, Oxford University Press.

Hoskin, K. (1993) Education and the Genesis of Disciplinarity: The Unexpected Reversal, in Knowledges: Historical and Critical Studies in Disciplinarity (eds E. Messer-Davidow et al), University of Virginia Press, Charlottesville, 271-304.

Latour, B. (1990) Drawing Things Together, in Representation in Scientific Practice (eds M. Lynch and S. Woolgar), MIT Press, Cambridge, MA, pp. 19-68.

Lowerson, J. (1989) Golf, in Sport in Britain (ed, A. Mason), Cambridge University Press, Cambridge.

Lowerson, J. (1993) Golf and the Making of Myths, in Scottish Sport in the Making of the Nation, Ninety-Minute Patriots? (eds, G. Jarvie and G. Walker), Leicester University Press, Leicester.

Mangan, J. (1981) Athleticism in the Victorian and Edwardian Public School. Cambridge University Press, Cambridge.

Stoddart, B. (1990) The Social Context of Golf: A Preliminary Framework, in Science of Golf (ed A.J. Cochran), Chapman and Hall, London, 303-308.

92 Golf, media and change in Australia

B. Parker
Australian Golf Digest, Sydney, Australia

Abstract
This paper will discuss the relationship between golf and the media, specifically in Australia, and what are the underlying reasons for its change and the consequences for its delivery to the golfing public. Firstly the paper will discuss the changes in the way golf has been reported and what affect this has had on its delivery. It will then analyse the relationship between television and golf - who has access, at what cost and what coverage is given to golf. Finally the paper will assess who controls the media in golf and discuss whether it is accessible and do the public get the full picture.
Keywords: Australia, Media, Journalists, Newspapers, Television, Sponsorship

1   Growth of golf reportage

Prior to and immediately after World War II little coverage had been given to golf in Australian newspapers. During the late 1940s and the early 1950s most coverage that was given to golf concentrated mainly in Sydney with Jack Simons or in Melbourne with Jack Dillon. These were only part-time writers but respected as specialist golf writers. Most sporting writers, golf included, had to spread their time among a number of other popular sports such as rugby and cricket (Tresidder, 1993). At this time Australian golf was dominated by the likes of Norman von Nida, Ossie Pickworth, Eric Cremin and, later, Peter Thomson and Kel Nagle. Despite the success of these players in Australia and, to some extent, overseas their performances did little to grab headlines in the major metropolitan newspapers. Reporting these tournaments was made easier, compared to today, because golfing talent was reasonably scarce. Golf writers would walk the fairways and watch the leading players' every movement, safe in the knowledge that the winner would most likely come from one of the two final groups (Tresidder, 1993).

Science and Golf II: Proceedings of the World Scientific Congress of Golf. Edited by A.J. Cochran and M.R. Farrally. Published in 1994 by E & FN Spon, London. ISBN 0 419 18790 1

The style of their stories reflected this form of reporting. Their stories would relate where, how and what shots were played by everyone in contention. The stories relied on the journalists' interpretation of the day's play as well as their observations, opinions and criticism. Journalists would then head back to the media centre at the close of play where they would write their stories then dictate it to a copy-taker back at the newspaper. The stories were generally smaller by today's standards because of the cost of dictating the stories back to the paper.

2   The increase in coverage

The crucial turning point in Australian golf, and with it media coverage, came in the early 1960s when the big three of world golf, Nicklaus, Palmer and Player regularly v sited Australia. Sporting goods company Slazenger signed the trio to make three appearances every five years (Tresidder, 1993). By this time a number of golf writers such as Phil Tresidder, Terry Smith, Bob Wilson and then Tom Ramsay had emerged. Golf's popularity rode on the back of the name players who had entered the game and upon the successes of local players such as Peter Thomson and Kel Nagle.

In 1956 television was introduced into Australia and this opened golf to an even wider market, though golf reporting would never be the same again. The golf writer was forced to change writing style because most people knew the result long before the paper came out.

3   Current practice

Today, golf writers are bound to the media centre, watching the television for most of the day's play without ever finding the first tee. If they were to follow the play, as in pre-television days, they would risk missing a good score from someone in an earlier group. Most stories now have a higher percentage of quotes than before. This has diminished the role of the specialist golf writer. This situation was no more evident than in a recent example involving a major tournament in Australia. The journalist watched the tournament at home, and gave the photographer a mobile phone so that players might ring the reporter after the round in order to provide a few quotes.

Until recently golf writing flourished given the explosion in interest created by overseas and local players as well as the healthy competition between the morning and afternoon papers. Under this competition, newspapers realised the importance of having their golf writer at every tournament. By the late 1970s the seeds for the demise of the specialist golf writer had been planted. People's working conditions were starting to change and so, too, were their buying habits. Newspapers were starting to

suffer declining sales figures while media magnates such as Rupert
Murdoch were starting to build newspaper empires by buying up
metropolitan dailies.

4   Changes in ownership

In 1986 there were 18 capital city dailies in Australia. The Herald and
Weekly Times Group owned eight papers, Melbourne's Sun Pictorial and
Herald, Brisbane's Courier Mail and Telegraph, the Adelaide Advertiser,
two Perth papers the West Australian and Daily News, and Hobart's
Mercury. Rupert Murdoch had six papers, The Australian, The Sydney
Daily Telegraph and Mirror, The Sun in Brisbane, the Adelaide News and
the Northern Territory News. Fairfax had four papers, The Sydney
Morning Herald, the Sydney Sun, the Financial Review and the
Melbourne Age (Bowman, 1988).

By 1988 Murdoch had bought the Herald and Weekly Times so that,
after a number of papers closed, he owned nine, Fairfax three and a
selection of smaller operators, including the Brisbane Sun and the
Adelaide News management, owned the five remaining papers. Over this
time four papers closed, ten others changed hands twice and two others
had been sold. This was quickly followed by the merger of four Murdoch
papers into two (Bowman, 1988).

By 1993 every major paper in the country, except The Canberra Times,
was owned by Murdoch's New Limited or by Canadian media baron
Conrad Black who bought Fairfax after an unsuccessful attempt by
Warwick Fairfax to privatise the company. There were now no afternoon
papers in the country, except the so-called 24 hour Murdoch papers while
the morning papers, the Sydney Telegraph Mirror and Melbourne's Herald
Sun, were controlled by two people, an American and a Canadian.

5   Consequences of change

David Bowman (1988), former editor of The Sydney Morning Herald and
The Canberra Times, wrote of the perilous position that the press was in
after this period:
> It follows that, while the press has a vital part to play in society, it is
> not in a condition to meet its responsibilities. There is a chasm
> between the state of the industry and what it should be if it is to
> serve the reasonable needs of a healthy democratic society.

The consequences of the shake-up of Australian newspapers are felt
strongly by golf writers today. In basic terms there are fewer papers, fewer
owners and less money.

In 1993 Brendan Moloney resigned as The Age's golf writer when conditions at the newspaper became untenable for him:

When I first went to The Age, the golf writer was really the golf writer, who was sent to all the good tournaments and the expense really wasn't a consideration. They wanted the stories and they realised to do the job properly we had to be there. Sadly the paper is now run by accountants and with the rationalisation of ownership of newspapers in Australia it's easy for an organisation to say why send x, y and z when one person could do the job of three.

This left much of the power for the success or failure of a tournament in the hands of one person. The golf writers left on those papers are limited to little more than a weekly golfing gossip column. With the size of the Murdoch and Black newspaper empire, journalists are being sent less often to overseas tournaments because their stories can be picked up from one of the overseas affiliates.

6   Decline of specialist golf writers

With the decrease in the number of papers and the concentration of ownership there are now fewer specialist golf writers and their work is done increasingly by journalists with little knowledge of the game. Some papers now have a policy of not keeping a journalist in the same job for longer than three years. This has made the standard of golf writing drop dramatically in the opinion of many.

Moloney says, "Its a joke, it's basically scores with a few verbs thrown in. There's no writing involved at all." (Moloney, 1993)

News Limited's Tom Ramsay believes the change has decreased the number of authentic critics in the game:

They all want to be friends with Greg Norman. I couldn't care a stuff about Greg Norman, whether I was friends with him or not. I think it's nice not to have to run after him like a dog, unlike a lot of others who seem to do. They all run after him like a dog on heat. (Ramsay, 1993)

While print coverage was once the yard stick to the success of a tournament, television has become the key to having a tournament at all. Sponsors no longer are even prepared to think about pouring money into a tournament if there is no television coverage.

7   The impact of television

Initially television was not a welcome partner in professional golf. In the first year of television in Australia, TCN 9 in Sydney televised the Pelaco tournament at The Australian Golf Club, making it the first live telecast of a sporting event in Australia. While this gave instant exposure to the tournament and access for its sponsor to a wider market, crowd figures instantly dropped. This became a major sticking point with tournament promoters as they relied on gate takings as major part of their income from the tournament. It was later resolved that the television companies had to pay the tournament organisers a rights fee which eventually became a substantial amount (de Groot and Webster, 1991).

Throughout the 1960s and 1970s television and professional tournaments co-existed with the television networks paying rights fees to the tournament organisers. But just like their newspaper colleagues, television fell on hard times. By the late 1980s two of the four stations were in receivership, another was up for sale after its owner (Alan Bond) went into bankruptcy, while the last, the government-owned ABC, was suffering from huge funding cuts.

This signalled the end of an era in the televising of golf and sporting events in general. Apart from the highest profile tournaments on the professional golf calendar, the Australian Open and the Australian Masters, no rights fees would be paid. In a reversal of fortune all other tournaments now had to pay the television stations to turn up. This was understandable as the current budget for the major tournaments on the Australian tour is in the vicinity of $1.4 million.

This led to a dramatic decrease in the quality of golf telecasts. When there was plenty of money to go around, the stations had funds to spend on providing a quality telecast. Now that the tournament organisers had to foot the bill they were unable to afford the costs of such high quality telecasts. The stations now offer the organisers a number of packages at different prices for the coverage of their tournament. At the ABC the lowest level coverage, the final two rounds, will cost $200,000, while the commercial networks charge a slightly higher amount. This is a far cry from the days when the ABC was paying the Australian Golf Union $50,000 a year, up until 1987, to cover the Australian Open (Pridmore, 1993).

8   The importance of sponsorship

This situation is in stark contrast to the mid eighties when there was an abundance of Japanese sponsorship in Australian golf. While the Japanese were in a financially sound position they could afford to pay the television networks for the best coverage possible. Moreover, many of their tournaments were televised on the ABC where there were no commercials. This not only gave the viewers a superior coverage but also helped the Japanese promoters to edit the tape to suit Japanese networks. By doing this they could recoup some of their outlay to the Australian networks and also gave publicity to their Australian resorts which were not only potential destinations for Japanese tourists but were, in some cases, listed on the stock exchange (Gee, 1993). Even for some of the smaller Australian promoters, selling the rights of their tournament to overseas cable networks went some way to off-setting the cost of buying television coverage, even though this rarely fetches more than $10,000 (O'Donohue, 1993).

But money alone will not guarantee air time. A stringent process exists before a tournament can get to air - even if the organiser has the ready cash. Firstly, the organisers have to write to the networks submitting an expression of interest in the network covering the tournament. Then the head of the sports department will approach the management meeting to discuss the possibilities and if accepted the network will start to talk about the financial details. But contrary to popular belief many stations do not sell air time, the tournament still has to create interest, no matter how much money the organiser is prepared to pay (Pridmore, 1993).

9   Importance of audience type

If ratings alone determined an event's existence, golf may not even get on television. In the US the highest rating golf tournament, the US Masters, reached 9.9/24 in 1987 and slid to even lower rating in the following years. While in comparison for a comedy or drama to survive on television it needs to attract a rating of 15 per cent or more (Wenner, 1989). Even if ratings did not reach any great number, the reason that most networks persist with golf is that they are heavily supported by advertisers. Surveys show that golf telecasts attract a specific market audience that advertisers are often keen to reach.

As Lawrence Wenner (1989) notes:
Sports - especially the major team sports plus golf, tennis, and Olympic Sports - tended to attract the types of educated, affluent, and consumption-oriented audiences that many major advertisers fantasize about.

10   Technology and coverage

Despite the increasing cost of producing a telecast, technology has led networks to produce a better telecast at the same price. With the advent of micro-wave technology, cameras can now be packed up and moved to a new hole in a matter of minutes, thus reducing the number of cameras needed to cover an event. Prior to this, when each camera was connected by cables, once the final groups had passed fixed camera positions that was the end of those cameras' usefulness. Now the final groups can have up to five cameras on the one hole all giving a different angle to the coverage.

Steven Barnett says in *Games and Sets - The Changing Face of Sport*:
Golf is traditionally the hardest of sports to televise. Courses are spread over a wide area, and little white balls have a habit of disappearing into the most inaccessible greenery. A poor shot into the bushes may have unfortunate consequences for the golfer; for the cameraman, it can be a positive nightmare. (Barnett, 1990)

11 Television and other coverage

In the 1993-94 Australasian tour of the 11 tournaments held in Australia, all were televised thus proving the point that no tournament can have Order of Merit status without television coverage. The ABC made a comeback covering five, plus the one ladies tournament, while the other six were shared by two commercial networks.

The organisers of these tournaments on the major Australian tour have few problems in obtaining press coverage these days, though television is a different story. Some tournaments, such as the year ending Coolum Classic, still offer free accommodation to entice journalists to cover the event. A similar arrangement exists for the only ladies professional tournament and privately funded amateur tournaments such as the BMW Cup and Holden Scramble. This situation will probably increase in the coming years as the proposed merger of the Asian and Australasian tours tees off. From 1994 the two tours will merge to make the one tour. To ensure its success inducements will most probably be offered to journalists, otherwise tournaments won't get covered. This was certainly the case two years ago when the first moves into Asia began where all journalists' expenses were paid.

But the opportunity for approaches to individual journalists is probably decreasing as the number of specialist golf writers decline. Most journalists are tied to their editors, whereas previously some determined individually where and when they would travel to tournaments previously. Despite some papers saying they never accept these inducements, even the holiest of newspapers still do. With limited golf specialists and the fate of many tournaments resting with so few, the incidence of inducements will only increase as sponsors often judge the value of their sponsorship by the square inches they receive in the media. As this situation increases more emphasis may be placed on the two major golf magazines that are more open to positive bias in return for an advertising commitment from the sponsor. In the media wash up, the role of the specialist golf magazine may hold a greater importance, as they deliver to the direct market and offer up to five times the amount of coverage a newspaper can offer.

12 Conclusion

The future of golf and the media lies in the fate of the media in general. Now, as golf writing has almost turned the full circle back to being dominated by part-timers the freedom to cover golf specifically will be determined by the financial state of newspapers.

David Bowman (1988) believes the only solution can be government intervention:

Only government can restore the conditions that are essential if the press is to be free. It is no good saying that private enterprise must be left alone to cure the evils of gross concentration of press ownership. Private enterprise brought about these evils - with government encouragement - because that is nature of private enterprise.

The same situation applies in television. As long as the promoters have to pay exorbitant fees to get the television networks to attend the tournaments, the standard of coverage will continue at its current low level. The only bright light on the horizon for this could be introduction of cable television into Australia. With the ABC guaranteed one licence, and two others being sold to private interests, the future of golf coverage could be brighter. Most commentators are predicting at least one of the cable stations to be sport which would help golf because of the length a golf tournament takes to complete.

Susan Eastman & Timothy Meyer (1989) believe cable television will also be assisted by the advertisers, who have been the main supporter of golf telecasts:

Most changes will result from cable channel's competition for telecast rights and major advertisers' reluctance to pay ever-higher rates for network commercial time when smaller but more targeted audiences are available at much lower advertising rates than the networks command.

While cable has yet to be proved as the savour of television coverage of golf, the overall state of the newspaper industry will continue to dog the golf industry. As journalists continue to be so badly paid, golf writers will continue to look for other public relations work to supplement their paltry incomes. And as a result we will still see journalists continue to pass off as editorial public relations stories of the highly financed Queensland resorts.

References

Barrett, Stephen (1990). *Games and Sets: the Changing Face of Sport on Television*. British Film Institute, London.

Bowman, David (1988). *The Captive Press.*

de Groot, Colin and Webster, Jim (1991). *Pro Golf - Out of the Rough.* PGA Australia, Sydney.

Eastman, Susan and Meyer, Timothy (1989)

in Wenner, Lawrence ed. (1989), *Media Sports and Society.* Sage, Newbury Park, CA.

Gee, Peter (1993). Interview.

Moloney, Brendan (1993). Interview.

O'Donohue, Terry (1993). Interview.

Pridmore, Alan (1993). Interview.

Ramsay, Tom (1993). Interview.

Tresidder, Phil (1993). Interview.

Wenner, Lawrence (1989). *Media, Sports & Society.* Sage, Newbury Park, CA.

Index

This index is based on keywords assigned to the individual chapter as its basis. The numbers are the page numbers of the first page of the relevant chapter.

Acid copolymer   383
Aerodynamics (ball)   340, 348
Age   127
Ageing   210
Agrostis capillaris   461
Agrostis palustris   471, 477, 489, 505
Agrostis stolonifera   461
Air gun   302
Anoxic conditions   449
Anti-golf   611
Arousal   127
Attention   127, 144
Australia   109, 626
Automaticity   144

Back pain   20
Backswing, start of   103
Balance point (shaft)   278
Balata   334
Ball
   aerodynamics   340, 348
   coefficient of restitution   334
   comparisons   362
   compression   334
   construction   334
   construction, market survey   369
   cover   334, 376, 383
   deformation   302, 309, 315
   dynamic characteristics   302
   launch conditions   327, 348
   launch machine   348
   performance, historical   355
   size   334
   spin rate   296, 327, 334, 340, 348
   velocity measurement   327, 348
Ball–club impact   296, 302, 309, 315
Ball–green impact   409, 431
Bend point (shaft)   278
Bending stiffness (shaft)   247
Benfluralin   511
Bensulide   511
Bentgrass   471, 477, 489, 505

Bioclimate pocket   467
Biomechanics   3, 14, 26, 33, 40, 71, 91
Borrow, under-estimating   180
Breathing   46
Bunker sand   483

Catchment area   589
Cations   383
Centrifugal force (swing)   59
Centrifugal loading (shaft)   259
Change   611
Civilizing process   620
Clearance angle   97
Club–ball impact   296, 302, 309, 315
Club design   390
Clubhead
   inertia ellipsoid   290
   market surveys   369
   moment of inertia   290, 321
   size   321
   velocity   84
Coaching   109
Coefficient of restitution   296
Compaction of greens   425
Competitions   109
Compression (ball)   334
Computer-aided club design   390
Computer-aided course design   534
Computer simulation of swing   71
Computers in teaching   123
Consumer research (golf facilities)   546
Contact force (ball–club)   302
Contrast sensitivity   168
Correlation coefficient   84
Course design, computer aided   534
Cover (ball)
   coatings (paint)   376
   hardness   334
   materials   383
Cultivation   437
Culture   611

DCPA   511
Deformation of ball   302, 309, 315
Dermal 'no effect' values   505
Development appraisal of facilities   554
Diagrammatic specification of swing   77

Digital ground modelling (DGM)   534
Digital terrain modelling (DTM)   534
Disciplinarity   620
Double pendulum swing   59
Downswing   259
Drag coefficient of ball   340
Drainage   437, 467
Drive
  accuracy   362
  distance   284, 355, 362
Driver heads   321
Dynamic characteristics of ball   302
Dynamic modelling of swing   71
Dynamic programming in putting   186

EEG   46, 127
Elite golfers   109
EMG   3
England (municipal courses)   602
Environment   497, 527, 540
  evaluation   540
  impact assessment   540
  quality   399
Epistemic orientation   117
Equipment, future trends   369
European golf market (courses)
  589
European PGA Tour   205
Evapotranspiration   505
Exclusiveness   602
Exceptional tournament scores   228
Eye–hand preference   168

Face mapping   321
Fairy rings   455
Feasibility studies (courses)   589
Fertilizer   489, 497
Finance for municipal courses   602
Fine sports turf   455
Finite element analysis   271
Fitness   127
Fixation disparity   168
Flex point   278
Flight testing of ball   355
Flow (psychological)   156, 162
Foot pressure   26, 33, 40
Foot torque   33
Forward bending   50
Frequency (shaft)   278
Frequency resonance (shaft)   284
Future trends in equipment   369

Geodemographics   589
Geometry of swing   77
Goal orientations   156
Goals   144
Golf development   109

Golf facilities
  database   205
  development   546, 554
  European market   589
  feasibiilty studies   589
  location   205, 554, 576
  market database   576
  market research   546, 554, 569
  marketing   569
  municipal   602
  supply and demand   205, 546,
    554,562, 569, 576
Golf market   237
  applications   576
Grain shape (sand)   483
Grasses   399, 443, 471, 477, 489
Greens   180, 409, 419
  classification   419
  compaction   425
  construction   409
  hardness   409
  impact of ball   409, 431
  maintenance   409
  playing quality   409, 419
  reading   180
  speed   409, 425
Greens-in-regulation statistic   210
Ground modelling   534
Ground reaction forces   3, 26, 33, 40
Ground water   497
Growth of golf   546

Half swing   14
Handicap   216, 222, 228
  accuracy   222
  competition   228
  reduction   228
Health   399, 505, 527
Heat/noise abatement   399
High speed camera   302
Hip rotation   50
Historical comparison, golf balls   355
Historical comparison, players   193
History of golf in USA   546

Impact
  ball–club   296, 302, 309, 315
  ball–green   409, 431
  normal   309
  oblique   309, 315
Indoor test range   348
Inertia ellipsoid   290
Inertia matrix   290
Infiltration   425
Inhalation 'no effect' values   505
Injury   14
Insects   461

Integrated pest management   519
Ionomer   334, 383
Iron sulphate   449
Irrigation   443

Japan, golf course development   562
Journalists   626
Junior golfers   109

Kick point   278
Kinematics of swing   3, 65, 71, 91
Kinematics, 3-D   91
Kinetics of swing   3, 71
Knowledge accessing mode   117
Korea, use of pesticides   527

Land   602, 611
Large clubhead   321
Launch angle   327
Launch conditions   327
Launch machine   348
Leaching   497, 511
Lift coefficient of ball   340
Literature   611
Load cell   302
Localized dry spots   477
Lower body stability   103

Management planning (environment)
   540
Marasmius oreades   455
Market
   development (golf facilities)   546
   research (golf facilities)   546, 554, 569
   surveys (club types)   369
Marketing
   golf projects   569
   sport   596
Markov decision model   186
Mathematical modelling
   ball   302
   ball aerodynamics   340, 348
   impact   302, 309, 315
   shaft   265
Mechanical golfer   321
Media   626
Membership market   562
Mental strategies   162
Meta scientific analysis   620
Metal woods   321
Middle class and golf   602
Moment of inertia
   ball   334
   clubhead   290, 321
Motivation   156
Multivariate analysis   419
Municipal authorities   602

Muscle activity   3
Mycorrhiza   461

Natural contours   467
Natural frequency of shaft   259
Newspapers   626
Nitrogen   471, 477, 489
Noise abatement   399
Normal forces on ball   296
Normal impact   309
Normal model (handicaps)   222
Novice golfers   20
Nutrient fate   443

Oblique impact   309, 315
Overland flow   489
Oxadiazon   511

Packing density (sand)   483
Part trajectory analysis   348
Partial swing   14
Participation in golf   546
Particle size distribution (sand)   483
Peak performance   162
Pendimethalin   511
Perceived competence   156
Performance
   enhancement   174
   management   162
   measures   193
   statistics   193, 199, 205, 210, 237
Permeability   437
Pesticide   497, 519, 527
   application   519
   fate   505
   management   519
Pests (turf)   461
pH   449
Phosphorus   489
Photogrammetry   65, 271, 327
Pixels   327
Planar motion (swing)   59
Plumb-bobbing   180
Poa annua   461
Polyurethane coating   376
Posture   103
Pre-performance routines   144
Preferential flow (irrigation)   443
Psychological skills   138
Psychology   150
Psychomotor skills   138
Putting   127, 174, 180, 186, 210

Quality of life   399
Quantitative analysis   216

Reading greens   180

Redox potential   449
Regression analysis   199
Rehabilitation   14
Respiratory pattern   46
Retroreflector   327
Rolling (greens)   425
Routines   127, 144
Royal and Ancient Golf Club   237
Rules of Golf   237
Ryder Cup teams   205
Rye grass   489

Sand (bunker)   483
Scientific design of equipment   237
Scotland (municipal courses)   602
Seaweed extract   449
Self-regulation   150
Shaft   247, 271
   deflection   259, 265
   flex   278
   frequency   278
   market surveys   369
   materials   247
   stiffness   247, 265
   torque   247, 278
   torsional stiffness   247, 278
   vibration   284
Shoes   26, 40
Shot-making skills   138
Shoulder turn   103
Side bending   50
Site selection (golf course)   554
Skills   138
Social factors   602, 611
Social organization of golf   620
Soil
   conditioning   437
   stabilization   399
   water repellent   455
Spectator research   596
Spin rate   296,. 327, 334
Spin rate decay   340
Spine rotation   50
Sponsorship   626
Sport marketing   596
Sport psychology   150, 162
Sports Institutes   109
Sports turf   455
Stability (lower body)   103
Standards for performance   216
Statistics (performance)   193, 199, 205,
   210, 216, 237
Stepwise multiple regression   84
Stereopsis   168
Strategic Plan (course provision)   546
Strobe   327
Stroke value   216

Strokes per round   205
Sulphide   449
Supply and demand (golf facilities)   554,
   562
Surface runoff   489
Swing   59, 77, 271
   arc widening   97
   categorization   65
   characteristics   84
   geometry   77
   keys   84
   kinematics   3, 65, 71, 91
   kinetics   3, 65, 71, 91
   kinetics   3, 71
   measurement   50
   partial   14
   plane   97, 103
   tendencies   103
   time   50

Tactics (putting)   186
Takeaway   97, 103
Tangential force on ball   296
Teaching methods   117
Television   626
Thatch   511
Theoretical profile shape method   505
Timing   77
Torque (shaft)   247, 278
Torsional stiffness   247, 278
Training   109
Trajectory   278, 340, 355
Trajectory analysis   340, 355
Trifluralin   511
Trimer   376
Turf pest management   519
Turfgrass   443, 455, 471, 477, 505

Ultra-violet absorber   376
Under-estimation of borrow   180
United States Golf Association   237
US LPGA Tour statistics   199
US PGA Tour statistics   199, 205, 237
US Senior tour statistics   199

Vectograms   40
Velocity
   ball   327, 348
   clubhead   84
Video for teaching   123
Video monitoring of ball launch
   327
Viscosity   296
Vision   168
Visual acuity   168
Visual performance   168
Volcanic material   467

Water quality   399
Water repellent soil   455
Watson, Tom   210
Wild life habitat   399
Wind tunnel measurements   340, 355
Working class and golf   602

X-factor (swing mechanics)   50

Yotaku Deposit   562

Coaching Children in Sport

Principles and practice

M Lee, Institute for the Study of Children in Sport, Bedford College of Higher Education, UK

Children participate in sport at all levels, from school involvement to international competitions. With the growing concern about the mental and physical pressures which can be exerted on a child, the coaches' traditional role is developing and expanding. They now need to be aware of how problems like depression, anxiety, sports injuries, etc occur and how they can be prevented.

This book has arisen out of a need for a text which tackles the special issues relating to coaching children (from 6 - 16) in sport. Academics (many with coaching experience) and practitioners have been commissioned to write on their specialist areas. The book contains clear, accessible information divided up into five parts: children in the world of sport, developmental changes in children, psychological aspects of participation, applications to the coaching process, and good practice in coaching. In these parts the theory behind the need for good communication, counselling, training, dealing with injuries, nutrition, etc is given with ample examples of how to put these ideas into practice.

Contents: Children in the world of sport. Developmental changes in children. Psychological aspects of participation. Applications to the coaching process. Good practice in coaching. Appendices. Index.

June 1993: 234x156: 328pp, 54 line drawings and 11 halftone illus
Paperback: 0-419-18250-0: £16.95

E & F N SPON
An imprint of Chapman & Hall

New and forthcoming books on Sports Science

Science and Racket Sports

T Reilly, Liverpool John Moores University, UK, and **M Hughes**, Cardiff Institute, UK

This volume contains papers presented at the first World Congress of Science and Racket Sports which have since been edited and revised. Keynote and invited addresses by a series of internationally renowned scientists provide a balanced view of theory and application.

July 1994 234x156 c.480 pages, 120 line illustrations
Hardback 0-419-18500-3 c. £50.00

Drugs in Sport
2nd Edition

D Mottram, Liverpool John Moores University, Liverpool, UK.

The 2nd edition of *Drugs in Sport* reflects new advances and trends. New chapters cover firstly, the basic principles of pharmacology which gives the reader an insight into how drugs work, and secondly, a more comprehensive overview of the problems associated with drug use and misuse in sport.

October 1994 234x156 c.208 pages, 20 line illustrations
Paperback 0-419-18890-8 c. £15.95

Sports Turf
Science, construction and maintenance

V I Stewart, Science and Sports Turf Consultant and Honorary Research Fellow, University of Wales, UK

A detailed, practical guide (produced in association with the National Playing Fields Association) to the construction and maintenance of sports grounds.

November 1993 246x189 312 pages, 56 line illustrations
Hardback 0-419-14950-3 £32.50

Kinanthropometry IV

Edited by **J W Duquet**, Free University of Brussels, Belgium and **J A P Day**, University of Lethbridge, Canada

The International Society for the Advancement of Kinanthropometry holds a major international conference every four years.

This volume contains the papers presented at the fourth such event, held at the World Congress on Youth, Leisure and Physical Activity in Brussels.

October 1993 234x156 320 pages, 5 line illustrations, 1 halftone illustration
Hardback: 0-419-16770-6 £45.00

⧓⧓⧓⧓⧓⧓⧓⧓⧓⧓⧓⧓⧓⧓⧓⧓⧓⧓⧓⧓⧓⧓⧓⧓⧓⧓⧓⧓⧓⧓⧓⧓⧓⧓⧓⧓⧓

Please send me further information on:

....

Name: .... Department: ....

Organisation: ....

Address: ....

....

Tel: .... Fax: ....

Send to: Mari Lewis, Dept JSPSC, Chapman & Hall, 2-6 Boundary Row, London, SE1 8HN, UK
Tel: +44 (0) 71 865 0066 **Fax:** +44 (0)71 522 9623

 # E & F N Spon
An imprint of Chapman & Hall